C All-in-One Desk Reference For Dummies®

Cheat Sheet

C Language Operators

Operator	Category	Duty
=	Assignment	Equals
+	Mathematical	Addition
–	Mathematical	Subtraction
*	Mathematical	Multiplication
/	Mathematical	Division
%	Mathematical	Modulo
>	Comparison	Greater than
>=	Comparison	Greater than or equal to
<	Comparison	Less than
<=	Comparison	Less than or equal to
==	Comparison	Is equal to
!=	Comparison	Is not equal to
&&	Logical	AND
||	Logical	OR
!	Logical	NOT
++	Mathematical	Increment by 1
--	Mathematical	Decrement by 1
&	Bitwise	AND
|	Bitwise	Inclusive OR
^	Bitwise	Exclusive OR (XOR or EOR)
<<	Bitwise	Shift bits left
>	Bitwise	Shift bits right
~	Bitwise	One's complement
+	Unary	Positive
–	Unary	Negative
*	Unary	Pointer
&	Unary	Address
sizeof	Unary	Returns the size of an object
.	Structure	Element access
->	Structure	Pointer element access
?:	Conditional expression	Funky if operator

Sacred Order of Precedence

Operators							Read from
Unary operator (typecast)							Left to right
*							Right to left
–							Left to right
								Left to right
								Left to right
==							Left to right
&							Left to right
^							Left to right
|							Left to right
&&							Left to right
||							Left to right
?:							Right to left
=	+=	-=	*=	/=	%=		Right to left
&=	^=	|=	<<=	>=			
,							Left to right

Comparisons and Their Opposites

If Comparison	Else Statement Executed By	This Condition
<	>=	Greater than or equal to
==	!=	Not equal to
>	<=	Less than or equal to
<=	>	Greater than
>=	<	Less than
!=	==	Equal to

C Language Keywords

auto	double	int	struct
break	else	long	switch
case	enum	register	typedef
char	extern	return	union
const	float	short	unsigned
continue	for	static	void
default	goto	sizeof	volatile
do	if	signed	while

For Dummies: Bestselling Book Series for Beginners

C All-in-One Desk Reference For Dummies®

Cheat Sheet

Conversion Characters

Conversion Character	Displays
%%	The percent character, %
%c	Single character (char) value
%d	Integer (int, short int, long int) value
%e	Floating-point (float or double) value in scientific notation with a little E
%E	Floating-point (float or double) value in scientific notation with a big E
%f	Floating-point (float or double) value in decimal notation
%g	Either %f or %e is used, depending on whichever is shorter
%G	Either %F or %E is used, depending on whichever is shorter
%i	Integer (int, short int, long int) value
%o	Unsigned octal value (no leading 0)
%p	Memory location or address in hexadecimal (pointer)
%s	String constant or variable (char *)
%u	Unsigned integer (unsigned int, unsigned short int, unsigned long int) value
%x	Unsigned hexadecimal value, lower case a–f, no leading 0 or x
%X	Unsigned hexadecimal value, upper case A–F, no leading 0 or X

Escape Sequences

Escape Sequence	Character
\a	Bell (speaker beeps)
\b	Backspace (non-erase)
\f	Form feed/clear screen
\n	New line
\r	Carriage return
\t	Tab
\v	Vertical tab
\\	Backslash
\?	Question mark
\'	Single quote
\"	Double quote
\x$nn$	Hexadecimal character code nn
\o$nn$	Octal character code nn
\nn	Octal character code nn

Assignment Operators

Operator	Shortcut for
+=	Addition
−=	Subtraction
*=	Multiplication
/=	Division
%=	Modulo
<<=	Shift left (bitwise)
>>=	Shift right (bitwise)
&=	Bitwise AND
|=	Bitwise inclusive OR
^=	Bitwise exclusive OR

C Language Variable Types

Type	Value Range	Comments
char	−128 to 127	
unsigned char	0 to 255	
int	−32,768 to 32,767	16-bit
	−2,147,483,648 to 2,147,483,647	32-bit
unsigned int	0 to 65,535	16-bit
	0 to 4,294,967,295	32-bit
short int	−32,768 to 32,767	
unsigned short int	0 to 65,535	
long int	−2,147,483,648 to 2,147,483,647	
unsigned long int	0 to 4,294,967,295	
float	1.17×10^{-38} to 3.40×10^{38}	6-digit precision
double	2.22×10^{-308} to 1.79×10^{308}	15-digit precision

For Dummies: Bestselling Book Series for Beginners

C

ALL-IN-ONE DESK REFERENCE

FOR

DUMMIES®

C
ALL-IN-ONE DESK REFERENCE
FOR
DUMMIES®

by Dan Gookin

WILEY

Wiley Publishing, Inc.

C All-in-One Desk Reference For Dummies®

Published by
Wiley Publishing, Inc.
111 River Street
Hoboken, NJ 07030-5774

WILEY

About the Author

Dan Gookin has been writing about technology for 20 years. He has contributed articles to numerous high-tech magazines and written more than 90 books about personal computing technology, many of them accurate.

He combines his love of writing with his interest in technology to create books that are informative and entertaining, but not boring. Having sold more than 14 million titles translated into more than 30 languages, Dan can attest that his method of crafting computer tomes does seem to work.

Perhaps Dan's most famous title is the original *DOS For Dummies,* published in 1991. It became the world's fastest-selling computer book, at one time moving more copies per week than the *New York Times* number-one best seller (although, because it's a reference book, it could not be listed on the *NYT* best seller list). That book spawned the entire line of *For Dummies* books, which remains a publishing phenomenon to this day.

Dan's most recent titles include *PCs For Dummies,* 9th Edition; *Buying a Computer For Dummies,* 2005 Edition; *Troubleshooting Your PC For Dummies; Dan Gookin's Naked Windows XP;* and *Dan Gookin's Naked Office.* He publishes a free weekly computer newsletter, "Weekly Wambooli Salad," and also maintains the vast and helpful Web site www.wambooli.com.

Dan holds a degree in communications and visual arts from the University of California, San Diego. He lives in the Pacific Northwest, where he enjoys spending time with his four boys in the gentle woods of Idaho.

Publisher's Acknowledgments

We're proud of this book; please send us your comments through our online registration form located at www.dummies.com/register/.

Some of the people who helped bring this book to market include the following:

Acquisitions, Editorial, and Media Development

Project Editor: Rebecca Whitney

Acquisitions Editor: Greg Croy

Technical Editor: Greg Guntle

Editorial Manager: Carol Sheehan

Editorial Assistant: Amanda M. Foxworth

Cartoons: Rich Tennant, www.the5thwave.com

Composition

Project Coordinator: Maridee Ennis

Layout and Graphics: Karl Brandt, Denny Hager, Joyce Haughey, Stephanie D. Jumper, Michael Kruzil, Melanee Prendergast, Jacque Roth, Julie Trippetti, Mary Gillot Virgin

Proofreaders: Arielle Carole Mennelle, Dwight Ramsey, Brian H. Walls

Indexer: Infodex Indexing Services Inc.

Publishing and Editorial for Technology Dummies

    Richard Swadley, Vice President and Executive Group Publisher

    Andy Cummings, Vice President and Publisher

    Mary Bednarek, Executive Editorial Director

    Mary C. Corder, Editorial Director

Publishing for Consumer Dummies

    Diane Graves Steele, Vice President and Publisher

    Joyce Pepple, Acquisitions Director

Composition Services

    Gerry Fahey, Vice President of Production Services

    Debbie Stailey, Director of Composition Services

Contents at a Glance

Table of Contents

Introduction

Congratulations on your purchase of *C All-in-One Desk Reference For Dummies* — a tome that not only sits fat and looks impressive on your computer bookshelf, but also teaches you a heck of a lot about the C programming language.

Because few people read book introductions, I have decided to fill the following six pages with filthy limericks, most of which are patronizing to immigrants and women.

Seriously, now that I have your attention, I thought that I would ramble on briefly about this book and what you can expect from its contents.

This book provides a solid overview of the C programming language, from the basics on up through advanced concepts and topics that third-year university students would pay real money to have someone else suffer through.

Despite the *For Dummies* text on the cover, this book takes a swifter approach to learning the C language than my book *C For Dummies,* 2nd Edition. This massive work assumes, for example, that you may have a wee bit of programming experience or are just more eager to find out more about the C language or perhaps need that extra training in those advanced topics that are skimpily covered in other programming books. If that's you, you have found your book! If that's not you, you should still buy this book because three of my kids need braces badly.

Above all, the bottom line in this book is about having fun. I take things easy, introducing the C language one tidbit at a time. Rare is the long, involved program in this book. Short, punchy (and often silly) programs make finding out about C quick and easy. After all, you need only a few lines of text to see how a function or concept in C works. And, everything is peppered with a modicum of irreverence and a dash of humor. Or, could it be the other way around? Anyway, you get the idea.

Why Bother with C When C++ Is Obviously Blah-Blah-Blah?

The C programming language is like the Latin of the computer world. As with Latin, if you know C, learning other programming languages is a snap. Each of the following programming languages (and many more) has its base in C:

- ✦ C++

- ✦ Perl

- ✦ Java

- ✦ Python

When you know C, learning any of these languages is simple and painless.

Unlike Latin, however, the C language is far from dead. As one of the older computer languages, C has a rich history and a full library of routines, programs, documentation, help, and other whatnot — a rich treasure of resources for you to draw on. Rare is the program that cannot be written using simple C programming. From graphics to games and from networking to building new operating systems, you have no limitation on what you can do in C.

Most of my C language students use my books as a foundation for leaping into C++ programming — mostly because many C++ books lack the gentle hand-holding approach that my books have. In fact, if you read this book from cover to cover, I promise you that any C++ (or other programming language) book will be that much easier for you to grasp. It may not be written with my dynamic wit, but the concepts will be easier to understand.

The bottom line, of course, is *programming*. Becoming a programmer means that you have ultimate control over your computer. *You* are finally in charge, telling the dang thing exactly what to do with itself. And, like the fast idiot it is, the computer dutifully obeys your every whim.

Plus, programming gives you instant feedback. Some folks find that benefit so addicting that they end up growing beards; wearing sandals and Hawaiian shirts; consuming coffee, stale doughnuts and Doritos; and never leaving the confines of their house. And that's just the women!

About This Here Dummies Approach

Don't you hate buying a programming book and having to read through 50 pages of this and that, background information, trivia, why the author thinks he's important, and all that other crap, only to discover that the first program in the book is five pages long and really (honestly) doesn't teach you one single thing about programming?

Yeah! I hate that too!

You know what else I hate? Those burr stickers that get into your socks and you can't pull them out because they poke into your fingertips. And, how about stockbrokers?

Unlike other programming books, this one starts out right away with something to do, something to type, something to learn. You want to get started right away. I can't blame you. Right away, this book has you doing things — right there on Page 11, you're typing something and finding out how to program.

Also unlike other books, this book keeps programs small and tidy. The best way to learn about something is one piece at a time. Baby steps! Therefore, you won't find me cramming several topics into one program or putting things into the demo programs that I don't discuss until "later."

Small program. Easy to type. Quick feedback. Instant response. That's the best way to figure out how to program. This book tells you how.

To keep you on your toes, I give you various exercises. Some chapters have many exercises, and some chapters have few or none. The idea is to see whether you can go off on your own and use your programming skills to solve a puzzle or come up with something new. Answers or suggested solutions are all offered in the back of this book — in Appendix C. I think.

How This Book Works

This book covers the C programming language, which is an activity that is, for the most part, independent of your computer's operating system. Therefore, this book covers both Windows and Unix computers.

Whether you have Linux (any flavor), FreeBSD (or any *BSD), Mac OS X, or any other flavor of Unix, I refer to it as Unix in this book.

Note that I do not cover Sun's Solaris here. That's because Sun has never sent me a free computer despite years of my never having asked for one.

The most important thing you need to do to work the examples in this book is *read Appendix A*. It covers the details on how you need to set up your computer for programming, selecting and using a text editor, and then fixing up the compiler.

Note that information on choosing a compiler is available on this book's companion Web page: www.c-for-dummies.com.

Generally speaking, stuff in this book that appears on the screen looks like this :

```
I am text on the screen. La-di-da.
```

This is how text appears in a program listing:

```
Remove soiled diaper.
Clean baby.
Apply clean diaper.
```

Line numbers aren't specified or used in C. Your editor should have a line number command or let you jump to line numbers, however. (It depends on the editor.) That way, when I refer to line 36 in the text, for example, you can use your editor to find and view that specific line.

Because this book is only so wide, some lines in a program may *wrap*. They look like this:

```
This is an example of a very long line that was painfully
    split in two by this book's cruel typesetters.
```

When you see that, *don't* type two lines. Just keep typing, and everything will fit on one line in your editor.

Elements of a program or source code may appear in a special `monospaced font`. I use it so that you understand that `a`, for example, is a part of the program and not a rogue article my editor ignored after imbibing too much wine.

If you need to press a certain key combination on your keyboard, it's listed like this: Press Ctrl+C. Ctrl is the name of the control key on your keyboard. C is the C key. A + (plus sign) means to press both keys together. Note that Ctrl+C and Ctrl+Shift+C are two different key combinations.

Source code files are available from this book's companion Web site, `www.c-for-dummies.com`. Go there to download all the source code files at one time or individually. The files are organized by "books," just as this entire volume is organized into books.

Note that many programs are updated throughout this book. Although you will update the same source code, I keep each source code file separate. For example, the OZ.C series of source files starts with OZ.C in this book. But, in the source code file reference on the Web, you find OZ1.C for the first update, OZ2.C for the second, OZ3.C for the third, and so on. This file-naming scheme is used in Appendix C too.

Icons Used in This Book

 Technical information you can merrily skip over like something brown and smoldering on the sidewalk.

 Something you should remember to do, like check for lettuce on your teeth before that job interview.

 Something you should remember not to do, like rip off a toenail with your teeth in court.

 A healthy suggestion, like *get out and exercise!*

Final Thots

Noli nothis permittere te terere.

Learning C is a journey. Enjoy it! Discover new things. Try new ways of doing things. Give yourself a challenge. *Remember:* If you can imagine it happening on your computer screen, you can program it. It may not run as fast as you imagine, but it will work!

Above all, keep on trying! You can explore so many different pockets of programming, from graphics to operating systems to networking to games — the variety is endless.

Occasionally, in your quest for knowledge, you may meet some arrogant member of what I call the Programmer Priesthood. Its members are people who are knowledgeable, but unwilling to help — almost to the point of cruelty. If you find people like that, in real life or on the Internet, quickly pass them by and seek out someone else for help. Not everyone who holds the keys is a jerk.

For myself, I can offer you this book's companion Web page:

`www.c-for-dummies.com`

This Web page has more information about programming, some excellent books I recommend, plus bonus programs and materials from myself as well as feedback from other readers. Check it out when you have time.

I make myself available to answer questions via e-mail. I view this as part of my duty to you as a reader of my books. My e-mail address is

`dan@c-for-dummies.com`

I'm willing to help with some programming stuff, but I won't write your programs for you, and I cannot help you with university assignments (especially stacks or binary trees) or C++ programming. But I am willing to return your message and say "Hello!"

Good luck with your C programming!

Book I

Hello, C

The 5th Wave   By Rich Tennant

Re·al Pro·gram·mers

Real Programmers think an eight hour day is for sissies.

Contents at a Glance

Chapter 1: Your Basic C Program

*L*earning a programming language is like trying to eat an entire banquet in one bite: You have so much to swallow at once, even to understand the most basic stuff, that it isn't a question of where to start, but rather what not to eat so that you don't get too sick too quickly.

This chapter provides a quick and dirty introduction to a single C language program. The chapter doesn't even explain why things are necessary because, honestly, at this point in the game you're probably more interested in accomplishing something than truly figuring out why something works. Don't worry: That comes later. For now, this chapter offers a small taste of the feast to come.

Remember to use the basic folder or directory for the source code and program files in this book.

The Section Where the Author Cannot Resist Describing the History of C

In the beginning was Charles Babbage and his Analytical Engine, a machine he built in 1822 that could be *programmed* to carry out different computations. Move forward more than 100 years, where the U.S. government in 1942 used concepts from Babbage's engine to create the ENIAC, the first modern computer.

To program Babbage's computer, you had to literally replace stacks of gears. To make the ENIAC carry out different tasks, it had to be rewired by hand.

By the early 1950s, computer programming had evolved from rewiring to entering instructions using rows of switches. The process began with Professor John von Neumann, who in 1945 developed the concept of the *function* (or *subroutine*), the *IF-THEN* choice statement, and the repeating *FOR loop*. By 1949, Von Neumann had come up with a binary programming language he called Short Code. Then, in 1951, Grace Hopper developed the first *compiler*, which allowed the computer to be programmed using words and symbols rather than binary ones and zeroes. Computers could then be programmed with written instructions rather than by rewiring or throwing switches.

In the mid-1950s, the first major programming language appeared. Named FORTRAN, for *formula trans*lating system, it incorporated *variables* and introduced logical conditions to the art of programming. Then, in 1959, the COBOL programming language was developed as businesses began to adopt computers. COBOL was the first programming language with a truly English-like grammar.

The Algol language was developed at about the same time as COBOL. From Algol, many programming techniques were introduced that are still used today.

In 1968, Zurich professor Niklaus Wirth used Algol as a basis for the Pascal programming language. Pascal was designed as a teaching tool because it didn't allow for sloppy programming and forced users to follow the rules of structured programming.

Meanwhile, over at the AT&T Bell Labs, in 1972 Dennis Ritchie was working with two languages: B (for Bell) and BCPL (Basic Combined Programming Language). Inspired by Pascal, Mr. Ritchie developed the C programming language.

The C language was used to write the Unix operating system. Ever since that first version of Unix in the early 1970s, a C compiler has always been a part of the operating system — even with Unix variations like Linux and Mac OS. It also explains why Unix comes with so many programming utilities. (Indeed, Unix is often called the "programmer's operating system.")

In 1983, C programmer Bjarne Stoustroup developed object oriented programming (OOP) extensions to the C language and created the C++ programming language. Even though it's often taught as a separate subject, C++ is really about 95 percent original C. Even so, some purists stick with the original C language and don't bother to discover that extra 5 percent of C++ — despite the power and flexibility it offers.

Branching off from C in the 1990s was another programming language: Java, from Sun Microsystems. Originally developed for interactive TV, the Java language truly found a home on the Web in 1994 and has been a popular Web programming language ever since.

Time to Program!

The C language has a certain structure to it — a form, a visual look, a feeling. Unlike in more freeform languages, you must obey traditions and rules to put together the most basic of C programs. That's what gives the C language its look and feel.

The following sections introduce you to the basic structure of a simple C program — the skeleton. Each section builds on the next, so read them in order.

Ensure that you have read through Appendix A, which discusses how to set up the C language compiler on your computer and the basic steps for editing, compiling, and running a program.

One suggestion: Please save all the source code files for this book in the `basic` folder on your hard drive (`prog/c/basic`).

The basic, simplest C program

When you program a computer, you tell it exactly what to do. The instructions are given in a particular language — in this case, the C language. Those instructions are then compiled into object code. The object code is then linked with a C language library, and the result is an executable file or a program you can run on your computer. It's just like magic!

I save the boring specifics for the next chapter. For now, consider the most basic of all programs:

Yes, that's a blank line. Open your editor and type a blank line. Just press the Enter key: *Thunk!* That's it.

Save the file to disk with the name DUMB.C. Remember to add to the end of the filename that .C part, which is what tells most modern compilers that you have created a C language file and not a C++ file.

Compile the source code for DUMB.C. Here's the command for most C compilers:

```
gcc dumb.c -o dumb
```

No, it doesn't compile. You get some sort of error message. That's for two reasons.

The first obvious reason is that your source code file is *blank!* It contains no instructions for the computer! With some programming languages, that would be acceptable, and the resulting program would also do nothing. But C is more structured than that.

The second reason is that the program needs a place to start. That place in all C language programs is the `main()` function.

The `main()` *function*

All C language programs must have a `main()` function. It's the core of every program. It's required.

A function is like a machine that does something. In C, built-in functions do things like compute the sine of an angle, display text on the screen, or return values from the computer's internal clock. You can also create your own functions that do wondrous things.

The `main()` function doesn't really have to do anything, other than be present inside your C source code. Eventually, it contains instructions that tell the computer to carry out whatever task your program is designed to do. But it's not officially *required* to do anything.

When the operating system runs a program, it passes control of the computer over to that program. This is like the captain of a huge ocean liner handing you the wheel. Aside from any fears that may induce, the key point is that the operating system needs to know *where* inside your program the control needs to be passed. In the case of a C language program, again, it's the `main()` function that the operating system is looking for.

At a minimum, the `main()` function looks like this:

```
main() {}
```

First comes the function's name, `main`. Then comes a set of parentheses. Finally comes a set of braces, also called curly braces.

Use your text editor to reedit the DUMB.C source code. In that file, on the first line, copy the `main()` function I just showed you. Copy it exactly as shown. Press the Enter key to end that line. (Many compilers require a blank line after the last bit of course code.)

Compile the program again:

```
gcc dumb.c -o dumb
```

This time, it compiles.

Run the program. Type **dumb** or **./dumb** at the prompt to run the resulting program.

Nothing happens.

That's right. And that's perfect because the program doesn't tell the computer to do anything. Even so, the operating system found the main() function and was able to pass control to that function — which did nothing and then immediately returned control right back to the operating system. It's a perfect, flawless program.

Inside the main() *function*

All C language functions have the same decorations. First comes the function name, main, and then comes a set of parentheses, (), and, finally, a set of braces, {}.

The name is used to refer to, or *call,* the function. In this case, main() is called by the operating system when the program runs.

The set of parentheses is used to contain any *arguments* for the function — stuff for the function to digest. For example, in the sqrt() function, the parentheses hug a value; the function then discovers the square root of that value.

The main() function uses its parentheses to contain any information typed after the program name at the command prompt. This topic is covered in a later chapter. For now, you can leave the parentheses blank.

The braces are used for organization. They contain programming instructions that belong to the function. Those programming instructions are how the function carries out its task or "does its thing."

By not specifying any contents, as was done for the main() function in the DUMB.C source code, you have created what the C Lords call a *dummy function* — which is kind of appropriate, given this book's title.

"Am I done?"

Note that the basic, simple dummy function main() doesn't require a specific keyword or procedure for ending the program. In some programming languages, an END or EXIT command is required, but not in C.

In the C language, the program ends when it encounters the last brace in the main() function. That's the sign that the program is done, after which control returns to the operating system.

Now you have various ways to end a program before the last brace is encountered. You can use the `return` keyword in addition to the `abort()` and `exit()` functions. You find out about the functions later; the `return` keyword is a key part of the `main()` function, as described in the next section.

Declaring `main()` *as an* `int`

When a program starts, it can optionally accept information from the operating system. Likewise, when the program is done, it can return information to the operating system. These return codes, called *errorlevels* in DOS and Windows and *exit codes* in Unix, can then be evaluated by the operating system or some shell script or batch file language.

To accommodate that evaluation, and to further define `main()` as a function, you need to declare the function as a specific type. The type is based on the kind of information the function produces. There are five basic variable types, and please don't memorize this list:

✦ `void`: A function that doesn't return anything

✦ `int`: A function that returns a whole number or *integer* value

✦ `char`: A function that returns text

✦ `float`: A function that returns a non-whole number or value with a fractional part

✦ `double`: The same as float, but more precise

For example, a function that reads a character typed at the keyboard is a `char` function; it returns a character. The function to calculate the arctangent of an angle would return a `float` or `double` value — some obnoxious number with a decimal part.

In the case of the `main()` function, what it can return to the operating system is a value, usually in the range of zero on up to some huge number (depending on the operating system). That makes `main()` qualify as an integer function, or `int`. Here's the proper way to define the `main()` function:

```
int main() {}
```

This line means that the `main()` function returns an integer (a whole number) value when it's done. How? By using the `return` keyword. `return` is responsible for sending a value back from a function. Here's how it looks:

```
return(0);
```

`return` is a C language keyword. It's followed by an optional set of parentheses and then the value to `return`, which is shown as `0` in the preceding line. Because this is a C language statement, it ends in a semicolon, which serves the same purpose as a period does in English.

Because the `return(0);` statement belongs to the `main()` function, it must be placed in the braces; thus:

```
int main() {return(0);}
```

Now you have a function that's properly defined to return an integer value and does in fact return the value 0 to the operating system.

Summon your editor again and bring up the source code for DUMB.C. Edit the first line so that it looks like the one I just showed you.

Save the change to disk, and then compile. Run.

The output is no different; the program runs and basically does nothing other than cough up the value 0 for the operating system to evaluate. (Because you're not evaluating the program, you have no way to tell, but the 0 is still produced.)

A little sprucing up

The C language compiler doesn't really care how pretty your source code is. There is value, of course, in presenting your source code in a readable format. This subject is directly addressed in another chapter. For now, return to your editor and add some space by changing your source code to look more like this:

```
int main()
{
    return(0);
}
```

The `int main()` function declaration appears on a line by itself, sort of "announcing" the function to the world.

The braces are kept on a line by themselves, as are the statements belonging to the function; however, the statements inside the braces are indented one tab stop. That keeps the statements visually together and helps align the braces so that you know that they are a pair.

By putting the `return(0);` statement on a line by itself, you can confirm that it ends in a semicolon.

Save back to disk the changes you have made to your source code. You can recompile the program if you like, but nothing has really changed as far as the compiler is concerned.

Finally, making `main()` *do something*

To breathe some life into the DUMB program, you need to employ the C language to direct the computer to *do* something. That's what programming is all about. Although the program already returns a value to the operating system, that just isn't enough.

The things that a program can do are limitless. The problem with that vast scope is that it takes a lot of "talking" in a program language to make the computer do impressive things. On the other hand, a simple thing you can direct the computer to do is display text on the screen. To do that, you can use the simple `puts()` function.

I suppose that *puts* stands for put string, where a string is a bit of text you put to the screen. Something like that. Here's how it works:

```
puts("Greetings, human!");
```

The text to display — the string — is enclosed in the function's parentheses. Furthermore, it's enclosed in double quotes, which is how you officially make text inside the C language, and how the compiler tells the difference between text and programming statements. Finally, the statement ends in a semicolon.

Here's how `puts()` fits into the DUMB.C source code:

```
int main()
{
    puts("Greetings, human!");
    return(0);
}
```

The `puts()` function works inside the `main()` function. It's run first, displaying the text `Greetings, human!` on the screen. Then the `return(0);` statement is run next, which quits the program and returns control to the operating system.

Save the changes to DUMB.C. Compile the program and then run the result. Unlike the previous renditions of DUMB.C, this one displays output on the screen:

```
Greetings, human!
```

One more thing!

As with the main function, you should also declare the puts() function, formally introducing it to the compiler. In fact, not doing this in some compilers generates an error.

Fortunately, the job of formal introductions has already been done for you. That information is contained inside a *header file* that was installed along with your compiler.

You find out more about header files in Book I, Chapter 2, but for now, to complete the task of formal introduction to the puts() function, add the following line at the top of your DUMB.C source code:

```
#include <stdio.h>
```

#include isn't a word in the C programming language. Instead, it's an instruction for the compiler to *include* another file on disk, inserting the text from that file into your source code at that specific point in the program. In this case, the text is grabbed from the file named STDIO.H, which is the standard input/output header file for the C language. It's also where the puts() function is formally introduced.

With the inclusion of that line, the final complete source code for DUMB.C should now look like this:

```
#include <stdio.h>

int main()
{
    puts("Greetings, human!");
    return(0);
}
```

Spruce up the source code in your compiler so that it resembles what you see here. Save it to disk. Compile and run:

```
Greetings, human!
```

Just about any time you use a function in C, you have to specify a header file to be included with your source code. It needs to be done only once; so, if you're using two functions that are both defined in the STDIO.H header file, you need only one #include <stdio.h>. But other functions use other header files, such as MATH.H, STDLIB.H, and numerous others. Again, it's all covered in Book I, Chapter 2.

The C Skeleton

Most C language source code listings start with a basic skeleton that looks like this:

```
#include <something.h>

int main()
{
    statement;
    statement;
    return(0);
}
```

Obviously, the skeleton will have more "meat" on it eventually — including various other braces and interesting whatnot. That's what comes with later chapters of the book, but at its most basic, C language source code looks like what you see here.

Chapter 2: How It All Works

In This Chapter

✔ Getting to know the parts of the C language

✔ Creating source code in an editor

✔ Building a program

✔ Understanding compiling and linking

*P*rogramming a computer is simply the official, professional method of telling the machine exactly what it can do with itself. If you can imagine it on the screen, you can make it happen.

At its simplest level, programming is merely communications. It's your instructions directing the microprocessor to interact with other hardware inside the computer to get some specific thing done. This chapter provides an overview of that process in the C language, describing how a text file full of cryptic terms and jargon is translated into instructions the computer can understand, and then how the computer carries out those instructions.

How to say "Hello" to a computer

All computer programming languages work in a similar manner. They provide you with tools for communicating directly with the computer's operating system or hardware. Unlike the rewiring or switch-throwing of decades past, this communication takes place using instructions in a language similar to a human language. By properly wording those instructions, you can make the computer do just about anything.

Unlike human languages, however, computer languages lack a rich vocabulary and are quite formal. You're given only a smattering of words or instructions, but typically that's enough to build on and get what you want. The real challenge, however, is keeping within the formalities; that's where most errors happen.

Your Computer Programming Bag of Tools

Here are the tools you need to communicate with your computer and tell it to do things:

+ A programming language

+ An editor, to create source code files

+ A compiler and linker, to create program files

The programming language is how you translate your intentions into instructions for the computer. You use the words and tools of the language to communicate with the computer's hardware and operating system.

Because the computer is generally bad at listening to you, you have to type the programming language instructions. Rather than enter them interactively (as in a conversation), the instructions are kept in text files known as *source code* files.

Finally, it's the compiler's job to convert the source code files into a program. Granted, the process is more complex than that. I divulge the details throughout this chapter.

The C Programming Language

The C language is one of many you can use to tell the computer what to do. The language consists of three major parts:

+ Keywords

+ Functions

+ Operators

You mix and match these items as needed to create your programs.

You use, beyond that language itself, other tools and gizmos to help make your programs purr. These items are all covered in the sections that follow.

Keywords

The C language has 32 keywords. Some are specific programming commands directing the computer to do something, some are used in conjunction with other keywords to make up commands, some are used to create things your program uses, some are antique, and a couple of them are never used! Regardless, they're all listed in Table 2-1 and in Appendix D.

Table 2-1	C Language Keywords		
auto	double	int	struct
break	else	long	switch
case	enum	register	typedef
char	extern	return	union
const	float	short	unsigned
continue	for	signed	void
default	goto	sizeof	volatile
do	if	static	while

Don't memorize the keywords! This book introduces you to them as needed.

Functions

Functions are small routines or software machines that do specific tasks. In the C language, most of the work is done by these functions, not by the C language keywords.

Despite only 32 keywords, the C language, has hundreds of functions. Most programs use a common set of about 50 or so. But — and this is a good thing — there are dozens and dozens of additional functions, many of which do amazing and specific things that you can incorporate into your programs.

Functions work in several ways. First, they can be used to immediately carry out a task. For example, the `abort()` function is used to quit your program. It doesn't generate a result, nor does it process any value or information:

```
abort();
```

This command immediately ends a program (assuming that some error condition has occurred). More importantly, it's a rare example of a C language function that doesn't process information. Otherwise, functions are used in C to process information; they either produce something or digest something, or a combination of both.

The second function example is one that sends information to the computer's hardware or operating system. For example, the `puts()` function is used to display a bit of text on the screen, as shown in Book I, Chapter 1:

```
puts("Hello!");
```

Functions can also return information from the computer, telling you what's going on. As an example, the `getchar()` function returns a character typed at the keyboard:

```
key = getchar();
```

Unlike `puts()`, `getchar()` doesn't require anything between its parentheses. Instead, it merely returns a value that must be stored. In the preceding line, the value is stored or assigned to the `key` variable. This type of assignment, as well as the concept of variables, is introduced later in this book.

Finally, some functions take something and give back something in return. The `sqrt()` function, for example, takes a value and returns that value's square root:

```
root = sqrt(27);
```

The `sqrt()` function takes the value 27 and returns that value's square root, which is then stored in the `root` variable.

TIP

Looking up functions

Functions may be listed in your compiler's online help system, though you have two other handy ways to look up information about functions.

The first way is to visit the gcc home page on the Internet: `http://gcc.gnu.org/`. You can find ample documentation on that Web site.

If your compiler has its own home page on the Web, consider visiting that site to peruse the documentation.

Remember to bookmark the pages you find!

Finally, as a bonus, users of Unix-like operating systems (FreeBSD, Linux, Mac OS X) can use the `man` command to look up functions by name; for example:

```
man sqrt
```

This command displays the manual entry for the `sqrt()` function, including its options, common uses, and related or similar functions.

Note that some C functions can also be Unix commands, such as `exit` or `log`. The C language functions are defined in Section 3 of the man pages. As an example, to look up the C language `log` function, use this command:

```
man 3 log
```

Note that not every Unix installation may include C language documentation. If your version of Linux is missing the C language man pages, for example, refer to the System Configuration utility for your version of Linux to add that information.

Alas, all the C language functions just aren't listed in one place any more. In the old days, the C compiler's manual would have a full listing. Today, most of that information is kept in the compiler's online help system. The key to knowing which function to use is merely experience.

Operators

In addition to the words in the C language, it has various symbols and whatnot. They're nothing mysterious; for example:

```
sum = first + second;
```

This C language statement contains two symbols: = and +. The + is used for addition and the = for assignment; the statement just listed adds the values of the variables first and second, saving the result in variable sum.

I assume that they could have made the C language more English-like by using the word plus rather than the + operator and equals rather than =, as in

```
sum equals first plus second;
```

That line may make more sense to a beginner, but they just didn't do it that way, for whatever reason.

The full list of C language operators is in Appendix D. You don't need to memorize the list. This book begins discussing the operators when I expose you to the horrors of math programming in Book I, Chapter 4.

Variables and values

Your programs also use various numbers and bits of text called *strings*. They're known collectively as *values* or *variables*, depending on whether the contents are known ahead of time.

For example, the string Hello! is a string value used in the puts() function:

```
puts("Hello!");
```

The number 27 is a value used in the sqrt() function:

```
root = sqrt(27);
```

The word root is a variable. That's a storage place you create in your program for placing values or text. When the program is written, the value of root is unknown. It can vary, hence the word *variable* — just like from those hated days of your youth when you learned algebra. (And it explains why programming is often not taught until after kids learn algebra.)

You find out more about variables in Book I, Chapter 4. Though it's possible to have a program that doesn't use variables (like the DUMB.C program, from Chapter 1), most programs have variables and they are a part of the C programming language.

Other C language goodies

To properly glue the C language words, functions, and operators together, you must obey the rules of C language syntax.

No, syntax isn't a levy on booze and cigarettes. It refers to the way a language is put together. The English language has a syntax, though a rather lax one. C has a syntax too, albeit very strict.

For example, in C you use braces, { and }, to group things together.

All statements in the C language end with a semicolon character, similar to the way English sentences end in a period.

Putting It Together in the Editor

In the old days, you entered programs one line at a time by throwing switches on the computer's console. Early astronauts had to manually punch numbers ("nouns" and "verbs") into their on-board computers to program them to do things. Things still happen much the same way now, but all that throwing and punching is done ahead of time in a text file.

The first step in creating a program is to fire up a text editor. Into the editor you type the programming instructions for the computer. You start with a basic C language skeleton, as shown in Book I, Chapter 1, and then you pad it in with the pieces and parts of the C language that direct the computer to carry out some task.

Just to keep from getting bored in this rather wordy chapter, consider typing this source code file:

```c
#include <stdio.h>

#define TOTAL 300

int main()
{
    int count;

    for(count=0;count<TOTAL;count++)
        printf("I think I'm going to be sick! ");
}
```

Be sure to type everything carefully, exactly as shown. Use lowercase and uppercase as shown. Pay attention to parentheses versus braces. Double-check your spelling. Note that a space appears after the exclamation point following sick in Line 10.

When you're done writing your instructions, save the text file back to disk. Use your editor's file-saving command to save this file as SICK.C.

Because this text file contains programming instructions, it's referred to as a *source code* file. In the C language, all such files end with the .C filename extension. This extension helps keep those files organized (and separate from plain text, or TXT files), plus the .C is recognized by the compiler as well as by other programming books. (C++ source code files often end in .CC or .CPP rather than in .C, which is how some C compilers know which language to use.)

C language source code is merely text in a file. It doesn't contain instructions for the computer directly. No, it contains instructions for the *compiler*. Using the compiler is the next step in creating a program.

Making a Program

After using the programming language to create the source code, the next step is to convert the source code in the text file into a program that the operating system can run. To do that, you must *compile* and *link* the source code.

The compiler

The *compiler* is a program. Its job is to read the source code file and convert that source code into *object* code. The compiler may also link the object code, creating the final program, but for this discussion I'm splitting the tasks into two: compiling and then linking.

When you compile your source code, the compiler opens up the source code document and first peruses it for any special instructions called *precompiler directives*. In the C language, these commands start with the # character and appear on a line by themselves (that is, they don't end with a semicolon, like C language statements).

The sample program, SICK.C, has two precompiler directives: #include <stdio.h>, found at Line 1, and #define TOTAL 300, found at Line 3.

The #include <stdio.h> directive tells the precompiler to load in the text from the header file STDIO.H, inserting that text into your source code at that point in the program. This is done to configure basic input and output routines common to most C programs. By keeping the information in the STDIO.H file, it saves you from having to retype that information over and over for every program you write. (See the nearby sidebar, "Finding header files," for more information.)

Figure 2-1 illustrates how the #include directive inserts a header file into your source code. Note that this is done by the compiler as it reads the text from your source code file; it doesn't modify the source code file itself.

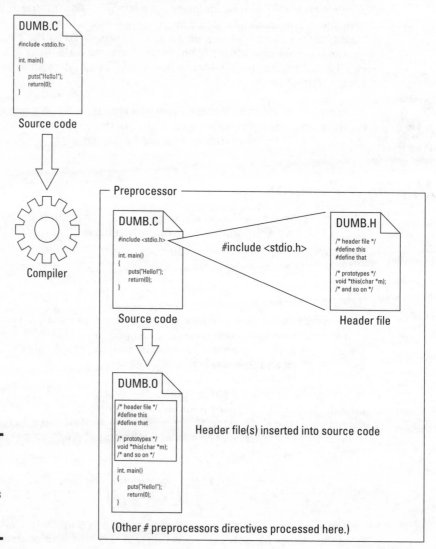

Figure 2-1:
The preprocessor includes a header file.

Finding header files

The #include directive directs the compiler to insert special files into your source code. These header files help define the functions you use, as well as other routine C language stuff — things that would make you go crazy if you had to type them in otherwise.

All header files end in .H, where the H stands for header. The files are a part of the C language compiler package installed on your computer. They were installed with the computer, and the compiler knows in which folder they're kept. In Windows, this is a folder named include branching beneath the main folder where the compiler is installed, such as \MinGW\include. In the Unix-like operating systems, the folder is /usr/include.

You don't need to specify the full path to the header file when you use the #include directive; the compiler knows where to find the files. However, some header files exist in subdirectories. For them you must specify the subdirectory name, as in:

    #include <sys/termios.h>

This directive looks for the TERMIOS.H header file in the sys subdirectory (/usr/include/sys).

You can also create your own header files, which is covered elsewhere in this book. In that case, you can keep the header file in the current directory and use double quotes rather than angle brackets to specify the header filename:

    #include "myown.h"

This command directs the compiler's preprocessor to look for the file named MYOWN.H in the current directory. If found, the text from that file is inserted into the source code. If it's not found, you get one of them ugly error messages.

Header files are plain text and can be read using any text editor or text-viewing command. For example, you can visit the include directory on your computer and view the contents of the STDIO.H file to see what's inside. Most of it is simply C language code, declarations, and such. It's helpful to view that information, but please look and do not touch!

In the SICK.C source code, a second preprocessor directive, #define, is used to create a constant value labeled TOTAL. What the compiler does here is search for that text, TOTAL, and replace it with whatever is specified. So, in Line 9 of the source code, the word TOTAL would be replaced with the value 300 by the preprocessor.

After preprocessing the source code, the compiler checks for common errors or, more specifically, things it just doesn't understand. These include missing semicolons, braces, parentheses, and other items awry or misplaced. If errors are found, the compiler stops and reports the errors, giving you a chance to reedit your source code and fix things.

The object code file

If the compiler finds that everything is up to snuff, it creates an object code file. This file has the same name as the source code file, but ends in .O rather than in .C; the O stands for object code.

An object code file isn't a program file. What the compiler has done is translate, or *parse,* the C language you typed, converting the instructions into a type of shorthand.

Figure 2-2 shows how the compiler creates the object code file based on a source code file. (Though it presents a rather simplistic view, the illustration helps you form a mental image of what's going on.)

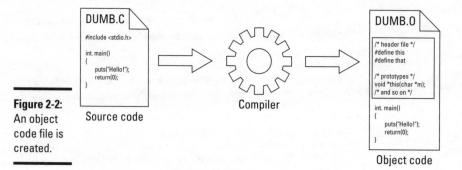

Figure 2-2:
An object code file is created.

Source code   Compiler   Object code

The next step is for that object code file to be linked, which is how the final program is created. This topic is covered in the next section.

Normally, the gcc command creates an object code file and then automatically links that file to create a program. The object code file is then deleted. (If you have an undelete utility, you can see all the little lifeless .O files in your programming directory.) You can, however, direct gcc to create an object code file and not link it. Here's the command to do so for the SICK.C source code you create earlier in this chapter:

```
gcc -c sick.c
```

Type that command and press Enter. Assuming that the SICK.C source code has no errors in it, the compiler should preprocess the source code and assemble it into object code.

Use the `dir` or `ls -l` command to view the contents of the directory. You see two files: SICK.C and SICK.O. SICK.O is the object code file. Notice that the object code file is a bit larger than the source code file. That's because of the parsing process, where the compiler massages the source code to prepare it for linking. (At this point, the English-language text of C programming departs into the low-level realm of the machine language that the computer's hardware understands.)

It may seem like creating an object code file is a useless step. Indeed, modern C compilers perform both the job of compiling and linking with a single command; rarely do you see an object code file (unless an error occurs). But other reasons exist for the intermediate object code step.

For example, large programs are often created by combining several smaller source code files. In those cases, each source code file is merely a piece of the larger whole. The compiler creates the pieces as separate object code files. Then the linker puts them all together, creating the final program.

For the SICK.C program, I merely showed you what object code looks like. Most of the time when you program, you use the gcc command to both compile and link in one step.

The linker

The *linker* builds the program file. It's what puts the guts into the program that makes the thing work. This is a point of confusion for many budding programmers because they don't really understand how text files containing programming languages are translated into binary (nontext) files that are programs.

To make a program work, the linker pulls in executable code from a *library* file. Normally, this is the standard C library, which contains the computer instructions for the functions in your program. Without that library to link in, the C language functions wouldn't work.

For example, if your source code uses the puts() function, that function must be both defined and executed. The definition takes place in the header file. The execution is a small bit of programming code inside the library file. But in addition to defining puts(), the standard C library file contains the code defining dozens of common (standard) C language functions.

Figure 2-3 illustrates how the linker adds in a library file to complete your program. The final step is, of course, an executable program, one that the computer obeys (you hope) and that does something constructive.

With the gcc compiler, linking takes place along with compiling in a single command:

```
gcc sick.c -o sick
```

In this command line, SICK.C is the name of the source code file. Without any other options (and as long as it has no errors), gcc compiles SICK.C, links in the standard C library, and creates the program named A.EXE or A.OUT.

When you specify the `-o` switch, gcc is directed to name the program file SICK.

Type the command to compile the SICK.C source code you create earlier in this chapter.

After compiling, you can run the program by typing **sick** or **./sick** at the command prompt.

You may also want to use the `dir` or `ls -l` command to view the final program's file size. Note that it's much larger than either the source code or object code file. That bulk you notice is the size of the library file that's linked in.

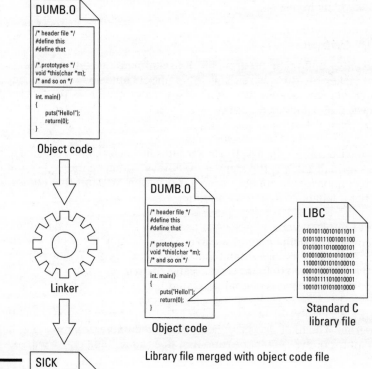

Object code

Linker

Figure 2-3:
An object
code file is
linked to
create a
program.

SICK

Program file

DUMB.O

Object code

LIBC

Standard C
library file

Library file merged with object code file

Finding library files

It's the linker's job to find C language library files and link them in with your object code to create the final program file.

C has many library files used for creating different types of programs in different environments. These are all kept in the lib directory. In Windows, the lib directory is found beneath the directory where your compiler is installed. In the Unix operating systems, it's the /usr/lib directory.

The standard C library is linked in by most compilers without specifying its name. This library contains the code required to use the standard C functions, though some libraries may contain fewer definitions and others may contain more. It all depends on the compiler.

Occasionally you may be required to link in a specific library. In that case, the library must be specified when you type the gcc command to compile and link. For instance, to compile some high-level math function you must specifically link in a math library. The man page for sqrt() in FreeBSD, as an example, explains that the option you must type is -lm to include the math library:

```
gcc -lm math_program.c -o
    math_program
```

In this command, the -lm switch directs the linker to fetch and include the math library (named m). That library includes the instructions necessary for the sqrt() function to work.

The size of the library file directly affects the size of the final program you create. In the olden days, users would fuss about this. After all, if you're using only one function from the library, why link in all the other functions that aren't being used? Today it's not much of an issue, though you should note that each of the different C language libraries has a different size and is used for different types of programs. As you find out more about C, you can decide which libraries you really need and customize your programs accordingly.

Finally, one important point: C language functions live in the libraries, not in the header files. Merely grabbing a GRAPHICS.H header file doesn't suddenly enable your program to use those graphics routines. No, to use the routines, you must both use the proper header file *and* link in the appropriate library for your compiler.

Chapter 3: More Basics, Comments, and Errors

In This Chapter

✔ Putting text up on the screen

✔ Displaying hard-to-type characters

✔ Adding comments to your code

✔ Avoiding nested comments

✔ Understanding different types of errors

✔ Fixing problems and errors

✔ Displaying even more error messages

I'm a firm believer in learning by doing. Enough with the blah-blah of programming. It's time to start doing stuff. Although you may not fully understand what's going on, you get a certain thrill from typing computer programs and having the dumb thing *finally* obey you. Most of us enjoy such positive feedback.

This chapter lists several small, useless programs that are easy to type and utterly give you the fulfilling satisfaction that you're finally making progress in your attempt to understand the C programming language. You still have lessons to learn here, mostly about comments and how to find and fix errors in your programs. And I assume that you have read through Appendix A and at least skimmed over Chapters 1 and 2 in this book to get a good idea of some basics. Beyond that, crack your knuckles and get ready to *code*!

Simple "Hello" Programs

Most C programming books start out with a simple program that merely displays text on the screen. They do this for many reasons: It's simple; it gives you instant feedback; and all programming books and courses do the same thing. Why should I be different?

The STOP program

Carefully type the following source code into your editor:

```
#include <stdio.h>

int main()
{
    puts("Stop: Unable to stop.");
    return(0);
}
```

This program uses the `puts()` function to display a string of text to the screen. Simple.

Save the source code to disk as STOP.C. Compile and run the program:

```
Stop: Unable to stop.
```

Ha! Get it? You type `stop` like it's a command, but the program seems to spit out some type of error message, like the program is unable to run. Ha-ha. Hope this doesn't hurt your sides too much from all the laughing.

Reediting your source code

A lot of basic programming involves going back and reediting your source code. You do this to fix errors (which you're exposed to before the end of this chapter) and to expand your programs. After all, no one sits down and writes an entire finished programming opus in one sitting. Programs are built one piece at a time.

Reedit the source code for STOP.C. Add a second `puts()` function below the first:

```
puts("Missing fragus found in memory.");
```

This is the *verbose* line. A normal error message is quick and to the point — often, just a number. But a verbose error message explains what's going on.

Save the modified STOP.C source code to disk; no need to give it a new name. Recompile and run it again. Here's the new output:

```
Stop: Unable to stop.
Missing fragus found in memory.
```

Ouch! How can you contain your laughter?

Printing text with `printf()`

Another C language function that displays text on the screen is `printf()`, which is far more powerful than `puts()` and used more often. Although the `puts()` function merely puts text to the screen (put-screen), the `printf()` function prints formatted text (print-formatted). This gives you more control over the output, as I demonstrate in later chapters.

The following source code is for HELLO.C, which is traditionally the name given to the first C language program you write — but not in this twisted tome:

```
#include <stdio.h>

int main()
{
    printf("Sorry, can't talk now.");
    printf("I'm busy!");
    return(0);
}
```

Type this code into your editor. Be careful how you spell `printf`; it's an easy name to "typo."

Save it to disk as HELLO.C. Compile. Run.

```
Sorry, can't talk now.I'm busy!
```

Often, your intentions as a programmer (or even a computer user) are one thing, yet the computer, because it's very specific, sees reality instead. This is a case of "Do what I mean!" You probably assumed that by putting two `printf()` statements on separate lines, two different lines of text would be displayed. Wrong!

Introducing the newline, `\n`

The newline character, `\n`, is "displayed" when you press the Enter key on your keyboard. It's not really a displayable character, but rather a control code or control character. When you display a newline character, it causes the cursor to drop down to the start of the next line.

The `puts()` function automatically appends a newline character at the end of any text it displays. The `printf()` function does not. Instead, you must manually insert the newline character into your text. This begs the question of how to stick the Enter key press into your source code.

You see, the problem of entering nonstandard characters is an old one, and the wise folks who created the C language have already thought of the solution: an escape sequence.

An *escape sequence* begins with the seldom-used \ (backslash) character. It signals to the C language output mechanism that the character that follows is special. In this case, \n is the escape sequence for a newline or Enter key press. The compiler doesn't see \n as two characters, but rather as one.

Reedit the HELLO.C source code. Change Line 5 as follows:

```
printf("Sorry, can't talk now.\n");
```

The escape sequence \n is added after the period. It's before the final double quote because the newline character needs to be part of the string that's displayed.

If you have a color-coded editor, notice that the \n takes on its own, unique color, illustrating that it's a special character and isn't displayed like the rest of the text.

Save the change to disk. Recompile HELLO.C. Run. Now the output is formatted more to your liking:

```
Sorry, can't talk now.
I'm busy!
```

Other escape sequences exist as well, allowing you to insert a variety of special characters and controls into any bit of text (not just in printf() functions). They're all listed in Appendix F, and many of them are introduced elsewhere in this book.

Adding Comments, Remarks, and Suggestions

A part of the C language doesn't do anything as far as programming is concerned. Like other programming languages, C gives you the ability to insert comments in your code. The comments are skipped over by the compiler, but remain in the source code as a way for you to jot down notes, your intentions, general information, or rude remarks about your customers.

/* C language comments */

In the C language, comments are enclosed between two sets of characters. The first is /* and the last is */. Everything between those two is ignored by the compiler:

```
/* The compiler will ignore this. La-di-da! */
```

Note that both characters are required. Unlike other programming languages, C doesn't limit comments to a single line or from a certain position to the end of a line. No, comments in C are more like a marked block (or selected text) in a word processor; the comment has a beginning and an end. This can cause some confusion, especially if you're not using a color-coded editor. (In a color-coded editor, commented text shows up as one color, making it easy to see where a /* or */ is misplaced.)

The most basic form of comment is a source code heading, which they make you add in school mostly to help identify who you are and because university professors enjoy comments more than some employers do in the real world.

The following program is a reworking of the STOP.C program from earlier in this chapter. Load up STOP.C into your editor and add the comments shown here:

```
/* STOP.C source code. By Dan Gookin. February 26, 2009 */

#include <stdio.h>

int main()
{

/* NOTE: added a beep to the following line
   The \a is the Alert or bell character */

    puts("\aStop: Unable to stop.");
    puts("Missing fragus found in memory.");

    return(0);
}
```

Two major chunks of comments have been added. The first is at the top of the source code. This heading is used to identify the program, the programmer, and the date. Often, other information is put in there as well, depending on the circumstances under which the program was written. It's just basic information, perhaps useful later, when you may be perusing the source code and wonder what the heck you were thinking. (It may even be a good idea to list in the comments what medications you're on.)

The second comment chunk is at Lines 8 and 9. By having the /* start at one line and the */ end at another, the single comment is able to span the two lines. Note what the comment says: The puts() function in Line 11 has been modified by prefixing the \a escape sequence to the start of the text.

Compile and run the program. Notice that the output is nearly the same, except for the BEEP! The comments don't add anything to the size of the program, nor do they slow down the code. They're just notes or suggestions for you or any other programmer who may work on the code again later.

Using comments to disable code

Because the compiler ignores anything flagged as a comment, you can use comments to disable portions of your code. For example:

```c
#include <stdio.h>

int main()
{
    printf("The First Soloist\n\n");   /* Extra blank line */
    printf("Vocalist Mary McDiva\n");
/*  printf("Song, "Under the Sea."\n"); */
    return(0);
}
```

Enter this source code into your editor. Double-check everything because you can make plenty of potential errors with all the comments and different ways to spell `printf`. Save the source code to disk as SOLOIST.C

Compile and run:

```
The First Soloist

Vocalist Mary McDiva
```

Because the third `printf()` in Line 7 is *commented out*, it doesn't display its text. The compiler just hops right over that code and discovers the `return(0);`, which ends the program.

In real life, Line 7 most likely produced an error. Because the programmer didn't know what caused the error (or didn't have time to fully investigate), he chose instead to comment out that line. Here's a more appropriate method of doing it:

```c
/* The following line doesn't work for some reason:
    printf("Song, "Under the Sea."\n"); */
```

Note that in this example, the line is still commented out, but extra text was added to explain why — a useful example of a descriptive comment.

Exercise 1.3.1

Write a program named MINE. This program displays the text `This com-puter belongs to` followed by your name, address, and phone number. Be sure to include a comment heading to list your name and the date, but also to describe why you think such a program would be necessary.

Watch out for nested comments!

Because C's comments start and end with specific characters, you cannot put one comment inside another. This is known as "nesting."

For example, Figure 3-1 shows how the compiler sees the source code for SOLOIST.C (from the preceding section). Note how the commented parts of the code are grayed out? That's the part the compiler ignores as a comment.

Figure 3-1:
Comments
are ignored
by the
compiler.

```
#include <stdio.h>

int main()
{
        printf ("The First Soloist\n\n");        /* Extra blank line */
        printf ("Vocalist Mary McDiva\n");
/*      printf ("Song, "Under the Sea."\n"); */
        return(0);
}
```

Now suppose that the programmer goes back and adds a reason for the comment — and pay special attention to what is done:

```
#include <stdio.h>

int main()
{
    printf("The First Soloist\n\n");   /* Extra blank line */
    printf("Vocalist Mary McDiva\n");

/* Can't get this following line to compile:
 * /*  printf("Song, "Under the Sea."\n"); */
 * displays some kind of error
 */

    return(0);
}
```

Despite the fancy, lined-up asterisks at the start of each line, the block of four lines is *not* a comment. The programmer probably intended for that entire section to be a comment and to be ignored by the compiler, but Figure 3-2 illustrates what really happens.

In Figure 3-2, you see that the first time the compiler encounters the */ characters, it assumes that the commented section is over, so it continues to compile the text that's left. That's where the errors happen.

```
#include <stdio.h>

int main()
{
        printf ("The First Soloist\n\n");          /* Extra blank line */
        printf ("Vocalist Mary McDiva\n");

        /* Can't get this following line to compile:
         * /* printf ("Song, "Under the Sea. "\n"); */
         * displays some kind of error
         */

        return(0);
}
```

Figure 3-2:
The nested comment doesn't work as intended.

Comment start

Ack!
Oop!
Eeek!

Comment end

The moral of the story is to remember that the /* starts a comment and */ ends the comment. If you stick one comment inside another, called *nesting* the comments, something bad happens.

By the way, this situation is easy to see when your editor color-codes your text. For example, in the VIM editor, comments appear blue on my screen. If I forget to end a comment or accidentally nest a comment, I can see the blue text spill over into areas where I don't want it. That way, those types of errors are easy to spot and fix.

Another way to comment text

In C++, a comment begins with two slashes, //, and extends to the end of the line. It's good for only one line, but like the /* and */ comments in C, everything after // in C++ is considered a comment and is ignored by the compiler. For example:

```
printf("The First
    Soloist\n\n");   // Extra
    blank line
```

The double-slash characters mark the beginning of the comment, and the end of the line is the end of the comment:

```
// Can't get this following
    line to compile:
```

```
//   printf("Song, "Under the
    Sea."\n"); */
// displays some kind of error
```

Each of these lines is a comment, ignored by the compiler. This example shows how you can disable code by using the C++ style of comments.

Most C compilers I have used support this C++ convention. The problem is that some may not. So, until all C compilers understand the // comment convention, avoid using them. (I stick with traditional-style comments in this book.)

Fixing a double-quote problem

The problem with the SOLOIST program is that the programmer is trying to display a double-quote character inside a string of text:

```
/* printf("Song, "Under the Sea."\n"); */
```

If you have a text editor that displays the code in color, you can instantly see what's wrong; the double quotes are used to mark the beginning and end of the text string. By putting double-quote characters *inside* the string, it ends prematurely. Figure 3-3 illustrates how it looks in case you don't have a text editor that displays color-coded text.

Figure 3-3:
How double quotes can goof up a string of text.

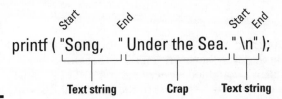

In C, strings of text are enclosed in double quotes. The double quotes aren't part of the string, but are used to mark the beginning and end. To stick a double quote into the middle of that string, you need to use the same trick you used for inserting the newline (the Enter key press): an escape character.

In the case of the double quote, the escape character is \". Those two characters combine to stick a rogue double quote in the middle of a string without affecting the characters used to mark the beginning and end of the string.

Bring up into your text editor the source code for SOLOIST.C. Edit Line 7 to read:

```
printf("Song, \"Under the Sea.\"\n");
```

First, remove the comment characters. Second, insert a backslash before the double-quote characters inside the text string. If you have a color-coded editor, notice that the complete string is now in one color. Furthermore, the \" escape sequences may be marked as such, indicating that they're a single character and not the \ and " characters separately.

Save the changes to disk. Compile and run the completed program.

Debugging

The art of fixing a broken program is generally referred to as *debugging,* as in "getting the bugs out." This is something that happens often; specifically, as you start to create your own programs and venture into new programming areas, such as networking and graphics. The more complex the program, the more likely debugging is required.

You have to deal with four types of errors in your programs:

✦ Compiler errors

✦ Linker errors

✦ Runtime errors

✦ Bugs

These errors happen to *everyone.* Only the most experienced, clever programmers can lie that they have written code that works perfectly and is done the first time it's compiled. Otherwise, the rest of us must accept and deal with errors continually — almost to the point that it should be called debugging and not programming.

Compiler error: This type of error is caught before the program is created, even before object code is made. A compiler error is typically caused by a typo or bad syntax, such as a forgotten semicolon, comma, or parenthesis or a misplaced quote mark. The good news is that this type of error is easy to fix. The bad news is that it's the most common.

Linker error: This type of error occurs as a program is being built. The linker cannot find the function you mentioned, which means that either a module is missing or — most likely — you mistyped some function name. Like a compiler error, this type of error is easy to fix.

Runtime error: This type of error happens when you run the program. Your source code compiles and links, but when the program runs, it does something unpredictable or perhaps even locks up the computer. The bad news is that this type of error (often a flaw in your program flow or thinking) is common. The worse news is that it's hard to fix.

Bugs: A bug is a minor quirk or unexpected thing that occurs when you run your program. Bugs are as common as runtime errors, and can be easy to fix if they're predictable. Then again, some bugs have eluded programmers for years.

Prepare to fail

I have purposely chocked the following source code full of errors. Type it as written — despite what you see — so that you can get a feel for the major types of errors that occur in C programming:

```
#include <stdio.h>

int main()
{
    print("Hello, geek!\n")
    return;
}
```

Type this code *exactly* — even if something appears wrong. The idea is to learn by making mistakes, so mistakes are being made! Save the code to disk as OOPS.C.

Compile. Yes, you have errors. You have compiler errors, which happen first because compiling happens first (refer to Chapter 2). The specific messages differ, depending on the compiler. Here are the samples from my office:

```
oops.c: In function `main':
oops.c:6: parse error before "return"
```

Over on the FreeBSD machine, the message reads:

```
oops.c: In function `main':
oops.c:6: syntax error before `return'
```

Both messages mean the same thing. A *parse* error means that a required (or expected) part of the C language is missing. A syntax error is essentially the same thing. Even so, both error messages are full of useful information.

The first line tells you in which function the error was found. Because your program is small, it's the main() function. As your programs grow larger, and you create more functions, this information is useful in helping you track things down.

Even more important, the second line gives the line number in your source code where the error was discovered: Line 6. Further, the error is described as occurring before return. Unlike your seventh-grade math teacher, the compiler is being precise about when your thinking fell apart.

Reedit the OOPS.C source code. Use your editor to jump to Line 6, as described by the error message. (In VIM, type **6G** to jump to Line 6.) But Line 6 isn't where the error is; the message says before 'return', so the error is, in fact, on Line 5. This is okay; at least the compiler was close.

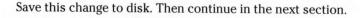

The error is a missing semicolon at the end of Line 5. Go ahead and add the semicolon, making the line look like this:

```
print("Hello, geek!\n");
```

Save this change to disk. Then continue in the next section.

Often, the error that's reported occurs on the line before the line number given in the error message.

Dealing with linker errors

To continue from the preceding section, compile the fixed source code for OOPS.C. Again, you get an error, but this time, it's a linker error:

```
ccmIaaaa.o(.text+0x36):oops.c: undefined reference to 'print'
```

Here's another version of the same error message:

```
/tmp/ccJnx8c3.o: in function `main':
/tmp/ccJnx8c3.o(.text+0xf): undefined reference to `print'
```

The key is the .o in the message — .O for *o*bject code file. Because gcc deletes the object code file, a temporary filename is used — so you may have to look hard to find the .o in there. But the result is fairly plain: The linker has looked for and not found any function named print. Yes, it's a typo.

Other types of linker errors are possible, but typos are the most common. To fix them, simply reedit the source code and fix the misspelling. Note that no line number is given (because object code files don't have them), so you may have to use the editor's Search command to find the booboo. In OOPS.C, edit Line 7 to fix the error:

```
printf("Hello, geek!/n");
```

The proper function name is printf(), not print(). Fix this mistake, and then save the source code back to disk. Compile. At last, the program compiles. But does it run? Keep reading in the next section.

Runtime errors and bugs

Most programmers get that waxing glow after a successful compile. But it's a mistake! The true test is if the sucker *runs*. You may survive a slew of compiler and linker errors, only to discover that your program is riddled with bugs — or, worse, runtime errors.

At this stage in your budding C programming career, I don't saddle you with a runtime error on purpose. You get enough later. But I do include a bug in the OOPS.C source code.

Go ahead and run the OOPS program, created in the preceding section:

```
Hello, geek!/n
```

Obviously, the /n was not intended as part of the text to be displayed. This is a bug. It's not fatal, but it needs to be fixed.

Open your editor again and fix the OOPS.C source code. Change the slash in Line 5 to a backslash. This change properly creates the newline escape sequence, \n:

```
printf("Hello, geek!\n");
```

Save the change to disk. Compile. Run. It should be — dare I say it? — perfect!

Error messages subtle and gross

Several degrees of errors are possible when you're writing C programs. You can make minor and major offenses as well as warning errors and fatal errors.

Warning errors are violations of protocol or, often, questionable acts that may or may not affect how a program runs.

Fatal errors prevent the program from being compiled because the errors are just too terrible to behold! This type of error is illustrated in the previous sections.

Some warning errors are nitpicky, so the compiler doesn't display them unless you demand that it does. In gcc, you can use the -Wall option to display all the warning errors that are possible when you compile your code.

For example, you use this command line to compile the original OOPS.C source code:

```
gcc -Wall oops.c
```

These error messages are generated:

```
oops.c: In function `main':
oops.c:5: warning: implicit declaration of function `print'
oops.c:6: warning: `return' with no value, in function
    returning non-void
```

These warning messages literally say "Warning." The first one tells you that the function `print` has no prototype in the source code (because it's a misspelling). Even so, prototyping `print()` doesn't work because it's a misspelling, not a reference to a function that merely lacks a prototype.

The second error recommends that `return` truly return a value, which is a good idea, but not one that causes your computer any brain damage.

Serious programmers heed these warning errors, often keeping the `-Wall` option (or whatever setting is required for their compiler) permanent. Even though they're mere warnings, it's still good programming practice to create code that's as trouble-free as possible.

Chapter 4: Introducing Numbers and Variables

In This Chapter

✓ Using and understanding integers

✓ Dealing with floating-point values

✓ Declaring `int` variables

✓ Knowing when to use `float` variables

✓ Declaring multiple variables

✓ Immediately assigning values to variables

✓ Mathematical operator summary

The computer has the desktop calculator as one of its ancestors, so one of the major aspects of programming a computer has to deal with numbers. This isn't anything scary; just like the calculator, the computer figures the result. You merely need to supply the numbers and the proper equation for the computer to do its thing. As a B- math student, I can promise you that doing math on a computer isn't an ordeal.

Programming in C does involve using numbers. To make things easier on the computer, different types of numbers are used in C, and it's important — but not difficult — to know which is which. Besides the numbers, things called *variables* are used, which are storage places for values unknown. As with numbers, different types of variables are used, depending on what's being stored inside them. This chapter introduces you to the basic concepts of numbers and variables.

Going Numb with Numbers

There are numbers large and small. If you're lucky, you may remember terms from high school math class, like whole number and fraction and decimal part. If you stayed awake in your later school years, you may even recall rational numbers and irrational numbers and maybe even imaginary numbers. Happily, you can freely ignore all that crap here.

In C, you use only two different types of numbers: integers and floating-point.

The joys of integers

Integers are whole numbers. They have no fractional or decimal parts. Back in math class, these were referred as whole numbers, though on the computer, integers can be negative, positive, or zero.

Type this source code into your editor. Save it to disk as INTEGER.C. Compile and run:

```
#include <stdio.h>

int main()
{
    printf("Here's your integer value %d.\n",123);
    return(0);
}
```

Here's the output:

```
Here's your integer value 123.
```

The `printf()` function displays the integer value 123. You could have written it like this:

```
printf("Here's your integer value 123.\n");
```

Here, 123 is part of a text string — not a value. In C, there's a difference. To make 123 a value, it must be specified without double quotes. The compiler then recognizes 123 as an *immediate* value, or a number that's just used right away for convenience sake.

The `%d` in the `printf()` statement's string is an *integer placeholder*. This is a glimpse into the power of `printf()`; the `%d` is replaced by an integer value specified later in `printf()`'s parentheses. For example:

```
printf("formatting string with %d in it",value_for_%d);
```

In this line, the text that `printf()` displays is merely a *formatting string*. If it has a `%d` in it, the `printf()` function looks beyond the formatting string (and a comma) for the value to substitute for `%d`.

Return to your editor and modify the `printf()` statement (Line 5) in INTE-GER.C so that it reads:

```
printf("Here's your integer value %d.\n",123+543);
```

You see 123+543 as the value for %d to display. But 123+543 isn't a value — it's a math problem. The compiler sees *two* values: 123 and 543. But because the + operator is sandwiched between them, the computer adds both values, comes up with a result, and then substitutes that result for %d. This is known as *immediate addition*. In C, that happens first, and then the value is used in printf() second.

Save the changes to disk. Compile and run. Here's the output:

```
Here's your integer value 666.
```

Quick! Call the Vatican!

Seriously, the value 666 is the result of adding 123 and 543, which the computer does without complaining. The result is then displayed.

Subtracting values in C makes as much sense as adding them. Consider the following modification to the INTEGER.C source code:

```
#include <stdio.h>

int main()
{
    printf("Shakespeare lived %d years.\n",1616-1564);
    return(0);
}
```

This time, the printf() statement contains some immediate math: integer subtraction. The minus sign is used to subtract the value 1564 (Shakespeare's birth year) from 1616 (the year he died). Compile and run the program to see the result.

(The full list of placeholder characters is kept in Appendix G.)

Exercise 1.4.1

Modify the INTEGER.C program again. This time, have it calculate when Sigmund Grockmeister will be 75 years old. He was born in 1952. Fix the printf() text string to reflect the new calculation.

Flying high with floating-point numbers

Although integers deftly handle the realm of whole numbers, for fractions and decimals you need to use floating-point numbers. It isn't that tough; merely entering a number with a fractional part tells the compiler that a floating-point value is being used rather than an integer, such as in the following program:

```
#include <stdio.h>

int main()
{
    printf("It's %f miles to the crematorium.\n",13.5);
    return(0);
}
```

Save the source code to disk as CREAM.C. Compile and run. Here's the output on my monitor:

```
It's 13.500000 miles to the crematorium.
```

The %f placeholder is used in printf() to display floating-point, or fractional, values, such as 13.5. (Don't let the extra zeroes bother you; I show you a fix in Book II, Chapter 2.)

As with integers, you can do math with floating-point numbers. You can add, subtract, multiply, and divide them, you can do it immediately, as shown here:

```
#include <stdio.h>

int main()
{
    printf("Two trips to the crematorium is %f
    miles.\n",13.5*2);
    return(0);
}
```

Edit the source code for CREAM.C, and make these modifications to Line 5. (In this book, the line "wraps"; in your editor, be sure to type it all on the same line.) The math performed is 13.5 multiplied by 2. In C, the symbol for multiplication is the asterisk (*), not the X character or ×.

Save the changes to disk, and then recompile and run.

```
Two trips to the crematorium is 27.000000 miles.
```

The result displayed is still a floating-point number. It could be an integer because 27 is an integer. But internally, the value is represented inside the computer as a floating-point number. (To prove it, replace the %f in the program with %d, used to display integers. Recompile and run to see a different result.)

The real difference between integers and floats (and when to use one or the other)

If a floating-point value can also be a whole number, why bother using integers in your programs? The reason is that floating-point values and integers are handled differently inside the computer.

An integer exists inside the computer as a true binary value. For example, the value 123 is stored in modern computers as a 32-bit value:

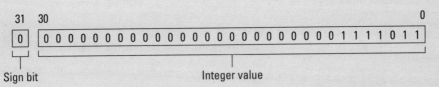

The sign bit determines whether the value is positive or negative (0 is positive, and 1 is negative). The rest of the 31 bits are used to represent the value.

A floating-point number, however, cannot exist in a computer that uses binary (1s and 0s). Don't be silly! So, the floating-point number is cleverly faked. Using the same 32 bits, a floating-point value of 13.5 might look like this:

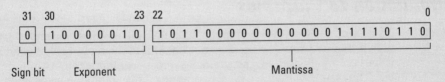

First comes the sign bit: 1 for negative or 0 for positive. The exponent is used with the mantissa in a complex and mystical manner to fake floating-point values in binary. (If you're curious, you can search for *floating-point binary* on the Internet and find some excellent tutorials that may or may not clear it up.)

The bottom line is that it takes more work for the computer to figure out binary problems than it does for the computer to work in integers. So, wherever possible, use integer values and use the floating-point numbers only when necessary.

(In the early days of C programming, you often had to link in a special floating-point library if your program used floating-point values. Most compilers now can handle floating-point numbers without this extra step.)

Finally, you come face to face with division. To do division in C, you use the / symbol. Like the * for multiplication, it's common to other programming languages and spreadsheets (besides, the keyboard has no ÷ symbol):

```
#include <stdio.h>

int main()
{
    printf("I'm halfway to the crematorium, %f
    miles.\n",13.5/2);
    return(0);
}
```

Use your editor to make the changes to CREAM.C. Save. Compile. Run.

```
I'm halfway to the crematorium, 6.750000 miles.
```

Note that whenever you divide any two numbers, regardless of whether they're integers or floats, the result is most often a float.

Exercise 1.4.2

To handle the overflow after flu season, they just built a new crematorium on the other side of town. It's 19.2 miles away. Write a program that calculates how much farther away the new crematorium is from the old one.

Introduction to Variables

It's no surprise that the computer can do math. The simple examples earlier in this chapter prove the point somewhat. But in the real world, immediate values are rarely used in a program. Instead, programmers use variables to hold the results of mathematical operations. This technique helps add flexibility to the program, and it can also help make the source code more readable.

Creating variables

A *variable* is a storage place in memory. It's like a cubbyhole in which you can store a value. The value stays in the cubbyhole and can be used at any time, or the value can be replaced with another value. Because the values can vary, the storage place is called a variable.

To make a variable in C, you must tell the compiler to set aside a chunk of memory for storage. Specifically, you must tell the compiler what type of value will be stored, and then a storage place is created specifically for that type of value.

Suppose that your program needs to store your age in years. Because your age in years is a whole number — an integer type of value — you need an integer variable to store that value. In C, you do it with the int command:

```
int age;
```

This statement directs the compiler to set aside storage for an integer variable and give it the name `age`. The line ends in a semicolon because it's a complete C language statement.

```
float distance;
```

This statement directs the compiler to set aside storage for a floating-point value. The variable is named `distance`.

Variables are traditionally declared at the start of your source code. This isn't a necessity; but you must declare a variable *before* it's used. One of the most common errors programmers make is to use a variable and then forget to declare it:

```
#include <stdio.h>

int main()
{
    int age;
    float distance;

    printf("The alien is %d years old and\n",age);
    printf("comes from a planet %f microns
    away.\n",distance);
    return(0);
}
```

This source code declares two variables: `age` and `distance`. It then uses them in the `printf()` statements to display their values. This example works just like the ones earlier in this chapter — rather than use immediate values, though, the contents of the variables are used.

Save this file to disk as ALIEN.C. Compile and run. The results should surprise you!

Assigning values to variables

Unlike some other programming languages, when the C compiler sets aside storage for a variable, it doesn't *initialize* that storage. It's up to you to assign a value to the variable before it's used. Otherwise, the variable contains whatever random junk was in memory when the compiler set aside the storage space. The preceding section demonstrates.

In the ALIEN.C program from the preceding section, the variables `age` and `distance` are declared, but never initialized or assigned values. For this reason, random data or garbage is used for the values. Obviously, this isn't the type of program you want to write.

In the C language, an equal sign is used to assign a value to a variable, as in

```
age = 27;
```

In this line, the value 27 is assigned to the integer variable `age`.

The value 319.125 is assigned to the floating-point variable `distance`:

```
distance = 319.125;
```

Reedit the source code for ALIEN.C so that it looks like this:

```
#include <stdio.h>

int main()
{
    int age;
    float distance;

    age = 27;
    distance = 319.125;

    printf("The alien is %d years old and\n",age);
    printf("comes from a planet %f microns
away.\n",distance);
    return(0);
}
```

In this source code, two statements are added (Lines 8 and 9) that assign values to the variables used. Save it to disk, and then compile and run.

Alas, in this particular example, there is little difference between using variables and using immediate values. The real benefit to using variables is to hold unknown or changing values until the program runs.

Using an `int` variable

You can use the awesome power of the computer to figure out how much older you will be in five years. Witness this potent program:

```
#include <stdio.h>

int main()
{
    int age;

    age = 43;                 /* put your age here */
    printf("You are %d years old.\n",age);
    printf("In five years you'll be %d years old!\n",age+5);
    printf("But today you're still %d years old.\n",age);
```

```
    return(0);
}
```

Copy this source code into your editor. Be sure to enter your own age on Line 7. Save the thing to disk as AGE.C. Compile and run. Here's what I saw:

```
You are 43 years old.
In five years you'll be 48 years old!
But today you're still 43 years old.
```

Note that adding 5 to `age` at the end of the second `printf()` function doesn't affect the value stored in `age`. As with immediate values, 5 was merely added to the value stored in `age`, and the calculation's results are displayed by `printf()`. The third `printf()` statement proves that the `age` variable's value hasn't changed.

Changing a variable's contents

Variables are variable! Their contents can change. To prove it, consider the following source code, which is a modification of AGE.C from the preceding section:

```
#include <stdio.h>

int main()
{
    int age;

    age = 43;               /* put your age here */
    printf("You are %d years old.\n",age);
    age = age + 5;
    printf("In five years you'll be %d years old!\n",age);
    return(0);
}
```

Copy this source code into your editor. Be sure to enter your own age on Line 7. Save the thing to disk again, and then compile and run:

```
You are 43 years old.
In five years you'll be 48 years old!
```

In this example, the value of variable `age` is increased by 5 in Line 9:

```
age = age + 5;
```

First comes the math: The computer adds 5 to the value stored in `age` with `age + 5`. In the example, the math works out to 48. That value is then stored in the `age` variable. Because the computer works out the math on the *right* side of the equal sign first, nothing explodes.

Explosions or not, the point is that variables can be used over and over and their values can change throughout the program.

Exercise 1.4.3

Write a program that subtracts 20 pounds from your weight and displays the result humorously.

Using a float variable

Suppose that the moon is now 378,921.46 kilometers from the Earth. (According to the Moon People I have met, the moon's true distance varies). How long would it take to drive that distance if your car can do 140 kilometers per hour?

Never mind! Let the computer do the work:

```
#include <stdio.h>

int main()
{
    float duration;

    duration = 378921.46 / 140;

    printf("It would take %f hours to drive to the
moon.\n",duration);
    return(0);
}
```

Note that you type the value 378,921.46 without a comma. Remember that! Numbers don't have commas in your source code! If you forget and stick them in there, the compiler barfs.

Save the source code to disk as MOON.C. Compile and run.

```
It would take 2706.581787 hours to drive to the moon.
```

Better pack a snack.

Using multiple variables

Rather than use the immediate values in MOON.C, you could just specify variables. Despite the fact that the immediate values don't change, using variables does make the code more readable; for example:

```
float duration;
float distance;
float speed;
```

```
distance = 378921.46;
speed = 140;

duration =  distance / speed;
```

In this example, two new `float` variables are created, `distance` and `speed`, which are then assigned values. Finally, the new variables are used to calculate the value of `duration`, which helps make the program more readable. But that's not the entire lesson.

As you often discover, the C language is full of shortcuts. Here, you can save yourself some lines by combining the `float` variable declarations all on one line, as in

```
float duration,distance,speed;
```

This declaration tells the compiler to set aside space for three `float` variables, named `duration`, `distance`, and `speed`. (Multiple `int` variables can also be declared this way.)

Here's the modified program:

```
#include <stdio.h>

int main()
{
    float duration,distance,speed;

    distance = 378921.46;
    speed = 140;

    duration = distance / speed;

    printf("It would take %f hours to drive to the
    moon.\n",duration);
    return(0);
}
```

The source code now declares three variables on one line; plus, by using well-named variables rather than immediate values, you make the equation (Line 10) more readable: `duration = distance / speed;`.

Reedit the source code for MOON.C and make the preceding modifications. Save to disk, and then compile and run:

```
It would take 2706.582031 hours to drive to the moon.
```

Time to discuss precision

You may have observed that it took 2,706.581787 hours to drive to the moon with the first version of MOON.C and then, for some reason, it took 2,706.582031 hours in the second version. Why the two different values?

The answer is *precision*. If you have read the earlier sidebar in this chapter, "The real difference between integers and floats," you should recall that the computer must use binary to keep track of floating-point values. This technique is only so accurate. The precision of the number is considered to be only six or seven digits long. The result of any floating-point operation is accurate, therefore, to only six or seven digits. The rest of the result is meaningless crap.

For example, in the MOON program, only 2706.58 (six digits) of the number is correct. The rest is silly stuff made up by the computer. Generally speaking, that's considered okay. Float variables are precise to six or seven digits, which often is enough. If you need more, you can use other variable types, which I introduce later in this book. For now, six digits is enough.

By the way, the programs produced two different results because of the way the distance value was handled. First, it's used as an immediate value. Second, it's stored in a variable and then used. This subtle difference is enough to change the "noise" that appears at the end of the floating-point result.

Immediately declaring a variable's value

In C, you can have the luxury of often doing several things in a single statement. You have already seen this feat earlier in this chapter:

```
printf("Here's your integer value %d.\n",123+543);
```

You could have written this line using a variable total, as in

```
int total;

total = 123+543;
printf("Here's your integer value %d.\n",total);
```

Instead, immediate values were used. The result is the same, but it shows how C can combine statements to save space.

Another way to do this is to assign variables values as they're declared; for example:

```
float duration;
float distance = 378921.46;
float speed = 140;
```

Rather than declare everything on one line (as shown in the preceding section), the variables in this example are individually declared. As a bonus for declaring the variables on separate lines, the distance and speed variables can be preassigned their known values. This idea is optional, but it saves a few steps. (And you can do this with ints or any C language variable declaration.)

This example shows you the improved MOON.C source code, which also shows some sprucing up:

```c
#include <stdio.h>

int main()
{
    float duration;
    float distance = 378921.46;
    float speed = 140;

    duration =  distance / speed;

    printf("The moon is %f km away.\n",distance);
    printf("Traveling at %f kph, ",speed);
    printf("it would take %f hours to drive to the
moon.\n",duration);
    return(0);
}
```

Reedit your MOON.C source code to look like what's shown here. Save. Compile. Fix any bugs. Run.

```
The moon is 378921.468750 km away.
Traveling at 140.000000 kph, It would take 2706.582031 hours
    to drive to the moon.
```

Refer to the nearby sidebar "Time to discuss precision" for information on the bogus values that appear in the fractional part of the moon's distance.

Exercise 1.4.4
Redo the last incarnation of the MOON.C program, and this time also display how many days the trip would take. *Hint:* There are 24 hours in a day.

The Official Introduction to Basic Math Operators

This chapter uses basic math operators without officially introducing them. Here's your introduction!

There are four basic mathematical operations and four C language operators that go with them, according to Table 4-1.

Table 4-1	Basic C Language Math Operators	
Operator	*Performs*	*Programming examples*
+	Addition	`result=45+60;` `total = test1 + test2 + test3;`
-	Subtraction	`age = 1616 - 1564;` `difference = finish - start;`
*	Multiplication	`pixels = 600 * 800;` `roll = dice1 * dice2;`
/	Division	`portions = 255 / 13;` `score = points / time;`

The operators can be used on variables or immediate values.

In C, the math is performed first, and then the result is used for the rest of the statement; for example:

```
printf("Here's your integer value %d.\n",123+543);
```

In this line, the addition of 123 and 543 is performed first. The result, 666, is then used in the `printf()` statement:

```
age = age + 5;
```

The calculation of `age+5` is done first, and then the result is saved into the `age` variable. Because this calculation is done in two steps, the compiler doesn't explode or get confused about which value should be stored in the variable `age`. (A shortcut for this form of equation is presented in Book I, Chapter 9.)

Chapter 5: More Variables and Basic I/O

In This Chapter

- ✔ Using single characters
- ✔ Introducing the `char` variable type
- ✔ Displaying characters with `putchar()`
- ✔ Creating tiny integer variables with `char`
- ✔ Using the `getchar()` function
- ✔ Reading the keyboard with `gets()`
- ✔ Understanding the `scanf()` function

Chapter 4 introduces two types of C language variables, the `int` and the `float`, which are both numeric types of variables. But the C language isn't all about math. Another type of variable comes in handy when you're dealing with text. That's the good old `char`, or character, variable type, which I introduce in this chapter.

When you start dealing with character variables in C, you must inevitably stumble into the garden of I/O, or input/output. The computer's primary input device is the keyboard. The primary output device is the monitor, or screen. Chapters 1 through 4 show you how to output text to the screen. In this chapter, and thanks to the ability of the `char` variable to hold characters, you can now read input from the keyboard.

The Good Ol' `char` Variable

Whether you pronounce it "car" or "care" (but not "char"), the `char` variable type is used in the C language to define storage space for one itty-bitty character. That may seem silly, but you did learn the alphabet one character at a time. As in real life, small things in a computer are used to build bigger things. If you ever plan to use a program that deals in words or language, the `char` variable sooner or later becomes your friend.

Presenting the single character

A single character is quite a powerful beast in C. Unlike regular life, where single people are forced to meet each other through awkward introductions, blind dates, or old when-I-was-thin images on Internet dating systems, single characters inside the computer can be quite popular.

Elsewhere in this book, you can see strings of text defined by double quotes, as in

```
puts("I am a string of text, la-di-da.");
```

Single characters, on the other hand, are embraced by single quotes:

```
'A'
```

The single character A is specified. Or, consider this:

```
'\n'
```

The escape sequence \n is specified as a single character. That's the escape sequence for newline, which is equivalent to the Enter key. (The '\n' may be used in some program to check whether the Enter key was pressed.)

But, just like strings of text in double quotes, the character must be used somewhere; for example:

```
#include <stdio.h>

int main()
{
    printf("This program is sponsored by the letter
    %c\n",'P');
    return(0);
}
```

Enter this source code into your editor. Save it to disk as SPONSOR.C. Compile and run.

```
This program is sponsored by the letter P
```

The printf() statement uses the %c — c for *char* — to display the single character P (or, officially, the *immediate character value* P).

Note that although P is enclosed in single quotes, those single quotes don't show up in the output. That's because the format string part of the printf() statement doesn't include them.

Exercise 1.5.1

Fix the SPONSOR.C source code so that the output displays single quote marks around the letter P.

Single quotes are holy too

Double quotes are used to hug strings, and single quotes are used to hug single characters. And, just as the double-quote character is special inside a string, the single-quote character is special as a single character; for example:

```
printf("Song, \"Under the Sea.\"\n");
```

The \" escape sequence is used to place a double-quote character in the middle of a string. Similarly, if you want to use a single quote character, you specify it as

```
'\''
```

That's the \' escape sequence inside single quotes. This modification to the SPONSOR.C program demonstrates:

```
#include <stdio.h>

int main()
{
    printf("This program is sponsored by the letter
    %c%c%c\n",'\'','P','\'');
    return(0);
}
```

Don't let the cryptic looking printf() statement bother you. This example displays three single characters and uses three %c placeholders in a row to show them. Each of the single characters is specified in single quotes, with a single comma to separate the lot.

I have noticed in several versions of the VIM editor that the sequence '\'' isn't properly color coded, although the sequence ''' is. Ignore this error. If you use ''' to represent a single quote character, the compiler gets cross with you.

Save the modified SPONSOR.C program to disk. Compile and run:

```
This program is sponsored by the letter 'P'
```

See Appendix F for the full list of escape sequences and which characters they represent. Note that any of them can be specified in single quotes to represent a special character in your programs.

Here a char, *there a* char, *everywhere a* char char

Setting aside storage for a single character is done by the char keyword in the C language, just as int sets aside storage for an integer value and float sets aside storage for a floating-point value. The following program demonstrates how to create and use a char variable:

```
#include <stdio.h>

int main()
{
    char oz;

    oz = 'O';       /* the letter O */
    printf("This book covers subjects from %c",oz);
    oz = 'Z';
    printf(" to %c.\n",oz);
    return(0);
}
```

Save the source code to disk as OZ.C. Compile. Run.

```
This book covers subjects from O to Z.
```

(If you see from Oto Z in the output, you forgot the space before to in Line 10.)

The character variable oz is created in Line 5. But, like creating a numeric variable in C, the compiler doesn't initialize the value. You must *assign* the variable a value; oz is assigned the letter O in Line 7.

The variable's value is displayed by the printf() statement, but then it's changed in Line 9. The new value is displayed by the printf() statement in Line 10. This example demonstrates that, like numeric variables, char variables can also change their values.

Exercise 1.5.2

Modify the source to OZ.C so that the variable oz is declared *and* assigned the value O all on one line.

Displaying characters one at a time with putchar( )

If you need to display characters one at a time, you can use this variation of the printf() statement:

```
printf("%c",ch);
```

The char variable ch has its value displayed. But the printf() statement uses lots of overhead. A better, and more direct, method is to use the putchar() function, which "puts" a single character to the display, as this program demonstrates:

```
#include <stdio.h>

int main()
{
    putchar('H');
    putchar('e');
    putchar('l');
    putchar('l');
    putchar('o');
    putchar('!');
    putchar('\n');
    return(0);
}
```

Save the source code to disk as HI.C. Compile. Run.

```
Hello!
```

In real life, of course, it's just easier to display the entire string using one command, such as puts("Hello!");, which does the same thing. Then again, that wouldn't be showing you how to use the putchar() function, which is almost unmatched in its ability to display individual characters.

Using char *as a tiny integer value*

Sadly, no such thing as text inside a computer exists. Nope. Trust me on this one: I opened up a computer once and never found one gizmo or doodad that processes text. It's all numbers.

The special nature of the char is that its *value* is displayed as a character. Internally, the computer codes all displayable characters using the ASCII or UNICODE schemes. (Older computers used other schemes.) For example, when you display the letter *A,* internally the computer is using the value 65. According to the ASCII standard, value 65 represents the letter *A.* So, you see an A on the screen, but internally the computer is using old ho-hum value 65.

This program's source code offers a bit of insight into how this internal type of coding works:

```
#include <stdio.h>

int main()
```

```
{
    char alpha = 'A';

    printf("Character %c has code %d.\n",alpha,alpha);
    alpha = 'B';
    printf("Character %c has code %d.\n",alpha,alpha);
    alpha = 'C';
    printf("Character %c has code %d.\n",alpha,alpha);
    return(0);
}
```

Save this source code to disk as AVALUE.C. Compile and run.

```
Character A has code 65.
Character B has code 66.
Character C has code 67.
```

The char variable alpha is used twice in each printf() statement. The first
time, its value is displayed using %c, a character. The second time, its value
is displayed using %d, an integer. Again, internally the computer uses only
values to keep track of variables. What matters is how the char variable is
displayed.

To drive this point home further, make the following modifications to the
source code for ALPHA.C:

```
#include <stdio.h>

int main()
{
    char alpha = 'A';

    printf("Character %c has code %d.\n",alpha,alpha);
    alpha = alpha + 1;
    printf("Character %c has code %d.\n",alpha,alpha);
    alpha = alpha + 1;
    printf("Character %c has code %d.\n",alpha,alpha);
    return(0);
}
```

The only changes are in Lines 8 and 10. There, the variable alpha is merely
increased by a value of 1: First, alpha + 1 adds 1 to the value of alpha.
Then, that new value is assigned to the variable alpha. The printf() statement that follows displays the results as both a character and a value.

Save the changes to disk. Compile and run. The output is the same.

Mr. Integer has a first name

Although Chapter 4 introduces the int variable type and discusses briefly how it's used, one important fact is omitted: Like cars, planets, boxes of laundry detergent, and people, integer variables come in different sizes.

An integer in the C language can be one of two sizes: short or long. Technically, these sizes refer to the number of bits used to store the integer value; specifically:

A short integer uses 16 bits to store values from –32,768 through 32,767.

A long integer uses 32 bits to store values from –2,147,483,648 through 2,147,483,647.

On a modern computer, when you declare an int variable, it's typically the long type. On older computers (PCs before 1993 or so), int variables were of the short type. You can use short or long in the variable declaration if you want to be specific; for example:

```
short int age;
```

This example creates a short integer variable. The next example creates a long integer variable:

```
long int lotto_prize;
```

Some sources say that you can save space or increase program efficiency by specifically declaring short ints when you need them. Then again, I have heard that inside the computer's memory, all short ints are stored using four bytes rather than two, so that may be just bunk. My advice is merely to use int.

(Refer to Book II, Chapter 1 for more information on signed and unsigned integer values. Appendix E lists all C language variable types and their storage capacities.)

Although you can store values directly in a char variable, remember that it has a size limitation. The range of values you can store in char is only from –127 through 128. If you need to store values greater than those, use a regular int. (Information on the range of sizes for integers is provided in the preceding sidebar "Mr. Integer has a first name.")

Note that although this trick works with char variables, I don't recommend attempting to store characters in int or float variables, nor should you attempt to use them for displaying characters with %c. This trick is unique to the char variable.

Exercise 1.5.3

Dig up the AGE.C program from Book I, Chapter 4. Change it so that the age variable is declared a char rather than an int. Compile and run.

Getting Input from the Keyboard

Computers are all about the old I/O, input and output. You have seen a lot of output so far; therefore, it's about time to discover input. On the modern PC, you do that via the keyboard, which is also known as the *standard input device*. (The monitor is the *standard output device*.)

The C language has a few handy functions for reading text from the keyboard. The first half of this chapter introduces the char variable, which is important if you plan on storing the information read from the keyboard. This section divulges the details.

Reading the keyboard one key at a time

In C, the getchar() function reads characters from the keyboard one key at a time. It makes sense: After all, you type only one character at a time (unless you're angry and start beating the keyboard with your fists). And, if you have waded through the first half of this chapter, you may recognize that getchar() is the syntactical sibling to the putchar() function. Dare I say that the C language is starting to make sense?

Type this code into your editor:

```
#include <stdio.h>

int main()
{
    char t;

    printf("Please type a character:");
    t = getchar();
    printf("Thank you for typing the '%c' character.\n",t);
    return(0);
}
```

The getchar() function in Line 8 reads a key from the keyboard. That key's value is stored in the char variable t, which is then used in the printf() statement to display the character. Save this code to disk as TYPECHAR.C.

Compile and run.

```
Please type a character:
```

Press a letter key, such as **Y**, and then press Enter:

```
Thank you for typing the 'Y' character.
```

Note that you must press Enter to end input for `getchar()`. Although I would prefer a function that immediately reads and returns any key pressed at the keyboard, sadly, that's not the way `getchar()` works. More on this in the next section.

The problem with `getchar()`

I'm not quite pleased with the `getchar()` function. It doesn't really read one character from the keyboard. No, it reads the *first* or *next* character from the input stream. Sounds scary, but it's not.

Run the TYPECHAR program you create in the preceding section:

```
Please type a character:
```

Go ahead and type **ishkabible**, and then press the Enter key:

```
Thank you for typing the 'i' character.
```

By typing ishkabible and pressing Enter, you were creating an *input stream,* a given length of characters that are terminated by the Enter key. It's `getchar()`'s job to read only the *next* character from the stream. In this program, that makes one difference: The remaining characters are discarded by the operating system when the program quits. But consider this program:

```
int main()
{
    char t;

    printf("Please type a character:");
    t = getchar();
    printf("Thank you for typing the '%c' character.\n",t);
    t = getchar();
    printf("Thank you for typing the '%c' character.\n",t);
    t = getchar();
    printf("Thank you for typing the '%c' character.\n",t);
    t = getchar();
    printf("Thank you for typing the '%c' character.\n",t);
    return(0);
}
```

I have modified the TYPECHAR.C source to repeat Lines 8 and 9 four times. It's just the same two lines, but, this way, you can see how `getchar()` reacts to the input stream.

Save the changes to TYPECHAR.C, and then compile and run the resulting program:

```
Please type a character:
```

Type **Bob** and then press Enter:

```
Thank you for typing the 'B' character.
Thank you for typing the 'o' character.
Thank you for typing the 'b' character.
Thank you for typing the '
' character.
```

The first `getchar()` waits for you to type something. So, you type Bob and press Enter, placing four characters into the input stream: B, o, b, and Enter. The first B is read by `getchar()` and stored in variable t.

The next `getchar()` then reads the o from the input stream.

The next `getchar()` reads the b from the input stream.

The last `getchar()` finally reads the Enter key from the stream — and displays it, which is why the last line appears split in two.

Run the program again:

```
Please type a character:
```

Type **T** and press Enter:

```
Thank you for typing the 'T' character.
Thank you for typing the '
' character.
```

The first `getchar()` reads the T from the input stream, which is then displayed.

The second `getchar()` reads the Enter key from the input stream, which is then displayed.

The third `getchar()` function isn't waiting for you to type another key. Input ain't done!

Type **H** and press Enter:

```
Thank you for typing the 'H' character.
Thank you for typing the '
' character.
```

Isn't this frustrating? Fortunately, a solution is available. It doesn't improve on `getchar()`, but it does help you clear out the input stream when you need to. This subject is covered in the next section.

Clearing the input stream

The following program illustrates the problem with `getchar()` leaving characters in the input stream:

```
#include <stdio.h>

int main()
{
    char letter,number;

    printf("What is your favorite letter?");
    letter = getchar();
    printf("What is your favorite number?");
    number = getchar();
    printf("Thank you!\n%c is your favorite letter and %c is
    your favorite number.\n",letter,number);
    return(0);
}
```

Deftly type this source code into your editor. Note that the `printf()` statement in Line 11 is kinda long and wraps in this book; don't type it on two
separate lines. Save the code to disk as FAVES.C. Compile and run:

```
What is your favorite letter?
```

Type a **Q**, for example, and press Enter. You see:

```
What is your favorite number?Thank you!
Q is your favorite letter and
 is your favorite number.
```

The Enter key, because it's part of the input stream, is read by the second
`getchar()` function and displayed in the output. Bad. Bad. Bad. Well, maybe
it's not "bad," but it's not what you intended.

To clear out the input stream, you must use a function to clear the input
stream. On Windows computers, that's the `fflush()` function; in Unix,
Linux, and Mac OS X, it's the `fpurge()` function. Both do the same thing:
clear out any loitering text.

Here's the repaired program:

```
#include <stdio.h>

int main()
{
    char letter,number;

    printf("What is your favorite letter?");
```

```
    letter = getchar();
    fflush(stdin);              /* fpurge(stdin) for Unix */
    printf("What is your favorite number?");
    number = getchar();
    printf("Thank you!\n%c is your favorite letter and %c is
    your favorite number.\n",letter,number);
    return(0);
}
```

Insert the new Line 9, as shown here — either `fflush(stdin)` for Windows or `fpurge(stdin)` for Unix. In both examples, `stdin` represents the standard input device on the computer. (`stdin` is defined as standard input inside the STDIO.H header.) The input stream is flushed immediately after the first value is plucked out via the `getchar()` function. Things then start afresh with the next `getchar()` function.

Save the changes to disk. Recompile and run. This time, the output works as expected.

Reading a chunk of text with `gets()`

Reading text one character at a time is one of the basic building blocks of any program, but it's tedious. Recognizing that, the C gurus added the `gets()` function to the C library. You use the `gets()` function to read in, or *get,* an entire string of text at a time.

```
To store a string of text, you need to jump ahead in your C
    language learning curve and say Hello to the character
    array. You see, C has no such thing as a string variable.
    Instead, strings are stored in character arrays. Don't let
    that fact frazzle your brain right now; you discover
    arrays and strings in more detail in Book 2. For now, a
    string variable is defined this way:char name[20];
```

This variable declaration defines `name` as storage for 20 characters of text, or a string up to 19 characters long. (This last character in the string is special; more on that in Book II.) Is that room enough? Who knows! For now, it will do, as shown in this program:

```
#include <stdio.h>

int main()
{
    char name[20];

    printf("What is your name?");
    gets(name);
    printf("Pleased to meet you, %s!\n",name);
    return(0);
}
```

WARNING!

gets() now, but not later

The gets() function is no longer considered kosher. The fault lies in that gets() continues to read text from the keyboard without properly checking to see how many characters have been read. This is known as *bounds checking*. Therefore, it's possible that gets() could read 50 characters and your string variable (also called a *buffer*) can hold only 30. If so, the extra 20 characters get dumped directly into memory, which can either crash the computer or be exploited as a security flaw.

For your own programs, as well as for understanding C, using the gets() function is just fine. But if you plan on writing code for others, especially code that could be exploited by the bad guys, write your own input routines and don't use gets().

Type this source code and then save it to disk as YOUARE.C. Compile. Run. Obey:

```
What is your name?
```

Type your name, such as **Bill**. Press Enter:

```
Pleased to meet you, Bill!
```

Three things are going on here!

1. Storage is set aside for the text the user types: A character array is created with char name[20]; in Line 5. That gives the user 19 characters to store input.

2. The gets() function is used to read text from the keyboard and store it in the name variable.

3. The printf() function displays the contents of the name variable by using the %s (s for *string*) placeholder.

As I mention earlier in this section, you find out more about strings and such in Book 2. Strings can be quite fun, and many handy C functions are used to manipulate them. Read why gets() is flawed in the nearby sidebar "gets() now, but not later."

Exercise 1.5.4

Modify the YOUARE.C source code so that it asks for both your first name and last name, storing each one in separate variables. The final printf() statement prints both first and last names in the proper order.

How to input numeric values

There's a difference between numbers and strings in C. All text input from the keyboard comes in as text, so, to convert it to a number, you need to know two handy functions:

✦ The atoi() function converts text (or ASCII text) to integer values. Remember it as *ASCII-to-i*nteger, or *atio*. Say "A to I."

✦ The atof() function converts text to floating-point values. Remember it as *ASCII-to-f*loating point, or *atof*. Say "A to F."

Both functions require you to include the STDLIB.H (standard library) header file with your source code. (If you don't, things get screwy.)

This program demonstrates both functions:

```
#include <stdio.h>
#include <stdlib.h>

int main()
{
    char input[20];
    int age;
    float height;

    printf("Enter your age in years:");
    gets(input);
    age = atoi(input);

    printf("Enter your height in inches:");
    gets(input);
    height = atof(input);

    printf("You are %d years old\n",age);
    printf("and %f inches tall.\n",height);
    return(0);
}
```

Type this source code into your editor. Note that the input variable is used twice; there is no point in creating a new string variable when you can just reuse an old one. (Reusing old ones is common in many programs.) Save the code to disk as YOURDATA.C. Compile it. Run it.

Nothing surprising is in the output — yet! But before modifying the output, here's a tip: You can often condense some multiline statements in C so that they sit all on the same line. Sometimes, this strategy makes the code less readable, but it often improves readability. For example:

When strings don't contain numbers

In the YOURDATA series of programs, the user is assumed to be typing numbers and not text for the input. That's also what the `atoi()` and `atof()` functions assume. If they encounter a string that begins with text, or a character other than 0 through 9, they assume that the value of the input string is 0 — even if a real value appears elsewhere in the string.

```
gets(input);
age = atoi(input);
```

These two lines can be combined to read

```
age = atoi(gets(input));
```

In C, things on the right side of the equal sign are done first, from the inside of the parentheses outward. Here, `gets(input)` is worked out first. Then that string of text is passed directly into the `atoi()` function, with the result saved in the `age` variable. It's a handy shortcut to know.

Exercise 1.5.5
Modify the YOURDATA.C source code so that Lines 11 and 12, as well as Lines 15 and 16, are combined into single lines.

Exercise 1.5.6
Further modify YOURDATA.C so that the program displays the user's age in months and height in centimeters. An inch measures 2.2 centimeters.

Directly reading values with scanf()
Another way to read input from the keyboard is with the `scanf()` function. The `scanf()` function is to formatted input as the `printf()` function is to formatted output.

For example, both `printf()` and `scanf()` use the % placeholders, or conversion characters. These % placeholders help specify the type of data `printf()` displays and the type of data `scanf()` reads from the keyboard. By using scanf() with the proper conversion character, you can dispense with the atoi() and atof() functions and read values directly into variables:

```
#include <stdio.h>

int main()
{
    char subname[32];
    int iq;
    float wages;

    printf("Input subject name:");
    scanf("%s",&subname);
    printf("Input subject IQ:");
    scanf("%d",&iq);
    printf("Input subject hourly wage:");
    scanf("%f",&wages);

    printf("Subject\tIQ\tWage\n");
    printf("%s\t%d\t%f\n",subname,iq,wages);
    return(0);
}
```

Save this code to disk as SUBJECTS.C. Compile and run:

```
Input subject name:Phil
Input subject IQ:127
Input subject hourly wage:7.25
Subject IQ      Wage
Phil    127     7.250000
```

Each scanf() statement has two parts in its parentheses. First comes the format string — just like printf(), but in scanf() the conversion character is used to read a specific type of value. (See Appendix G for the variety.) That string is followed by a comma and then the name of the variable in which the value is stored. The variable must be prefixed by an ampersand. It tells the compiler that the variable itself is being manipulated. If you forget the ampersand, scanf() may function unpredictably (and the compiler may moan about it).

Note how silly the printf() statement looks with its tossed green salad of conversion characters and escape sequences:

```
printf("%s\t%d\t%f\n",subname,iq,wages);
```

The \t escape sequence is the tab character, which helps line up the program's output. But intermingled are conversion characters for the three variables being displayed. That makes the printf() statement look more complex than it is (and may be a source of errors when you typed the code).

Exercise 1.5.7

Modify the source code for YOURDATA.C *one more time!* (Use the results of Exercise 1.5.5.) This time, replace the gets()/atoi() and gets()/atof() functions with their scanf() counterparts. Don't forget those ampersands!

Summary of Basic Text I/O Functions

Table 5-1 lists a quick summary of the C language text input and output functions, reviewing what's covered in this chapter. Table 5-2 lists a few other common functions you can use to help read information from the keyboard.

Table 5-1		C Language Text I/O Functions
Function	*Format*	*Description*
getchar()	[*ch* =]getchar();	Reads a single character from the keyboard. The character is displayed and, optionally, stored in the char variable *ch*.
gets()	gets(string);	Reads a string of text from the keyboard (terminated by the Enter key). The text is stored in the variable *string*.
printf()	printf("*format*"[,var[,var...]]);	Displays formatted text according to the *format* string. Optional values or variables, *var*, can be specified to match placeholders or conversion characters in the format string. (See Appendix G for the full list.)
putchar()	putchar(*ch*);	Displays the character *ch* on the screen, where *ch* is a single character (or escape code) in single quotes or the name of a char variable.
puts()	puts(*string*);	Displays a text string on the screen, where *string* is a literal string of text (enclosed in double quotes) or the name of a string variable.
scanf()	scanf("format",&var);	Reads information from the keyboard according to the conversion character in the *format* string. The information is then stored in the variable *var*, which must match the type of conversion character that's used (int, float, or char, for example).

Table 5-2	Other Helpful Text I/O Functions	
Function	*Format*	*Description*
atof()	[numvar =]atof(string);	Converts a floating-point value found in *string* into a floating-point number, which can be stored in a variable, *numvar*, or used immediately. Requires the STDLIB.H header file to be included.
atoi()	[numvar = atoi](string);	Converts an integer value found in *string* into an integer, which can be stored in a variable, *numvar*, or used immediately. Requires the STDLIB.H header file to be included.
fflush(stdin)	fflush(stdin);	Removes characters from the input stream (keyboard).
fpurge(stdin)	fpurge(stdin);	Removes characters from the input stream (keyboard). This function must be used in Unix rather than `fflush(stdin)`.

Chapter 6: Decision Time

To really use the power of the computer, your programs need to make decisions. I don't mean that the computer does any thinking — it can't; computers do only what you tell them. But a computer can make comparisons, evaluating the results of the comparisons and then acting on that information.

This chapter introduces the `if` and `else` keywords, which are used in C programming to make comparisons and control the flow of your program. It's decision time!

Making Decisions with `if`

The `if` keyword is used in C to make a comparison: A variable is compared to a value, or two variables are compared to each other. If the result of that comparison is true, one or more statements are executed. If the comparison is false, the statements are skipped over like a 3-month-old box of Chinese take-out food you find in the back of your refrigerator.

In English, the `if` comparison looks like this:

```
if(I_am_hungry == yes)
{
    go_to(kitchen);
    snack = make(food);
    eat(snack);
}
```

if is followed by a comparison in parentheses. This is a mathematical comparison. The operators shown in Table 6-1 are used for comparing the values of two variables or the values of one variable and an immediate value.

Table 6-1	C Language Comparison Operators	
Operator	*Meaning*	*Example*
==	Is equal to	`decade == 10`
<	Is less than	`negative < 0`
>	Is greater than	`century > 100`
<=	Less than or equal to	`little_kid <= 12`
>=	Greater than or equal to	`millionaire >= 1000000`
!=	Not equal to	`odd != 2`

No semicolon follows the if statement's parentheses.

Following the parentheses is one or more statements, enclosed in braces. Those statements are executed only if the condition (in parentheses) is true. If the condition is false, the statements are skipped. The next statement, following if's final brace, is then executed.

Most of the operators in Table 6-1 should be familiar to you from elementary school math class. Note however, that an equal comparison is done with *two* equal signs, not one. Also, "less than or equal to" is written as it's pronounced: <= and not =<; ditto for "greater than or equal to," which cannot be written =>.

Not-equal is written !=. The character for *not* in the C language is the exclamation point. (This topic pops up elsewhere as you find out more about C.) As with less-than or equal-to and greater-than or equal-to, not-equal must be written != and not =!.

It helps to remember == for a comparison if you pronounce it "is equal to" and not "equals." The single equal sign, =, is used in C for assignment.

Are they equal?

The following source code demonstrates using an if comparison to see whether two single characters are equal:

```
#include <stdio.h>

int main()
{
    char fav;

    printf("Enter your favorite character:");
```

```
        fav = getchar();
        if(fav == 'Q')
        {
            printf("That's my favorite character, too!");
        }
        return(0);
}
```

Save this source code to disk as MYFAV.C. Note that the comparison being made is a single character. If the user types Q (and it must be uppercase to match), the statement belonging to if — between the braces — is executed. Otherwise, it's skipped over.

Compile and run:

```
Enter your favorite character:
```

If you type anything other than Q, nothing happens. But if you press **Q** and Enter, you see

```
That's my favorite character, too!
```

If must be a big Q; that's a perfect match. No other character matches.

Although you can compare two single-character values with if, you cannot compare strings of text. To compare strings, you must use special functions, such as strcmp(). These are covered in Book III, Chapter 2.

Exercise 1.6.1
Reedit the source code for MYFAV.C so that it asks for your favorite number from 1 through 10. Choose your own favorite for the computer's number. If the numbers match, a similar message is displayed. *Hint:* Use integers, not characters.

The old less-than, greater-than puzzle
The following program demonstrates the less-than and greater-than comparisons:

```
#include <stdio.h>

int main()
{
    int age;

    printf("How old are you?");
    scanf("%d",&age);
    if(age > 64)
```

```
    {
        printf("You're %d years old.\n",age);
        printf("How's your retirement?\n");
    }
    return(0);
}
```

Save this source code as RETIRE.C. Compile and run. If you're younger than 65, you need to lie about your age to see the extra text displayed.

Exercise 1.6.2

Modify the source code for RETIRE.C so that the greater-than-or-equal-to operator, >=, is used instead.

Even more comparisons!

The following program uses if to make a less-than comparison. See whether you can tell how it differs from the other if programs shown earlier in this chapter:

```
#include <stdio.h>

int main()
{
    float temp;

    printf("What is the temperature outside?");
    scanf("%f",&temp);
    if(temp < 65)
        printf("My but it's a bit chilly out!\n");
    return(0);
}
```

Something missing? Yes! No braces appear after the if statement. That's fine; when only one statement belongs to if, the braces are optional. The statement still ends in a semicolon, which makes it the last (and only) statement belonging to if.

Note that the statement belonging to if is indented in the preceding example. This is purely for readability; the compiler doesn't care how the code is indented. In fact, you can also write the statement on one line, as in

```
if(temp < 65) printf("My but it's a bit chilly out!\n");
```

Save this code to disk as CHILLY.C. Compile and run. Try out a few temperatures to get the program to do its tricks.

else, *the Anti-*if *Statement*

More often than not, your programs react to an if comparison in two ways. First, they execute statements when a condition is true, but what happens when the situation is false? For example, consider the following code, a modification of CHILLY.C, from the preceding section:

```
#include <stdio.h>

int main()
{
    float temp;

    printf("What is the temperature outside?");
    scanf("%f",&temp);
    if(temp < 65)
        printf("My but it's a bit chilly out!\n");
    if(temp >= 65)
        printf("My how pleasant!");
    return(0);
}
```

Save these changes to CHILLY.C to disk, and then recompile and run. The first time, enter a value less than 65. The second time, enter a value 65 or greater.

The code works because the first if statement catches all values less than 65. The second if statement catches all values 65 or greater. But, you have a better way to weave this solution in the C language, as I describe in the following section.

Or Else!

Many decisions in your programs are of the either-or type. The program takes one course of action if the condition is true, and if the condition is false, the program takes another course of action. The CHILLY.C source code from the preceding section attempts to do this in a clumsy way with two if statements. But C has a better solution: Use the else keyword, as shown in this source code update:

```
#include <stdio.h>

int main()
{
    float temp;

    printf("What is the temperature outside?");
    scanf("%f",&temp);
```

```
if(temp < 65)
{
    printf("My but it's a bit chilly out!\n");
}
else
{
    printf("My how pleasant!");
}
return(0);
}
```

Here's another modification to the most recent incarnation of the CHILLY.C program (from the preceding section). I have added the braces back in for readability, and the second if statement was replaced with else.

Both if and else work together; you cannot use else without an if statement immediately before it. What happens is that when the if condition is true, statements belonging to if are executed. But when the condition is false, the statements belonging to else are executed instead.

Make the necessary changes to CHILLY.C and save the source code to disk. Compile and run.

The output is no different from the preceding program, but the source code has become more readable and logical; figuring out the opposite condition isn't necessary when you can just use else.

Exercise 1.6.3

Modify the source code for RETIRE.C. Add an else plus a group of statements to display when the user's age is less than 65.

Making Multiple Decisions

Occasionally, a decision is made in a program based on more than two possible outcomes. For example, consider a modification to the CHILLY.C program that also displays the text My but it's hot out when the temperature is higher than 80. How can that be done?

else if *to the rescue!*

Say Hello to the else if combination. By using else-if, you can have several if statements piled on top of each other, narrowing a complex decision tree into various possible outcomes:

```
#include <stdio.h>

int main()
{
    float temp;

    printf("What is the temperature outside?");
    scanf("%f",&temp);
    if(temp < 65)
    {
        printf("My but it's a bit chilly out!\n");
    }
    else if(temp >= 80)
    {
        printf("My but it's hot out!");
    }
    else
    {
        printf("My how pleasant!");
    }
    return(0);
}
```

Modify your CHILLY.C source code so that it resembles this construction. This is one way to handle multiple conditions in C.

The first comparison is made by if in Line 9. If the value of the variable temp is less than 65, those statements belonging to if are executed; the rest of the construction (Lines 13 through 20 inclusive) is skipped.

When the first comparison is false, the comparison is made by else if in Line 13. When that comparison is true, the statements belonging to else if are executed; Lines 17 through 20 (inclusive) are skipped.

Finally, when both if and else if comparisons are false, the statements belonging to else (Line 17) are executed.

Save this monster to disk. Compile. Run it three different times, each time with a high, middle, and then low temperature. It may seem like the computer is smart, but it's just making a comparison and controlling the program flow to match.

Get the order right!

When you're performing multiple comparisons, it's important to get the order right. Often, this requires a visual image, as shown in Figure 6-1, because, if you cannot visualize the comparisons and the way they eliminate the outcome, the program doesn't do what you intended. (This is a "bug" type of error.)

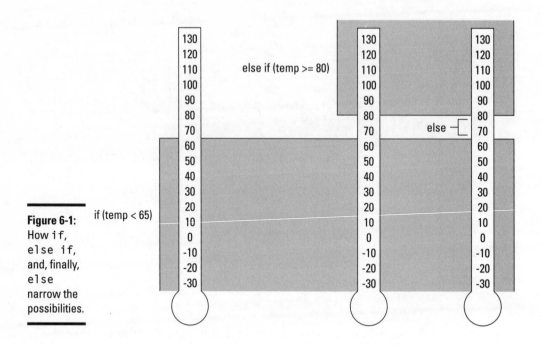

Figure 6-1:
How if,
else if,
and, finally,
else
narrow the
possibilities.

In Figure 6-1, you see how the first if statement eliminates any temperatures lower than 65. Next, the else if statement eliminates all temperatures 80 and higher. When you get to the final else, the temperatures that remain are in the range from 65 through 79.99.

Now assume that someone wasn't thinking and the three statements appear as shown in Figure 6-2. In that example, nothing is left for else to represent, and the program most likely yields an improper answer. (Note that the compiler doesn't point out this type of mental error.)

Exercise 1.6.4

Modify the CHILLY.C source code again. This time, add another decision to the source code, one that displays the message "It's perfect out!" when the temperature is *exactly* 72 degrees.

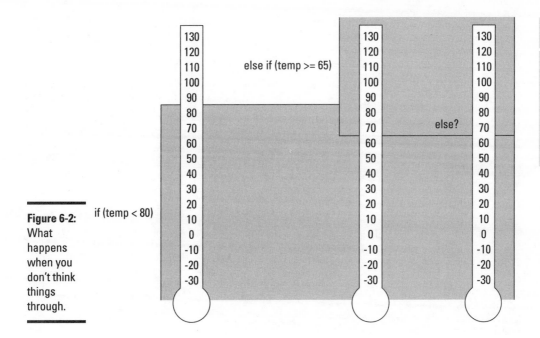

else if (temp >= 65)

else?

Figure 6-2:
What
happens
when you
don't think
things
through.

if (temp < 80)

Chapter 7: Looping

In This Chapter

✔ Repeating statements with a `for` loop

✔ Looping a given number of times

✔ Monitoring values in the loop

✔ Dealing with endless loops

✔ Using the `break` keyword

✔ Putting one loop inside another (nesting)

✔ Making a `for` loop with multiple conditions

*E*ver get stuck in a loop? That typically means that you repeat something over and over. The same situation or event or circumstance is repeated over and over — often, seemingly without end. But it's exactly that kind of drudgery that the computer really doesn't mind. When it comes to loops, your computer not only is an expert, but it also truly *enjoys* repeating itself.

The core of most modern programs is the loop. It gives a program the ability to repeat a group of statements over and over, sometimes for a given count or duration, or, often, until a certain condition is being met. The C language gives you many ways to create loops in your code. The one presented in this chapter is the `for` loop, created with the C language keyword `for`.

Presenting the `for` Loop

A loop has three parts:

✦ A setup or initialization

✦ The part that loops, which is the statements that are repeated

✦ The condition on which the loop finishes

In the C language, the `for` loop can handle these conditions in one handy statement, which makes it easy to understand, despite how complex it looks.

When I was in the third grade, my teacher made me write "I shall refrain from calling my friends names" on the chalkboard 100 times. The following program does the same thing on a computer screen in less than one second:

```
#include <stdio.h>

int main()
{
    int c;

    for(c=0;c<100;c=c+1)
    {
        puts("I shall refrain from calling my friends
    names.");
    }
    return(0);
}
```

I don't even bother describing this example yet. Just be careful how you type Line 7. Nothing in there is new, but the arrangement looks rather strange. Save the source code to disk as BIGEARS.C. Compile and run:

```
I shall refrain from calling my friends names.
I shall refrain from calling my friends names.
I shall refrain from calling my friends names.
```

And so on, for 100 lines.

(I called a kid Big Ears. I told my teacher that Big Ears had just called me Fatso, but she didn't buy that.)

Dissecting the for *loop*

The for keyword is followed by a set of parentheses. Inside the parentheses are three separate items that configure the loop. I call them "init or setup," "as long as," and "do this." Consider the for loop from BIGEARS.C:

```
for(c=0;c<100;c=c+1)
```

The c variable is already defined as an int. It's used by the for loop to control how many times the loop — the statements belonging to for — is repeated. First comes the init or setup:

```
c=0
```

The variable c is assigned the value 0. The for statement does this first, before the loop is ever repeated, and then only once. Note that starting at 0 rather than 1 is a traditional C language thing. Zero is the "first" number. Get used to that.

Next:

```
c<100
```

The loop repeats itself *as long as* the value of variable c is less than 100. This is the *exit condition* for the loop, or what I call the "as long as," as in "repeat the loop as long as c < 100." This condition is examined at the start of the loop, every time the loop is repeated.

Finally, here's the do this part of the loop:

```
c=c+1
```

After the loop is repeated, the for statement executes this statement. It must be a real C language statement, one that you hope somehow manipulates the variable that's set up in the first step. Here, the value of variable c is increased, or *incremented*, by one.

All told, the for statement basically says "Take variable c and make it equal to 0. Then, as long as the value of c is less than 100, keep incrementing c by 1."

The long and the short of it is that the loop is repeated 100 times.

The loop itself consists of the statements following for. These are enclosed in braces:

```
for(c=0;c<100;c=c+1)
{
    puts("I shall refrain from calling my friends names.");
}
```

Or, as in the if statement, when there is only one statement after for, you don't need the braces:

```
for(c=0;c<100;c=c+1)
    puts("I shall refrain from calling my friends names.");
```

Counting to 10

The following source code demonstrates how a for loop ticks. For each turn of the loop, the statement that is repeated explains the value of the variable used in the loop:

```
#include <stdio.h>

int main()
{
    int tick;
```

```
    printf("Variable tick is uninitialized.\n");
    for(tick=0;tick<10;tick=tick+1)
    {
        printf("\tIn the loop, tick = %d\n",tick);
    }
    printf("After the loop, tick = %d\n",tick);
    return(0);
}
```

Type this source code into your editor. Note the \t (tab) escape character at the start of the `printf()` string in Line 10. Save the source code to disk as TICK.C. Compile and run:

```
Variable tick is uninitialized.
        In the loop, tick = 0
        In the loop, tick = 1
        In the loop, tick = 2
        In the loop, tick = 3
        In the loop, tick = 4
        In the loop, tick = 5
        In the loop, tick = 6
        In the loop, tick = 7
        In the loop, tick = 8
        In the loop, tick = 9
After the loop, tick = 10
```

Compare the program's output with the loop itself. Before the loop runs, the variable `tick` is uninitialized.

As the loop runs (or turns), 10 lines are printed. The \t indents the lines so that you can see which are produced inside the loop and what the value of variable `tick` is.

At first, variable `tick` equals 0. This means that `tick<10` is true, so the loop is repeated. As it repeats, `tick=tick+1` is executed, incrementing the value of `tick`. That's proven on the second line displayed in the loop, which says that `tick` is now equal to 1.

The loop continues to repeat until `tick=tick+1` sets the value of variable `tick` to 10. At that point, the loop stops. The final line proves that `tick` is equal to 10, but note that the loop wasn't repeated an eleventh time.

Exercise 1.7.1

Modify the source code to TICK.C so that the variable `tick` starts at 1 but the loop still is repeated 10 times.

Counting by twos

No rule says that a for loop must count by ones using something like
tick=tick+1. No, you can put just about any statement in the for loop as
its do-this part. Of course, it's nice to have that statement somehow play a
role in stopping the loop. Consider this example:

```
#include <stdio.h>

int main()
{
    int b;

    printf("Here is your two's table:\n\n");
    for(b=2;b<=20;b=b+2)
        printf("%d\n",b);
    return(0);
}
```

This loop is repeated 10 times, but does so in steps of 2. Save the source
code to disk as TWOS.C. Compile and run:

```
Here is your two's table:

2
4
6
8
10
12
14
16
18
20
```

Exercise 1.7.2

Devise a for loop that works by counting backward. Have the loop repeat
itself 10 times, each time displaying a value from 10 down to 1, and then
have the code display 0 and Blastoff! Name the source code BLASTOFF.C.

Endless Loops

When you get into programming loops, you discover the joys and dreads of
endless, or *infinite,* loops. These loops continue forever because either the
programmer forgot to include a way to exit from the loop or the exit condition is just never met. Either way, endless loops are a pain.

Your first endless loop

The following program demonstrates an endless loop. You can easily cause one by simply making a typo, as this example demonstrates:

```c
#include <stdio.h>

int main()
{
    int packet;

    printf("Processing 1000 packets:\n");
    for(packet=0;packet=1000;packet=packet+1)
    {
        printf("Doing amazing things with packet#%d\n",
    packet);
    }
    return(0);
}
```

Carefully type this code into your editor. Can you see the typo? (It's in the `for` statement, on Line 8.) Type it that way regardless. Save the code to disk as ENDLESS.C.

Compile and run.

And run. And run. And run. . . .

Press Ctrl+C to stop the program.

What happens is that the as-long-as condition is always true; the compiler evaluates assignments like `packet=1000` as true. As you can see by the output, the value of `packet` is always 1000 and, because the `for` loop lacks an ending condition, it loops forever.

Exercise 1.7.3

Fix the ENDLESS.C program so that it loops 1,000 times and then stops.

Exercise 1.7.4

Here's a task some project manager may give you someday. Suppose that you have a program similar to ENDLESS.C, which processes a given number of items. You like your loops to start at 0, but the project manager wants the output to display the number 1 instead. Rewrite the code for ENDLESS.C and keep the `for` statement the same, but adjust the output so that packets numbers 1 through 1000, rather than 0 through 999, are displayed.

A forever loop on purpose

Often, a program contains an endless loop on purpose. This type of construct may seem odd, yet the basis of many modern programs is that they sit and spin while they wait for something to happen. The loop may look like this:

```
for(;;)
{
    check_Keyboard();
    check_Mouse();
    check_Events();
    check_System();
}
```

I call the (preceding) empty `for` statement "for ever." The conditions inside the parentheses are missing, which is okay. The result is an endless loop where the statements are checked repeatedly, one after the other: The program is looking for activity somewhere. When activity is found, the program goes off and does something interesting. But most of the time, the program just sits in this type of loop, waiting for something to happen. (The typical word processor may perform thousands of these loops as it waits between keystrokes as you're typing.)

Enter this source code and save it to disk as TYPING.C. Compile and run the program:

```
#include <stdio.h>

int main()
{
    char ch;

    puts("Typing Program");
    puts("Type away:");
    for(;;)
    {
        ch=getchar();
    }
    return(0);
}
```

Yes, you can type. And you can see your text on the screen. But how do you stop?

To stop, you have to break the endless loop, which can be done by pressing Ctrl+C. That's not the way I want my programs to work, though. Instead, an exit condition must be defined for the loop, which is where the `break` keyword comes into play.

Breaking out with break

The C language developers knew that, in some instances, a loop must be broken, based on conditions that could not be predicted or even set up inside the for statement. So, in their wisdom, they introduced the break keyword.

What break does is to immediately quit a loop (any C language loop, not just for loops.) When the computer sees break, it just assumes that the loop is done and continues as though the loop's ending condition was met:

```
#include <stdio.h>

int main()
{
    char ch;

    puts("Typing Program");
    puts("Type away; press '~' to quit:");
    for(;;)
    {
        ch=getchar();
        if(ch=='~')
        {
            break;
        }
    }
    return(0);
}
```

I have fixed the TYPING.C source code so that an exit condition is defined. The if comparison in Line 12 checks to see whether a ~ (tilde) character is entered. If so, the loop is halted by the break statement.

Change your TYPING.C source code so that it matches what was just shown. Compile and run. Now, you can halt the program by typing the ~ character.

Note that the if statement can also be written without the braces:

```
if(ch=='~') break;
```

This line may be a bit more readable than using braces, as shown earlier.

Exercise 1.7.5

Modify the source code for TICK.C (see the section "Counting to 10," early in this chapter) so that when the value of the variable tick is greater than 5, the loop is halted with break.

Nesting Loops

Unlike nesting comments, putting one loop inside another is not only permissible, but also quite common inside the C language:

```c
#include <stdio.h>

int main()
{
    char a;
    int x;

    for(x=1;x<10;x=x+1)
    {
        for(a='A';a<='I';a=a+1)
        {
            printf("%d%c   ",x,a);  /* 3 spaces after %c */
        }
        putchar('\n');                  /* end of the line */
    }
    return(0);
}
```

Carefully copy this source code into your editor. Save it to disk as GRID.C. Compile and run:

```
1A    1B    1C    1D    1E    1F    1G    1H    1I
2A    2B    2C    2D    2E    2F    2G    2H    2I
3A    3B    3C    3D    3E    3F    3G    3H    3I
4A    4B    4C    4D    4E    4F    4G    4H    4I
5A    5B    5C    5D    5E    5F    5G    5H    5I
6A    6B    6C    6D    6E    6F    6G    6H    6I
7A    7B    7C    7D    7E    7F    7G    7H    7I
8A    8B    8C    8D    8E    8F    8G    8H    8I
9A    9B    9C    9D    9E    9F    9G    9H    9I
```

Two `for` loops are nested in GRID.C. The outer loop counts from 1 to 9 using variable x. That loop is responsible for each of these rows.

The inner `for` loop counts from A to I using variable a. That loop is responsible for the columns.

After the inner loop is done, the `putchar('\n');` statement ends each line of text so that the outer loop can start again on a new line.

Remember that the inner loop completes its job each time the outer loop is repeated once. If that isn't what you wanted, you have nested the loops wrong!

Counting by letters

The source code for GRID.C makes it appear that the inner loop counts by using letters rather than numbers. Of course, this isn't true.

Book I, Chapter 5 points out that `char` variables are simply tiny integers. It's how that value is displayed that makes the `char` a character. In the inner `for` loop, the value of variable a is set to `'A'` — a simple assignment. But, internally, and according to Appendix C, the ASCII value of character A is really 65. Similarly, the ASCII value of character I is 73. So, the `for` loop could have been written as

```
for(a=65;a<=73;a=a+1)
```

Yet, because the compiler automatically translates the `'A'` into 65 and the `'I'` into 73, you can specify those letter values instead. As long as you understand that the letters are really shorthand for the values, everything works out fine.

The 17,576 Names of God

In the short story *The Nine Billion Names of God*, author Arthur C. Clarke writes about a group of monks who are determined to figure out the name of God. They have devised a phonetic alphabet and have written down various combinations of sounds, but they can work only so fast. So, they hire a computer company to install a system that can quickly create 9 billion permutations of the sounds, one of which is likely to be the Name of God. The idea is that, after God's name is known, the world will end.

It's a charming story, all the more so because desktop computers can now also calculate the name of God, as long as you properly code them with the monk's alphabet, write the program, and then sit and wait for the output to compile.

The following program uses three nested loops to generate every possible 3-letter combination using the common English alphabet. This example isn't sufficient to produce the Name of God, so the world doesn't end when you run the program:

```c
#include <stdio.h>

int main()
{
    char a,b,c;

    for(a='A';a<='Z';a=a+1)
```

```
        for(b='A';b<='Z';b=b+1)
            for(c='A';c<='Z';c=c+1)
                printf("%c%c%c\t",a,b,c);
    return(0);
}
```

Save the source code as NAMES.C. Compile. Run. Be amazed.

This example shows a triple nested loop. I removed the braces from the source code because the indented for statements have a sort of elegance all their own.

Incidentally, the program produces 17,576 results, which is where this section gets its title. That pretty much covers every 3-letter acronym ever invented by the government.

Exercise 1.7.6
Modify the source code for NAMES.C so that it generates names that are five, rather than three, letters long.

Multiple for *Conditions*

Here's a rarity you don't find in many other C books. The for statement's format *really* looks like this:

```
for(init[,...];as_long_as;do_this[,...])
```

Yeah, that looks confusing. Anyway, my point is that a for statement can contain multiple initiations for the loop as well as multiple *do_this* parts.

The only restriction is that the extra conditions must be separated with a comma. This example shows an update to the TWOS.C source code presented earlier in this chapter:

```
#include <stdio.h>

int main()
{
    int a,b;

    printf("Here is your two's table:\n\n");
    for(a=1,b=2;b<=20;a=a+1,b=b+2)
        printf("2 * %d = %d\n",a,b);
    return(0);
}
```

Save these changes to disk. Compile and run. The output is a bit more clear, thanks to the extra a variable used in the output. Instead of that, gander at the for statement in Line 7:

```
for(a=1,b=2;b<=20;a=a+1,b=b+2)
```

Two variables are initialized:

```
a=1
b=2
```

The "as long as" part remains unchanged: b<=20. But the code has two *"do this"* parts:

```
a=a+1
b=b+2
```

Each of these is executed when the loop completes.

By compacting everything into the loop, you make the source code shorter, albeit at the cost of readability. The following example is a rewrite of the source code without loading up on the for statement:

```
#include <stdio.h>

int main()
{
    int a,b;

    printf("Here is your two's table:\n\n");
    a=1;
    for(b=2;b<=20;b=b+2)
    {
        printf("2 * %d = %d\n",a,b);
        a=a+1;
    }
    return(0);
}
```

You don't need to type this source code; it merely illustrates how the same thing can be done without monkeying with the for statement.

Chapter 8: Using Constants

In This Chapter

✔ **Understanding constants**

✔ **Dealing with changes in immediate values**

✔ **Declaring a constant**

✔ **Using constants**

✔ **Abusing the** #define **directive**

M ost programming books I have ventured into seldom cover the concept of constants. The books spend time discussing variables, naturally, because variables are an alien concept to most folks and form the core of most programming activities. But constants are either glossed over or mentioned in passing. That's not true in this book.

I find constants to be particularly valuable in a program. I learned this lesson the hard way, but it's one that I want to pass along to you for your own programming enrichment. Therefore, say Hello to a sweet little chapter covering the subject of constants in your programs.

Are Constants Necessary?

In C, you can use three types of values: values stored in variables, immediate values, and constants. Of the three, constants may seem like the least important. Yet they can play a handy role.

A program example to drive home the point

The following program doesn't use constants. Instead, it uses immediate values and variables, which is typical of the programs demonstrated in most other programs in this book:

```
#include <stdio.h>

int main()
{
    int total,fine,speeding;

    puts("Speeding Tickets\n");
```

```
/* first ticket */

    speeding = 85 - 55;        /* mph over limit */
    fine = speeding * 15;      /* $ fine per mph over limit */
    total = total + fine;
    printf("For going 85 in a 55 zone: $%d\n",fine);

/* second ticket */

    speeding = 95 - 55;        /* mph over limit */
    fine = speeding * 15;      /* $ fine per mph over limit */
    total = total + fine;
    printf("For going 95 in a 55 zone: $%d\n",fine);

/* third ticket */
    speeding = 100 - 55;       /* mph over limit */
    fine = speeding * 15;      /* $ fine per mph over limit */
    total = total + fine;
    printf("For going 100 in a 55 zone: $%d\n",fine);

/* Display total */

    printf("\nTotal in fines: $%d\n",total);
    return(0);
}
```

The code may seem long (and it's one of the longer ones in this book), but it's mostly one chunk of code that's copied and pasted twice. Save it to disk as TICKETS.C. Compile. Run.

But then, something changes!

Suppose that you have completed the program, as promised. But you find out that the speed limit has changed from 55 miles per hour to 60 miles per hour. Also, the fine has jumped from $15 to $26 for every mile per hour you speed over the limit. That may seem like no big deal: Just search and replace inside the program, and it's done. Even so, by using constants, you can fix it up even quicker.

How? Consider that constants were defined at the start of the program, something like this:

```
SPEEDLIMIT = 55
RATE = 15
```

And even

```
FIRST_TICKET=85
SECOND_TICKET=95
THIRD_TICKET=100
```

"Aren't constants the same thing as immediate values?"

Yes and no. The answer is Yes in that neither immediate values nor constants change. Only the *value* of variables can change. But the answer is No in that, unlike with immediate values, you can manipulate a constant's declaration and affect the constant throughout your program. Otherwise, you would have to do a search and replace operation for every immediate value. That can be hard because you may not want to change *every* immediate value, as would be done in a global search-and-replace operation.

Had these "constants" been available, changing values throughout the program would be cinchy; just change the line that defines the constant. Hold that thought!

Chickening out and using variables instead

You can, of course, merely use variables and just chuck the idea of constants. This strategy works, of course. It wastes memory, but that's not a big deal any more. (Back in the 1980s, it was a huge deal!) So, why not? In fact, I made it an exercise for you.

Exercise 1.8.1

Modify the source code to TICKETS.C so that five new `int` variables are declared:

`speedlimit`, `rate`, `first_ticket`, `second_ticket`, and `third_ticket`

Each one is assigned values as listed, in the earlier section "But then, something changes!" Edit the source code so that those variables are used at every instance in which the immediate values were used in the original TICKET.C code.

Constants: The Anti-Variable!

I suppose, if constants weren't available, using variables as constants would be a practical solution. But, alas, constants *are* available.

My advice is to use constants for any value that is repeated in your program. Even if you don't think that the value will ever change, using a constant is preferred. For example, in my programs, I have declared the following types of values as constants:

+ The number of times certain loops need to repeat

+ The size of a storage location or buffer

+ The maximum number of items a character in a game can carry

+ The number of tries someone has to retype a password

+ The number of seconds of inactivity before the program hangs up the modem

+ The size of the screen

+ And so on

Declaring these types of information as constants in your program just makes using those values — and maybe changing them later — handier. It also has the side effect of making your code more readable if you name the constant properly.

Declaring a constant

Constants are declared in a manner similar to declaring variables. However, constants are declared using the C language preprocessor and not the compiler. Here's the format:

```
#define VOTING_AGE 18
```

The #define directive is a preprocessor command. It's followed by the name of the symbol being defined, VOTING_AGE. These symbols are named like variables, though I use ALL CAPS for constants, which lets me easily identify constants versus variables elsewhere in my source code.

The symbol is all one word. You can use an underline to connect multiple words, as shown here.

Following the symbol is a space and then the value that the symbol represents. *There is no equal sign!*

The line ends with a press of the Enter key. Don't include a semicolon, unless you want the semicolon to be a part of the constant (and you probably don't).

It's the preprocessor's duty to take the symbol and do a search-and-replace operation throughout your code, substituting the symbol with whatever it represents. In the end, the "constant" becomes an immediate value. And, by using #define to create the constant, you give yourself the flexibility to easily change it later.

Using constants in your code

Constant definitions typically follow the #include directives at the top of your source code; for example:

```
#include <stdio.h>

#define SPEEDLIMIT 55
#define RATE 15
#define FIRST_TICKET 85
#define SECOND_TICKET 95
#define THIRD_TICKET 100

int main()
{
    int total,fine,speeding;

    puts("Speeding Tickets\n");

/* first ticket */

    speeding = FIRST_TICKET - SPEEDLIMIT;
    fine = speeding * RATE;
    total = total + fine;
    printf("For going %d in a %d zone: $%d\n",
    FIRST_TICKET,SPEEDLIMIT,fine);

/* second ticket */

    speeding = SECOND_TICKET - SPEEDLIMIT;
    fine = speeding * RATE;
    total = total + fine;
    printf("For going %d in a %d zone: $%d\n",
    SECOND_TICKET,SPEEDLIMIT,fine);

/* third ticket */
    speeding = THIRD_TICKET - SPEEDLIMIT;
    fine = speeding * RATE;
    total = total + fine;
    printf("For going %d in a %d zone: $%d\n",
    THIRD_TICKET,SPEEDLIMIT,fine);

/* Display total */

    printf("\nTotal in fines: $%d\n",total);
    return(0);
}
```

What about the `const` keyword?

The ANSI C standard introduced the `const` keyword to the C language in the 1990s. The `const` C++ convention isn't used in C to create constants. Instead, you use `#define`, as described in this chapter.

You may see `const` used when certain functions are prototyped inside header files. Beyond that, feel free to avoid `const` in your C language code.

Make these changes to your source code for TICKETS.C. Save to disk. Compile. Run. The output is the same, but the control you have gained over your source code is incredible.

Exercise 1.8.2

Modify the program with these changes:

✦ The speed limit is really 65 miles per hour.

✦ The fine is now $26 for every mile per hour over the limit.

✦ The third ticket was really 110, and not 100, miles per hour.

Exercise 1.8.3

Edit the source code for the final rendition of MOON.C, from Chapter 4. Specify constants rather than variables for the values of `distance` and `speed`.

Other Things You Can #define

The #define directive doesn't necessarily limit its scope to merely creating constants for you. You can define anything by using the #define directive, essentially replacing major pieces of your program with whatever you want — if you want to carry it that far. For example:

```
#include <stdio.h>

#define BEGIN int main()
#define HELLO {
#define WRITELN printf
#define END_CODE return(0);
#define BYE }

BEGIN
HELLO
```

```
WRITELN("What the heck is going on?\n");
END_CODE
BYE
```

Scribble down this source code in your compiler. Mind your typos! Save it to disk as WEIRD.C. Compile. Fix the typos you missed. Then recompile and run:

```
What the heck is going on?
```

Well, the #define directive is being used to replace literal chunks of the program. This situation can happen, though how useful it is in the WEIRD.C example is questionable.

A better example may be something like this:

```
#define ASK_PROMPT printf("Please enter Yes or No (Y/N)?");
```

This way, the programmer can just type ASK_PROMPT in the code, which is globally replaced with the printf() statement when the code is compiled. (As a bonus, the programmer can universally fix every prompt by simply modifying the single #define.)

Chapter 9: Mysterious Math

In This Chapter

✔ Recognizing C's math operators

✔ Understanding which operators work first

✔ Changing signs with unary operators

✔ Using ++ to increment variables

✔ Using -- to decrement variables

✔ Pre-incrementing versus post-incrementing

✔ Manipulating variables with more cryptic operators

I ended up changing majors in college because I couldn't hack math. Throughout high school, I was a mediocre math student. The highest grade I ever got was a B+ in geometry. That's because I had an excellent teacher. (Thank you, Mrs. Jones!) But, in college, my professors were horrible, and with my wobbly math background I squeaked by with a C in Calculus 1A and a D in Calculus 2A. (I took Calculus 2A over again and got an F! That was the last math class I ever took.)

I don't worry about math much now, unless it's reconciling my checking account with the Evil Bank. Generally, I don't worry because the computer does the math. Even for programming, computers do math wonderfully and without complaint. Even so, a few math doohickeys are still good to know. This chapter covers them all, courtesy of a college math dropout.

Math Review

Yes, indeedy, the computer can manage basic math operations. No sweat. Just like with a calculator, you punch in the values or variables, plus the proper mathematical symbols, and the computer does the rest.

As a review (or an introduction, depending on where you are in this book), Table 9-1 lists the basic mathematical operators used in the C language. These common symbols are used for math in most computer languages, spreadsheets, PC calculators, and so on.

Table 9-1		C Language Basic Mathematical Operators
Operator	*Function*	*Example*
+	Addition	`caravan = car1 + car2;`
-	Subtraction	`profit=income-expenses;`
*	Multiplication	`hotel = houses * 4;`
/	Division	`distribution = insects/square_feet;`

You can use the mathematical operators in C with immediate values, variables, or constants.

The mathematical operation always goes on the right, as in

```
seconds = days * 24 * 60 * 60;
```

The result can be stored, as shown here, or it can be used as an immediate value, as in

```
printf("The plot is %d square feet.\n",60*90);
```

The Sacred Order of Precedence

Math problems can get ugly. That's one reason for disliking math; the larger reason is that it's not easy to always get the right result. Even in the C language, this can be true. Consider this problem:

```
4 + 5 - 2 * 6 / 3
```

What's the right answer? *Don't even bother trying to figure it out!* Use the computer instead!

```
#include <stdio.h>

int main()
{
    int answer;

    answer = 4 + 5 - 2 * 6 / 3;
    printf("The answer is %d\n",answer);
    return(0);
}
```

Save the code to disk as ANSWER.C. Compile and run:

```
The answer is 5
```

Really now! Run it again to be sure:

```
The answer is still 5!
```

(Just kidding! The text still reads `The answer is 5`.)

My Dear Aunt Sally

English-reading humans tend to do things from left to right. As such, when faced with a problem such as

```
4 + 5 - 2 * 6 / 3
```

people tend to work the problem from left to right: 4+5 is 9. Minus 2 is 7. Multiplied by 6 is 42. Divided by 3 is 14.

How about cultures that would work the problem from right to left? In that case, 6 divided by 3 is 2. Multiplied by 2 is 4. Minus 5 is –1. Plus 4 is 3.

Or even this: 4 plus 5 is 9. Six divided by 3 is 2. Nine minus 2 is 7, times 2 is 14 (again).

But in the computer, things are done in *order of precedence*. That is, the computer scans a long equation and decides to perform certain operations first. In the case of basic math, the order is

1. Multiplication

2. Division

3. Addition

4. Subtraction

The mnemonic for this sequence is MDAS, or My Dear Aunt Sally. That tells you how the computer calculates things. When you apply MDAS to this equation:

```
4 + 5 - 2 * 6 / 3
```

here's what you get: First, 2 times 6 equals 12; second, 12 divided by 3 equals 4; third, 4 plus 5 equals 9; and, fourth and finally, 9 minus 4 equals 5. Figure 9-1 also illustrates how this order works.

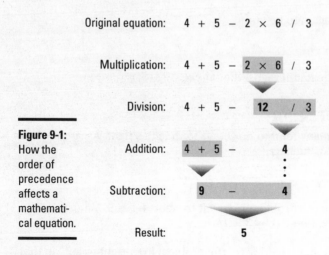

Figure 9-1:
How the order of precedence affects a mathematical equation.

Exercise 1.9.1

Take these numbers:

7 4 3 2 8

and these operators:

* / + -

and concoct a program similar to ANSWER.C that displays 9 as the result. (Try not to have the code create fractions or `float`s.)

What about multiple multiplications?

My Dear Aunt Sally tells you that the math operators have a certain priority over each other. But what about multiple math operators? Consider this ugly monster:

```
unknown = 5 * 2 * 6 / 6 / 2;
```

Can you figure it out? Oh, why bother! Let the computer do the work:

```
#include <stdio.h>

int main()
{
    int unknown;

    unknown = 5 * 2 * 6 / 6 / 2;
```

```
    printf("The unknown value is %d.\n",unknown);
    return(0);
}
```

Save this source code to disk as UNKNOWN.C. Compile and run.

```
The unknown value is 5.
```

Faced with multiple operators — either *, /, + or - — the C language figures things from left to right, just as you read.

In the example, multiplication comes first: 5 times 2 is 10, and then 10 times 6 is 60. Next comes division — in order, from left to right: 60 divided by 6 is 10. Finally, 10 divided by 2 is 5.

The official order of precedence is multiplication first and then division, addition, and, finally, subtraction, in order from left to right.

Fooling old Sally with parentheses

You can, and sometimes have to, override the order of precedence. For example, if you're trying to calculate triple profits, you would want to use a program like this:

```
#include <stdio.h>

int main()
{
    int profits,profits3;
    int income = 120;
    int expenses = 27;

    profits = income - expenses;
    profits3 = income - expenses * 3;
    printf("Garage Sale profits were $%d.\n",profits);
    printf("Triple profits would have been $%d.\n",profits3);
    return(0);
}
```

Save this source code to disk as PROFITS.C. Compile and run:

```
Garage Sale profits were $93.
Triple profits would have been $39.
```

In the order of precedence, expenses * 3 is calculated first, tripling expenses, not profits. The secret is to use parentheses to tell the compiler what to do first.

Reedit the source code for PROFITS.C. Modify Line 10 to read:

```
profits3 = (income - expenses) * 3;
```

The compiler always looks inside parentheses to see what happens there first. Here, it calculates income - expenses immediately. Then it multiplies the result by 3.

Save the changes to PROFITS.C. Recompile and run again:

```
Garage Sale profits were $93.
Triple profits would have been $279.
```

Exercise 1.9.2

Use parentheses to change the equation in the original ANSWER.C source code so that the program displays 14 as the result.

Say It Out Loud: Unary Operators!

There's a difference between *unary* and *urinary.* One applies to *urine,* the word that makes boys of all ages giggle. The other applies to math. In the C language, unary operators are used to perform math on a single value.

Going negative

Several unary operators are used in C, but I'm showing only two of them here: unary + (plus) and unary - (minus). Of the two, the only one worth knowing is unary - (minus). Simply put, the unary minus in front of a value makes that value negative:

```
#include <stdio.h>

int main()
{
    int t;

    t = 50;
    printf("You may think it's cold at %d,\n",t);
    printf("but at %d it's colder!\n",-t);
    return(0);
}
```

Save this source code to disk as COLDER.C. Compile and run:

```
You may think it's cold at 50,
But at -50 it's colder!
```

The tiny unary - sign at the end of the second `printf()` statement reverses the sign of the value in variable t, producing a negative.

Getting silly

The + unary operator isn't really necessary, just as you don't use + when you're writing out numbers normally. Only the - unary operator is truly useful. (They say that the + was added for "symmetry" reasons.)

So, theoretically, you could change Line 7 from the source code COLDER.C (in the preceding section) to read:

```
t = +50;
```

Even so, the result doesn't change the outcome. But what about this line:

```
t = -50;
```

Reedit the source code for COLDER.C, making this change to Line 7. Recompile and run to see the silly output:

```
You may think it's cold at -50,
But at 50 it's colder!
```

In this output, you can see how the first unary minus in Line 7 created the negative value 50. But the second unary minus, at the end of Line 9, *reversed* that state, resulting in a positive number.

The negative of a negative is positive.

Better yet, don't remember that sentence; negative numbers were annoying back in math class, and there's no point in reviving those memories here.

Incrementing and Decrementing and Loving It

The C language is full of shortcuts, and they're *wonderful* things. First, they save you typing time. More importantly, the shortcuts let you express some ideas in fun and cryptic ways. They help you make your code look more mysterious to casual users, which is okay; C programmers can still read your code — no problem.

The first two cryptic operators I want to introduce you to are ++ and --. These incrementing and decrementing operators are described in this section.

Just add one to it

Often in programming, you come across a situation where a value needs to be incremented. Whatever the value is, you have to add 1 to it. This happens a lot in loops, but it can occur elsewhere in programs as well.

For example, you have variable `count` and you need to add 1 to its value. You can do it like so:

```
count = count + 1;
```

Because C works out the math first, the current value of `count` is incremented by 1. Then that new value is stored in the `count` variable. So, if `count` now equals 6, `count` +1 results in 7, and 7 is then stored back into the `count` variable. `count` then equals 7. But it can also work like this:

```
count++;
```

The ++ operator tells the computer to increment the value of `count` by 1. Click-click! Or, inc-inc! Or, plus-plus! Whatever the value of `count` was, it's now one greater, thanks to ++. Here's a demo program:

```c
#include <stdio.h>

int main()
{
    int age;

    printf("Enter your age in years:");
    scanf("%d",&age);
    printf("You are %d years old.\n",age);
    age++;
    printf("In one year you'll be %d.\n",age);
    return(0);
}
```

Oh, golly. It's another "how old are you?" program. Bear with me and type it into your editor. Save the source code to disk as YEAROLD.C. Compile and run.

```
Enter your age in years:
```

Who enters their age in months any more? How about your age in leap years? Anyway, I typed **24**, dreaming of that day when I was 24:

```
You are 24 years old.
In one year you'll be 25.
```

The mystery of C++

The ++ operator means to "add 1" to whatever is in front of it. When it came time to name the variation of C that Bjarne Stoustroup developed in 1983, he chose to call it C++, as in "one more added to C." Very clever, these humans.

On the other hand, when Microsoft came up with its implementation of Sun Microsystems'

Java language, they chose to call it C#, or "C sharp." It's a musical term; the # has nothing to do with the C programming language — and many C# detractors point out that C# has little to do with the C programming language either.

Yee-haw! The value of the variable age is changed by age++. Afterward, the value is increased by 1. That's incrementation!

Exercise 1.9.3

Now that you know about the ++ operator, fix up the program BIGEARS.C from Chapter 7. Modify the for statement so that the ++ operator is used.

Just take one away from it

To keep the world in harmonic balance, a -- operator counters the ++ operator in C. You could call it "minus minus," but I call it "dec dec" because what it does is decrement, or subtract, 1 from the variable it modifies. For example:

```
count--;
```

This statement subtracts one from the value of variable count. It's the same as

```
count = count - 1;
```

Exercise 1.9.4

Modify the source code to BLASTOFF.C from Exercise 1.7.2 (Book I, Chapter 7). Change the for statement to use the -- operator to modify the countdown variable.

Pre-incrementing and post-incrementing

Here's a puzzle. If variable alpha equals 5, what's the value of variable beta after this statement:

```
beta = alpha++;
```

The answer is 5. The reason is that the ++ is a post-incrementing operator. It increments the value of the variable *after* the variable is used. Here's the code to prove it:

```
#include <stdio.h>

int main()
{
    int alpha,beta;

    alpha=5;
    beta = alpha++;
    printf("Alpha = %d\n",alpha);
    printf("Beta = %d\n",beta);
    return(0);
}
```

Name the source code PREPOST.C. Compile and run:

```
Alpha = 6
Beta = 5
```

If you think that this example is odd and it makes you uncomfortable, remember that you can always split Line 8 in two:

```
alpha++;
beta = alpha;
```

Or, you can take advantage of the fact that the ++ operator can go on either side of the variable. When ++ appears before the variable name, as in ++alpha, it's pre-incrementing the value of alpha.

Edit the source code for PREPOST.C and change Line 8 to read

```
beta = ++alpha;
```

Save to disk. Recompile and run. Observe the output:

```
Alpha = 6
Beta = 6
```

The value of alpha was incremented *first,* and then its value was assigned to variable beta.

You can do the same thing with the -- operator. If it appears after a variable, the variable is decremented after being used. Here's how that modification looks on Line 8:

```
beta = alpha--;
```

Or, if the - - operator appears before the variable name, the value is decremented and then used:

```
beta = --alpha;
```

Note that this construction isn't allowed:

```
++alpha++;
```

This isn't "double incrementing." In fact, the compiler gets angry with you if you attempt such a thing.

Exercise 1.9.5
Modify the source code for PREPOST.C again. By changing only Line 8, have the answers come out so that alpha equals 4 and beta equals 5.

Other Cryptic Math Shortcuts

When it comes to cryptic shortcuts, C is full of them! You would think that ++ and - - would be enough. But, no! There have to be more. After all, more types of equations are similar to the following:

```
count = count + 1;
```

The variable count is incremented, which is done by using the ++ operator. But what about this operation:

```
count = count + 5;
```

Or, what do you do when this happens:

```
inf = inf * 10;
```

These examples are variables modifying their own values. This type of thing seems to happen often in programming, so the C language offers you a smattering of shortcuts to deal with it. (Using the shortcuts is optional; if they confuse you, ignore them!)

Incrementing by more than one
Here's one of the variations of the AGE.C program, from Chapter 4 in this book:

```
#include <stdio.h>

int main()
```

```
{
    int age;

    age = 43;                /* put your age here */
    printf("You are %d years old.\n",age);
    age = age + 5;
    printf("In five years you'll be %d years old!\n",age);
    return(0);
}
```

This program contains a variable, age, and that variable's value is increased by 5:

```
age = age + 5;
```

Here's another way you can do that:

```
age++;
age++;
age++;
age++;
age++;
```

Here's another:

```
age += 5;
```

I read this operation as "Add 5 to the value of variable age." The += symbol is merely a mathematical shortcut, a sort of hyperincrementing operator.

Summon the most recent incarnation of the AGE.C program from your computer's hard drive, or just enter the preceding source code. Modify the program so that age=age+1 is replaced by age+=5. Save. Compile. Run.

Exercise 1.9.6

Modify the source code for AGE.C again. This time, add code so that the user's age is entered from the keyboard (a trick I present in Chapter 5). Then tell the user what their age will be in 25 years. If the user's age is over 100, tell them that they will probably be dead. (Use the if statement that I introduce in Book I, Chapter 6.)

Multiplying a variable by itself

The =+ mathematical shortcut can be used with all C math operators. For each time a variable is added, subtracted, multiplied, or divided by itself, there is an operator. Table 9-2 lists the lot.

Table 9-2   **C Language Cryptic Shortcut Operators**

Operator	Function	Example
++	Increment by 1	`age++;`
--	Decrement by 1	`beauty--;`
+=	Add a value to a variable	`weight += 10;`
-=	Subtract a value from a variable	`income -= 100;`
*=	Multiply a variable by a value	`taxes *= 2;`
/=	Divide a variable by a value	`divorce /= 3;`

The mathematical symbols for the cryptic shortcut operators must be on the left and not on the right. The easy way to think of this rule is that the wrong way can look like an equation missing a value, as in

```
age =+ 5;
```

It looks like a value should appear between the = and the +. But if you do it right, it doesn't really look like anything is missing:

```
age += 5;
```

The following source code demonstrates using the *= operator for multiplying a variable by its own value:

```
#include <stdio.h>

int main()
{
    int distance = 2;

    printf("You have to walk only %d miles to school.\n",
distance);
    distance *= 25;
    printf("But when I was a kid, I walked %d miles to
school!\n",distance);
    printf("Both ways!\n");
    printf("In the snow!\n");
    printf("Up hill!\n");
    return(0);
}
```

Save the source code to disk as SCHOOL.C. Compile and run. Have a laugh.

Chapter 10: It's Only Logical

In This Chapter

✔ **Making multiple comparisons in C**

✔ **Using the logical OR operator, ||**

✔ **Using the logical AND operator, &&**

✔ **Dealing with multiple logical operators**

Comparisons happen all over in the C language. The `if` statement is the primary dwelling place for the comparison; `if` makes its living by comparing different things and having the program perform different actions based on the results. Similarly, a comparison is made in a `for` loop as well as in the `while` loop.

Most of the time, comparisons can be rather simple, deftly handled by the smattering of operators shown over in Table 6-1, in Chapter 6. But more complex comparisons are possible. To help you deal with them, the C language employs a pair of logical operators. This chapter introduces you to the logical AND and OR operators, which can be used to help hone your C language decision-making and comparison processes.

Comparisons from Hell

How many ways are there to handle the following problem? The computer asks a question to which you must answer Yes or No. You can press the Y key for Yes or the N key for No. Press any other key and the computer asks the same questions again.

You can handle the Yes-or-No question in C in about a zillion ways. This section mulls over some possibilities.

YORN.C, attempt number 1

The following code attempts to solve the Yes-or-No question puzzle:

```c
#include <stdio.h>

int main()
{
```

```
char ch;

printf("Would you like me to send your password to the
bad guys?\n");
printf("Enter Y or N (Y/N)?");
ch = getchar();
if(ch=='N')
{
    printf("Well, then: your password is safe!\n");
}
else
{
    printf("Okay. Sending your password!\n");
}
return(0);
}
```

Save this source code to disk as YORN.C. Compile. Run.

```
Would you like me to send your password to the bad guys?
Enter Y or N (Y/N)?
```

Press **n** and then press Enter:

```
Okay. Sending your password!
```

Whoops. Run the program again, and this time press **N** (Shift+N) and then press Enter:

```
Well, then: your password is safe!
```

YORN.C, attempt number 2

The original YORN.C code, shown in the preceding section, has a serious flaw. The if statement is used to check only one condition when, in fact, *four* conditions should be checked:

```
ch == 'N'
ch == 'n'
ch == 'Y'
ch == 'y'
```

This example covers all keyboard possibilities for pressing the Y or N keys. As a programmer, you can never assume that Caps Lock is on or off or that users take you literally and press Y (rather than y) whenever they see a "Press Y" prompt.

The program should not only check the preceding four conditions, but also loop and ask the question again when none of the conditions is met.

In programming, you should solve one puzzle at a time. So, the first step in repairing YORN.C is to ensure that all four conditions inside the code are met:

```
#include <stdio.h>

int main()
{
    char ch;

    printf("Would you like me to send your password to the
bad guys?\n");
    printf("Enter Y or N (Y/N)?");
    ch = getchar();
    if(ch=='N')
    {
        printf("Well, then: your password is safe!\n");
    }
    else if(ch=='n')
    {
        printf("Well, then: your password is safe!\n");
    }
    else if(ch=='Y')
    {
        printf("Okay. Sending your password!\n");
    }
    else if(ch=='y')
    {
        printf("Okay. Sending your password!\n");
    }
    else
    {
        printf("You must enter Y or N!\n");
    }
    return(0);
}
```

This example is a solution to the YORN.C puzzle, one that involves multiple else if statements to handle the four possible conditions. The final else displays the warning that Y or N wasn't pressed. (You can add the loop later.) For now, try to see how well this code works: Update the YORN.C source code in your editor. Save the code to disk again. Compile it.

Run the program five times. The first four times, try keys **N**, **n**, **Y**, and **y**. The fifth time, try some other key. This process confirms that the program properly filters the correct keys. But — admit it — the code isn't the most elegant thing.

YORN.C, attempt number 3

The final fix-up to the YORN.C code (from earlier sections in this chapter) is to add a loop. The loop repeats as long as none of the proper keys — N, n, Y, or y — is entered. You can do this in multiple ways in C. The method I settled on for the following code is to use an infinite `for` loop with `break` statements that are used when someone presses the proper key:

```c
#include <stdio.h>

int main()
{
    char ch;

    printf("Would you like me to send your password to the
bad guys?\n");
    for(;;)
    {
        printf("Enter Y or N (Y/N)?");
        ch = getchar();
        if(ch=='N')
        {
            printf("Well, then: your password is safe!\n");
            break;
        }
        else if(ch=='n')
        {
            printf("Well, then: your password is safe!\n");
            break;
        }
        else if(ch=='Y')
        {
            printf("Okay. Sending your password!\n");
            break;
        }
        else if(ch=='y')
        {
            printf("Okay. Sending your password!\n");
            break;
        }
        else
        {
            printf("You must enter Y or N!\n");
            fflush(stdin);   /* Eliminate other keys */
            /* no break here; keep looping! */
        }
    }
    return(0);
}
```

Make these modifications to your YORN.C source code. Remember to substitute `fpurge(stdin);` in Line 35 if you're using a Unix-like operating system. Save the changes to disk. Compile and run.

First, try the four good keys: **Y**, **y**, **N**, and **n**. Then, try other keys to see how the program handles them.

Although this strategy may appear to work fine, a better, more elegant solution is available: Use logical operators to help boost the power of your comparisons.

Here Are Your Logical Operators, Mr. Spock!

When you deal with multiple comparisons in a programming language, you must stumble into the land of logical operators. They just make things easier. And, despite the reputation of "logic" as being a demanding category of mathematics, I have found that it makes sense, especially if you sound things out. For example:

```
if(ch=='Y' OR ch=='y')
```

This `if` statement makes two comparisons and uses a logical OR to weigh them. This line reads "If the value of variable `ch` is equal to big Y or the value of variable `ch` is equal to little y." If either comparison is true, the `if` statement is also true.

The companion for logical OR is logical AND. It works like this in an `if` statement:

```
if(temp > 75 AND skies==SUNNY)
```

This `if` statement makes two comparisons with a logical AND connecting them. It reads "If the value of variable `temp` is greater than 75 and the value of variable `skies` is equal to the constant SUNNY." In this case, both comparisons must be true for the `if` statement to be true.

Of course, the C language doesn't use OR or AND as logical operators. Instead, special symbols are used, as shown in Table 10-1.

Table 10-1		C Language Basic Logical Operators	
Operator	*Meaning*	*Example*	*Explanation*
`&&`	Logical AND	`a==10 && b<75`	Both comparisons must be true for the entire statement to be true.
`||`	Logical OR	`ch=='Z' || ch=='z'`	Either comparison can be true for the entire statement to be true.

Introducing Mr. Logical OR

When you're connecting two comparisons with a logical OR, either condition must be true for the entire statement to be true. Here's a sample program:

```
#include <stdio.h>

int main()
{
    int age;

    printf("Please enter your age in years:");
    scanf("%d",&age);
    if(age<=18 || age>=65)
        puts("Enjoy life while you can!");
    else
        puts("Get back to work!");
    return(0);
}
```

Enter this code into your editor. Save it to disk as LIFE.C. Compile.

Run the program three different times, trying three different ages: one younger than 18, one older than 65, and one in the middle.

Two comparisons are made by the if statement in Line 9. The first is age<=18, and the second is age>=65. If either one is true, || (logical OR) makes the entire statement true. Only when neither is true does the || fail the test and the else statement get executed.

Table 10-2 helps explain how logical OR evaluates comparisons.

Table 10-2	**Results of Various Logical OR Operations**		
Comparison 1	*Logical OR*	*Comparison 2*	*Entire Statement Result*
TRUE	||	TRUE	TRUE
TRUE	||	FALSE	TRUE
FALSE	||	TRUE	TRUE
FALSE	||	FALSE	FALSE

Exercise 1.10.1

Modify the last rendition of the TYPING.C program (from Book I, Chapter 7). Change Line 12 so that either the ~ or ` character quits the program. (Both characters are on the same key.)

Say hello to Mr. Logical AND

Good morning, programmer! Your job is to devise the secret password system by which agents can log in to the company's computer and thereby play endless games of FreeCell. Here's the code you have so far:

```c
#include <stdio.h>

int main()
{
    int agent;
    char code;

    printf("Enter your agent number:");
    scanf("%d",&agent);
    fflush(stdin);
    printf("Enter your single-digit code key:");
    scanf("%c",&code);
    if(agent == 7 && code=='B')
    {
        puts("Welcome aboard, James Bond.");
        puts("You may commence with operation FreeCell.");
    }
    else
    {
        puts("The authorities have been notified");
        puts("of this illegal access.");
    }
    return(0);
}
```

Save the world! But first, save your source code to disk as AGENT.C. Unix users, remember to substitute `fpurge(stdin)` in Line 10. Compile and run:

```
Enter your agent number:
```

Type **007**. This input is okay; the `scanf()` function ignores leading zeroes, but still accepts input as a value:

```
Enter your single-digit code key:
```

Press **B** and then Enter:

```
Welcome aboard, James Bond.
You may commence with operation FreeCell.
```

REMEMBER

"Is equal to" versus "equals"

When you're coding complex, multiple comparisons using logical operators, you can easily forget that == means "is equal to" and = means "equals." You must remember the difference because the compiler *does* evaluate the single = sign as a TRUE comparison.

For example, to see whether two values are equal, this comparison is made:

    a==b

This line is a comparison. It reads "If variable a *is equal to* variable b." The result is either TRUE or FALSE. Now consider this example:

    a=b

This line is an assignment. It reads "The value of variable a equals, or is assigned, the value of variable b." The result of this operation is *always* TRUE.

You may one day have a maddening bug in your code that is caused by a subtle mistake, such as forgetting to use == or using = instead. Remember the difference!

The logical AND operation in Line 13 ensures that both conditions that the if statement is evaluating are TRUE: The agent number must be equal to 7 && ("and") the single-digit code key must be equal to the letter B. B for Bond. James Bond. When either or both conditions are FALSE, the entire thing is false, so if fails the test. Table 10-3 describes the various results of logical AND operations.

Table 10-3	Results of Various Logical AND Operations		
Comparison 1	*Logical AND*	*Comparison 2*	*Entire Statement Result*
TRUE	&&	TRUE	TRUE
TRUE	&&	FALSE	FALSE
FALSE	&&	TRUE	FALSE
FALSE	&&	FALSE	FALSE

Exercise 1.10.2

Write another rendition of the CHILLY.C program (introduced in Chapter 6). This time, have the program ask for the current temperature, and if the temperature is between 68 and 75 degrees, have the program say My how pleasant. Otherwise, the program displays the message The temperature could be better.

YORN.C, attempt number 4

Now that you know a bit about logical operators, it's time to reign in some of the bulk in the YORN.C series of programs. By using the logical OR operator, you can test for either Y or y, or N or n, in a single if statement. Here's the modified code:

```c
#include <stdio.h>

int main()
{
    char ch;

    printf("Would you like me to send your password to the
    bad guys?\n");
    for(;;)
    {
        printf("Enter Y or N (Y/N)?");
        ch = getchar();
        if(ch=='N' || ch=='n')
        {
            printf("Well, then: your password is safe!\n");
            break;
        }
        else if(ch=='Y' || ch=='y')
        {
            printf("Okay. Sending your password!\n");
            break;
        }
        else
        {
            printf("You must enter Y or N!\n");
            fflush(stdin);   /* Eliminate other keys */
            /* no break here; keep looping! */
        }
    }
    return(0);
}
```

Make the necessary changes in your YORN.C code so that it resembles what's shown here. The program's size is really reduced — but its efficiency is increased. Save the changes to disk, recompile, and run.

Run the program five times, first checking **Y**, **y**, **N**, and **n** for input and then checking other characters to be certain that they're caught.

Multiple Madness with Logical Operators

Oh, that silly James Bond. After you wrote that wonderful program AGENT.C (from earlier in this chapter), Mr. Bond refuses to type a capital B and instead often types a lowercase B. Rather than falsely alarm the authorities, agent M is asking whether you can modify the program so that lowercase B can also be accepted. Are you up to it?

Load the source code for AGENT.C into your editor. Modify Line 13 to read:

```
if(agent==7 && code=='B' || code=='b')
```

Save this change to disk. Compile. Pray that it works. Run:

```
Enter your agent number:
```

Type **007** and press Enter:

```
Enter your single-digit code key:
```

Whew! So far, so good. Now press (lowercase) **b** and press Enter:

```
Welcome aboard, James Bond. You may commence with operation
    FreeCell.
```

Yeah!

You can group any number of comparisons with logical operations. According to the order of precedence (refer to Book I, Chapter 9), && and || operate from left to right. But, like the math operators, you can use parentheses to override. In fact, I often use parentheses to clear up some involved statements, such as

```
if(input=='Y' || input=='y' && code=='Z' || code=='z')
```

This statement seems like a mess, but basically it's checking upper- and lowercase values for input and code. Another way to write it is

```
if((input=='Y' || input=='y') && (code=='Z' || code=='z'))
```

The inner sets of parentheses can help make the statement more readable. Here, input is first tested against Y and y; and then code is tested against Z and z; and, finally, a logical AND operation is performed between the results.

Book II

Middle C

Contents at a Glance

Chapter 1: Variables from Beyond Infinity

In This Chapter

✔ Using long **and** short ints

✔ Introducing double **precision**

✔ Going positive with unsigned **variables**

✔ Typecasting

✔ C language variable summary

Welcome to the unknown! It's the mysterious letter *X*, the cattle brand of unknown things. Who knows what it could be? Strange. Unexplained. Enigmatic. The secret depths of the variable are left for only the most intrepid of programmers to explore! Bwaa-ha-ha!

Seriously. Although on one hand it seems unearthly and mysterious to have a storage place for values unknown, on the other hand you need this type of exotic cubbyhole for holding unknown solutions inside a program. Those storage places make your programs deal with unknown information and unpredictable outcomes.

This chapter fully uncovers the possibilities of all the C language variable types — from int to float and from char to double and all the pit stops between. This chapter is your journey to the unknown and back!

Remember to use the middle folder or directory for the source code and program files in this book.

Review of C Language Variable Types

Book 1 introduces the basic three types of variables used in C: the int, the float, and the char. Here's a quick review:

✦ int: C language int variables are used for storing integer, or whole number, values. They can range from the negative millions, including zero, on up through positive values in the millions. Because most simple math and programming operations take place quickly with int variables, this numeric variable type is preferred in C.

+ **float:** The float variable type is used to handle all numbers, including values with decimal or fractional parts. The range of values a float can handle is huge, including just about any number the mind can imagine — including incredibly small values. The limitation with the float, however, is that the displayed number is precise to only six or seven digits.

+ **char:** The char variable type is used in the C language to store single characters and special escape-sequence characters (such as \n). char can also store integer values in a small range, but mostly it's used for storing characters and building strings of text.

The following silly program demonstrates each of the three basic variable types:

```
#include <stdio.h>

int main()
{
    int number;
    float iq;
    char first;

    puts("IQ Calculator");
    printf("Enter your house or apartment number:");
    scanf("%d",&number);
    fflush(stdin);            /* use fpurge(stdin) in Unix */
    printf("Enter the first letter of your last name:");
    scanf("%c",&first);
    puts("Calculating your IQ...");
    iq = number/first;
    printf("This computer guesses your IQ to be %f.\n",iq);
    return(0);
}
```

Type this source code into your text editor. The operations used in this example are all described in Book 1; refer to it if you see anything here that you're unfamiliar with.

If you're using Linux or Mac OS X or Unix, then remember to use fpurge(stdin); in Line 12.

Save the source code to disk as IQ.C. Compile the source code and then run the program. Here's a sample:

```
IQ Calculator
Enter your house or apartment number:
```

I live at **714**, so I type that:

```
Enter the first letter of your last name:
```

I type **G** and press Enter:

```
This computer guesses your IQ to be 10.000000.
```

Wonderful.

Note that the program uses the char variable type to store a character (in Line 14) and as a value (in Line 16). That's allowed when you're using the char variable. Also note that there's no logic in dividing a street address by a letter of the alphabet.

Exercise 2.1.1

Note that the IQ.C program spits out low IQ values for low street numbers. Concoct a fix in the program so that when the value of the iq variable is less than 50, the program automatically adds 100 to that value, or, when the value of iq is between 51 and 80, the value is doubled.

The long *and the* short *of it*

The C language uses two sizes for integers: long and short. These terms relate to the size of the memory chunk used to hold the integer value.

+ short integers use 16 bits, which can store values from –32,768 through 32,767.

+ long integers use 32 bits to store values from –2,147,483,648 through 2,147,483,647.

On modern computers, whenever you declare an int, it's automatically of the long type. When PCs were first introduced, ints were automatically of the short type. And, that may still be true in some compilers.

The point is that if you want to be specific, you must use the word short or long when declaring the int variable, as in

```
short int paycheck;
long int cost_of_living;
```

These commands specifically direct the compiler to create an integer-storage cubby of a given size. Of course, this begs the question "How much money would you make if you could roll 32,000 on the dice in Monopoly?"

Enter the following source code into your editor:

```
#include <stdio.h>

#define ROLL 32000
#define SPACES 40          /* 40 spaces on the Monopoly board */

int main()
{
    short int dice;
    long int money = 0;

    puts("Monopoly Money Calculator");
    for(dice=0;dice<ROLL;dice+=SPACES)
    {
        money+=200;
        printf("Roll %d\r",dice);    /* display on one line */
    }
    putchar('\n');           /* add newline for last roll */
    printf("You made a total of $%d!\n",money);
    return(0);
}
```

Save the code to disk as MONOPOLY.C. Compile and run to see how much money you would make by rolling 32000 on the dice and rounding the board several thousand times.

The \r in Line 15 may be new to you. That escape character represents the carriage return, which moves the cursor to the beginning of the line. Unlike the newline \n, the cursor neither advances nor scrolls the screen. This handy trick redisplays a line of text. In fact, to see it work better, change Line 4 so that the value of constant SPACES equals 2.

Not long *enough*

The MONOPOLY.C program just doesn't quite sate my greed. A long int is defined, yet the program on my computer calculated only a measly $160,000 — a pittance!

Modify the MONOPOLY.C source code. Increase the ROLL value by changing Line 3 to read

```
#define ROLL 3200000
```

(That's 3,200,000.)

Save that change to disk, and then recompile:

```
warning: comparison is always true due to the limited range
    of data type.
```

Oh, bother. It's just a silly *warning* error. The program really did compile, so go ahead and run it!

If you were superhuman, you could see that the display on the screen modulates between –32,000-something and 32,000-something — eternally. That's what the warning error was trying to explain: A `short int`, which is what the `dice` variable is, cannot hold a value larger than 32,767, yet the `for` loop tries to stuff a larger value into that variable. The result is that the variable overflows.

**Book II
Chapter 1**

**Variables from
Beyond Infinity**

For example, when the value of `dice` equals 32,767 and one more is added, the next value is–32,768. That's simply the range the variable has to deal with and how it handles values internally.

You can choose from two solutions. First, you can reset the value of ROLL back to 32000, or you can redefine `short int dice` as `long int dice`.

Press Ctrl+C to halt the program run amok.

Reedit your source code. Change Line 8 to read

```
long int dice;
```

Save the source code to disk. Recompile. Run.

That's more like it!

Exercise 2.1.2
Modify the MONOPOLY.C source code by declaring both variables as plain `int`s. See whether it still works on your compiler.

Float me to the moon
The C language uses floating-point variables to store very large values, very small values, and values with fractional parts. The official numerical range for a `float` in C is from 1.17×10^{38} to 3.40×10^{38} with 6-digit precision. To put that in nonmathematical terms, the `float` covers a large swath of numbers. Only

in some backroom laboratory on a college campus is some übergeek whimpering because he can't make a proper calculation with a float, like this:

```
#include <stdio.h>

#define DISTANCE 378921.46      /* in kilometers */
#define PI 3.141

int main()
{
    float orbit;

    orbit = DISTANCE * 2 * PI;
    printf("The moon travels %f km in one orbit.\n",orbit);
    return(0);
}
```

Oh, gosh! Ugly! Math! But don't fret. I assume that the distance from the earth to the moon is about 378,921.46 kilometers. (Its true distance varies, depending on the moon's mood.) To figure out how far the moon travels as it orbits the earth, you double the distance and multiply it by π (pi). It's a delicious problem for a float to solve.

Save the source code to disk as MOON.C. Compile and run:

```
The moon travels 2380384.500000 km in one orbit.
```

Or does it? Remember that float variables are accurate to only six digits of precision, and 2380384 is *seven* digits long! Should you pack more, or less, granola trail mix for the moon-loop hike? Hmmm.

Exercise 2.1.3

You're a foolish American who still thinks in *miles*. Recraft the MOON.C program to have it calculate and display the results in miles. One kilometer equals 0.621371192 miles. (Rename the source code MOONM.C to keep this exercise's answer separate from the other MOON.C programs in this chapter.)

Double or nothing!

Don't despair! When more precision is required than a float can muster, the C language comes through with a more precise, larger type of floating-point variable.

Say hello to double, which is sort of the long int type of float. The double variable type has a much higher range of values and a more precise degree of precision than the mere mortal float. With a double variable, you can have values from 2.22×10⁻³⁰⁸ to 1.79×10³⁰⁸ and 15-digit precision. That's more than enough to handle even the most obnoxious calculations you can think of. Whimper no more!

Modify the source code to MOON.C, changing only Line 8 to read

```
double orbit;
```

You're declaring `orbit` as a `double` rather than as a `float`. That makes the answer more precise. Save the change to disk, and then recompile and run:

```
The moon travels 2380384.611720 kilometers in one orbit.
```

Using 15 digits of precision, you can be assured that the result is dead-on. Or is it? After all, PI is defined to only 3.141. Would it make that much difference? (See Exercise 2.1.4.)

As with using `ints` over `floats`, the disadvantage of the `double` is that the computer takes more time to deal with it than it does with other types of variables. For today's fast computers, that difference is moot, but when you can, try to use a `float`. Save the `double` for only when it's required or necessary.

Exercise 2.1.4

Would you like more π with that? When you're talking rocket science, you should be as accurate as possible. The precision of π is known to billions of digits, so why not exploit some of that accuracy in your program? Even so, modify the MOON.C program again. This time, define the constant PI to 15 digits: that is, 3.14159265358979.

Signed, Unsigned, Soap, No Soap, Radio

Whenever you declare an `int` or `char` in the C language, the compiler assumes that you want to deal with both positive and negative numbers. This assumption makes sense: If you're doing math and the result is minus-something, it's breezy to store it in any old integer variable.

The only time the negative numbers may throw you for a loop is in a loop. Check this out:

```
#include <stdio.h>

int main()
{
```

```
    char c;

    for(c=0;c<128;c++)
        printf("%d\t",c);
    return(0);
}
```

Type this source code into your editor. Save it to disk as GOOFY.C.

Compile the program. You may see a warning error. That's puzzling because you should know that the value for a `char` "integer" ranges from –128 through 0 and up to 127. In the preceding `for` loop, the value of c should never be greater than 127, right? Well. Whatever. After all, it's only a *warning* error, and the program was created anyway.

Run the program.

Press Ctrl+C to halt the program.

Oh, yeah! Value out of range. I get it! Duh!

Greetings, O Unsigned One

The `int` and `char` variables you use in your programs are really *signed* variables. That is, they can hold negative values. You read about this when you first find out the range of values that can be stored in a variable. To review:

◆ `char`: Values from –128 to 127

◆ `short int`: Values from –32,768 to 32,767

◆ `int` (or `long int`): Values from –2,147,483,648 to 2,147,483,647

In fact, you omit a C language keyword when you declare these variables: `signed`. That's because these variables carry both negative and positive values. So, this example:

```
int number;
float iq;
char first;
```

could have easily been

```
signed int number;
signed float iq;
signed char first;
```

And the program would have run the same. For this reason, the `signed` keyword is rarely, if ever, used. It's merely included for symmetry with the `unsigned` keyword.

Unsigned variables lack a negative part. Figure 1-1 illustrates how signed and unsigned integers get their values.

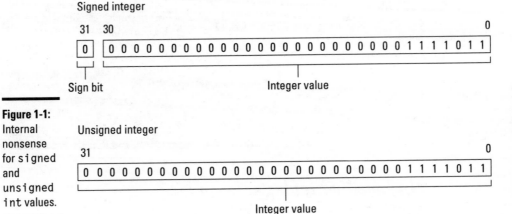

Figure 1-1:
Internal
nonsense
for `signed`
and
`unsigned`
`int` values.

In a signed integer, one bit is the sign, negative or positive. The other 31 bytes are the value itself. But an unsigned integer uses all its bits for the value. Because one extra bit is available and each bit is a power of two, an unsigned variable can hold values twice as large as the positive values of signed integers. To wit:

+ `unsigned char`: Values from 0 to 255

+ `unsigned short int`: Values from 0 to 65,535

+ `unsigned int` (or `long unsigned int`): Values from 0 to 4,294,967,295

Yes, `unsigned` means no negative values. So, whenever you need a larger integer value or you just know that you're not using negatives, unsigned integers are the way to go.

Bring up into your editor the source code for GOOFY.C. Modify Line 5 to read

```
unsigned char c;
```

Save to disk. Recompile. (Note that you see no more warnings now.) Then run it.

TIP

The proper order of things

If this signed/unsigned and short/long stuff is new to you, you may be concerned about which words go first. After all, declaring an int is easy:

    int cinchy

But what if it's a long unsigned int? Is it:

    long unsigned int

or

    unsigned long int

The answer is (thankfully) *both!* The C compiler doesn't care whether signed/unsigned or short/long comes first. The variable type, int or char, must come last. But, otherwise, the order isn't important.

To keep consistent in my own code, however, I specify unsigned first and then short or long if needed.

Unsigned variables seem to lack that negative-attitude problem

Quickly type the source code for the following stupid, silly, little program:

```
#include <stdio.h>

int main()
{
    /* keep values small with short */
    short unsigned int a,b,u;
    short int s;

    a=150;
    b=300;
    u=a-b;
    s=a-b;

    printf("Unsigned variable u = %d\n",u);
    printf("Signed variable s = %d\n",s);
    return(0);
}
```

Save the program to disk as NONEGS.C. It demonstrates the signed and unsigned nature of integers and what happens during the struggle to avoid negative numbers.

Compile the program and run it. Here's what the output should look like:

```
Unsigned variable u = 65386
Signed variable s = -150
```

You *can* try to stuff a negative value into an unsigned variable. In Line 11, someone attempted to place the value -150 into unsigned variable u. But because the value is unsigned, it becomes 65368, which is displayed.

(If the variables were not defined as ints, the result would be 4,294,967,146 for unsigned long int variable u.)

Essentially the same value is stored in both variables u and s, but being declared signed or unsigned makes all the difference.

One last twisty turn

Don't dispense with that NONEGS source code just yet!

In NONEGS, the printf() statements use the %d, integer, placeholder to display the values of variables s and u. However, you can use a special %u, unsigned integer, placeholder as well:

```
#include <stdio.h>

int main()
{
    /* keep values small with short */
    int a,b,u,s;

    a=150;
    b=300;
    u=a-b;
    s=a-b;

    printf("Unsigned variable u = %u\n",u);
    printf("Signed variable s = %d\n",s);
    return(0);
}
```

Modify NONEGS.C as shown. Note that no unsigned variables are created. You merely use the %u placeholder to *display* a variable's value as though it were unsigned. Save the changes to disk.

Compile and run:

```
Unsigned variable u = 4294967146
Signed variable s = -150
```

The %u placeholder displays the value of the u variable as though it were unsigned. The problem is that %u assumes that the value is a long int, not a short. For this exercise, the value appears larger than when the original NONEGS.C was run, but it's really the same type of reinterpretation of the value –150, but in an unsigned variable. (Or something like that.)

This example may not seem so strange to you. Book I, Chapter 5 demonstrates how the char variable type displays characters when the %c placeholder is used and displays integer values when %d is used. With %u, it's pretty much the same thing: The variable may be of one type, but the placeholder determines how and which type is displayed.

Fair and Unfair Variables

There's no such thing as fair and unfair variable types. Neither are there holy or unholy variables. No, not in this C language.

Typecasting and Other Acting Problems

Remember Adam West? He was TV's Batman (and the only person who could ever play Batman, in my humble opinion). Poor Adam. He did such a good job that no one would hire him for anything other than "Batman"-like roles. Because of *typecasting,* he was doomed to endless nights of dinner theater and "Love Boat" cruises for unappreciative audiences (who still thought of him as Bruce Wayne).

Typecasting definitely happened to lots of actors over the years: Johnny Weissmuller as Tarzan, Bela Lugosi as Dracula, and Bob Denver as Gilligan. It almost happened to Sean Connery, who was *the* definitive James Bond. It can also happen to your variables in the C language, though it doesn't ruin anyone's acting career.

Pretending that a variable is something it's not

In the C language, *typecasting* works by placing a variable type declaration before a variable of another type. Suppose that variable i is an integer:

```
(float)i
```

This typecast makes variable i look like a float. Of course, this typecast would appear in a function or mathematical statement; you can't just typecast a statement by itself — it's like standing in the shower without the water running. But you can get the idea from a program I demonstrate earlier in this chapter.

Bring up the source code for the program GOOFY.C, the original version, which looks like this:

```
#include <stdio.h>

int main()
{
    char c;

    for(c=0;c<128;c++)
        printf("%d\t",c);
    return(0);
}
```

The fix for this example is to redeclare variable c as an unsigned char. But what if, everywhere else in the program, the variable had to be signed? In that case, you would whip out a typecast merely for the one instance that c needed in order to be unsigned. Modify Line 7 to read

```
for(c=0;(unsigned)c<128;c++)
```

The (unsigned) cast is used to make variable c unsigned temporarily — just in that one place in that one statement. Save the change to disk. Compile and run.

The program doesn't burp or warn or produce an error. It simply does its job, thanks to the typecast.

Typecasting is temporary. It doesn't change a variable's type at all. Only for the brief moment that the typecast appears is the variable treated as another type.

Exercise 2.1.5

Write a program that uses the long integer variable humongous in a loop to count from 65 through 90. In each loop, the value is typecast as a char variable and saved in the char variable chuck. A putchar() function then prints to the screen the value of the char variable chuck. Name the source CHUCK.C.

Cast away!

A type casting problem occurred in the IQ.C program, presented earlier in this chapter. The problem is this:

```
iq = number/first;
```

Variable iq is a float. Variable number is an int. Variable first is a char. Now, there's nothing morally wrong here; you can perform that type of math. But remember that in C the calculation is done *on the right first*. Then the result is put through to the variable. In this example, the calculation is all-integer. Any fractional part is lopped off. That explains why all the IQ values printed by the program end in .000000.

Typecasting to the rescue!

To make the operation's result a floating-point value, typecast. But you don't have to cast each variable — just the equation:

```
iq = (float)number/first;
```

Make this change to the IQ.C source code on your computer. Save the change to disk, recompile, and run. Note how the output is a more proper floating-point number, thanks to the typecast.

You may find yourself using this type of typecast in programs that involve lots of math. Don't worry about that now; just recognize the typecast when you see it and understand what's going on.

C Language Variable Reference

The full gamut of C language variable types, including their various and sundry modifiers, ranges and comments, are all listed in Table 1-1.

Table 1-1	C Language Variable Types	
Type	*Value range*	*Comments*
char	−128 to 127	
unsigned char	0 to 255	
int	−32,768 to 32,767	16-bit computers
	−2,147,483,648 to 2,147,483,647	32-bit computers
unsigned int	0 to 65,535	16-bit computers
	0 to 4,294,967,295	32-bit computers
short int	−32,768 to 32,767	
unsigned short int	0 to 65,535	
long int	−2,147,483,648 to 2,147,483,647	
unsigned long int	0 to 4,294,967,295	
float	1.17×10^{-38} to 3.40×10^{38}	6-digit precision
double	2.22×10^{-308} to 1.79×10^{308}	15-digit precision

Chapter 2: The Madness of Printf()

In This Chapter

- Understanding numbering systems
- Beginning binary
- Using hexadecimal
- Displaying hex values
- Ignoring octal
- Nerding it with scientific notation
- Using `printf()` to format **floats**
- Controlling the width of numeric output
- Justifying text with `printf()`

The `printf()` function is one of the first you find out about in C and one of the last you fully understand. In modern documentation, I have never seen anything fully describe the power available in `printf()`; it's almost like the writer is too busy to get through the information to bother to fully explain it. Either that, or I just have so much to explain that it's impossible to describe all that `printf()` can do in one chunk.

This chapter is primarily about how `printf()` can format output. Part of that format involves `printf()` displaying information in non-base 10 numbering systems. Because of that, this chapter also covers those non-base 10 number systems, for your fun, frolic, and amusement.

Going Numb with Numbering Systems

Long before humans could write, they could count. The earliest form of document we have is some clay tablet that inventories sheep or water buffalo or some other creature.

After a while, humans realized that pressing one tick into a clay tablet per water buffalo was rather inefficient, so shortcuts and abbreviations were made. For five water buffalo, the symbol of a hand was used; the hand meant five, probably because there are five fingers on a hand. Eventually, shortcuts for other values were used: 10, 20, 50, 100, and whatever the system employed as shortcuts for representing large numbers. And, from all that evolved the counting systems we use now.

Counting bases has nothing to do with baseball

Suppose that you have these 50 alien pods you have to deliver to San Francisco for the end of human life as we know it. Do you have 50 pods? Or maybe 32 pods? Or 62? Or even 110010? How about L pods? How many? The number is still 50, but it's represented in different ways. Those ways are referred to as a *counting base*.

The counting base humans use is *base 10*, called the *decimal* system. The reason is probably that we have 10 fingers (and, of course, most Vikings have 12 fingers, so they use counting base 12).

Fifty pods in base 10 is written like this: 50. It figures out to 5×10 to the power of 1, which is 50. Each position in the number is a multiple of 10.

If you had to deliver 375 pods to Marin County, that would be 3×100 plus 7×10 plus 5. This stuff all makes sense because it's the way you were taught how to count.

All numbers used in C programming are base 10. You don't need to specify them that way; it's how the compiler accepts things. Check out this example:

```
#include <stdio.h>

#define PODS 50

int main()
{
    puts("Base 10:");
    printf("I must deliver %d pods to San Francisco.\n",
    PODS);
    return(0);
}
```

Enter this source code into your editor. Save it to disk as BASES.C. (I know, it should be named PODS.C, but the program isn't about pod people taking over the world, which is inevitable anyway.) Compile and run:

```
Base 10:
I must deliver 50 pods to San Francisco.
```

Base 2, or binary

Computers aren't human. They're inhuman! As such, they don't count in base 10 or decimal. Computers don't have 10 fingers. No, they have only themselves to count, so they use only 0 and 1 — two digits — which form the binary counting system.

Inside the computer, when you specify 50 pods, the number looks like this:

110010

That's what 50 looks like in base 2. You don't need to go into base 2 here; the printf() function lacks a method for displaying base 2 — probably because few programs require binary output and few humans would know what to do with it. No, for now, keep binary inside the computer.

(The C language does have various tools for manipulating *binary digits,* or *bits.* Book III, Chapter 4 covers binary information in C.)

Book II
Chapter 2

The Madness of Printf()

Base 16, or hexadecimal

Counting base 16 is called the *hexadecimal* system. The word *hex* comes from the Greek *hexe,* which means "witch" or 16 of something. In hexadecimal, you count like this:

1, 2, 3, 4, 5, 6, 7, 8, 9, A, B, C, D, E, F, 10, 11, 12, 13, 14 . . .

The letters A through F are used to represent values 10 through 15. And the hex value 10 is 16, 11 is 17, and so on.

You can easily spy a hex number because it usually contains a letter, as in C800. Even so, to avoid confusing hex numbers with decimal, the numbers are prefixed by a 0 and an x, as in

0xC800

0x10

0xFFFF

In the computer world, hexadecimal programmers use a nifty shortcut for binary values. As you may someday discover, the computer is just crawling with binary values, which makes the hex shortcut all the more useful.

Often, binary values are divided into chunks of four bits (*binary digits*) for easy reading. This example:

1011101000111100

becomes

1011 1010 0011 1100

Programmers, however, prefer hexadecimal, which can easily substitute any 4-bit binary chunk because binary values 0000 (0) through 1111 (15) correspond well with hex values 0x0 (0) through 0xF (15), as shown in Table 2-1.

Table 2-1		Hexadecimal, Binary, and Decimal Values			
Hex	*Bin*	*Dec*	*Hex*	*Bin*	*Dec*
0	0000	0	8	1000	8
1	0001	1	9	1001	9
2	0010	2	A	1010	10
3	0011	3	B	1011	11
4	0100	4	C	1100	12
5	0101	5	D	1101	13
6	0110	6	E	1110	14
7	0111	7	F	1111	15

So, the binary value

1011 1010 0011 1100

becomes this number in hex:

0xBA3C

1011 is B.

1010 is A.

0011 is 3.

1100 is C.

What is value 0xBA3C? Why not let the computer tell you:

```
#include <stdio.h>

#define PODS 50
#define LOCATIONS 0xBA3C

int main()
{
```

```
    puts("Base 10:");
    printf("I must deliver %d pods to %d locations.\n",PODS,
LOCATIONS);
    return(0);
}
```

Modify the source code to BASES.C so that it looks like what's shown here. You're adding a new constant, `LOCATIONS`, defined as hex value 0xBA3C. The `printf()` statement in Line 9 displays the hex value using %d, which displays the value in decimal. (Remember that, internally, all values are binary; `printf()` chooses the output format based on the placeholder you use.)

Save the changes to disk. Compile and run:

```
Base 10:
I must deliver 50 pods to 47676 locations.
```

Better pack a sack lunch.

Displaying hex values with `printf()`

As I say many times throughout this book, values are held inside the computer in binary form and are displayed in whatever manner you choose by using the proper conversion characters (placeholders) in `printf()`.

Earlier in this chapter, you used the %d placeholder to display the hex value 0xBA3C in decimal. Similarly, `printf()` has the %x placeholder, which is used to display any value in hexadecimal. Here's an example:

```
#include <stdio.h>

#define PODS 50
#define LOCATIONS 0xBA3C

int main()
{
    puts("Base 10:");
    printf("I must deliver %d pods to %d locations.\n",PODS,
LOCATIONS);
    puts("Base 16:");
    printf("I must deliver %x pods to %x locations.\n",PODS,
LOCATIONS);
    return(0);
}
```

Make the necessary changes to your BASES.C source code so that these modifications are included. Basically, you're repeating the `puts()` and `printf()` statements, modifying `printf()` so that the %x placeholder is used and the output is displayed in hexadecimal and not in decimal (%d). Save the changes to disk.

Other ways to represent hex

Assembly language is a close cousin to the C language, though on a much lower level. Unlike C, however, hexadecimal values in assembly language aren't prefixed with an x or 0x. Instead, hexadecimal values are suffixed with an h, as in

C800h

10h

FFFFh

A big H may also be used. In fact, hex can be spelled out, as in C800 hex.

Another way hex values can be written is with a $ (dollar sign) prefix:

$C800

$10

$FFFF

Note that hexadecimal numbers A through F can also be written in lowercase:

0xc800

0x10a

0xffff

In my programs, I use uppercase for consistency, but the compiler doesn't care — just remember to prefix the values with 0x.

Compile and run:

```
Base 10:
I must deliver 50 pods to 47676 locations.
Base 16:
I must deliver 32 pods to ba3c locations.
```

As promised, the final line displays values in hexadecimal. 32 is the hex way of writing 50 decimal; ba3c, you have already met, at 0xBA3C.

Exercise 2.2.1

Fix up the BASES.C program. Modify the output so that 0x is prefixed before the hexadecimal numbers that are displayed. Also, replace the %x placeholder with %X so that the hex numbers A through F are displayed in uppercase.

Exercise 2.2.2

Write a program that asks for the user's age and then displays the age in hexadecimal. Name the program AGEHEX.C.

Escape in hex

Hexadecimal values are the preferred way of representing information inside the computer — so much so that a handy escape sequence was devised so that your C programs can find single characters using hex rather than decimal.

In C, the \xnn escape sequence is used to represent a single character by its hex value. First comes \x and then the hex value *nn* as a 2-digit number. Because most character charts specify hex values (in addition to decimal), you can use this shorthand method to easily represent characters that are otherwise not readily typed on the keyboard:

Book II
Chapter 2

The Madness of Printf()

```c
#include <stdio.h>

#define POUNDS 0x9C
#define YEN 0x9E

int main()
{
    float amount,bp,jy;
    float d2p = 0.5407;      /* dollars per pound */
    float d2y = 106.79;      /* dollars per yen */

    printf("Enter the amount in dollars: $");
    scanf("%f",&amount);
    bp = amount * d2p;
    jy = amount * d2y;
    puts("Currency Conversion:");
    printf("%c%f\n",POUNDS,bp);
    printf("%c%f\n",YEN,jy);
    return(0);
}
```

Enter this source code as CURRENCY.C. It's a legitimate program! If you enter the current dollars-per-pound and dollars-per-yen figures into Lines 9 and 10, you can use the code to calculate the value of U.S. currency in both the United Kingdom and Japan. Save the source code to disk.

Compile and run:

```
Enter the amount in dollars: $
```

Suppose that you just bought your own Oompa Loompa for $450. How much would that be in pounds or yen? Type **450** and press Enter:

```
Currency Conversion
£243.315002
¥48055.500000
```

The hexadecimal escape characters are displayed as the pound and yen symbols. They're defined as character constants with the #defines on Lines 3 and 4 and then displayed using the %c placeholder on Lines 17 and 18.

Hexadecimal escape characters can be used anywhere that single characters would otherwise appear, such as in a putchar() function.

(Appendix C lists all ASCII characters and their codes in decimal and hexadecimal.)

Base 8, or octal

The C language uses decimal, binary, and hexadecimal, and the final sibling of the C language counting base family goes to *octal*. Fortunately, this counting system is now rarely used. It's included in the C language (as well as other programming languages) primarily to be backward-compatible with older programs and computer systems.

The octal system is counting base 8. The word *oct* means eight, which is easy to remember because an octopus has eight tentacles and the month of October isn't the eighth month of the year. Here's how you count in octal:

> 1, 2, 3, 4, 5, 6, 7, 10, 11, 12, 13, 14, 15, 16, 17, 20, 21, 22 . . .

Octal came about because earlier computers counted bits in groups of three. So, like hexadecimal for groups of four bits, octal became a popular shortcut.

And that's about as far as I need to get into octal, other than to show you the printf() placeholder for octal, which is %o (little letter *o*, not a leading zero).

Again, the source code for BASES.C is modified, this time to add octal output:

```
#include <stdio.h>

#define PODS 50
#define LOCATIONS 0xBA3C

int main()
{
    puts("Base 10:");
    printf("I must deliver %d pods to %d locations.\n",PODS,
LOCATIONS);
    puts("Base 16:");
    printf("I must deliver 0x%X pods to 0x%X locations.\n",
PODS, LOCATIONS);
    puts("Base 8:");
```

```
    printf("I must deliver %o pods to %o locations.\n",PODS,
LOCATIONS);
    return(0);
}
```

The only change is in the way `printf()` displays the values, this time using the %o (little *o*) placeholder. Update your source code. Save. Compile. Run:

```
Base 10:
I must deliver 50 pods to 47676 locations.
Base 16:
I must deliver 0x32 pods to 0xBA3C locations.
Base 8:
I must deliver 62 pods to 135074 locations.
```

One way to recognize an octal number — though it's not entirely reliable — is to notice that it lacks the digits 8 and 9.

The C language also has an octal escape sequence, either \onn (little *o*), or, because octal predates hexadecimal, \nn, where *nn* is an octal value. Again, this sequence is now rarely used, though some older, crusty programs may have it and even older and crustier programmers may still be fond of octal. If you meet one of these people, be polite, but then run away.

It's not a counting base — it's scientific!

`printf()` supports another number format, but it's not a counting base. No, it's *scientific*, as in scientific notation. You probably recall sleeping through math class when this type of numbering system was discussed.

In a nutshell, scientific notation prevents those guys in white lab coats from standing around saying "zero" all the time. For example, rather than say

6,000,000,000

(or "six billion"), scientists can say

6E+09

Rather than some infinitesimal value like this:

.000000000097531

they can say instead:

9.7531E-11

This is known as scientific, or E, notation. It works by taking a value and converting it into the *n.nnnnnE±mm* format. The number *n.nnnnn* is shifted left (–) or right (+) by *mm* number of decimal places. That's about all I need to say; if this format is one that you need to use, you probably know how to use it already. The following program does help a tad:

```
#include <stdio.h>

#define BIG 2468000000000.0         /* 9 zeros before the . */
#define TEENSY 0.00000000097531   /* 9 zeros after the . */

int main()
{
    puts("Using %f:");
    printf("Big %f\tTeensy %f\n",BIG,TEENSY);
    puts("Using %E:");
    printf("Big %E\tTeensy %E\n",BIG,TEENSY);
    puts("Using %G:");
    printf("Big %G\tTeensy %G\n",BIG,TEENSY);
    return(0);
}
```

You must specify the large values in Lines 3 and 4 as floating point. To do so, the value must contain a decimal, as shown in this example for both BIG and TEENSY. If you don't specify a decimal, the value is assumed to be an integer.

The preceding program uses three conversion characters for printf() to display the two values in three different ways:

%f displays the values as floating point.

%E displays the values using scientific notation.

%G displays the values using the shortest size possible (%f or %E).

Save the program to disk as SCI.C. Compile and run. Here's a sample of the output:

```
Using %f
Big 2468000000000.000000         Teensy 0.000000
Using %E
Big 2.468000E+012         Teensy 9.753100E-010
Using %G
Big 2.468E+012    Teensy 9.7531E-010
```

Note that the first display of TEENSY lists 0 as the value. That's because the number is out of range for %f to display. This example shows why scientific notation is necessary.

The C language also uses the %e and %g placeholders, which work just like their big brothers %E and %G, except that a little *e,* rather than the big *E,* is used in the scientific notation output. They're similar to the %x and %X placeholders, which determine whether hexadecimal values are displayed using lowercase or all-caps A through F values.

Exercise 2.2.3

Finish up the BASES.C series of programs by adding output in scientific notation. Have puts() say scientific notation, and use the %G placeholder for the final printf() statement.

Scientific notation is for floats only

If you just completed Exercise 2.2.3, you noticed that the output is rather bizarre, something like:

```
I must deliver 1.01168E-309 pods to 1.78006E-307 locations.
```

Because computers don't make mistakes, it's obviously *you* who screwed up. Rather than let you stew, let me explain that the %f, %E, and %G conversion characters work with *only floating-point values.* In BASES.C, the PODS and LOCATIONS constants are integers (no decimals). Thanks to typecasting (refer to Book II, Chapter 1), you can quickly fix that in Line 15 for when it's needed:

```
printf("I must deliver %G pods to %G locations.\n",
    (float)PODS,(float)LOCATIONS);
```

Make this change to your BASES.C source code. (If you didn't do Exercise 2.2.3, see Appendix B for the up-to-date source code.) Save! Compile! Run!

```
Base 10:
I must deliver 50 pods to 47676 locations.
Base 16:
I must deliver 0x32 pods to 0xBA3C locations.
Base 8:
I must deliver 62 pods to 135074 locations.
Scientific notation:
I must deliver 50 pods to 47676 locations.
```

Nope — nothing is wrong: %G just chose the shortest format for the values, which is what it does. To really see scientific notation, reedit the source code and replace the two %G conversion characters with %E. Save. Compile. Run again:

```
I must deliver 50 pods to 47676 locations.
Base 16:
```

Book II
Chapter 2

The Madness of Printf()

```
I must deliver 0x32 pods to 0xBA3C locations.
Base 8:
I must deliver 62 pods to 135074 locations.
Scientific notation:
I must deliver 5.000000E+001 pods to 4.767600E+004 locations.
```

Using immediate scientific notation values

Just as you can specify values in hex or octal in C, you can also specify values by using scientific notation. So, if your documentation says that a value is 6.27E-4, you can assign that value to a variable:

```
float var = 6.27E-4;
```

Or, declare it as a constant:

```
#define DELTA_V 6.27E-4
```

Enough with that.

Putting Printf( ) to the Test

The f in printf( ) means *formatting*. Much of that formatting is handled by the conversion characters, several of which I introduce in this chapter. The rest of the formatting is meat between those buns. To put it another way, printf( ) lets you wiggle lots of stuff between the % and the conversion-character letter that follows it.

This section demonstrates several of the more useful printf( ) formatting tricks.

Formatting floating-point numbers

The most useful formatting command I have found is %.2f for printing floating-point values as dollars and cents. The .2 between % and f tells printf( ) to output the value with only two places after the decimal point. So, this value:

123.4500000

becomes

123.45

Bring up the CURRENCY.C source code, presented earlier in this chapter. Modify Lines 17 and 18 to read

```
printf("%c%.2f\n",POUNDS,bp);
printf("%c%.2f\n",YEN,jy);
```

Save these changes to disk. Recompile and run:

```
Enter the amount in dollars: $450
Currency Conversion
£243.32
¥48055.50
```

The output is not only truncated to two places after the decimal point, but it has also been rounded: The original value in pounds was 243.315002.

Exercise 2.2.4

Can you figure it out? Modify the CURRENCY.C program again, this time to display the results using *three* places after the decimal.

Setting the output width for values

The output from CURRENCY.C looks funky:

```
£243.32
¥48055.50
```

Wouldn't it be better if the values lined up on the decimal place? Try this modification to Lines 17 and 18:

```
printf("%c%9.2f\n",POUNDS,bp);
printf("%c%9.2f\n",YEN,jy);
```

Stick a 9 before the .2 so that the conversion character looks like %9.2f. (If you did Exercise 2.2.3, change the .3 back to .2.) Save. Compile. Run:

```
Enter the amount in dollars: $450
Currency Conversion
£    243.32
¥  48055.50
```

The value 9 means that the number displayed is nine characters wide (including the decimal place), right-justified, with spaces padded on the left. As shown by the preceding output, both values line up on the right. Because .2 was used, they each display only two values after the decimal place, with the 9 allowing for six other characters to be displayed to the left of the decimal place. Figure 2-1 explains it better.

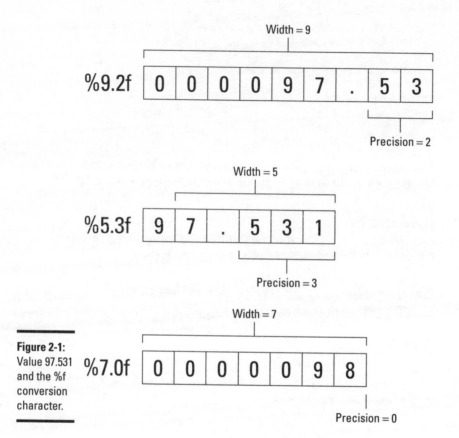

Figure 2-1:
Value 97.531
and the %f
conversion
character.

Note in the figure that the precision value affects the number of places shown after the decimal. On the other hand, the width value doesn't truncate a large number. Because of that, it's good to know how large your numbers will be before you set a proper width value.

Exercise 2.2.5

Modify CURRENCY.C again. Observe how changing the width value from 9 to 12 affects the output. Then change the width value to 5 to see what happens. Which value works best?

Padding integers

You can also specify a width for the %d, integer, placeholder. Though there's no decimal part, a value you put between the % and the d specifies how many character places are to be used to display the value. The value is right-justified, and spaces pad any extra room on the left.

For example, the placeholder %3d specifies that all values be displayed using three characters, right-justified, with spaces padding the left:

```
  9
 27
125
 34
```

Exercise 2.2.6

From Book I, Chapter 7, update the program TWOS.C so that the printf() statement displays its integers using two character places.

A handy hex trick

Dig up the source code for AGEHEX.C that you wrote for Exercise 2.2.2. Change your printf() statement so that it reads

```
printf("You are %#X years old!\n",age);
```

Put a # between the % and the X. Save that change to disk. Compile and run:

```
Enter your age in years:
```

Lie and say that you're **29**.

```
You are 0X1D years old!
```

The # character is a modifier for the %x, %X, and %o placeholders. For %x, it prefixes 0x to the output; for %X, it prefixes 0X; and for %o, it prefixes an 0.

Justifying text with printf()

Just as you can justify numbers using special placeholder formats, you can also justify strings of text. Here's an example:

```
#include <stdio.h>

int main()
{
    char name1[] = "George Washington";
    char name2[] = "John Adams";
    char name3[] = "Thomas Jefferson";

    printf("%17s\n",name1);
    printf("%17s\n",name2);
    printf("%17s\n",name3);
    return(0);
}
```

Save this program as TEXT.C. Compile and run:

```
George Washington
      John Adams
 Thomas Jefferson
```

The %17s placeholder directs printf() to set the output size for the string to 17 characters, right-justified.

Other formatting options

Many combinations of width, justification, and prefix options are available in the printf() function — far too many to list them all here and all their combinations. I have squeezed as many of these as I could into later chapters of this book, primarily in places where they're most useful. Be on the lookout for them!

Chapter 3: Maniacal Math Functions

In This Chapter

✔ **Getting the square root of a value**

✔ **Raising a number to a certain power**

✔ **Getting the cubed root of a value**

✔ **Doing trigonometry in C**

✔ **Converting between radians and degrees**

✔ **Using the** `sin()`, `cos()` **and** `tan()` **functions**

✔ **Computing the absolute value**

*P*oor math students, unite! The computer is as big of a blessing to your bruised ego as the calculator. Heck, I would have failed statistics for a *fourth* time in college had I not had with me a tiny Radio Shack handheld "computer." After all, I knew the formulas — it was computing the proper result that killed me. Thankfully, with that trusty handheld, I punched in the proper formulas and proudly earned a C, thus passing the course and moving on to greatness.

The C language uses so many math functions that the mind boggles to think of them all. Those who find themselves in the rarefied air of high-level math know what functions to pick and choose. The rest of us have this chapter, which introduces a few of the more common math functions — sort of like the typical stuff you stumble into in a spreadsheet, but not as dorky.

 If you have a Unix, Linux, or Mac OS X computer, you can review all the C language math functions in one swipe! Type **man 3 math** at the terminal prompt, and you should see the lot of them (as long as you have the C language documentation installed on your computer).

 'Nuther Unix tip: In some versions of Unix, you must link in the math library to get some of the math functions to work. I mention one method of doing so in this chapter, but you should really bone up with your own compiler to find out what it specifically requires; the **man 3 math** command lists the library and linking command you need.

The Symbols That C Forgot

If you're familiar with other programming languages — or even math in general — you may notice a few symbols missing from the C smorgasbord. For example, where's the square root symbol? Or the power symbol? Where's the symbol for the natural logarithm? And, who really cares?

For those who do care, this section describes how some common math operations are performed in C — without those special symbols that other programming languages may have.

The root of the square

Here's something they don't teach you in math class: The square root of a number is literally the root of the square that the number makes. Figure 3-1 explains it graphically. If you know the Pythagorean theorem, you can kind of grasp what's going on. If not, fugghedaboutit.

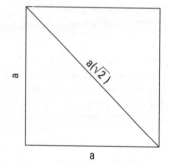

Figure 3-1:
The root of
the square.

Now that you're totally confused, what is that sacred value, the square root of 2? Better find out:

```c
#include <stdio.h>
#include <math.h>

int main()
{
    double sqroot2;

    sqroot2 = sqrt((double)2);
    printf("The square root of 2 is %f.\n",sqroot2);
    return(0);
}
```

A few things to note as you type this source code:

✦ Yes, you must add #include to the MATH.H header file. It's required so that the compiler doesn't barf when it sees the sqrt() function.

✦ The sqrt() function calculates the square root of an immediate value or variable. The result is returned as a double variable.

✦ The sqrt() function requires a double as its input; hence, the typecast of (double) before the immediate value 2.

Save the source code to disk as SQRT2.C. Compile it.

For some versions of Unix, you may be required to link in the math library to make the program run. You do this by adding the -lm option to the compiling command, as in **gcc -lm sqrt2.c -o sqrt2**. (See your compiler's documentation for the proper option to link in the math library.)

Run:

```
The square root of 2 is 1.414214
```

A holy math number! Om!

Oh, yeah: Don't try to calculate the square root of a negative number. Although the program compiles, the answer isn't correct, at least not according to those pointy-headed math guys.

Exercise 2.3.1
Rewrite the source code to SQRT2.C. Figure out a way to specify the value 2 in Line 8 so that the (double) typecast isn't needed.

Exercise 2.3.2
What is the square root of 3?

Pow to the power of pow
Most programming languages have a symbol or shortcut for figuring "the power of." For example, if you want to calculate 4 squared, or 4^2. In many programming languages, the ^ symbol is used to "raise the power to," as in

4^2

which is 4^2 or 16.

But, no — not in C!

For such a thing, you use the C language pow( ) function, as in

```
result = pow(4.0,2.0);
```

The pow( ) function raises the value 4 to the power of 2, the *exponent*. The result is stored in the double variable result. Note that both 4 and 2 must be double types (or typecast double):

```
#include <stdio.h>
#include <math.h>

int main()
{
    double two;
    int exponent;

    puts("Power of 2's Table");
    for(exponent=0;exponent<=10;exponent++)
    {
        two = pow(2.0,(double)exponent);
        printf("2 to the %2d power is %.0f\n",exponent,two);
    }
    return(0);
}
```

Type this source code. Like the sqrt( ) function, the pow( ) function requires the MATH.H header file (and library) to work. Don't forget it! Save the code to disk as 2POWER.C.

Compile. (Remember to link in the math library, if you must.) Run:

```
Power of 2's Table
2 to the  0 power is 1
2 to the  1 power is 2
2 to the  2 power is 4
2 to the  3 power is 8
2 to the  4 power is 16
2 to the  5 power is 32
2 to the  6 power is 64
2 to the  7 power is 128
2 to the  8 power is 256
2 to the  9 power is 512
2 to the 10 power is 1024
```

Exercise 2.3.3
What is 5 to the 399th power? Call the source code WHATEVER.C.

Exercise 2.3.4

Square roots are common enough that C sports a `sqrt()` function. Or does it? After all, isn't the square root of some number the same thing as raising that value to the ½ power? In other words:

$$\sqrt{5} \ == \ 5^{1/2}$$

Is this true? Write a program that displays the results of both calculations, $\sqrt{5}$ and $5^{1/2}$. Name it FIVE.C.

Ah, the root of the cube!

The cube root is written with a teensy three above the root symbol, as in the cube root of 27, or $\sqrt[3]{27}$. And, for your amusement, I have graphed the cube root equation in Figure 3-2, just as I graphed the square root in Figure 3-1. Trivia for you!

Book II
Chapter 3

Maniacal Math
Functions

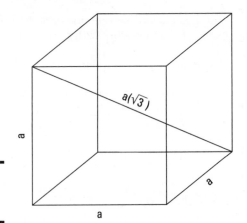

Figure 3-2:
The root of
the cube.

Just as C has a function for squaring the root, `sqrt()`, it has a function for cubing the root, `cbrt()`. Here's another silly little program:

```c
#include <stdio.h>
#include <math.h>

int main()
{
    double cube;

    cube = cbrt(2.0);
    printf("The cube root of 2 is %f\n",cube);
    return(0);
}
```

Enter this source code. Save it to disk as CUBE3.C. Compile and run to see the thrilling result:

```
The cube root of 2 is 1.259921
```

Exercise 2.3.5

Rewrite the CUBE3.C source code so that the pow() function is used to calculate the cubed root of 2.0.

Logarithms

I'm really, really, *really* not into logarithms. The C language has a smattering of log functions, most of which confuse me. But I can mention two of them:

✦ The log() function computes the natural logarithm of a value.

✦ The log10() function computes the base 10 logarithm for a value.

Values must be double, and these logarithm functions return double values. (Note that some C language log functions work with float types.)

The following source code calculates the natural logarithm for a series of values from .1 through 6:

```
#include <stdio.h>
#include <math.h>

int main()
{
    double ln,x;

    for(x=0.1;x<6.0;x+=0.1)
    {
        ln = log(x);
        printf("ln(%3.1f) = %f\n",x,ln);
    }
    return(0);
}
```

(Okay — it seems dumb. But suppose that these are values for plotting a graph. It could happen! Work with me here.) Save the source code to disk as E.C.

Compile. Run. The output is several screens long. Ho-hum.

That's enough of that.

Trigonometric Functions

C is loaded with your standard "trig" functions. As with other non-operator math things in C, you have to include the MATH.H header file to make the functions digestible, plus you have to link in the math library if your version of gcc requires it.

The looming terror of radians and degrees

Before diving into the trig functions, you need to have one further disappointment: Computers measure angles in *radians,* not degrees. If you're a human (and I can only guess), you're probably used to figuring angles and such as so-and-so degrees. Tough luck here!

Consider your typical circle, beheld in Figure 3-3. To humans, it has 360 degrees. But, to the computer, a circle has 2π, or 6.28318531, radians. Both values measure the same thing; they just use different approaches to get there.

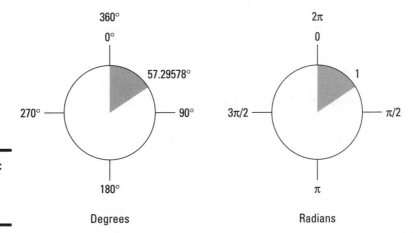

Figure 3-3:
Around
the circle
we go!

If you want to work in degrees, you need to convert your degrees into radians and then convert back from radians into degrees to display the result so that a human can read them. Here's the math (and refer to Figure 3-3):

π radians = 180 degrees

1 radian = $180/\pi$ degrees, or 180/3.14159265

1 radian = 57.2957795 degrees

And, going the other way:

1 degree = 0.0174532925 radians

Why bother doing math to figure out what the computer can do so well? Two programs are in order — real programs to help you!

```c
/* convert radians to degrees */

#include <stdio.h>

#define RAD 57.2957795

int main()
{
    float radians,degrees;

    puts("Convert radians to degrees");
    printf("Enter a value in radians: ");
    scanf("%f",&radians);

    degrees = radians*RAD;

    printf("%.5f radians is %.3f degrees.\n",
    radians,degrees);
    return(0);
}
```

Type this useful source code. Save it to disk as RAD2DEG.C. Compile and run:

```
Convert radians to degrees
Enter a value in radians:
```

Enter the value for π: **3.14159265**. Press Enter:

```
3.14159 radians is 180.000 degrees.
```

It checks out!

Exercise 2.3.6
Modify the RAD2DEG.C source code so that it converts degrees to radians. This process involves swapping variables, rewriting text, and making a simple math correction in Line 15 to make it work. Can you do it? Name the code DEG2RAD.C.

Why bother with radians?

It may seem like working in radians is a kooky idea, but it makes many operations quite easy for the computer. Basically, when you work with radians, you're working with values of π. So, some common angles become relatively easy to calculate:

$180° = \pi$ radians $90° = \pi/2$ radians

$60° = \pi/3$ radians $45° = \pi/4$ radians

$30° = \pi/6$ radians $15° = \pi/12$ radians

Triangle hell

Yes, I dislike trigonometry as much as the next joker. So, let me breeze through this subject and give you only one example so that you can quickly move on to the next, less painful section.

I cover only the basic trig functions:

+ `sin()`, for calculating the sine

+ `cos()`, for calculating the cosine

+ `tan()`, for calculating the tangent

For each function, and in the examples that follow, consider these variables declared as `double` values:

```
double angle, opposite, adjacent, hypotenuse;
```

Additionally, a `ratio` variable is used for simply returning the function's effect on an angle. But that's O so boring.

Sine time: The *sine* of an angle is the ratio of the side opposite the angle to the hypotenuse. Figure 3-4 illustrates this concept for your viewing pleasure.

If you know Angle *A*, you can compute the ratio of the length of the *opposite* side to the length of the *hypotenuse:*

```
ratio = sin(angle);
```

If you know the length of the side *opposite* and the *angle*, you can calculate the length of the *hypotenuse* as

```
hypotenuse = opposite / sin(angle);
```

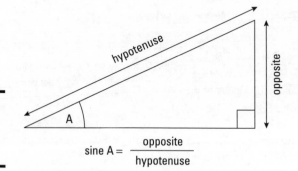

Figure 3-4:
Computing
the sine of
an angle.

$$\text{sine } A = \frac{\text{opposite}}{\text{hypotenuse}}$$

If you know the angle and the length of the *hypotenuse*, you can calculate the *opposite* side's length with

```
opposite = sin(angle) * hypotenuse;
```

Finally, if you know both the lengths of the *hypotenuse* and the *opposite* sides, you can divine the angle by using this equation:

```
angle = asin(opposite/hypotenuse);
```

Of course, that's the *arcsine* function, `asin()`, but I thought I would just throw that one in.

Cosine away your life: The *cosine* of an angle is the ratio of the length of the side adjacent to an angle to the length of the hypotenuse. This concept is beautifully illustrated in Figure 3-5.

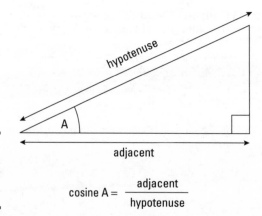

Figure 3-5:
Computing
the cosine
of an angle.

$$\text{cosine } A = \frac{\text{adjacent}}{\text{hypotenuse}}$$

The first equation worthy of note is the simple ratio produced by the `cos()` function when you feed it an angle:

```
ratio = cos(angle);
```

That's so ho-hum. How about when you know the length of the *adjacent* side and the *angle* and want to know how long that silly *hypotenuse* is?

```
hypotenuse = adjacent / cos(angle);
```

Or, suppose that you know the *angle* and the length of the *hypotenuse* and want to know the length of the *adjacent* side. Then you use

```
adjacent = cos(angle) * hypotenuse;
```

And, if you know the lengths of the *adjacent* side and the *hypotenuse* and want to find the angle, you go off the map and use the `acos()` function:

```
angle = acos(adjacent/hypotenuse);
```

In this example, you're calculating the *arc cosine,* or using the ratio of the sides to figure out what the angle is. Weird.

Off on a tangent: I envision something tangential as breaking away at a 90-degree angle, which is illustrated in Figure 3-6. Officially, a *tangent* is the ratio of the length of the side opposite an angle to the length of the side adjacent and blah-blah-blah.

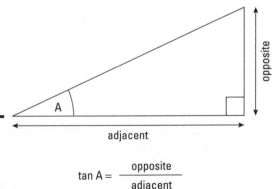

Figure 3-6:
Computing
the tangent
of an angle.

$$\tan A = \frac{\text{opposite}}{\text{adjacent}}$$

If you're just itching to see that tangent ratio for a given *angle,* you can compute it with this statement:

```
ratio = tan(angle);
```

If you know the *angle* and the length of the *opposite* side, you can calculate the *adjacent* side's length with this statement:

```
adjacent = opposite / tan(angle);
```

Finally — a program! Here's the way to discover how tall that tree is in your backyard. You measure the distance between you and the base of the tree (assuming that the backyard is flat) and then point up at the top of the tree. Using the distance — *adjacent* — and the angle — *angle* — you can calculate how tall the tree is by using this program:

```
#include <stdio.h>
#include <math.h>

#define RAD 57.2957795

int main()
{
    double opposite,angle;
    float degrees,adjacent;

    puts("How tall is that tree?");
    printf("How far away is the tree in feet?");
    scanf("%f",&adjacent);
    printf("What angle is it to the tree top?");
    scanf("%f",&degrees);

/* Convert degrees to rads */

    angle = (double)degrees/RAD;

/* Get the tree height */

    opposite = tan(angle) * (double)adjacent;

    printf("That tree is %.2f feet tall.\n",opposite);
    return(0);
}
```

Carefully type this source code. Be alert! The program does something truly useful. Save it to disk as TREETALL.C. Compile and run:

```
How tall is that tree?
How far away is the tree in feet?
```

Suppose that the tree is 20 feet away; type **20** and press Enter:

```
What angle is it to the tree top?
```

I would guess 60 degrees or so. Type **60** and press Enter:

```
That tree is 34.64 feet tall.
```

Amaze your friends!

Before you enter hippopotamus land, here's the formula for finding the *angle* when you know the lengths of the *adjacent* and *opposite* sides:

```
angle = atan(opposite/adjacent);
```

The `atan()` function calculates the *arctangent* of the ratio of the side opposite to the adjacent side, which gives you the angle in question. Fine and dandy.

Other Handy Math Functions

As I said at the top of this chapter, C has many math functions. Sadly, I'm so much of a math dweeb that I couldn't think of any fun or interesting programs for most of the functions, some of which I have never heard of, so I knew that there was no sense in wasting time on them.

From the rest I chose a few math leftovers that I thought you may find useful in some of your programs. This chapter ends with a tiny parade of those functions, demonstrated in this section.

Working on your `abs()`

As a programmer, the first time I heard someone speak of *abs,* I figured that they were talking about the absolute value of some number. Wrong! It has something to do with your tummy, mostly about it not being in a round shape. But that's another issue for another day.

The *absolute value* of a number is its non-negative value. Simply put, the `abs()` function removes the negative sign from a number, making it positive. `abs()` has no effect on zero.

For input, `abs()` requires an integer value. The `abs()` function also requires the STDLIB.H header file to be included in the source code.

Suppose that you write a square root program. Now, everybody knows that you cannot have the square root of a negative number. Here's how you use `abs()` to ensure that such a thing doesn't happen:

```
#include <stdio.h>
#include <math.h>
#include <stdlib.h.>

int main()
{
    int value;
    double root;

    printf("Enter a value: ");
    scanf("%d",&value);
    value = abs(value);
    root = sqrt((double)value);
    printf("The square root of %d is %f.\n",value,root);
    return(0);
}
```

Hunt and peck in this source code. Save it to disk as ROOT.C. Compile and run:

```
Enter a value:
```

Type **16** and press Enter:

```
The square root of 16 is 4.000000.
```

Well, you knew that! Or, maybe you didn't. But what's the square root of –16? Who knows? Ask the computer by running the program again:

```
Enter a value:
```

Type **-16** and press Enter:

```
The square root of 16 is 4.000000
```

The computer isn't fooled! The abs() function makes the negative number positive, thus avoiding any lengthy discussion of the value *i* in this book.

Exercise 2.3.7
Modify the source code for ROOT.C so that Lines 12 and 13 are combined into one line.

Exercise 2.3.8
Modify the source for ROOT.C again, and this time don't use the abs() function; instead, create an if-else structure to catch the input of negative values.

Don't bother reading this information on the imaginary number *i* because there's nothing here to read

Getting the abs() of a float

What if you want to find the square root of 7.5? The problem with the ROOT.C series of programs is that they accept only integers as input. That's because the abs() function requires an integer as its value. What happens if you type-cast? Consider this code:

```c
#include <stdio.h>
#include <math.h>
#include <stdlib.h>

int main()
{
    float value;
    double root;

    printf("Enter a value: ");
    scanf("%f",&value);
    value = abs((int)value);
    root = sqrt((double)value);
    printf("The square root of %f is %f.\n",value,root);
    return(0);
}
```

This source code shows several modifications to the original ROOT.C program. Make these changes in your editor, and then compile and run the resulting program:

```
Enter a value:
```

Type **7.5** and press Enter:

```
The square root of 7.000000 is 2.645751.
```

Uh-oh! By type casting a float to an int, the number is truncated; the decimal portion of the value is removed so that only the whole number part remains. Obviously, there must be another way!

Change Line 12 to read

```
value = fabs(value);
```

The fabs() function is used to compute the absolute value of a floating-point number. It requires only the MATH.H header file, so you can now remove the line that includes STDLIB.H. Save the source code back to disk. Recompile and run:

```
Enter a value:
```

Type **7.5** and press Enter:

```
The square root of 7.500000 is 2.738613.
```

Even try this:

```
Enter a value:
```

Type **-7.5** and press Enter:

```
The square root of 7.500000 is 2.738613.
```

Ta-da!

Chapter 4: Not Truly Random

In This Chapter

✔ Understanding what is truly random

✔ Generating random numbers

✔ Seeding the randomizer

✔ Calculating the modulus

✔ Using the modulo % operator

✔ Rolling the dice and flipping coins

"**H**ey, Mom! Look at this!"

I remember being just a lad and first discovering how to program. I finally created code worthy enough to show my folks: a program that displayed 100 random numbers. My mother was obviously baffled, but passed on parental kudos and quickly moved on to something else.

What is random?

Random. What is it? Sometimes, I think that the mutterings of my teenage son are random. But truly random things have no pattern, design, or purpose and cannot be predictable. Sadly, inside your computer, just about everything can be predicted (with enough time and patience). Because of that, it's said that a computer cannot predict truly random numbers. Instead, computers generate pseudorandom numbers.

A *pseudorandom* number is as random as the C compiler's designers can make it. In fact, the old function for producing random numbers in C was rand(). But rand() just isn't random

enough — not to satisfy our current data encryption standards. So, the better random() function was developed.

Alas, some gcc compilers lack the random() function. If so, you can use the older rand() function instead.

Regardless of whichever function you use, rand() or random(), in this chapter I refer to the values that are generated as *random*. Even so, they're still pseudorandom. (I also do this to keep snooty college sophomores from sending me "You're wrong!" e-mail.)

The nonprogrammer may not see the value of random numbers, but the value is there. Random numbers add a layer of unpredictability to your programs, especially games. Imagine how dull it would be to battle an electronic opponent whom you knew would behave in exactly same manner during every turn of the game. If you know "the pattern," the game lacks zest.

This chapter is about another math function, random(). It returns a pseudo-random number you can use to enliven your programs. It's the basis for nearly all computer games. This chapter also covers other functions that help make random() useful, including the mysterious modulus operator.

Introducing the random() *Function*

Hey! Pull a number out of my hat:

```
hat = random();
```

The random() function yanks a pseudorandom number at large from within the bowels of the computer, pooping it out as a long integer value. In the preceding example, that random value would be stored in the long int variable, hat. What is its value? For that, you need a program:

```
#include <stdio.h>
#include <stdlib.h>

int main()
{
    long int hat;

    hat = random();        /* alt: use rand() */
    printf("%d is a random number.\n",hat);
    return(0);
}
```

Note that the STDLIB.H header file is required for the random() function not to offend the compiler. Beyond that, curiosity must be burning a hole in your cerebrum, so save the source code to disk as RANDUMB.C. Compile. Run:

```
1804289383 is a random number.
```

When I use rand(), which generates a short int (or int) value, I get

```
41 is a random number.
```

I'll bet you do too! So, is that truly random? Hmmm.

Exercise 2.4.1

Write a program that displays 100 random numbers. Call it RAND100.C.
Optional: Show it to your mom.

"Give me 100 really random numbers"

Run the RAND100 program (created in Exercise 2.4.1) two or three times.
Notice anything? Although each of the numbers is displayed differently,
every time you run the program the output is the same. That's not very
random. In fact, it's not random at all: It's predictable! Yikes!

To truly make the computer churn out random numbers, you need the sran-
dom() function. The *s* in srandom() stands for seed. What you can do with
srandom() is seed the randomizer gears inside the computer, shifting them
subtly so that each time the program runs, you get different random results.
This may sound strange, so why not put it into practice with a program:

```
#include <stdio.h>
#include <stdlib.h>

int main()
{
    long int hat;
    int loop;
    long int seed;

    printf("Enter a seed number:");
    scanf("%d",&seed);
    srandom(seed);

    for(loop=0;loop<100;loop++)
    {
        hat = random();
        printf("%10d\t",hat);
    }
    return(0);
}
```

Here's a modification to the program RAND100.C. This time, a prompt is added
to fill variable seed with a value. That value is then fed into the srandom()
function to seed the randomizer.

If your version of gcc lacks the random() function, you need to make these
adjustments to the preceding source code:

✦ srand() requires only an unsigned int, so delete long in Line 8.

✦ Substitute srand() for srandom() in Line 12.

✦ Replace `random()` in Line 16 with `rand()`.

✦ Use `%5d` in the `printf()` statement, in Line 17.

Save these changes to RAND100.C. Compile the program and run:

```
Enter a seed number:
```

Type any value — or just slap the numeric keypad with your open palms — and then press Enter. You see a screen of deliciously random numbers.

Try it again, this time using a different seed. You discover a fresh batch of 100 new and different random numbers.

Of course, if you use the same seed over again, you see the same predictable random numbers. Hmmm.

"Give me 100 really random numbers without much effort on my behalf this time"

The last time I played a computer game, I didn't notice a prompt that asked for a random number seed. That's because those programmers have figured out how to find a seed all by themselves. They use a value inside the computer that is constantly changing, a value that's different from one second to the next — that is, the value of the computer's clock.

Because a program may start at any given time, chances are that time will never be exactly the same twice. Therefore, it's a good bet that the computer's clock can be a good source of random number seeds. To get at the clock, you need to venture into one of the C language's time functions.

Rather than dig into the `time()` function here, I just pass along the method for extracting a seed using the timer. Here's the C language statement:

```
srandom((unsigned)time(NULL));
```

The `time()` function returns a special time value, which I don't get into here. The `NULL` in this example is basically a special type of value that the `time()` function eats; it's required so that the compiler doesn't get angry. And, `(unsigned)` is required by `srandom()`; seed values must be unsigned. Add the TIME.H header and you never have to manually seed the randomizer again:

```
#include <stdio.h>
#include <stdlib.h>
#include <time.h>
```

```
int main()
{
    long int hat;
    int loop;

    srandom((unsigned)time(NULL));

    for(loop=0;loop<100;loop++)
    {
        hat = random();
        printf("%10d\t",hat);
    }
    return(0);
}
```

Conjure up the source code for RAND100.C. Make modifications to the code so that it resembles what you see here. Save the code back to disk. Compile and run.

Then, run it again. Are the numbers different? As long as you don't repeat the program too quickly, the numbers are always different. At last! You're truly (pseudo) random!

The Diabolical Dr. Modulus

I could dream up wonderful programs all day, but not fully get you to understand the modulus operator without the random number stuff that comes first in this chapter. That's because the modulus, although an easy concept to explain, is quite a scoundrel to understand.

Introducing the modulo operator

The *modulus* is basically the remainder. You divide 16 by 5, and you get 3 with 1 remainder. So, 16 *modulo* 5 is 1. Cool people say "mod" rather than modulo, so it's really 16 *mod* 5 is 1.

In C, the % operator is the modulo, or "mod," so

$$17 \% 5 = 2$$

$$18 \% 5 = 3$$

$$19 \% 5 = 4$$

$$20 \% 5 = 0$$

When the modulo is 0, it means that the values divide out evenly, with no remainder.

Order is important with the modulo operator. *The big number must come first.* If not, the result always equals the first number, as in

5 % 18 = 5

3 % 55 = 3

5 % 20 = 5

Putting the small value first in this manner can be okay, for example, in a loop. And, the values make sense in that case. But, if you really want to find the remainder of 5 going into 18, you say 18 % 5 and not 5 % 18.

Here's a silly program for you:

```
#include <stdio.h>

int main()
{
    int m,c;

    for(c=0;c<100;c++)
    {
        m = c % 10;
        printf("%d\t",m);
    }
    return(0);
}
```

Save this source code to disk as MOD100.C. Compile and run.

On most 80-column displays, you see 10 rows of 10 numbers, going from 0 through 9. Those are the modulus values of 10 from 0 through 99.

What does all this have to do with random numbers?

Random numbers in the C language are all over the map. Rerun your RAND100 program. See? On my screen, I find values ranging from 78-million-something to values over 2 billion.

Now, consider the roll of a die or the flip of a coin. Obviously, playing a game of Parcheesi when the program generates a roll of 210,668,040 is time-consuming.

Dr. Modulus to the rescue!

By adding the right modulo function, you can trim a random number from what the computer generated into something more manageable.

Open up the last revision to the RAND100.C source code. In the `for` loop, after Line 14, add this line:

```
hat = hat % 10;
```

No, better yet, make it this line:

```
hat %= 10;
```

That's the same thing, but it's taking advantage of one of these cryptic C language math shortcuts (refer to Book 1, Chapter 9).

Save the change to RAND100.C to disk. Compile. Run.

On my screen, I see 100 random numbers, all in the range of 0 to 9. That's much more manageable; much more visually random. Indeed.

Exercise 2.4.2

Modify the RAND100.C program again, this time to ensure that the numbers displayed are in the range from 1 through 10. This isn't a modulus puzzle, but, rather, just a normal math problem. Suppose that your supervisor simply directs you to have the output display values 1 through 10 rather than 0 through 9. That's the issue to address.

Roll them bones!

Here's a program that simulates the rolling of a pair of dice:

```
#include <stdio.h>
#include <stdlib.h>
#include <time.h>

int main()
{
    int d1,d2,total;

    srandom((unsigned)time(NULL));

    d1 = random() % 6 + 1;
    d2 = random() % 6 + 1;
    total = d1 + d2;
    printf("You rolled %d and %d: Total %d\n",d1,d2,total);
    return(0);
}
```

Save this source code to disk as DICE.C. Compile. Run:

```
You rolled 6 and 2: Total 8
```

The math operation in Lines 11 and 12 may throw you:

```
d1 = random() % 6 + 1;
d2 = random() % 6 + 1;
```

According to the sacred order of precedence — MDAS — the % operator works between division and addition (refer to Book 1, Chapter 9 and Appendix C). So, it's really MDMAS, or *m*ultiplication, *d*ivision, *m*odulo, *a*ddition, and *s*ubtraction (My Dear Mother's Aunt Sally?). Therefore, in the preceding statements, the result of the `random()` function is modulo 6 first, and 1 is added to the result.

I have often seen such statements written like this:

```
d1 = (random() % 6) + 1;
d2 = (random() % 6) + 1;
```

The parentheses aren't needed for the compiler, but are added by the programmer only for readability. They confirm to the observer that the result of `random()` modulo 6 is done *first* and then 1 is added to the result.

Exercise 2.4.3

Modify the DICE.C program so that 16 rolls are made in a row. (Basically, you add a loop to the thing.)

What number is rolled most often?

I was going to make this section an exercise, but I just have too many goodies to show you. The following program is *another* modification to the DICE.C program. This time, the dice are rolled 1,000 times, and then the average roll is calculated and displayed. If you think that you can do this exercise on your own, do so. Then compare your results with what I have here:

```c
#include <stdio.h>
#include <stdlib.h>
#include <time.h>

#define ROLLS 1000

int main()
{
    int d1,d2,total,loop;
    int running_total = 0;
    float average;

    srandom((unsigned)time(NULL));
```

```
for(loop=1;loop<=ROLLS;loop++)
{
    d1 = random() % 6 + 1;
    d2 = random() % 6 + 1;
    total = d1 + d2;
    running_total += total;
    printf("You rolled %d and %d: Total %d\n",
d1,d2,total);
}
average = (float)running_total/ROLLS;
printf("The average roll for %d rolls was %3.1f\n",
ROLLS,average);
return(0);
}
```

Book II
Chapter 4

Not Truly Random

Update your DICE.C source code so that it looks like what's shown here. Here are the highlights:

✦ I set the number of rolls as a #define constant in Line 5. This way, you can easily adjust the number of rolls. (The constant ROLLS is used in several places in the program.)

✦ The running total is kept in the aptly named running_total variable, declared in Line 10. Note that this variable must be initialized to 0. If not, whatever value lurks in that memory space is used later on. (Always remember to initialize variables, either by assigning them to a value directly or to the result of some functions.)

✦ Line 20 calculates the running total by adding the value of total to running_total. The += shortcut is used.

✦ The average is calculated in Line 23. Note that the division is typecast as a float. Although you can do this without typecasting, my experience is that whenever you divide numbers, chances are that you don't always end up with an integer. Therefore, the result is typecast, and the variable average is declared as a float.

✦ Finally the printf() statement in Line 24 displays the results. The %3.1f placeholder limits the results to a 0.0 type of display.

Save the changes to disk. Then, recompile DICE.C and run.

Most of the time, you discover that the average roll is 7. But, occasionally, the results are on the high or low side of 7 (hence, the 0.0 display).

Come on, baby! Daddy needs a new pair of shoes!

TIP

Floating-point random numbers

If the random() function returns integers, how can you get a floating-point random number? All I know is that there doesn't seem to be an absolute, or absolutely correct, answer to that question. Here's what I do:

```
f = (rand)r/100000;
```

Variable f is a float. Variable r is the value returned from the random() function. And,

100000 is the value I chose for division. After the preceding statement, variable f contains a random number that has a decimal part, large or small, depending on the original random number, r. It's definitely a float. Whether that works for you or not, I can only guess. But it's what I use.

Flip a coin 1,000 times

I was going to make this section an exercise, just as I was in the preceding section, but you have too much to discover in this example.

Just as you can roll dice with random numbers and the modulus, you can also flip coins. The following program flips a single coin 1,000 times, displaying heads or tails as each flip comes up. The result of each flip is counted, and then the program displays the percentages for heads and tails when it's done. Does it always come out 50/50? Find out:

```c
#include <stdio.h>
#include <stdlib.h>
#include <time.h>

#define FLIPS 1000

int main()
{
    int coin,loop;
    int total_heads = 0;
    float hpercent,tpercent;

    srandom((unsigned)time(NULL));

    for(loop=1;loop<=FLIPS;loop++)
    {
        coin = random() % 2;
        /* assume 1 is heads, 0 is tails */
```

```
        total_heads += coin;
        if(coin)
            printf("Heads\t");
        else
            printf("Tails\t");
    }
    hpercent = (float)total_heads/FLIPS * 100;
    tpercent = 100.0 - hpercent;
    printf("Total Flips: %d\nHeads: %.2f\nTails: %.2f\n",
    FLIPS,hpercent,tpercent);
    return(0);
}
```

Name this source code COINFLIP.C. Here are some highlights and lowlights:

+ The total number of coin flips is set up as the FLIPS constant by #define. That way, you can easily change it later to see what effects it has on the program.

+ As with the last DICE.C example, the running tally total_heads must be initialized to 0. It's handy to do this when you declare the variable in Line 10.

+ Line 17 is the coin-flipping statement. The value returned by random() modulo 2 is either 0 or 1. As the comment in the code states, the program assumes that heads is 1 and tails is 0. You don't need to further modify this number — in fact, the 1 and the 0 come in handy on the next line.

+ The total number of heads is kept by merely counting all the 1s that the random number generator produces. Because 0s (for tails) don't increase that amount, you can get away with a simple addition statement: total_heads+=coin.

+ The comparison that if makes in Line 20 may seem odd, but remember that all comparisons evaluate to TRUE or FALSE. Internally, that's 1 or 0. Again, the advantage of the coin toss being 1 or 0 is used here. If a 1 (heads) appears, the result of the if statement is true, and Heads is displayed. If not, it's assumed that coins==0, and Tails is displayed.

+ The percentage of heads is calculated in Line 25. As with the DICE.C program, the results of division are typecast as a float. The formula is the standard percentage formula: the number of times heads came up in the total number of flips.

+ Line 26 calculates the percentage of tails by simply subtracting the heads value from 100.0. Note that 100.0 is specified, which makes the compiler treat it as an immediate floating-point value.

Save these changes to disk. Then, compile and run that sucker:

```
. . .
Heads    Tails    Tails    Heads    Heads    Tails    Heads
Total Flips: 1000
Heads: 50.60
Tails: 49.40
```

Remember that the average *tends toward* a 50/50 split. They do say, however, that, over time, heads prevails because that side of the coin is heavier by a mite. (Then again, recently it has been proved that what really matters is whether the coin was heads-up or tails-up before it was flipped. But I'm not going to go there.)

Chapter 5: While Going Loopy

In This Chapter

✔ **Understanding the** `while` **loop**

✔ **Reducing lines in your code**

✔ **Enjoying a** `while(!done)` **loop**

✔ **Using the** `do while` **loop**

✔ **Creating an endless** `while` **loop**

✔ **Introducing the** `continue` **keyword**

✔ **Nesting** `while` **loops**

There's more than one way to skin a cat. You knew that. You probably didn't know why it was necessary to skin the cat. No one really eats kitties — at least I know of no foreign land where *catus* is a delicacy. The only reason I can imagine to skin the cat would be out of pure cruelty. Yet we continue to use the saying to demonstrate that you can use more than a single method to accomplish some task. (At least I *hope* that's what is meant.)

In the C language, there's more than one way to spin a loop — no skinning involved. The `for` loop is the most ancient and traditional of the looping types. More modern is the `while` loop. It's similar to the `for` loop in that it has its three parts; unlike the `for` statement, though, where everything can appear in one place, a `while` loop has a more carefree, *la-di-da* style.

The `while` Loop

The `while` loop is the second major looping command in C, right after `for`. I personally find `while` easier to look at and a bit easier to set up. There's more of a potential, though, for endless loops with `while` — if you don't keep track of things.

Constructing a basic while *loop*

All loops have three parts:

✦ A setup, or initialization

✦ The part that loops — the statements that repeat

✦ The condition on which the loop finishes

In the for loop, these three parts are all pretty much in the for statement itself. With a while loop, only the condition on which the loop finishes is included with the while statement. The other parts of the loop must happen elsewhere in the program. To wit:

```
some sort of setup;
while(condition==true)
{
    statement;
    statement;
    /* more statements... */
    something to modify the condition and end the loop;
}
```

The only part of the loop included with the while statement is the part that must be true for the loop to repeat. As long as that statement is true, the loop repeats. Therefore, something inside the loop must affect that condition and eventually cause the loop to stop.

Note that the setup is kind of optional; as long as you can get the loop spinning and eventually stop it, that's great:

```
#include <stdio.h>

int main()
{
    int c;

    c = 10;
    while(c>0)
    {
        printf("%d\n",c);
        c--;
    }
    return(0);
}
```

With building anticipation, eagerly type this source code. Save it to disk as LOOP.C. Compile and run:

```
10
9
8
7
6
5
4
3
2
1
```

BOOM!

The while loop continues to spin as long as the value of the variable c is greater than 0. Inside the loop, the printf() statement displays the current value of c. Note that c starts out as 10 (in the output). Then, the next statement decrements the value of c. The loop continues to repeat until c decrements to 0, in which case the loop statements are skipped and the rest of the program runs.

Like an if statement, when the condition that while evaluates is not (or is no longer) true, the statements belonging to while are skipped. This means that some while loops may not even be executed.

Turn on the incredible shrinking ray!

The program LOOP.C, from the preceding section, is rather wordy. I wrote it that way to show you the pieces' parts. Normally, you could write this type of program with a modicum of brevity, as this example shows:

```
#include <stdio.h>

int main()
{
    int c = 10;

    while(c>0)
        printf("%d\n",c--);
    return(0);
}
```

Here, I have scrunched some things together. That makes the program a tad bit less readable, but it also shows you a few nifty things. Primarily, it illustrates that as with the for loop and the if statement, if only one line is repeated in a while loop, you don't need the curly braces.

Make these changes to your LOOP.C source. Recompile and run. The output is shockingly the same! Goodness!

Exercise 2.5.1

Concoct a program that displays numbers 1 through 100 by using a while loop. Name the program WHILE100.C.

1 could while *away the hours*

This while loop works similarly to the for(;;) loop in the TYPING.C program, from Book 1, Chapter 1. The deal here is that an endless loop isn't necessary to solve the problem:

```c
#include <stdio.h>

int main()
{
    char ch;

    puts("Press ~ and Enter to stop");
    while(ch != '~')
    {
        ch=getchar();
    }
    return(0);
}
```

Enter this source code and save it to disk as TYPING.C. (This example doesn't erase the TYPING.C program from Book 1 if you're using separate folders or directories for each book, as I mention in Appendix A.)

Compile and run.

Type at the console! Press ~ (the tilde) and then Enter to leave the program.

You can make the loop even tighter, if you wish. Lookee this:

```c
#include <stdio.h>

int main()
{
    puts("Press ~ and Enter to stop");
    while(getchar() != '~')
        ;
    return(0);
}
```

Make these modifications to TYPING.C. Save. Compile. Run.

The program works the same as the original TYPING.C program. That's because — as I say over and over again — C works from the inside out. First, the getchar() function generates a value. In this example, that's an immediate character value, which is compared with the ~ tilde character. As long as the characters don't match, the loop spins. The single semicolon is the while loop's "statement."

The popular while(!done) *loop*

One type of while loop you see and use a lot is what I call the while(!done), or "while not done," loop. This loop spins and spins until some unknown condition or conditions are met. So, in a way, it's like an endless loop, but with a single simple escape hatch.

For example, a variable named done or finished is created. It's set equal to 0, or FALSE. The while(!done) loop is then interpreted as while(TRUE), and the while loop spins and spins.

Eventually, some condition inside the loop is met. At that point, the done variable is set to TRUE. Therefore while(!done) works out to while(FALSE) and the loop stops.

You may think — especially if you're capable of thinking — that this type of loop is silly. After all, the C language break command can also stop a loop amidst a spin. But, unlike with break, you can reset the value of done inside a loop *and the rest of the loop's statements continue to run*. This can be important and is often necessary, as this source code demonstrates:

```c
#include <stdio.h>
#include <stdlib.h>
#include <time.h>

#define FALSE 0
#define TRUE !FALSE
#define OMEGA ('Z' - 'A')

int main()
{
    int done;
    long int r;
    char alpha;

    srandom((unsigned)time(NULL));

    done=FALSE;
    while(!done)
    {
```

```
        r = random() % OMEGA;
        alpha = 'A' + (char)r;
        if(alpha=='Q') done=TRUE;
        putchar(alpha);
    }
    putchar('\n');
    return(0);
}
```

Carefully type this source code into your editor. Here are the highlights and explanations:

✦ Lines 5 and 6 define TRUE and FALSE. FALSE is interpreted as 0 by the compiler. The value of TRUE is merely defined as !FALSE (not false), which is always correct. (Generally speaking, compilers see non-zero values as TRUE, and !0 works out to a nonzero value for the compiler.)

✦ Line 7 is used to calculate the number of letters in the alphabet without any mental effort on your behalf. The ASCII value of character A is subtracted from character Z so that random letters of the alphabet can be generated later.

✦ The value of 'Z'-'A' is 25. That works later in the program because C starts counting at 0. Had you merely set the value 26, for 26 letters in the alphabet, the program wouldn't work. That's why the 'Z'-'A' construction is used.

✦ Line 15 seeds the randomizer. Refer to Book II, Chapter 4 for more information.

✦ Remember to use srand() in Line 15 if your version of gcc lacks the srandom() function. Ditto for Line 20: Use the rand() function rather than random().

✦ Line17 is easy to understand if you read it like this: Is the loop done? The answer: FALSE!

✦ Line 18 ensures that the loop continues to run as long as the value of the done variable is FALSE. But it really reads "while not done," which is useful.

✦ Line 20 uses the random() or rand() function to generate a random number. The number is modulo 25 so that the value of variable r is in the range of 0 through 25. (Book 2, Chapter 4 covers this operation.)

✦ Character variable alpha is assigned to a random letter of the alphabet. The value of 'A' is added to whatever result is returned from the random() function. Note that variable r is typecast as a char to keep all variables on that line as character variables.

✦ All the random words that the program generates end in *Q,* so Line 22 ensures that. It reads that if the letter *Q* is generated, the loop is finished: `done=TRUE`.

✦ In Line 23, the character that is generated is displayed.

✦ Line 25 caps the output with a newline.

Save this source code to disk as BABELON.C — the program that generates unique and difficult-to-pronounce words, all ending with the letter *Q.* Compile and run:

```
LEFNWFCQ
```

Run again:

```
IYJSBVPTODYWTLVBGFUVWYEOGOFPSCTGFPNSFGGMJKTECABQ
```

Now you know where Microsoft gets its product keys!

What if the `done=TRUE` statement is replaced with `break`? In that case, Line 23 isn't executed and the Q isn't displayed — which may be what you want. In more complex programs, it's useful to have the remaining statements in the `while(!done)` loop continue to be executed and then have the loop stop on the `done=TRUE` condition.

Book II
Chapter 5

While Going Loopy

Exercise 2.5.2
Modify the BABELON.C source code so that the output is in lowercase letters.

The do-while *Loop*

A `do-while` loop is basically an upside-down `while` loop. It looks like this:

```
do
{
    statement;
    statement;
    /* more statements... */
}
while(condition==true);
```

A few subtle differences exist between the typical `while` loop and this one. The main difference is that a `do-while` loop is always executed at least once. Unlike a `while` loop, the *condition* is looked at *after* the loop spins. So, those statements after `do` really *do* get executed.

The other subtle differences are that initialization and a condition to end the loop are more or less optional. Because the loop always spins once, those conditions need not apply (but they usually do).

Note that the final while statement ends in a semicolon.

One way I like to implement a do-while loop is for confirming input. The input prompt is stated once and then repeated if the desired input isn't received. Sounds ideal for a do-while loop:

```c
#include <stdio.h>

int main()
{
    int value;

    do
    {
        printf("Enter a value greater than 20: ");
        scanf("%d",&value);
    }
    while(value <= 20);

    printf("Thank you. You entered %d\n",value);
    return(0);
}
```

Save this source code to disk as YORN.C. Compile and run.

A change in formatting for do-while

Occasionally, you may see a do-while loop written like this:

```c
do
{
    something;
    something;
} while(condition);
```

The while statement ending the loop is placed on the same line as the final brace ending the loop's statements. This is done, especially in larger programs, so that the lone while on a line by itself isn't mistaken as the start of a new loop.

To be consistent, in this book I put the while statement on a line by itself. But, note the preceding alternative and remember the reasons that it's used. (Keep in mind that source code formatting is for the human eye only; the compiler really doesn't care how it looks on the screen or page.)

Messing with Loops

You can do interesting, strange, and useful things with `while` loops, just as you can do them with other loops in the C language. This section highlights some of the more useful manipulations.

The endless `while` loop

`while` loops can easily become infinite loops. If there's no exit condition, the loop spins and spins, running amok like a Ferris wheel with a stoned carny manning the controls.

Sometimes, endless loops can be necessary. For example, if you don't know how many times a loop needs to be repeated, you must construct an endless loop, just in case. You merely need to provide a method for breaking free — ideally, by using the `break` keyword:

**Book II
Chapter 5**

While Going Loopy

```c
#include <stdio.h>
#include <stdlib.h>
#include <time.h>

#define RANGE 100

int main()
{
    int guess,number;

    srandom((unsigned)time(NULL));

    puts("Guessing Game!");

    number=random() % RANGE + 1;   /* value from 1 to RANGE */

    printf("I'm thinking of a number from 1 to %d.\n",RANGE);
    printf("Can you guess what it is?\n");

    while(1)
    {
        printf("Enter guess: ");
        scanf("%d",&guess);
        if(guess == number)
        {
            puts("You got it!");
            break;
        }
        else if(guess < number)
            puts("Too low!");
        else
```

```
        puts("Too high!");
    }
    printf("The number was %d\n",number);
    return(0);
}
```

Carefully enter this source code. Note that while(1) sets up an infinite loop. Only by guessing the correct number does a break statement end the loop.

Save the source code to disk as GUESS.C. Compile and run.

Here's a sample run:

```
Guessing Game!
I'm thinking of a number from 1 to 100.
Can you guess what it is?
Enter guess: 50
Too high!
Enter guess: 25
Too high!
Enter guess: 12
Too high!
Enter guess: 6
Too low!
Enter guess: 9
Too low!
Enter guess: 10
Too low!
Enter guess! 11
You got it!
The number was 11
```

For more information on the break keyword, refer to Book I, Chapter 7.

Exercise 2.5.3

Modify the source code for GUESS.C. This time, make it so that the user has fewer than six guesses to find the correct number. If the user can't guess the number in fewer than six guesses, the computer stops the game and displays the value.

Continuing loops

The C language is full of symmetry, some of which is there just to be symmetrical. For example, the signed keyword balances the unsigned — even though no one uses signed. I suppose, to be symmetrical with the break keyword, the C language has the continue keyword.

The `continue` keyword is used inside a loop to jump immediately to the top and repeat the loop; any statements in the loop following `continue` are skipped.

Yeah, it's weird. That's why it's rarely used. Here's a dorky program example:

```
#include <stdio.h>

int main()
{
    int count = 0;

    while(count<100)
    {
        count++;
        if(count%5 == 0)
            continue;
        printf("%d\t",count);
    }
    return(0);
}
```

Clickity-clack this code on your keyboard and type it into your editor. Save the source code to disk as CONT.C.

Compile. Run.

The output displays numbers from 1 through 99, merrily skipping over any multiple of 5. Yeah, silly. I could show you other examples, but they tend to be longer and more boring. Suffice it to say that there's a place for the `continue` statement.

Exercise 2.5.4

Rewrite the source for CONT.C so that it does the same thing without the `continue` statement. Do this by changing one character and deleting one line from the original source code.

Nested `while` *loops*

Like `for` loops, `while` loops can be nested — though I must admit that this practice isn't as common as nesting `for` loops. I think that most programmers find that nesting `for` loops looks better visually because all the items that control the `for` loop are listed in the `for` statement. With a `while` loop, discovering how the nesting works is tougher. But it can be done:

```
#include <stdio.h>

int main()
```

```
{
    int x = 1;
    char a;

    while(x < 10)
    {
        a = 'A';
        while(a < 'J')
        {
            printf("%d%c\t",x,a);
            a++;
        }
        putchar('\n');
        x++;
    }
    return(0);
}
```

Save this source code to disk as GRID.C. Compile and run.

Yes. Another grid program. La-di-da.

For kicks, compare this GRID.C source code with the `for` loop version from Book I, Chapter 7. It should become apparent why `for` loops are preferred for nesting.

Chapter 6: More Decision Making

In This Chapter

✓ Using `switch-case`

✓ Curing the `if-else-if-else-if-else` **syndrome**

✓ **Halting fall-through with** `break`

✓ **Avoiding the odd** `?:` **construct**

✓ **Playing Craps**

T he `if` statement isn't the end-all of C language decision making. You have two other ways to make decisions in C. One is a helpful solution to the endless `if-else` problem, and the other is perhaps the most bizarre and cryptic C language thing you may ever see. This chapter covers them both.

The Old `Switch Case` Trick

When I think of `switch case`, I have to remember the classic screwball comedy *What's Up, Doc?* — a wild film based on the premise of several identical cases, all of which get switched between the craziest characters this side of a Mel Brooks film. It was the movie that taught me the word *igneous*.

The C language lacks the `igneous` keyword. But it does have two useful words from the plot of *What's Up, Doc?* — `switch` and `case`. They're used together to make the same thing, or structure. It's not a loop. No, it's a `switch-case` *thing*. And it's a handy way to have your programs handle multiple outcomes from a single event.

The else-if else-if else-if else-if disease

As error numbers grow more complex, some error number program needs to let you decipher the various error numbers and help to figure out what it all means. The following is just such a program:

```
#include <stdio.h>

int main()
{
```

```
    int code;

    printf("Enter the error code number\n");
    printf("Range 1 through 5: ");
    scanf("%d",&code);

    if(code == 1)
    {
        puts("San Andreas Fault");
        puts("Solution: Move your house.");
    }
    else if(code == 2)
    {
        puts("Illegal Operation");
        puts("Solution: Find another doctor.");
    }
    else if(code == 3)
    {
        puts("Bad Filename");
        puts("Solution: Spank the filename and put it to bed
without any supper.");
    }
    else if(code == 4)
    {
        puts("Missing Socket");
        puts("Solution: Look in the dryer.");
    }
    else if(code == 5)
    {
        puts("Divide by Zero");
        puts("Solution: Mess with the numbers until it
works.");
    }
    else
    {
        puts("Error code value out of range");
        puts("Solution: Read the directions next time.");
    }
    return(0);
}
```

Type this source code into your editor. It's a bit long, but you can easily create much of it by using copy-and-paste in your editor. Save it to disk as ERRORS.C. Compile and run.

Oh, ha-ha! This program is *funny!*

On the other hand, the program is a mess! Look at all those else-if statements! Imagine if you were writing this type of program for real and had dozens of conditions to test for. There has to be a better way!

Introducing the cure: switch case

In C, the `switch-case` structure is used to handle multiple decisions, similar to the endless `else if` structure shown in the preceding section. Here's how it looks:

```
switch(expression)
{
    case value1:
        statement(s);
        break;
    case value2:
        statement(s);
        break;
    case value3:
        statement(s);
        break;
    default:
        statement(s);
}
```

Book II
Chapter 6

More Decision Making

Complex, eh? But it's not really because most of the structure is repeated. What comes first?

```
switch(expression)
```

The `switch` statement evaluates an *expression,* which is typically just a variable. The value of that variable is examined by the multiple `case` statements that follow, warmly hugged by `switch`'s braces:

```
case value1:
    statement(s);
    break;
```

The keyword `case` is followed by an integer value. It must be an immediate value or constant. *case does not examine variables!* If the integer value is equal to the expression (both items match), the statements that follow are executed.

Note that `case`'s value is followed by a colon. The statements belonging to `case` end in semicolons.

The last statement to follow `case` is traditionally a `break` command. This command leaves the `switch` structure and continues program execution with the next statement after `switch`'s final brace.

Optionally, the switch structure can end with a `default` item:

```
default:
    statement(s);
```

This group of statements is executed when no `case` match is made — kind of like the last `else` in a long `else-if` structure. Keep in mind that `default` is optional, though it's almost too handy to give up.

`switch case` is ideally used to examine multiple possibilities or conditions in a program, handily replacing awkward `else-if` combinations.

The `switch case` *solution*

The following code is the elegant `switch case` version of the ERRORS.C source code. Observe its grace:

```c
#include <stdio.h>

int main()
{
    int code;

    printf("Enter the error code number\n");
    printf("Range 1 through 5: ");
    scanf("%d",&code);

    switch(code)
    {
        case 1:
            puts("San Andreas Fault");
            puts("Solution: Move your house.");
            break;
        case 2:
            puts("Illegal Operation");
            puts("Solution: Find another doctor.");
            break;
        case 3:
            puts("Bad Filename");
            puts("Solution: Spank the filename and put it to
bed without any supper.");
            break;
        case 4:
            puts("Missing Socket");
            puts("Solution: Look in the dryer.");
            break;
        case 5:
            puts("Divide by Zero");
```

```
            puts("Solution: Mess with the numbers until it
works.");
            break;
        default:
            puts("Error code value out of range");
            puts("Solution: Read the directions next time.");
    }
    return(0);
}
```

Modify your ERRORS.C source code to match what's shown here. From the ugly duckling of else if the handsome swan of switch case is born! Save the changes to disk. Recompile and run.

The output is the same, but the program is designed to show off the elegance of the switch case structure. Yet, you can do more with this type of thing than just replace ugly else-if statements.

Aghgh! No breaks!

Mostly, the statements that follow case end with break. If not, the program would continue executing the statements belonging to the next case statement. This is known as "falling through" and sometimes it can be used to an advantage. This source code demonstrates:

```c
#include <stdio.h>

int main()
{
    char c;

    puts("Available packages:");
    puts("A - Transportation, Hotel and Meals.");
    puts("B - Transportation and Hotel.");
    puts("C - Transportation only.");
    printf("Select your package: ");
    c = getchar();

    switch(c)
    {
        case 'A':
        case 'a':
            puts("You get the Meals and");
        case 'B':
        case 'b':
            puts("You get the Hotel and");
        case 'C':
        case 'c':
```

```
            puts("You get transportation.");
            break;
        default:
            puts("You don't get nuthin!");
    }
    return(0);
}
```

Save this source code to disk as TRIP.C. Compile and run:

```
Available packages:
A - Transportation, Hotel and Meals.
B - Transportation and Hotel.
C - Transportation only.
Select your package:
```

If you choose A (press **a** or **A** on the keyboard), you see

```
You get the Meals and
You get the Hotel and
You get transportation.
```

case matches A and falls through to display the results for matching B and C. The break at the end of the case 'c' statement prevents the statement belonging to default from executing.

Notice how falling through works as an advantage to match multiple items:

```
case 'A':
case 'a':
```

Both upper- and lowercase answers are dealt with in two case statements; the first one simply falls through to the next.

Run the program a few more times to get an idea of how falling through works.

If a break isn't found in the last case statement, the program falls through and executes the default statements as well. Just because they're default statements doesn't protect them from the rest of the structure.

Exercise 2.6.1

Write a program named PARTY.C that asks the user for their political party affiliation. Have the program use a switch case structure to confirm the single-character input.

The switch case while(!done) *trick*

I have often seen switch case structures used inside while loops as part of a menu system or other repeating contraption that attempts to extract information.

The following code is an update to the YORN.C series of programs I present in Book 1. This time, the loop has been updated to a while(!done) loop and switch case is used to replace the various if statements:

```c
#include <stdio.h>

#define FALSE 0
#define TRUE !FALSE

int main()
{
    int done;
    char ch;

    done = FALSE;
    printf("Would you like me to send your password to the
bad guys?\n");
    while(!done)
    {
        printf("Enter Y or N (Y/N)?");
        ch = getchar();
        switch(ch)
        {
            case 'N':
            case 'n':
                printf("Well, then: your password is
safe!\n");
                done = TRUE;
                break;
            case 'Y':
            case 'y':
                printf("Okay, Sending your password!\n");
                done = TRUE;
                break;
            default:
                printf("You must enter a Y or N!\n");
                fflush(stdin);
        } /* end switch */
    } /* end while */
    return(0);
}
```

**Book II
Chapter 6**

More Decision Making

Carefully type this source code into your editor. In Line 31, use fpurge(stdin) if you're using a Unix type of operating system.

Note that I added comments to the single braces in Lines 32 and 33. You often do this with longer source code files to help match up which brace belongs to which function. Believe me, with some programs, that can get hairy.

Save the file to disk as YORN.C.

Compile and run.

The program repeatedly asks you the yes-or-no (hence, YORN) question until you press **Y** or **N** (or **y** or **n**). The `while(!done)` loop makes that possible. The `switch case` structure helps eliminate the wrong keys.

This type of structure is often used in menu systems: The system displays a series of options and waits for input to see which commands to run. For example:

```
1 - Word processing
2 - E-mail
3 - Browse the web
4 - Quicken
5 - Manage Windows
6 - Quit
```

The program keeps looping with a type of `while(!done)` loop. A `switch case` structure examines input.

Refer to Book II, Chapter 5 for more information on `while(!done)` loops.

The Weird and Creepy ? : Construct

I have saved the weird thing for last in this chapter: It's the scary ? : *ternary operator.* Even its official name is scary. What *is* ternary? Then again, it's also called the *conditional operator.* I like to think of it as the ugly way to write an `if` statement.

The traditional example is the "max" function, which sets variable z equal to the value of variable a or b, whichever is larger. Here's how to write that as an `if-else` statement:

```
ff(a > b)
    z = a;
else
    z = b;
```

Here's the ?: method:

```
z = (a > b) ? a : b;
```

First comes the comparison, a > b. If it's true, z = a; otherwise, z = b. You can look at it this way:

```
z = comparision ? if_true : if_false;
```

Here's my sample-program contribution to the cryptic conditional operator:

```
#include <stdio.h>

int main()
{
    int grade;

    printf("Enter your grade on the last test (0 to 100): ");
    scanf("%d",&grade);
    printf("The computer says you: ");
    printf("%s\n",(grade >= 60) ? "Passed!" : "Failed");
    return(0);
}
```

Book II
Chapter 6

**More Decision
Making**

Type this code into your editor. Save it to disk as GRADE.C. Compile and run.

The conditional operator in Line 10 evaluates the grade variable. If the value is greater than or equal to 60, the text Passed! is used to replace %s in the printf() formatting string. Otherwise, the text Failed is used.

And that's enough of that!

Dog-ear this page or put a PostIt(tm) note here so that you can refer to it when the ?: crosses your path. My recommendation is *not* to use it and stick with if-else instead. The people who read your code will appreciate that.

Bonus Program!

Does anyone understand the game of Craps? Yeah, it's a dice game. And if you have ever been to Las Vegas, you have probably seen the Craps table, surrounded by wildly cheering crowds.

I love the game of Craps. I think I like it because there isn't a bet you cannot make: You can bet that the human will win, bet that the house will win, or bet on any combination that could possibly come up on the dice. If you feel that a 6 is coming up, bet on the 6 and win money.

It's because of all those bets that Craps can be confusing to learn. The basic game, however, is rather simple:

1. You roll two dice.

2. If the roll comes up 7 or 11, you win! Yeah! You're done.

3. If the roll comes up 2, 3 or 12, you lose. That's Craps, and you're done.

4. But when the roll comes up another number (4, 5, 6, 8, 9 10), that becomes your *point*. The object of the game now is *not* to roll a 7. Instead, you try to roll your point number before a 7 comes up. If you can roll the point number again, you win. But when that 7 comes up, you lose.

It's that dual nature of Craps — 7 can win and 7 can lose — that confuses a lot of people. Fine! Let them play the slots! You and I can enjoy Craps, even on the computer with your limited knowledge of C programming:

```c
#include <stdio.h>
#include <stdlib.h>
#include <time.h>

int main()
{
    int bet,roll,point;
    char c;

    srandom((unsigned)time(NULL));

    printf("Enter your bet: $");
    scanf("%i",&bet);

    puts("Rolling them bones....!");
    roll = random() % 11 + 2;

    printf("%d ",roll);
    switch(roll)
    {
        case 7:
        case 11:
            printf("- You win!\n");
            bet *= 2;
            break;
        case 2:
        case 3:
        case 12:
            printf("- Craps! You lose!\n");
            bet = 0;
            break;
        default:
```

```
        point=roll;
        printf("- Your point is now %d.\n",point);
        while(1)
        {
            roll = random() % 11 + 2;
            printf("\tYou rolled %d, point is
%d.\n",roll,point);
            if(roll==point)
            {
                printf("\tYou win!\n");
                bet *= 2;
                break;
            }
            if(roll==7)
            {
                printf("\tSeven out, you lose!\n");
                bet = 0;
                break;
            }
        }
    }
    printf("You now have $%d.\n",bet);
    return(0);
}
```

Carefully type this source code. Save it to disk as CRAPS.C. Here are the highlights:

✦ Remember to use srand( ) in Line 10 if your version of gcc lacks the srandom( ) function. This line is used to seed the randomizer.

✦ Line 16 generates the random roll of the dice. The value is modulo 11 because you cannot roll a 1 with two dice. That produces random values between 0 and 10, which is then increased by two so that it's in the range from 2 through 12 — like a roll of the dice. (Remember to change random( ) to rand( ) if you need to.)

✦ The switch case thing is the heart that beats in the bosom of the CRAPS.C code. For a 7 or 11, you win! For a 2, 3, or 12, you lose!

✦ The default condition of the switch case structure handles the odd "point" situation. Note how elegantly it does so without having to specify the point values individually.

✦ An endless while(1) loop in Line 35 ensures that the dice are rolled (Line 37) over and over until either the point is met (Line 39) or a 7 comes up (Line 45). All other numbers are just noise (though in the real game of Craps, you can continue to bet on the *action*).

✦ break commands are used to bust out of the endless loop when either the point is made or a 7 comes up.

Compile and run the program!

```
Enter your bet: $100
Rolling them bones....!
8 - Your point is now 8.
         You rolled 5, point is 8.
         You rolled 12, point is 8.
         You rolled 8, point is 8.
         You win!
You now have $200.
```

Of course, not every time do you win. Enjoy!

Chapter 7: The Goto Chapter

In This Chapter

✔ **Understanding** goto

✔ **Avoiding** goto

✔ **Using** goto **only when you really need to**

*O*ne C language keyword is despised over all others. Hated so much is this word that you would think college sophomores would e-mail away to Dr. Ritchie and accuse him of being a fool for including it in the C language to begin with! (Even college sophomores are too respectful to do that.)

The word is goto. It's a legitimate C language keyword and command. Its use is shunned, however, because the goto command is just too darn useful, and overusing it leads to sloppy code that's difficult to read. University professors rail against goto. C language gurus roll their eyes at its mention. And, mere mortal programmers dare not touch it for fear of public shame and humiliation.

Because of all that, I present you with an entire chapter on goto, the C language's orphan command, which does have a place and isn't as evil as others may lead you to believe.

What Now? Go To!

Yes, Dr. Ritchie himself invented the C language goto statement. But even he calls it "infinitely abusable." There's just no circumstance under which you can use goto that you cannot do more elegantly and properly with another C language looping statement. But, in one situation, goto can get you out of a pinch. More on that in a few pages.

The Basic goto Thing

The goto statement is used to redirect program execution to a label elsewhere in the program; for example:

```
printf("Prepare for vital information on world peace:\n");
goto somewhere
printf("Love your neighbor as yourself\n");
```

```
somewhere:
printf("There! Remember it!\n");
```

When the program sees the goto in the second line, it immediately looks for and jumps to the somewhere label in the fourth line. (*Labels* are single words ending with a colon.) Then, program execution continues with the following line. The third line is never executed.

Mostly, goto is abused to instigate a loop. This example can get you thrown out of any computer science graduate program:

```
#include <stdio.h>

int main()
{
    int naughty = 0;

loop:
    puts("Naughty, naughty");
    naughty++;
    if(naughty < 10) goto loop;
    return(0);
}
```

Enter this heinous source code into your editor. Save it to disk as OHNO.C. Compile and run:

```
Naughty, naughty
Naughty, naughty
...
```

(You get the idea.)

In OHNO.C, the goto command is used to create a loop. The condition is evaluated by an if statement; when the value of variable naughty is less than 10, if passes the test and program execution branches back to the loop label.

Oh, but it's such a crime.

Exercise 2.7.1

Rewrite OHNO.C so that the program performs the same actions, but with a for loop instead.

Goto: The ugly truth!

Professors (and the graduate students who teach their classes) rail against goto, but few of them remember the utter chaos involved in the old days. You see, goto is one of the oldest programming instructions around. It's very useful. The problem with it is abuse.

Back in the old days, rank programmers would use goto to branch all over a program with neither motive nor sanity. Often, they did this on purpose to *obfuscate* the code, rendering it unreadable by others and therefore semi-secure. But most often, they did it simply because they were lazy and didn't think the whole thing through.

Here's an ugly truth: Deep inside your computer, when that C language object code is translated into machine language, it becomes *full of goto instructions!* The most basic and powerful microprocessor instruction is a *jump*. It's used just like goto to branch program execution to a specific spot in memory. So, although the professors (and the graduate students who teach their classes) shun the use of goto, probably not one single program deep inside your computer lacks a microprocessor-level goto or jump instruction. But keep that between you and me, okay?

Where goto *Is Perhaps Needed*

In one instance, goto can be useful: in the midst of a nested loop. The break statement is normally used to bust out of a loop, but break stops only the loop it's in; if the loop is nested, the outer loop continues to turn. In this case, only goto can save your butt from the middle of a nested loop.

Granted, this type of situation is rare. In fact, unless you foresee a complete disaster, it may be a good idea to simply set a specific variable that can be examined after the nested loop is complete. For example:

```c
#include <stdio.h>

int main()
{
    int x = 1;
    char a;

    while(x < 10)
    {
```

```
a = 'A';
while(a < 'J')
{
    printf("%d%c\t",x,a);
    a++;
}
putchar('\n');
x++;
}
return(0);
}
```

This source code is a modification to the GRID.C source code from Book II, Chapter 5. I added a condition whereby matching x==5 and a=='E' causes the program to panic (well, pretend to). At that point, supposedly, the program needs to stop and bail out of both loops. You can do this only with goto, as shown in the preceding example.

Save. Compile. Run:

```
1A    1B    1C    1D    1E    1F    1G    1H    1I
2A    2B    2C    2D    2E    2F    2G    2H    2I
3A    3B    3C    3D    3E    3F    3G    3H    3I
4A    4B    4C    4D    4E    4F    4G    4H    4I
5A    5B    5C    5D    5E
```

Now, you could handle this example another way, so goto isn't utterly vital. For example, you can have an error variable available. If a "bad" condition deep inside nested loops is met, you can do this:

```
error=TRUE;
```

After exiting the nested loops, the program can examine the error variable to see whether things are okay. That's one way around the problem, and I'm sure that you can find many more when you sit down and think about it.

If you can imagine a programming problem where goto is used in a manner that cannot be duplicated in any other way, please feel free to let me know. I will publicly post any such situations on the *C For Dummies* Web site, at www.c-for-dummies.com.

Book III

Above C Level

AT THE REAL PROGRAMMERS DATING BAR

Whoa! Look at the pocket protectors on this one!

Contents at a Glance

Chapter 1: Asking for Arrays

In This Chapter

*I*t was easy for the evil emperor Bartholomew to conquer the world. After all, he had his marvelous cloned flying-monkey army. He didn't start out that way. One flying monkey does not make an army. Only with *many* flying monkeys was Bartholomew able to strike terror in the hearts of his enemies.

The C language variable types are powerful enough by themselves. But one of the real strengths of variables comes from their ability to be multiplied into arrays. This ability opens the door a crack into the land of the database, increasing the scope of the mere mortal variable to near army-size proportions.

You should save source code and programs created for this part of the book in the ABOVE folder or directory on your computer's hard disk.

Beyond Normal Variables

Array is one of those words that loses its meaning the more you say it. Array. A ray. Air ray. Hairy. Hooray!

An *array* is nothing more than an organized collection of stuff. A computer programmer would look at a row of cars in a parking lot and see it as an array of cars. A line (or *queue*) of people at the grocery store is an array. A list of your daughter's friends that she's inviting to her birthday party is an array. An array is merely a collection of stuff.

Making an array in C

In the C language, an array is a collection of variables, all of the same type. You can have an array of `int`, `char`, `float`, `double`, or any type of variables.

Suppose that a bunch of football jocks are standing in line at Starbucks. Never mind that they can't decide on what to drink, and forget those child-ish impulses that make you think that they will suddenly turn on you and stick you into the trash can through the swinging Thank You lid. No, instead, you notice the numbers on their jerseys:

16, 88, 45, 99, 6, 33

To store these numbers in a computer program (without using an array), you need six separate `int` variables. It can be done! But, like that double caramel frappé-machiato, it's messy.

Instead, you can handily store each of the numbers in an array, created thusly:

```
int jocks[] = {16, 88, 45, 99, 6, 33};
```

This example is an *integer array*. It's declared just like a single variable would be (`int jocks`), but note the two braces. They tell the compiler that the variable being declared is an array containing multiple integer values.

The values in the array are assigned immediately in the preceding statement. Each value appears between a set of curly braces separated by commas. Each value is an *element* of the array. The preceding example has six ele-ments in the `jocks[]` array, numbered 0 through 5 (again with the 0!).

Here's how each of the elements is referenced:

```
jocks[0] = 16
jocks[1] = 88
jocks[2] = 45
jocks[3] = 99
jocks[4] = 6
jocks[5] = 33
```

In this example, the variables are listed individually, and they can be treated as individual `int` variables: everything works the same. But they're still ele-ments in an array.

The most important thing to remember about an array is that the first element is numbered 0, not 1. That's fine because a lot of the craziness in the C language also starts with 0. So if you have been working through this book from front to back, you should be used to the starting-with-0 theme by now.

Using an array

Here's a sample program that uses an array to store a series of digits — in this case, the combination to a safe:

```
#include <stdio.h>

int main()
{
    int combination[] = { 36, 24, 12 };

    printf("The combination for the safe:\n");
    printf("Turn left to %d\n",combination[0]);
    printf("Turn right to %d\n",combination [1]);
    printf("Turn left to %d, open.\n",combination [2]);
    return(0);
}
```

Save this source code as SAFE.C. Note how each element in the array is referenced — 0 is first! The elements behave just like individual `int` variables, though each is part of an array.

Compile and run:

```
The combination for the safe:
Turn left to 36
Turn right to 24
Turn left to 12, open.
```

Here's another program example:

```
#include <stdio.h>

int main()
{
    char grades[] = { 'A', 'A', 'B', 'C', 'A',
                      'B', 'C', 'C', 'B', 'A',
                      'D', 'D', 'B', 'B', 'A',
                      'A', 'A', 'B', 'A', 'B',
                      'A', 'F', 'B', 'B', 'B' };
    int student;

    puts("Class Grades");
    for(student=0;student<25;student++)
    {
```

```
        printf("Student #%d, %c\n",student+1,
grades[student]);
        }
    return(0);
}
```

Save this source code to disk as GRADE.C. Compile and run to see how poorly the class did!

Note that I have "pretty printed" the grades[] array across several lines in the program. As long as each element is properly defined and separated by commas, that's okay. Remember that the last element doesn't have a comma after it; the compiler sees that as a "something is missing" type of error.

This program also shows you how you can use char variables in an array.

See how student+1 is used in the printf() statement so that the student numbers range from 1 to 25 and not 0 through 24.

Finally, note how the for loop is used to display each array element's values. The construction grades[student] evaluates to a different element for each turn of the loop.

Exercise 3.1.1

Devise a program that contains a float array of five elements. Each element is the IQ of a co-worker at your job. Have the program spin a for loop to display each worker's IQ value. Name the program COWORKER.C (**Hint:** Use GRADE.C as a starting point.)

Declaring an empty array

Not every array you use starts out filled. Most of them are, in fact, empty when the program starts. You simply size up the array for however many elements you think it will have and let the program fill in the values. For example:

```
int chairs[12];
```

This declaration tells the compiler to set aside space for an integer array, name it chairs, and have room inside for 12 elements, numbered 0 through 11.

Because the size of the array may change, it's often declared by using a constant. For example:

```
#define GAMES 26
```

And then, later in the code:

```
int team[GAMES];
```

GAMES can even be used in a `for` loop or other part of the program that manipulates the array. The idea is that you can resize the array by simply changing the constant GAMES instead of doing a search and replace.

One other important note: You cannot dynamically resize an array in C. After the size is set, it's unchangeable. Lots of beginning C programmers want to resize arrays while a program is running — and I wish that it could be done — but it cannot. So there.

Carefully type this source code:

```
#include <stdio.h>
#include <stdlib.h>
#include <time.h>

#define COUNT 100

int main()
{
    int r[COUNT];
    int c;

    srandom((unsigned)time(NULL));

/* initialize the array */

    for(c=0;c<COUNT;c++)
        r[c] = random() % 100 + 1;

/* display the array */

    puts("100 Random numbers:");
    for(c=0;c<COUNT;c++)
        printf("%d\t",r[c]);

    putchar('\n');
    return(0);
}
```

Remember that for some versions of gcc, you must substitute the `srand()` and `rand()` functions for `srandom()` and `random()` in Lines 12 and 17. (Refer to Book II, Chapter 4 for more information on random numbers in C.)

Save the source code to disk as RAND100.C Compile and run. You see 100 random numbers displayed, each in the range of 1 through 100.

Exercise 3.1.2

Write a program that stores the daily high temperatures for the past five days. Create a `float` array of five elements for it. Have the user manually enter each day's temperature. Then have the program display the results *and* list the average temperature of the past five days. Call this program TEMPS.C.

Refilling an array

Arrays are basically chain-gang variables. And, as with any variable, you can change their contents at any time. You can replace individual array elements with new values, or you can reinitialize the entire array. Witness this source code, a modification to the RAND100.C program presented a scant few pages back:

```c
#include <stdio.h>
#include <stdlib.h>
#include <time.h>

#define COUNT 100

int main()
{
    int r[COUNT];
    int c;

    srandom((unsigned)time(NULL));

/* initialize the array */

    for(c=0;c<COUNT;c++)
        r[c] = random() % 100 + 1;

/* display the array */

    puts("100 Random numbers:");
    for(c=0;c<COUNT;c++)
        printf("%d\t",r[c]);

    putchar('\n');

/* Reinitialize the array */

    for(c=0;c<COUNT;c++)
        r[c] = random() % 100 + 1;

/* display the array again */

    puts("100 NEW Random numbers:");
```

```
for(c=0;c<COUNT;c++)
    printf("%d\t",r[c]);

putchar('\n');
return(0);
}
```

This update is easy to make: Just copy the text from Lines 14 through Line 25, and then paste it back in to create the second run-through shown here. Save the monster back to disk. Recompile and run.

The output this time shows two separate batches of random numbers, proving that the array is a variable and its contents can be changed. But you probably could have guessed that anyway.

Sorting an Array

When people deal with arrays, they inevitably ask the question "How do I sort an array?" The answer to this question, of course, is, "Yes! You can sort an array. Thank you for asking. Good day!" And then you walk away.

This section shows you how to sort an array using the simple (and excruciatingly slow) *bubble sort*. Better and faster sorts are available, none of which is covered in this book.

Sort me, quickly!

Even though Lotto balls may be drawn in random order, they're always listed in ascending order in the next day's paper. Sounds like a complex job — something the paper probably has an intern do. But your computer is better than any old intern.

Carefully type this source code into your editor. Save it to disk as SORTME.C. Compile and run:

```
#include <stdio.h>

#define SIZE 6

int main()
{
    int lotto[] = { 10, 48, 1, 37, 6, 24 };
    int c,a,b,temp;

    puts("Here is the array unsorted:");
    for(c=0;c<SIZE;c++)
```

```
            printf("%2d ",lotto[c]);
        putchar('\n');

/* sort the array */

    for(a=0;a<SIZE-1;a++)
        for(b=a+1;b<SIZE;b++)
            if(lotto[a] > lotto[b])
            {
                temp=lotto[b];
                lotto[b] = lotto[a];
                lotto[a] = temp;
            }

/* display the result */

    puts("Here is the sorted array:");
    for(c=0;c<SIZE;c++)
        printf("%2d ",lotto[c]);
    putchar('\n');
    return(0);
}
```

Here's a sample of the output:

```
Here is the array unsorted:
10 48  1 37  6 24
Here is the sorted array:
 1  6 10 24 37 48
```

Exercise 3.1.3

Can you figure it out? Change only one character in the SORTME.C source code so that the lottery numbers are sorted in *descending* order.

Sorting things out

Sorting anything involves making comparisons. When you sort an array, you're comparing one value with every other value in the array. An if command and various symbols, such as <, >, ==, <=, and => make it all happen. And, two for loops ensure that every value is compared to every other value in the array.

Hey! A figure would sure help!

Figures 1-1 through 1-5 graphically illustrate how the SORTME.C program goes about its business. In each progressing figure, the first (outer) for loop's variable a points to the first element of the array, and the second (inner) for loop's variable b points to the next (and subsequent) elements in the array. At each step of the process, a comparison is made: "Is 10 greater than 48?" If so, the numbers are swapped, which is what happens in the second step in Figure 1-1.

As soon as variable b equals the last element, the first (outer) for loop spins again, starting at the array's second element (see Figure 1-2). Again, each item in the array is compared with the second element, and, if one is greater than the other, they're swapped.

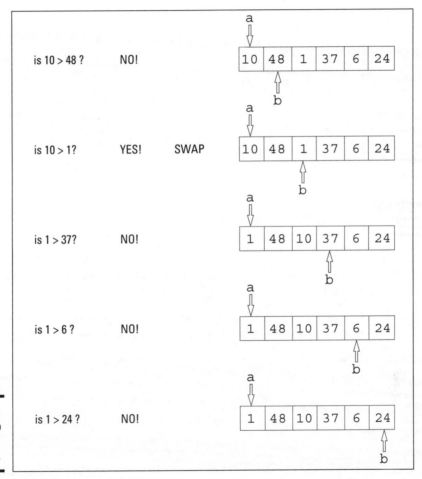

Figure 1-1:
Bubbling up through a bubble sort.

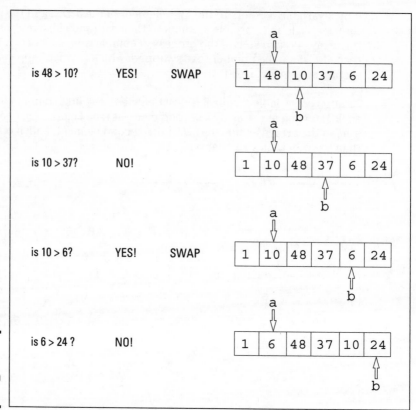

Figure 1-2:
The second
time through
the array.

Figure 1-3 shows the next turn of the first `for` loop. More comparing. More swapping.

Figures 1-4 and 1-5 show the final two turns of the first `for` loop. Everything wraps up nicely — a fine denouement, if you ask me.

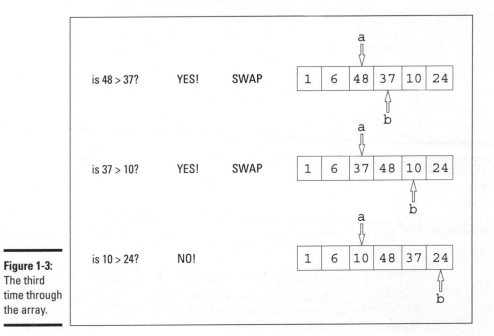

Figure 1-3:
The third
time through
the array.

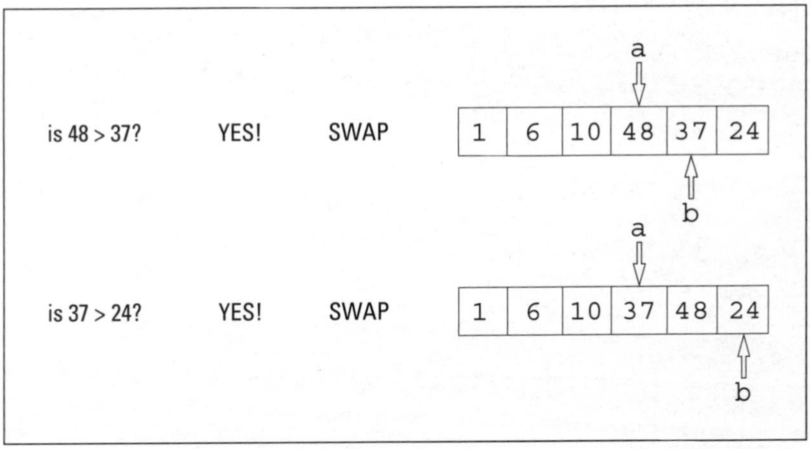

Figure 1-4:
Wrapping
things up
with this
sorting stuff.

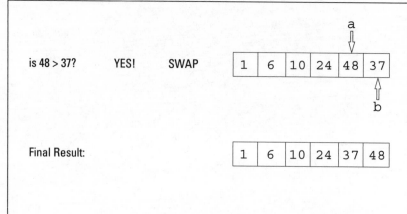

Figure 1-5:
The final trip
through and
the final
result.

Sorting an obscenely huge series of numbers

The problem with the bubble sort demonstrated in the preceding section is
that it's slow. As I say earlier in this chapter, you have better ways to sort
arrays. And, nothing drives that home like trying to sort a huge swath of
numbers. Such number crunching (as it's called) really prompts you to go
out and buy Sedgewick's *Algorithms in C* (Addison-Wesley) and learn about
the QuickSort routine:

```
#include <stdlib.h>
#include <time.h>
#include <stdio.h>

#define SIZE 100

int main()
{
    int r[SIZE];
    int c,a,b,temp;

    srandom((unsigned)time(NULL));

    puts("Here is the array unsorted:");
    for(c=0;c<SIZE;c++)
    {
        r[c] = random() % 100 +1;
        printf("%3d\t",r[c]);
    }
    putchar('\n');

/* sort the array */

    for(a=0;a<SIZE-1;a++)
```

```
        for(b=a+1;b<SIZE;b++)
            if(r[a] > r[b])
            {
                temp = r[b];
                r[b] = r[a];
                r[a] = temp;
            }

/* display */

    printf("Press Enter to see the sorted array:");
    getchar();

    for(c=0;c<SIZE;c++)
        printf("%3d\t",r[c]);
    putchar('\n');
    return(0);
}
```

As a tip, you can start out by editing the source code to RAND100.C, which is what this source code is based on. Note the addition of the bubble sort routine. (Remember whether you use the `random()` or `rand()` function, which should have been taken care of when you first wrote RAND100.C, earlier in this chapter.)

Save the source code to disk as SORTBIG.C.

Compile and run.

Not so bad, eh? That's because I use an old trick: The array is sorted while you're still gawking at the first display. On a slow computer, there's a brief pause before the `Press Enter to see the sorted array` prompt appears. To prove this on a faster computer, just sort more numbers:

```
#define SIZE 1000
```

Change Line 5 as shown. That's 1,000 random numbers in the array. Save. Compile. Run.

Maybe you notice it running slower on your computer; maybe you don't. If not, change the `SIZE` value to 10,000 or even 100,000. Eventually, you see the pause as the computer slugs through the bubble sort. (On my computer, I noticed the pause at 10,000 numbers.)

Arrays from Beyond the First Dimension!

All the arrays you have seen in this chapter are of the one-dimensional variety. They're all basically a bunch of numbers, one after the other. That's

1-dimensional — like the characters in a Steven Seagal movie. But C is capable of more: It also uses 2-dimensional arrays. Ta-da!

Declaring a 2-dimensional array

A *2-dimensional* array is essentially a grid. For example, a chess board is a 2-dimensional array. It has eight squares going across and eight going up and down — a giant grid of 64 squares ($8 \times 8 = 64$).

In C, you declare such an array this way:

```
int chessboard[8][8];
```

This line reads: "Create an array of integers that has two dimensions — eight rows of eight items each."

So, if the queen is located at King's Bishop 3, she could be at location `chessboard[5][2]`. Figure 1-6 helps you visualize it. It also helps if you remember that each dimension starts with Element 0.

Zero! Zero! Zero!

All array elements must be of the same variable type. You cannot have a 2-dimensional array with one `int`s dimension and one `char`s dimension. In that case, what you need is a *structure,* which is covered in Book III, Chapter 4.

Initializing a 2-dimensional array

C programmers get all fancy-schmancy when they declare an initialized 2-dimensional array. It's time to show off your prowess with the Tab key and curly brackets!

The dirty secret about multidimensional arrays

There's no such thing as a multidimensional array in C. All arrays are basically single dimensions — just one long line of numbers or letters. The 2-dimensional notation is simply a shortcut to reference elements that appear to be two dimensional, but are in fact 1-dimensional. Honestly, it makes no difference to the compiler.

For example, the 2-dimensional array `chessboard[8][8]` is really seen by the compiler as a single 64-element array. When you reference element `chessboard[5][2]`, the compiler internally translates that to element 42 in the array. As far as it's concerned, they're the same thing. Two-dimensional notation is merely for the ease of the programmer.

And now you know. So don't tell anyone else!

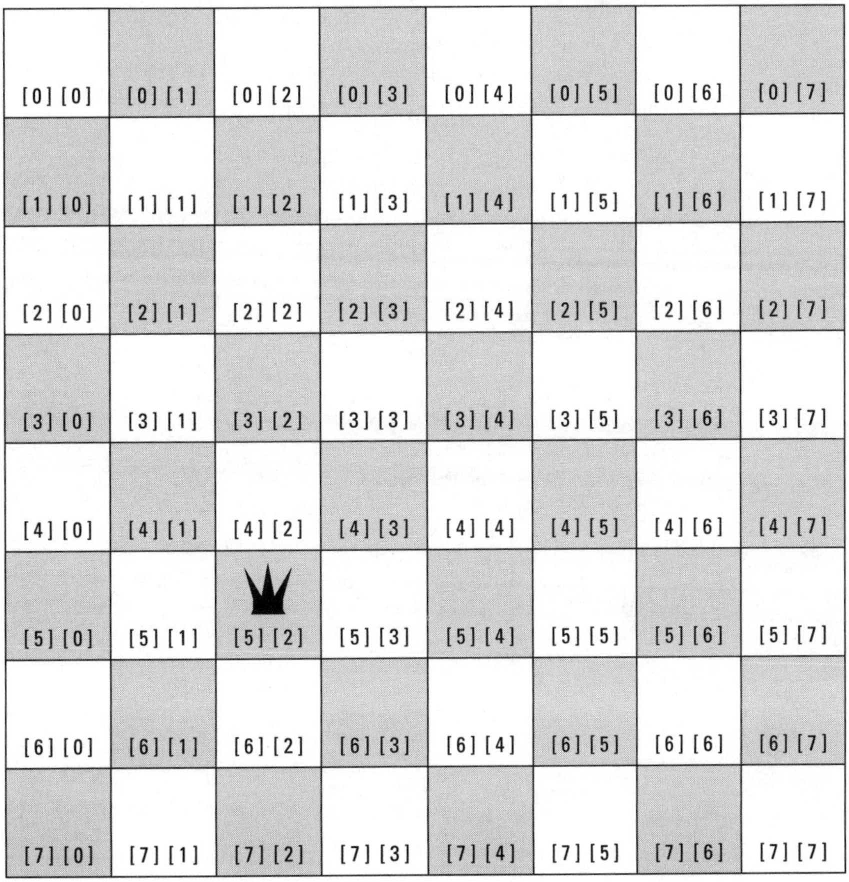

Figure 1-6:
Finding
the Queen
in a 2-
dimensional
array.

Essentially, the declared 2-dimensional array is splayed out in the source code to look like a grid, as in

```
int array[3][3] = {
    8, 1, 6,
    3, 5, 7,
    4, 9, 2
    };
```

You could easily declare the array like this:

```
int array[3][3] = { 8, 1, 6, 3, 5, 7, 4, 9, 2};
```

Still, that's kind of confusing, especially if you're copying something from a book and trying to double-check the numbers. It also ruins the spirit of the 2-dimensional array, which has been known to induce missing } errors in some compilers.

Wantonly type the source code for this program into your editor. Save it to disk as MAGIC.C. Compile and run:

```c
#include <stdio.h>

int main()
{
    int r,c;
    int m[3][3] = {
        8, 1, 6,
        3, 5, 7,
        4, 9, 2
        };

    puts("Presenting the Magic Square:\n");

    for(r=0;r<3;r++)
        printf("%d   %d   %d\n",m[r][0],m[r][1],m[r][2]);
    putchar('\n');

    for(r=0;r<3;r++)
        printf("Sum for row %d is %d\n",
    r+1,m[r][0]+m[r][1]+m[r][2]);

    for(c=0;c<3;c++)
        printf("Sum for column %d is %d\n"
    ,c+1,m[0][c]+m[1][c]+m[2][c]);

    printf("Sum for diagonal NW/SE is %d\n",
    m[0][0]+m[1][1]+m[2][2]);

    printf("Sum for diagonal SW/NE is %d\n",
    m[0][2]+m[1][1]+m[2][0]);

    return(0);
}
```

The magic square is a grid of numbers that has the same totals up and down for all rows, even diagonally:

```
Presenting the Magic Square:

8   1   6
3   5   7
4   9   2

Sum for row 1 is 15
Sum for row 2 is 15
Sum for row 3 is 15
Sum for column 1 is 15
Sum for column 2 is 15
```

```
Sum for column 3 is 15
Sum for diagonal NW/SE is 15
Sum for diagonal SW/NE is 15
```

When declaring an initialized array, you don't always have to specify a count between the array's brackets, as in

```
int jocks[] = {16, 88, 45, 99, 6, 33};
```

The same holds true for multidimensional arrays to a certain degree. For example:

```
int array[][3] = {
    8, 1, 6,
    3, 5, 7,
    4, 9, 2
    };
```

The compiler guesses that the first value should be three because the total number of items divided by three is equal to three. I recommend against setting up arrays like this because they tend to make people scrunch up their faces when they read your source code.

Arrays in the twilight zone

Just as 2-dimensional arrays are rare in C, 3-dimensional arrays are almost unheard of. I don't know whether you can have four or more dimensions in an array. I haven't seen one in any book, and, honestly, I'm too tired to test it now.

If you can reenergize those dozen or so brain cells that you have left over from high school geometry, you probably remember that a 2-dimensional square becomes a cube in the third dimension. That's exactly what happens in C when you create a 3-dimensional variable. It's mind-boggling, as this declaration proves:

```
int boggle[3][3][3] = {
   1, 2, 3,
   4, 5, 6,
   7, 8, 9,

   10, 11, 12,
   13, 14, 15,
   16, 17, 18,

   100, 101, 102,
   103, 104, 105,
   106, 107, 108,
   };
```

Keeping in mind that Element 0 thing, you should know that the variable `boggle[1][0][2]` refers to the second "page" of numbers — first row, last item, or the value 12.

Egads!

Bonus Program!

Here's a handy program that uses an array in a special way to help you draw Lotto numbers.

Normally, you would just think that plopping out five or six random numbers would give you a Lotto program. But the problem there is that the random-number generator has a habit of spewing out the same number two times in a row. After all, this week's Lotto winner could not possibly be

```
2 15 17 30 30 30
```

The solution is to devise a method for keeping track of the numbers that are drawn. The following source code does that by tracking the numbers in an array. That way, any number of Lotto balls can be drawn and the computer will never reproduce a number that has already been picked:

```c
#include <stdio.h>
#include <stdlib.h>
#include <time.h>

#define RANGE 50
#define BALLS 6

int main()
{
    int numbers[RANGE];
    int c,ball;

    puts("L O T T O   P I C K E R\n");

    srandom((unsigned)time(NULL));

/* initialize the array */

    for(c=0;c<RANGE;c++)
        numbers[c]=0;

    printf("Press Enter to pick this week's numbers:");
    getchar();

/* draw the numbers */
```

```
        puts("Here they come:");
        for(c=0;c<BALLS;c++)
        {

/* see if a number has already been drawn */
            do
            {
                ball = random() % RANGE;
            }
            while(numbers[ball]);

/* Number drawn */

            numbers[ball] = 1;

            printf("%2d ",ball+1);
        }

        printf("\n\nGood luck in the drawing!\n");
        return(0);
}
```

Enter this source code into your editor. Here are the highlights:

✦ The program picks six numbers from 1 to 50 as your lucky Lotto numbers this week. You can change the range of numbers by entering a new value for RANGE, and you can choose more or fewer numbers by changing the value of BALLS, both at the beginning of the source code.

✦ This Lotto program works the same way any computer card game works. Like cards in a deck, balls in a lottery machine can be drawn only once. The object isn't to generate the same random number twice. That is, you can't draw the same Lotto ball, bingo ball, or card from a deck in the real world, so you shouldn't be able to do that in a computer program either.

✦ The solution is to use an array to keep track of the numbers (cards or whatever) that are drawn. The array is initialized with all zeroes to start, which is done in Lines 19 and 20:

```
        for(c=0;c<RANGE;c++)
            numbers[c]=0;
```

✦ As the random numbers are drawn, a 1 is inserted into the array to indicate which numbers (cards or whatever) have already been used. This snippet makes that happen:

```
        do
        {
            ball = random() % RANGE;
        }
        while(numbers[ball]);
```

The `do-while` loop is repeated as random numbers are drawn. If that number's element in the array has a 1 in it, that number has already been drawn. So, the loop repeats, drawing another number. This process continues until a number not previously drawn is produced.

✦ When a fresh number is found, its position in the array is then marked as used:

```
numbers[b]=1;
```

✦ And, that number is displayed as a Lotto pick:

```
printf("%i ",b+1);
```

✦ The loop continues until the number of balls (represented by the short-cut word `BALLS`) has been drawn.

✦ All this nonsense is created to ensure that the same number isn't drawn twice. By sticking a 1 into the array, you ensure that that number isn't drawn again in your program.

Save the source code to disk as LOTTO.C. Compile and run:

```
L O T T O    P I C K E R

Press Enter to pick this week's numbers:
```

Press the Enter key:

```
Here they come:
35 11 49 34 26 37

Good luck in the drawing!
```

You can easily modify the LOTTO.C program to draw all 50 balls; just change the value of `BALLS` to 50 in the `define` statement. Notice that the program takes longer and longer to display the last few numbers as it waits for the random-number generator to produce a number that hasn't yet been drawn.

Now you can write that card game! You need an array of 52 elements, each of which represents a card in the deck. You can use a `do-while` loop similar to the one in LOTTO.C to determine which cards have already been drawn.

Chapter 2: 1 Sing of Strings

In This Chapter

✔ Understanding how strings work in C

✔ Avoiding common string boo-boos

✔ Using the character array

✔ Knowing about the NULL byte

✔ Copying, comparing, and concatenating strings

✔ Getting the length of a string

✔ Working with arrays of strings

*B*eyond math, computer programs can also mess with text. In programming, text comes in the form of a *string*, as in string of text or string of characters. You can read strings of text input from the keyboard, display strings on the screen, and, using the proper functions and other tools, mess with strings inside your programs to do fun and amazing things. Computers aren't all math.

This hefty chapter is all about strings. It's your official introduction into everything stringy in C programming.

The Strings Review

You can't have gotten this far in your C programming without some experience with strings. After all, didn't the first program you wrote in C display some text on the screen, something like `Now you're in for it!`?

This section may or may not be review for you. In any case, you're required to read it; this stuff *is* on the test.

Declaring strings

In C, strings are declared using the `char` variable type. If the string of text is known, it's assigned as follows:

```
char greeting[] = "Good morning, fellow geeks!";
```

Here, the string variable `greeting` is declared. Its contents consist of the string that follows the text enclosed in double quotes. The text can include any character plus special characters entered as escape sequences. (See Appendix F for the lot.)

If a string's value is unknown, you can declare an empty string variable, as in

```
char first_name[25];
```

Here, the string variable `first_name` is declared. It has room to store 24 characters. (Later in this chapter, you find out why string storage is always one character less than specified.)

Reading and writing strings

Inside your programs, strings can be swallowed whole by using the `gets()` or `scanf()` function:

```
gets(excuse);
```

Here, the `gets()` function reads the keyboard and stores the text typed into the `excuse` string variable. Input stops with a press of the Enter key, though the Enter key press isn't saved as part of the string.

Here, the screwy format of `scanf()` is used to read text into the string variable `complaint`:

```
scanf("%s",&complaint);
```

`%s` is the string placeholder. The & is required, helping `scanf()` to properly find the location of the `complaint` variable in memory.

Strings are displayed on the screen by using functions like `puts()` or `printf()`.

The `puts()` function displays an immediate string or string variable, adding a newline character to the end:

```
puts("Petition of Grievances");
puts(foolishness);
```

In the first `puts()` function, the immediate text string `Petition of Grievances` is displayed on the screen, followed by a newline. In the second example, `puts()` displays the contents of the `foolishness` variable, again adding a newline to the output.

The `printf()` function has many ways to display a string of text:

```
printf("I should have taken the blue pill.");
printf(caustic_comment);
printf("%s",caustic_comment);
```

The `printf()` function can display an immediate string of text, or string constant. It can also display a string variable directly. Note that in both these cases, a newline is *not* appended to the string. Finally, `printf()` can use the `%s` placeholder in its format string to display a string variable (or string constant). Here's some code to illustrate:

```
#include <stdio.h>

int main()
{
    char prompt[] = "Please enter your first name:";
    char gratis[] = "Thanks!";
    char first[25];

    printf(prompt);
    gets(first);
    puts(gratis);
    printf("Pleased to meet you, %s!\n",first);
    return(0);
}
```

Carefully type this source code into your editor. Save it to disk as GREETINGS.C. Compile and run.

```
Please enter your first name:
```

Type your name. I typed **Dan**:

```
Thanks!
Pleased to meet you, Dan!
```

Exercise 3.2.1

Modify the source code GREETINGS.C so that the `last` string variable is declared and the program asks for the user's last name. Use the `scanf()` function to read in the last name. Have the final `printf()` statement display both the `first` and `last` variables.

What you may think you can do,
but cannot do, with strings

Every budding C language programmer attempts, at one time or another, to make one of two common string boo-boos. Here's the first:

```
#include <stdio.h>

int main()
{
    char yours[25];
    char mine[25];

    printf("What is your name?");
    gets(yours);
    mine = yours;
    printf("My name is %s just like your name is %s!\n",
mine,yours);
    return(0);
}
```

Type this source code as BOOBOO1.C. Compile. Don't even bother to run it, because you get an error message. Basically, the error message tells you that you cannot assign string variables to each other, at least not by using an equal sign.

You can assign any two variables the same value by using an equal sign. This works for `int`, `float` and `char` variables, but it doesn't work for strings.

Here's the second mistake made with strings:

```
#include <stdio.h>

int main()
{
    char yours[25];
    char mine[] = "Henry";

    printf("What is your name?");
    gets(yours);
    if(mine == yours)
        printf("We both have the same name!\n");
    return(0);
}
```

Save this source code to disk as BOOBOO2.C. Compile. Yes! It compiles! Run it:

```
What is your name?
```

I typed **Dan** and pressed Enter — but nothing happened.

Try entering **Henry** as the name.

Still, nothing happens. That's because you cannot compare two string values with the == operator. The program doesn't explode because variables `mine` and `yours` evaluate to something, but what they evaluate to isn't the strings they contain. And, the evaluation is always false.

Later in this chapter, you find out how to copy and compare string variables in C. Before that, you have to understand that a variable in C isn't a variable at all.

The Truth about Strings

There are no string variables in C.

Huh?

All strings in C are basically single-character arrays. They're special arrays, to be sure. But they're not variables in the sense that strings don't behave like int, float, or char variables. That's why you cannot do assignments or comparisons with strings in C.

Deep inside the character array

Consider this text:

```
sushi is mooshi
```

You can view this text as a sentence or a string of text or a character array. As a human, you see it as a sentence. As a programmer, you may view it as a string, as in

```
char phrase[] = "sushi is mooshi";
```

To the compiler, it's a character array, which looks like this:

```
char phrase[] = { 's', 'u', 's', 'h', 'i', ' ', 'i', 's',
    ' ', 'm', 'o', 'o', 's', 'h', 'i', '\0' };
```

The string is still referred to by its name, `phrase`. But it can also be referred to as an array. You can further reference, in the array form, individual characters inside the string, just as you can reference elements inside an array.

(Refer to Book III, Chapter 1 for more information on arrays.)

Terminating a string (the NULL character)

Strings in C aren't really the same as single-character arrays. That's because strings have a special character tacked on to the end, like the caboose on a train. I showed it to you in the preceding section:

```
char phrase[] = { 's', 'u', 's', 'h', 'i', ' ', 'i', 's',
    ' ', 'm', 'o', 'o', 's', 'h', 'i', '\0' };
```

See the last character of the string? It's the \0 escape sequence, which, according to Appendix B, is the NULL character. In this case, the NULL character is ASCII code 0.

NULL characters are used in C to mark the end of a string. That way, text strings in C can contain other characters, such as Tab, Enter, Escape, Backspace, and even random and meaningless control codes. They all can be a part of the string except for ASCII code 0, which is the NULL character, and that marks the end of the string.

This NULL character also explains why you need to define string storage to be one character greater than is required for the string:

```
char first_name[25];
```

Here, 25 characters are set aside for string storage. Twenty-four of them are used to store the string text itself, and the 25th is for the NULL character, or *terminator,* as it's also known.

As another example, consider this lesson's silly string *du jour:*

```
sushi is mooshy
```

This string is composed of 15 characters, including alphabetic characters and space characters. Although the string is 15 characters long, it occupies *16* bytes in memory. That's because the string has a NULL character living at its end, right after the y in mooshy.

Q: If the NULL character is also known as the terminator, is Arnold Schwarzenegger also a NULL character?

A: Yes.

Messing with strings

Given your gullibility in this book, by now you may have accepted the truth that strings are really special character arrays. As such, you can do various array-like things with strings, as these programs demonstrate:

```
#include <stdio.h>

int main()
{
    char phrase[] = "sushi is mooshi";
    char ch;
    int x = 0;

    do
    {
        ch = phrase[x];
        putchar(ch);
        x++;
    }
    while(ch != '\0');

    putchar('\n');
    return(0);
}
```

Save this source code to disk as SUSHI.C. Compile and run:

```
sushi is mooshi
```

The program wades through the character array one letter at a time, and the do-while loop continues to process characters until the NULL character (\0) at the end of the string is found.

Here's another variation:

```
int main()
{
    char phrase[] = "sushi is mooshi";
    char ch;
    int x = 0;

    while(ch = phrase[x])
    {
        putchar(ch);
        x++;
    }

    putchar('\n');
    return(0);
}
```

Make these changes to your SUSHI.C source code. Save. Compile. Run:

```
sushi is mooshi
```

The `while` statement evaluates the character generated by `ch=phrase[x]`. The NULL character works out to 0, which is interpreted by the compiler as FALSE, so the loop stops.

Here's a fun variation that takes advantage of a string's dual nature as an array:

```
int main()
{
    char phrase[] = "sushi is mooshi";
    char ch;
    int x = 0;

    puts(phrase);
    phrase[9] = 's';
    puts(phrase);
    return(0);
}
```

Save this change to the SUSHI.C source code. Compile. Run:

```
sushi is mooshi
sushi is sooshi
```

The `m` in the string is the tenth character, or ninth element, in the array. The `m` is replaced by the letter `s` in Line 10 of the code.

Exercise 3.2.2

Modify the SUSHI.C program again, and this time write code that replaces the spaces in the phrase with hyphens.

Lovely and Handy String Functions

C isn't the best language for manipulating strings. The Perl language has better and more powerful string functions, as do BASIC and other popular languages. Even so, I have often found that by using C's armada of string functions, I can do anything with strings that can be done in those other programming languages. Perhaps the code isn't as elegant, but C does get the job done.

An overview of all the string functions

Table 2-1 lists all the string functions available in the standard C library. Some C compilers may have more and different functions; see your compiler's documentation for the gamut.

Table 2-1	Various C Language String Functions
Function	*Painfully Brief Description*
strcat()	Sticks two strings together, one at the end of the other
strncat()	Sticks only a given number of characters from one string to the end of another string
strchr()	Returns the location of a certain character in a string, from the string's start
strrchr()	Returns the location of a certain character in a string, from the string's end
strcmp()	Compares one string to another; returns 0 if both match
strcasecmp()	Compares two strings, ignoring upper- and lowercase differences; returns 0 when both strings match
strncasecmp()	Compares only a given number of characters between two strings, ignoring case
strcpy()	Copies or duplicates one string into another string
strncpy()	Copies only a given number of characters from one string to another
strlen()	Returns the length of a string (but doesn't count the NULL character at the end of the string)
strstr()	Locates one string inside of another string

The remainder of this section highlights several of these string functions. Refer to your compiler's documentation for more string functions.

A few of the string functions aren't mentioned in Table 2-1 because they assume a knowledge of *pointers*. This subject is covered in Book IV. I highly recommend that you know what pointers are and how to manipulate them before attempting to work with string and pointer functions.

Copying a string

Strings are arrays, and, just as you cannot duplicate an array by using an equal sign, you cannot copy a string. You have two choices.

First, you can duplicate a string by copying each element from one string into another. A loop like this works this way:

```
while(copy[x] = org[x])
    x++;
```

Assuming that copy[] is a string array of a size equal to or greater than the string org, this loop copies each character from the first string to the second, including the NULL at the end. (You can use this loop to duplicate other arrays also.)

If you're in a hurry, however, you can use the strcpy(), or string copy, function instead. Here's the format:

```
strcpy(copy,org);
```

Both copy and org are strings of equal size. The strcpy() function duplicates the contents of string org into string doop. Both strings are then identical, containing the same text or characters.

You must include the STRING.H header file in your source code for the strcpy function to work:

```
#include <string.h>
```

If you don't, the compiler goes bonkers.

This example shows you the fix to the program BOOBOO1.C, introduced earlier in this chapter:

```
#include <stdio.h>
#include <string.h>

int main()
{
    char yours[25];
    char mine[25];

    printf("What is your name?");
    gets(yours);
    strcpy(mine,yours);
    printf("My name is %s just like your name is %s!\n",
mine,yours);
    return(0);
}
```

Make the modifications to the source code so that it looks like what was just shown. Save it to disk. Compile and run:

```
What is your name?
```

Type your name, such as **Jerry**:

```
My name is Jerry just like your name is Jerry!
```

Exercise 3.2.3

Rewrite the preceding code for BOOBOO1.C so that the while loop method of copying strings is used rather than strcpy().

Comparing two strings

Another fun string function is `strcmp()`, the string compare function. When the two strings it examines are equal, `strcmp()` oddly returns the value 0, or FALSE. That takes some getting used to. Anyway, here's the official format:

```
result = strcmp(gumby,pokey);
```

This statement compares the contents of the strings `gumby` and `pokey`. Both can be string variables, or one can be a string constant. If both strings contain exactly the same information and are exactly the same length, the function returns 0, which is saved in the preceding `result` variable.

As with other string functions, if you want the `strcmp()` function to please the compiler, you have to include the STRING.H header file at the tippy-top of your source code, as is done in this example:

```
#include <stdio.h>
#include <string.h>

int main()
{
    char string[16];
    char password[] = "please";
    int result;

    printf("Enter your secret password:");
    gets(string);

    result = strcmp(string,password);

    if(result==0)
        puts("Entry granted!");
    else
        puts("Sorry. Wrong password.");
    return(0);
}
```

Type this source code. Save it to disk as PASSWORD.C. Compile and run:

```
Enter your secret password:
```

Type **please** (in lowercase) and press the Enter key.

```
Entry granted!
```

If you type something other than `please`, the program spits out the message `Sorry. Wrong password.` (Ignore for now the password that appears on the screen in full view of God and everybody.)

Exercise 3.2.4

Eliminate the `result` variable from the PASSWORD.C program. See whether you can code it so that the `if` statement directly evaluates the `strcmp()` function's result.

Comparing two strings of unequal case

Run the PASSWORD program from the preceding section. This time, enter **Please** as your password. Or, you could enter **PLEASE**. It's the same word, but the program doesn't match. That's because `strcmp()` is an exact-match function.

Often, you may want to match strings that could be typed in mixed case. After all, who's to trust a user's capitalization skills or know whether the Caps Lock key is on?

To compare two strings that may contain the same text but not in the same case, you use the `strcasecmp()` function. It works just like `strcmp()`, but the case of the text is ignored.

Reedit the source code for PASSWORD.C. Change Line 13 to read

```
result = strcasecmp(string,password);
```

Save. Compile. Run.

Try to type variations of please: **Please**, **PLEASE**, and **PlEaSe**, for example. Each one matches, thanks to `strcasecmp()`.

Note that some C compilers may use the `strcmpi()` or `stricmp()` function rather than `strcasecmp()` for comparing strings while ignoring case. Refer to your compiler's documentation for details.

Sticking two strings together

Suppose that you want to stick one string on the end of another string. If so, you may use the word *append*. It's techy. Normal humans may say "glue," as in "Glue two strings together" (or maybe "tie two strings together"). Then there's the word *stick* and its past tense, *stuck*. I like those myself. In C, though, the word is *concatenate*.

Gads — isn't *concatenate* an ugly word? "Kon-KAT-un-ate." Could you ever see Uncle Vern use the term? "Come help me concatenate the trailer to my truck." Nope. In computer science, however, especially Unix-like things, such as the C language, you get to *concatenate* a bunch of things — primarily strings.

If you're into all this `cat` nonsense, you can probably guess that the C language function used to stick one string on the end of another is `cat`-something. Specifically, it's `strcat()`. Here's the format:

```
strcat(start,end);
```

The `strcat()` function sticks the contents of the string `end` at the end of the string `start`. The string `start` then contains the contents of both strings, one after the other. The string `end` is unchanged.

You must ensure that enough room has been set aside for the `start` string to hold both itself and the contents of whatever string you append, or concatenate, to it.

As with other string functions, you must add `#include` to the STRING.H header file in your source code to prevent the compiler from going all verklempt:

```
#include <stdio.h>
#include <string.h>

int main()
{
    char command[64];
    char response[] = "You think I know how to ";
    char new[128];

    while(strcasecmp(command,"quit"))
    {
        printf("C:\\>");
        gets(command);

        strcpy(new,response);
        strcat(new,command);
        strcat(new,"?");
        puts(new);
    }
    puts("Well, maybe I do...");
    return(0);
}
```

**Book III
Chapter 2**

I Sing of Strings

Carefully type this source code into your editor. Note that two backslashes are used in the `printf()` statement, in Line 12. The `\\` is the escape sequence for a single `\`. Also note how the `strcpy()` and `strcat()` functions are used to build a string. Save this source code to disk as RUDEDOS.C.

Save. Compile. Run:

```
C:\>
```

It's the DOS prompt! Type **run**

```
You think I know how to run?
```

Type a command, such as **dir**. Press Enter:

```
You think I know how to dir?
```

Try **exit**:

```
You think I know how to exit?
```

Try **quit**:

```
You think I know how to quit?
Well, maybe I do...
```

Note that you can type **quit** in mixed case and it still works to stop the program; refer to Line 10 and the use of strcasecmp() in the while loop. Remember that strcasecmp() returns 0 when a match occurs — the ideal way to stop a while loop.

How long is that string?

Often, you have to know how long a string is — especially if that string is entered from the keyboard or otherwise generated in a manner where it's difficult to determine the string's length. Fortunately, a string function helps: strlen(), which works like this:

```
size = strlen(text);
```

strlen() takes the length of string text and returns its size in the integer variable size. The size value is the exact number of characters in the string, not counting the NULL character at the end. If the string is a constant in double quotes, the double quotes aren't counted either:

```
#include <stdio.h>
#include <string.h>

int main()
{
    char input[64];
    int size,c;

    printf("Enter a common Earth phrase:");
```

```
    gets(input);

    puts("Here is how we say that on Backward Planet:");
    size = strlen(input);
    for(c=size-1;c>=0;c--)
        putchar(input[c]);
    putchar('\n');
    return(0);
}
```

Type this source code into your editor. Save it to disk as REVERSE.C. Compile and run:

```
Enter a common Earth phrase:
```

Type **Just Do It** and press Enter:

```
Here is how we say that on Backward Planet:
tI oD tsuJ
```

The string's length is returned by the `strlen()` function in Line 13, saved in the `size` variable. Note that the `for` loop subtracts 1 from `size` in Line 14. That's because array elements start with *zero*. So, if the string is 15 characters long, `input[14]` is the last character; `input[15]` would be the NULL character, \0.

The Boggling Concept of Arrays of Strings

Strings were born for two-dimensional arrays. A string by itself is a one-dimensional array. It's just plain unfair that it can't be more. After all, think of the things you can do with multiple strings — things like the tepid little game I dreamt up, named DWARFS.C. It's something Disney should have included on its *Snow White and the Seven Dwarfs* CD-ROM, but somehow overlooked:

```
#include <stdio.h>
#include <string.h>

int main()
{
    char dwarf[7][8] = {
        "bashful",
        "doc",
        "dopey",
        "grumpy",
        "happy",
        "sneezy",
        "sleepy"
    };
```

```
        char input[64];
        int named=0;
        int x;

        puts("See if you can name all seven dwarfs:");

        while(named<7)
        {
            if(named==1)
                printf("\nSo far you've named %d dwarf.\n",
named);
            else
                printf("\nSo far you've named %d dwarfs.\n",
named);

            printf("Enter a name:");
            gets(input);

/* check for no input */
            if(strcmp(input,"")==0)
                break;

            for(x=0;x<7;x++)
            {
                if(strcasecmp(input,dwarf[x])==0)
                {
                    printf("Yes! %s is right.\n",input);
                    named++;
                }
            }
        }
        return(0);
}
```

Use your best typing fingers to enter this source code into your editor. Beware the long lines in the listing; they may be split in two here, but you should type them as one line in your editor. Save the mess to disk as DWARFS.C.

Compile. Fix any errors, and don't forget doodads and missing semicolons.

Run:

```
See if you can name all seven dwarfs:

So far you've named 0 dwarfs.
Enter a name:
```

Go ahead and play the game. Press Enter by itself to quit if you get bored.

Here are some things worth noting:

✦ A 1-dimensional character array is a single string. A 2-dimensional character array is a set of several strings.

✦ You can declare a 2-dimensional character array as empty or full. The DWARFS.C program declares a full or initialized 2-dimensional string array.

✦ An empty string array is declared like this:

```
char newideas[4][128];
```

This string array has room for four strings, each of which can be as long as 127 characters (plus one extra item for the NULL at the end of the string).

✦ Generally speaking, with a 2-dimensional string array, the first item in square brackets tells you the number of strings in the array, and the second item tells you how long each string can be.

✦ You reference the string by mentioning only the first array element:

```
puts(states[49]);
```

Assume that `states` is a 2-dimensional array. Here, `states[49]` refers to the 50th string in the array. (Remember that `states[0]` is the first string in the array.)

✦ Do not reference strings in a 2-dimensional array like this:

```
puts(uhoh[9][0]);
```

You may assume that `uhoh[9][0]` refers to the tenth string in the array — but it does not! It refers to the first *character* of the tenth string — a single-character variable, not a string. When you use the two brackets with the array name, you're treating the array like a 2-dimensional character array, not an array of strings.

✦ The following variable refers to a specific character in a 2-dimensional string array:

```
pickypicky[3][4]
```

This variable represents the fifth character of the fourth string in the array.

3-dimensional string arrays

String arrays are already 2-dimensional. If you add a third dimension, you're basically creating a grid of strings — like the answer squares in *Jeopardy!*

The following program example shows you how to declare a 3-dimensional array of strings, how to reference them, and how to drive yourself nuts trying to use them in a program:

```
#include <stdio.h>

int main()
{
    char names[4][3][10] = {
        "Bob",     "Bill",  "Bret",
        "Dan",     "Dave",  "Don",
        "George",  "Harry", "John",
        "Mike",    "Steve", "Vern"
    };
    int a,b;

    for(a=0;a<4;a++)
        for(b=0;b<3;b++)
            printf("%s\n",names[a][b]);
    return(0);
}
```

Type this program into your editor. Watch the quotes and commas in the 3-dimensional string array. Save this mess to disk as NAMES.C:

Compile and run:

```
Bob
Bill
Bret
Dan
Dave
Don
George
Harry
John
Mike
Steve
Vern
```

When you create a multidimensional array of strings, the first and second items are the rows and columns. The last item is the maximum size for every string in the array. For `names[4][3][10]`, the array holds four rows of three strings, and each string can be no more than nine characters long (plus the NULL character).

As with an array of strings, you don't specify the last number in square brackets when you reference the array. To reference `John`, you specify `names[2][2]` and not `names[2][2][0]`.

Exercise 3.2.5

Rewrite the code to NAMES.C so that the output looks like this:

```
Bob
Dan
George
Mike
Bill
Dave
Harry
Steve
Bret
Don
John
Vern
```

Fixing the dwarfs

A bug in the DWARFS program introduced earlier in this chapter enables a sharp-witted user to simply type the same dwarf's name over and over to win the game. Obviously, it would be nice if the program somehow kept track of which names had already been guessed.

Welcome to 3-dimensional array land! It's just behind Cinderella's castle in Disneyland. To get there, you just have to make a few modifications to your DWARFS.C source code. First, a brief discussion.

To keep track of which names have been guessed, each name grows another element, which is a short string containing either a question mark or an exclamation point. If the string contains a question mark, it means that the name hasn't been guessed. If the string contains an exclamation point, the name has already been guessed. That should foil the rascals!

Here's how to redeclare the dwarf array in three dimensions:

```
char dwarf[7][2][8] = {
  "bashful", "?",
  "doc",     "?",
  "dopey",   "?",
  "grumpy",  "?",
  "happy",   "?",
  "sneezy",  "?",
  "sleepy",  "?"
  };
```

The dwarf array has seven [7] lines with two [2] strings. Each string can have as many as eight [8] characters in it. (Although this technique wastes some space because the second string is only one character long, I think that most computers can handle a few extra bytes of program bloat.)

The if statement that uses the strcasecmp() function to compare a user's input with the dwarves' names must be changed to reflect the added dimension:

```
if(strcmpi(input,dwarf[x][0])==0)
```

Now, dwarf[x][0] refers to the row represented by variable x and then the first string in that row. You don't write this example as dwarf[x][0][0], which points to a single character and not to a string.

Finally, an if-else structure must be added (or modified from the existing if statement) to determine whether a name has already been guessed:

```
if(dwarf[x][1][0]=='!')
    printf("You already named that dwarf!\n");
else
{
    printf("Yes! %s is right.\n",input);
    named++;
    dwarf[x][1][0]='!';
}
```

The reference dwarf[x][1][0] is acceptable here; it's a single character, and the if statement compares it to a single character, '!' (the exclamation point). If the first character [0] of the second string [1] for name [x] is an exclamation point, the user has already guessed that name.

The final line in the else part of the if-else structure sets the character to an exclamation point when a user guesses a name. It's a simple variable assignment, just like you would find in a 1-dimensional array:

```
dwarf[x][1][0]='!';
```

This line reads "Set the first character [0] of the second string [1] for name [x] to an exclamation point. (Single quotes are used for single-character variables.

This code is the finished, touched-up source code for DWARFS.C:

```
#include <stdio.h>
#include <string.h>

int main()
{
    char dwarf[7][2][8] = {
        "bashful",  "?",
        "doc",      "?",
        "dopey",    "?",
        "grumpy",   "?",
        "happy",    "?",
```

```
        "sneezy",   "?",
        "sleepy",   "?"
    };
    char input[64];
    int named=0;
    int x;

    puts("See if you can name all seven dwarfs:");

    while(named<7)
    {
        if(named==1)
            printf("\nSo far you've named %i dwarf.\n",
named);
        else
            printf("\nSo far you've named %i dwarfs.\n",
named);

        printf("Enter a name:");
        gets(input);
/* check for no input */
        if(strcmp(input,"")==0) //no input, end
            break;

        for(x=0;x<7;x++)
        {
            if(strcmpi(input,dwarf[x][0])==0)
            {
                if(dwarf[x][1][0]=='!')
                    printf("You already named that
dwarf!\n");
                else
                {
                    printf("Yes! %s is right.\n",input);
                    named++;
                    dwarf[x][1][0]='!';
                }
            }
        }
        if(named==7)
            puts("You got 'em all! Snow would be proud!");
        else
            puts("Try again:");
    }
    return(0);
}
```

Make the proper changes to the source code on your computer. Be wary of
long lines split in two in the DWARFS.C source code listing. You don't have to
split those lines in your editor.

Chapter 3: Messing with Characters

In This Chapter

✓ **Using the C language CTYPE functions**

✓ **Testing characters**

✓ **Converting characters to upper- and lowercase**

*I*t's only fair! The C language has a whole library of functions to manipulate, squish, and squirm numbers. So, it makes sense that C has an almost equal and imposing armada of text-manipulation functions. I talk about them in Book III, Chapter 2.

On a smaller, molecular level, C has a battalion of functions that operates specifically on the single character. You can use these single-character functions to turn and tug an entire string, as long as you thread the string through a `for` loop. The functions are properly introduced to the compiler through the CTYPE.H header file. Therefore, I call them the CTYPE functions.

Introducing the CTYPE Functions

To help you examine or change a string, or just mess with a single character, the C language provides a smattering of functions or macros, which are all defined in the CTYPE.H header file.

There are two types of CTYPE functions. The first type is used to examine individual characters. The function takes a character and returns a logical TRUE or FALSE depending on what the function is examining.

For example, the `isalpha()` function (pronounced "is alpha") returns TRUE if the character, or `char`, variable between its parentheses is a letter of the alphabet, either upper- or lowercase.

This type of function is listed in Table 3-1.

The second type of CTYPE function is used to change individual characters, modifying them. For example, the `tolower()` function ("to lower") changes any uppercase character to its lowercase equivalent. Any non-uppercase characters aren't affected. This type of CTYPE function is listed in Table 3-2.

Table 3-1	CTYPE.H Test Functions
Function or Macro	*Returns TRUE When Character Variable c Is This*
isalnum(c)	A number or letter of the alphabet, either case
isalpha(c)	A letter of the alphabet, either case
isascii(c)	A character whose ASCII code value is less than 128
isblank(c)	A tab or space
iscntrl(c)	A control character, ASCII code 0 through 31 and code 127
isdigit(c)	A number character 0 through 9
isgraph(c)	A printable character (basically, all the characters on your keyboard except for the space)
ishexnumber(c)	(See isxdigit(c))
islower(c)	A lowercase letter (*a* through *z*) only
isprint(c)	A printable character, including the space
ispunct(c)	A punctuation character (basically, all non-alphanumeric characters on the keyboard except for the space)
isspace(c)	A "white space" character: space, tab, vertical tab, return, newline, form-feed
isupper(c)	An uppercase letter, *A* through *Z*
isxdigit(c)	A hexadecimal digit character, *A* through *F,* *a* through *f,* and 1 through 9

Table 3-2	CTYPE.H Character-Changing Functions
Function or Macro	*Changes Character Variable c to This*
toascii(c)	A true ASCII code (basically lops off the top bit in any 8-bit character code — techy stuff)
tolower(c)	A lowercase letter (other characters are ignored)
toupper(c)	An uppercase letter (other characters are ignored)

The logical FALSE in C is expressed as 0. Logical TRUE is non-zero. (It's not specifically 1, but rather !0, or "not zero.")

I mention that some functions are *macros*. That is, they aren't really functions, but, rather, #define shortcuts, typically combining other functions or certain C language tricks. If you examine the text of the CTYPE.H file, you can see exactly what's going on.

Characters That Tell the Truth

The bulk of the CTYPE functions can be used to help you narrow input, extracting just the information you want and tossing the rest away. The gamut of the CTYPE functions, specifically those listed in Table 3-1, in the preceding section, are best suited for this purpose.

Just a Trivial Program Example

Suppose that you have this dying urge to count up the total number of letters and spaces in a sentence. Well, then, this is the program to do it!

```c
#include <stdio.h>
#include <ctype.h>

int main()
{
    char input[128];
    int x,spaces,letters;

    x = spaces = letters = 0;

    printf("Enter the first line of a poem:");
    gets(input);

/* scan the text */
    while(input[x])
    {
        if(isspace(input[x]))
            spaces++;
        if(isalpha(input[x]))
            letters++;
        x++;
    }
    printf("That sentence has %d spaces and %d letters.\n",
    spaces,letters);
    return(0);
}
```

Carefully type this source code. Save it to disk as POEM.C. Compile and run:

```
Enter the first line of a poem:
```

Type a poem. Something from memory. Something other than Roses Are Red:

```
She walks like beauty in the night
That sentence has 6 spaces and 28 letters.
```

The program uses two CTYPE tests: isspace() and isalpha(). Both return a TRUE result and pass the if test when either a space or letter of the alphabet is scanned into the string.

Did you get a load of Line 9? Yes, you can initialize several variables to the same value — as long as each variable is of the same type and they all equal the same value when the statement is done.

Exercise 3.3.1

Write a program that has the user enter a street address. Then report back how many digits (numbers) are in the address. Call it WASTEOFTIME.C.

Altering Text

The CTYPE testing functions are useful, but hard to demonstrate merely by themselves. Coupled with the CTYPE changing functions, they can yield some pretty handy programs, some of which are demonstrated in this section.

The droll "make me uppercase" program

Changing characters from upper- to lowercase in a string is a handy thing to do. For example, you may be using one of the string-comparing functions (introduced in Book III, Chapter 2) to make sure that what a user types is proper. One way to do that is to make the entire string uppercase and compare it to other uppercase strings. (In fact, that's what Microsoft used to do with the old DOS prompt.)

This source code is for SHOUT!.C, a program that uses the toupper() function to convert characters in a string to uppercase:

```
#include <stdio.h>
#include <ctype.h>

int main()
{
    char string[] = "You don't have to shout!";
    char c;
    int x;

    x = 0;

    puts(string);

    do
    {
        c = string[x];
        c = toupper(c);
```

```
        string[x] = c;
        x++;
    }
    while(c);

    puts(string);
    return(0);
}
```

Carefully type that code into your editor. Save the file to disk as SHOUT.C. Compile and run:

```
You don't have to shout!
YOU DON'T HAVE TO SHOUT!
```

Notice how the `toupper` function converts only letters of the alphabet? The punctuation marks and spaces aren't changed.

A `do-while` loop is chosen here because a `while(c)` loop may not run. Variable c is uninitialized in the program, so its value could be 0. In that case, `while(c)` would be FALSE and the loop's statement skipped. The `do-while` loop, on the other hand, always runs. And, because strings in C have at least one character (the terminating NULL), the program doesn't crash.

Yorn again?

It's the longest-running program in this book! YORN.C. It asks a yes-or-no question and only now — now that you know about the CTYPE functions — can you finally put it to bed. Witness this, one last modification to the YORN.C program:

```
#include <stdio.h>
#include <ctype.h>

#define FALSE 0
#define TRUE !FALSE

int main()
{
    int done;
    char ch;

    done = FALSE;
    printf("Would you like me to send your password to the
bad guys?\n");
    while(!done)
    {
        printf("Enter Y or N (Y/N)?");
        ch = tolower(getchar());
        switch(ch)
```

```
        {
            case 'n':
                printf("Well, then: your password is
safe!\n");
                done = TRUE;
                break;
            case 'y':
                printf("Okay, Sending your password!\n");
                done = TRUE;
                break;
            default:
                printf("You must enter a Y or N!\n");
                fflush(stdin);
        } /* end switch */
    } /* end while */
    return(0);
}
```

Modify your source code from Book II, Chapter 6 to what's shown here, or, if you're lucky, type it for the first time! Here's what has changed:

✦ The program now includes the CTYPE.H header in Line 2.

✦ The character retrieved by `getchar()` in Line 17 is converted to lower-case. It could just as easily be uppercase, but I haven't yet used the `tolower()` function in this chapter. This narrows the searching choices to 2: `'y'` and `'n'`.

✦ The `case` statements for capital Y and N have been removed from the program.

Save the source code to disk as YORN.C. Compile and run:

```
Would you like me to send your password to the bad guys?
Enter Y or N (Y/N)?
```

You can type **Y** or **y** or **N** or **n** or any character. Anything you type in upper-case is converted to lowercase so that the program has fewer options to examine.

Exercise 3.3.2

Write a program similar to POEM.C, earlier in this chapter. Have the program convert the input string to all lowercase and have it remove any characters that aren't letters or numbers. Call this program STRIPPER.C.

Chapter 4: Stinkin' Structures

In This Chapter

- ✔ Storing multiple values in structures
- ✔ Declaring structures
- ✔ Using structure variables
- ✔ Creating an array of structures
- ✔ Copying one structure to another
- ✔ Dealing with nested structures

The C language gives you many weapons to tackle the battle of storing information or data. You can break down just about anything into the molecular tidbits of the int, char, and float variables. When you need to handle multiple quantities of something, you can reach out and grab an array. But even arrays can't handle everything.

This chapter introduces you to what I call the C language's multivariable. It's officially known as the lumbering structure monster. If you're new to structures, note that this is a major turning point for your experience with the C language. I recognize this because of all the e-mail I get; it's structures that mark the starting point for when things turn tough. So I'm as gentle as possible.

Life without Structures

Imagine how dull life was before the invention of the 3 x 5 card:

"Oh, here's that meat loaf recipe you wanted. I just knotted it out using Morse code on this piece of rope."

"Card catalog? No, you just stand here and shout out the name of the book you want. We have librarians stationed throughout the building. See? Just say 'Anyone know where Mark Twain is?' and then someone will shout 'He's over here!' and you just follow that person's voice."

"Are you the new applicant? Just tell me your name and employment history. I remember everything."

In the C language, structures are similar to 3 x 5 cards. They hold a combination of information tidbits — like a fill-in-the-blank something-or-other. They keep related information together and easily accessed — yes, just like a database.

Part 1: The Oz database

Not knowing anything about structures, you may one day sit down and start that *Wizard of Oz* database you have always dreamed of. The following program, OZ.C, is a step in this direction: It keeps tabs on actors and their roles and ages at the time they appeared in the film *The Wizard of Oz,* made in 1939 B.C. (Before Computers):

```c
#include <stdio.h>

#define LINE_LENGTH 35

int main()
{
    char actor[] = "Judy Garland";
    int age = 17;
    char role[] = "Dorothy";
    int line;

    puts("Wizard of Oz Database!\n");

/* draw the table heading */
    printf("%-15s\t%3s\t%-15s\n","Actor","Age","Role");
    for(line=0;line<LINE_LENGTH;line++) putchar('-');
    putchar('\n');

/* display the data */
    printf("%-15s\t%3d\t%-15s\n",actor,age,role);

    return(0);
}
```

Type this source code into your editor. Save it to disk as OZ.C. Compile and run:

```
Wizard of Oz Database!

Actor           Age     Role
-----------------------------------
Judy Garland     17     Dorothy
```

Ho-hum.

You may find the `printf()` statements interesting. They make full use of the f-for-formatting in `printf()`. Although it looks confusing in the code, here's how `printf()`'s formatting breaks down:

`%-15s`: This formatting chunk is really the `%s`, string, placeholder, but on steroids. The 15 sets the width to 15 characters and the `-` sign left-justifies the string.

`\t`: It's a tab.

`%3d`: This placeholder displays an integer value using only three characters. If the value is less, it's right-justified.

`\t`: It's a tab.

`%-15s`: Again, the text uses 15 characters and is left-justified.

All told, the output from this `printf()` statement fits neatly on the screen. Figure 4-1 may help you to visualize things.

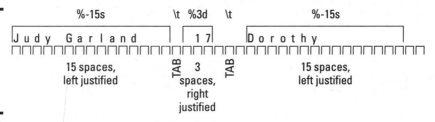

printf ("%-15s\t%3d\t%-15s", actor, age, roll)

Figure 4-1: How the printf() statement formats its output.

The tabs can also be removed; for example:

```
printf("%-15s %3d    %-15s\n",actor,age,role);
```

Spaces replace the `\t` tab escape characters. Make this change to Line 20 in the program and change Line 15 to read

```
printf("%-15s %3s    %-15s\n","Actor","Age","Role");
```

Save these changes to disk. The output is the same, but you may find that by specifying spaces directly, you get more control over the output.

Part II: The Oz database grows

Finish up the OZ database by adding information about the other actors. Each chunk of information is referred to as a *record* in the database. So, in this next step, you're adding three records, one each for the three male leads in *The Wizard of Oz:*

```c
#include <stdio.h>

#define LINE_LENGTH 35

int main()
{
    char actor1[] = "Judy Garland";
    int age1 = 17;
    char role1[] = "Dorothy";

    char actor2[] = "Ray Bolger";
    int age2 = 35;
    char role2[] = "Scarecrow";

    char actor3[] = "Bert Lahr";
    int age3 = 44;
    char role3[] = "Cowardly Lion";

    char actor4[] = "Jack Haley";
    int age4 = 40;
    char role4[] = "Tin Woodsman";

    int line;

    puts("Wizard of Oz Database!\n");

/* draw the table heading */
    printf("%-15s\t%3s\t%-15s\n","Actor","Age","Role");
    for(line=0;line<LINE_LENGTH;line++) putchar('-');
    putchar('\n');

/* display the data */
    printf("%-15s\t%3d\t%-15s\n",actor1,age1,role1);
    printf("%-15s\t%3d\t%-15s\n",actor2,age2,role2);
    printf("%-15s\t%3d\t%-15s\n",actor3,age3,role3);
    printf("%-15s\t%3d\t%-15s\n",actor4,age4,role4);

    return(0);
}
```

Modify the OZ.C source code and, using a great deal of copy and paste, create the following output. Save it to disk.

Compile. Fix any errors. This is Missing Semicolon Season, so double-check for any statements that have lost their semicolons.

Run:

```
Wizard of Oz Database!

Actor           Age     Role
-----------------------------------
Judy Garland    17      Dorothy
Ray Bolger      35      Scarecrow
Bert Lahr       44      Cowardly Lion
Jack Haley      40      Tin Woodsman
```

This program is just a fount of information. Go ahead: Stun your neighbors with it.

Still, it could use some improvement. For example, weren't you just itching to have a `for` loop display the data? Yet that wouldn't work, would it? You cannot specify a variable in a variable name, right?

```
for(r=1;r<=4;r++)
    printf("%-15s\t%3d\t%-15s\n",actorr,ager,roler);
```

Nope! The compiler would see `actorr`, `ager`, and `roler` and think that you just made up variables without declaring them. Specifying (`r`) also wouldn't work. Hmmm.

Part III: Arrays are not the answer

You may think that you can solve the *Wizard of Oz* program's problems by sticking everything into an array. (Or, just give the wizard the witch's broomstick and be done with it.)

Unfortunately, arrays are a half-solution, really. The following source code shows you how you would work it if you tried to stuff all the information into arrays:

```
#include <stdio.h>

#define LINE_LENGTH 35

int main()
{
    char actor[4][16] = {
        "Judy Garland",
        "Ray Bolger",
        "Bert Lahr",
        "Jack Haley"
    };
```

```
    int age[4] = { 17, 35, 44, 40 };
    char role[4][16] = {
        "Dorothy",
        "Scarecrow",
        "Cowardly Lion",
        "Tin Woodsman"
    };

    int line,x;

    puts("Wizard of Oz Database!\n");

/* draw the table heading */
    printf("%-15s\t%3s\t%-15s\n","Actor","Age","Role");
    for(line=0;line<LINE_LENGTH;line++) putchar('-');
    putchar('\n');

/* display the data */
    for(x=0;x<4;x++)
        printf("%-15s\t%3d\t%-15s\n",
    actor[x],age[x],role[x]);

    return(0);
}
```

Modify OZ.C again, making these changes. Watch your typing! Lots of jots and tittles can get lost. Save the thing to disk. Compile. Run.

The output is the same, but are three separate arrays really useful for storing this kind of information? A multidimensional array doesn't work because the data is of different types. (You could specify the ages as text, but why go through all that extra work?) And, doesn't array notation get clumsy after a while? What if you want to sort the list? How do you keep track of three (or more) arrays?

There must be a better solution. . . .

Exercise 3.4.1

Honestly, I haven't really taught you anything yet, so there's no point in giving you an exercise. Merely consider this one *busy work:* Add the following information to your OZ.C program. You use it later in this chapter:

```
Margaret Hamilton, 37, Wicked Witch
Frank Morgan, 49, The Wizard
```

Multivariables!

Why, what you need is an electronic, C language 3 x 5 card!

In real life (remember that?), you probably would store complex information on a 3 x 5 card. As any computer salesperson can tell you, computers are just big 3 x 5 card things anyway. Remember the old advertisements? You could store your recipes on the computer, put your CD collection there, organize your checkbook, yada-yada, and so on.

Presenting the structure

In the C language, a 3 x 5 card is known as a *structure*. It's a collection of variable types all stored in one compact unit. Each unit is similar to a record in a database, which you can access and tweak just like any other variable in C.

Rather than bore you with the format right away, observe this source code:

```
#include <stdio.h>

int main()
{
    char input[10];

    struct stuff
    {
        char letter;
        int number;
    };

    struct stuff my;

    puts("Your Own Stuff");

    printf("Enter your favorite letter: ");
    my.letter = getchar();

    printf("Enter your favorite number: ");
    scanf("%d",&my.number);

    printf("Your favorite letter is %c\n",my.letter);
    printf("and your favorite number is %d.\n",my.number);
    return(0);
}
```

Double-check your typing because some new doohickeys that you haven't seen are in there. Save it to disk as MYSTUFF.C. Compile and run:

```
Your Own Stuff
Enter your favorite letter:
```

Type a **Q** and press the Enter key:

```
Enter your favorite number:
```

Type **17** and press the Enter key:

```
Your favorite letter is Q
and your favorite number is 17.
```

This program probably should win the Big Deal award for the whole book. After all, what it did could easily be done without structures. As usual, that's not the point.

The point is covered in the next section.

The lowdown on structures

A *structure* is a collection of differing variable types — any number or combination, including arrays — all of which describe something similar. For example, your name, address, weight, and favorite cartoon character could be stored in a structure.

The `struct` keyword is used to create a *structure,* a single unit that holds several different variable types. Here's the format:

```
struct name {
        type name;
        type name;
};
```

`name` is the name of the structure.

Within the structure's curly braces are one or more variable declarations — just as you would have at the start of a program: `type` is a variable type (`char`, `int`, or `float`, for example), and `name` is the name of that variable. There's nothing new here, except that the variables that are declared belong to the structure, not to the entire program. Officially, the variables are "members" of the structure, just as obsessively skinny people are members of a gym.

When you define a structure, you create a new type of variable named after the structure. In the program MYSTUFF (from the preceding section), you define the `stuff` structure. Note that this definition alone doesn't create any new structure variables. For that, another line in the program is required:

```
struct name variable;
```

The keyword `struct` is followed by the name of a declared structure, `name`, and then the name of the structure variable itself, `variable`.

You can also define structure variables "on the fly," by using this format:

```
struct name {
        type name;
        type name;
} variable;
```

And, you can declare multiple structure variables like this:

```
struct name {
        type name;
        type name;
} var1, var2, var3;
```

where `var1`, `var2`, and `var3` are each variables of the `name` type of structure.

To access the elements of a structure, the dot format is used:

```
name.var
```

The `name` is the name of a structure variable. That's followed by a dot (or period) and then the variable name `var` as declared inside the structure.

Variables inside a structure are used just like any other variables in C. Just because a `char` variable is named `person.name` doesn't mean that it's any weirder or different from a `char` variable named `orville`.

Whither `typedef`?

It's usually at this point in your C language voyage that you encounter the joys and sorrows of the `typedef` keyword. Bad move.

I strongly suggest that you work through this entire chapter before even thinking about `typedef`. If you already know `typedef`, keep it out of your mind for now.

Book III, Chapter 7 covers `typedef`. If you try to get ahead of yourself now — especially on the advice of college professors (and the graduate students who teach their classes) — you get into trouble.

Structures must be defined and then variables for that structure created. *Two steps!* Only after a structure's variables have been created can you store information in the structure. Merely creating the structure is only half the job.

More stuff

By itself, the MYSTUFF.C program's job could be done without a structure, but not when you try to juggle a second set of information, as shown in this code:

```c
#include <stdio.h>

int main()
{
    char input[10];

    struct stuff
    {
        char letter;
        int number;
    } my, his;

/* Here is his info */

    his.letter = 'Y';
    his.number = 199;

    puts("Your Own Stuff");

    printf("Enter your favorite letter: ");
    my.letter = getchar();

    printf("Enter your favorite number: ");
    scanf("%d",&my.number);

    printf("Your favorite letter is %c\n",my.letter);
    printf("and your favorite number is %d.\n",my.number);
    printf("His favorite letter is %c\n",his.letter);
    printf("and his favorite number is %d.\n",his.number);
    return(0);
}
```

Load the MYSTUFF.C program into your editor and make these changes, which add a second variable of the stuff structure type.

Save the program to disk. Compile and run.

Type your favorite letter and number again. In the last part of the output, you see the preset information for the his stuff structure variable as well:

```
Your favorite letter is Q
and your favorite number is 17.
His favorite letter is Y
and his favorite number is 199.
```

You see similar information, but from two different structure variables.

This example could also be written as

```
struct stuff
{
    char c;
    int n;
};

struct stuff mystuff;
struct stuff hisstuff;
```

Or, you can combine the last two lines:

```
struct stuff mystuff, hisstuff;
```

Exercise 3.4.2

Modify the MYSTUFF.C source code again, this time adding a new `stuff` structure variable named `her`. Her favorite letter is *A,* and her favorite number is 21.

Declaring and defining a structure

As with every other type of variable in C, you can also create a structure variable that contains predefined data. The part to remember here is that you must define the structure first and then declare a structure variable filled with data. This source code shows how it's done:

```
#include <stdio.h>

int main()
{
    struct month
    {
        char name[16];
        int age;
        char likes[64];
        char dislikes[64];
        float iq;
    };
```

```
struct month march = {
    "Kelly",
    23,
    "Books, scented candles, macramé, handguns",
    "Bureaucrats, locked doors, guys named Milton",
    139.8
    };

puts("Mensa Playmate of the Month Data");
printf("%9s %s\n", "Name:", march.name);
printf("%9s %d\n", "Age:", march.age);
printf("%9s %s\n", "Likes:", march.likes);
printf("%9s %s\n", "Dislikes:", march.dislikes);
printf("%9s %5.1f\n", "IQ:", march.iq);
return(0);
}
```

Type this source code into your editor. Save it to disk as MARCH.C:

Compile and run.

```
Mensa Playmate of the Month Data
    Name: Kelly
     Age: 23
   Likes: Books, scented candles, macramé, handguns
Dislikes: Bureaucrats, locked doors, guys named Milton
      IQ: 139.8
```

Note how the %9s formatting string lines up the prompting text right-justified? Interesting trick, no?

You cannot define the structure *and* assign variables to it at the same time. Defining the structure is merely telling the compiler, "Hey! Here's a strange, new type of variable." Only after that's done can you declare variables of that type of structure and, optionally, initialize them with data.

Now you can, if you like, declare everything together; for example:

```
struct month

{
    char name[16];
    int age;
    char likes[64];
    char dislikes[64];
    float iq;
} march = {
    "Kelly",
    23,
    "Books, scented candles, macramé, handguns",
    "Bureaucrats, locked doors, guys named Milton",
```

```
    139.8
    };
```

This example essentially combines both steps into one statement: The month structure is defined and then the march variable declared *and* filled with data. This method works, but it's ugly. It also limits you to initializing only one variable. My advice: Don't bother.

Arrays of Structures

A database program isn't truly useful unless you have more than one record. In C, a structure is similar to a record. An array of structures — well, that's looking more and more like a database.

Creating an array of structures is cinchy. After all, struct variables are just like any other in C; the only difference is that you define the variable — the *multivariable* — yourself. Then you can declare a structure variable as an array just as you would declare a char or int array. For example:

```
struct stuff
{
    char letter;
    int number;
};
```

Here, the stuff type of structure variable is defined. To create an array of similar structures, you would use this declaration:

```
struct stuff mystuff[20];
```

An array of 20 stuff structures named mystuff is created.

To access the elements in the array, you also use a similar format:

```
mystuff[0].letter
```

In this example, character letter of the first element (the first structure) in the array is accessed. The array notation comes first, and then the period, and then the variable in the structure:

```
mystuff[x].number
```

Here, variable x represents an element in the mystuff structure array. Whatever element that is, the preceding variable represents the x integer value of that structure thing.

The first element of any array is always 0.

Meanwhile, back in Oz . . .

The following source converts the Wizard of Oz database from arrays to
structures. Note how the structures are filled by using strcpy(). Remember
that you cannot copy strings with an equal sign!

```
#include <stdio.h>
#include <string.h>

#define LINE_LENGTH 40

int main()
{
    struct oz {
        char actor[18];
        int age;
        char role[16];
        };

    struct oz cast[6];
    int line,x;

    strcpy(cast[0].actor,"Judy Garland");
    cast[0].age = 17;
    strcpy(cast[0].role,"Dorothy");

    strcpy(cast[1].actor,"Ray Bolger");
    cast[1].age = 35;
    strcpy(cast[1].role,"Scarecrow");

    strcpy(cast[2].actor,"Bert Lahr");
    cast[2].age = 44;
    strcpy(cast[2].role,"Cowardly Lion");

    strcpy(cast[3].actor,"Jack Haley");
    cast[3].age = 40;
    strcpy(cast[3].role,"Tin Woodsman");

    strcpy(cast[4].actor,"Margaret Hamilton");
    cast[4].age = 37;
    strcpy(cast[4].role,"Wicked Witch");

    strcpy(cast[5].actor,"Frank Morgan");
    cast[5].age = 49;
    strcpy(cast[5].role,"The Wizard");

    puts("Wizard of Oz Database!");

/* draw the table heading */
```

```
        printf("%-18s\t%3s\t%-15s\n","Actor","Age","Role");
        for(line=0;line<LINE_LENGTH;line++) putchar('-');
        putchar('\n');

/* display the data */
    for(x=0;x<6;x++)
        printf("%-18s\t%3d\t%-15s\n",
            cast[x].actor,\
            cast[x].age,\
            cast[x].role);
    return(0);
}
```

Type this source code into your editor. It's very messy, so please be careful.
Save it to disk. Compile. Fix any errors. Compile again. And so on.

Run:

```
Wizard of Oz Database!
Actor               Age  Role
----------------------------------------
Judy Garland         17  Dorothy
Ray Bolger           35  Scarecrow
Bert Lahr            44  Cowardly Lion
Jack Haley           40  Tin Woodsman
Margaret Hamilton    37  Wicked Witch
Frank Morgan         49  The Wizard
```

The output is the same as the preceding incarnation of OZ.C, but it was produced by structures.

You must use strcpy() to copy strings. You cannot use the equal sign, as
you can with other variables.

Note how the long printf() at the end is split between several lines. Ending
a line in C with a single backslash tells the compiler that the line is split. It's
a good way to space out a complex statement and make it more readable, as
just shown.

Predefining an array of structures

If it's elegance you're into and if you know what's in your structure array,
you can, of course, preload it. This source code shows you how it looks:

```
#include <stdio.h>

#define LINE_LENGTH 40

int main()
{
```

```
struct oz {
    char actor[18];
    int age;
    char role[16];
    };

struct oz cast[6] = {
    "Judy Garland", 17, "Dorothy",
    "Ray Bolger", 35, "Scarecrow",
    "Bert Lahr", 44, "Cowardly Lion",
    "Jack Haley", 40, "Tin Woodsman",
    "Margaret Hamilton", 37, "Wicked Witch",
    "Frank Morgan", 49, "The Wizard"
    };
int line,x;

puts("Wizard of Oz Database!");

/* draw the table heading */
printf("%-18s\t%3s\t%-15s\n","Actor","Age","Role");
for(line=0;line<LINE_LENGTH;line++) putchar('-');
putchar('\n');

/* display the data */
for(x=0;x<6;x++)
    printf("%-18s\t%3d\t%-15s\n",
        cast[x].actor,\
        cast[x].age,\
        cast[x].role);
return(0);
}
```

Pretty spiffy, eh? Gone is the STRING.H header file plus all those seemingly endless `strcpy()` functions. *Good riddance!*

Type this source code into your editor, modifying the preceding incarnation of OZ.C as you go. Save to disk. Compile. Run.

As usual, the output is the same; the program itself, however, is much more elegant.

Welcome to the way things typically work in the C language. Whenever you find your source code growing messy, repetitive, or ugly, a better solution for your problem probably exists.

In real life, information is loaded into a structure array either by a user, who types merrily at the keyboard, or by reading the information from a file on disk. Rarely do you pack a structure array as just shown.

All arrays begin with element 0.

Copying one structure element to another

You know, Frank Morgan played *five* characters in the *Wizard of Oz*. In addition to the title role, he was Professor Marvel, the doorman, the cabbie, and the Wizard's guard. So, his estate wants to know why he's listed *last* in the OZ program's database. He should at least be ahead of the witch, don't you think?

But how do you swap elements in a structure array? In a regular array, you would just use a `temp` variable of the same type:

```
temp = b[x];
b[x] = a[x];
a[x] = temp;
```

Fortunately, the solution is just that obvious. In the case of the OZ program, the variable type is `oz`, a structure variable. You simply declare a new structure variable to hold the temporary value:

```
struct oz temp;
```

Variable `temp` is a structure variable. Like `cast`, it has `actor`, `age`, and `role` part. Swapping elements of a structure array can now be done just like with any other array. Witness this, hopefully, final update to OZ.C:

```
#include <stdio.h>

#define LINE_LENGTH 40

int main()
{
    struct oz {
        char actor[18];
        int age;
        char role[16];
        };

    struct oz cast[6] = {
        "Judy Garland", 17, "Dorothy",
        "Ray Bolger", 35, "Scarecrow",
        "Bert Lahr", 44, "Cowardly Lion",
        "Jack Haley", 40, "Tin Woodsman",
        "Margaret Hamilton", 37, "Wicked Witch",
        "Frank Morgan", 49, "The Wizard"
        };
    struct oz temp;
    int line,x;
```

**Book III
Chapter 4**

Stinkin' Structures

```
/* Swap Margaret and Frank */
    temp = cast[4];
    cast[4] = cast[5];
    cast[5] = temp;

    puts("Wizard of Oz Database!");

/* draw the table heading */
    printf("%-18s\t%3s\t%-15s\n","Actor","Age","Role");
    for(line=0;line<LINE_LENGTH;line++) putchar('-');
    putchar('\n');

/* display the data */
    for(x=0;x<6;x++)
        printf("%-18s\t%3d\t%-15s\n",
            cast[x].actor,\
            cast[x].age,\
            cast[x].role);
    return(0);
}
```

It almost seems too innocent to work, right? Make these modifications to
your OZ.C source code. You're declaring a new struct oz variable named
temp and then adding three lines to swap elements 4 and 5 of the cast array.
Save it to disk. Compile!

Run it to see whether it worked:

```
Wizard of Oz Database!
Actor               Age   Role
------------------------------------
Judy Garland         17   Dorothy
Ray Bolger           35   Scarecrow
Bert Lahr            44   Cowardly Lion
Jack Haley           40   Tin Woodsman
Margaret Hamilton    37   Wicked Witch
Frank Morgan         49   The Wizard
```

Amazingly enough, the simple action of assignment (using an equal sign) is
powerful enough to duplicate elements in a structure array.

You can even use this technique to copy information from one structure variable to another. As long as the variables are of the same structure type, this
trick works; the elements of one structure are duplicated into the next.

Exercise 3.4.3

Now that you know how to swap to variables in a structure, go ahead and
modify OZ.C *one last time*. Have your program sort the array of structures,

listing the cast in order by their ages, from youngest to oldest. (Don't bellyache — I could have had you sort the list by last name!)

Structures for the Birds (Nested Structures)

Defining a structure is just like creating another type of variable, a multi-variable. If your insanity level has been keeping up with the C language, you may have assumed that one structure can live inside another structure.

Then again, you may be a stable person and not used to thinking like the C language. (Me? I try not to imagine what other horrors this programming language could possibly dream up.)

Consider this structure:

```
struct date {
    int month;
    int day;
    int year;
            };
```

This example is simple enough: It's a structure that contains information about a birth date. This structure could also be a part of a larger structure:

```
struct family {
    char name[20];
    struct date birthday;
            };
```

Don't go running from the computer! All you're doing is sticking a structure variable of type date into the family structure. This example shows you what's known as a *nested structure*.

A nested structure variable is declared just like any other variable:

```
struct family people;
```

The structure variable people is created.

The only craziness with a nested structure comes when you're referring to the nested variables. These printf() statements display the contents of each item in the people family structure:

```
printf("Your name = %s\n",people.name);
printf("Birth month = %d\n",people.birthday.month);
printf("Birth day = %d\n",people.birthday.day);
printf("Birth year = %d\n",people.birthday.year);
```

It's just more dots! The variable people.birthday.day is the structure people, member birthday (which is a structure), and then day (which is a member of the birthday structure). Whew!

Here's all that in a program you can type into your editor and delight over:

```
#include <stdio.h>
#include <string.h>

int main()
{
    struct date {
        int month;
        int day;
        int year;
        };

    struct family {
        char name[20];
        struct date birthday;
        } me;

/* Fill in your own data here */

    strcpy(me.name,"Dan");
    me.birthday.month = 10;
    me.birthday.day = 19;
    me.birthday.year = 1960;

    printf("%s was born on %d/%d/%d\n",\
        me.name,\
        me.birthday.month,\
        me.birthday.day,\
        me.birthday.year);
    return(0);
}
```

Substitute your own vital statistics for those shown here (enter your name and birthday information). Save the code to disk as MYBDAY.C:

Compile and run:

```
Dan was born on 10/19/1960
```

(Your output should reflect your information, of course, and not mine.)

You have to use the strcpy() function to copy a string constant into a structure's string variable!

Yes, you can easily avoid nested structures. For example, the `family` structure could be redefined this way:

```
struct family {
  char name[20];
  int month;
  int day;
  int year;
          };
```

I have never seen a circumstance in which a nested structure has been used (other than in a book about C), but that doesn't rule them out of existence.

The structure you nest inside must be declared as a variable; for example:

```
struct family {
  char name[20];
  struct date;
          };
```

This declaration is wrong. The `struct date` item must have a variable name after it. This statement makes sense when you also observe that the `char name[20]` variable isn't written as just `char`. Variables must be named inside structures.

Chapter 5: Creating Your Own Functions

In This Chapter

✓ Writing your own functions in C

✓ Using functions in C

✓ Prototyping functions

✓ Working with variables inside functions

✓ Understanding local and global variables

✓ Passing values to functions

✓ Returning a value from a function

✓ Avoiding the function prototype

The C language is composed of keywords, operators, variables — blah, blah, blah — and functions. If you have done any C programming at all, you have already used many functions: `printf()`, `getchar()`, `scanf()`, `strcpy()`, and the lot. All told, the C language and all its libraries have hundreds of functions that do many various and miraculous things for you. But they don't do everything.

To cover all the bases, you can create your own functions in C. These functions are created using the C language and they work just like the C language library functions. You can use your own functions to optimize your source code, carry out repetitive tasks, or just because. The function can do anything you want, as long as you read through this chapter and understand how to do functions in C.

Your Typical Function

It's entirely possible to code without functions. But it's also an insane thing to do. At some point, you rewrite the same chunk of code over and over. It may be a long chunk of code, or something tiny. But you have to copy and paste and soon your source code is five or seven screens long.

I'm fond of saying that when things look redundant or awkward in your C language source code that a better way of programming looms on the horizon. This is especially true with repetitive code, and possibly the motivation for early programmers in the 1950s to dream up the function — or *procedure* or *subroutine*, as it's called in other programming languages.

Some functions optimize code. Some merely hide the dirty work to keep the main part of the program clean. Some functions produce output. Some functions require input. And some functions do neither input nor output. It's all up to the programmer who created the function.

This section gives you the whirlwind tour of functions in C. Sorry, no examples this time through. So read it all, and then be prepared to do some coding for the remainder of this chapter.

Making a function in C

Every C language program has at least one function, the main() function. Every program in this book has it, and if you have been working this book front-to-back, you have probably written dozens of programs with dozens of different main() functions.

The good news is that all functions in C look like main() and have the same parts:

```
type name(type)
{
    statement(s);
}
```

Like variables, functions must be declared of a specific *type*. The *type* is one of the standard variable types in C, plus a special void type:

+ char (signed, unsigned)

+ double

+ float

+ int (long, short, signed, unsigned)

+ void

This declares the function just as a variable is declared. It tells the compiler what type of value the function returns. For example, the getchar() function is a char function. It generates (or returns) a single character. The random() function returns a long int. If the function doesn't return a value, it's a void function.

The function is named like a variable in C; the same rules apply. You cannot duplicate function names. For example, `puts()` is already taken, so your `puts()` function would have to be renamed to something else — ditto for `main()`, which is reserved. Function names can contain letters and numbers and they're mostly written in lowercase.

Don't use spaces in your function names. Instead, use underlines. For example, this isn't a function name:

```
get the time()
```

But this could be:

```
get_the_time()
```

You can also resort to using an upper-lowercase combination when you're naming your functions:

```
getTheTime()
```

Keep your function names short and descriptive. A function named `f()` is permissible yet ambiguous — it's like saying "nothing" when someone asks you what you're thinking.

All functions are declared with a set of parentheses:

```
float hugs(char you);
```

Between the parentheses are any values the function requires, such as the `char` variable `you` in the preceding line. These are the variables the function eats. If the function doesn't need any values, the word `void` is sandwiched between the parentheses.

Finally, after the function declaration comes a set of braces. Between them are the statements that do what the function sets out to do:

```
void blah(void)
{
    puts("blah void blah void blah void");
    puts("void blah void blah void blah");
    puts("blah void blah void blah void");
    puts("void blah void blah void blah");
}
```

Using functions

To use a function, you *call* it. Yoo-hoo! You have seen this a bazillion times:

```
heyyou();
```

This statement "calls" the heyyou( ) function, and the computer goes off and does whatever it's instructed to do in that function. Then program control returns to the next statement following heyyou( );

Some functions require information in their parentheses. For example, puts:

puts("Rhymes with foots not nuts.");

Some functions *return* a value. That is, they produce something your program can use, examine, compare, whatever. The getchar( ) function returns a character typed at the keyboard, which is typically stored in a character variable, thus:

thus=getch();

Creating a function doesn't really add a new word to the C language. However, you can use the function just like any other function in your programs; printf( ), getchar( ), and so on.

The importance of prototyping

The compiler has a right to know! Specifically, the compiler wants to know about the functions you're using to make certain that they're used properly. Because of this, every function you use is prototyped.

But I don't remember any prototyping for printf( )!

All functions are prototyped, even the library functions. That happens when you add the header file required for a function; the prototype is inside the header file. printf( )'s prototype is in the STDIO.H header file.

For your own functions, you have to add the prototype at the top of your source code, before the main( ) function (or before your function is used), and usually after any #include or #define directives. For example:

#include <stdio.h>

#define REPEAT 100

void bleep(int volume);

int main()
{
/* and so on... */

Before the function is used, and before the main( ) function, the prototype is listed. This is simply a restating of the function's declaration. It tells the compiler the function name, type, and what if any variables are required. All functions in your program must be prototyped this way:

```
#include <stdio.h>

void blorf(int count);
float rootbeer(void);
int frink(double mhey);

int main()
{
/* and so on... */
```

The compiler notes the prototypes and automatically flags you if the function is misused in the code later on.

There's only one way around prototyping: write your functions first, before they're used. Then specify the main() function last, at the bottom of the code. An example of this approach is offered later in this chapter.

Functions That Don't Func

Some functions require no input nor return any output. I call them functions that don't func, but they're still valuable and useful.

Here's an example:

```
#include <stdio.h>
#include <string.h>

void showprompt(void);        /* prototype */

int main()
{
    char input[64];

    do
    {
        showprompt();         /* call the function */
        gets(input);
        puts("Someday I must implement that function.");
    }
    while(strcasecmp("quit",input));
    puts("Oh! Apparently I did!");

    return(0);
}

void  showprompt(void)
{
    printf("What is thy bidding? ");
}
```

What? No return?

Yes, the `showprompt()` function in the DSHELL.C source code does not end with a `return(0);` statement, as the `main()` function does. The reason? `main()` is a `int` function, and it must return an integer value or the compiler gets grumpy. The `showprompt()` function, on the other hand, is a `void` — `showprompt()` doesn't return anything. Therefore no `return` is necessary.

Type this source code into your editor. Save it to disk as DSHELL.C. Compile and Run. Have fun with it. (Note it's similarity to RUDEDOS.C, from Book III, Chapter 2.)

The `showprompt()` function is called only once, and produces no input or output — though it does display information on the screen. (That's not input nor output from the *function* however.) The best functions are those that are called repeatedly.

The function prototype ends in a semicolon. The function declaration does not! If you typed:

```
void  showprompt(void);
{
    printf("What is thy bidding? ");
}
```

The computer would suspect something was wrong — and rightfully so. Function declarations are followed by braces.

Using Variables in Functions

Each function can have and use its own set of variables, separate from the variables declared and used in the `main()` function. In fact, variables are all *local* to the functions they're created in. This is a concept that may take some getting used to.

The concept of local variables

Contemplate this source code:

```
#include <stdio.h>
#include <stdlib.h>
#include <time.h>
```

```
void separator(void);

int main()
{
    long int r;
    srandom((unsigned)time(NULL));

    puts("Here are today's secret number values:");
    separator();
    r = random();
    printf("%d\n",r);
    separator();
    r = random();
    printf("%d\n",r);
    separator();
    r = random();
    printf("%d\n",r);
    return(0);
}

void separator(void)
{
    int r;

    for(r=0;r<10;r++)
        putchar('*');
    putchar('\n');
}
```

Carefully type this code and save it to disk as SECNUM.C.

Some versions of gcc use `srand()` and `rand()` rather than `srandom()` and `random()`. Make the necessary changes to the preceding source code. Also refer to Book II, Chapter 4 for information on random numbers in C.

Compile and run.

```
Here are today's secret number values:
**********
263130901
**********
220147721
**********
10386019
```

Of course, your random numbers will vary, but that's not the point of the program. Look at your source code, Line 9:

```
long int r
```

Now look at Line 27:

```
int r
```

Two variables are named r. That works because each variable lives in its own function. Inside a function, variables are insulated from the rest of the program. Outside forces don't corrupt them.

Variables in different functions can share the same name. If you're fond of using x for your `for` loops, feel free to define and use it in every function.

Exercise 3.5.1

Quite a few statements are repeated in the SECNUM.C source code. Aren't functions about eliminating that? Modify the `separator()` function so that it also generates and displays the random number (you have to use a different variable name). Have the `main()` function then call `separator()` three times.

Using global variables

Sometimes, you do have to share a variable between two or more functions. Most games, for example, store the score in a variable that's accessible to a number of functions: the function that displays the score on the screen; the function that increases the score's value; the function that decreases the value; the function that stores the score on disk; and so on. All those functions have to access that one variable. That's done by creating a global variable.

A *global variable* is one that any function in the program can use, change, examine, modify, do whatever. No problem.

Global variables are declared *outside* of any function, typically right above the main function, as in

```
#include <stdio.h>

int score;

int main()
{
/* and so on */
```

That `int score;` declaration may seem like it's floating in space, but it's really part of the entire program. The value of `score` can be set, changed, modified, used, or abused by any function in the program. That one declaration is *global*.

"Global" or "external"?

I refer to them as global variables, which is common in other programming languages. But in C, they're often referred to as *external* variables or the *external storage class*. As such there is a C language keyword used to reference the variables.

The `extern` keyword is often included in a function to identify a global variable. For example, from the source code MODLINE.C nearby, the function `dashes()` could declare the `linelen` variable as:

```
extern int linelen
```

This tells the compiler that variable `linelen` is to be found between the functions. However,

it's not necessary here; that's because the global variable is defined first in the code, before the functions that use it. Similar to prototyping, as long as you define the variable before it's used, you don't have to bother with the `extern` keyword or redeclare the global variable that way.

Where `extern` is necessary is when creating separate source code modules for a larger program. In that case, `extern` is required to identify global variables created in other modules. You see this demonstrated at the end of Book IV.

The opposite of a global variable is a *local variable*. It's what you have seen so far. A local variable exists inside only one function — like the variable r in the SECNUM sample program.

You can also declare a group of global variables at one time, such as:

```
int score,lives,powerups;
```

And you can preassign values to global variables if you want:

```
float temperature=98.6;
```

Global variable names must be unique! If you give your global variable a name already used by some local variable somewhere (or vice versa), your program gets serious willies.

An example of a global variable in a real, live program

The following program uses not one but *two* global variables. It also is the first program in this chapter to sport two functions, one of which calls another. A function calling a function! What has society decayed into?!

```c
#include <stdio.h>
#include <string.h>

void showline(void);
void dashes(void);

char line[81];
int linelen;

int main()
{
    puts("Enter a line of text:");
    gets(line);
    linelen = strlen(line);

    puts("Here is the line you entered:");
    showline();
    return(0);
}

void showline(void)
{
    dashes();
    puts(line);
    dashes();
}

void dashes(void)
{
    int x;

    for(x=0;x<linelen;x++)
        putchar('-');
    putchar('\n');
}
```

Type in this source code. Save it to disk as MODLINE.C.

Compile and run.

```
Enter a line of text:
Help me, Obiwan Kenobi. You're my only hope.
Here is the line you entered:
---------------------------------------------
Help me, Obiwan Kenobi. You're my only hope.
---------------------------------------------
```

Try it again. The output always frames the sentence with dashes, no matter how long or short the sentence is. Amazing. Here's the lowdown of what's going on:

✦ The two functions are prototyped in lines 4 and 5, `showline()` and `dashes()`.

✦ The two global variables are specified in lines 7 and 8, `line` and `linelen`. Note how they look just like regular variable declarations? They are! But they're accessible to the entire program.

✦ Global variable `line` is assigned text using the `gets()` function in Line 13 in `main()`.

✦ Line 14 in the `main()` function assigns a value to global variable `linelen`. The `strlen()` function returns the length of the string stored in variable `line`.

✦ In the `showline()` function, Line 24, the global variable `line` is used again.

✦ Note how the `showline()` function calls the `dashes()` function? Functions are free to call any other function defined in the program.

✦ The `dashes()` function uses the global value of `linelen` to calculate how many hyphens to display.

You can pull off one of these for a global variable just like a local variable:

```
int x = 0;
```

But you cannot do this for a global variable:

```
x = cos(angle);
```

That's because global variables can only be declared or assigned immediate values. Such assignment as shown here can be done only where programming can be done: inside a function.

Exercise 3.5.2

Modify MODLINE.C so that another function is added. This function, `shout()`, displays the line in uppercase. (Refer to Book III, Chapter 3 on the CTYPE functions.) Name the source code LINEMOD.C so as to keep it separate from the original MODLINE.C code.

Functions That Eat Values

Hungry functions eat values! Sometimes they chew on one value, sometimes they chew on many values. You just have to tell the function what kind of value to expect and then it has a dandy old time working that value over.

Note that sending a value to a function isn't the same thing as using a global variable. See the previous few sections for information on global variables.

Here it comes!

Sending a value to a function is as easy as getting a sunburn. Just follow these steps:

1. Know what kind of value you will send to the function.

It can be any normal C variable type: `int`, `float`, `char`, and so on.

2. Define the variable in the function's parentheses.

Suppose that you want an integer value. Go ahead and declare it in the parentheses following the function's name:

```
void adnauseum(int repeat)
```

Don't follow the variable name with a semicolon! This is one of those rare times. Otherwise, you declare the variable as you normally would. In the preceding line, the integer variable `repeat` is declared. This means that the `adnuaseum()` function requires an integer variable, which it names `repeat`.

3. Somehow use the variable in your function.

The compiler doesn't like it when you declare a function that eats a variable and then that variable isn't used in the function. It's assumed that if the value is passed, it must be used.

Inside the function, the variable uses the same name as declared in the function's definition:

```
void feed_the_kitty(int quantity)
```

The compiler expects you to reference and use the `quantity` `int` variable inside the `feed_the_kitty()` function.

4. Properly prototype the function.

No sweat.

5. Remember to send the proper values when you're calling the function.

As Hammurabi would say, and `int` for an `int` and a `char` for a `char`.

The following code is a modification to the SECNUM.C program, presented earlier in this chapter. It has been modified so that a value is sent to the `separator()` function. Observe:

```
#include <stdio.h>
#include <stdlib.h>
#include <time.h>
```

```
void separator(int repeat);

int main()
{
    srandom((unsigned)time(NULL));

    puts("Here are today's secret number values:");
    separator(10);
    separator(15);
    separator(20);
    return(0);
}

void separator(int repeat)
{
    int x;
    long int r;

    for(x=0;x<repeat;x++)
        putchar('*');
    putchar('\n');
    r = random();
    printf("%d\n",r);
}
```

Update the source code to SECNUM.C as shown here. The preceding code reflects modifications from Exercise 3.5.1, but this time the function accepts an integer value.

Save the changes to disk. Compile. Run.

```
Here are today's secret number values:
*********
109031362
***************
127741022
********************
91068301
```

Here are the changes worth noting:

✦ The separator() function is now declared (and prototyped) to accept an integer variable as input.

✦ When separator() is called, in Lines 12, 13, and 14 of the program, an integer value is specified in the parentheses. Like any other C function that eats an int, this could be an integer variable or an immediate value, as shown in the code.

◆ Inside the `separator()` function, the `repeat` variable is used to reference the value passed. Note that `repeat` is declared inside the function's definition. There's no need to redeclare it; simply use the variable, which represents any value passed to the function.

◆ Essentially the value passed to the function behaves like a local variable in the function.

◆ The variable in a function's parentheses is referred to as an *argument*. This gives you a tiny taste of C's combative nature.

Exercise 3.5.3

Modify the source code to MODLINE.C so that the `dashes()` function accepts a single `char` variable. That character is then used to draw the lines that `dashes()` produces.

How to send more than one value to a function

You can pass along any number of items to a function. All you have to do is declare them inside the function's parentheses. It's like announcing them at some fancy diplomatic function; each item has a variable type and a name and is followed by a lovely comma dressed in red taffeta with an appropriate hat. There's no semicolon at the end because this is a formal occasion.

Avoiding variable confusion

The variable name defined for a function need not be the same as any variables passed to that function. Don't reread that. Just take a for instance:

Suppose that you're in the `main()` function where a variable named `count` is used. You want to pass along its value to the `geek()` function. You would do so this way:

```
geek(count);
```

This tells the compiler to call the `geek()` function, sending it along the value of the `count` variable. Because `count` is an integer variable, this works just fine; `geek()` accepts `int` values. But keep in mind that it's the variable's

value that is passed along, not its name. The name `count` is just a name in the `main()` function.

In the `geek()` function, the value is referred to by using the variable name `repeat`. This is how the `geek()` function was set up:

```
void geek(int repeat)
```

Whatever value is sent, however it was sent, always is referred to as `repeat` inside the function.

In summary: You can call any function with any variable name. Only inside that function is the function's own variable name used.

For example:

```
void bloat(int calories, int weight, int fat)
```

This function is defined as requiring three integer values: `calories`, `weight`, and `fat`.

```
void separator(int repeat, char c)
```

Here you see a modification of the `separator()` function, which now requires two values: an integer and a character. These values are referred to as `repeat` and `c` inside the `separator()` function:

```c
#include <stdio.h>
#include <stdlib.h>
#include <time.h>

void separator(int repeat, char c);

int main()
{
    srandom((unsigned)time(NULL));

    puts("Here are today's secret number values:");
    separator(10,'*');
    separator(15,'-');
    separator(20,'#');
    return(0);
}

void separator(int repeat, char c)
{
    int x;
    long int r;

    for(x=0;x<repeat;x++)
        putchar(c);
    putchar('\n');
    r = random();
    printf("%d\n",r);
}
```

Modify the source code for SECNUM.C to match what was just shown. There are only a few modifications:

- ✦ Line 5 to change the prototype for `separator()` to accept two variables, and `int` and a `char`.

- ✦ Lines 12 through 14 to specify which `char` to send to the function.

- ✦ Line 18 to redefine the declaration of `separator()`.

♦ Line 24 to use the character variable c rather than the immediate character '*'.

Save. Compile. Run:

```
Here are today's secret number values:
**********
109031362
---------------
127741022
#####################
91068301
```

Sending structures to functions

Alas, you just can't pack a structure variable into a trunk that goes on a journey to a function. Witness this modification to the MYSTUFF.C program from Book III, Chapter 4:

```c
#include <stdio.h>

void showstuff(struct stuff the);

int main()
{
    char input[10];

    struct stuff
    {
        char letter;
        int number;
    } my;

    puts("Your Own Stuff");

    printf("Enter your favorite letter:");
    my.letter = getchar();

    printf("Enter your favorite number:");
    scanf("%d",&my.number);

    showstuff(my);

    return(0);
}

void showstuff(struct stuff the)
{
    printf("Your favorite letter is %c\n",the.letter);
    printf("and your favorite number is %d\n",the.number);
}
```

Another way to argue with a function

This book teaches you the modern, convenient way of declaring variables (or "arguments") shuffled off to a function. To wit:

```
void jerk(int repeat, char c);
```

You can also use the original format:

```
void jerk(repeat, c)
int repeat;
char c;
```

This declaration does the same thing, but it's a little more confusing because the variable name is introduced first and then the "what it is" comes on the following line (or lines). Otherwise, the two declarations are the same; the next line would contain the first curly bracket, and then comes the function's statements.

My advice is to stick with the format used in this book and try not to be alarmed if you see the other format used. Older C references may use the second format, and certain fogey C programmers may adhere to it. Beware!

Modify the source code to MYSTUFF.C — if you have the time — and save it back to disk. Compile. Don't even bother running it; just observe the error messages. To summarize:

Structures cannot be passed to nor returned from functions.

Unless . . . you declare the structures are a global variable. Defining the structure outside the bounds of any particular function does work. Here's the correct MYSTUFF.C source:

```
#include <stdio.h>

struct stuff
{
    char letter;
    int number;
};

void showstuff(struct stuff the);

int main()
{
    char input[10];
    struct stuff my;

    puts("Your Own Stuff");

    printf("Enter your favorite letter:");
    my.letter = getchar();
```

```
        printf("Enter your favorite number:");
        scanf("%d",&my.number);

        showstuff(my);

        return(0);
}

void showstuff(struct stuff the)
{
        printf("Your favorite letter is %c\n",the.letter);
        printf("and your favorite number is %d\n",the.number);
}
```

Fix your source code so that it matches what's shown here. Note that the structure is declared externally, outside of any functions. I could have also declared the my structure variable external as well, but I wanted to show you how a variable can be passed, as well as how to declare a structure variable for a function (showstuff()) that uses one.

Save the source code to disk. Compile and Run. The output is unchanged from the original MYSTUFF program.

Incidentally, this solution also shows you how you "return" structure values from a function. Again, you cannot do that directly, but you can do it handily by using a global variable.

How to send strings (or arrays) to a function

Strings are arrays, not variables. As such you don't send them to a function directly. You can send individual elements of an array using the techniques described in the previous two sections. But to send an array or a string you must understand the C concept of *pointers*.

Pointers are covered in Book IV. They're a heavy duty part of the C language that is at the same time mysterious and confusing, while being very powerful. Fortunately they're explained rather well in Book IV, so I leave you to understand that definition before you begin to use pointers to send arrays and strings to functions.

Sending strings off to functions is tricky stuff. It encroaches on a C language topic called *pointers,* which everyone agrees is kind of scary (but primarily because it's never properly explained).

Besides: I have way too much information in this chapter already!

Functions That Return a Value

I would guess that the majority of functions return a value. Some may eat a value as well, but most typically send some value back — a valuable value to value. Or I could say a valuable variable value to value.

Returning a value with the `return` keyword

To return a value, a function must obey two rules:

Warning! Rules approaching.

✦ The function has to be *defined* as a certain type (`int`, `char`, `float`, etc. — just like a variable). Something other than `void`, because `void` functions (by their definition) don't return values.

✦ The function has to return a value.

The function type tells you what type of value it returns. For example:

```
double nationalDebt(void)
```

The `nationalDebt()` function returns the national debt of the United States as a `double` value. No input is required. Even if input were offered, Congress would most likely ignore it.

```
int birthday(int date);
```

The function `birthday()` is defined. It's an integer function that returns an integer value. (It also requires an integer parameter, `date`, which it uses as input.)

How does a function return a value? Well, that's where the handy return keyword comes into play.

You have been typing `return(0)` in every `main()` function in every program you have been writing. That's because `main()` is an `int` function and it's required to return an integer value back to the operating system when it's done.

The operating system doesn't really use the value returned by a program, but it makes that value available for other programs to examine. You can see how to do this in Book V, Chapter 2, in the section about dealing with the exit status.

Here's your official introduction to the `return` keyword:

```
return(something);
```

The *something* is a value the function must return. What kind of value? Depends on the type of function. It can be an integer, character, string (which is tricky), floater — whatever. And you can specify either a variable name or a constant value.

In this line, the value of the variable `total` is returned from the function:

```
return(total);
```

Here, the function returns a value of 0:

```
return(0);
```

By the way, the `something` is optional. For the `void` type of functions, you can use the `return();` or merely `return;` statement by itself to cause the program to return, for example, in the middle of something. More on that in Book III, Chapter 6.

Functions can return only a single value. So unlike sending a value to a function, in which the function can receive any number of values, they can cough up only one thing in return. I know. Sounds like a gyp.

(Functions *can* return several values, but only by using global variables or taking advantage of an array of pointers — advanced stuff. Shhh!)

Roll 'dem bones!

The following is a modification to the CRAPS.C program used in Book II. In this modification I have created a function `roll()` which is used to "roll" the dice. The `roll()` function returns a value in the range of 2 to 12, simulating the throw of a dice — a natural type of function for a program such as this:

```
#include <stdio.h>
#include <stdlib.h>
#include <time.h>

int throw(void);

int main()
{
    int bet,roll,point;
    char c;
```

```
srandom((unsigned)time(NULL));

printf("Enter your bet: $");
scanf("%i",&bet);

puts("Rolling them bones....!");
roll = throw();

printf("%d ",roll);
switch(roll)
{
    case 7:
    case 11:
        printf("- You win!\n");
        bet *= 2;
        break;
    case 2:
    case 3:
    case 12:'
        printf("- Craps! You lose!\n");
        bet = 0;
        break;
    default:
        point=roll;
        printf("- Your point is now %d.\n",point);
        while(1)
        {
            roll = throw();
            printf("\tYou rolled %d, point is
%d.\n",roll,point);
            if(roll==point)
            {
                printf("\tYou win!\n");
                bet *= 2;
                break;
            }
            if(roll==7)
            {
                printf("\tSeven out, you lose!\n");
                bet = 0;
                break;
            }
        }
}
printf("You now have $%d.\n",bet);
return(0);
}
```

Book III
Chapter 5

Creating Your
Own Functions

```
int throw(void)
{
    int die1,die2,total;

    die1 = random() % 6 + 1;
    die2 = random() % 6 + 1;
    total=die1+die2;
    return(total);
}
```

Modify your source code for CRAPS.C so that it looks like what's shown here. Basically, I have added the new function throw() prototype and inserted it twice in the program where the dice are rolled, Lines 18 and 39. The new function is also added. Save the changes to disk.

Compile and run.

```
Enter your bet: $1000
Rolling them bones....!
10 - Your point is now 10.
        You rolled 4, point is 10.
        You rolled 5, point is 10.
        You rolled 12, point is 10.
        You rolled 12, point is 10.
        You rolled 7, point is 10.
        Seven out, you lose!
You now have $0.
```

Yes the program still works! But note how the throw() function operates:

✦ throw() requires no input, so void is specified between the buns. Also note how when throw() is called, no value is specified there either. The compiler knows this, thanks to the prototype.

✦ Inside throw() three int variables are declared. These are local variables to the function.

✦ First a random value from 1 to 6 is placed in die1. Then a random value from 1 to 6 is placed into die2. The total is calculated and then sent back using the return keyword.

✦ In the main() function, the throw() function generates a roll of two dice, producing a value in the range of 2 through 12.

The throw() function could find its way into multiple programs. Consider all the dice games out there! You're on your way to writing a suite of games!

Exercise 3.5.4

Write a new program called ROLLEM.C. Have the program ask the user how many dice they want to roll, in the range of 1 to 12. Make a function like `throw()` from CRAPS.C that rolls one die and returns the result. Use your best `printf()` formatting skills to present the throws to the user in as pretty a format as possible, something like this:

```
R O L L ' E M !
How many dice would you like to roll (1 to 12)? 10
Rolling 10...
Here they come!
  1   2   3   4   5   6   7   8   9  10
+---+---+---+---+---+---+---+---+---+---+
| 4 | 6 | 4 | 5 | 5 | 6 | 5 | 6 | 4 | 4 |
+---+---+---+---+---+---+---+---+---+---+
Total = 49
```

Functions That Do Both

Yes, functions can both accept input and generate output. The majority of the C language's math functions do this. You want to the know the square root and then pass the `sqrt()` function a value and squirt back the result. *Quid pro quo*, agent Starling.

There's nothing weird or complex with such functions. You merely combine information from earlier in this chapter to weave together a function that both eats and poops. Let's call this function `baby()` and see how it works in the following source code, also called BABY:

```c
#include <stdio.h>

float baby(float food);

int main()
{
    float input,output;

    printf("Enter quantity you plan on feeding baby:");
    scanf("%f",&input);

    output = baby(input);

    printf("According to the computer, baby will\n");
    printf("produce %.2f material as output.\n",output);
    return(0);
}
```

```
float baby(float food)
{
    float poop;

    poop = 1.217*food;
    return(poop);
}
```

Carefully enter this source code. Save it as BABY.C. Compile and run.

```
Enter quantity you plan on feeding baby:
```

Type **3**. I don't know why. It seems like a good quantity to feed baby.

```
According to the computer, baby will
produce 3.65 material as output.
```

Amaze your friends who are new parents!

The Land of No Prototyping

To weasel out of prototyping, you merely must introduce the entire function to the computer before that function is used. I call this "upside down" programming. Here's an example of how this looks using the source code BABY.C (from the preceding section) as an example:

```
#include <stdio.h>

float baby(float food)
{
    float poop;

    poop = 1.217*food;
    return(poop);
}

int main()
{
    float input,output;

    printf("Enter quantity you plan on feeding baby:");
    scanf("%f",&input);

    output = baby(input);

    printf("According to the computer, baby will\n");
    printf("produce %.2f material as output.\n",output);
    return(0);
}
```

I don't know any programmer who starts out programming this way. Basically they write `main()` first. Then as they need functions, they write them *before* `main()` rather than after.

Personally I think this format is less readable than the traditional method. The only advantage is that you don't need to prototype. Then again, I *like* the prototypes, as they tell me which functions are defined in the program. Otherwise I may believe those functions to be library functions with which I am unfamiliar.

Chapter 6: Quitting Before You're Done

In This Chapter

- ✔ Using `return` to end the `main()` function
- ✔ Understanding the `abort()` function
- ✔ Gracefully leaving with the `atexit()` function

*W*inners never quit and quitters never win!

Yeah, but what about the *cheater?* Huh? And, what about those who say that it's just best to walk away? Or run away if you're young enough to still do so?

Despite your best efforts, at times you may need to get out of a sticky situation. Or, perhaps you're just done early and you want to leave. As with real life, these types of situations often arise in your programs. I call such a thing *bailing out,* as in jumping out of an airplane that's still flying. This type of activity isn't only possible in your code, but often it's necessary. This chapter shows you the whys and hows of leaving early.

Abruptly Leaving the `main()` Function

Well, it's time to say goodbye . . . for the summer.

It's the height of propriety to know when to leave. In your programs, the deft use of the `return` keyword makes leaving quick and proper. Two other ways out are the `exit()` and `abort()` functions. All three sorties are covered in this section.

Note that `return` and `exit()` are covered in Book V, Chapter 2.

Many happy `returns`

Does every function need a `return`?

No: void functions don't need a return. But, if the other types of functions need a return, do they need only one? What about two?

```c
#include <stdio.h>
#include <ctype.h>

char ask(void);

int main()
{
    char key;

    printf("Would you like to see the menu?");
    key = ask();
    if(key=='Y')
    {
        puts("Someday the menu will appear here");
        /* finish this later */
    }
    return(0);
}

char ask(void)
{
    char c;

    printf(" (Y/N)? ");
    fflush(stdin);
    c = toupper(getchar());
    if(c == 'Y')
        return(c);
    else
        return('N');
}
```

Type this source code. Save it to disk as MENU.C. Compile and run.

The output is blah, so I just concentrate on the ask() function.

First, note how ask() converts the input to uppercase by using the toupper() CTYPE function. That narrows down the options to one as far as the function is concerned: If someone typed **Y**, return Y. Otherwise, N is returned.

If you're using a Unix-like operating system, be sure to substitute fpurge(stdin); in Line 25.

Two returns! Two different values! What will those humans think of next?

If you're done, you can use return to leave a function early.

You can use return to leave early even when return doesn't necessarily return a value:

```
void dashes(char c)
{
    int x;

    if(c == ' ')
    {
        putchar('\n');
        return;
    }
    for(x=0;x<linelen;x++)
        putchar(c);
    putchar('\n');
}
```

This snippet is from the source code for MODLINE.C, from Book III, Chapter 5. (You don't need to see the entire program.) The function displays a string of characters equal to the value of the global variable linelen. In this example, if the character requested is a space, ' ', the function displays a newline and "leaves early" with a return statement.

Exercise 3.6.1

Modify the source code to MODLINE.C. Change one of the calls to the dashes() function so that a space is specified, and then modify the dashes() function as shown in the preceding code.

Sending in your return early

In all those programs you have written, have you ever wondered, if all main() functions end in return(0); why isn't it just assumed?

For one, you can pass values other than 0 back to the operating system. For another, return doesn't have to be at the end, and you definitely don't need one of them. Consider this, a modification to the MENU.C program presented earlier in this chapter:

```
#include <stdio.h>
#include <ctype.h>

char ask(void);

int main()
```

```
{
    char key;

    printf("Do you want to quit before you see the menu?");
    key = ask();
    if(key=='Y') return(0);

    printf("Would you like to see the menu?");
    key = ask();
    if(key=='Y')
    {
        puts("Someday the menu will appear here");
        /* finish this later */
    }
    return(0);
}

char ask(void)
{
    char c;

    printf(" (Y/N)? ");
    fflush(stdin);
    c = toupper(getchar());
    if(c == 'Y')
        return(c);
    else
        return('N');
}
```

Make these modifications to the MENU.C source code. Save 'em to disk. Compile that source code into a program. Run!

```
Do you want to quit before you see the menu?
```

Press **Y** and . . . the program quits — right then and there!

The `return` statement need not be the last thing in a function!

Finding the nearest `exit()`

Another way to leave a program is by using the `exit()` function. Unlike `return`, which may merely toss you out of a function somewhere deep within a program, `exit()` *always* quits the program and returns control over to the operating system — even from the deepest function, inside the darkest nested loop.

Officially, the `exit()` function "terminates a process." Scary words. It's almost as though the function should be named `kevorkian()` or something!

Does exit() clean up your mess?

I have been in debates with programmers over the extent of what the exit() function does. As far as I can tell, and have read in all my documentation, when you call exit(), it attempts to cleanly leave your program and return to the operating system.

By *cleanly,* I mean that the exit() function attempts to empty or flush all open buffers; any

text in the input stream, or any information waiting to be written to open files is processed. Furthermore, exit() properly closes any open files. So, if you call exit() deep within your program, rest assured that any lingering files or data are safely written to disk by that call.

But seriously, exit() is the best way to quit a program, especially in case of error.

See Book V, Chapter 2 for more information on how to use the exit() function.

Abort! Abort! Abort!

C has a special function, named abort(), that's reserved for use whenever a program must *abnormally* terminate. What's abnormal? Inside a computer? Beats me!

In many respects, abort() is similar to exit(). Though exit() can be used to successfully leave a program, abort() is used only when something has gone wrong. Granted, the abort() function still tries to clean up after itself, but it's assumed that the reason abort() is being used is that major booboos have occurred.

To make abort() work, you must add #include to the STDLIB.H header file.

Here's a small program example:

```
#include <stdio.h>
#include <stdlib.h>
#include <math.h>

int main()
{
    float value;
```

```
      double answer;

      printf("O! Computer, find me the square root of: ");
      scanf("%f",&value);

      if(value < 0.0) abort();

      answer = sqrt((double)value);
      printf("The computer says the answer is %f\n",answer);
      return(0);
}
```

Type this source code into your editor. Save it to disk as ABORT.C. Compile and run.

Some versions of Unix require that the math library be linked in to compile this program. The command is **gcc -lm abort.c -o abort**.

The first time through, enter a positive value to ensure that it works. (It does.) Then, try entering a negative number. Here's what Windows XP told me:

```
This application has requested the Runtime to terminate in an
    unusual way.
Please contact the application's support team for more
    information.
```

(The "support team" says "Don't use a negative number next time!")

Here's what Unix said:

```
abort trap (core dumped)
```

Oops! That's *serious*. Better save the abort() way out for only the gravest of dangers!

A Most Graceful Exit

When your programs grow larger and take on more tasks, you find that you need to run special initialization as well as shutdown routines. Who knows what they are! But the initialization routines come first, and you want those shutdown routines to come last.

Who knows where exactly your program will exit? What if you use an exit() function deep down somewhere? How can you be sure that your special bailing-out functions get run?

Say Hello to the graceful `atexit()` function. It registers certain special functions that are run whenever your program quits. Any time. From any place. Via any regular exiting method (`return` or `exit()`). All you need to do is add #include to the STDLIB.H header file to make `atexit()` work. This section shows you the details.

If we ever get out of here. . . .

Pretend that the following source code is much, much longer and extensive. It's merely a part of a bigger program to show you the advantage of the `atexit()` function:

```c
#include <stdio.h>
#include <stdlib.h>

void finish(void);

int main()
{
    atexit(finish);

    puts("Press Enter to begin shutting down this program");
    getchar();
    return(0);
}

void finish(void)
{
    puts("This is the function that looks under");
    puts("the hard drive for any missing bits...");
}
```

Book III
Chapter 6

Save this source code to disk as BAIL.C. Compile and run:

```
Press Enter to begin shutting down this program
```

By looking at the preceding code, you may assume that after the `getchar()` function, the `return(0);` simply tosses you back to the operating system. Not so! Press Enter:

```
This is the function that looks under
the hard drive for any missing bits...
```

The `atexit()` function registers the `finish()` function to be run when the program quits. It doesn't matter where the program quits, or whether it quits with a `return` or an `exit()`. At the point where the program quits, the function registered with `atexit()` runs.

Note that the function is registered by using its name — no parentheses. Also note that only double-void functions can be specified with `atexit()`; the functions cannot accept or return any values.

In the BAIL.C source code, the program is assumed to be rather huge and the `finish()` function is designed to accomplish some necessary task that is required before you can quit the program. Rather than have you guess at things, the `atexit()` function assures you that `finish()` will be run when the program quits.

Registering multiple functions

What if you have multiple functions that you want to run whenever a program quits? If so, you can register them by specifying each function — which must be `void-void` functions — with separate `atexit()` statements.

Suppose that you want to run these three functions whenever the program quits:

```
finish()

spiffy()

animation()
```

Furthermore, you want to run them in that order. If so, here's the source code you need:

```
#include <stdio.h>
#include <stdlib.h>

void finish(void);
void spiffy(void);
void animation(void);

int main()
{
    atexit(animation);
    atexit(spiffy);
    atexit(finish);

    puts("Press Enter to begin shutting down this program");
    getchar();
    return(0);
}

void finish(void)
{
```

```
        puts("This is the function that looks under");
        puts("the hard drive for any missing bits...\n");
}

void spiffy(void)
{
        puts("This function cleans up the keyboard.\n");
}

void animation(void)
{
        puts("As a final trick, the Taco Bell dog will dance");
        puts("across your monitor with this function.\n");
}
```

Update your BAIL.C source code so that it resembles what's shown here. Note that I have added \n newlines to the last of each function's puts( ) statement (or statements). Save it to disk. Compile and run:

```
Press Enter to begin shutting down this program
```

Press Enter:

```
This is the function that looks under
the hard drive for any missing bits...

This function cleans up the keyboard.

As a final trick, the Taco Bell dog will dance
across your monitor with this function.
```

The important thing to remember is that atexit( ) registers each function from first to last. So, if you have three functions, as in the preceding source code, register the last one first and the first one last.

Chapter 7: More Variable Nonsense

In This Chapter

✔ **Understanding Hungarian notation**

✔ **Using and abusing** `typedef`

✔ **Creating a variable type with** `typedef`

✔ **Dealing with** `auto`, `const`, `register`, `volatile` **and others**

✔ **Working with enumerated values**

✔ **Creating a** `static` **variable**

✔ **Understanding unions**

✔ **Using unions inside structures**

*I*n the C programming language, variables are declared up front and right away, never leaving to doubt in anyone's mind which variables your program uses and of what type they are. Or, is it really that clear?

Declaring variables up front assumes that everyone reads code from the top down, and, specifically, that they pay attention to the variable declarations. If not, who really knows whether the variable `age` is an `int`, an `unsigned int`, or a `float`? Maybe it's a `char`!

This chapter covers something called Hungarian notation, which is a method for naming variables that removes all doubt. It's especially handy for those who need to share their code with other programmers.

Also covered here are even more C language spells and incantations used to declare, modify, or abuse variables — including the mysterious `typdef`.

The Joys of Hungarian Notation

Hungarian notation is a way of naming variables with consistency and readability in mind. It was pioneered by programmer Charles Simonyi in 1972. It's called Hungarian either because Charles is Hungarian or the notation makes variables look like they're Hungarian words — or merely because programmers are fond of Liszt's *Hungarian Rhapsody*.

What Hungarian notation (also known as the Hungarian naming convention) states is that variables should be given consistent names so that the programmer, as well as others reading the source code, can recognize the variable type by looking at its name.

For example:

```
temp
```

What is variable `temp`? In Hungarian notation, you could say

```
fTemp
```

The little `f` prefix identifies `fTemp` as a `float`.

Table 7-1 lists common Hungarian notation prefixes used by many C (and C++) programmers. Note that the exact prefixes may vary; some programmers may use their own set of prefixes. (Also, Windows programming uses a whole set of prefixes not listed in Table 7-1.)

Table 7-1	Common C Language Hungarian Notation Prefixes	
Type	*Prefix*	*Example*
int	n	nCount
float	f	fBaby
double	d	dRoot
char	c	cKey
string (null terminated)	sz	szInput[]
global	g_	g_nScore
pointer	p (always first)	*pnArray
struct	S	SCast
long	l	lHours
unsigned	u	uAge

Although I admire Hungarian notation, and I often use it, or my own variation, from time to time, I'm not a big fan. The problem I have with it is that there's no enforcement by the compiler; if you change a variable type in the middle of a program, the old name no longer applies. Although you could globally search-and-replace the name, few programmers bother. Therefore, without enforcement of the naming convention by the compiler, what's the point?

On the other hand, large projects with many folks working on them should have common ground. Even if you don't all use the examples from Table 7-1, and instead settle on your own naming conventions, this type of naming convention provides marvelous consistency and self documentation.

Beware the typedef *Statement!*

Oooh. I'm about to get in trouble.

There's a C language keyword, typedef. It's not really a command. It's more like the #define directive in that it tells the compiler to pretend that one thing is something else. Whereas #define can be used to create constants (and other mischief), typedef is used to add a new name for an existing type of variable. Keep reading.

Refer to Book I, Chapter 8 for more information on #define.

The silly way to use typedef

Some programmers often mistakenly believe that typedef is used to create a new type of variable. No. No. No. The typedef statement merely gives you a new word to use when you're referring to an existing type of variable:

```
#include <stdio.h>

typedef char byte;
typedef int word;

word main()
{
    byte a;

    for(a=65;a<=90;a++)
        putchar(a);
    putchar('\n');
    return(0);
}
```

**Book III
Chapter 7**

**More Variable
Nonsense**

Carefully type this source code. Save it to disk as ODDVAR.C. Compile and run:

```
ABCDEFGHIJKLMNOPQRSTUVWXYZ
```

In Line 3, typedef creates an alias for the char variable type. The new name is byte. Line 4 does the same thing, creating word for int. Then, byte and word are used inside the code.

Note that using typedef in ODDVAR.C doesn't redefine char and int; those two types still exist and could be used. But byte and word can also be used as alternatives.

As with #define constants, some programs choose to name their typedef variable names in ALL CAPS. In Windows programming, nearly all new variable types are in all caps; for example:

```
typedef unsigned long DWORD;
```

The new variable type DWORD is defined as an unsigned long (integer) variable. The typedef declarations are created in with the WINDEF.H header file.

Using typedef *with structures*

Most often, you find typedef used in creating structure variables. The typedef is used as a shortcut:

```
#include <stdio.h>

typedef struct stuff
{
    char letter;
    int number;
} junk;

void showstuff(junk the);

int main()
{
    char input[10];
    junk my;

    puts("Your Own Stuff");

    printf("Enter your favorite letter:");
    my.letter = getchar();

    printf("Enter your favorite number:");
    scanf("%d",&my.number);

    showstuff(my);

    return(0);
}

void showstuff(junk the)
{
    printf("Your favorite letter is %c\n",the.letter);
    printf("and your favorite number is %d\n",the.number);
}
```

This source code is a modification to one of many incarnations of the MYSTUFF.C program, from previous chapters in this book. Type it, if you dare. Compile and run, though the output isn't what's important here:

```
typedef struct stuff
{
    char letter;
    int number;
} junk;
```

Here, `typedef` *does not* create a new structure. Instead, it creates a shortcut name for the structure `stuff`. That name is `junk`. Just as `typedef int word;` creates `word` as a synonym for `int`, the preceding monster creates the `junk` synonym for

```
struct stuff
{
    char letter;
    int number;
};
```

To create a new structure variable of the `stuff` type, the program now uses this statement:

```
junk my;
```

Also, to identify the structure as a value used by the `showstuff()` function, `junk` is used:

```
void showstuff(junk the)
```

Book III
Chapter 7

More Variable
Nonsense

Where programmers get into trouble

Programmers get into trouble with `typedef` when they're using structures in something called a *linked list*. The problem is that the `typedef` structure cannot be used until it's defined. (Like, *duh!*) Look at this example:

```
typedef struct
{
    char name[25];
    president next;
} *president;
```

How can you use `typedef` on a structure and name that variable `president` when the structure contains the variable `president`? How does the compiler know what to do? Ugh.

The solution is simple: *Don't try to do everything at once!*

In this example, the structure is defined first, and then `typedef` creates the alternative word for it:

```
struct pres
{
    char name[25];
    struct pres *next;
};

typedef struct pres *president;
```

Or, you could also do it this way:

```
typedef struct pres *president;

struct pres
{
    char name[25];
    president next;
};
```

or even this way, if you dare to do it all at once:

```
typedef struct pres
{
    char name[25];
    struct pres *next;
} *president;
```

The idea is the same: Don't use the `typedef` definition until it has been defined.

Although Book VI covers linked lists, I don't use `typedef` there. I just feel that the shortcut gets in the way of things. After reading Book VI, you can decide on your own whether you need to use `typedef` to create structure pointers.

C is not C++! One reason that programmers get into trouble here is because the `typedef` operation on a structure in C++ is automatic. In C++, a structure name becomes a new variable type (or something like that). Keep that in mind when you're copying code from a C++ program.

Other Funky Variable Things

Who are these guys?

```
auto

const
```

```
enum

register

static

volatile

union
```

Rock stars? The newest generation of Power Rangers? Breakfast bars?

Not quite. These things comprise the mystery grab bag of C language key-words, some of which are used in the C language's struggle to help you define variables. Some of them are useful. Most of them can be ignored. I have docu-mented them here because readers of my original *C For Dummies* books (Wiley Publishing) were always curious. I hope that this section sates your curiosity.

Auto

A keyword named auto is in the C language's list of keywords. It's a reserved word, so you cannot name a function or variable auto. What does auto do? Nothing.

auto is a holdover from the B language, from which C was derived. auto was once used to describe a type of variable, but now it serves no purpose in C.

Const

The const keyword is a borrow-under from the C++ language. In that tongue, const is used to create constants. In C, however, you can best create con-stants by using the #define directive, covered in Book I, Chapter 8.

If you define a variable as a const in C, you merely create a read-only (non-changeable) variable. Unlike with a #define constant, you cannot use the variable to size an array or in any other spot where an immediate value or constant can be used (such as in a case statement). So . . . what's the point?

What about entry?

Another funky C language keyword is entry. Like auto, entry is a holdover from primitive times in the C language. I can only assume that entry marked the entry point into the code for the operating system, but that's just a guess.

(Some programming languages have a similar type of statement.)

Feel free to ignore and never use the entry keyword.

Enum

The enum keyword is used to enumerate, or assign sequential values, to a series of names, similar to what #define does. Don't get all excited! You can program for your entire life and never use enum.

Suppose that a program can evaluate a series of error conditions. Those conditions are assigned the numbers 0 through 5:

0. Out of money

1. Drowning in debt

2. No end in sight

3. Wife wants divorce

4. Car is broken

5. Cat peed on leg

These items are enumerated. In C, you can do the following with enum:

```
enum error {OUT_OF_MONEY, DROWNING_IN_DEBT, NO_END_IN_SIGHT,
    WIFE_WANTS_DIVORCE, CAR_IS_BROKEN, CAT_PEED_ON_LEG};
```

Here, enum takes each word and assigns it a value from 0 through 5. So, elsewhere in your program, you can use something like this:

```
switch(error_value)
{
    case OUT_OF_MONEY:
        /* do something here */
        break;
    case DROWNING_IN_DEBT:
        /* program goes on... */
```

You get the idea. Or, maybe you don't. Here's a real, live program example:

```
#include <stdio.h>

int main()
{
    enum days {Monday, Tuesday, Wednesday, Thursday, Friday,
    Saturday, Sunday};
    int x;

    for(x=Monday;x<=Sunday;x++)
        printf("X = %d\n",x);
    return(0);
}
```

Type this source code into your editor. Save it to disk as ENOCH.C. (Enoch is a Biblical character; `enum` is a C language keyword.) Compile and run:

```
X = 0
X = 1
X = 2
X = 3
X = 4
X = 5
X = 6
```

Surprised? Did you think that `Monday` through `Sunday` would be printed? *Not!* That's because enumeration assigns numbers to the shortcut words `Monday` through `Sunday`. It doesn't create string variables.

Exercise 3.7.1

Modify ENOCH.C so that Line 5 looks like this:

```
enum days {Monday = 100, Tuesday, Wednesday, Thursday,
Friday, Saturday, Sunday};
```

Can you guess the program's output?

Register

Another stinky, unusable keyword is `register`. I'm not sure whether it really works, but `register` tells the compiler to place an integer or `char` variable's value directly into one of the microprocessor's registers. That way, the variable can be manipulated more efficiently and it may even speed up your program. But, again, I'm not sure whether this ability is available on any modern C compiler.

Using `register` is often mentioned as a way to speed up a program. Therefore, some sources suggest dotting your code with `register` variable declarations wherever you can, such as

```
register int loop;
```

Whether it really works is debatable.

Static

The theory goes that whenever a function is called, the variables used in that function aren't initialized. When the function is done, whatever values were in the variables is considered lost; the compiler doesn't keep track of

Book III
Chapter 7

More Variable Nonsense

a variable's value after the function in which it was used is no longer active. What the `static` keyword does is retain a variable's value even after the function is done.

Believe it or not, I have even encountered a situation where I needed to declare a `static` variable. I even had to look up how to use it because I had never seen it done. This program poses a similar problem:

```c
#include <stdio.h>
#include <ctype.h>

void request(void);

int main()
{
    char ch;

    do
    {
        puts("\nMain Menu\n=========");
        printf("Press 1 enter new request, Q to quit: ");
        ch = toupper(getchar());
        fflush(stdin);
        switch(ch)
        {
            case '1':
                request();
                break;
            case 'Q':
                puts("Quitting Now");
                return(0);
            default:
                puts("\nNaughty Input!");
        }
    }
    while(ch != 'Q');
}

void request(void)
{
    char input[64] = "";

    puts("\New Request!");
    printf("\tPrevious request was \"%s\"\n",input);
    printf("\tEnter new request: ");
    gets(input);
    puts("\Thank you!");
}
```

Carefully type this source code into your editor. Note that the `return(0);` statement, normally found at the end of `main()`, is now inside the `switch` case structure (inside the `do-while` loop). That's okay! Read Book III, Chapter 6 for more information.

Remember to change Line 15 to `fpurge(stdin)` if you're using a Unix-like operating system.

Save the code to disk as STATIC.C. Compile.

What's being demonstrated here is that the string storage `input` doesn't remember what was typed when the function previously was called. Run the program and try this:

```
Main Menu
=========
Press 1 to enter new request, Q to quit:
```

Press **1** and then Enter:

```
New Request!
        Previous request was ""
        Enter new request
```

It's obvious that the previous request was blank because that's how the `input` string storage location is initialized. But, moving along:

Type **Hello!** and press Enter:

```
Thank you!

Main Menu
=========
Press 1 to enter new request, Q to quit:
```

Press **1** and then Enter:

```
New Request!
        Previous request was ""
        Enter new request
```

You could argue that the program doesn't remember the preceding request because of this line:

```
char input[64] = "";
```

But this argument is incorrect. The line doesn't *initialize* the variable. You can prove it by making the variable static, which means that the compiler retains its value between function calls.

Press **Q** to quit the program.

Modify the source code, changing Line 33 to read

```
static char input[64] = "";
```

This line doesn't create a constant! It merely tells the compiler to retain the value of `input` between function calls. Save the change to disk. Compile. Rerun the code to see what happens:

```
Main Menu
=========
Press 1 to enter new request, Q to quit:
```

Press **1** and then Enter:

```
New Request!
        Previous request was ""
        Enter new request
```

Type **Will this work?** and press Enter:

```
Thank you!

Main Menu
=========
Press 1 to enter new request, Q to quit:
```

Press **1** and then Enter again.

```
New Request!
        Previous request was "Will this work?"
        Enter new request:
```

Go ahead and type something else, and then quit the program.

You have three things to remember here: First, the values of a function's variable's aren't retained between function calls. Second, declaring a variable and assigning it a value doesn't make that variable a constant. Third, you can tell the compiler to remember a variable's value by declaring that variable as `static`.

Exercise 3.7.2

Modify STATIC.C so that an integer variable, rather than a string, is used in the `request()` function.

Do functions really forget their values?

Sometimes, it's difficult to prove that a function doesn't remember its values between calls. That's because, though the function's memory is released by the program, the data inside memory isn't necessarily cleaned up.

For example, consider this program:

```c
#include <stdio.h>
void a(void)
{
    int a; a = 5;
}
void b(void)
{
    int b;
    printf("B is %d\n",b);
}

int main()
{
```

```c
    a();
    b();
    return(0);
}
```

In function a(), the value of variable a is set to 5. Function b() comes along and declares variable b. Many times in a computer, that variable is declared in the same memory location as the old (and discarded) variable a. For this reason, without initializing variable b, its value is equal to variable a. This quirk happens often, but it's not predictable behavior or something your programs should rely on.

Always consider uninitialized variables to contain "garbage." Even if a trick like the one in this sidebar is possible on your computer, don't assume that it works on every computer, with every program. Consider it a fluke.

Volatile

The volatile keyword is similar to register in that it's an instruction for the compiler to optimize your code. Although you can easily write a bazillion programs without ever using volatile, is tells the compiler that the value the variable addresses will change often:

```c
volatile char *p;
```

A pointer variable, p, is created, the value of which probably changes drastically as the program runs. When you add volatile to the declaration, the compiler supposedly is better able to store and handle this type of variable.

Alas, I don't know of any proof that declaring a variable volatile makes any difference with today's compilers. Therefore, as with the register keyword, I would freely forget volatile.

(I introduce pointer variables in Book IV.)

The State of the union

Here's one that goofs some folks up: the union. It's a type of variable, similar to a struct, but different in the way it holds information. That's enough to confuse most people. Well, that and not that many programs out there use unions. But they do come up a lot when you access system calls and do various operating system chores. So, it's worth a few pages to cover it here.

A simple union

Use a union when you're not sure what type of data will be stored or when you have options for different types of data to be stored. For example:

```
union height {
    float centimeters;
    int inches;
};
```

A type of union named height is created. It can hold either an int value or a float — not both. The compiler allocates enough space for only whichever variable is largest.

As with a structure, the height *type* of union variable is created. To create an actual variable, you need a statement like this one:

```
union height doris;
```

The doris variable is created. It's a union variable of the height type. It can contain either an int value *or* a float value. To assign doris an integer value, you use this statement:

```
doris.inches = 65;
```

To assign height a float, you use this statement:

```
doris.centimeters = 165.1;
```

Note that both values cannot be kept at the same time. If you try to access doris.inches after assigning a value to doris.centimeters, you get junk. Here's one of them thar demo programs:

```
#include <stdio.h>

#define CENT_PER_INCH 2.54

int main()
{
    union measure
    {
```

```
     float centimeters;
     int inches;
  };
  union measure you;
  union measure paul;

  paul.inches = 70;

  printf("Paul is %d inches tall.\n",paul.inches);
  printf("How tall are you in inches? ");
  scanf("%d",you.inches);

  you.centimeters = CENT_PER_INCH * (float)you.inches;
  paul.centimeters = CENT_PER_INCH * (float)paul.inches;
  printf("You are %f.1 centimeters tall.\n",
you.centimeters);
  printf("Paul is %f.1 centimeters tall.\n",
paul.centimeters);
  return(0);
}
```

Save this source code to disk as UNPAUL.C. Compile and run.

```
Paul is 70 inches tall.
How tall are you in inches?
```

Type your height. I'm **72** inches tall:

```
You are 182.9 centimeters tall.
Paul is 177.8 centimeters tall.
```

`you.inches` and `you.centimeters` *is the same variable!* You can get away with a statement like this:

```
you.centimeters = CENT_PER_INCH * (float)you.inches;
```

because C figures out the value on the right first. After that's done, the variable `you.centimeters` replaces `you.inches`. To demonstrate, edit the source code so that Lines 23 and 24 read like this:

```
printf("You are %f.1 centimeters tall.\n", you.inches);
printf("Paul is %f.1 centimeters tall.\n", paul.inches);
```

In both cases, you're changing `%f.1` to `%d` and `centimeters` to `inches`. Save, recompile, and rerun the program:

```
Paul is 70 inches tall.
How tall are you in inches?
```

I enter **72** again:

```
You are 1127670088 centimeters tall.
Paul is 1127337165 centimeters tall.
```

The numbers you see are merely the result of the compiler trying to interpret a floating-point value as a long integer. (Refer to Book I, Chapter 4 for information on how floats and ints are stored inside the computer.) That's because the you and paul variables are in their floating-point modes.

Again, unlike a structure, a union can have only one value active or usable at a time.

Unions buried inside structures

Unions often wiggle their way into a structure to allow flexibility when representing different types of information:

```
struct person
{
    char name[50];
    int age;
    union
    {
        struct
        {
            char game[25];
            int jersey_number;
        } sports;
        struct
        {
            char instrument[25];
            int years_practice;
        } music;
        struct
        {
            int hours_week;
        } television;
    } hobby;
};
```

This structure for person contains a union. The union has three structures as members: sports, music, and television. For each variable of the struct person type that's created, only one of the union items (sports, music, or television) can be used. Consider this code snippet:

```
struct person a;
struct person b;
struct person c;
```

First, three `person` variables are created. Next, you can assign values to the new structures, but when it comes to the `hobby` variable, you can choose only one of the three types — `sports`, `music`, or `television`:

```
a.hobby.sports.jersey_number = 23;

b.hobby.television.hours_week = 60;

strpcy(c.hobby.music.instrument,"Viola");
```

Here's the program to prove that it all works. It's hefty; type it at your leisure:

```
#include <stdio.h>
#include <string.h>

int main()
{
    struct person
    {
        char name[50];
        int age;
        union
        {
            struct
            {
                char game[25];
                int jersey_number;
            } sports;
            struct
            {
                char instrument[25];
                int years_practice;
            } music;
            struct
            {
                int hours_week;
            } television;
        } hobby;
    };
    struct person a;
    struct person b;
    struct person c;

    strcpy(a.name,"Alex");
    a.age = 17;
    strcpy(a.hobby.music.instrument,"Guitar");
    a.hobby.music.years_practice = 4;
```

```
strcpy(b.name,"Jerry");
b.age = 22;
strcpy(b.hobby.sports.game,"Football");
b.hobby.sports.jersey_number = 66;

strcpy(c.name,"April");
c.age = 37;
c.hobby.television.hours_week = 60;

printf("Person A is %s, who is %d years old.\n",
a.name,a.age);
printf("A has played %s for %d years.\n\n",
a.hobby.music.instrument,\
        a.hobby.music.years_practice);
printf("Person B is %s, who is %d years old.\n",
b.name,b.age);
printf("B has plays %s and is number %d.\n\n",
b.hobby.sports.game,\
        b.hobby.sports.jersey_number);
printf("Person C is %s, who is %d years old.\n",
c.name,c.age);
printf("C watches TV %d hours a week.\n",
c.hobby.television.hours_week);

return(0);
}
```

After breathlessly typing this code, save it to disk as HOBBIES.C. Compile. Fix those booboos that always creep into long source code files. Then recompile. Run:

```
Person A is Alex, who is 17 years old.
A has played Guitar for 4 years.

Person B is Jerry, who is 22 years old.
B has plays Football and is number 66.

Person C is April, who is 37 years old.
C watches TV 60 hours a week.
```

Amazing. It works!

As I mention earlier in this chapter, you encounter unions mostly when you deal with programming the operating system or some device driver. Just remember that unions are accessed like structures and that they can hold only one type of data at a time.

Book IV

Advanced C

The 5th Wave   By Rich Tennant

Re'al Pro·gram·mers

Real Programmers drink lots of coffee, but never know how to use the coffee machine.

Contents at a Glance

Chapter 1: Introduction to Evil Pointers

In This Chapter

✔ Understanding variables and computer memory

✔ Using sizeof

✔ Finding memory locations with the & operator

✔ Creating pointer variables

✔ Storing memory locations in pointers

✔ Doing pointer math

There's this bug. It's called a fly in English. That's also what the bug does — it *flies*. So, a *fly flies*. Most people don't find that confusing, probably because everyone has had their share of flies buzzing around their heads. Saying that a fly flies makes perfect sense, and no one goes into brain lock (unless you get into the idea that a flea flees).

There's this thing in C. It's a variable called a *pointer*. That's also what the variable does — it *points* at something. *Pointers point*. Therein lies the rub: If pointers were called something else, budding C programmers would probably not sit and stew and suffer from brain lock over the concept.

This chapter begins to take a look at what many people consider to be the most awkwardly presented part of the C programming language: *pointers*. Besides their funny name, pointers are misunderstood because many folks who teach the C language don't fully understand pointers. Therefore, this is the first of several chapters on pointers, designed to ease you into the concept one baby step at a time.

You should save source code and programs you create for this part of the book in the advanced folder or directory on your computer's hard drive.

Basic Boring Computer Memory Stuff

Before you can understand pointers, you need to know about memory inside your computer.

You probably know that memory is also called RAM, or random access memory. The "random access" part means that the contents of memory can change. The other type of memory is ROM, or read-only memory, which cannot be changed. The computer's BIOS is an example of read-only memory.

Computer memory is used for information storage, for *data*. That's where programs run. The microprocessor directly accesses memory, either reading instructions or data, depending on whatever task is taking place.

Finally, computer memory is measured by the byte. A modern computer has millions of bytes of memory. Each byte lives at a specific location or address, just like houses on a street or apartments in a block.

That's good enough for today's memory lesson. I hope that most of it was review for you. Now, on to C language things.

Truly random memory

Here's an odd little program:

```
#include <stdio.h>

int main()
{
    char c;
    short int i;
    long x;
    float f;
    double d;

    printf("char variable c = %c\n",c);
    printf("int variable i = %d\n",i);
    printf("long variable x = %l\n",x);
    printf("float variable f = %f\n",f);
    printf("double variable d = %f\n",d);
    return(0);
}
```

Blindly type this source code into your editor. Name it ODDLITL.C. Compile. Run.

Your output may look something like this:

```
char variable c = w
int variable i = 0
long variable x = 4008344
float variable f = -1.499881
double variable d = -0.124941
```

You may see other, random values there, or you may just see zeroes. That's the whole point: The values are meaningless and random. Why? And, why didn't the program crash? After all, the variables were used, but never assigned anything. Doesn't that vex the compiler? Answers are coming up!

Buying the land, but not building the house

When you declare a variable in C, you're telling the compiler to set aside space for whatever value that type of variable stores. This process works just like building your dream house: First, you buy a piece of land, and then you build the house. You can't build the house first without the land, just as you can't assign a value to an undeclared variable.

In your computer, the land is memory.

When you need variables, you tell the compiler how many and of what type. The computer then builds a program that goes out and talks to the computer's real estate agent, who dishes up the proper portions of memory for your program.

✦ Variables must be stored somewhere. Computer memory is that *somewhere*. It's designed to hold information.

✦ Memory also holds the program while it's running.

✦ Memory is also referred to as RAM.

✦ Most people use the term RAM when they're writing a song about their computer, because more words rhyme with *RAM* than with *memory*.

Refer to the ODDLITL.C source code. Variables are created, but no value is assigned to them, which is similar to buying a lot and not building a house on it. What do you have in that case? You may call it a vacant lot, but something is always there: trees, scrub, a garbage, muck, radioactive waste — whatever. The same thing holds true for your computer's memory.

When your program assigns a variable some memory space, it doesn't clear out whatever information may already be stored there. Instead, the variable *assumes* whatever random information already exists, whether it's from a program you just ran or data that was previously in memory, just as a vacant lot *assumes* the scrub and trees that are already there. That's what the ODDLITL.C program displays: the random data already stored in your computer's memory. What that could be is anything.

The moral of the story is that you should always assign data to your variables *before* you use them. Otherwise, they assume random information in your PC, which is different from computer to computer. And, that's not the end of the story.

**Book IV
Chapter 1**

**Introduction to
Evil Pointers**

The compiler doesn't initialize new variables to 0. In other programming languages, variables that are declared may be assigned 0 to begin with, but not in C.

Some variables are greedier than others

Each variable you declare in your program consumes one or more bytes of memory. Sure, your program may start out innocently enough, but eventually those little bytes add up to kilobytes and megabytes, and then you're writing real programs and apologizing to your project manager about how the software needs 512MB of RAM just to load. But, enough about the next edition of Windows.

Make modifications to the ODDLITL.C source code so that it looks like what's shown here:

```
#include <stdio.h>

int main()
{
    char c;
    short int i;
    long x;
    float f;
    double d;

    puts("Variable sizes:");
    printf("Size of char variable c = %d\n",sizeof(c));
    printf("Size of int variable i = %d\n",sizeof(i));
    printf("Size of long variable x = %d\n",sizeof(x));
    printf("Size of float variable f = %d\n",sizeof(f));
    printf("Size of double variable d = %d\n",sizeof(d));
    return(0);
}
```

You're adding the handy `sizeof()` function to the code. What `sizeof()` does is covered in a few paragraphs. For now, save the changes to disk, compile, and run:

```
Variable sizes:
Size of char variable c = 1
Size of int variable i = 2
Size of long variable x = 4
Size of float variable f = 4
Size of double variable d = 8
```

The program no longer displays uninitialized variables. Instead, ODDLITL now divulges how much memory each variable is allocated by the compiler.

It uses the `sizeof` operator to determine how many bytes each variable sucks up. The program's output tells you the values: one byte for a `char`, two bytes for a `short int`, and so on (refer to the preceding code).

Note that `sizeof` is an *operator*, not a function, as I said earlier. (I claimed that it was a function because it looks like one, but also I didn't want to throw you.) In fact, `sizeof` is a C language keyword, according to Appendix D. So there!

The lowdown on `sizeof`

Here's how `sizeof` works:

```
i = sizeof(something);
```

The `sizeof` operator is followed by a set of parentheses, inside of which is a C language variable. It can be a traditional variable (`int` or `char`, for example), a `typedef` variable, a structure, a union, or any of the bits and pieces described as a variable in the C language. `sizeof` returns the number of bytes (the size) of the *something* variable. The value that's returned can be used directly or stored in an integer variable (`i`, in the preceding example).

Because `sizeof` is a keyword, it doesn't require a header file in order to work properly.

Note that `sizeof` works only with variables in C. It doesn't return the size of your program in memory, or the total amount of memory available to your program, or the entire amount of memory in your computer, or the entire amount of memory in Donna's computer.

The `sizeof` operator is necessary because not every computer uses the same storage space for its variables. Although this may not be an issue with desktop computers, it certainly is with mainframe and other computers. Be careful of what you assume when you write programs!

The `sizeof` operator is used mostly for allocating memory with the C language `malloc()` function. You use `sizeof` a lot when you're working with pointers and structures — specifically, the terrifying area of *linked lists*.

Calculating the size of an array

Aside from single variables, you can use the `sizeof` operator to return the size of an array. Here's the ODDLITL.C source code, now updated with an array declaration:

```
#include <stdio.h>

int main()
```

```
{
    char c;
    short int i;
    long x;
    float f;
    double d;
    char temp[8];

    puts("Variable sizes:");
    printf("Size of char variable c = %d\n",sizeof(c));
    printf("Size of int variable i = %d\n",sizeof(i));
    printf("Size of long variable x = %d\n",sizeof(x));
    printf("Size of float variable f = %d\n",sizeof(f));
    printf("Size of double variable d = %d\n",sizeof(d));
    printf("Size of the temp array = %d\n",sizeof(temp));
    return(0);
}
```

Make these changes to your ODDLITL.C source code. You're adding two lines — one to declare the array and a `printf()` to display its size.

Save your changes to disk. Compile and run. The last line of output now reads:

```
Size of the temp array = 8
```

An array of eight characters is eight bytes long — which follows because character variables measure one byte each.

What about short integer arrays?

Edit the ODDLITL.C source code and change the array to an array of short integers:

```
short int temp[8];
```

(You don't have to edit the `printf()` statement because it measures only the size of the array and doesn't use the array's data.)

Save. Compile. Run. You see a new amount for the size of the array:

```
Size of the temp array = 16
```

Integers — even short ones — are bigger than character variables. On your screen right now, in fact, you should see that a short integer is two bytes in size:

```
Size of int variable i = 2
```

Therefore, the array of integers requires 16 bytes of storage; an array of eight 2-byte integers (2×8 elements in the array) is 16 bytes long.

Although `sizeof` determines the size of an array, you must still rely on the `strlen()` function to get the size of a string in memory. Don't use `sizeof` as some kind of `strlen()` shortcut or alternative.

Exercise 4.1.1

Modify the ODDLITL.C source code again — this time, to discover how much memory is used when the `temp` variable is declared as a double.

Location & location & location

The compiler knows four things about any variable:

✦ Its name

✦ Its type (`char` or `int`, for example)

✦ Its size (in bytes)

✦ Its location in memory (its address)

You, O, program creator, know the variable's name and type because you were the one who entered that information (into your editor) when you first molded the program from clay. You can use the `sizeof` keyword to find out the variable's girth in memory, but, to find out where in memory the variable lives, you need the & unary operator.

Unary operators you probably already know about are `++` and `--` to increment and decrement, respectively, and the unary `-`, which makes a value negative. When the & operator is prefixed to a variable name, it returns the memory address of the variable. Here's another modification to the ODDLITL.C source code, to prove it:

```
#include <stdio.h>

int main()
{
    char c;
    short int i;
    long x;
    float f;
    double d;
    double temp[8];

    puts("Variable sizes:");
    printf("Memory location of char variable c = %p\n",&c);
```

```
printf("Memory location of int variable i = %p\n",&i);
printf("Memory location of long variable x = %p\n",&x);
printf("Memory location of float variable f = %p\n",&f);
printf("Memory location of double variable d = %p\n",&d);
for(i=0;i<8;i++)
    printf("Memory location of temp[%d] = %p\n",
i,&temp[I]);
return(0);
}
```

Modify ODDLITL.C, making the changes as shown here. Note the following:

✦ The variables in the `printf()` statement are prefixed by the & operator, which returns the variable's location or address in memory.

✦ The `printf()` placeholder %p is used to display the address value in hex. %p is the *pointer* placeholder. The only type of variable that can properly hold a memory location is a pointer.

✦ Note how variable i is used in the `for` loop. That way, you can see the memory location for each element in the array.

Save the changes to disk. Compile and run. The results you see on your computer are different from mine, but the flavor is similar:

```
Variable Sizes:
Memory location of char variable c = 0022FF87
Memory location of int variable i = 0022FF84
Memory location of long variable x = 0022FF80
Memory location of float variable f = 0022FF7C
Memory location of double variable d = 0022FF70
Memory location of temp[0] = 0022FF28
Memory location of temp[1] = 0022FF30
Memory location of temp[2] = 0022FF38
Memory location of temp[3] = 0022FF40
Memory location of temp[4] = 0022FF48
Memory location of temp[5] = 0022FF50
Memory location of temp[6] = 0022FF58
Memory location of temp[7] = 0022FF60
```

First, note how the variables are stored sequentially in memory, from higher locations through lower locations. The specific address is unique to each computer.

Second, note how each variable is of a proper size. This is harder to tell in hex, with the exception of the `double` array; the values in that array are each 8 bytes long, so the memory locations reflect that well in hex.

Third, there are gaps in memory. The reason is that the compiler likes to align variable values at specific locations. That may seem like a waste of space, but it lets the microprocessor more efficiently access the variables. (You don't have to worry about the gaps; with &, `sizeof`, and pointer variables, you have all the tools you need to work with memory.)

Finally, I have added Figure 1-1, which illustrates how the preceding output maps into memory. It helps to recall the values returned by `sizeof` when you look at how each variable type is stored in memory.

In your computer, a location is a spot in memory — called an *address*. Everything in your computer's memory has its own address, which tells everything else in the computer where that something lives and keeps things from living in the same spot.

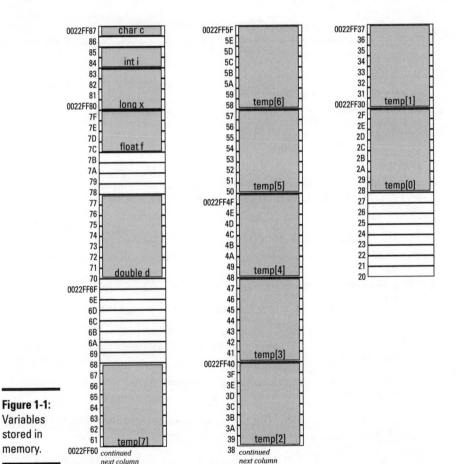

Figure 1-1: Variables stored in memory.

continued next column

Book IV Chapter 1

Introduction to Evil Pointers

How & works in `scanf()`

You have likely been using the `scanf()` function for some time now, blindly remembering to put an & before the variable's name or suffer some horrid error. But now you can open the door a bit on understanding why the ampersand is needed.

The `scanf()` function requires an ampersand to be used with its variables to help store values. In this case, the & operator works the same as described in the text; it returns the variable's memory location and not its value. That's because internally, `scanf()` relies on pointers to set the values it reads from the keyboard. Therefore, the real argument you're passing to the `scanf()` function isn't a variable name, but, rather, its location in memory. The placeholder that `scanf()` uses then determines the type and size of variable to place at that location in memory.

The & unary operator must be prefixed to the front of a variable type. If you put a space between & and the variable, & becomes a logical bitwise operator. I cover that subject elsewhere in this book, but for dealing with pointers, remember this: `&address` and not `& address`.

Exercise 4.1.2

Modify ODDLITL.C again. This time, change the `temp` array type back to `short int` and see how it changes the memory locations.

It all boils down to this

The compiler really saves you a great deal of work. Look what it does so far:

✦ Sets aside a certain chunk of memory for each variable you declare

✦ Knows exactly how much memory to set aside for the variable

✦ Knows how to organize an array so that it can find variables in the array — even though not every type of array holds variables of the same memory size

✦ Accesses the information stored in the variables and interprets that data properly (`chars` are characters, and `ints` are integers)

✦ Never calls you dirty names or says nasty things about you behind your back

So far, you have only half the equation. You know how much real estate (computer memory) variables and arrays require. You also know the real estate's address. But, what can you *do* with all that information? I cover this subject starting in the next section.

Some Pointers

The C language has tools that let you name a variable, set the variable type, find the size of the variable in memory, and determine the variable's location. To bring all that information together — and make it useful — the C language uses a tool called a *pointer*.

The simple definition of a pointer

A *pointer* is a variable that holds a memory address. Although that may be fun enough, the pointer variable is also custom designed to manipulate values stored at those memory addresses.

At first scare, pointers may seem silly. Why bother with pointers and memory locations when a variable's value can be affected with a simple statement that even nonprogrammers can easily understand:

```
a = b;
```

But, pointers can do more than just change values. Because they manipulate memory directly, they give you a power that other programming languages lack. This ability takes some time to understand — and it's important not to get ahead of yourself — so this book uncovers pointer details one step at a time.

A boring program that's suitable as an example

You never know when the United States may suddenly convert to the metric system. My guess: never. If we ever succumb to world pressure, you have this program ready to help you make the switch:

```c
#include <stdio.h>

#define KPM 1.609344

int main()
{
    float miles,kilometers;

    printf("Enter a value in miles:");
    scanf("%f",&miles);

    kilometers = miles*1.609;

    printf("%.2f miles works out to %.2f kilometers.\n",
    miles,kilometers);
    return(0);
}
```

Save the dopey thing to disk as METRIC.C. Compile and run.

```
Enter a value in miles:
```

Try to impress your metric-literate friends by telling them how long your commute is every day. Suppose that you trek 8½ miles every day. Type **8.5** and press the Enter key:

```
8.50 miles works out to 13.68 kilometers.
```

Wow. Much impressive. Put this program on the back burner for later.

Making Mr. Pointer

In the final incarnation of ODDLITL.C (earlier in this chapter), you use the & operator to divine the location in memory for a slew of variables. The & produces an immediate value, however, displayed by using `printf()`'s %p placeholder. To save the memory address, however, you need a pointer variable. That's because:

A *pointer* is a variable that holds a memory address.

Pointer variables are declared just like any other variable — with one exception: Pointer variable names are prefixed with an * (asterisk). Here's the format:

```
type *pointervar;
```

`type` is any type of variable: `char`, `int`, `double`, `float`, or `long`, for example.

`pointervar` is the name of the pointer, which is named just like any other variable in your programs. Pointer variables are always prefixed by an asterisk when they're declared. That's what identifies the variable as a pointer.

You may think that pointer variables need not be of a certain type. After all, pointers contain memory addresses, and all memory addresses are integer values right? But it's not the memory address that's important to the pointer. No, it's what *lives* at that address.

Just as you would need a special type of radio to hear the short-band frequency, you need special types of pointers to view specific types of variables.

Suppose that your program needs a pointer to examine a `short int` variable in memory. Here's how to create such a pointer:

```
short int *arrow;
```

In this line, a pointer variable named `arrow` is created. It can be used to store the address of any `short int` variable in your program. It cannot be used to store the address of any other type of variable. If you attempt such a thing, you get a "pointer mismatch" or some such error.

You can use this pointer to examine a `double` variable:

```
double *rainbow;
```

The type of pointer must match the type of variable it examines. The reason is that each variable's value is stored differently in memory. (I demonstrate this concept in the first part of this chapter.)

So, if you have these variables declared:

```
char c;
short int i;
long x;
```

you would need the following pointers to "play" with the preceding variables:

```
char *ptr2c;
short int *p2i;
long *pointer_to_x;
```

Note that each pointer variable name is unique, though in the preceding example I have included clues in the names to which variables the pointer is examining. (Also refer to Book III, Chapter 7 for information on Hungarian notation.)

Although you need the asterisk when you declare a pointer variable, whenever you *use* the pointer variable, it may or may not have its asterisk. Don't let that bother you now. Just remember that pointers need asterisks whenever they're declared.

Exercise 4.1.3

Write the four C language statements that would be required to make pointers for these variable declarations:

```
char key;
int start,end;
float seat_cushion;
```

The converted metric-conversion program

Summon the source code for METRIC.C back into your editor. Modify the program so that it looks like this:

```c
#include <stdio.h>

#define KPM 1.609344

int main()
{
    float miles,kilometers;
    float *pmiles;

    printf("Enter a value in miles:");
    scanf("%f",&miles);

    kilometers = miles*1.609;

    printf("%.2f miles works out to %.2f kilometers.\n",
    miles,kilometers);

    pmiles = &miles;                /* initialize pointer */
    printf("Variable 'miles' is %d bytes long at %p
    address\n",sizeof(miles),pmiles);
    return(0);
}
```

Here are the changes that are made:

✦ The pointer variable pmiles is declared in Line 8. It's a float pointer, which means that it's good for examining float-type variables. That makes sense because the only two other variables in the programs are floats.

✦ Note how the pointer variable is declared by using the * (asterisk). This is a must; it means that pmiles is a pointer variable, not a float. pmiles contains a memory address, the address of a float, but pmiles itself isn't a floating-point value.

✦ Like all variables, a pointer must be initialized before it's used. In Line 17, pmiles is assigned to the location of the variable miles in memory. The & is used to extract the address (memory location) of miles, not the value of miles.

✦ The asterisk is *not* used when a pointer variable is initialized.

✦ The printf() statement in Line 18 makes use of sizeof to get the size of the float variable miles in memory. Then it uses the %p placeholder to display the address of miles in memory.

+ Note that Line 18 works just like the printf() statements in the final incarnation of ODDLITL.C. The difference is that the memory address is stored in the pmiles pointer variable and isn't extracted by using an immediate value.

Save the changes to METRIC.C. Compile and run:

```
Enter a value in miles:
```

Type **10** and press the Enter key:

```
10.00 miles works out to 16.09 kilometers.
Variable 'miles' is 4 bytes long at 0022FF8C address
```

The float variable miles is 4 bytes in size and resides at memory address 0x0022FF8C. (You most likely see a different address on your screen.)

And now, an experiment. First, take note of the address that's returned for the miles variable. (Write it down, if necessary.) Next, modify the METRIC.C source code. Change Line 7 to read:

```
float kilometers,miles;
```

(You're just swapping miles and kilometers.) Save this change to disk. Then, compile and run. Specify the same input as you did the preceding time you ran the program:

```
Enter a value in miles: 10
10.00 miles works out to 16.09 kilometers.
Variable 'miles' is 4 bytes long at 0022FF88 address
```

Simply by changing the order in which the variables were declared, the program now reports that miles lives at address 0022FF88. In the preceding run, the program put miles at address 0022FF8C. The point is that memory locations vary, which is why pointer variables are needed to keep track of things in memory. But that's not the only reason for pointers. No, no, no, no!

This summary shows how pointers are used in a program:

+ Declare the pointer; it must exist before you can use it. It must also match the type of variable being examined: int for int or char for char, for example.

+ Initialize the pointer. Assign the pointer an address in memory; like other variables, it must be equal to something, or else it contains "garbage."

+ Use the pointer.

Pointers are one area where it's just too darn easy to get confused. I don't know how many times I have done this myself, but it's just plain wrong:

```
*m_address = &miles;
```

This operation works in C, but you get a warning error. That's because such a thing is most likely *not* what you intended. To initialize a pointer, you *do not* use the asterisk.

Pointers hold memory addresses. They literally *suck* them out of other variables.

Exercise 4.1.4

Modify the METRIC.C source code so that the pointer variable k_address is created. Assign to k_address the memory location of the kilometers variable. Print the result, similar to what was done for the miles variable.

Snagging the address of an array

Arrays aren't the same as regular variables in C. They're special. As such, you have special ways to deal with them when it comes to pointers. This is one of many exceptions with pointers that help drive beginning programmers mad. Pay close attention:

```
#include <stdio.h>

int main()
{
    char array[] = "Hello!\n";

    printf("%s",array);
    return(0);
}
```

This program is one of the simplest of all C programs. If you have been reading this book from the front cover to where your eyeballs are looking now, you can properly guess what the program does without even compiling it. That's fine because it's this contraption that I want you to observe closely:

```
#include <stdio.h>

int main()
{
    char array[] = "Hello!\n";
    char *a;

    printf("%s",array);
    a = array;
```

```
    printf("Array 'array' is %d bytes long and lives at %p
address.\n",sizeof(array),a);
    return(0);
}
```

Type this code into your editor as is. Don't make any smart-alecky adjustments. Just type, and then save it as HELLO.C. Compile and run.

What! No errors?

```
Hello!
Array 'array' is 8 bytes long and lives at 0022FF88 address.
```

To examine the string, or `char` array, a `char` pointer is needed. Before a pointer can be used, it must be initialized, which is done in Line 9, but note that this format is *not* used:

```
a = &array;
```

The missing ampersand is another one of those few weird exceptions in the C language — not as many exceptions as you get in French, but an exception anyway. For some reason, the compiler knows that an array name is an address already, so the ampersand becomes unnecessary. Here's the rule all spelled out:

If you don't need an & to read an array's address in C, why does `scanf()` still need an & in order to read a string?

As I mention earlier in this chapter, the `scanf()` function uses pointers to access variables. As such, the information you pass to `scanf()` is a variable's location in memory, not its name or value. But, in the section about snagging the address of an array, you find out that pointers don't need the & when obtaining the address of an array. If so, why does `scanf()` still need the & when reading in a string?

The answer is cryptic. (What else?) It has to do with how arrays are treated internally by the compiler. Deep down inside the compiler's bowels, arrays are really cleverly disguised pointers. The compiler makes the distinction when you declare and use an array in your code. But, internally, and specifically with `scanf()`, the & operator is still needed when working with a string variable name.

You may grow to understand this difference as you work with pointers — especially in later chapters. Until then, just chalk it up as *another* exception.

When you snag the address of an array into a pointer, you don't need the & operator before the array's name.

This rule holds true for all types of arrays, not just for char arrays. For a secret reason that you read about in Book IV, Chapter 4, the array's name is enough for the pointer to get what it needs. (You still need an & when you use an array in a scanf( ) function, but that's another story.)

Note that this type of assignment applies to only the full array itself. For individual elements, just like individual variables, the & is still needed. Here's another modification to the program:

```
#include <stdio.h>

int main()
{
    char array[] = "Hello!\n";
    char *a,*e;

    printf("%s",array);
    a = array;
    e = &array[1];
    printf("Array 'array' is %d bytes long and lives at %p
    address.\n",sizeof(array),a);
     printf("The second element of 'array' is %d bytes long
    and lives at %p address.\n",sizeof(array[1]),e);
     return(0);
}
```

Make these modifications to HELLO.C. Save the changed code to disk. Compile and run:

```
Hello!
Array 'array' is 8 bytes long and lives at 0022FF88 address.
The second element of 'array' is 1 bytes long and lives at
    0022FF89 address.
```

Exercise 4.1.5

Write a program based on HELLO.C where the address of each element of a character array is displayed. *Hint:* Use a for loop to stomp through each element of the array. Only one pointer variable needs to be used.

The Insanity of Pointer Arithmetic

Once again with the math! And, once again, I remind you: The computer does the math. You just plug in the numbers properly, and the program does the rest. This is true even when you do math with pointers, though, with pointers, a strange spice is added.

Elementary pointer math

I hope that you went through Exercise 4.1.5 because it points out one interesting and (another) difficult concept to grasp about pointers. Here's the encapsulation:

Pointers work in chunks the same size as their variable type.

Don't bother rereading it or trying to understand it now. Instead, quickly type this code:

```
#include <stdio.h>

int main()
{
    short int array[] = { 2, 3, 5, 7, 9 };
    int *pa;
    int x;

    for(x=0;x<5;x++)
    {
        pa = &array[x];
        printf("array[%d] at %p = %d\n",x,pa,array[x]);
    }
    return(0);
}
```

Save this to disk as PADD.C. Compile and run:

```
array[0] at 0022FF78 = 2
array[1] at 0022FF7A = 3
array[2] at 0022FF7C = 5
array[3] at 0022FF7E = 7
array[4] at 0022FF80 = 9
```

The output should make sense to you: Each array element takes up 2 bytes of memory; the value returned by `sizeof` for a `short int` is 2 bytes (on desktop computers). The address values returned by the `pa` pointer confirm it. Plus, I have illustrated it in Figure 1-2.

Now, make the following addition to the code. Place these lines just after the for loop's last curly brace and before the `return(0)` statement:

```
pa = array;
for(x=0;x<5;x++)
{
    printf("array[%d] at %p\n",x,pa);
    pa++;
}
```

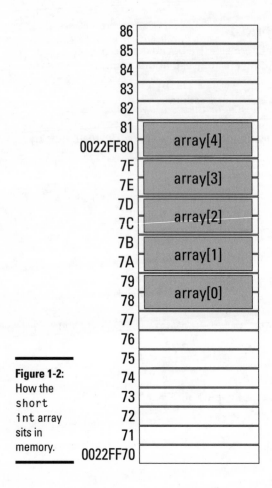

Figure 1-2:
How the
`short`
`int` array
sits in
memory.

This code adds a second loop. First, the pointer variable pa is initialized to the start of the array. Then, the loop increments pa five times. Save the program to disk. Recompile and run:

```
array[0] at 0022FF78 = 2
array[1] at 0022FF7A = 3
array[2] at 0022FF7C = 5
array[3] at 0022FF7E = 7
array[4] at 0022FF80 = 9
array[0] at 0022FF78
array[1] at 0022FF7A
array[2] at 0022FF7C
array[3] at 0022FF7E
array[4] at 0022FF80
```

At the start of the new `for` loop, the variable `pa` contains the address `0022FF78` (see the preceding code). In your normal brain, you would assume that adding 1 to `pa`, or `pa++`, would make the value `0022FF79`. But, no!

When you increment a `short int` pointer, the pointer then contains the next address of the next `short int` in memory.

Math with pointers isn't at all like math with numbers. Because pointers deal with memory, adding, subtracting, multiplying, dividing, or doing any math with pointers makes calculations for whatever variable size the pointer is examining. Figure 1-3 tries to explain this concept visually.

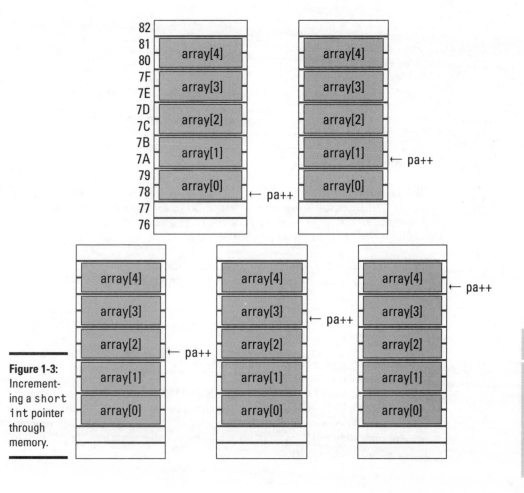

Figure 1-3: Incrementing a `short int` pointer through memory.

More to the pointer

If you can accept that pointers work in the same chunk size as their variable type, you can almost guess the answer to the next programming puzzle. If you can, you're free to move on to Book IV, Chapter 2:

```
#include <stdio.h>

int main()
{
    float rootbeer;
    float *pr;

    pr = &rootbeer;
    printf("The address of variable rootbeer is %p\n",pr);
    printf("The next float in memory will be at ??\n");
    return(0);
}
```

Type this bit of code. Save it to disk as PFLOAT.C. Compile and run:

```
The address of variable rootbeer is 0022FF8C
The next float in memory will be at ??
```

Can you guess?

Okay, then: I'll try. A `float` is 4 bytes in size on my computer, according to the `sizeof` operator's report way earlier in this chapter, in the ODDLITL.C program. So, if `rootbeer` is 4 bytes in size at `0022FF8C`, the next `float` in memory would sit 4 bytes away from that location.

Ah! To heck with it. Because the pointer variable `pr` is a `float`, the easiest way to calculate the value is just to add 1 to the variable `pr`! Modify Line 10 to read:

```
printf("The next float in memory will be at %p\n",pr+1);
```

```
The address of variable rootbeer is 0022FF8C
The next float in memory will be at 0022FF90
```

If you still find it odd that `pr + 1` equals `0022FF90` and not `0022FF8D`, you're normal. That's because you have been using real math and not pointer math. Once again: When you do math with a pointer, the chunks that are involved are the same size as the type of variable the pointer examines. In the preceding example, that's 4 bytes for a `float`.

Internally, I suppose that the compiler sees `pr + 1` as `pr + 4`. But, most likely, what happens is this:

```
pr + (1 * sizeof(float))
```

The compiler converts the number into the variable size. So, if you were working with `long` integers, it would be

```
pr + (1 * sizeof(long))
```

The point to remember is that pointer math isn't incremental, like regular math; rather, the pointer is manipulated in chunks. The size of the chunks are equal to the variable size. And, that's about all your brain needs to know right now.

Hoppity, skippity, hoppity, skippity.

Chapter 2: Getting to the *Point

In This Chapter

✔ Using the * with a pointer

✔ Spying on a variable's values

✔ Changing values with a pointer

✔ Sharing one pointer with several variables

*P*ity the pointer. The sad little guy has so much potential, yet so few friends. Being misunderstood can be emotionally painful. To his allies, and to those who understand him, the pointer is a hero. He's indispensable. To those who don't know him, sadly, he's an unapproachable mystery. Socially awkward. Clumsy. Prone to error. Give him time, dear reader, give him time.

Book IV, Chapter 1 was just a warm-up to the concept of pointers. The true power of the pointer variable has yet to be revealed. Beyond that — the place in C where pointers aren't only valuable but also necessary — is yet to come. Still, like Book IV, Chapter 1, this chapter takes things one step at a time. So, sit back, take it easy, and relax with a cup of a soothing beverage. And, continue your odyssey into the land of the point.

Pointer Review

Make sure that you know the following things. If you're fuzzy on any one of them, review the preceding chapter until you have this stuff pretty much inside your head:

✦ Variables take up different amounts of space in memory. The `sizeof` operator tells you how much space each variable hogs up.

✦ The & operator is used to obtain the address, or location in memory, of a variable.

✦ A *pointer* is a variable that contains a memory address.

✦ Pointer variables are declared to be of the same type as the variables they examine: `char` for `char` and `int` for `int`, for example.

✦ Pointer variables are declared and named like any other variable, though the name is prefixed with an * (asterisk).

- Pointer variables must be assigned an address before they can be used. They must be *initialized.*

  The preceding point gets C programmers in more trouble than anything, so let me repeat it:

  Pointer variables must be assigned an address before they can be used. They must be *initialized.*

- To get the address of any variable, you need the & (address-of) operator. The address is then given to the pointer variable, like any assignment in C:

  ```
  pvar = &whatever;
  ```

- You don't use the * when you're initializing a pointer, as shown here.

- You don't need the & when you're assigning a pointer to an array.

- You do need the & when you're assigning a pointer to an array element.

- The value contained inside the pointer is a memory address, which can be displayed with the printf() function and the %p placeholder.

- When pointers are incremented or decremented, they point at the next chunk of memory, not at the next memory location. If the pointer is a float and you increment the pointer's value, it points at the next memory address that would hold a float, usually 4 bytes away.

And Now, the Asterisk, Please

To add even more confusion to the pointer variable (if Book IV, Chapter 1 wasn't enough), know that there are two modes of operation for the typical pointer variable: with or without the asterisk.

In Book IV, Chapter 1, pointer variables were used without the asterisk. That's how pointers are initialized. By name only, pointers hold a memory address. But, adding the asterisk? That opens up a whole new aspect of how pointers are used.

Pointers that point and peek

Consider the pointer variable arrow:

```
arrow
```

By itself, pointer arrow represents a memory location — if it has been properly initialized. Otherwise, like any other uninitialized variable, it holds garbage:

```
arrow = &oblio;
```

After the pointer has been initialized, it holds the memory location of some variable. In this example, the arrow pointer holds the address of variable oblio.

After the pointer is initialized, it can be prefixed with the * unary operator, also known as the pointer operator:

```
*arrow
```

The * used here isn't the same as the * multiplication operator. For that, you need a space between * and arrow. But, when the * touches the variable name and the variable is a pointer, a new mode of operation is entered.

Like an open eye, a pointer variable with an asterisk is used to peek into a memory location, divulging the contents thereof. So, *arrow tells you what value dwells at the memory location stored in arrow, which is the value of the variable oblio.

I like to think of the asterisk as an eye. Other programs pronounce the * as "Show me what lives at. . . ."

The pointer is a snoopy mailman

The following silly demo program shows how a pointer variable is used with an asterisk. It shows the pointer used both with and without an asterisk — merely more confusion to stir into the soup:

```c
#include <stdio.h>

int main()
{
    int teeny;
    int *t;

/* initialize variables */
    teeny = 1;
    t = &teeny;

/* use and abuse variables */
    printf("Variable teeny = %d\n",teeny);
    printf("Variable t = %p\n",t);
    printf("Variable *t = %d\n",*t);
    return(0);
}
```

Type this source code into your editor. Save this trivial little program as TEENY.C. Compile and run. Here's a sample of the output:

```
Variable teeny = 1
Variable t = 0022FF8C
Variable *t = 1
```

First comes the value of the variable `teeny`. Assigning a value to a variable is one of the first things you find out about in C, so this should make sense.

Second comes the value of variable `t`, which is equal to the address, or location in memory, of the variable `teeny`.

Third comes the contents found at the memory location referenced by the pointer variable `t`. The value is properly interpreted as an integer because that's the type of pointer that's used.

To sum it all up: The pointer with its asterisk shows you what value lives at an address in memory.

When you initialize a pointer to look at a specific variable in memory:

```
t = &teeny;
```

this line is true:

```
*t == teeny
```

This line assumes, of course, that `teeny` has been initialized. Otherwise, `*t` would point to the same random garbage that uninitialized `teeny` would contain.

Exercise 4.2.1

Modify the source code for TEENY.C. Change the variable types for `teeny` and `t` from `int` to `float`. Modify the conversion characters in the various `printf()` statements. Finally, change the value assigned to `teeny` equal to `1.414213`.

Using *pointers to Modify Variables

After being initialized, as in

```
p = &var;
```

referring to the pointer variable with an asterisk is the same as referring to the original variable:

```
*p == var
```

If you change *p, var changes. Likewise, if you change var, *p changes. That may make pointers seem redundant — and it does! But, you have to know this trick first, before you discover more powerful pointer ploys.

Changing a variable's value with a pointer

When the contents of a variable change, the pointer to that variable reflects the change. So, if the TEENY.C program (from the preceding section) is modified so that the value of teeny changes, the *t pointer reflects that new value as well. This bit of code demonstrates:

```
#include <stdio.h>

int main()
{
    int teeny;
    int *t;

/* initialize variables */
    teeny = 1;
    t = &teeny;

/* use and abuse variables */
    printf("Variable teeny = %d\n",teeny);
    printf("Variable t = %p\n",t);
    printf("Variable *t = %d\n",*t);

    teeny = 64;
    printf("Variable teeny = %d\n",teeny);
    printf("Variable t = %p\n",t);
    printf("Variable *t = %d\n",*t);

    return(0);
}
```

Save the modified source code to disk. Compile and run.

Here's the output:

```
Variable teeny = 1
Variable t = 0022FF8C
Variable *t = 1
Variable teeny = 64
Variable t = 0022FF8C
Variable *t = 64
```

This shouldn't be a surprise. But, how about this? Change Line 17 to read

```
*t = 64;
```

Save. Compile. Run.

The output is the same. Why? Because you didn't really change anything. Using the variable *t is the same as using teeny in the program. That's basically the point of pointers.

In the equation *t = 64, you're placing the value 64 into the memory location referenced by the pointer variable t. It doesn't change or reinitialize the address, but it *does* change the value stored at that address.

Don't do this:

```
t = 64;
```

This example attempts to stick memory location 64 into the variable t. The compiler coughs and hacks at such a thing; the action initializes a pointer to a specific address. What lives at address 64? I don't know, but it's probably very creepy.

C gurus say that *t accesses the contents of variable teeny "indirectly." That makes sense: The pointer snuck around the neighborhood, found out teeny's address, and then peeked in the window to see what value was there.

One pointer for everyone to share

You don't need a pointer for every variable. Pointers can be shared. As long as the pointer's type matches the type of variable (int for int or char for char, for example), you can reuse old pointers just as Grandma reuses old pie tins. Here's a sample program:

```c
#include <stdio.h>

int main()
{
    int start,finish;
    int *examine;

    start = 100;
    finish = 9;

    examine = &start;
```

```
    printf("%d little old ladies started the race.\n",
*examine);
    examine = &finish;
    printf("But only %d little old ladies finished.\n",
*examine);
    return(0);
}
```

Save this source code to disk as LOLS.C. Compile and run:

```
100 little old ladies started the race.
But only 9 little old ladies finished.
```

The same variable, *examine, is used in both printf() statements. But, the value of *examine differs because it's used to look at two different variables — first start and then finish. As with other types of variables, the contents of a pointer variable — and what the pointer points at — can change.

Here's a subtle modification to the LOLS.C source code:

```
#include <stdio.h>

int main()
{
    int start,finish;
    int *examine;

    examine = &start;
    *examine = 100;
    printf("%d little old ladies started the race.\n",
start);
    examine = &finish;
    *examine = 9;
    printf("But only %d little old ladies finished.\n",
finish);
    return(0);
}
```

Save this update to disk. Compile and run.

The output is unchanged, but the program certainly is changed! Observe how neither start nor finish is initialized directly. Indirectly, though, the pointer variable examine is used to initialize both start and finish. It works flawlessly, as the preceding code demonstrates.

Exercise 4.2.2

Here's the MOON.C program from Book I, Chapter 4:

```c
#include <stdio.h>

int main()
{
    float duration;
    float distance = 378921.46;
    float speed = 140;

    duration =  distance / speed;

    printf("The moon is %f km away.\n",distance);
    printf("Traveling at %f kph, ",speed);
    printf("it would take %f hours to drive to the
moon.\n",duration);
    return(0);
}
```

Modify this source code so that a pointer variable, d, is created. Redesign the program so that the `printf()` statements use only the variable d to display the same results as the original code, just shown.

Chapter 3: Binary Bits

In This Chapter

✔ Understanding base two, binary

✔ Using bits, bytes, words, and long words

✔ Shifting bits left or right

✔ Shortcutting hexadecimal for binary

✔ Performing bitwise logical operations

✔ Displaying binary values

✔ Manipulating bits in unusual ways

*B*inary is the true language of the computer. Forget this C language stuff! The computer *lives* for binary! All the programming you do, all that language and source code, it eventually ends up as binary inside the computer. That's because, deep down, binary is all the computer understands: ones and zeroes.

One blessing of the C language is that it's pretty good at dealing with binary information. The only language I know of that's better is assembly language, which is sadly neglected in today's multimegabyte, gigahertz, I-need-the-software-this-afternoon world.

If you have been reading this book sequentially, you know darn well that it's time for a break from pointers! What better way to soothe your aching brain than by taking a dive into the highly logical realm of the binary digit or bit? Believe it or not, some of this stuff is quite useful! Forget your fingers and toes for an hour or so, and be prepared to immerse yourself in the gentle waters of ones and zeroes.

Say Hello to Mr. Bit

Bit is a contraction of *binary dig*it. There are only two binary digits: 0 and 1. So, a bit itself can be only one or zero. If you're more creative, you can also think of a bit as true or false, up or down, in or out, off or on, male or female, night or day, good or evil, yin and yang, and so on.

Counting by twos

Remember this guy.

I remember him as the Little Man with the Stupid Hat, and he taught me how the decimal system works.

The Little Man with the Stupid Hat has 10 fingers — just like you and me, boys and girls! That makes sense. But the real reason that he has 10 fingers is to show you how the 1s, 10s, and 100s positions work to help represent big numbers.

In Figure 3-1, you see the Little Man with the Stupid Hat helping to represent the value 379. That's three 100s, seven 10s, and nine 1s. Put it together, and you get 379. Not that such a trick lets you truly recognize 379 of something, but it clues you in to how the number is represented in decimal.

Figure 3-1:
The number 379 in decimal, care of the Little Man with the Stupid Hat.

Okay! You either get it or you don't.

I want to use a similar idea to present the binary counting system. Presenting *Binary Man!*

Unlike the Little Man with the Stupid Hat, Binary Man has only one finger. He can only count to one. Well, he can count to both zero and one; zero fingers shows zero, and one finger shows one. Toss in a few brothers, and, just like the decimal counting system with the Little Man with the Stupid Hat, Binary Man and his brothers can also count up to large values.

With only one finger, Binary Man counts by twos, not by tens. The first position is 1s, the second is 2s, and then come 4s, 8s, 16s, and up, each time double the amount of the previous Binary Man (see Figure 3-2). It may seem weird, but it's quite effective.

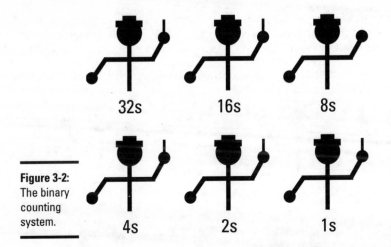

Figure 3-2:
The binary counting system.

Then again, what is a value? Humans have 10 fingers, 5 on each hand. But what is 10? Figure 3-3 illustrates how the value 10 is written in a variety of languages by a variety of cultures. Which is right? Which is 10 of anything?

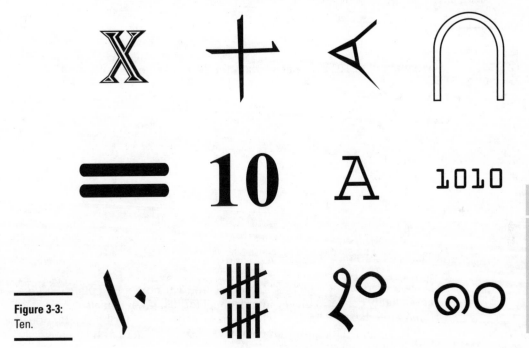

Figure 3-3:
Ten.

The binary representation for 10 is 1010. Figure 3-4 shows how Binary Man would illustrate this concept. Ten turns out to be 8 plus 2 in binary lingo, or 1010. Do you need to memorize that? Nope! But, you should understand how it works.

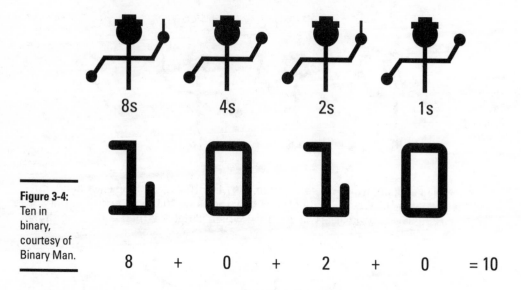

Figure 3-4:
Ten in binary, courtesy of Binary Man.

$$8 \quad + \quad 0 \quad + \quad 2 \quad + \quad 0 \quad = 10$$

What about 1010110? That's binary for 86. Here's how it works out:

1×64

0×32

1×16

0×8

1×4

1×2

0×1

That's 64 + 16 + 4 + 2. Add 'em up and you get 86.

Do you need to know all this? Of course not! The computer counts for you and handily converts binary into decimal for display. It can also convert binary into hexadecimal, which is kind of a shorthand for binary. But, deep inside, you need to know that computers use this binary system natively. That's important to understand.

Forget the math! Accept that computers use and understand binary.

Bits and bytes and words and long words

Bits don't just drift around inside your computer like rubber ducks in a pond. Nope, they're organized. In a modern desktop computer, bits are packed 8 to a *byte,* with the byte the basic measurement of storage inside a computer.

Two bytes can be referenced together to form a *word.* This is the same size chunk of memory that's used to denote a `short int` value. Conveniently, a word composed of 16 bits can represent values from –32,678 through 32,767 or from 0 to 65,535 unsigned. It's freaky how that works.

Finally, 4 bytes are referenced in a single chunk to represent a *long word,* which is also conveniently a `long` integer or the same size chunk of memory used to store a `float`.

Figure 3-5 illustrates how bits are organized into bytes, words, and long words. These are also the convenient chunks by which the computer's microprocessor can access memory. And, despite the fact that the microprocessor can easily digest a long word chunk, memory is still measured by the byte (kilobyte, megabyte, and gigabyte).

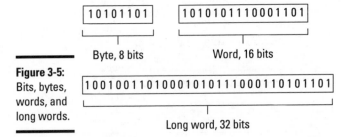

Figure 3-5:
Bits, bytes, words, and long words.

Not every computer uses 8 bits to the byte. Some older mainframes operate on 7 bits per byte. And, I believe that one series of computers had 9, 10, or even 12 bits per byte. Though these systems are uncommon, they may still exist. So, if you want your code to run on a wide variety of computers, don't assume that there are always 8 bits in a byte.

**Book IV
Chapter 3**

Binary Bits

Expressing binary values by using hexadecimal

Normally, programmers don't write down information in raw binary. It's just too easy to mess things up. This isn't unique to binary; writing long numbers in decimal is just as ugly:

What value is that? Well, it helps to break things up with commas or periods or however one's culture does it. In the United States, commas are used to split large values into 3-digit chunks:

```
200,049,623
```

The same holds true for binary values, though they can get long quickly:

```
10111110110010000011111010111
```

Yikes! What programmers do first is to split up the binary value into *nybble*-size chunks. A nybble is half a byte, or 4 bits. (Ha-ha. Get it?)

```
1011 1110 1100 1000 0011 1101 0111
```

In this line, the same binary value is a little easier to read. In fact, some geek at some university may even be able to understand the preceding value and tell you instantly what its decimal counterpart is. (If so, they probably don't let that guy out much.)

The best solution at hand, however, is to use hexadecimal as a type of binary shorthand. I mention this briefly in Book II, Chapter 2. If you break up binary numbers into 4-bit chunks, 16 combinations are possible for the ones and zeroes. They correspond directly with the 16 digits in the hexadecimal counting system. Table 3-1 illustrates this relationship.

Table 3-1		Hexadecimal and Binary Conversion Table	
Hex	*Bin*	*Hex*	*Bin*
0	0000	8	1000
1	0001	9	1001
2	0010	A	1010
3	0011	B	1011
4	0100	C	1100
5	0101	D	1101
6	0110	E	1110
7	0111	F	1111

Return to the binary value.

If you replace each 4-bit chunk with its corresponding hexadecimal match, you end up with

```
1011 1110 1100 1000 0011 1101 0111
B    E    C    8    3    D    7
```

or the value 0xBEC83D7.

Here's your Question of the Day: As a programmer, which is easier to bandy about?

```
1011 1110 1100 1000 0011 1101 0111
```

or

0xBEC83D7

Even though hexadecimal may make that letter home to Mom shorter, remember that inside the computer, it's all binary.

Exercise 4.3.1
What's the decimal equivalent for 0xBEC83D7? Name the program BEC83D7.C.

Basic Bit Twiddling

The C language comes replete with a smattering of operators that let you manipulate integer values at the bit level. In programmer's parlance, it's known as *bit twiddling*. The infamous C language bitwise operators are listed in Table 3-2.

Table 3-2	C Language Bitwise Operators
Operator	*What It Does*
<<	Shifts bits to the left
>>	Shifts bits to the right
&	Bitwise AND operator
|	Bitwise OR operator
^	Bitwise Exclusive OR operator
~	Bitwise one's complement

The values that are manipulated must be integers. Why? Because integers fit 0 so nicely into bytes, words, and other handy-size chunks that are well-suited for binary manipulation. Floating-point values are binary in nature, but they're not stored in the same straightforward binary manner as integers. Therefore, they're not useful for bitwise operators to manipulate.

The << and >> operators are, in fact, the same as the put-to and get-from operators (*inserters* and *extractors*) in the C++ language. The C++ IOSTREAM library merely adds input-output functionality to the existing bitwise operators.

Doing the bit hula

The >> operator is used to shift the bits in a value to the right. Conveniently, the >> operator also points to the right, so that should help remind you about the direction of the shift.

Here's a simple right-shift of one bit:

1101 0110

This value is one byte. In hex, it's 0xD6 or 214 in decimal. Shifting the bits to the right one notch yields this value:

0110 1011

That's 0x6B or 107 in decimal. Each bit from the original value was marched one place to the left. The bit on the far right? It was blasted off into infinity. The bit on the far left? It's always 0. This is a bitwise *shift*, not a *cycle*. (In a cycle, or rotate, the bit hopping off the end on the right would reappear on the left.)

Did you notice anything else about the bit shift?

Yes: The original value is *cut in half* by the shift. This is just the nature of binary; shifting any value one notch to the right cuts the value in half.

This type of division isn't perfect; dividing an odd number in half yields a whole number integer result (for example, 15 divided by shifting equals 7, not 7.5). Still, dividing a value in this manner is much quicker than using division. That's because the microprocessor can shift bits several hundred times faster than it does division. It's time for a sample program!

```
#include <stdio.h>

int main()
{
    int v,r;

    printf("Enter an integer value: ");
    scanf("%d",&v);
    r = v >> 1;      /* shift bits one notch right */
    printf("%d cut in half is %d\n",v,r);
    return(0);
}
```

Save this source code to disk as SHIFTR.C. Compile and run:

```
Enter an integer value:
```

Be fair the first time. Type **300**. Press Enter:

```
300 cut in half is 150
```

Smart computer! Good computer!

Run the program again and enter 99:

```
99 cut in half is 49
```

Oh, well. So much for the division speed shortcut.

The official >> format

One mistake I often make — probably from my years of programming in assembly language — is thinking of >> as always shifting *one* place to the left. But here's the official format for the >> operator:

```
result = value >> steps;
```

`value` is the immediate value or variable being manipulated. `steps` is the number of steps to the right the bits in value are shifted. The `result` is, like, the result!

Rather than just shift everything over 1 spot, you can do leaps of 2 or 3 — or more. In fact, there's no checking; you could shift a `short int` value to the right 99 places. The value of such a thing is dubious, of course, but you can do it.

There's also the shortcut format:

```
value >>= steps;
```

In this format, the `value` is shifted over a given number of `steps` and the result stored back in `value`. This is quite close to the exact machine language instruction that shifts bits inside the microprocessor.

Exercise 4.3.2

Modify the source code to SHIFTR.C so that the value is quartered rather than halved. Be sure to change the output to reflect this.

**Book IV
Chapter 3**

Binary Bits

Exercise 4.3.3

No, integers don't have fractional parts, so bit-shifting doesn't truly divide some values in half. Even so, would bit-shifting work on floating-point values and yield a proper result when they're divided by 2 or 4?

Shifting to the left

Just as >> marches bits off to their death on the right, the << marches bits out of a value to their death on the left. Any bits falling off the edge are lost and forgotten. To make up for the missing bits, zeroes are inserted on the right; for example:

```
0101 0110
```

This value is 0x56 or 86 in decimal. Shifting this value to the left one notch yields

```
1010 1100
```

Now, the value is 0xAC, or 172 in decimal — double the original value.

Shifting bits to the left *doubles* an integer value, one double per shift. As with shifting to the right, this math operation is much faster and more efficient for the microprocessor than trying to use multiplication. How about a demo program?

```c
#include <stdio.h>

int main()
{
    int v,r,x;

    printf("Enter an integer value: ");
    scanf("%d",&v);
    for(x=1;x<8;x++)
    {
        r = v << x;
        printf("%d << %d = %d\n",v,x,r);
    }
    return(0);
}
```

Save this source code to disk as LEFTR.C. Compile and run:

```
Enter an integer value:
```

Type **2** and press Enter:

```
2 << 1 = 4
2 << 2 = 8
2 << 3 = 16
2 << 4 = 32
2 << 5 = 64
2 << 6 = 128
2 << 7 = 256
```

Ah! The holy numbers of computing! *Om!*

Try some other values too.

Exercise 4.3.4

Is your interest in assembly language piqued? Would you like to become an assembly language programmer for a few minutes — even though you're using C? Remember that C is kind of a low-level language, or at least it's capable of such stuff. In any case, I can grant your wish if you complete one small task.

No, forget about the witch's broomstick. Instead, write a program that multiplies a value by 10 using the << operator to perform the multiplication. Don't use a loop or the * symbol!

Yes! It can be done! But you must *think* like an assembly language programmer, not a C programmer.

Please give this a try before you peek in Appendix C to uncover the answer.

The Utter Inanity of Binary Logic

Binary logic is the same as the AND/OR logic you can use when you're comparing things in C. Rather than use the && for a logical AND, you use & for a bitwise AND. Rather than use the | | for a logical OR, you use | for a bitwise OR. The comparisons are the same, but they're conducted at the bit level.

Yes, this does seem utterly useless. But you can do some cool tricks with logical binary operations. (Sadly, most of the really cool tricks happen with graphics, but I have to save those for another time.)

Using the AND mask

I prefer to think of the bitwise logical AND operation as a mask — a way of filtering or testing certain bits. Logically, the AND operation works as described in Table 3-3.

Table 3-3	The Results of Logical AND on Bits		
Bit	*AND*	*Bit*	*Result*
1	&	1	1
1	&	0	0
0	&	1	0
0	&	0	0

Obviously, you need to get dirty with bits if you want to make sense of bit-wise logical AND. But I'm not totally dry on ideas here.

For example, consider whether you want to split a 16-bit word into its two 8-bit byte values. The first step, as shown in Figure 3-6, is to use a logical AND to mask off the upper 8 bits of the 16-bit word, which leaves you with just the lower half.

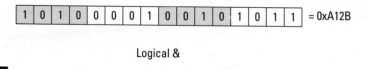

= 0xA12B

Logical &

Figure 3-6:
Splitting a word into two bytes: the lower byte.

= 0x00FF

=

= 0x002B

The second step, as shown in Figure 3-7, is to use a logical AND to mask off the lower 8 bits and then right-shift the upper 8 bits into the lower 8 bits. The result is two 8-bit values from one 16-bit value. In many places, this type of operation may be necessary, and if you hear of any, please e-mail me at the address listed in the Introduction to this book.

Here's the code:

```c
#include <stdio.h>

int main()
{
    unsigned short int hex,upper,lower;

    printf("Enter a four-digit hex value: ");
    scanf("%x",&hex);
```

```
lower = hex & 0x00FF;
upper = hex & 0xFF00;
upper >> = 8;

printf("0x%04X is composed of %02X and %02X\n",
hex,upper,lower);

return(0);
}
```

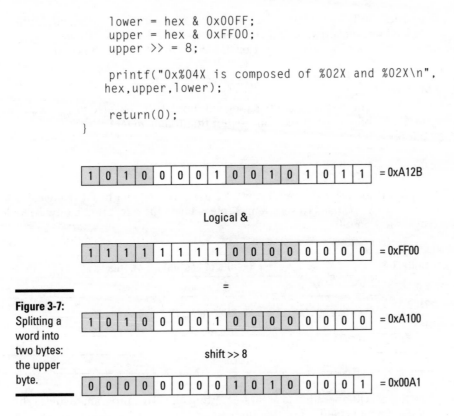

Figure 3-7:
Splitting a
word into
two bytes:
the upper
byte.

Save this source code to disk as SPLIT.C. Compile and run:

```
Enter a four-digit hex value:
```

Type something interesting, such as **FACE**. Press Enter:

```
0xFACE is composed of FA and CE
```

Some things to note:

Book IV
Chapter 3

Binary Bits

+ `unsigned short int` values were used to avoid weirdness that occurs
  with signed `short int`s. Don't bother asking me what; just remove the
  `unsigned` if you want to see the weirdness.

+ The `%x` placeholder in `scanf()` is used in entering hexadecimal numbers.

+ The `%X` placeholder in the `printf()` function ensures that the hex numbers appear as output in ALL CAPS. This helps identify them as hex numbers and not some random pointer garbage.

✦ The 0 and 4 or 2 between the %X placeholders do two things. First, the leading 0 ensures that leading zeroes pad the number. That way, the value 1 is displayed as 0001 or 01. The 4 and the 2 set the width.

Exercise 4.3.5

Modify SPLIT.C so that it splits a long word or 32-bit unsigned integer value into four 8-bit values. (Come on! It's not that tough. In fact, it's rather pretty source code.)

One OR in the water

Where the logical AND operator can be used to mask out bits, the logical OR operator can be used to set them. Table 3-4 lists the effect that a bitwise logical OR has on bits.

Table 3-4		The Results of Logical OR on Bits	
Bit	*OR*	*Bit*	*Result*
1	|	1	1
1	|	0	1
0	|	1	1
0	|	0	0

The logical OR operation is great for setting bits. This program divulges this, though I admit that it's not that impressive:

```c
#include <stdio.h>

int main()
{
    int twos[] = { 1,     2,     4,      8,
                   16,    32,    64,     128,
                   256,   512,   1024,   2048,
                   4096,  8192,  16384,  32768 };
    int x,r;
    unsigned short int v = 0;

    for(x=0;x<16;x++)
    {
        r = v | twos[x];
        printf("0x%04X | %5d = 0x%04X\n",v,twos[x],r);
    }
    return(0);
}
```

Type this source code, saving it to disk as OAR.C. Compile and run.

```
0x0000  |      1 = 0x0001
0x0000  |      2 = 0x0002
0x0000  |      4 = 0x0004
0x0000  |      8 = 0x0008
0x0000  |     16 = 0x0010
0x0000  |     32 = 0x0020
0x0000  |     64 = 0x0040
0x0000  |    128 = 0x0080
0x0000  |    256 = 0x0100
0x0000  |    512 = 0x0200
0x0000  |   1024 = 0x0400
0x0000  |   2048 = 0x0800
0x0000  |   4096 = 0x1000
0x0000  |   8192 = 0x2000
0x0000  |  16384 = 0x4000
0x0000  |  32768 = 0x8000
```

Yawn.

Yup: It's boring. But, you come back to it later. *Heh, heh.*

Exercise 4.3.6
Rewrite the code to OAR.C so that the twos[] array isn't needed.

Displaying Binary Values

Sadly, the printf() function lacks any ability to output values in binary format. But that doesn't mean that you can write your own function to display binary values! Of course! Now that you know how to shift bits and the logical & operation, it's a snap!

The BinString() function

Submitted for your approval:

```
#include <stdio.h>

void binString(int n);

int main()
{
```

```
    unsigned short int value;

    printf("Enter an integer value, 0 to 65,535: ");
    scanf("%d",&value);

    printf("Decimal value is %d\n",value);
    printf("Hexadecimal value is 0x%X\n",value);
    printf("Binary value is ");
    binString(value);
    putchar('\n');
    return(0);
}

void binString(int n)
{
    char bin[17];
    int x;

    for(x=0;x<16;x++)
    {
        bin[x] = n & 0x8000 ? '1' : '0';
        n <<= 1;
    }
    bin[16] = '\0';
    printf("%s",bin);
}
```

Carefully type this code. The important part is the binString() function, which displays a value using binary digits. I tell you more about that in a second. Save the source code to disk as BINBIN.C.

Compile. Run:

```
Enter an integer value, 0 to 65,535:
```

Type your favorite short int value. Mine is **30000**. Press Enter:

```
Decimal value is 30000
Hexadecimal value is 0x7530
Binary value is 0111010100110000
```

Holy smokes! It works. But, how? Ponder these notes:

+ binString() is designed specifically around the 16-bit integer value. That's why the string variable has room for only 17 elements; 16 binary characters and then the NULL byte.

✦ Line 27 uses one of those weirdo ?: contraptions — which I swore that I would never use in this book! But, in this instance, it was just too clever to pass up. Here's the code that Line 27 replaces:

```
if(n & 0x8000)
    bin[x] = '1';
else
    bin[x] = '0';
```

✦ See Book II, Chapter 6 for more information on ?:.

✦ Line 27 fills the array with a binary digit depending on the outcome of n & 0x8000. That evaluation checks to see whether the leftmost bit in value n is a 1 or a 0. The bin[x] array is then filled accordingly.

✦ Line 28 shifts the bits in value n to the left so that the loop can repeat and still evaluate the leftmost bit with n & 0x8000.

✦ Although the bits in the value n shift left, the placeholder for the binary string, bin[x], shifts to the right. This makes for lots of leading zeroes with some values, but the string is always fixed at 16 digits.

✦ The function should, of course, merely return the string that's produced. Alas, the subject of returning a string from a function is covered in Book IV, Chapter 6. (I'm assuming that you're reading this book from front to back, like most humans do.)

Revisiting the logical OR

Empowered with the binString() function from the preceding section, you can now more visibly see how the OAR.C program produces its results. Here's a revised version of the source code:

```
#include <stdio.h>

void binString(int n);

int main()
{
    int twos =  1;
    int x,r;
    unsigned short int v = 0;

    for(x=0;x<16;x++)
    {
        r = v | twos;
        printf("0x%04X | %5d = 0x%04X or ",v,twos,r);
```

```
            binString(r);
            putchar('\n');
            twos += twos;
        }
    return(0);
}

void binString(int n)
{
    char bin[17];
    int x;

    for(x=0;x<16;x++)
    {
        bin[x] = n & 0x8000 ? '1' : '0';
        n <<= 1;
    }
    bin[16] = '\0';
    printf("%s",bin);
}
```

Modify the source code for OAR.C to include the additions shown here. Save! Compile! Run! The output is a wee bit more interesting, no?

```
0x0000 |     1 = 0x0001 or 0000000000000001
0x0000 |     2 = 0x0002 or 0000000000000010
0x0000 |     4 = 0x0004 or 0000000000000100
0x0000 |     8 = 0x0008 or 0000000000001000
0x0000 |    16 = 0x0010 or 0000000000010000
0x0000 |    32 = 0x0020 or 0000000000100000
0x0000 |    64 = 0x0040 or 0000000001000000
0x0000 |   128 = 0x0080 or 0000000010000000
0x0000 |   256 = 0x0100 or 0000000100000000
0x0000 |   512 = 0x0200 or 0000001000000000
0x0000 |  1024 = 0x0400 or 0000010000000000
0x0000 |  2048 = 0x0800 or 0000100000000000
0x0000 |  4096 = 0x1000 or 0001000000000000
0x0000 |  8192 = 0x2000 or 0010000000000000
0x0000 | 16384 = 0x4000 or 0100000000000000
0x0000 | 32768 = 0x8000 or 1000000000000000
```

Two Stragglers: ^ and ~

Sleepy yet? Good! I have two more binary operators to unmask. I keep this quick.

The exclusive OR

I'm sorry, but your name isn't on the list. Next!

No. The Exclusive OR isn't *that* kind of exclusive. As a logical operation, it differs from the regular OR (sometimes called an Inclusive OR) because Exclusive OR gets excited only when two bits are different. Table 3-5 explains.

Table 3-5		The Results of Logical Exclusive OR on Bits	
Bit	*XOR*	*Bit*	*Result*
1	^	1	0
1	^	0	1
0	^	1	1
0	^	0	0

This may seem silly, but it's a necessary function. The most magical thing about it is demonstrated in this program:

```c
#include <stdio.h>
#include <string.h>

int main()
{
    char input[64];
    int len,x;

    printf("Enter tonight's pass phrase: ");
    gets(input);
    len = strlen(input);

    for(x=0;x<len;x++)
        input[x] = 0x7F ^ input[x];

    puts("Press Enter to see the encrypted text:");
    getchar();
    for(x=0;x<len;x++)
        putchar(input[x]);

    for(x=0;x<len;x++)
        input[x] = 0x7F ^ input[x];

    puts("Press Enter to see the text recovered:");
    getchar();
    for(x=0;x<len;putchar(input[x++]))
```

```
    ;

    return(0);
}
```

This program demonstrates how you can use the Exclusive OR to both encrypt and decrypt text. Don't get excited! Every programmer knows this trick, so it's considered to be extremely *weak* encryption. Save the source code to disk as SECRET.C.

You may notice that I got a little carried away in Line 26. Basically, I combined the entire `for` loop on one line. (It's the same `for` loop as shown in Lines 18 and 19.)

Compile and run:

```
Enter tonight's pass phrase:
```

Type something clever, like **Kiss me, Titus!** and press Enter:

```
Press Enter to see the encrypted text:
```

Press Enter:

```
Seemingly random characters are displayed.
Press Enter to see the text recovered:
```

Press Enter:

```
Kiss me, Titus!
```

Note that the same string, input, is used to display the text in the program. In the first pass, the Exclusive OR with `0x7F` changes every character. With the next pass, Exclusive OR with `0x7F` changes every character back to the original.

The Exclusive OR is also known as an XOR, or EOR, in some circles. That's how programmers can tell the difference between the standard OR (what I call the *either* OR) and the Exclusive OR.

The one's complement

The final dojobbie to tackle on the bitwise level is the ~ operator. It's a unary operator, like ++, -- and the - (minus sign). What it does is easy to understand: It takes all the 1 bits in a value and turns them into zeroes and vice versa. So, if the variable `unf` holds this binary value:

11010110

the value of ~unf would be

00101001

What treasure does this behold? Nothing notable, sadly. In the preceding line, the value 214 becomes 41. Now, it's true that 214 + 41 = 255, but that doesn't earn you a standing ovation from the MIT faculty.

Here's the silly demo program:

```
#include <stdio.h>

void binString(int n);

int main()
{
    unsigned short int value;

    printf("Enter an integer value, 0 to 65535: ");
    scanf("%d",&value);

    printf("The binary value is\t");
    binString(value);
    putchar('\n');

    value = ~value;

    printf("One's complement is\t");
    binString(value);
    putchar('\n');

    return(0);
}

void binString(int n)
{
    char bin[17];
    int x;

    for(x=0;x<16;x++)
    {
        bin[x] = n & 0x8000 ? '1' : '0';
        n <<= 1;
    }
    bin[16] = '\0';
    printf("%s",bin);
}
```

Type this source code into your editor. Save it to disk as BITFLIP.C. Then compile and run. You know the drill:

```
Enter an integer value, 0 to 65535:
```

I type **12345**:

```
The binary value is      0011000000111001
One's complement is      1100111111000110
```

Cool. Whatever. Binary bits? *You're done!*

A *complement* is something that completes, balances, or harmonizes something else. A *compliment* is a note of appreciation or praise.

Chapter 4: The Myth of the Array

In This Chapter

- ✔ Replacing arrays with pointers
- ✔ Filling an array with a pointer
- ✔ Marching through an array
- ✔ Changing an array's elements
- ✔ Using pointers rather than array notation

Behold the mystery of pointers! If you have been reading this book front to back, you have just graduated from binary land in Book IV, Chapter 3. It should have been a nice break. But now, it's back to the mythology and mastery of pointers, perhaps the most devilishly complicated part of the C language, but also the most powerful.

In this chapter, I burst the myth of the array in C. You may have already accepted the fact no such thing as multidimensional arrays exist in C (refer to Book III, Chapter 1). Now, be prepared to find out that this whole array nonsense is nothing but an illusion — like the concept of "caring government" or the notion of the "sympathetic ex-spouse."

This chapter assumes that you have already read through and understand the concepts I present in Book IV, Chapters 1 and 2.

Pointers and Arrays

The array thought that he had it all. Fame. Glory. A place up there with the primary variable declarations. Multiple copies of himself. The good life.

Then one day, the pointer walked into town. He asked the array whether there was anything the array could do that the pointer couldn't. Try as he could, the array couldn't think of anything. Every time the array thought of something new and clever, the pointer would comment "I can do that too!"

The array was heartbroken. The pointer had won, but array wasn't totally down and out; the only thing the pointer cannot do that the array can do is declare and size an array. But beyond that, the poor array was crushed.

Even though pointers can effectively replace most things an array can do, don't forget array notation! Most programmers find array notation more comfortable to deal with than remembering all the subtle nuances of using pointers. Nothing is wrong with using array notation rather than pointers! I know many long-time programmers who prefer array notation simply because it's more readable. There's no shame there!

Death to the Array!

Is there any trick you can pull with an array that you cannot pull off just as well with a pointer? That's a point to ponder.

This section describes the de-evolution of the array into pointer land.

Exercise 4.4.1

Write a program that has the first 10 prime numbers in an array, and then use a `for` loop to display those values. Here are the first 10 prime numbers:

```
2, 3, 5, 7, 11, 13, 17, 19, 23, 29
```

Name your program PRIMES.C.

Goodbye, array notation, Part 1

Displaying values in an array is easy. You use the array's name, some square brackets, and the array element number between the brackets. Heck, babies in the year 2040 will be doing this stuff in their sleep.

Sadly for the array, a pointer can do the same thing. My solution to the PRIMES.C source code uses a pointer to display the array elements rather than the bracket-thing:

```c
#include <stdio.h>

int main()
{
    int primes[] = { 2, 3, 5, 7, 11, 13, 17, 19, 23, 29 };
    int *p;
    int x;

    p = primes;
    for(x=0;x<10;x++)
    {
        printf("%d\n",*p);
```

```
        p++;
    }
    return(0);
}
```

Four modifications to the source code are necessary:

✦ The pointer variable p is declared in Line 6.

✦ p is initialized to the start of the array in Line 9. Remember that the &
  isn't needed for array names — only for array elements.

✦ *p is used in Line 12 to represent the value of the array at location p.

✦ p is incremented in Line13. Remember that incrementing a pointer variable doesn't add 1 to the memory location value, but, rather, adds the
  chunk size of the pointer variable. In this case, p is hopped up one
  integer-size chunk in memory, which conveniently points to the next
  array element.

Save this source code to disk as PRIMES.C, or merely update your PRIMES.C
source code from Exercise 4.4.1. Compile and run:

```
2
3
5
7
11
13
17
19
23
29
```

Using pointers to display an array's elements doesn't change the values that
are displayed. Pointers merely provide another path to reach the same result.

A *prime number* is any number that can be divided evenly by only 1 and itself.
Five is a prime number, for example, because when you divide it by any numbers other than 1 or 5, you get severe decimal-place action. The number 12
isn't a prime number because it can be divided evenly by 2, 3, 4, and 6.

Using a pointer to fill an array

I don't make you toil here and come up with a program for generating prime
numbers (not yet, at least). The following code shows, though, how an array

can be filled by using pointers rather than array notation. First, the array notation example:

```
#include <stdio.h>

int main()
{
    int cent[8];
    int x;

    for(x=0;x<8;x++)
    {
        cent[x] = (x+1) * 100;
        printf("cent[%d] = %d\n",x,cent[x]);
    }
    return(0);
}
```

Save this source code to disk as CENT.C. Compile and run:

```
cent[0] = 100
cent[1] = 200
cent[2] = 300
cent[3] = 400
cent[4] = 500
cent[5] = 600
cent[6] = 700
cent[7] = 800
```

Nothing remarkable here. But. . . .

Exercise 4.4.2

Convert the source code for CENT.C so that a pointer variable, *c, is used to fill and display the array.

And now, something to truly drive you nuts

The pointer version of the original array source code PRIMES.C and CENT.C (from earlier in this chapter) do basically the same thing. In fact, the rules for converting between each program's original array notation and pointers goes something like this:

1. Declare the pointer to be of the same variable type as the array:

```
int *p;
int *c;
```

2. Initialize the pointer to the array's memory location:

```
p = primes;
c = cent;
```

3. Use asterisk notation to represent an array element:

```
*p
*c
```

4. Increment the pointer to the next element's address:

```
p++;
c++;
```

What happens if you want to pull a shortcut? What about this type of statement for the CENT.C program:

```
printf("cent[%d] = %d\n",x,*c++);
```

What the heck is *c++, and what does it do?

This type of construction shouldn't be entirely alien to you. You should recognize that *p is a pointer, which means that p contains a memory address.

You should also recognize the ++ operator for incrementing a value. So, the question really is "What gets incremented?" Does the memory address change, or does the value at that address change?

Oh, bother! Why not let the computer tell you?

Open the source code for PRIMES.C. Change the for loop to read

```
for(x=0;x<10;x++)
    printf("%d\n",*p++);
```

What you're doing is combining the *p with the p++ statement that follows it. Put them both in a vise, and it comes out like *p++.

Save. Compile. Run.

The program's output doesn't change. The *p++ statement increments the memory address, not the value stored at that address. The reason is that the ++ binds to the variable p more tightly than the * does. I bring this topic up because *p++ is used often in C, especially when chomping through arrays.

Pointers, like all variables, aren't islands unto themselves. They must be used somehow. This statement:

```
*p;
```

generates one of those annoying Lvalue required errors. It's just as silly as if you write

```
total;
```

You must *do* something with a variable or use it somehow. The statement *p++ is okay because the ++ is an operator that affects the variable p.

Exercise 4.4.3

Modify the source code to CENT.C so that the *c++ is used in the printf() statement and the c++; line is removed.

"What if I want to increment the value and not the memory location?"

The weird *p++ pointer thing from the preceding section brings up the Sacred Order of Precedence in C. First covered in Book I, Chapter 9, you may recall that certain operators in C take precedence over others. In the case *p++, the ++ operator is higher on the list, so it increments memory location p one chunk before the * operator fetches a value.

What if you want to increment the value at a memory location rather than the memory address? That's a tough one: Call up the source code for CENT.C again. Modify Line 13 to read

```
printf("cent[%d] = %d\n",x,++*c);
```

You're replacing *c++ with ++*c. Then add a new line:

```
c++;
```

The whole program should now look like this:

```
#include <stdio.h>

int main()
{
    int cent[8];
    int *c;
```

```
        int x;

        c = cent;
        for(x=0;x<8;x++)
        {
            *c = (x+1) * 100;
            printf("cent[%d] = %d\n",x,++*c);
            c++;
        }
        return(0);
}
```

Make these changes so that your source code looks like what's shown here. Save the updated file to disk. Compile and run:

```
cent[0] = 101
cent[1] = 201
cent[2] = 301
cent[3] = 401
cent[4] = 501
cent[5] = 601
cent[6] = 701
cent[7] = 801
```

Why did it work? Simple. Again, it's the order of precedence: A ++ on the left side of *c increments the memory contents, not the memory location. Furthermore, because the memory contents are on the left, they're incremented first.

This statement would also have worked:

```
printf("cent[%d] = %d\n",x,(*c)++);
```

With parentheses overriding the order of precedence, in (*c)++ the value at location *c is incremented. But, because ++ appears on the right, the value is incremented *after* the variable is used. The array would be changed, but the display wouldn't reflect that.

Isn't this maddening?

Keep in mind that pointers are variables and that you can manipulate them just like you can manipulate any other variable. They're also subject to two weird C language rules:

✦ The order of precedence

✦ The weird ++ or -- before or after the variable

Knowing both these rules tells you whether the pointer's memory location or variable is incremented and whether it's incremented before or after it's read. But why memorize rules when you can cheat?

When I want to know what's happening with a pointer variable and ++ or --, I just whip out Table 4-1. It illustrates many of the pointer knot problems you may encounter. Refer to this table whenever you're puzzled or you need a quick reference without hurting your brain.

Table 4-1	Pointers, Parentheses, ++, and --	
Pointer Thing	*Memory Address*	*Memory Contents*
p	Yup	Nope
*p	Nope	Yup
*p++	Incremented after value is read	Unchanged
*(p++)	Incremented after value is read	Unchanged
(*p)++	Unchanged	Incremented after it's used
*++p	Incremented before value is read	Unchanged
*(++p)	Incremented before value is read	Unchanged
++*p	Unchanged	Incremented before it's used
++(*p)	Unchanged	Incremented before it's used
p*++	Not a pointer	Not a pointer
p++*	Not a pointer	Not a pointer

Table 4-1 tells you whether the pointer's memory location or variable (memory content) is being manipulated. It also explains whether the contents are manipulated before or after a value is read from memory. Note that the same operations for -- hold true for ++, which is why I use only ++ in the table.

A great way to always ensure that a pointer behaves the way you want is to enclose the vital parts of it in parentheses; for example:

```
*(p++)
```

The value at address p is read, and then p is incremented. No argument. No right-to-left reading. As long as you remember that p is incremented *after* it's used, you're okay.

Whatever appears in the parentheses happens first.

The Weird Relationship between Pointers and Array Brackets

Pointers can march through an array like army ants through a cheesy 1950s black-and-white horror film. Or, was that an episode of the old *Tarzan* TV show? Anyway, you may think that there's one place pointers can't compete. Take this example:

```
array[5];
```

How can you use pointers to steal away that notation? It's a good thing you asked! Type this source code:

```
#include <stdio.h>

int main()
{
    int primes[] = { 2, 3, 5, 7, 11, 13, 17, 19, 23, 29 };

    printf("The fifth prime number is %d\n",primes[4]);
    printf("and the seventh is %d\n",primes[6]);

    return(0);
}
```

Remember that in an array, the first element is 0. So, in this example, `primes[4]` is the fifth prime number and `primes[6]` is the seventh. Save these changes to disk, and then compile and run the result:

```
The fifth prime number is 11
And the seventh is 17
```

Now, do the same thing without using array notation. In fact, I make it an exercise. *Ha!*

Exercise 4.4.4

Modify the PRIMES.C program presented in the preceding section so that a pointer is used rather than array notation.

Goodbye, array notation, Part II

Don't worry about getting the program from Exercise 4.4.4 right or wrong. If you succeeded, great. But it probably would have been better if you knew about the trick presented in Table 4-2 before you set off to modify the program. The table shows a straight-across way of replacing any array-thing with a pointer-thing in a program.

Table 4-2	Pointers and Array Brackets
Array Notation	*Pointer Equivalent*
`array[0]`	`*a`
`array[1]`	`*(a+1)`
`array[2]`	`*(a+2)`
`array[3]`	`*(a+3)`
`array[x]`	`*(a+x)`

In the table, `array` is the name of any array in C and `a` is a pointer variable. It's assumed that `a` is initialized to point to the `array` as follows:

```
a = array;
```

Each element in the array can be accessed by using pointers, as shown in the table. (Although Table 4-2 shows only elements 0 through 3, you can access any array element as shown here.)

The final item in Table 4-2 shows how to access an element based on a variable, *x*, rather than on a constant. It all really works the same.

Here's the update to the latest incarnation of the PRIMES.C source code — the better answer for Exercise 4.4.4:

```c
#include <stdio.h>

int main()
{
    int primes[] = { 2, 3, 5, 7, 11, 13, 17, 19, 23, 29 };
    int *p;

    p = primes;

    printf("The fifth prime number is %d\n",*(p+4));
    printf("and the seventh is %d\n",*(p+6));

    return(0);
}
```

Make these changes to your PRIMES.C source code. Save, compile, and run.

One big reason for preferring the *(a+x) type of notation is that you don't mess with the array's starting location in memory. If you initialize the pointer, as in

```
p = primes;
```

you can always rely on the pointer variable p equaling the starting address of the array in memory. That way, p+n always points to element n in the array (the first element is 0 [now you know!]). And, in the same format, *(p+n) equals the value of the array element n.

The parentheses are important here. What happens inside the parentheses happens first in C, so

```
*(p+2)
```

Two memory chunks are added to the address stored in p (making it equivalent to array[2]). The two chunks are added first. Then, whatever value lives there is fetched by the * that lives outside the parentheses.

Removing all vestiges of array notation

The CENT.C program's conversion to pointers from array notation was rather clumsy. To make a better stab at it, you should replace the old array notation directly with the pointer notation shown earlier in this chapter, in Table 4-2.

Open up your editor and load CENT.C once again.

Restore the for loop to its original state, but with pointers rather than with array notation. Here's how it should look:

```
for(x=0;x<8;x++)
{
    *(c+x) = (x+1) * 100;
    printf("array[%d] = %d\n",x,*(c+x));
}
```

You're replacing the array[x] from the program's original listing with *(a+x) from Table 4-2. Here's the complete code listing:

```
#include <stdio.h>

int main()
{
    int cent[8];
    int *c;
```

```
int x;

c = cent;
for(x=0;x<8;x++)
{
    *(c+x) = (x+1) * 100;
    printf("cent[%d] = %d\n",x,*(c+x));
}
return(0);
}
```

Save the source code to disk. Compile and run. The program's output remains the same.

Proof for disbelievers

You can thank your friends the parentheses for ensuring that the value fetched by pointer notation comes from the proper place. Witness this flashback to beginning algebra:

```
*(a + 5)
```

If `a` is the address of the array's starting point in memory, `a + 5` is the fifth integer-size chunk (*element*) in the array. No problem. If you omit the parentheses, you get something else:

```
*a + 5
```

Then, it works out to whatever value lives at `*a` plus 5. If `*a` points at the first array element and that element is 0, for example, `*a +5` evaluates to 5 — not the fifth array element.

This may seem strange, until you work another demo program.

Load the source code for CENT.C into your editor. Change the `printf()` statement to read

```
printf("cent[%] = %i\n",x,*a+x);
```

You're removing the parentheses from the `*(a+x)` at the end of the statement. Rather than display the value stored at element `x`, the program should now just do some math.

Save. Compile. Run:

```
cent[0] = 100
cent[1] = 101
cent[2] = 102
```

```
cent[3] = 103
cent[4] = 104
cent[5] = 105
cent[6] = 106
cent[7] = 107
```

These results are misleading. The array holds the same values as it did before. What you see here is the result of *a + x, which simply adds the value of *x* to 0 for each loop in the array.

More proof!

Load the source code for CENT.C from the preceding section into your editor again. Change the printf() statement once more:

```
printf("cent[%d] = %d\t%d\n",x,array[x],*a+x);
```

The output displays the array element number, the contents of that array element using array notation, and then the results of *a + x. Save it to disk.

Compile and run:

```
cent[0] = 100    100
cent[1] = 200    101
cent[2] = 300    102
cent[3] = 400    103
cent[4] = 500    104
cent[5] = 600    105
cent[6] = 700    106
cent[7] = 800    107
```

The array's elements still hold their so-far traditional values. The result of *a + x is completely different.

See? Your friends the parentheses truly are your pals.

Arrays and Pointers Summary

Although many similarities exist between pointers and arrays, they have one key difference: An array isn't a variable.

Pointers are variables. You can change their contents and change whatever lives at the memory addresses they point to. Arrays, on the other hand, are pretty much stuck in memory. You can't move them. You can't reassign them. You can't add more elements. What you can do is to change their variables, but that's about it.

In a way, this situation makes pointers a more versatile method of accessing arrays in memory. You see this concept demonstrated especially with character arrays (strings), as covered in Book 4, Chapter 5. Keep these points in mind when you're dealing with arrays and pointers:

✦ Even though pointers can replace array notation, you still have to declare an array as you always have.

✦ Pointers cannot be used to declare an initialized numeric array:

```
int *p = { 1, 2, 3, 4, 5 };
```

✦ Pointers *can* be used to initialize a special type of string:

```
char *name = "Elbert Funklemeyer";
```

More on this oddity in Book IV, Chapter 5.

✦ Pointers cannot be used to declare an empty array:

```
int *p[8];
```

This example declares an array of *pointers*, not integers. (Gadzooks!) Nope, you *must* declare your arrays the old-fashioned way. Then, declare a pointer and assign it to the array.

Chapter 5: Pointers and Strings

In This Chapter

✔ **Zipping through a string using a pointer**

✔ **Using a pointer to read characters in a string**

✔ **Understanding compiler documentation**

✔ **Declaring strings by using a pointer**

There really is no such thing as a string in C. It's just not a variable type. You may have read this statement elsewhere or discovered it on your own. I don't know how many C programmers out there have tried to compare strings with == or used a single = to assign a string a value. It just doesn't work.

The only time strings tend to make sense in C is when you discover pointers. Finding out about strings and pointers tends to make more sense than finding out about either one alone. Pointers and strings have a special relationship, which buds from the cozy pointer-array thing (covered in Book IV, Chapter 4). Pointers don't just love strings — they *love* strings.

Using Pointers to Display Strings

You should know two basic things about strings in C:

✦ Strings aren't variables; they're single-character arrays.

✦ The last character in a string or array is the NULL character.

When you combine those simple truths with the power of a pointer, you're starting to get to something really big.

The boring way to display a string

Honestly! Displaying a string is simple. If you want the string to be on a line by itself, use the puts() function. Otherwise, you can display the string without an extra newline by using printf(). This stuff should be old hat.

What's even more boring is traipsing through a string character by character and then using `putchar()` to display the string. Boring. Waste of time. Why not show a demo program?

```c
#include <stdio.h>

int main()
{
    char string[] = "Is it supposed to smell that way?";
    char ch;
    int x;

/* initialize variables */
    ch = 'a';
    x = 0;

    while(ch != '\0')      /* NULL character ends string */
    {
        ch = string[x];
        putchar(ch);
        x++;
    }
    return(0);
}
```

Save this stinker to disk as STINKER.C. Compile and run:

```
Is it supposed to smell that way?
```

The program uses a simple `while` loop to scan through and display each character in the string. Boring!

Note that both the variables `ch` and `x` must be initialized. `ch` must be because, otherwise, whatever random garbage is already in memory may be the NULL character, halting the loop before it starts. Therefore, either `ch` must be initialized or a `do-while` loop used instead. (You still have a better option; keep reading.)

The variable `x` is initialized to help track through the array.

Overall, this technique is a truly clunky way to do things in C. True, the program works, but things can be made to work much more efficiently by employing pointers.

A better way to display a string

Reload the source code for STINKER.C into your editor. Change it so that it resembles this pointer-improved version of the program:

```
#include <stdio.h>

int main()
{
    char string[] = "Is it supposed to smell that way?";
    char *s;

/* initialize the pointer */
    s = string;

    while(*s != '\0')      /* NULL character ends string */
    {
        putchar(*s);
        s++;
    }
    return(0);
}
```

Many things have changed: Gone are the ch and x variables. Also, the clunky array notation is missing. And, the program is shorter, sweeter, and more to the pointer.

Save your changes to disk.

Compile. Run:

```
Is it supposed to smell that way?
```

Here's a rundown of the program's improvements:

✦ The program's pointer variable, s, is initialized to be equal to the start of the array in memory:

```
    s = string;
```

Remember that the & isn't required here because string is the name of an array.

✦ The nature of the while loop's condition changes as well:

```
    while(*s != '\0')
```

You have no need to initialize *s; unlike the char variable ch, *s already points at the first character in the string. That saves the step of setting ch equal to a in the first version of the program. By using a pointer, you're already set up and ready to loop.

✦ The putchar function displays the character to which the s variable points:

```
    putchar(*s);
```

The variable s contains a memory location, and *s represents the character stored at that location.

✦ Then, the address of the s variable is incremented to the next character-size chunk of memory:

```
s++;
```

✦ The program continues to loop through the string until the NULL byte is encountered.

Is this the only improvement you can make?

No!

More tricks!

The NULL byte is 0. Zero is interpreted by the compiler as FALSE, so you can rewrite the while loop:

```
while(*s)
```

This line reads "While the value represented by pointer s isn't equal to 0 (the NULL character), keep looping." As long as the character at the memory location s isn't the NULL, the while loop repeats.

Make the preceding modification to the STINKER.C source code. Save your work to disk, and then compile and run it.

Even more tricks!

Consider these two lines in the program:

```
putchar(*s);
s++;
```

If you have read through Book IV, Chapter 4, you have agonized over the fact that these two lines can really be combined:

```
putchar(*s++);
```

No, that's not pretty to look at, but it still works: The value stored at memory location s is read and displayed, and then the memory location s is incremented.

Edit the STINKER.C source code again, replacing the existing while loop with

```
while(*s)
  putchar(*s++);
```

You don't need the curly braces because only one statement is in the `while` loop.

Save. Compile. Run.

Of course, you're pondering any further improvements. So, it's time for . . .

One last, crazy trick

Those insurance company diet charts are all screwed up. For example, a person of my height — a big-boned, large-frame type of person (really big-boned, I mean) — I should weigh in at 179 pounds. I haven't weighed 179 since I was 17. Doctors tell me that it's always possible to lose more weight, but it has been my experience that most doctors are scrawny people, so how can they understand what it's like to be big-boned as I am?

Losing weight is also possible for STINKER.C, even though it's big-boned and looks skinny enough already.

Here's one last, final notch on the belt for STINKER.C:

```
while(putchar(*s++))
    ;
```

Never mind why or how this is possible; just make this change to your source code. Save, compile, and run.

Amazing. The program still works.

Here's the final version of STINKER.C, which little resembles how the program began at the beginning of this lesson:

```
#include <stdio.h>

int main()
{
    char string[] = "Is it supposed to smell that way?";
    char *s;

/* initialize the pointer */
    s = string;

    while(putchar(*s++))
        ;
    return(0);
}
```

TIP

I wouldn't seriously expect any beginning programmer to write something like `while(putchar(*s++));` off the top of his head. Even experienced programmers start out the long way and work things back together as they mess with the program.

As you get more comfortable with pointers, don't worry about including a chestnut like `while(putchar(*s++));` in your code. I recommend documenting it somehow, though.

Exercise 4.5.1

Write a program that accepts your name as input. The program then uses a `char` pointer to display what you enter by using a `while` loop. Name the source code GETNAME.C.

Distinguishing Strings from Chars

I find it insanely easy to get tripped up when it comes to the difference between strings and characters. Especially when you deal with pointers, you can easily become confused and, often, screw up some program with some tiny, subtle mistake — especially if you read the C language library documentation.

The lowdown and letdown of library documentation

The source code for STINKER.C (presented earlier in this chapter), shows a great example of the C language working from the inside out:

```
while(putchar(*s++))
```

The character at location `s` is grabbed first. Location `s` is incremented second. `putchar()` displays the character next, and then the `while` loop spins on the outside.

How exactly does the compiler know what's *inside*? Or, better: How would you as a programmer know that `putchar(*s++)` not only displays a character but also returns that same character for `while` to evaluate?

The answer is in your C language library documentation. It lists all C language functions and how they're defined. On a Unix system, the library documentation is usually kept in part 3 of the man function. In Windows, you have to refer to the documentation from your compiler's source.

The documentation shows what the library functions require as input and produce as output. For example, here's the format for the `putchar` function:

```
int putchar(int c);
```

The putchar() function requires an integer value c, which is the character to be displayed. (Most libraries use int when they may mean char, because a char is like a tiny int — don't ask me why.)

The putchar() function also returns an integer value, which is the character that's displayed. Therefore, you can use putchar() in a while or if comparison because it returns what it displays.

Consider this definition:

```
char *gets(char *str)
```

The gets() (get string) function requires one string as input and generates another string as output. char *str is the same thing as a string; it's a character pointer to a string in memory. Same thing. The function is prototyped as a string with char * because it returns a string.

Here's the definition for puts(), the put-string function:

```
int puts(const char *string);
```

The puts() function displays a string. The const variable type is used, showing that the string isn't (or cannot be) modified. The int return value is equal to 0 on success or EOF if there's a problem. (EOF, the end-of-file character, is defined in STDIO.H.)

Given the definition of puts(), which you just saw, you may think that you can get away with this in your source code:

```
#include <stdio.h>

int main()
{
    char text[] = "Going! Going! Gone!";
    char *t;

/* initialize the pointer */
    t = text;

/* display the string */
    puts(*t);

    return(0);
}
```

Type this source code into your editor. This wee li'l program represents some code that you may create on your own someday. Confidently save the code to disk as STRING.C.

Compile and . . . er, uh?

```
string.c:12: warning: passing art 1 of `puts' makes pointer
    form integer without a cast
```

Wait-ho!

What the error message means is that you fed a function one thing when it was expecting another. In this case, you fed the function what it looked like it wanted: *t, which is what char *string looks like in the library definition. But, it just ain't so.

In a library definition, char *string refers to a string in memory — a character array. Your variable *s is a single character, an element of the array — not the whole string. A *big* difference exists between a single variable and an array, as your compiler just informed you.

To make amends, change Line 12 in the program to read

```
puts(t);
```

By itself, t is a memory location. Because the pointer has been initialized to point to the address of the string, it's really the *same doo-dah deal* as the string itself.

Save STRING.C to disk. Compile . . . and, no errors!

Run:

```
Going! Going! Gone!
```

This result really shouldn't be a surprise to you. First, if you declare a string as text, you should know that this statement displays that string:

```
puts(text);
```

Second, if you set the pointer t equal to text — which is done in the program — you should know that this line also displays the string:

```
puts(t);
```

After all, t = text. It says so right in your program.

Don't let the formats in your C language library reference confuse you. A char *string definition means a string of characters, not a single character.

And, while I'm on the subject of weird strings

A key item to remember about pointers is that they're variables. Because of that, you can mess with them, as shown by these modifications to the STRING.C program.

```c
#include <stdio.h>

int main()
{
    char text[] = "Going! Going! Gone!";
    char *t;

/* initialize the pointer */
    t = text;

    while(*t)
    {
        puts(t);
        t++;
    }
    return(0);
}
```

Whip the source code for STRING.C into your editor. Change the program to reflect the addition of a `while` loop, as shown here. Save the file back to disk, and then compile and run it.

Here's what the output should resemble:

```
Going! Going! Gone!
oing! Going! Gone!
ing! Going! Gone!
ng! Going! Gone!
g! Going! Gone!
! Going! Gone!
 Going! Gone!
Going! Gone!
oing! Gone!
ing! Gone!
ng! Gone!
g! Gone!
! Gone!
 Gone!
Gone!
one!
ne!
e!
!
```

The `while` loop scans through the `text` array one character at a time. Each time it scans, it displays the string. Because the `t` variable is incremented, the string gets shorter and shorter with each iteration of the loop.

Declaring a String by Using a Char Pointer

Here's a trick that I dare not show you because it has a tendency to be abused. It's the old declaring-a-string-with-a-char-pointer trick, and it works like this:

```
char *hello = "Your computer sends you greetings.";
```

It's almost the same as this declaration, but not quite:

```
char hello[] = "Your computer sends you greetings.";
```

First, this demo program proves where the two declarations are similar:

```
#include <stdio.h>

int main()
{
    char *hello = "Greetings from your computer!";
    char byebye[] = "So long now!";
    char *b;

/* initialize the pointer */
    b = byebye;

    puts(hello);
    puts(b);

    return(0);
}
```

Hunt and peck this source code, saving it to disk as THING.C. Compile and run:

```
Greetings from your computer!
So long now!
```

No biggie here. But, you must be careful. Here's the warning:

When you declare a string by using a pointer, you cannot modify the string.

You can mess with the `hello` pointer variable, if you like. And, you can use `*hello` to represent individual characters within the string. But, you cannot use the variable to modify or change the string. If you do, the program crashes. (In Unix, you get a `segmentation fault` type of error.)

In fact, you should borrow a trick from C++ here and assert any such pointer or string declarations as `const` variables:

```
const char *hello = "Greetings from your computer!";
```

The `const` keyword enforces the compiler to ensure that nothing modifies the string or the variable, guaranteeing that bad code doesn't compile. Note that such a thing doesn't prevent you from incrementing the `hello` variable, like this:

```
while(*hello)
{
    puts(hello);
    hello++;
}
```

(If you will change the value of `hello`, as just shown, you should save it first. Create a second `char` pointer, `h`, and then use `h = hello;` to save the start of the string early in the code.)

This trick also doesn't prevent you from accessing individual characters with something like this:

```
f = *(hello+10);
```

But, it prevents you from committing this transgression:

```
gets(hello);
```

Such a thing just isn't allowed. No. No. No. No. No. No. No.

Don't worry about this type of shortcut yet. I'm not quite done exploiting the pointer and string. Chapters 6 and 7 in Book IV also describe how you can use, and abuse, this thing.

Chapter 6: Crazy Arrays of Pointers

In This Chapter

✔ Saving space with string pointer arrays

✔ Using pointers to find characters in arrays

✔ Understanding arrays of pointers

✔ Eliminating array notation for pointer arrays

✔ Sorting string arrays with pointers

Oh, really! Don't be silly: The pointer string-declaration shortcut demonstrated at the end of Book IV, Chapter 5 isn't a pointer array. It's a string declared by using a pointer, a topic also covered in this chapter. But the true subject here is a monster you may not have conceived of, even in your strangest, late-night-eating and too-much-alcohol generated night-mares. I speak of the `pointer array`.

(Cue the creepy music and sound of woman screaming.)

Introducing the Pointer Array

The Nothing Surprises Me Any More chapter of your programming career isn't yet finished. After all, you have yet to encounter this beast:

```
int *nifty[6];
```

At first glance, it looks like you have created an integer array of six elements and a pointer to that array, all at the same time.

Wrong. Wrong. Wrong. Such an explanation would be too easy. Too simple. Too . . . inappropriate.

An array of pointers contains a list of memory addresses.

A *pointer* is a C language variable that holds a memory address, usually the location of some other variable in memory. An array of such beasts simply means that more than one pointer is created at a time:

```
#include <stdio.h>

int main()
{
    int a,b,c,d,e,x;
    int *variables[5];

    a = 1;
    b = a * 2;
    c = b * 2;
    d = c * 2;
    e = d * 2;

    variables[0] = &a;
    variables[1] = &b;
    variables[2] = &c;
    variables[3] = &d;
    variables[4] = &e;

    for(x=0;x<5;x++)
        printf("Variable %c = %d\n",'a'+x,*variables[x]);

    return(0);
}
```

This program may seem silly, but bear with me: Type this source code. Save it to disk as ABCDE.C. Compile it. Can you guess what the output is? Run it!

```
Variable a = 1
Variable b = 2
Variable c = 4
Variable d = 8
Variable e = 16
```

Here are the highlights:

✦ Line 6 declares an array of 5 pointers. Each pointer is an `int` pointer, which means that it can contain the address of an `int` variable — five of 'em.

✦ Lines 8 through 12 initialize variables a through e.

✦ Lines 14 through 18 initialize the five pointers in the `variables` array.

✦ The `for` loop's `printf()` statement is used to display each variable, a through e, and its value.

This program is the best way to display such information. The other solution is five different `printf()` statements, one for each `int` variable that's declared.

Saving Some Space with String Pointer Arrays

Pointers can also be used to help represent multidimensional arrays. This process becomes a wee bit more twisted than single-dimension arrays — by one full dimension! But the tricks you can do with pointers and 2-dimensional arrays are quite nifty — if you can fathom the strange notation.

Wasting space with string arrays

In Book 3, Chapter 2, you were introduced to a multidimensional string array that holds the names of the seven dwarfs:

```
char seven[7][8] = {
    "bashful",
    "doc",
    "dopey",
    "grumpy",
    "happy",
    "sneezy",
    "sleepy"
};
```

The seven strings sit in a 2-dimensional character array — a giant grid that's seven rows by eight columns. That's what's needed because the longest dwarf name (`"bashful"`) is seven characters long, and you need an extra character for the NULL at the end of the string.

Figure 6-1 illustrates the character array grid that the DWARFS.C program creates and how it's filled.

The array is a grid of 56 bytes (7×8, as declared in the program). Yet, because the longest string needs 8 bytes of storage, the rest of the strings waste space. It's not much space — 11 bytes total — but imagine how bad it could be for this array:

```
char prompts[3][16] = {
    "Type something:",
    "C:\>",
    "."
};
```

Three (`[3]`) strings of 16 (`[16]`) characters each must be declared in order to properly initialize this array. Figure 6-2 shows how that wastes space in your computer's memory.

b	a	s	h	f	u	l	\0	
d	o	c	\0					
d	o	p	e	y	\0			
g	r	u	m	p	y	\0		
h	a	p	p	y	\0			
s	n	e	e	z	y	\0		
s	l	e	e	p	y	\0		

Figure 6-1:
Two-dimensional string arrays can be inefficient.

T	y	p	e		s	o	m	t	h	i	n	g	:	\0
C	:	\	>	\0										
.	\0													

Figure 6-2:
Lots of space is wasted in this array.

The point here really isn't wasted memory. Your PC has bazillabytes of RAM in it, so being sloppy with a string array is forgivable. As is often the case with C, however, you can just find better ways to do things. In this case, you should create a string array with pointers rather than create a multidimensional array.

Making a string pointer array

The compiler lets you get away with this:

```
char *dame = "Snow White";
```

Shouldn't it also let you get away with this?

```
char *seven[] = {
    "bashful",
```

```
        "doc",
        "dopey",
        "grumpy",
        "happy",
        "sneezy",
        "sleepy"
};
```

You bet! Just as you can declare a character pointer string, you can get away with declaring an array of character pointers to a whole bunch of strings.

Make the variables constant, to avoid some common boo-boos:

```
const char *dame = "Snow White";
const char *seven[] = {
    "bashful",
    "doc",
    "dopey",
    "grumpy",
    "happy",
    "sneezy",
    "sleepy"
};
```

The declaration *seven[] tells the compiler to do two things. First, a character pointer array is created, as shown in Figure 6-3. The pointers each take up two bytes of memory and can hold the addresses of strings stored elsewhere in memory. Whatever. It's all done by the compiler, so you don't have to think about it.

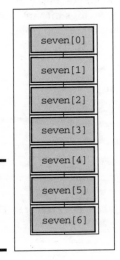

Figure 6-3:
A string pointer array in memory.

Figure 6-3 shows how the compiler allocates the array, creating storage space for seven pointers to hold the address of seven strings elsewhere in memory.

The second thing the `*seven[]` declaration tells the compiler is to initialize the pointers to hold the addresses of the seven strings declared in the array — two steps in one. What's really created in memory looks like Figure 6-4.

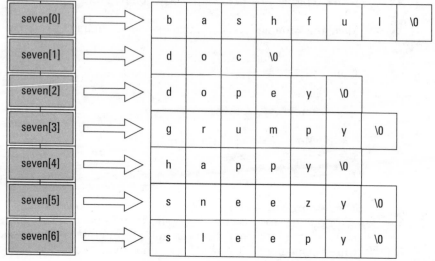

Figure 6-4: A string pointer array and its strings.

The initialized string pointer array works because you can use a pointer to create a string. The compiler simply sticks the strings into memory and then plugs those strings' addresses into the proper pointer variable slots.

Exercise 4.6.1

Convert this declaration into a pointer version:

```
char prompts[3][16] = {
    "Type something:",
    "C:\>",
    "."
};
```

A redundant demo program to prove that it works

Re*dun*dant (*ri-dun'dent*) *adj.* 1. *See* redundant.

The following program uses both array notation and pointer notation to declare an array of strings. It illustrates how both methods work similarly, which is kind of redundant, but that has sort of been the point of the sample programs in this book:

```c
#include <stdio.h>

int main()
{
    char dwarf[7][8] = {
        "bashful",
        "doc",
        "dopey",
        "grumpy",
        "happy",
        "sneezy",
        "sleepy",
    };

    const char *seven[] = {
        "bashful",
        "doc",
        "dopey",
        "grumpy",
        "happy",
        "sneezy",
        "sleepy"
    };
    int x;

    for(x=0;x<7;x++)
        printf("%10s - %-10s\n",dwarf[x],seven[x]);

    return(0);
}
```

Save this source code to disk as SEVEN.C. Compile and run:

```
bashful - bashful
    doc - doc
  dopey - dopey
 grumpy - grumpy
  happy - happy
 sneezy - sneezy
 sleepy - sleepy
```

The program displays the contents of both arrays, showing that pointer and array notation are basically the same.

TIP

The placeholder `%10s` sets the width of the string output to 10 characters, right justified. The placeholder `%-10s` sets the width of the string output to 10 characters, left justified.

Finding Characters in a Pointer String Array

After getting AOL broadband for the cottage, Snow decided to dole out an e-mail account to each dwarf. To be efficient, she would use only the first three letters of each dwarf's name.

Rather than use a new array, Snow decided to use the traditional pointer array that she found out how to create earlier in this chapter:

```
const char *seven[] = {
    "bashful",
    "doc",
    "dopey",
    "grumpy",
    "happy",
    "sneezy",
    "sleepy"
};
```

Along the way, Snow discovered some interesting things about the C language. Most notably, she found that performing this trick wasn't as easy as it looks.

More puzzles, more problems

Welcome to the time when most budding programmers forget everything that they have learned about pointers. This situation is quite common because you can *easily* confuse the `*array[]` creature with a regular pointer, `*a`. But they're not the same. One is an array of pointers, and the other is a memory location.. In other words:

```
*a != *array[];
```

On the left, you have a single pointer to a single memory location containing a single value. On the right, you have a pointer to an array of pointers. That should be a big hint, but maybe not. Consider this program:

```
#include <stdio.h>

int main()
{
    const char *seven[] = {
        "bashful",
```

```
            "doc",
            "dopey",
            "grumpy",
            "happy",
            "sneezy",
            "sleepy"
    };
    int x;

    for(x=0;x<7;x++)
        printf("%s\n",seven[x]);

    return(0);
}
```

Busily type this code into your editor. Busily save it to disk as SNOW.C. Busily compile it. Busily run it.

There's no point in busily divulging the output here; it's pretty straightforward.

Exercise 4.6.2

Rewrite the source code for SNOW.C so that the `printf()` statement doesn't use array notation. *Do not peek ahead!* Really, try it. See whether you remember all that stuff you read about pointers.

Finding the pointer array without array notation

Oh, how soon they forget! If you have an array of integers:

```
int primes[] = { 2, 3, 5, 7, 11, 13, 17, 19, 23, 29 };
```

and a pointer:

```
int *p;
```

initialized to the start of the array:

```
p = primes;
```

you can walk through the array using this format:

```
*(p + n)
```

where *n* is the array element and the entire thing translates to:

```
primes[n] == *(p + n);
```

If you don't remember it, go to Book IV, Chapter 4, and, specifically, Table 4-2. It's all right there in black and white, plain as the nose on my face.

If you did remember it, *great!* Then you answered Exercise 4.6.2 with code that looks like this:

```
#include <stdio.h>

int main()
{
    const char *seven[] = {
        "bashful",
        "doc",
        "dopey",
        "grumpy",
        "happy",
        "sneezy",
        "sleepy"
    };
    int x;

    for(x=0;x<7;x++)
        printf("%s\n",*(seven+x));

    return(0);
}
```

Even though `seven` is an array of pointers, the `*(seven+x)` thing evaluates the same as `seven[x]`. Again, this was just shown, and you can see it in Table 4-2. The fact that `seven` is an array of pointers could throw you, but it shouldn't. Again, it's just a basic array issue. But that's not your problem.

Your problem is figuring out how you reference a single character in the string. In other words, Snow would write this code if she got stuck using array notation:

```
#include <stdio.h>

int main()
{
    const char *seven[] = {
        "bashful",
        "doc",
        "dopey",
        "grumpy",
        "happy",
        "sneezy",
        "sleepy"
```

```
    };
    int x,c;

    for(x=0;x<7;x++)
    {
        for(c=0;c<3;c++)
            printf("%c",seven[x][c]);
        putchar('\n');
    }
    return(0);
}
```

Update your SNOW.C program to resemble this bit of code. Note that %s is changed to %c in printf(); you're printing characters, not strings here.

Save the update to disk. Compile it. Congratulate your compiler if it finds an error; most compilers are too forgiving to find it. Run the beast:

```
bas
doc
dop
gru
hap
sne
sle
```

Excellent. Then again, Snow is cheating because she's using array notation. There must be some way to squeeze that into pointer notation, right?

Exercise 4.6.3
Oh, never mind!

Pointers that point at pointers
Think about this one:

```
*(seven+x)
```

This notation represents a *memory location*. It goes counter to your training, where seven by itself would be a memory location. Therefore, your human brain assumes that *seven must be the contents of that memory location.

Right!

In this case, though, seven is an array of pointers, or *pointers to pointers*. Figure 6-5 may help explain this strange concept.

Boring old array notation

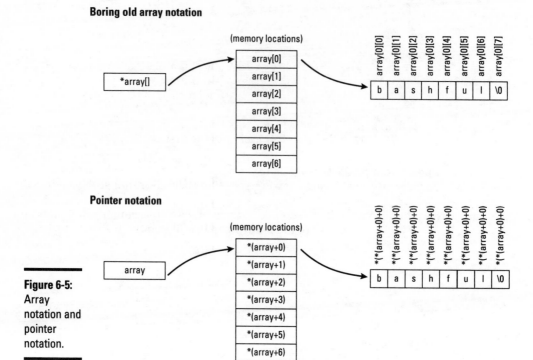

Pointer notation

Figure 6-5:
Array
notation and
pointer
notation.

In the program SNOW.C, `seven` is declared as an array of pointers or a list of memory locations:

```
const char *seven[] = {
    "bashful",
    "doc",
    "dopey",
    "grumpy",
    "happy",
    "sneezy",
    "sleepy"
};
```

Variable `seven` itself is a memory location. It marks the start of the array in memory. But the first item in the array is *not* `bashful`. No, it's a *pointer* to the location of `bashful`. So:

```
seven[0] == *(seven + 0) == memory location of "bashful";
```

When you use `*(seven+x)` in the SNOW.C program, you're using the string's address in memory. This statement seems obvious, but, for some reason, it's easy to forget.

To access the first character in the string, you need to use another offset:

`*(seven+x)+c`

This thing is a *memory location*, not a value at that location. First, `*(seven+x)` represents a memory location; for example, the start of the string `bashful` in memory. Then, by adding `c`, you get another memory location, one that's offset inside the string:

> `*(seven+x)+0` = Memory location of the first character in the string
>
> `*(seven+x)+1`= Memory location of the second character in the string
>
> `*(seven+x)+2` = Memory location of the third character in the string
>
> `*(seven+x)+3` = Memory location of the fourth character in the string
>
> `*(seven+x)+4` = Memory location of the fifth character in the string
>
> `*(seven+x)+5` = Memory location of the sixth character in the string

And so on.

Again, those are all memory locations. `*(seven+x)` is a memory location. Adding a value to the memory location offsets the memory location by a given chunk (the size of the pointer).

Keep these thoughts warm!

Exercise 4.6.4
If `*(seven+x)+0` is a memory location, how do you convert it into a thing that represents the `value` at that location?

Replacing the `array[a][b]` notation with pointers
I present to you the solution to the SNOW.C problem using pointers and not array notation:

```
#include <stdio.h>

int main()
{
    const char *seven[] = {
        "bashful",
        "doc",
        "dopey",
        "grumpy",
        "happy",
        "sneezy",
        "sleepy"
```

```
    };
    int x,c;

    for(x=0;x<7;x++)
    {
        for(c=0;c<3;c++)

            printf("%c",*(*(seven+x)+c));
        putchar('\n');
    }
    return(0);
}
```

Save these changes to disk. Compile and run:

```
bas
doc
dop
gru
hap
sne
sle
```

The program effectively found a character after following a pointer to a pointer.

And now, for a disa-pointer. *(Oh, ha!)*

This format:

```
*(*(array+x)+c)
```

is *not* the same as

```
**(array+x)+c
```

Honestly, I can't figure out what this beast is. This thing:

```
**(array+x)
```

is a shortcut reference to the first character of the string x in an array. And, you may see the ** notation used when fetching values from an array of integer pointers. But, with strings, the proper notation is

```
*(*(array+x)+c)
```

They're the same thing, though I swear that the ** (pointer-pointer) prefix really terrifies beginning C programmers. All it means is that you're referencing a pointer to a pointer — typically, a pointer array. The ** thing references individual items inside the array, and it's loosely similar to the multidimensional array notation array[][].

When in doubt, whip out Table 6-1.

Table 6-1	How the Ugly ** Notation Works Itself Out	
Pointer Notation	*Array Notation*	*What It Is*
array	*array[]	Location of an array of pointers
array+1	N/A	Second element of the array (a pointer)
*(array+1)	array[1]	The string at address (array+1)
((array+1))	array[1][0]	An element of the array at address array[1]
**(array+1)	array[1][0]	An element of the array at address array[1]
((array+a)+b)	array[a][b]	An element of the array at address array[a]
**(array+a)+b	array[1][0] + b	Value at array[1][0] + value of b

Exercise 4.6.5

Modify SNOW.C so that it uses *(*(array+a)+b) pointer notation to display each of the strings in the array.

Sorting Strings with Pointers

The subject of sorting arrays is covered in Book III. Numbers were sorted, and I think I wrote a section on sorting structures. But I presented nothing on sorting strings. That's because you have to be completely insane to sort strings in C without using pointers. I'm certain that it can be done, and some grizzled programmer probably shows off glorious no-pointer-string-sorting routines to his small group of hygiene-challenged friends — but I don't want to know about that.

The most effective way to sort entire strings in C isn't to move the clunky character arrays around in memory. No! Rather, you create an array of pointers to the strings and then sort that array of pointers. It's much, much more civilized; the strings themselves don't even move!

A simple, though incorrect, string-sorting program

The following program sorts eight characters. (It really sorts eight strings, but the strings happen to be the names of Disney cartoon characters). To accomplish this task, the program borrows the bubble-sort technique that I introduce in Book III:

```c
#include <stdio.h>

#define SIZE 8

int main()
{
    char *names[] = {
        "Mickey",
        "Minnie",
        "Donald",
        "Daisy",
        "Goofy",
        "Chip",
        "Dale",
        "Pluto"
    };
    char *temp;
    int x,a,b;

    for(a=0;a<SIZE-1;a++)
        for(b=a+1;b<SIZE;b++)
        {
            if(*names[a] > *names[b])
            {
                temp = names[a];
                names[a] = names[b];
                names[b] = temp;
            }
        }

    for(x=0;x<SIZE;x++)
        printf("%s\n",names[x]);
    return(0);
}
```

Save this program to disk as PSORT.C. Compile and run:

```
Chip
Daisy
Donald
Dale
Goofy
```

```
Minnie
Mickey
Pluto
```

It works! Well, sort of. The program did effectively swap the pointers in the array so that the array now points to the strings in alphabetical order — but only alphabetical order as far as the first character of each string is concerned. See how the *D* names and *M* names aren't in alphabetical order?

What went wrong

The PSORT.C program uses a bubble sort to sift through each string in the array. Strings are swapped based on an `if` comparison — which is all standard stuff. Because pointers are being swapped, this `if` statement is used:

```
if(*names[a] > *names[b])
```

You may think that this line would produce an error, but it doesn't. (And, forget about the `strcmp()` function for now.) The comparison works, and it makes sense: `names[a]` is the address of one string in the array, and `names[b]` is the address of another string. The `*` is used to represent the contents of the strings. Alas, `*names[a]` and `*names[b]` are *character* variables. They're not entire strings.

A string is a *character* array. The C compiler references the string by the memory location of the first character. The variable `*names[a]` is a character variable, not a string.

When you put an asterisk before an element in a pointer array, you're using a pointer to a pointer. In the case of strings, you get a single character and not the entire string. So:

```
*names[a]
```

is really the same as

```
names[a][0]
```

But, you can't do that in this program. This is a `pointer` array program, and the preceding line is a no-no.

To sort the strings, you must make comparisons beyond the first character in the string. That means that the program requires more digging.

Exercise 4.6.6

My first advice for cleaning up the PSORT.C source code is to remove the ugly array notation. That only serves to fool people. So, please rework the original PSORT.C source code so that array notation is gone and pointer notation is used exclusively. Don't worry about solving the sort problem just yet; merely clean up the code.

Digging for characters

The secret to comparing two strings is to march through each string one character at a time, comparing individual characters from each string. You do that until you find one character "greater than" another, there's no use in swapping the values. So, the search must continue deep into both strings until a mismatch occurs. This process is more easily shown than written about:

```c
#include <stdio.h>

#define SIZE 8

int main()
{
    char *names[] = {
        "Mickey",
        "Minnie",
        "Donald",
        "Daisy",
        "Goofy",
        "Chip",
        "Dale",
        "Pluto"
    };
    char *temp;
    int x,a,b;

    for(a=0;a<SIZE-1;a++)
        for(b=a+1;b<SIZE;b++)
        {
            x = 0;
            while(*(*(names+a)+x))
            {
                if(*(*(names+a)+x) > *(*(names+b)+x))
                {
                    temp = *(names+a);
                    *(names+a) = *(names+b);
                    *(names+b) = temp;
                    break;
                }
                else if(*(*(names+a)+x) < *(*(names+b)+x))
                    break;
                else
```

```
                x++;
            }
        }
    for(x=0;x<SIZE;x++)
        printf("%s\n",*(names+x));
    return(0);
}
```

Save this update to PSORT.C to disk. Compile it. Fix any errors; considering that the program has many, many semicolons and curly braces to goof up. And, those parentheses! Miss one of them, and the compiler gags. It's ugly. Make sure that all your parentheses match up.

Run:

```
Chip
Daisy
Dale
Donald
Goofy
Mickey
Minnie
Pluto
```

The program successfully sorts all the strings. Look at the *D*s. Even `Daisy` and `Dale` are sorted correctly.

More sorting, more strings

Yes, it *is* a heck of a lot easier to use the `strcmp()` function to compare strings. But, there's power in the array. One more example I want to show you is how to use an array of pointers to sort an array of strings. In this example, the strings are left untouched; only the pointer array is "sorted." This trick is a common one to pull in C.

I have coded the following program in array notation. It's likely the way that most programmers would approach the problem: Take 10 strings as input, and then sort the strings by using pointers to the strings rather than sort the original character arrays. The net effect is that the original list is unchanged. Observe:

```
#include <stdio.h>
#include <string.h>

#define SIZE 10

int main()
{
    char input[SIZE][64];
```

```
    char *isort[SIZE];
    char *temp;
    int x,a,b;

/* Get the SIZE number of strings */
    printf("Enter %d types of fruit:\n",SIZE);
    for(x=0;x<SIZE;x++)
    {
        printf("#%d: ",x+1);
        gets(input[x]);
        isort[x] = input[x];
    }

/* Sort the strings via pointers */
    for(a=0;a<SIZE-1;a++)
        for(b=a+1;b<SIZE;b++)
            if(strcasecmp(isort[a],isort[b]) > 0)
                {
                    temp = isort[a];
                    isort[a] = isort[b];
                    isort[b] = temp;
                }

/* print the results */
    printf("Sorted list:\tOriginal list:\n");
    for(x=0;x<SIZE;x++)
        printf("%12s\t%12s\n",isort[x],input[x]);

    return(0);
}
```

Enter this beastly source code into your editor. It's long because it does three things: asks for you to enter 10 strings, sorts those strings by using a pointer array, and then displays the original and sorted result. Save the beast to disk as SORTER.C.

Compile and run.

Here are some fruit names you can use. I'm writing them here because, after apples, grapes, and bananas, most folks have to power up that brain to remember other fruit names:

Apples	Cantaloupe	Grapes	Oranges	Pineapple
Avocados	Cherry	Guava	Papaya	Plums
Bananas	Coconuts	Mango	Peaches	Raspberries
Blackberries	Cranberry	Marionberries	Pear	Strawberries
Boysenberries	Cumquats	Melon	Persimmons	Watermelon

The program's output, of course, depends on the fruits you enter. But, what is sorted isn't the original array; rather, they're pointers to the original array.

Now imagine how horrible this task would be if you swapped the arrays themselves and not the pointers. This type of nightmare is one of the main motivations for using pointers in the first place.

Exercise 4.6.7

Modify SORTER.C so that numbers (integers), rather than strings, are entered and sorted.

Chapter 7: Functions and Pointers

In This Chapter

✔ Making a function eat a pointer

✔ Returning a pointer from a function

✔ Sending an array to a function

✔ Making a function modify an array

✔ Returning arrays from functions

✔ Sending a string to a function

✔ Making functions that return strings

As with any variable, you can pass a pointer to a function. O, but why? The pain! The pain!

Honestly, pointers passed to functions are no big deal. As long as you keep in mind the basics — a pointer is a memory address — you never get goofed up. Then, you find out about one of the true power of pointers: By using them, you can pass diverse and unusual values to a function, such as an array or a string, and never have to worry about cheating by using global variables or many of the other dodges that rank C programmers use to entirely avoid the subject.

Passing a Pointer to a Function

Why is passing a pointer to a function considered scary? Probably because pointers are misunderstood as scary themselves — especially when you get into pointers to pointers (see Book VI). But, honestly, a pointer is just a variable. As with any other variable, it flits off to a function just fine. The key is to remember that the variable is a memory location or address. That seems simple enough.

Basic pointer-nonsense review

Don't let your head spin 'round like a possessed 13-year-old. You can easily get overwhelmed by pointers and functions and such. I have seen programmers go through their source code and randomly place asterisks and ampersands to try to get things to work right. As long as you keep in mind the basic rules of pointers, you're okay:

✦ Initialize a pointer before you use it.

✦ Without the asterisk, the pointer is a memory address.

✦ With the asterisk, the pointer represents what lives at that address.

Those are the pointer basics from bonnet to boot. Passing a pointer to a function? Allow this program to help explain it:

```
#include <stdio.h>

void peasoup(int green);

int main()
{
    int turn;

    turn=13;
    peasoup(turn);
    return(0);
}

void peasoup(int green)
{
    while(green--)
        puts("Blech!");
}
```

Okay, this source code has no pointers. Yet. Just copy this code into your text editor and save it to disk as PUKE.C. Compile and run.

The program passes the value 13 to the `peasoup()` function, which spews out the word `Blech!` that many times.

I would bet that a pointer could do the same thing. . . .

Exercise 4.7.1

Modify the PUKE.C source code so that the `head` integer pointer variable is declared in the `main()` function. `head` is initialized to the `turn` variable and, finally, passes the value of `head` to the function. Can you do that on your own? See whether you can.

Know the differences between pointers and values

Exercise 4.7.1 should have been easy for you — especially if you followed the instructions listed in the preceding section.

First, the pointer is declared:

```
int *head;
```

Next, it must be initialized:

```
head = &turn;
```

(Note that this can happen before or after the value is assigned to the variable turn.)

Finally, the value is passed to the function, per instructions:

```
peasoup(*head);
```

You may have screwed up here, which is plausible. This line doesn't work:

```
peasoup(head);
```

This line passes to the function the memory location stored in head, not the value at that location. The compiler should flag this as a boo-boo, thanks to the peasoup() prototype, which says that an int value is required and not a memory address. Also:

```
peasoup(&head);
```

This line passes the address of the pointer variable to the function — again, not what you want.

Exercise 4.7.1 may have been challenging, but it still didn't pass a pointer to a function. It *used* a pointer to pass a value, but the function itself merely swallowed that value as an integer, the same as though an immediate value had been used. That's nothing new.

Functions that eat pointers

To eat a pointer, the function must be declared as requiring a pointer as input. It's nothing fancy: pointers are variables. Just as float, int, and char variables are declared in a function, so are pointers declared:

```
void peasoup(int *green);
```

This prototype tells the compiler that the peasoup() function requires a pointer as input — a memory address. The variable green is used inside the peasoup() function to point at the address of an integer in memory. The most important part is this:

Functions that accept pointers accept memory locations, not values.

This statement is most important. The declaration int *green defines a pointer variable, not an integer value. If the function needs an integer value, it's declared as this:

```
void peasoup(int green);
```

But, if the function requires a pointer or memory location, it's declared like this:

```
void peasoup(int *green);
```

It's time to modify PUKE.C yet again:

```
#include <stdio.h>

void peasoup(int *green);

int main()
{
    int turn;

    turn=13;
    peasoup(&turn);
    return(0);
}

void peasoup(int *green)
{
    while(green--)
        puts("Blech!");
}
```

Update your PUKE.C source code to reflect these changes. Note that there's no need to declare a pointer variable in the main() function; simply passing the address of the turn variable suffices. Save the changes to disk. Compile and run:

```
Blech!
Blech!
Blech!
Blech!
Blech!
```

And on and on. . . .

Obviously, there's a flaw in logic. To help fix it, I use a special trick.

The following source code is a modification of the PUKE.C program. It uses a trick to determine how pointers are interpreted, either as an *ADDRESS* or a *VALUE*. This helps to ensure that the pointer variable is being used consistently throughout the program. Observe this bit of code, but *don't type it*:

```
#include <stdio.h>

void peasoup(int ADDRESS);

int main()
{
    int turn;

    turn=13;
peasoup(ADDRESS);
    return(0);
}

void peasoup(int ADDRESS)
{
    while(ADDRESS--)
        puts("Blech!");
}
```

In Line 16, `while(green--)` decrements the value of the variable `green`. But `green` is an *ADDRESS*, not a value. This can be determined by looking at the preceding modified code. As an ADDRESS, the program obviously doesn't work properly. In that case, the pointer must be used as a VALUE instead.

In your editor, modify Line 16 in the PUKE.C source code to read

```
while(*green--)
```

Save that one change to disk. Recompile. Run:

```
Blech!
```

Hmmm. Wasn't that supposed to be printed 13 times?

The problem here isn't pointer-related. No, it's an order of precedence problem. You see, the `--` binds more tightly to `green` than the `*` does. A simple insertion of parentheses solves the problem:

```
while((*green)--)
```

Make this change to your PUKE.C source code. Save to disk. Compile. Run.

This time, the output is 13 lines long, as expected.

The glorious advantage of passing a pointer

When you pass a pointer to a function, it's more than a variable. It's a peep-hole into a variable that can be anywhere in memory. That means that the variable's value can be manipulated inside the function and it affects the value all over the program.

Consider this, another modification to the PUKE.C series:

```
#include <stdio.h>

void peasoup(int *green);

int main()
{
    int turn;

    turn=13;
    peasoup(&turn);
    printf("Oh, no, it's %d!\n",turn);
    return(0);
}

void peasoup(int *green)
{
    while((*green)--)
        puts("Blech!");
    *green = 13 * 51 + 3;
}
```

Make these modifications to your PUKE.C source code. Save it to disk. Compile and run:

```
Blech!
Blech!
Blech!
Blech!
Blech!
Blech!
Blech!
Blech!
Blech!
Blech!
Blech!
Blech!
Blech!
Oh, no, it's 666!
```

When the value of the variable `*green` is modified in the `peasoup()` function, the value is changed all over the program, not just locally. By using a pointer, the variable itself — even though it's inside `main()` — is changed.

Even without returning the pointer from the function, the value is returned. That's one of the key powers of using a pointer rather than (or in addition to) a regular variable.

Returning a pointer from a function

There's no big deal to remember about returning a pointer from a function, other than that the value that's returned is a memory address and *not* a value. How does the compiler know? Because the function is prototyped; for example:

```
float catweight(float pounds)
{
    return(pounds*0.453592);
}
```

This function, catweight(), translates pounds into kilograms. The value that's returned is a float — a variable. Now, consider a pointer variation:

```
int *greatest(int a, int b, int c)
{
    int *g;

    if(a > b && a > c) g = &a;
    else if(b > a && b > c) g = &b;
    else g = &c;
    return(g);
}
```

This function returns a memory address — a pointer — in the variable g. The variable g is initialized according to which value that's passed along is larger. Note the similarities between int *greatest to define the function and int *g, which is the value returned. They're both pointers.

Here's the full-on program for you:

```
#include <stdio.h>

int *greatest(int a, int b, int c);

int main()
{
    int *p;

    p = greatest(5, 25, 16);
    printf("The greatest value is %d\n",*p);
    return(0);
}

int *greatest(int a, int b, int c)
```

```
{
    int *g;

    if(a > b && a > c) g = &a;
    else if(b > a && b > c) g = &b;
    else g = &c;
    return(g);
}
```

Type this code into your editor. Save it to disk as PRETURN.C. Compile and run:

```
The greatest value is 25
```

Faced with such a monster as PRETURN.C, most C programmers go through what I call the *pointer guessing game*. First, they try using the pointers alone, and then with ampersands, and then with asterisks, guessing the whole while until they get the function correct.

But it has been my experience that what works even better is to use my trick of replacing pointer variables, and the & and * notation, with the words *ADDRESS* and *VALUE;*. That way, you can easily check the way pointer variables are being used to determine where the problem lies.

Observe this sample, but *don't type it* or modify your PRETURN.C code:

```
#include <stdio.h>

int *greatest(int a, int b, int c);

int main()
{
    int *p;

    ADDRESS = ADDRESS;
    printf("The greatest value is %d\n",VALUE);
    return(0);
}

int *greatest(int a, int b, int c)
{
    int *g;

    if(a > b && a > c) ADDRESS = ADDRESS;
    else if(b > a && b > c) ADDRESS = ADDRESS;
    else ADDRESS = ADDRESS;
    return(ADDRESS);
}
```

In this example, I have replaced the following:

✦ Pointer variable g with *ADDRESS*

✦ Pointer variable *g with *VALUE*

✦ Any non-pointer variable prefixed by & with *ADDRESS*

Note how it all makes sense that way: *ADDRESS = ADDRESS* and so on. If you get confused, you may encounter something like this:

```
p = greatest(5, 25, 16);
```

Recognize that the variable p is a pointer and that pointers are variables which hold memory locations. So, p is an *ADDRESS*:

```
ADDRESS = greatest(5, 25, 16);
```

Also recognize that greatest() is a pointer function. Therefore, it too returns an *ADDRESS*:

```
ADDRESS = ADDRESS;
```

Suppose that you get confused and do this:

```
*p = greatest(5, 25, 16);
```

and then work it out:

```
VALUE = ADDRESS;
```

Wrong!

Or, maybe you do one of these (which makes no sense, but that doesn't stop beginners from trying it):

```
&p = greatest(5, 25, 16);
```

What's &p? It's the address *of* a pointer variable. It's a common mistake, and one that the compiler catches. This mistake is easy to make because pointers hold addresses. But, unlike other variable types, they do so without the &.

Pointers are variables that hold memory locations.

Arrays to and from Functions

To pass any array to a function, you pass its memory address. Specifically, you pass the address of the array's first element. That's done by using a pointer. In fact, the only tricky part about passing an array to a function is properly declaring the function. But, even that part isn't hard — as long as you have been paying attention!

Passing an array to a function

Functions can eat arrays just as they can eat any other value in C. Because of the similarities between arrays and pointers, you have a choice: You can use array notation to pass arrays to a function, or you can use pointer notation.

Here's the array notation example:

```
#include <stdio.h>

void showArray(int array[]);

int main()
{
    int primes[] = { 2, 3, 5, 7, 11, 13 };

    showArray(primes);
    return(0);
}

void showArray(int array[])
{
    int x;

    for(x=0;x<6;x++)
        printf("Element %d: %d\n",x,array[x]);
}
```

Type this source code into your editor. Save it to disk as ARRAY.C. Compile and run:

```
Element 0: 2
Element 1: 3
Element 2: 5
Element 3: 7
Element 4: 11
Element 5: 13
```

This type of program can be understood by any beginning C programmer who knows about arrays and understands functions. The only pointer-related issue is how the function is called:

```
showArray(primes);
```

Array notation isn't used with primes here because it's only the starting address of the array that's passed to the function, not the first element of the array.

If you had used &primes to call the function, the compiler would have barfed. That's because &primes is improper notation. When you're dealing with arrays and pointers, the array name by itself is used to represent the starting address for the array. Only when you reference individual elements in the array do you bother with the &.

If you need to brush up on this subject, refer to Book IV, Chapter 4. But, note that the program works if you *properly* use the &. Change Line 9 to read

```
showArray(&primes[0]);
```

Save this change to disk. Compile and run. The output is the same, thanks to the way arrays function in memory. In fact, you could even do this:

```
showArray(&primes[2]);
```

But, the showArray() function spits out random values for the fourth and fifth elements because they're not defined. I tell you more on fixing that problem in a few pages.

Reedit the program so that Line 9 reads as it was originally written:

```
showArray(primes);
```

Down with array notation!

If you can recall from Book IV, Chapter 4, C has no such creatures as arrays, so the entire ARRAY.C source code (introduced in the preceding section) is a sham.

Load ARRAY.C back into your editor. Edit Line 3 to read

```
void showArray(int *array);
```

And change Line 13 to

```
void showArray(int *array)
```

Save this change back to disk. Recompile and run.

The output is the same. That's because you have replaced ugly array nota-tion with pointer notation, which is what the compiler prefers to use inter-nally. So, secretly, somewhere deep inside the computer, the compiler is thanking you.

Exercise 4.7.2

Modify the original source code for ARRAY.C (shown in the section "Passing an array to a function") so that pointer notation rather than array notation is used in Line 18.

How big is that array?

One flaw that the ARRAY.C program has is that the size of the array is hard coded into the showArray() function. In real life, a function like showArray() can be used to display arrays of different sizes, so a size variable should be passed to the array to ensure proper output.

Here's the modified code:

```
#include <stdio.h>

void showArray(int *array, int size);

int main()
{
    int primes[] = { 2, 3, 5, 7, 11, 13 };

    showArray(primes,6);
    return(0);
}

void showArray(int *array, int size)
{
    int x;

    for(x=0;x<size;x++)
        printf("Element %d: %d\n",x,*(array+x));
}
```

Make the modifications to your ARRAY.C source code so that it resembles what's shown here. Save these changes to disk, and then recompile and run. The output is the same — but, as you would suspect, you're not done yet.

Exercise 4.7.3

Can you think of any way to modify the ARRAY.C source code so that the pro-gram can figure out the size of the array by using the sizeof keyword?

Modifying the array in a function

One of the key bonuses to using pointers is that they allow you to modify the original variable without the program necessarily having direct access to that original variable. In light of that, here's another modification to the ARRAY.C source code:

```c
#include <stdio.h>

void showArray(int *array, int size);
void modArray(int *array, int size);

int main()
{
    int primes[] = { 2, 3, 5, 7, 11, 13 };

    puts("Original Array:");
    showArray(primes,6);
    modArray(primes,6);
    puts("Modified Array:");
    showArray(primes,6);
    return(0);
}

void showArray(int *array, int size)
{
    int x;

    for(x=0;x<size;x++)
        printf("Element %d: %d\n",x,*(array+x));
}

void modArray(int *array, int size)
{
    int x;

    for(x=0;x<size;x++)
        *(array+x) *= 2;        /* double the value */
}
```

Save this, the final change to ARRAY.C, to disk. Compile. Run:

```
Original Array:
Element 0: 2
Element 1: 3
Element 2: 5
Element 3: 7
Element 4: 11
Element 5: 13
```

```
Modified Array:
Element 0: 4
Element 1: 6
Element 2: 10
Element 3: 14
Element 4: 22
Element 5: 26
```

The point here is that the modArray() function can manipulate the array declared in the main() function via pointers.

Returning an array from a function

Normally, functions don't return arrays — unless they're character arrays or strings, but that's the subject of the latter half of this chapter. Functions that generate and return number arrays are rather rare, but they can be done. The key to winning here is *not* to think in array notation. For example, you may concoct something like this program:

```c
#include <stdio.h>

#define SIZE 5

int *odds(void);

int main()
{
    int numbers[SIZE];
    int x;

    numbers = odds();

    for(x=0;x<SIZE;x++)
        printf("Element #%d = %d\n",x,numbers[x]);
    return(0);
}

int *odds(void)
{
    int o[SIZE];
    int x;

/* fill the array */
    for(x=0;x<SIZE;x++)
        o[x] = 2*x+1;
    return(o);
}
```

Carefully type this source code into your editor. Save it to disk as ODD.C. Compile. Oh, boy! Errors abound!

The main problem with the program is that it uses array notation thinking, and that fouls things up. Stick to pointer notation when you're working between functions that manipulate arrays. That's the first problem to work on.

The `odds()` function is declared as an integer pointer function. That means that it returns a *memory location* — specifically, the address of an integer. In this case, it's the starting address of an array — whatever.

So, the first problem with the program is that the memory address that's returned is stuffed into an array. Why doesn't that work? Because you cannot use = to assign values to an array. Consider this:

```
alpha = beta[];
```

That doesn't work either. Now, if n were an integer pointer variable, this would work:

```
n = numbers;
```

But, it doesn't work the other way around. Similarly:

```
&numbers = odds();
```

This contraption is doomed to failure as well. The &numbers thing generates an address, and odds() returns a memory location. So, what is assigned to what? *Nothing!* And the compiler throws up all over the floor.

No. No. No. No. No.

If a function returns a memory address, the best place to store that address is a . . . .what? Anyone?

Of course! A pointer variable! Here's a rewrite of the program's main() function:

```
int main()
{
    int *n;
    int x;

    n = odds();

    for(x=0;x<SIZE;x++)
        printf("Element #%d = %d\n",x,*(n+x));
    return(0);
}
```

First, the `numbers[SIZE]` array is done away with. You don't need it. All you need is a variable to hold the location of an integer, such as `*n`.

Second, the new variable is used to retrieve the address returned by the `odds()` function.

Finally, pointer notation is used in the `printf()` statement to display the offset values inside the array returned by `odds()`.

Make the preceding modifications to the ODD.C source code. Save it to disk. Compile and. . . .

```
odd.c:27: warning: function returns address of local variable
```

Whatever. It's only a warning error, so run the program anyway and you see

```
Element #0 = 254100227
Element #1 = 254100667
Element #2 = 6455
Element #3 = 304858
Element #4 = 654824
```

Garbage! The problem here is an old one: Functions discard their variable's values when the function is done. To retain the values, you must make the variable `static`.

Don't make the variable a `const`. If you do, the variable changes into a constant, which doesn't work! You need `static`, which simply tells the compiler *not* to discard the variable's value when the function is done.

Edit Line 21 in the ODD.C code to read

```
static int o[SIZE];
```

Save this change to disk. Compile — now with no errors. And run it:

```
Element #0 = 1
Element #1 = 3
Element #2 = 5
Element #3 = 7
Element #4 = 9
```

Strings, Functions, and Pointers

I have more fun in my programs with strings than with numbers every day. The problem is that, inevitably, strings bump into pointers and the fun dries up like a fallen Popsicle on a hot summer sidewalk. It gets even more complex when you deal with functions. Passing a string to a function isn't that terrible, but functions that return strings have been known to tie those strings into all sorts of knots.

Sending a string to a function

The following program, ULINE.C, contains a function, `underline()`, that swallows a string — which is the same as any other array in C. See whether you can figure out what it does before you run it:

```
#include <stdio.h>

void underline(char *string);

int main()
{
    underline("This Year's Starting Line-Up");
    return(0);
}

void underline(char *string)
{
    puts(string);
    while(*string)
    {
        putchar('=');
        string++;
    }
    putchar('\n');
}
```

Carefully hunt and peck in this source code. Save it to disk as ULINE.C.

Compile and run:

```
This Year's Starting Line-Up
=============================
```

The `underline()` function displays a string and then underlines it with a bunch of equal signs.

As input, `underline()` requires a string. The string variable that it eats is declared just like any other string, though pointer notation is used and not array notation:

```
void underline(char *string)
```

Internally, the function refers to the string as `string` — no ampersand. The `*string` format is used to read characters in the string.

You can call the function with a string variable or a string constant (as is the case in ULINE.C). Again, no ampersand is needed.

It helps if you think of the string existing in memory as a series of characters, all packed into an array with a NULL at the end. Rather than use all those characters themselves, only the string's address is used.

Whenever you see a `while` loop with `*string` (or something similar) as its condition, you can bet your bonnet that the loop is repeated until no more characters are in the string.

Exercise 4.7.4

Using the ugly `*string++` thing, create your own version of the `strlen()` function. Call your function `strlength()` to avoid confusing the compiler. Have that function return the length of a string of characters. Name the source code STRLEN.C.

Returning a string from a function

Passing a string back from a function is rather simple — as long as you're utterly open to the concept of strings, memory addresses, and pointer variables. As with functions that return other types of values, a function returning a string must be declared as such:

```
char *randName(void);
```

This prototype defines a function `rendName`. The function requires no input and returns a string as output. Or, to be more exact, it returns the address of a character array in memory.

As a real-life example of this type of function, I present to you this modification of the BINBIN.C source code from Book IV, Chapter 3. In this update, the `binString()` function now returns, rather than displays, the binary text string:

```
#include <stdio.h>

char *binString(int n);

int main()
{
    unsigned short int value;

    printf("Enter an integer value, 0 to 65,535: ");
    scanf("%d",&value);

    printf("Decimal value is %d\n",value);
    printf("Hexadecimal value is 0x%X\n",value);
```

```
        printf("Binary value is %s\n",binString(value));
        return(0);
}

char *binString(int n)
{
        static char bin[17];        /* must be static! */
        int x;

        for(x=0;x<16;x++)
        {
            bin[x] = n & 0x8000 ? '1' : '0';
            n <<= 1;
        }
        bin[16] = '\0';
        return(bin);
}
```

Aside from recasting the binString() function as a char pointer, the only
other changes are to the printf() statement, making the bin[] array
static, and a return at the end of binString():

```
printf("Binary value is %s\n",binString(value));
```

The immediate value returned by binString() is used in printf() to display the binary text string. I could have saved the value in a char pointer
and used it instead, but there was no need.

The address of the bin array is returned:

```
return(bin);
```

Note that bin[] must be declared as static; otherwise, its contents are lost
when the function returns.

Save these changes to BINBIN.C. Compile and run:

```
Enter an integer value, 0 to 65535: 54321
Decimal value is 54321
Hexadecimal value is 0xD431
Binary value is 1101010000110001
```

Exercise 4.7.5

Write a function that accepts a string as input and returns that string as
output, though reversed. Name your source code REVERSE.C.

Chapter 8: Structures, Pointers, and the Malloc Deity

In This Chapter

- ✔ Grabbing memory chunks with the `malloc()` function
- ✔ Resizing a memory chunk with `realloc()`
- ✔ Using the `free()` function to release memory
- ✔ Making a structure by using `malloc()` and pointers
- ✔ Working with a pointer structure

*T*his book is so full of pointer chapters that you would think that the subject has been run dry. But, no! If you have been following along from Book IV, Chapter 1, you have completely experienced the entire pointer roller coaster. The ups. The downs. The vomiting.

After seven (six, really) chapters of pointer nonsense, one more bothersome thing to point out remains. That's the structure — the old multivariable you may have first read about in Book III. The problem with pointers and structures, however, is that structures must have content. You can't just wish a structure out of thin air. Or, can you? This chapter explains how thin air can be transformed into the stuff of structures.

Making Sacrifices to Malloc

Mem'ries, like a PC full of RAM
Kil-o-bytes are full of memories
That's the way I am. . . .

Programming would be so much easier if you just knew what users wanted; for example:

```
#include <stdio.h>

int main()
{
```

```
    puts("42\n");
    return(0);
}
```

or:

```
#include <stdio.h>

int main()
{
    puts("You left your car keys on your dresser.\n");
    return(0);
}
```

Alas, as a programmer, you must anticipate every possible thing that could happen in your program. One of the hardest things to guess, especially in a program that fiddles with lots of data, is how much stuff a user types: How many records are needed in a database or how big a graphics image must be or how long a word processing document is.

The solution to the how-much-memory puzzle is to *allocate more memory.*

Allocating memory isn't the same thing as wishing more RAM from thin air. No, it's more like creating space for variables you haven't used yet. It's setting aside a chunk of memory for later use — a specific chunk, just the right size. All you need is the right command to find the memory and a pointer variable to return the location where the memory chunk starts.

In the C language, the malloc() function is used to set aside a chunk of the computer's memory for your program to use. malloc() is the *memory allocation* function, not a pagan god.

You tell the malloc() function how much memory you need, and if that memory is available, malloc() returns a pointer to the start of that memory.

Allocating memory and using malloc() may seem rather useless at this stage of the game. And, I agree: Only when you *need* memory does malloc() become necessary. Examples of needing memory are provided in the next section.

Your computer probably has many megabytes of RAM installed. When your program runs, it sets aside storage space for all the variables you have declared. Only if you need more variables do you have to go out and fetch the memory, allocating it to any new variables or arrays you create on the fly. That's all the malloc() function does. Please don't think that malloc() magically creates new RAM in your computer.

Know your ancient evil pagan deities

Abigor: An upper demon of hell, in charge of warfare and battle. He will sell the secrets of victory to any prince willing to sell his soul. He's often seen riding a winged horse followed by lots of guys in 3-piece suits.

Baal: A Semitic fertility god and also the sun god. Jezebel, the wife of Ahab, who was king of Israel, turned the country away from Yahweh to worship Baal. The prophet Elijah did battle with the priests of Baal, and, lo, they were smitten. Even so, eventually the kingdom of Israel switched to Baal worship, so Yahweh smote them and scattered them over the earth.

Beelzebub: The Lord of the Flies himself, this name is a contraction (or, can you say *concatenation?*) of Baal (*see* Baal) and zebul, which means *exalted*. In Milton's *Paradise Lost*, Beelzebub was second in command to Satan. In *Bohemian Rhapsody,* Beelzebub has a devil put aside for Freddie Mercury.

Belial: An evil spirit of darkness, wickedness, ungodliness, and so forth; often compared with Satan. According to Milton, he's on the executive board in hell.

Leviathan: The Ugaritic god of evil, often depicted as the chaos animal, a snake or other reptile, though it can also be a sea serpent. The Leviathan is a symbol of evil power that will be destroyed by the forces of good on Judgment Day, sometime after the halftime show.

Lilith: Adam's first wife, who aspired to be his equal. Defying Adam, she spoke the holy name of God and flew off to do evil and corrupt souls. Cursed to have all her own children die, Lilith is often accused of smothering young babies in their cribs. She is the first ex-wife.

Lucifer: Satan's original logon when he was prince of the angels. He rebelled against God and was cast out of heaven. Now rules hell and parts of Wall Street.

Moloch: A real monster; an Ammonite (and Phoenician) god who required children as sacrifices. Several of King Solomon's wives worshipped Moloch and eventually converted old King Solomon to that cult.

Molech: *See* Moloch.

Marduk: The chief Babylonian god. He gained prominence as a rival to Yahweh when the Hebrews were held captive in Babylon. He has no counterpart in the C programming language.

A poor example of not allocating any memory

When you create a variable, you give it a name and a type. The compiler dutifully responds by finding a location in memory for the variable, a location that's the exact size to hold the variable. That's the way it is for every variable, every time you declare something in C. Or, let me put it this way:

A variable in C cannot be used until it's created in memory, assigned storage space, and initialized.

If you dare not believe this, witness this program:

```
#include <stdio.h>
#include <string.h>

int main()
{
    char *string;

    strcpy(string,"Howdy! Howdy! Hi!");
    printf("%s\n",string);
    return(0);
}
```

Type this source code into your editor. Save it to disk as HOWDY.C, which is probably what Kernighan and Ritchie would have called HELLO.C had they lived in Texas and not in New Jersey. Compile.

What? Were you expecting an error? If you were paying attention, you probably guessed correctly that no memory storage has been allocated in the program. The pointer variable `string` is merely a pointer variable. Nowhere in the program is storage for the string set aside, but that's not cause for alarm to the compiler.

Run.

I have even seen compilers where the program works, which is amazing because it's not supposed to. On some computers, however, the program locks up tight and may even require you to strangle the console to regain control.

What went wrong? No space was set aside for the string. You can do that in two ways. The first is to create a string buffer and use it, such as by redefining the `string` variable to an array:

```
char string[80];
```

The second way is to use the `malloc()` function to allocate memory for the string on the fly.

Whenever you see the `null pointer` error, it means that a string or other variable was accessed through a pointer but that the pointer was never initialized to anything or was improperly initialized.

Grant me more space, O, Malloc!

The `malloc()` function is what gives you memory when you need it. You can even use the power of the computer to figure out exactly how much space you need.

The `malloc` function (pronounced "MAL-lock," for *memory allocation*) is used to grab a chunk of memory and assign it to a variable in your program. Here's the format:

```
pointer = (type *)malloc(size);
```

`malloc()` attempts to set aside a chunk of memory equal to `size`, which is the number of bytes that are needed. `size` can be a constant or the size of a variable or structure, determined by using the `sizeof` operator.

`(type *)` is a typecast, ensuring that the chunk of memory that's allocated is suited for a specific type of variable: `char` for character and string storage; `int` for integers; and `float` for floats; for example. This system ensures that `malloc()` returns the proper type of pointer for which you're allocating space.

What `malloc()` returns is either the address of the chunk of memory or NULL.

If NULL is returned, `malloc()` is unable to set aside enough memory. Maybe it means that memory is full, or maybe some other problem has occurred. Otherwise, `malloc()` returns a memory address. What type of variable holds a memory address? Anyone?

Yes! It's a *pointer* variable: `char` for string storage or a `struct` for new structure storage, for example.

Finally, to make the `malloc()` function behave itself, you must include the STDLIB.H file:

```
#include <stdlib.h>
```

Note that the memory allocated by `malloc()` isn't initialized or zeroed out; like any other memory allocated in C, the contents are garbage until you set them equal to something.

Essentially, `malloc()` does for you what it does for the compiler when a variable is declared. But, by using `malloc()`, you can set the memory size on your own.

Properly allocating space for "Howdy, Howdy, Hi"

The shocking news is that the HOWDY.C program can really work, or, if it worked for you the first time, it can be made to work *for real*. With `malloc()` in your pocket, though, you can create any old pointer, allocate memory for

it, and then use it like a normal variable. This update shows how it's done to
the HOWDY.C program:

```
#include <stdio.h>
#include <string.h>
#include <stdlib.h>

int main()
{
    char *string;

    string = (char *)malloc(80);
    if(string==NULL)
    {
        puts("Not enough memory");
        return(0);
    }

    strcpy(string,"Howdy! Howdy! Hi!");
    printf("%s\n",string);
    return(0);
}
```

Modify the source code for HOWDY.C in your editor, making the changes and
additions as just noted. Save it to disk using the same name, HOWDY.C:
Compile and run:

```
Howdy! Howdy! Hi!
```

HOWDY.C has no string storage. None! Not one byte! The storage for the
string is created by malloc():

```
string = (char *)malloc(80);
```

The 80 sets aside 80 *chunks* of storage. The chunk size is set by the typecast,
(char *), which means that malloc() is finding storage for 80 characters
of text. The value that's returned is a memory location, saved in the string
pointer variable.

You don't have to use #define to create the NULL value in the program;
NULL is already defined in the STDIO.H header file, and you can use it as a
NULL pointer (or the value 0) whenever you like. In fact, if you want to be
really safe with the NULL value, you could write the line like this:

```
if(string==(char *)NULL)
```

But this is unnecessary in modern compilers; the malloc() function should
have already typecast any NULL returned as a char.

Exercise 4.8.1

Modify the HOWDY.C program so that it accepts input from the user, allocates space for a duplicate of the string that's entered, and then displays that duplicate string.

Malloc's More Useful Relatives

malloc() is the father of a family of memory-allocation functions. You can view the entire malloc() horde in your compiler's documentation. Of the lot, two companion functions worthy of mention are realloc() and free().

The realloc() function is used to resize or re-allocate memory originally divvied up by malloc(). By using realloc(), you can modify your memory allocations on the fly, giving your data more memory when it needs it or trimming back to save memory.

The free() function is the un-malloc(); it takes memory allocated by malloc() and releases it, making that memory available.

Resizing memory chunks with realloc()

Consider a program that must accept input from the user. You don't know how much junk the user will type, but you don't want to overallocate memory and waste space. This bit of code presents a potential solution to this problem:

```c
#include <stdio.h>
#include <stdlib.h>
#include <string.h>

int main()
{
    char *input;
    int size;

/* Allocate "enough" memory */
    input = (char *)malloc(4069);      /* 4K input buffer */

    printf("Enter some text: ");
    gets(input);

/* resize input buffer to save space */
    size = strlen(input) + 1;          /* +1 for NULL */
    if(!realloc(input,size))
    {
        puts("Unable to reallocate memory");
        return(0);
```

**Book IV
Chapter 8**

Structures, Pointers, and the Malloc Deity

```
        }
        puts("Memory reallocation successful");
        printf("String is:\n\"%s\"\n",input);
        return(0);
}
```

Carefully type this code into your editor. If you have been reading this book from front to back, note that this program is the first to accept string input that doesn't allocate space for the string. Save the code to disk as INPUT.C. Compile and run:

```
Enter some text: Girls don't make passes at guys who pass
    gases
Memory reallocation successful
String is:
"Girls don't make passes at guys who pass gases"
```

The realloc() function is buried inside an if statement. Here's how it reads:

```
realloc(input,size)
```

The pointer variable input contains the start of the memory chunk previously allocated by malloc(). The value size is the new size. In the program, malloc() originally gave 4 kilobytes of memory to the string. After the preceding statement, the string is allocated only as much space as it really needs. The rest of the 4K buffer is released for later use.

realloc() returns a NULL if it fails. So, the ! in the if statement is used to catch that condition and then display the error message and exit the program.

Note that I didn't bother to do error checking for malloc() in this code. For this demo program, I decided that checking wasn't necessary and would just junk up the code. But, for real life, you should always confirm that memory was, in fact, allocated.

You can use this type of allocation technique to cough up space for any text the user enters. That way, you don't have to specify various character arrays for input in your program. Instead, use malloc() and realloc() inside your code to assign as much storage space as necessary for string input.

If you love your RAM, set it free()

The free() function is straightforward and simple: Pass it a pointer to memory that has been allocated with malloc() and that memory is gone. No longer available. DOA.

To continue with the INPUT.C program, consider the situation where, after the text string is used, its memory needs to be freed up so that some other part of the program can use it. Here's how you can use `free()` to make that happen:

```
#include <stdio.h>
#include <stdlib.h>
#include <string.h>

int main()
{
    char *input;
    int size;

/* Allocate "enough" memory */
    input = (char *)malloc(4069);      /* 4K input buffer */

    printf("Enter some text: ");
    gets(input);

/* resize input buffer to save space */
    size = strlen(input) + 1;          /* +1 for NULL */
    if(!realloc(input,size))
    {
        puts("Unable to reallocate memory");
        return(0);
    }
    puts("Memory reallocation successful");
    printf("String is:\n\"%s\"\n",input);
    free(input);
    puts("Memory has been released");
    printf("String is:\n\"%s\"\n",input);
    return(0);
}
```

Make these changes to your INPUT.C source code. Three lines have been added between the original's final `printf()` statement and the `return`. Save the changes to disk. Recompile. Run:

```
Enter some text: Now we have wrinkles on our face, but pruney
    has them everyplace.
Memory reallocation successful
String is:
"Now we have wrinkles on our face, but pruney has them
    everyplace."
Memory has been released
String is:
"p7="
```

Historical nonsense about `free()` that you shouldn't read

Contrary to rumor, the `free()` function doesn't make more memory available to your program, nor does it return how much memory is available inside the computer. Both are myths that I occasionally hear about.

It reminds me of the old `DIM` command in an ancient version of BASIC. Once upon a time, a programmer figured out that if you call the `DIM` function at certain key spots in your program, memory would be optimized and the code would run more efficiently.

Because anything that could speed up a BASIC program was desired, programmers would often litter their code with the occasional `DIM`

statement. The problem was that they misread the instructions: `DIM` had to be used specifically and precisely. By scattering `DIM` statements around their code, unwitting BASIC programmers made their programs run slower!

The bottom line is to double-check the rumor mill before you try something. There's usually a reason behind any madness. The myths around the `free()` function may be caused by programming on ancient computers with limited amounts of memory. Because those conditions don't exist any more, the myth — even if it were true — is no longer valid.

That last `printf()` statement, and the preceding output, is merely for demonstration purposes. The memory has been released, so there's no string to output. The random output sort of proves this.

By the way, the `free()` function really has no error exit condition to check; it returns no value.

Using Pointers and Malloc to Make New Structures

One shortcoming of C is that you cannot dynamically re-allocate arrays. You will try. You will yearn for it. You will e-mail me and ask how it can be done, even though I'm telling you that it cannot. (That's because you didn't read this part of the book.) But, no matter what, you cannot re-allocate an array. It just cannot be done, not in C, not even by using `malloc()`.

But, you try anyway. You do this:

```
int array[var];
```

Where you try to declare an array by using a variable (var in the preceding line), the compiler coughs and hacks and gleefully explains that arrays can be dimensioned only with constant values. The downside here is that you can guess too low and your program runs out of storage places. But, if you guess too high, you're just wasting memory.

The key to dynamically allocating space as needed isn't to use an array, but to use structures instead.

What you need in order to create a structure from thin electrons

All of a sudden, like one of those chest pains that you hope is just gas, you decide that your program needs a new structure. With the help of malloc(), you create it from all that excess RAM lying around inside your computer. Here's what you need in order to make that happen:

✦ The size of the structure so that malloc() can allocate the proper number of bytes

✦ A pointer variable of that structure type so that the address of the new structure can be known

✦ A way to access the members of a pointer-structure thing

The size of the structure is determined by using the sizeof operator. That way, malloc() gives you exactly the amount of storage you need — no more or less.

A pointer variable for a structure is no big deal. Structure pointers are declared just like any other type of pointer:

```
struct oz *toto;
```

Because toto has an asterisk before its name, it's defined as a pointer and not as a normal structure variable. You use the oz variable to store the address returned by malloc(), which tells the world the location of the new structure in memory.

Finally, you have to use the strange pointer structure notation. It looks like this:

```
toto->actor
```

Although that's normally toto.actor, when you use a pointer to a structure, the strange -> thing is used instead. Don't ask me why; I didn't make this stuff up. But, it's important to remember. Unlike other types of pointers, structure pointers *do not* use the asterisk notation. So, this is wrong:

```
*toto.actor
```

And this is just way out:

```
*toto->actor
```

Your first strange structure and pointer program

If you have worked through Book III, you may have already encountered the OZ series of programs, which create a database of structures. You can do the same with pointers and structures. The difference with pointers and structures is that you can continue to build the array and aren't limited by the size that was declared when you wrote the program.

Oh, bother! Why not just show you the example?

```
#include <stdio.h>
#include <stdlib.h>
#include <string.h>

#define LINE_LENGTH 40

int main()
{
    struct cast {
        char actor[18];
        int age;
        char role[16];
    };
    struct cast *star;        /* create structure pointer */
    int line;

/* Get memory chunk */
    star = (struct cast *)malloc(sizeof(struct cast));

    if(star == NULL)
    {
        puts("Memory allocation failed");
        return(0);
    }

    strcpy(star->actor,"Judy Garland");
    star->age = 17;
    strcpy(star->role,"Dorothy");
```

```
    puts("Wizard of Oz Database!\n");

/* draw the table heading */
    printf("%-18s %3s   %-15s\n","Actor","Age","Role");
    for(line=0;line<LINE_LENGTH;line++) putchar('-');
    putchar('\n');

/* display the data */
    printf("%-18s %3d   %-15s\n",
        star->actor,\
        star->age,\
        star->role);
    return(0);
}
```

Save the changes to the last rendition of the OZ.C source code, as just noted. Be careful! Lots of new doodads are in there. Save the changes back to disk, and then compile and run:

```
Wizard of Oz Database!

Actor             Age   Role
------------------------------------
Judy Garland       17   Dorothy
```

Pretty nifty, huh? That chunk of information was stored in space that the program allocated on the fly. With proper modifications, other structures and pointers can be created just like that, building the database without declaring an array and allocating space as needed. Here are the program's high points:

✦ The structure pointer is created like any structure variable, though it's prefixed with a * — like all pointers:

```
struct cast *star;
```

✦ In Line 18, the `star` pointer is assigned a chunk of memory equal to the size of the `cast` structure:

```
star = (struct cast *)malloc(sizeof(struct cast));
```

First, `malloc()` is typecast to be of the same variable type as the `cast` structure. Internally, `malloc()` uses `sizeof` to get the size of the `cast` structure and set aside that much memory for a new variable.

✦ Lines 20 through 24 handle the case when memory cannot be allocated. Honestly, this isn't necessary for such a small chunk of memory in a demo program. In real life, however, when you're allocating space for sockets or other vital things, checking for available memory is a must.

✦ With the pointer memory allocated, it can be filled with information. Note how the -> thing is used in lines 26, 27, and 28 to put data into memory via the pointer.

✦ The official name for the -> thing is *arrow pointer*.

✦ Finally, the -> thing is used in Line 38 (which includes Lines 39 through 41) to display values stored in the allocated structure.

✦ Beyond using pointers, this technique is really no different than creating a structure variable and filling it directly. Again, the advantage here is that you can create new structures on the fly.

Exercise 4.8.2

Modify the OZ.C source code so that typedef is used to create a new variable for the cast structure. Name the new variable OZ.

And now, the rest of the story

Using structures and pointers involves more than just allocating space for one structure. Most programs don't need only one new structure. They may need dozens of structures — new ones are created all the time. An array isn't the answer, and using malloc() to allocate individual structures is really only a half-solution.

To make a program allocate as many structures as it needs, C language scientists and others in white lab coats devised something called a *linked list*. This concept is really nuts, so I devote all of Book VI to the subject. You can find that book later in this reference.

Chapter 9: Does Anyone Have the Time?

In This Chapter

- Understanding how computers keep time
- Using TIME.H functions
- Getting the epoch seconds' value with `time()`
- Using the `tm` structure to display time-and-date bits and pieces
- Displaying the current date and time
- Pausing program execution for a second

Computers make lousy watches. They're not only too big to put on your wrists, but are also (the main thing) too busy doing other things to make accurate timekeeping a priority. If you ever get into low-level systems programming, you can understand why the clock is every so often interrupted or even, at times, suspended. But that's not the subject here.

As a timepiece, your computer may not always display the proper time, but it does know the time — or close to the current time. Thanks to tiny batteries inside the computer, the time is maintained even when the computer is off. This information is freely available to any program that wants it. All you need to know are the programming techniques covered in this chapter, and you too can take advantage of the computer's less-than-accurate watch.

No, Seriously: What Time Is It, Really?

You may recall the utter panic in the non-computer world about the Year 2000 (Y2K) problem. To save precious memory, early computers could accurately keep track of time for only a certain number of dates. For example, programmers would specify only the last two digits in a year just to save two bytes of RAM. That trick worked from 1986 until 1999, but at the year 2000, the computer would assume that it was 1900 and all sorts of chaos would ensue.

Of course, we all survived Y2K just fine. Few computers were subject to catastrophic problems, and the problems that did arise were mostly predicted and eventually fixed. No one died in a plane crash. No elevators plunged 40 stories. And, no chemical plants dumped toxic waste into our drinking water when they became confused about the date.

Even though Y2K has passed, computers still have issues with timekeeping. In a way, the Y2K problem will haunt us again, in several years and for the same reasons; the clocks on computers are tuned for only a given chunk of time. This section describes more about why this issue is a problem and covers some basic background about timekeeping on a computer.

Julian dates, Julienne fries

How does a computer keep track of time? If you have been reading this book from front to back, you know the answer: The computer keeps time in *binary*. For the most part, that's true. As long as the binary value can be translated into a date somehow, everything should work out hunky-dory. The problem is to determine how a binary value, or integer, works out to something non-binary, like a date.

One method for storing dates and times on a computer is the Julian date, named after the old Julian calendar, credited to Julius Caesar. Using this system, each day, starting with January 1, 4713 B.C. is given a number. Partial days, or hours and minutes, are given a fractional part of the number.

The Modified Julian Day (MJD) was developed in the 1950s and is pretty much the standard now. For example, Microsoft Excel uses it to express dates inside its worksheets.

In the MJD standard, the date January 1, 2000, has the value 51,544. Noon on that day would have been 51,544.5.

The computer can choose to store the Julian date as two integers — the date and then the fractional part — or as a floating-point number. Honestly, I don't know how Excel does it internally.

Julienne fries are potatoes cut into long strips, usually with a curled twist in them.

The Gregorian calendar

By the 1500s, the Julian calendar was showing signs of age — such severe signs that spring festivals were being celebrated in the early part of summer. Although old Julius was clever, there were certain facts about the earth's rotation about the sun that he wasn't quite aware of.

To fix the problem, Pope Gregory XIII established a new calendar. It took into account corrections for missing leap years — stuff that Julius couldn't predict. The calendar also leapt forward 10 days from October 4, 1582, directly to October 15, 1582, so as to realign seasonal festivals with their proper dates.

(Leaping forward 10 days was quite a catastrophic event, and Pope Gregory was gutsy to make the move. Many people blamed the church for purposely shortening their lives. In England, mobs accused the banks of using the new date system to shortchange them on interest payments.)

The Gregorian calendar is the timekeeping system we now use. So, no matter what the computer bases the time on internally, that value is eventually converted into the Gregorian calendar system for our use.

Greenwich Mean Time and UTC

The main parallel on the earth is the equator, which divides the globe in half from top to bottom. The prime meridian, which divides the world from east to west, rips through Greenwich, England. You can credit the British navy for having the most accurate charts of the oceans for such an honor.

After a prime meridian was established through Greenwich, other time zones could be created around the world: 24 of them, one for each hour in the day. Before that, local time was set at noon wherever you were. But, that made such things as train schedules impossible to keep, so the standard of having time zones came into play, with Greenwich again settled on as having the first time zone in the world. Greenwich Mean Time (GMT) became the world's standard for setting clocks.

With the adoption of atomic clocks — far more accurate than looking at the noon sun in Greenwich — Coordinated Universal Time, or UTC, was adopted as the successor to GMT.

Most sophisticated computers now set their clocks to UTC. So, no matter which time zone you live in, the computer keeps time according to the international standard. For local display, however, your time zone is noted. That's one reason that computer setup programs require you to enter your time zone. That way, the local time is what you see on the screen. But, internally, the computer uses UTC exclusively.

The UTC standard also explains why computers don't go nuts in areas that have daylight savings time.

"What is Zulu time?"

Zulu time is another name for UTC.

The epoch

Meanwhile, back in the computer, the struggle to represent time continued. Obviously, setting the date and time according to UTC and displaying it in the Gregorian fashion were tops. But, what about the binary format inside the computer itself?

Say hello to the *Unix epoch*.

TECHNICAL STUFF

What about Windows and timekeeping?

When you program in C on a Windows computer, you're using Unix epoch timekeeping, regardless of what Windows uses internally. I don't program Windows, so I really don't know the limitations of its internal clock or even whether Microsoft makes that information available. As long as the Unix functions work in C, it's really not an issue.

I do know, however, that all PCs, regardless of operating system, store the year as a 2-byte value deep down in memory. The first byte is

either 19 or 20 for the century (though they're really the 20th and 21st centuries). The second byte is the year, beginning with 1980 when the first byte is 19 and ranging from 0 through 99 when the first byte is 20.

By this reckoning, the PC can accurately track dates from 1980 through 2099. And, it seems that with a little extra work in modifying the first byte, the system could work well into the year 25,599. Sadly, by then, our robot slaves will have destroyed us, so the issue again will be moot.

Timekeeping on Unix computers begins at what its fans call the epoch. The *epoch* began at midnight (00:00:00) on January 1, 1970, and has ticked away, one bit per second, ever since. That's because the epoch is stored as a 32-bit (`long signed int`) number. That number's value is equal to the number of seconds that have elapsed since the start of the epoch. And, that's how most computers tell time.

Various functions exist that can translate the number of seconds past the epoch into a date-and-time format, something that programs *use*. That way, dates and times are kept consistent across all Unix systems.

The problem with the epoch is that it ends in the year 2038. That year will present another Y2K problem for all Unix computers. Because a 32-bit signed integer is used, at 3:14:07 a.m. on January 19, 2038, every Unix computer will suddenly believe it to be January 1, 1970, all over again.

TIP

Eventually, programmers will convert the storage space for epoch-seconds from a 32-bit value to a 64-bit value. For this reason, I highly recommend that you comment any code that uses the epoch-seconds value so that it can be handily updated in the future. A future version of yourself, or some descendant, will thank you for that.

Getting the Time

C has a small smattering of time functions, each of which is defined and massaged in the TIME.H header file. This section mulls over the more popular timekeeping functions.

Timekeeping is a function of the operating system. As such, more operating system functions are probably available to you that provide more interesting or detailed feedback than the standard C library functions presented in this section. For more information, refer to the developer's kit for your particular operating system.

What time is it right now?

The most common of the time functions is named, naturally, `time()`. Here's a quickie demo:

```
#include <stdio.h>
#include <time.h>

int main()
{
    time_t now;

    time(&now);
    printf("It is now %d\n",now);
    return(0);
}
```

Quickly type this source code before time runs out. Save it to disk as TODAY.C. Compile and run:

```
It is now 1082580966
```

The time you see varies, of course. Then again, you may think that I'm nuts because the preceding value doesn't look like any time you have ever seen. Well, *it's not!* It's the Unix epoch you see. In the preceding example, approximately 1,082,580,966 seconds have passed since midnight, January 1, 1970 UTC — adjusted for my local time zone.

To prove that the value is a certain number of seconds and not your computer's serial number, run the program again:

```
It is now 1082581104
```

Or, run the program a second later:

```
It is now 1082581105
```

Yup. It's the epoch. *As the Epoch passes. . . .*

The `time()` *function*

The `time()` function generates a copy of the epoch-seconds, saving it in a `time_t` variable type you create. You can do this in two ways:

Suppose that variable `t` is of the `time_t` type:

```
t = time(NULL);
time(&t);
```

In either case, a copy of the current time is saved in the variable `t`. Note that this is a copy of the time; because the epoch constantly moves forward, you see only a copy of it.

Exercise 4.9.1

Change the code in TODAY.C so that the `t = time(NULL)` format is used in Line 8.

What time is it right now, REALLY?

Few people walk around expressing the current time in terms of the Unix epoch. I'm sure that some hilarious geek at some university loves to bewilder college freshmen by responding with the epoch time rather than the common time of day. (Back in school, we referred to such clever people as jackasses.)

Fortunately, it's the `ctime()` function to the rescue. Seeing the need for knowing the real time versus the number of seconds that have elapsed since *Laugh-In* was live on TV, the `ctime()` function is a godsend:

```
#include <stdio.h>
#include <time.h>

int main()
{
    time_t now;

    time(&now);
    printf("It is now %s\n",ctime(&now));
    return(0);
}
```

Make the necessary modifications to the TODAY.C source code, as just shown. The only change is to Line 11, which now displays the string returned by the `ctime()` function. Remember the & before the `now` variable. Save these changes to disk, and then compile and run:

```
It is now Wed Apr 21 14:11:30 2004
```

Naturally, the time you see is current to whatever your computer believes the current time is. The `ctime()` function successfully converts the seconds in the epoch to the current, local time on your computer

Getting at the Individual Time-and-Date Pieces' Parts

Don't fret over peeling out individual time, day, month and other values from the number of seconds in the epoch or struggling with extracting strings of text from `ctime()`'s output and other nonsense. Some C language functions automatically let you pick and choose which time information you want. These functions are covered in this section.

What's the day today?

Here's some source code for you:

```c
#include <stdio.h>
#include <time.h>

int main()
{
    char *wdays[] = {
        "Sunday",
        "Monday",
        "Tuesday",
        "Wednesday",
        "Thursday",
        "Friday",
        "Saturday"
    };
    struct tm *t;
    time_t now;

    time(&now);                 /* get the current time */
    t = localtime(&now);        /* get the tm structure */
    printf("Today is %s.\n",wdays[t->tm_wday]);
    return(0);
}
```

Without thinking about anything, carefully type this code. Save it to disk as WEEKDAY.C. Compile. Run:

```
Today is Wednesday.
```

The output reflects the current day of the week. The soul of the program is the `tm` structure, described in the section that follows. That structure contains elements that represent all sorts of date-and-time aspects. Specifically, the element `tm_wday` is an integer that represents the current day of the week.

The following points explain the bowels of the WEEKDAY.C source code:

✦ The code begins by declaring a pointer array specifying the seven week-day names. That's okay: The strings are only displayed, not changed. This type of array is also the most efficient way to store this information in the program.

✦ The `struct tm *t` statement creates a pointer to a `tm` structure. That's the structure that contains all the individual tidbits about today's date and time.

✦ Review Book IV, Chapter 8 if you need to know more information about structures and pointers.

✦ In Line 18, `time(&now)` is used to get the current time — specifically, the number of seconds that have passed since the epoch. (Review the first part of this chapter for details.)

✦ The number of seconds is stored in the `now` variable, which is used by the `localtime()` function in Line 18. That function breaks the time into individual pieces, which are stored inside the `tm` structure.

✦ It helps if you read Line 20 from the inside out:

```
t->tm_wday
```

This line is a reference to the `tm_way` element inside the `t` structure. That element contains values 0 through 6, with 0 representing Sunday, 1 for Monday, and so on. This value is used as an index in the `wdays` array:

```
wdays[t->tm_wday]
```

The `wdays` array is set up so that Element 0 is "Sunday," 1 is "Monday," and so on. So, this operation evaluates to a string representing the current day of the week. That's finally used by the `%s` placeholder in `printf()` to display the weekday.

Exercise 4.9.2

Modify the WEEKDAY.C program so that the current day of the week is displayed as a 3-letter abbreviation of the full day name.

Introducing the `tm` structure

For digging down deep into the current date and time, you must use the `tm` structure. Here's how it's defined inside the TIME.H header file:

```
struct tm {
    int tm_sec;      /* seconds    [0 - 60]    */
    int tm_min;      /* minutes    [0 - 59]    */
    int tm_hour;     /* hours      [0 - 23]    */
    int tm_mday;     /* day        [1 - 31]    */
    int tm_mon;      /* month      [0 - 11]    */
```

```
    int tm_year;    /* year        [year since 1900] */
    int tm_wday;    /* weekday     [0 - 6]           */
    int tm_yday;    /* day of year [0 - 365]         */
    int tm_isdst;   /* DST         [-1,0,1]          */

/* there may be other definitions here,
   depending on the compiler */
};
```

This structure contains just about any possible date or time element you would ever want. Here, you see the standard elements and their ranges. I have some comments:

✦ The number of seconds ranges from 0 to 60, to account for one leap second. With some compilers, the value is 61, to account for two leap seconds.

✦ The year that's returned is relative to 1900. So, for the year 2006, a value of 106 would be returned. Be wary of this!

✦ The tm_isdst value is used for daylight savings time. When the value is 1, or greater than 0, daylight savings time is on. When the value is 0, standard time is on. When the value is -1 or less than 0, the computer really doesn't know what's going on.

✦ Your compiler may have additional elements in the structure. For example, some compilers may have a tm_gmtoff element to describe the local time zone, a tm_zone string element to give the name of the local time zone, plus other goodies. Refer to your compiler's docs for the details.

At the tone, the time will be. . . .

Here's a program that uses the tm structure to pull out the current time:

```
#include <stdio.h>
#include <time.h>

int main()
{
    struct tm *t;
    time_t now;

    time(&now);                 /* get the current time */
    t = localtime(&now);        /* get the tm structure */
    printf("It is now %d:%02d:%02d\n",
        t->tm_hour,
        t->tm_min,
        t->tm_sec);
    return(0);
}
```

Boring information on setting the time

Most C language time functions involve manipulating time or expressing the date and time in some manner. Setting the time is an operating system function, and on Unix that's a function that only the root account is allowed to run.

Even if some C language functions set the time or adjusted the date, I would recommend against their use. Timekeeping is important in a computer and is something not to be messed with lightly.

Write this source code in your editor. Save it to disk as TTIME.C. Compile. Run:

```
It is now 15:17:31
```

Note how I used the %02d placeholder in printf(). That way, each digit in the time output is always two places in size *and* prefixed with a 0 in case the number is only one digit long. (I didn't do that for the hour, though, because most people prefer 1:23:44 as opposed to 01:23:44.

Of course, changing the placeholder doesn't stop the computer from displaying the time in ugly 24-hour format. For that, you have to do some fixing on your own.

Exercise 4.9.3

Modify the TTIME.C source code so that the program outputs the time in a 12-hour format, with either the proper a.m. or p.m. suffix.

Exercise 4.9.4

Write a program that displays the date in this fashion:

```
mm/dd/yy
```

That's two digits each for the month, date and year, separated by slashes. Name the source code DDATE.C.

Just a Sec!

Here's a handy program that uses the difftime() function to calculate a 1-second pause:

```
#include <stdio.h>
#include <time.h>

#define DELAY 0.1

void pause(void)
{
            time_t then;

    time(&then);
    while(difftime(time(NULL),then) < DELAY)
        ;
}

int main()
{
            int x;

            for(x=10;x>0;x--)
    {
                    printf("%d\n",x);
                    pause();
    }
            printf("Blast Off!");
    return(0);
}
```

Enter this code into your editor. Save it to disk as WAITASEC.C. Compile and run.

The computer displays numbers from 10 through 1 with a 1-second pause between each value. That's thanks to `difftime()` inside the `pause()` function. Here's how it goes:

✦ Just to be handy, I have defined the constant `DELAY` to be equal to the pause that the program uses in seconds. This value must be floating point, though `difftime()` uses only the whole-number part.

✦ The first thing the `pause()` function does is to get the current time. This is done in Line 10, with the time saved in the `then` variable.

✦ The `difftime()` function in Line 11 compares the difference between two `time_t` type values. The first value is what's returned from the `time(NULL)` function (which is a `time_t` type of variable). That value is compared with the original time value, `then`. `difftime()` returns the time difference between the two values in seconds.

**Book IV
Chapter 9**

**Does Anyone Have
the Time?**

◆ Note that the recent value comes first. If you put the recent value second, `difftime()` returns negative numbers.

◆ The net effect of the `while` loop is that `difftime()` continues to spin the loop until the time values have passed the constant `DELAY`.

◆ By adjusting `DELAY`, you can make the `pause()` function pause for any length of time in your programs. Build suspense! Raise anticipation! Create programs with a . . . dramatic pause in them!

Chapter 10: Building Big Programs

In This Chapter

✓ Understanding big programs and multiple modules

✓ Creating object code files

✓ Linking object code files together

✓ Sharing global variables with `extern`

✓ Building the big Lotto program

✓ Creating your own header file

✓ Working with big projects

The largest program I have on my hard disk weighs in at 10,330 kilobytes. The smallest program I have measures a paltry 27 bytes. The larger program is obviously more versatile than my little program, but do you think that the big one was written using one source code document, like my little program?

You can bet a pot of Pooh's hunny that a 10MB program would have a source code file much larger than 10MB. If you could stick this type of document into a text editor, it would drive you, well, *insane* to make even the tiniest update. No, a better solution for creating a large program probably exists. The solution is program *modules*.

This chapter discusses program modules, which are the best way you can go about building huge, impressive, daunting programs in C.

Making Programs with Multiple Modules

This multiple-module stuff is about two things: building bigger programs and reusing common chunks of code. These concepts are similar because most of your big programs reuse the same chunks of code from previous big programs you have created. It's more like what Dr. Frankenstein did than cannibalism.

To build a big program, you need more source code. That source code most likely contains dozens and dozens of functions. Although you could stuff it all into a single file, it would be big and tough to manage. A better solution is to use smaller program chunks, or modules. Each chunk is compiled individually, creating an object code file. Then, the linker assembles all the object code files, creating the single, final program.

Banishment to the command prompt!

Truly, the best way to manage a large project and work with multiple programming modules is to use an IDE, or Integrated Development Environment. For example, you can use the Dev-C environment or Visual Studio, which Microsoft Visual C++ uses.

These IDEs allow you to build huge projects as well as manage and update all your individual modules and stuff like that. Sadly, each one of these IDEs works differently, so there's no point in my trying to document all that here. Instead, I show you how to create a multiple-module program the old-fashioned way, at the command prompt. It isn't as painful as it sounds, and it gives you the background information you need to better understand the IDEs and how to choose one that's best for you.

How it works

The key to creating a multiple-module program is knowing that despite the code existing in separate files, the program is still one unit. The code in MODULEA.C can easily call a function used in MODULEB.C. Likewise, global variables can be shared between modules by using the extern keyword. As long as you can call functions — and pass and return values to and from them — as well as use global variables, multiple modules make sense.

When you compile a module, you use a variation of the gcc command:

```
gcc -c module.c
```

The gcc command compiles the source code in MODULE.C, creating an object code file named MODULE.O (or MODULE.OBJ), but not a program file. Each module is compiled this way.

When it comes time to link everything, this command is used:

```
gcc  moda.o modb.o modc.o modd.o
```

When the gcc command sees all those .O files, it merely links them, creating the A.OUT or A.EXE file. If you want to name the final program, use this format:

```
gcc  moda.o modb.o modc.o modd.o -o prog
```

In this line, gcc links the four object code files and names the final program file PROG or PROG.EXE.

As is the case any time, gcc reports any linker errors it encounters. This is usually the common typo, though other flaws in program logic can occur or missing pieces can be caught.

The Tiny, Silly Examples

There's no point in plunging headlong into *the biggest program in this book* just to prove a point that can be made with smaller, sillier programs. So, this section demonstrates this multiple-module madness to you without rubbing too much skin off the end of your fingers.

A small, yet potent, example

Here are two bits of source code, two separate files, that you compile only into object code and then link to form one larger program. It's a demo of how things work:

```
#include <stdio.h>

int main()
{
    printf("Hello ");
    b();
    return(0);
}
```

Enter the preceding source code and save it to disk as ALPHA.C.

```
#include <stdio.h>

void b(void)
{
    printf("World!\n");
}
```

Start over with a new slate in your editor and enter the preceding source code. Save it to disk as BETA.C.

ALPHA.C and BETA.C are both modules in the same program. Granted, they're ridiculously tiny. But, they can be blended together — *linked*, in fact — to create one program. This way, the b() function in BETA.C can be called from the ALPHA.C source code.

To compile them both at once and then link them, use this command:

```
gcc alpha.c beta.c
```

The resulting program is named A.OUT or A.EXE. Run that program:

```
Hello World!
```

It works. Yeah!

How it works

If you understand how the C compiler works, all this stuff should make sense. Even so, consider this discussion a review.

The gcc command is both a compiler and a linker. For stand-alone code, it converts the source code file, SOURCE.C, into object code SOURCE.O. Then, the object code file is linked in with the C standard library file to create the final program. The object code file is then deleted. (Some compilers don't delete the object code file.)

For a detailed review of how the operation works, refer to Book I, Chapter 2.

In the case of multiple modules, gcc behaves a bit differently.

First, any source code files that are specified are compiled into object code. So, for this command:

```
gcc alpha.c beta.c
```

two object code files are created, ALPHA.O and BETA.O.

(If any errors occur during compiling, an appropriate error message is displayed.)

Next, the linker is called. It takes all the object code modules produced and links them in with the standard C library, producing the final program.

You could also do this one step at a time. It's commonly done with larger C programs and many modules; recompiling all the modules is time consuming. So, instead, only the updated module is compiled directly into object code. Here's the gcc command that does that:

```
gcc -c alpha.c
```

Here, gcc uses the -c switch to compile, but not link, the source code file ALPHA.C. If everything goes right, the object code file ALPHA.O is created.

The gcc command can then be used to link all the object code files and create the final program:

```
gcc alpha.o beta.o
```

Because gcc recognizes the .O extension as an object code file, the compile step is skipped and linking happens. If any errors occur, they're reported. Otherwise, the final program is created.

To name the program, the `-o` switch is used:

```
gcc alpha.o beta.o -o test
```

In this line, the two object code files are compiled and the result is a program named TEST.

Be careful not to screw up the `-o` and `-c` switches. They're easy to confuse because you may think that `-o` means "create object code." But, that's not the case. Think of `-c` as "compile" and `-o` as "output program."

Exercise 4.10.1

Add a third module to the sample program. Name it GAMMA.C and have it contain the function `c()`, which displays the text "I'm having fun now" five times.

Exercise 4.10.2

Modify the GAMMA.C and ALPHA.C modules. Make it so that the `c()` function requires an integer as input, the value of which determines how many times the loop is repeated.

Sharing variables between modules

The first example in this chapter proves that functions can be called between modules. What about sharing variables? Specifically, global variables are those variables you want available to every module in the program.

The secret to making global variables work is the `extern` keyword. `extern` assures the compiler that a global variable has been defined and exists in another program module. `extern` then informs the linker to go out to that module and find the variable at link time. Here's the format:

```
extern type name;
```

The external variable essentially is declared just like any other global variable except that the word `extern` precedes it. *Type* is a variable type, and *name* is the name of the variable — just like declaring any variable in C. Global arrays are declared and referenced the same way:

```
extern float recent_temps[31];
```

This declaration tells the module that the global array recent_temps exists and is declared in another module.

I generally declare global variables in the main, or first module, the one with the main() function in it. That way, I can keep track of where the variables really exist. The other modules then use extern to reference the global variable.

The following two program modules use global variables. Save the first bit of source code as FRED.C:

```
#include <stdio.h>

int age;

int main()
{
    printf("Enter your age in years: ");
    scanf("%d",&age);
    show();
    return(0);
}
```

Save the second bit of source code as BARNEY.C:

```
#include <stdio.h>

extern int age;

void show(void)
{
    printf("You're %d years old!",age);
}
```

Compile them both with the gcc fred.c barney.c command. Run:

```
Enter your age in years:
```

I lie and say that I'm **29**:

```
You're 29 years old!
```

(The computer will never know.)

Thanks to the extern statement, the age variable is shared between modules.

You need to declare the variable in only one module. Any other module that needs to use the global variable merely redeclares it with the `extern` keyword prefixed.

The Big Lotto Program

Most large programs are built from smaller pieces that may be lying around the hard drive. Back in my programming days, I had a directory full of such modules. One contained a text input program, for example. Another had routines for communicating with the serial port. Still another had the basic workings required for a full-screen text editor. And on and on. Whenever I needed to build a new project, I would pull those older routines out, dust them off, and stitch them together.

If you have been working through this book, you may already have the pieces of source code necessary to build the LOTTO.C program, both in Book III, Chapter 1:

+ LOTTO.C
+ SORTME.C

The source code for the big lotto program is created by using bits and pieces from those two programs.

Making a place for your work

Every multiple-module project I create has its own folder or directory. I like to keep the files separate and in one location, away from other projects, which not only keeps me organized but also helps me use some fancy programming tools that I cover later in this chapter.

If you have been following along in every chapter in this book, you have been building your projects in the ADVANCED folder or directory. For this project, create a LOTTO subdirectory inside the directory:

```
mkdir lotto
```

Then, change to that directory:

```
cd lotto
```

The LOTTO folder is now reserved for use solely by this project.

(Another advantage of the IDE is that it sets this type of thing up for you automatically.)

Building the main module

Every large project I create has one primary module, which I call MAIN.C. That's where the program starts and where the main() function lives. I like to keep this file rather small:

```
#include "lotto.h"

int ball[BALLS];              /* Global lotto ball array */

int main()
{
    init();
    select();
    sort();
    display();
    return(0);
}
```

Enter this source code to disk. Save it as MAIN.C in the LOTTO folder. Compile it to object code only; use the gcc -c main.c command.

Oops! An error has occurred; the LOTTO.H header file isn't found. That's because you haven't created it yet.

Note that the ball array is declared globally. It's available to every function and module that wants to use it — as long as it's referenced via the extern keyword.

It's the linker that finds typos, such as pirntf. The compiler just assumes that those functions are merely defined elsewhere. But when the linker encounters the typo and doesn't find a matching function, you get a fatal error.

Making your own header file

You can create your own header files in the C language. It's cinchy.

A *header file* is basically just source code. It contains definitions, prototypes, and other common things required to make the C compiler happy. For the lotto program, I have created a LOTTO.H header file. Here it is:

```
/* LOTTO.H Header File
 * For use with the LOTTO program and its modules
 * Written 4/21/04 by Dan Gookin
 */

/* PROTOTYPES */
/* This saves having to do this in each module */
```

```
void init(void);
void select(void);
void sort(void);
void display(void);

/* DEFINES */
#define RANGE 50
#define BALLS 6

/* TYPEDEFS */
/* I'm not using any, but they would go here as well */

/* END */
```

Copy this source code into your editor. Save it to disk as LOTTO.H — and remember that it's an H extension, not a C.

To include this file with your source code, you use double quotes rather than angle brackets. I show you this in the preceding section's listing of MAIN.C:

```
#include "lotto.h"
```

This directive tells the compiler to look for a file named LOTTO.H in the current folder or directory and stick all the instructions found therein into the source code file.

If you're following along sequentially (and you probably are, but my editor tells me that I need to say so), you can now recompile MAIN.C, as was attempted in the preceding section. This time, it works.

The result is three files in your LOTTO folder:

> MAIN.C, the main module's source code
>
> MAIN.O, the object code file for MAIN.C
>
> LOTTO.H, the project's header file

Some backup files may be in the folder as well. That's fine. These three are key, and provide the foundation for the larger program.

When you work with a large number of modules, ensure that no two modules use the same function name. Just as in a single source code file, no two functions in any program can share the same name.

Specifying modules in proper order

In the text in this chapter, I mention that it doesn't really matter how you specify source code files when you're linking multiple modules. This statement is true because the linker is smart enough to know where the program starts, and it shall create a proper program file no matter what the order of the modules. For certain larger programs, however, the order does, in fact, matter quite a bit.

For example, there may be an optimal way to link modules — a way that allows the linker to create the program with fewer "passes" over the source code. That may not make a bit of difference for a small program, but you can bet that for those multimegabyte monsters, the professional turnout, putting the modules in proper order can save them minutes or hours of linking time.

Creating the Init module

The INIT.C module is used to set up the program. In the case of LOTTO.C, it's rather simple. In some programs, however, it may require opening ports, initializing the screen or creating a window, allocating memory as necessary, or negotiating protocols, for example. Most large programs that I have written benefit from an INIT.C module. Even for the LOTTO program, this module may be simple, but it does have some tasks to fardel:

```
/* Init Module */
#include "lotto.h"
#include <stdio.h>
#include <stdlib.h>
#include <time.h>

void init(void)
{
/* seed the randomizer */
    seedRandomizer();

/* display startup text */
    puts("L O T T O   P I C K E R\n");
    puts("Press Enter to pick this week's numbers:");
    getchar();
}

void seedRandomizer(void)
{
    srandom((unsigned)time(NULL));
}
```

Type this source code into a new file.

If your compiler doesn't support the `srandom()` function, substitute `srand()` in Line 20 instead.

Save the source code to disk as INIT.C.

Before compiling, note that you have added a new function. Load the LOTTO.H header file into your editor and add the function prototype:

```
void seedRandomizer(void);
```

Place this line in the list of prototypes defined in LOTTO.H, and then resave LOTTO.H back to disk.

Now, you can compile the INIT.C module. (***Hint:*** Use the `gcc -c init.c` command.)

The program continues to grow more modules in the next section.

Creating the Select module

The SELECT.C module is where the lotto numbers are chosen. It uses a technique, covered in Book III, Chapter 1, which ensures that each ball is a unique number:

```
/* Select Module */
#include "lotto.h"
#include <stdio.h>

extern int ball[BALLS];          /* Global array */

void select(void)
{
    int numbers[RANGE];
    int c,b;

/* initialize the tracking array */
    for(c=0;c<RANGE;c++)
        numbers[c]=0;

/* draw the numbers */
    puts("Here they come:");
    for(c=0;c<BALLS;c++)
    {
        do
        {
            b = random() % RANGE;
        }
```

```
    while(numbers[b]);
                            /* number drawn */
    numbers[b] = 1;         /* number drawn lock */
    ball[c] = b + 1;        /* save number drawn */
  }
}
```

The idea in this module is to fill the global array `ball` with random values from 1 through RANGE. The extra code up there ensures that the same number doesn't get drawn twice. (Refer to Book III, Chapter 1 for more information.)

To reference the `ball` array, the `extern` declaration is used. That's followed by the original declaration of the global variable. This ensures that this module is fully aware of the global variable. When the linker glues this module together with the MAIN.C module, the final connection is resolved.

Save this code to disk as SELECT.C. Compile into object code. Then, get ready to move on to the next module.

Creating the Sort module

There really is no need to sort the lotto balls as they're drawn — but, what the heck! I'm sure that if the members of the Lotto Authority had it their way, they would love to draw the numbers sequentially. How long they could get away with such a thing is anyone's guess. Regardless, this lotto program uses this module to sort the results:

```
/* Sort module */
#include "lotto.h"

extern int ball[BALLS];

void sort(void)
{
    int a,b,temp;

    for(a=0;a<BALLS-1;a++)
        for(b=a+1;b<BALLS;b++)
            if(ball[a] > ball[b])
            {
                temp = ball[b];
                ball[b] = ball[a];
                ball[a] = temp;
            }
}
```

Type this source code into your editor. Save it to disk as SORT.C, and then compile it.

Moving right along. . . .

Creating the Display module

The task of the final module in the program is to display the lotto results.
Here's some code that does just that:

```
/* Display module */
#include "lotto.h"
#include <stdio.h>

extern int ball[BALLS];

void display(void)
{
    int c;

    for(c=0;c<BALLS;c++)
        printf("%2d ",ball[c]);
    puts("\nGood luck in the drawing!\n");
}
```

Gingerly enter this source code into your editor. Save it to disk as DISPLAY.C.
Compile.

There. That's the last module.

Putting the whole thing together

Your lotto directory should now contain at least these files:

> MAIN.C
>
> MAIN.O
>
> INIT.C
>
> INIT.O
>
> SELECT.C
>
> SELECT.O
>
> SORT.C
>
> SORT.O
>
> DISPLAY.C
>
> DISPLAY.O
>
> LOTTO.H

The object code files now need to be glued together to form the final program. Oddly enough, it doesn't matter how you specify them. Remember that the compiler merely searches for the main() function and uses it as the program's entry point. In the end, everything always turns up sunshiny. Even so, I'm a stickler for specifying modules in the order the program uses them:

```
gcc main.o init.o select.o sort.o display.o -o lotto
```

This command links the object code modules and creates the final program, named LOTTO.

If you see any errors, they're most likely typos. Fix 'em. Double-check the source code in this chapter, if necessary.

Good luck in the drawing!

Be sure to check out the section on the Make utility in Book IV, Chapter 11 for information on how to make this process amazingly simple.

Chapter 11: Help!

In This Chapter

✔ Fixing or debugging your code

✔ Using `printf()` statements to track problems

✔ Avoiding common problems

✔ Using various utilities to help you program

✔ Working with the make utility to build large projects

*Y*ou may be puzzled about why I would put the "Help!" chapter in the advanced book. Experienced C programmers, however, understand. The further you get into C, the more help you need, and, sadly, the fewer other programmers are available to help you.

TIP

Basic C programmer knowledge tidbits

Programmers have a lingo all their own. Most of these folks have been programming for years, weaned on ancient network systems in college. That experience gives them an insight that cannot be taught, but can be mimicked.

For starters, I recommend picking up *The New Hacker's Dictionary*, 3rd Edition, edited by Eric Raymond (The MIT Press, ISBN 0-262-68092-0). You may not get every tidbit in the book, but it helps you to understand a programmer's mindset.

In addition to the book, consider these suggestions:

✔ Be able to quote spontaneously from *Monty Python and the Holy Grail*.

✔ Use `foo` as a sample variable or filename (from *foobar*, or Fouled Up Beyond All Recognition).

✔ Always call storage space a *buffer*.

✔ Revere classic science fiction TV shows — the more obscure, the better. For example, you're esteemed among your peers if you can quote from *Red Dwarf*.

✔ Lose your hygiene skills (unless you want to keep your wife or girlfriend — or both!).

✔ Keep in mind that old food is still good. Pizzas are better the next morning. Doughnuts don't gain true favor with a programmer until you can audibly rap them on a tabletop.

✔ Discover 2:00 a.m.

You can always ignore these suggestions and start a trend of your own. Remember that I slipped into the programmer community quite easily, and — like you — I am self taught.

The key to being a productive, successful C programmer is to *practice*. If you can't impress them with a programming degree from a major university, you can certainly dazzle them with your code; I tell my readers that having a dozen or so useful and *working* programs may mean more to a future employer than guzzling beer at some college for five or six years.

For those dire times when you need help, I offer you this chapter. In it, you find my advice on debugging as well as some handy, helpful tools you can use to hone your C skills. Beyond that, there's always the Internet. And, of course, this reference continues with a few more books to help round out your C language education.

Debugging

Every programming project has warnings, errors, and bugs in it. Of the three, bugs are the most evil. They aren't typos. They aren't a user's fault. They're misjudgments in program logic, things you didn't think of, and misplaced or unfinished thoughts. They drive you bonkers.

In C, you see the warnings and errors when you compile and link. These problems are easy to fix because most compilers give you a clue about which line contains the offensive statement. If you're using an IDE, you may even experience the joy of highlighted errors in your code — a missing semicolon, parenthesis, or brace. Fixing is a snap.

Linker errors mean missing header files, or missing OBJ files, if you're making a multiple-module project. Again, this type of error is easy to fix.

Bugs are just frustrating. The program runs, but not *right*. Here are some hints for tracking down bugs:

Make liberal use of random `printf()` statements. At various spots where your program goes astray, stick in a `printf()` statement to display a variable's values. Use the exact variable format you're using in the program:

```
printf("\n***%d***\n",*var++);
```

In this example, the value of variable `*var++` is displayed. It may look something like this:

```
***245***
```

That number appears as your program runs, giving you an idea of whether the variable contains the proper value. If not, you know where to adjust the program.

Repeating the same `printf()` statement before and after a function call can also be used to illustrate what happens to values in the program.

Mind your parentheses. Especially in a complex `if` comparison, make sure that you have the proper number of parentheses and the right items between them. The compiler doesn't tell you when you have a goofy `if` comparison:

```
if(toupper(cheddar[i]=='H'))
```

In this example, the first right parenthesis should appear after the `cheddar[i]` variable, not after the `'H'`. The `if` comparison still works and probably would be TRUE all the time, but it's not what you intended.

Also, check `while` loop conditions for this same type of error.

If you use a color-coded editor, such as VIM or any of the editors included with an IDE, you can easily avoid this type of error. Most color-coded editors instantly flag an excess or absence of parentheses, brackets, or braces.

Remember the `break` **in a** `switch-case` **structure.** Your program continues to flow through every `case` item in a `switch-case` structure until a `break` is encountered; for example:

```
switch(ch)
{
  case 'A':
  case 'E':
  case 'I':
  case 'O':
  case 'U':
        puts("It's a vowel");
  case 'B':
// and so on....
  case 'Z':
        puts("It's a voiced consonant");
  default:
        puts("It's an unvoiced consonant");
}
```

If `ch` is a vowel, this is displayed:

```
It's a vowel
It's a voiced consonant
It's an unvoiced consonant
```

Granted, this error would be easier to see than some program in which math was done for various `case` statements. In some cases, such as A-E-I-O-U in this example, you want execution to flow through the `case` statements. Even so, don't forget the `break`s where you need them.

Don't mess up a `for` **loop.** Here's something the compiler never catches:

```
for(x=0;x=5;x++);
```

If you have ever been poisoned by the BASIC language, you may forget that the second item in a C language `for` loop is a condition, not a comparison. In the preceding example, it doesn't read "Keep looping `while` the value of `x` is equal to 5." It reads "Keep looping while TRUE because `x` equals 5 now." Remember that `x=5` is an assignment, not a comparison. Assignments usually are evaluated as TRUE in an `if` or `while` condition.

The second item in a `for` loop is usually a comparison, such as in an `if` statement, but, typically, with a less-than or greater-than operator.

Here's another problem with the preceding `for` statement: the semicolon! Any statements after `for` don't belong to it; the semicolon ends the loop right there. This problem is a maddening one that I have often overlooked.

While I'm on the subject of loops:

Beware of endless loops! They can creep up on you. Many programs need some type of endless loop, but then rely on some type of machine inside the loop to break out. Nothing is wrong with this technique, but make sure that the method for breaking the loop works!

Honestly, sometimes I think that endless loops are the only reason programmers insist on using computers with a manual Reset button.

A programmer maxim: The last 10 percent of a project takes 90 percent of the time to complete.

Helpful Utilities

One nice thing about the C language is that it has been around for more than 30 years. Few other programming languages have maintained such a history and (forgetting C++ for a moment) remained basically the same since inception.

Because of its long history, and specifically because of C's arm-in-arm standing with the Unix operating system, C programmers are blessed with an armada of wondrous utilities and tools.

If you're using a Unix-like operating system, you find all these tools — and many more — at the ready. Otherwise — and I'm talking to Windows users here — you have to find the tools online.

The MinGW compiler comes with a wonderful set of companion tools named MSYS. You can download MSYS binaries for Windows at www.mingw.org. If you're really into C programming, I highly recommend these tools (or just giving up on Windows and switching to a real operating system).

This section highlights what I feel are the most useful and practical tools to help you in your C language struggles.

ar

The ar tool may be used to build your own custom archives of commonly used routines. You can then link in these archives or libraries just as you would any standard C library. If someday you build a set of routines common to all your source code files, you can use ar to compile those modules into a custom library file that you can link into other source code files. In a way, this is how you can expand the C programming language for your custom needs.

The ar utility replaces the older lib, or library, program that did essentially the same thing.

gdb

The gdb utility is the GNU Debugger, which you can use to peel apart and examine your source code. It's complex, so I don't have room to do it justice here. Some additional information is available on this book's companion Web page, in Supplemental Linux Lesson 2: www.c-for-dummies.com.

grep and egrep

The grep utility, as well as its more powerful cousin, egrep, can be used to find text in one or more files. grep is very powerful and has a rich set of features, too many to mention here. But, suppose that you want to find which source code file in a directory contains your famous clearScreen() function. You would use this grep command:

```
grep -i "clearScreen()" *.c
```

The -i option tells grep to ignore text case when searching. "clearScreen()" is the text to search for. And, the grep utility searches in every file ending in .C — all your C source code files.

You can also use grep to report line numbers for text found in files. Here's the format:

```
grep -n "return" show.c
```

In this line, grep scans the SHOW.C source code file for the text `return`. The output lists the line numbers inside the code where that word is found.

Yeah, they could have thought of a better name for it. grep stands for Global Regular Expression Print — not very mnemonic, but that reflects its Unix background.

indent

The indent utility can be used to clean up your C language source code, formatting it with a consistent style. As an example:

```
#include <stdio.h>
int main(){int x;for(x=0;x<10;x++)printf("Ugly code!\n");
    return(0);}
```

Type this program into your editor just as it looks. Note that the program is really only two lines long; the second line "wraps," but it doesn't need to wrap inside your text editor. Save it to disk as UGLY.C. Compile and run:

```
Ugly code!
Ugly code!
Ugly code!
Ugly code!
Ugly code!
Ugly code!
Ugly code!
Ugly code!
Ugly code!
Ugly code!
```

You can fix the code with the indent program by using the following command. Note that it works on Unix systems that have the indent command installed or on Windows systems using a version of indent:

```
indent ugly.c
```

You can then view the new file using the `cat` command (or the `type` command in Windows). Here's what was shown on my screen:

```
#include <stdio.h>
int             main() {
        int             x;
        for (x = 0; x <  10; x++)
                printf("Ugly code!\n");
        return(0);
}
```

The indent utility has a whole boatload of options to customize output in a number of ways. In this example, you see only one interpretation of how indent can operate. You have to refer to the online documentation for the full complement of indent's options and how they affect source code formatting.

You can also direct indent to place its output into a new file by using this format:

```
indent ugly.c pretty.c
```

PRETTY.C would be the new formatted source code file based on instructions in UGLY.C.

Note that the compiler really doesn't care about the white space (tabs, spaces, blank lines) in a program. Even so, the indent utility tries to fix all that up for you.

ld

The GNU linker program, named ld, can be used to link your C language object code files into program files. Note, however, that the ld linker can be used with a number of programming languages; unlike the gcc command, ld doesn't automatically link in the standard C library. Therefore, I recommend using gcc instead (refer to Book IV, Chapter 10).

lint

The lint utility is a compiler warning and error-checking program. It scans your source code and looks for things that may go wrong: missing semicolons, nonportable pointers, and missing pairs of parentheses or curly braces.

Lint has fallen by the wayside, thanks to modern compilers' ability to find and warn against many of the things lint once caught. Even so, lint still finds some quirks and oddities that compilers occasionally overlook. If you're ever *really* stuck, consider running your source code through lint.

make

The make utility is one that many IDEs render to make obsolete, but can be invaluable when compiling at the command prompt. Most larger C projects are maintained by using the make utility.

What make does is to read a special makefile, or script. That script contains instructions for updating, compiling, and linking all the source code files in a project, keeping everything up to date. For example, you may be working on

**Book IV
Chapter 11**

Help!

some huge project, but not really keeping track of which source code files you have been updating. When you use make, only those source code files that have been modified since the last build are compiled, saving time.

Here's a sample makefile, one that can be used to compile the lotto program I present at the end of Book IV, Chapter 10:

```
#Makefile for lotto program

lotto: main.o init.o select.o sort.o display.o
    gcc main.o init.o select.o sort.o display.o -o lotto

main.o: main.c lotto.h
    gcc -c main.c

init.o: init.c lotto.h
    gcc -c init.c

select.o: select.c lotto.h
    gcc -c select.c

sort.o: sort.c lotto.h
    gcc -c sort.c

display.o: display.c lotto.h
    gcc -c display.c
```

If your computer system supports the make command, save this code to disk as `Makefile`; save it in the same folder or directory as the lotto program you create in Book IV, Chapter 10.

To recompile and update the lotto program, all you need to do is type the **make** command in the `lotto` directory and all the files are recompiled and updated as necessary.

The preceding Makefile is rather simple. The file basically tells the make utility to look out on disk and see which modules need updating. It works like this:

```
filename: depends_on
    command
```

First comes a *filename*, such as LOTTO. (I'm using uppercase here, but note that Unix operating systems are case sensitive.) That's followed by a colon and then the list of all the files that one file depends on. For LOTTO, that means that it depends on the MAIN.O, INIT.O, SELECT.O, SORT.O, and DIS-PLAY.O object code files for the LOTTO program to be created.

Second comes the *command* necessary to rebuild the file. It starts with a tab and then the command. For the LOTTO program, the command to rebuild things is the gcc command, which links all the object code modules together.

Further parts of the makefile list each object code file followed by the files it depends on. Note how the LOTTO.H header is included in the list. For example, if you update the LOTTO.H header file, you would then type the **make** command and all the modules that rely on LOTTO.H would be updated automatically and the LOTTO program rebuilt.

By using the make command, you can make a minor change in only one program and then just type **make** and the entire project is instantly rebuilt. (In fact, in many IDEs, the command to rebuild the entire project is Make or Make All.)

touch

The fun but strange touch program stamps every file in the current directory (or only those files you specify) with the current date and time or a date and time that you specify. This is one way you can synchronize all the files in your project, or specifically back-date files, forcing a utility like make to update them.

It's normally the operating system's job to date- and time-stamp each file you create or modify. What touch does is override that decision. The file itself is unchanged, but touch manages to update the file's date-and-time stamp.

You may notice that Microsoft uses this trick when it releases new software. The touch utility explains why, for example, most of the files in your Windows folder share the same exact date and time.

Book V

Disk Drive C

The 5th Wave   By Rich Tennant

Okay—you were right, I was wrong. F5 opens the garage door, and F6 backs the car out.

Contents at a Glance

Chapter 1: Just Your Standard I/O

In This Chapter

✔ **Understanding I/O**

✔ **Using** stdin **(standard input) and** stdout **(standard output)**

✔ **Reading and writing standard I/O with** fgetc() **and** fputc()

✔ **Redirecting input and output**

✔ **Piping output into input**

✔ **Creating filters**

✔ **Translating text into pig Latin**

I/O is input and output, the reason your computer lives. Without either input or output, your computer becomes useless. For example, goldfish barely have any I/O, which makes them a useless pet.

Okay, okay: Goldfish may still be pretty to look at. I suppose that they fall under the Entertainment category of pet-keeping. Even so, a C program can also look pretty and, having no I/O, still be next to useless.

This chapter begins your C language journey to the land of disk storage. Because disk storage is basically another form of I/O, the first city on the roadmap is the town of Standard I/O and the amazing twins who rule there, stdin and stdout.

You should save the source code and programs created for this part of the book in the Disk folder or directory on your computer's hard drive.

Programming without Any I/O

You have never, in your short C programming career, written a program without any I/O. Even this book's silliest program has some I or some O in it. Even so, I/O isn't a requirement of the C programming language, as this program demonstrates:

```
void main()
{
    int x;

    x=255;

    while(x)
    {
        x--;
    }
}
```

Type this program into your editor. Do not add the #include <stdio.h> directive. Note that main() is being cast as a void function.

Save the source code to disk as NOIO.C.

Compile. The compiler may warn that main() isn't an int function. That's okay here; a void main() function is acceptable for this demonstration.

Run. Here's what you see on your screen:

Yup. Nothing. The reason is that the program — and it's a program because it does something — has no I/O. There's no input. There's no output — not even a value returned to the operating system.

Technically speaking, C language keywords utterly lack any I/O abilities. The only way your programs can perform input or output is via the library functions.

Not all I/O is entered from the keyboard and output to the monitor. Although the tiny program that runs your PC's clock may not display text or read the keyboard, the program communicates with the PC's ticker. Although it's low-level I/O, it's still I/O.

But, What Is Standard I/O?

Many forms of I/O are in a computer. Just about every port, hole, or plug on the computer's front or rear is some type of I/O used to communicate with some device. As I say earlier in this chapter, computers are all about I/O. Standard I/O, however, is different.

Basically, *standard* I/O is the way your computer communicates with you, the human. Unless the computer is dedicated to some task — like the computer in an automobile — it must interact with a person. It does that through the two standard I/O devices:

✦ The keyboard is the standard input device, nicknamed stdin, for *standard in*put.

✦ The screen is the standard output device, nicknamed stdout, for *standard out*put.

Normally, the computer expects input to come from the stdin device, and it sends output to the stdout device. I say *normally* because you can change these devices and redirect the input or output to another device inside the computer. I tell you more on that in a few pages.

A third standard I/O device, the stderr device, is reserved for error output only, and, like stdout, its output is directed toward the screen. Unlike stdout, however, stderr cannot be redirected to another device. That way, error messages always show up on the screen (or other standard error device), despite any mangling of the stdout device.

Why use standard I/O devices?

You can thank the brilliance of the folks who originally designed computers and computer operating systems for standard I/O devices. Their notion was simple: Everything inside the computer is a file.

A *file* is a collection of stuff or data. It can be text, which means that you can read the contents of the file, or it can be binary data for the computer to digest.

Though you may think of files as living primarily on disk, accessing each input and output device as a file is an advantage: Primarily, input and output can be handled by using the same commands used to manipulate files regardless of which device is generating the input or handling the output.

For example, rather than use a keyboard function to read the keyboard, you can open the stdin device just as a file on disk would be opened. To produce output, you open the stdout device and "save" text to it, which appears on the screen. That's essentially what the I/O functions you have been using in your programs have done: putchar(), for example, sends one character of text to the stdout device; getchar() reads one character input from the stdin device.

How STDIO.H fits into the picture

The STDIO.H file in C is just a set of routines, customized for your computer, that handle all the standard I/O tasks. That's where the header file gets its name.

In addition to defining all the standard I/O functions (`printf`, `gets`, `fopen`, and `getchar`, for example), STDIO.H also defines `stdin`, `stdout`, and `stderr`, allowing you to use them for input, output, and error output inside your programs.

A Demonstration of Standard I/O

Because you were most likely weaned on a graphical operating system and not on a command-prompt system, the tutorial in this section should help you understand about files and standard I/O. First, here's some sample code:

```
#include <stdio.h>

int main()
{
    char ch;

    while((ch = fgetc(stdin)) != EOF)
        fputc(ch,stdout);
    return(0);
}
```

Type this source code into your editor. Save it to disk as IO.C. Compile the program and name the output file **IO**. Don't bother running it yet.

This code introduces two new functions, `fgetc()` and `fputc()`, which are the file equivalents of the `getchar()` and `putchar()` functions. Basically, they read information from or save information to a file one character at a time: `fgetc()` is the *file get* character function; `fputc()` is the *file put* character function.

In the IO.C source code, `fgetc()` is used to read a character from the "file" `stdin`, the *standard in*put device. This character is saved in the variable `ch`. The `fputc()` function "saves" the character `ch` to the "file" `stdout`.

`EOF` is defined in the STDIO.H header file as the *end-of-file* character. In Windows, that's Ctrl+Z (and Enter); in Unix, Ctrl+D is often the `EOF`. So, the program continues to loop until that character is encountered.

Run IO.

At first, it seems like nothing is happening. But that's because the program is waiting to read input. Type the word **Hello** and press Enter:

```
Hello
Hello
```

The IO program simply takes input from stdin and sends it back out through stdout.

Note that though the program is written to do this one character at a time, the output shows up only when you press Enter. That's because of the nature of how the operating system transfers information to and from disk: Doing so one character at a time is inefficient, so the operating system waits until a "chunk" of data is collected before reading or writing.

You use the fpurge() or fflush() command to force the operating system to immediately write all information to disk or read any pending information from disk.

Press the EOF control key combination to halt the program: In Windows, press Ctrl+Z and then Enter; in Unix, press Ctrl+D.

Input redirection with <

The operating system expects standard input to come from the standard input device unless you redirect input from another device or file. Redirection is done in both Windows and Unix by using the < symbol.

Where can input come from, besides the standard input device? Well, it can come from any device that produces output. But a common trick is to put the input text in a file.

Use your text editor to start a new file:

```
Hello. I am text in a text file.
```

Type the preceding line into your editor, and then save the line to disk as TEXT.TXT.

At the command prompt, you can use TEXT.TXT and the input-redirection symbol to supply input for the IO program. Here's the command:

```
io < text.txt
```

Press Enter after typing that command:

```
Hello. I am text in a text file.
```

Input is redirected from stdin to the TEXT.TXT file. That file's text is displayed just as though it were typed at the keyboard. The EOF in the file naturally ends the IO program.

Output redirection with >

You can redirect output as well as input. In this case, the symbol that's used is > for output redirection. Type this command:

```
io > sample.txt
```

This command redirects the standard output from the IO program to a file named SAMPLE.TXT. If the file doesn't exist, the operating system creates it. If the file already exists, it's overwritten.

Type a line of text, such as

```
Sample files smell so lovely this time of year.
```

Press Enter. Then press the EOF control key, either Ctrl+Z or Ctrl+D, for your operating system.

Note that unlike other times when you have run the IO program, this time the output is displayed on the screen only once. Actually, what you see on the screen is your echoed *input*. The output was sent to the SAMPLE.TXT file. To prove it, use input redirection to view the file's contents:

```
io < sample.txt
```

Press Enter after typing this command and you see this text displayed:

```
Sample files smell so lovely this time of year.
```

Piping output with |

The pipe character, |, takes the output of one command and supplies that output as standard input for another command. Most often, pipes are used with filters to massage the output of certain commands. Using pipes is more common in Unix than it is in Windows, though both operating systems have this ability.

Output redirection, append >>

Another symbol used at the command prompt is >>. It also redirects output, but with the effect of appending the redirected output to the end of any existing file. Unlike >, the >> redirection is nondestructive.

For example, to display a text file in Windows, you use the `type` command. In Unix, the `cat` command is used. Both commands, alas, display the entire file in one swoop. To pause the output after each screen of text, you can use the pipe:

```
cat longfile | more
```

In this example, the output from the `cat longfile` command is piped through the `more` command. Output from `cat longfile` becomes input for `more`. The same technique would work on a Windows computer, but with this command:

```
type longfile | more
```

You could use the pipe to send output from a command to the IO program you wrote. But the IO program doesn't really do anything to the text. So, what you need is a program that modifies standard input and then produces standard output. Then, you can demonstrate the pipe on your computer.

Exercise 5.1.1

Write a program using the same standard input and output commands found in the IO.C source code and replace all spaces with underlines. Name this program UNDERLINE.

Using | with the Underline command

Assuming that you have written the UNDERLINE program, it's time to put that tool to the test. First, try it alone at the command prompt. Run the UNDERLINE program, and then type a line of text:

```
My name is Gorath and I fear no mortal.
```

Now, press Enter:

```
My_name_is_Gorath_and_I_fear_no_mortal.
```

Not bad — if it works. If not, go to Appendix C and use my solution.

You can use the `underline` command with the pipe to modify the output of any other command. The pipe converts the other command's output into input for the `underline` command. For example, in Windows, you type this command to send the output from the `dir` command into the UNDERLINE program:

```
dir | underline
```

In Unix, the equivalent command is

```
ls -l | underline
```

Writing Filters

I refer to a program such as UNDERLINE, one that takes standard input, modifies it, and then produces standard output, as a *filter*. You can use it to filter the output of other commands, or even files; for example:

```
underline < sample.txt
```

In this line, the `underline` command gets its input from the text in the SAMPLE.TXT file, which it converts into underlined text on the standard output device.

By writing a program similar to UNDERLINE, one that merely accepts characters from `stdin`, modifies them, and then pumps characters out through `stdout`, you can make filters that do all sorts of fun and interesting things.

The rot13 filter

Rot13 is a tool that was once common in e-mail and public message forums on the early Internet. What it does is offer a simple form of encryption, one that can hide potentially off-color jokes. Only those who want to read the text can un-rot13 it.

The following source code creates a simple rot13 filter. This program uses `stdin` to read data from the standard input device (the keyboard). The program then modifies the text, by rotating the alphabetical characters 13 places. The results are then sent to the standard output device, `stdout`, by using the `fputc()` function:530

```c
#include <stdio.h>
#include <ctype.h>

int main()
{
    char ch;

    while( (ch = fgetc(stdin)) != EOF)
    {
        if(isalpha(ch))
        {
            if(toupper(ch)>='A' && toupper(ch)<='M')
                ch+=13;
```

```
        else
            ch-=13;
    }
    fputc(ch,stdout);
}
return(0);
}
```

Save the source code to disk as ROT13.C. Compile. Fix any errors and recompile if necessary.

Before you run the program, remember that it's a filter. It accepts standard input and generates standard output. So, you can pipe or redirect other input to the program. But, first, start with something simple.

Run the program and type something like this:

```
A pig fell in the mud.
```

Press the Enter key:

```
N cvt sryy va gur zhq.
```

Press the EOF control key to end the program (press Ctrl+Z and then Enter for Windows; press Ctrl+D for Unix.)

A better example is to filter a file. Use your text editor to create this:

```
There were these two nuns walking in the park. One of the
    nuns said to the other one, "I believe I have a pebble in
    my shoe." So they stopped and sat on a park bench, while
    the one nun removed her shoe, plucked out the pebble, and
    then put her shoe back on. The nuns then got up and
    continued walking through the park and enjoying the day.
```

Save the file to disk as NUNS.TXT.

Now, use the rot13 filter at the command prompt to process the file:

```
rot13 < nuns.txt
```

Press Enter, and you see the rotated copy of the text:

```
Gurer jrer gurfr gjb ahaf jnyxvat va gur cnex. Bar bs gur
    ahaf fnvq gb gur bgure bar, "V oryvir V unir n crooyr va
    zl fubr." Fb gurl fgbccrq naq fng ba n cnex orapu, juvyr
    gur bar aha erzbirq ure fubr, cyhpxrq bhg gur crooyr, naq
    gura chg ure fubr onpx ba. Gur ahaf gura tbg hc naq
    pbagvahrq jnyxvat guebhtu gur cnex naq rawblvat gur qnl.
```

It looks Dutch, but it's simply rotated English. You could save this example to a file and run it through the ROT13.C filter again, and the text would translate back to the original. In fact, here's the command to do that:

```
rot13 < nuns.txt | rot13
```

Remember that the key to using rot13 is to use it twice. The first time, it encrypts the text. The second time, it decrypts it. Be aware that most programmers know this trick, and it isn't considered a good way of encrypting your text.

Exercise 5.1.2

Write a filter that converts all text to uppercase. Name it CAPS.

The pig Latin filter

My 8-year-old was amazed that I could speak fluent pig Latin. That was until I pointed out to him how easy it is and that I was basically speaking English. Of course, now I can't get away with saying "itshay" around him any more, but that's not my point.

Like any other filter you want to dream up, a pig Latin filter does nothing more than modify standard input to create custom output. In this case, words are examined so that the first letter or letter combination is moved to the end of the word, and then *ay* is added. The words are all converted to lowercase with an initial capital letter:

```
/*
 * Pig Latin Filter
 */

#include <stdio.h>
#include <ctype.h>
#include <string.h>

void iglatinpay(char *english);
void strlower(char *string);

int main()
{
    char word[32];
    char *w;
```

```
        char ch;
        int count;

        while( (ch = fgetc(stdin)) != EOF)
        {
            if(isalpha(ch))              /* a word starts */
            {
                count=0;
                while(isalpha(ch))       /* read the word */
                {
                    word[count] = ch; /* store word */
                    count++;
                    ch = fgetc(stdin);
                }
                word[count] = '\0';      /* cap word with NULL */
                iglatinpay(word);        /* process the word */

/* This routine displays the word stored in word[] */

                w = word;
                while(*w)
                {
                    fputc(*w,stdout);
                    w++;
                }

/* Finally, original non-alpha character is displayed */

                fputc(ch,stdout);
            }
            else
                fputc(ch,stdout);        /* non-alpha char */
        }
        return(0);
}

/*
 * This function converts a word (all letters
 * terminated with a NULL) into pig Latin by
 * following some made-up rules. The word is stored
 * in the piglatin[] buffer. Various string routines
 * copy and concatenate parts of the reconstructed
 * word into that buffer. The original starting letter
 * is also saved in a buffer, append[], because only
 * strings, not single chars, can be concatenated to
 * each other.
 *
 * A pointer variable saves the original address of
 * the word being translated, so the word is sent and
 * returned as the same variable. This saves going
```

```
 * through the pains of returning a string from a
 * function.
 */

void iglatinpay(char *english)
{
    char piglatin[32];        /* temporary word sto. */
    char *e;
    char append[] = "h";      /* first letter sto. */
    char ch;

    e = english;              /* Save starting loc. */

    strlower(english);        /* make it all lowercase */
/*
 * RULES FOR TRANSLATING ENGLISH INTO PIG LATIN
 * As told to a switch-case loop
 *
 * First rule: Words starting with a vowel
 * are merely given the AY ending.
 *
 * Note how strcpy() is used first and then strcat()
 * is used to continue building the pig Latin word.
 *
 * Also: See how the case statements "fall through,"
 * enabling several of them to catch common
 * situations.
 */

    ch = *english;
    switch(ch)
    {
        case 'a':
        case 'e':
        case 'i':
        case 'o':
        case 'u':
            strcpy(piglatin,english);
            strcat(piglatin,"ay");
            break;
/*
 * Second rule: Words starting with SH, CH,
 * TH, PH, RH, WH, and QU have both letters
 * moved to the end before adding AY.
 */

        case 'c':
        case 'p':
        case 'r':
        case 's':
```

```
            case 't':
            case 'w':
                if(*(english+1)=='h')
                {
                    english+=2;
                    strcpy(piglatin,english);
                    append[0] = ch;
                    strcat(piglatin,append);
                    strcat(piglatin,"hay");
                    break;
                }
            case 'q':
                if(*(english+1)=='u')
                {
                    english+=2;
                    strcpy(piglatin,english);
                    append[0] = ch;
                    strcat(piglatin,append);
                    strcat(piglatin,"uay");
                    break;
                }

/*
 * Standard rule: Move the first letter to the
 * end of the word and add AY.
 */
                        /* continuing switch-case */
            default:
                english++;
                strcpy(piglatin,english);
                append[0] = ch;
                strcat(piglatin,append);
                strcat(piglatin,"ay");
                break;
        }

    strcpy(e,piglatin);
    *e = toupper(*e);
}

/*
 * Convert a string to lowercase. Uses pointers
 * to modify the string elsewhere in memory.
 */

void strlower(char *string)
{
    int len,x;

    len= strlen(string);
    for(x=0;x<len;x++)
        *(string+x) = tolower(*(string+x));
}
```

Carefully type the preceding source code. But, note that this code is available on this book's companion Web site: www.c-for-dummies.com, where you can easily download it. If you opt to type it, save it to disk as PL.C.

Compile. Fix any errors. You may have a few typos. Then run it.

Because it's a filter, the cursor just blinks at you. Type something clever and press Enter:

```
Something clever
Omethingsay levercay
```

Consider translating the NUN.TXT story into pig Latin.

Chapter 2: Interacting with the Command Line

In This Chapter

✔ Using the `main()` function's arguments

✔ Counting arguments with `argc`

✔ Viewing arguments with `*argv[]`

✔ Confirming the presence of command-line arguments

✔ Running other programs with `system()`

✔ Setting the exit status

✔ Evaluating the exit status

When the operating system launches your C program, it doesn't just hurl it off into space, flinging it away like some careless yuppie hurling a trash-filled fast food bag out the window of the Volvo. Like any responsible parent, the operating system leaves open the possibilities of sending a message to your program when it starts. Similarly, your program can deposit a small token of its esteem when it's finished, a value the operating system can scrutinize and keep.

Program and operating system communications may be crude, but they exist. This chapter covers the interaction between your programs and the command line, first by reading optional arguments passed at the prompt and ending with returning values from a program that had completed its task.

Reading the Command Line

The computer knows all, sees all!

When you type a command at the prompt, the operating system remembers what you typed. It also remembers what you type *after* that command, if anything. Suppose that you type

```
crack passwords -find "master password"
```

First, the operating system looks for an internal command or a program to run named CRACK. If the operating system finds it, it launches the program.

Second, the operating system sends along information about the items typed after the command, if any. In the preceding example, the operating system tells the CRACK program that three items, or three *arguments,* were specified:

✦ `passwords`

✦ `-find`

✦ `"master password"`

Note that the items in double quotes are treated as one argument by the operating system.

The operating system does this every time for every program you run. Whether your program pays attention to it is up to you as the programmer. You can freely choose to ignore the options or you can scrutinize them in depth.

The `main()` *function's arguments*

Like many other functions in C, `main()` has arguments. They need not be specified if you don't use them, which is why you don't see them elsewhere in this book. But the arguments are available if you want to use them.

(Some purists believe that you should always state `main()`'s arguments, even if they're not used. Whatever.)

`main()`'s arguments are

✦ `argc`

✦ `*argv[]`

The `argc` variable contains the number of items you type at the command prompt, or the argument count.

The `argv` variable is declared as a pointer array, but don't let that scare you. It's really an array of strings. Each string is a different argument or word typed at the command line.

Officially, you can declare the `main()` function this way:

```
int main(int argc, char *argv[])
```

You can use the variables `argc` and `*argv[]`inside the program — as long as `argc` reports that there are any arguments worthy of note to begin with.

Counting command-line arguments with `argc`

The `main()` function's `argc` variable counts the number of items typed at the command prompt. Here's a sample program for you to fiddle with:

```c
#include <stdio.h>

int main(int argc, char *argv[])
{
    printf("There were %d command line arguments typed.\n",
    argc);
    return(0);
}
```

This source code uses the `argc` argument to report how many things (arguments) are typed at the command prompt when the program is run.

Save the source code to disk as ARG.C. Compile. Run.

```
There were 1 command line arguments typed.
```

Yes. The name of the program is an argument! It's always the first argument.

Try typing this command:

```
arg barg carg darg farg garg
```

Press Enter:

```
There were 6 command line arguments typed.
```

Arguments 2 through 6 are the "optional parameters" for the ARG command. The program can read and examine them, but, to access what they are, you must use the `argv[]` variables.

Reading command-line arguments with `argv`

The `*argv[]` thing is an array pointer. It represents stuff you type at the command prompt.

The operating system *parses,* or chops up, the command-line arguments into individual elements. A pointer is assigned to each element, and those pointers are stored in the `*argv[]` array. The `argc` variable tells you how many elements the array contains.

From the preceding section, you may remember that `argc` is always at least 1 for the program name itself. That means that `argv[0]` is always the name of the program being run.

Type this source code into your editor. It's just a silly little program that displays all the options you type after the program name at the command prompt:

```
#include <stdio.h>

int main(int argc,char *argv[])
{
    int x;

    puts("Command line arguments:");
    for(x=0;x<argc;x++)
        printf("Argument #%d: %s\n",x,argv[x]);
    return(0);
}
```

Save the source code to disk as ARGV.C. Compile and run:

```
Command line arguments:
Argument #0: argv
```

Run it again, and this time type **I am not an argument** after the ARGV command:

```
Command line arguments:
Argument #0: argv
Argument #1: I
Argument #2: am
Argument #3: not
Argument #4: an
Argument #5: argument
```

Remember that the operating system treats text in double quotes as a single argument. Run the program again and type **"I am not an argument"** after the ARGV command:

```
Command line arguments:
Argument #0: argv
Argument #1: I am not an argument
```

Testing for command-line arguments

Programs that require a command-line argument have code inside that determines whether that argument is present. If the argument is found, the program proceeds. Otherwise, the program displays either an error or a help message. Here's how such a thing is done:

```
#include <stdio.h>

int main(int argc, char *argv[])
{
/* check for proper number of arguments */
    if(argc == 1)
    {
        puts("This program requires you to type");
        puts("some text after the program name.");
        return(1);
    }

/* Program continues here */
    printf("I shall now work on the \"%s\" option.\n",
    argv[1]);
    return(0);
}
```

Type this source code into your editor. Save it as REQUIRED.C. Compile and run:

```
This program requires you to type
some text after the program name.
```

Oops! Run the program again and type **something** after the program name:

```
I shall now work on the "something" option.
```

Clever!

Exercise 5.2.1
Write a variation on the REQUIRED.C program that warns the user if more than one argument is typed after the program name.

Exercise 5.2.2
Write another variation of REQUIRED.C; this time, one that requires two options for the program to do its thing.

Running Another Program with system()

The system() function gives your program its own little command prompt. Any command you normally type at the real command prompt can be issued from your program directly to the operating system via the system() function. So, one program can run another, or your program can run a shell or DOS command. Here's a sample:

```
#include <stdio.h>
#include <stdlib.h>

int main()
{
    puts("Press Enter to see a list of files:");
    getchar();
    system("dir");
    puts("Done!");
    return(0);
}
```

Type this source code into your editor. Note that the STDLIB.H header file is required in order to make the `system()` function "funct." If you're using Unix, change Line 8 to read

```
system("ls -l");
```

Save this source code to disk as SYSTEST.C. Compile and run. The program sends the **dir** or **ls -l** command to the operating system. The output of that command is what you see on the screen.

The `system()` function returns control to your program. It optionally returns any exit status as an integer value:

```
exit_status = system("dir");
```

You can read more about what an exit status is beginning with this chapter's next section.

Note that `system()` can accept an immediate string value, as shown in SYSTEST.C, or it can take a string variable.

Exercise 5.2.3
Write a program named ALPHA that asks for the user's name. Then have ALPHA call a program named BETA that displays the user's name.

Dealing with the Exit Status

When your program quits, it traditionally passes a small token of its esteem back to the operating system. This token is in the form of an integer value, ranging from 0 through about 255 or so.

The operating system can choose whether to evaluate the returned integer, also known as the *exit status*. If an evaluation is made, it's usually done in a shell script or batch file. Or, if the `system()` function is used, the calling program can examine the return code.

In any event, you have two popular ways to send the exit status back to the operating system. The first is by putting the value in a `return` statement inside the `main()` function. But, because you may not always leave a program from the `main()` function, you can also use the `exit()` function to send a value back to the operating system. This section demonstrates how this nonsense works.

Coughing up an exit status

The exit status is used by your programs to communicate with the operating system. Because only a single integer is returned, communication is rather limited. Therefore, only the most important information is typically sent back in the exit status. For most programs, the value that's returned is used to determine whether the task was successfully completed. (And this type of information also plays out well in the scripts and batch file programs that read the exit status value.)

If everything goes well, a program returns the value 0. If you're reading this book from front to back, you have seen this in every other program in this book:

```
return(0);
```

This statement, found at the end of the `main()` function, returns 0 to the operating system; the task was successfully completed.

Note the return statement used in the REQUIRED.C source code, earlier in this chapter:

```
return(1);
```

When the user neglects to type the proper number of arguments, the program returns a 1 to the operating system. For this program, that value means that an improper number of arguments were passed:

```
#include <stdio.h>

int main()
{
    int r;

    printf("Enter the exit status value: ");
    scanf("%d",&r);
    return(r);
}
```

Type this source code into your editor. Save it to disk as EXSTAT.C. Compile and run:

```
Enter the exit status value:
```

Type a number, such as **8**. Press Enter.

You get no feedback, but the exit status is set to 8. You have to refer to one of the following two sections (depending on your operating system) for a method of extracting the exit status value.

Outside the `main()` function, you can bail out of any program by using the `exit()` function (defined in the STDLIB.H header file). Like `return`, `exit()` also passes a value back to the operating system. But, unlike with `return`, you can use `exit()` anywhere in a program to cleanly and quickly quit. Refer to Book III, Chapter 6 for more information on using `exit()`.

C has no official list of exit status values. For this reason, most programs include in their documentation the list of return status codes and what they mean.

Reading the exit status in Windows

To obtain the exit status in Windows, you must use the arcane batch file command **if errorlevel *n***, where *n* is less than or equal to the return code generated by the previously run program.

Yes, I know: It's bizarre. Trust me — I made a mint selling books on batch file programming that explained how **if errorlevel** works:

```
@ECHO OFF
IF ERRORLEVEL 10 ECHO 10
IF ERRORLEVEL 9 IF NOT ERRORLEVEL 10 ECHO 9
IF ERRORLEVEL 8 IF NOT ERRORLEVEL 9 ECHO 8
IF ERRORLEVEL 7 IF NOT ERRORLEVEL 8 ECHO 7
IF ERRORLEVEL 6 IF NOT ERRORLEVEL 7 ECHO 6
IF ERRORLEVEL 5 IF NOT ERRORLEVEL 6 ECHO 5
IF ERRORLEVEL 4 IF NOT ERRORLEVEL 5 ECHO 4
IF ERRORLEVEL 3 IF NOT ERRORLEVEL 4 ECHO 3
IF ERRORLEVEL 2 IF NOT ERRORLEVEL 3 ECHO 2
IF ERRORLEVEL 1 IF NOT ERRORLEVEL 2 ECHO 1
IF ERRORLEVEL 0 IF NOT ERRORLEVEL 1 ECHO 0
```

Type this code into your editor. Save it to disk as ERRORLEVEL.BAT. Note the BAT extension, which identifies it as a Windows batch file program, not a C language source code file.

Unix error-code return values for system functions

Although no standard exists for a program's exit status values, specific codes match Unix system function calls. The documentation typically states that a function returns a code value, such as 0 for success and then `errno` on failure. These errors are defined in the man page for `errno` and in the SYS/ERRNO.H header file. Refer to it for all the gory, boring details.

Because of the limitations of Windows, this file can detect exit status values only to 10. If you want to detect higher values, you need to add to the preceding program — one line to detect for each return status value using the same format as just shown:

```
IF ERRORLEVEL n IF NOT ERRORLEVEL n+1 ECHO n
```

Yes, that can get intense, but it's how you must do things.

To use ERRORLEVEL.BAT with the EXSTAT.C program, first run the EXSTAT program:

```
Enter the exit status value:
```

Type **8** and press Enter.

Now, type **errorlevel** to run the ERRORLEVEL.BAT batch file program:

```
8
```

The batch file program properly reports the exit status returned by EXSTAT. That value remains available until another program is run and returns a different value.

Reading the exit status in Unix

In Unix shell scripting, the special $? variable is used to represent the exit status of the most recently completed program. The variable can also be displayed directly at the command prompt by using the **echo $?** command:

```
$ echo $?
0
```

In this line, the last program that was run coughed up a return status of 0, indicating successful completion.

Run the EXSTAT program that you create earlier in this chapter:

```
Enter the exit status value:
```

Type **8** and press Enter.

To view the exit status, you merely need to display the $? variable's value. You do that with the **echo $?** command:

```
$ echo $?
8
```

The exit status is stored in the special $? variable until you run another program that returns a value to the operating system, and then the new value is assumed by the $? variable.

Chapter 3: Hello, Disk!

In This Chapter

✔ Understanding disk access in C

✔ Opening a file

✔ Writing information to disk

✔ Reading information from disk

✔ Accessing files in binary mode

*N*estled deep in your PC's lexicon is a batch of jargon associated with saving stuff to and reading stuff from the disk drive. Mostly, the lingo for saving is the same: Save. That makes sense. But, for reading stuff from disk, the slang can be varied and complex: Load. Open. Read. In ancient Microsoft software, the superfluous word *transfer* was also used. Weird.

In the C language, the lingo for disk access is quite simple. You *open* a file on disk to either *read* from it or *write* to it. When you're done, you *close* the file. Open. Close. Read. Write. Simple. This chapter uncovers the grimy details.

Fopen the Ffile, Fplease

Accessing the disk drive in C is cinchy. Or, I should say fcinchy because the file access functions tend to all begin with the letter *f*. So, you don't really "open" or "close" a file on disk — you `fopen()` the file and then `fclose()` it.

Reading and writing disk information is done by commands you're already familiar with: `printf`, `gets`, `puts`, and the whole assortment of screen and keyboard commands have disk access counterparts: `fprintf`, `fgets`, `fputs`, and so on.

Sounds `fcinchy`. Could be `ffun`. Don't be `fridiculous`.

Writing a small smackerel of something to disk

If you're going to be a mad scientist, you need a lot of money. You had better inherit it. You may have inherited that Transylvanian castle on the craggy mountain, but the property taxes are eating you alive! Those electrical devices don't come cheap. Then you have to bribe the gravedigger's union and find decent help. Hunchbacks don't come cheap, you know.

Oh, forget it all! If you're going to create something, do it with the C language and create a small text file on disk. This program does the job nice and neatly, with no ugly suture marks or electrodes sticking out of anyone's neck:

```
#include <stdio.h>

int main()
{
    FILE *myfile;

    myfile = fopen("alive.txt","w");
    if(!myfile)
    {
        puts("Some kind of file error!");
        return(1);
    }

    fprintf(myfile,"I created a file! It's alive!\n");
    fclose(myfile);
    return(0);
}
```

Type this source code into your editor. You can probably guess how it works, but don't make such a bold move until after you have read the next section. Save this program to disk as CREATE.C.

Compile and run!

Nothing happens. Well, nothing you can see (unless you got a disk error). If the program worked properly, it created a new file on disk, ALIVE.TXT. Use your operating system's file-viewing commands to view the file's contents: **type alive.txt** in Windows or **cat alive.txt** in Unix:

```
I created a file! It's alive!
```

It works! You create a file all by yourself and without the help of an electrical storm and anyone named Igor.

To see the file listed in the directory, type the **dir alive.txt** or **ls -l alive.txt** command. It lives! It lives!

If the file ALIVE.TXT already exists on disk, your CREATE program overwrites it. Yes, you have ways to prevent that, which you can read about in a few pages.

How disk access works in C

When you want to talk to a file on disk, you *open* it. This is true no matter what's in the file, whether its text or binary information and whether you plan to create a new file, open an existing file for reading, or open an existing file for writing. The command is always the same, fopen(). What's different are the options specified in the fopen() command. Here's the format:

```
handle = fopen(filename,mode);
```

The fopen() function is prototyped in the STDIO.H header file. It requires two arguments in its parentheses: *filename* and *mode*. Both are strings, either constants (enclosed in double quotes) or variables.

Filename is the name of the file you want to open or create. It must be the full filename, including extension. It can also include the path if the file lives (or will be created) in another directory. Note that Windows doesn't care about upper- or lowercase filenames, but Unix is case sensitive.

Mode is a tiny string that tells fopen() how to open the file: for reading, writing, or appending or a combination of these. Table 3-1 lists all the various *mode* strings.

Table 3-1	Access Modes for the fopen Function		
Mode	*Opens a File for*	*File Created?*	*Existing File?*
"r"	Reading only	No	If not found, fopen() returns an error
"w"	Writing	Yes	Overwritten
"a"	Appending	Yes	Appended to
"r+"	Reading and writing	No	If not found, fopen() returns an error
"w+"	Reading and writing	Yes	Overwritten
"a+"	Reading and appending	Yes	Appended to

If all goes well, fopen() returns a value of the FILE type. FILE is a "type-def'd" variable defined in STDIO.H. It's a pointer variable that provides a shortcut reference, or *handle,* to represent the open file. When FILE is equal to NULL, the fopen() command has failed.

In CREATE.C, the file handle pointer variable myfile is declared as follows:

```
FILE *myfile;
```

Then, the file ALIVE.TXT is opened using the fopen() function:

```
myfile = fopen("alive.txt","w");
```

In this line, fopen() opens or creates the file alive.txt. The "w" means that the file is being opened in Write mode (refer to Table 3-1).

The handle returned by fopen() is stored in myfile. That file handle is then used by the program like a claim ticket you get for checking your coat in a fancy restaurant. The handle is how the file is referred to in your program; for example:

```
fprintf(myfile,"I created a file! It's alive!");
```

The fprintf() function works just like the printf() function, with two differences. First, the fprintf() statement sends its output to a file, not to the screen. Second, fprintf() requires an open file handle, like myfile in the preceding example. The file handle tells the operating system to which file the information must be sent.

Finally, when the program is done working with the file, the file is closed by using the fclose() function. Inside fclose(), the handle for the file is specified so that the operating system knows which file to close:

```
fclose(myfile);
```

Here, and in CREATE.C, the fclose() function closes the file represented by the handle myfile. The act of closing tells the operating system to finish writing all information to the file, properly saving the file to disk, and it makes the memory and resources associated with the file handle available for other programs to use.

Why bother with file handles?

One reason I believe that there are file handles is that it's just easier to refer to an open file by a handle reference as opposed to using the filename over and over. Even if you did use a filename rather than a handle inside your code, you would probably just use a pointer to the filename rather than the filename itself. If so, why not cut directly to the chase and use a file handle to begin with?

Another reason for having filenames is that it's possible to have one program open more than one file at a time. You can declare multiple file handles just as you would multiple copies of any variable in C:

```
FILE *first, *second, *third;
```

Each individual handle tells the operating system which disk file to access.

Internally, the FILE handle is a pointer that references a structure somewhere else in memory. The structure contains all sorts of trivial information about the file, mostly stuff to help the operating system recognize the file.

Finally, though a FILE handle variable is a pointer, note that you never use the asterisk or the ampersand. Only when the FILE variable is created is the asterisk specified. Otherwise, the handle is used only as an address; no asterisk.

Closing a file ensures that the last bit of information has been written to the file. Although your operating system may close files automatically whenever your program quits, it's still a good idea to issue an `fclose()` statement. That's especially helpful if you (or someone else) need to debug your code in the future.

Exercise 5.3.1

Write a program that asks for the user's name and saves that information to disk. Call the program YOURNAME.C and have it save the user's name in a file named YOURNAME.TXT.

Reading something from disk

Reading a file from disk is just as easy as reading text from the keyboard. You open the file, read the information, and then close the file. This source code shows you how to deal with all that — it's cinchy:

```
#include <stdio.h>

int main()
{
    FILE *myfile;
    char c;

    myfile = fopen("alive.txt","r");
    if(!myfile)
    {
        puts("ALIVE.TXT not found!");
        return(1);
    }

    do
    {
        c = fgetc(myfile);
        putchar(c);
    }
    while(c != EOF);

    fclose(myfile);
    return(0);
}
```

You can use the CREATE.C source code as a base and modify it to look like the preceding source code. Note that the file ALIVE.TXT is opened in "r" mode, read-only. Save this code to disk as ITLIVES.C.

Compile and run. The program reads in any text file named ALIVE.TXT. If you created this file using the CREATE program earlier in this chapter, you see

```
I created a file! It's alive!
```

Ta-da!

The program uses `fgetc()` to read individual characters from an open file until the end of file marker, EOF, is read from disk.

The `fgetc()` function works just like `getchar()`, except that a file handle is specified by `fgetc()` and any characters that are read come from that open file.

The EOF character is defined by STDIO.H. That character signals that the end of file has been encountered, which tells the program when to stop reading the file.

A better, albeit more cryptic, way to write the `do-while` loop could be

```
while((c=fgetc(myfile)) != EOF)
    putchar(c);
```

This method basically combines the several statements into one. It's harder to read, but it still works.

Exercise 5.3.2
Write a program named CONSUME.C whose job, when run, is to display its own source code.

Preventing an accidental overwrite
You must decide *how* you want to open a file. Earlier in this chapter, Table 3-1 lists all the various file-opening modes: reading, writing, appending, and various combinations. You can choose a mode that requires a file to already exist or one that utterly zaps any file from disk without so much as a whimper.

The CREATE.C program opens the file ALIVE.TXT using `"w"` mode. From Table 3-1, you can divine that `"w"` mode opens a new file for writing and also may destroy an existing file named ALIVE.TXT.

To prevent overwriting a file you may want to keep, you can run a test first by attempting to open the file for reading. If the file exists, you can ask the user whether he or she wants to overwrite it. Isn't that common courtesy?

This source code is for CREATOR.C, a much nicer version of CREATE.C and one that protects against accidentally overwriting a file on disk:

```
#include <stdio.h>
#include <stdlib.h>
#include <ctype.h>

int main()
{
    FILE *myfile;
    char c;

    myfile = fopen("alive.txt","r");

    if(myfile)        /* the file exists */
    {
        puts("ALIVE.TXT already exists!");
        printf("Overwrite it? [Y/N]");
        c = toupper(getchar());
        if(c!='Y')
        {
            puts("Okay. Good-bye.");
            fclose(myfile);
            exit(1);
        }
    }

    myfile = fopen("alive.txt","w");
    if(myfile==NULL)
    {
        puts("Some kind of error");
        exit(0);
    }

    fprintf(myfile,"I created a file! It's alive!\n");

    fclose(myfile);
    return(0);
}
```

Type this source code into your editor. Because it's a major modification to
the CREATE.C code, you can start with that, if you want. Save the final thing
as CREATOR.C.

Compile! Run!

```
ALIVE.TXT already exists!
Overwrite it? [Y/N]
```

Press **N** and then Enter:

```
Okay. Good-bye.
```

The file was not overwritten. Now, run it again:

```
ALIVE.TXT already exists!
Overwrite it? [Y/N]
```

Press **Y** and then Enter.

Nothing happens! Actually, the file was re-created. You can run the ITLIVES.C program to check.

If you don't see the `ALIVE.TXT already exists!` message, the file hasn't been created. Don't worry — CREATOR.C creates it automatically, with no feedback. Run CREATOR.C a second time to prove that it works.

The program discovers that ALIVE.TXT is already on disk because it first attempts to open the file in `"r"` mode. That way, `fopen()` doesn't overwrite the file, but merely returns a file handle. If so, the program asks whether you want to overwrite it. If you don't, the file is closed and an `exit()` function quits the thing. Otherwise, the file is closed and reopened in `"w"` mode, which overwrites it.

Notice how the file was opened and closed! This is very important. If you plan to change file modes, you must close the file and then open it again.

Exercise 5.3.3
Write a program named EVENMORE.C that appends the text `Alive, I tell you! Alive!` to the end of the ALIVE.TXT text file. Refer to Table 3-1 for the proper file-opening mode.

Would You Like Binary or Text with That?

If you have been using computers for some time, you probably have been brainwashed into thinking that dozens of types of files exist. Hoo, boy, do they have you fooled!

Honestly, there's only *one* type of file: *binary*. All files are binary because the computer itself is binary. Duh. But, strictly speaking, some files contain only readable text. So, if you separate text files from the morass, you get two file types: text or readable files, and then the rest of the lot are binary.

Your C compiler is probably tuned to open all files in text mode. Even so, you can specify — nay, *demand* — that a file be opened in text mode, if you like. Likewise, you can direct the computer to open a file in binary mode if that is your wont. All that matters is properly directing the `fopen()` function to access a file in one mode or another.

The C lords refer to binary files as *raw* and to text files as *cooked*. That reminds me of the tale of the grizzled programmer, eyes frazzled and wandering dazed into a nice steak house. After days of solid programming, he wasn't fully prepared to interact with a human. When the waiter asked how he wanted his steak, he said "Cooked!"

The View command

Nothing is as easy to program, or as necessary to a programmer, as a utility designed to help you view files — specifically your *code*, on disk — something like this:

```c
#include <stdio.h>
#include <stdlib.h>

#define BUFSIZE 255

void main(int argc,char *argv[])
{
    FILE *viewfile;
    char buffer[BUFSIZE+1];     /* storage */

/* check for proper no. of arguments */
    if(argc<2)
    {
        puts("Missing filename!");
        puts("Here is the format:");
        puts("VIEW filename");
        exit(1);
    }

/* Does the file exist? */
    viewfile = fopen(argv[1],"r");
    if(!viewfile)
    {
        printf("Error opening \"%s\"\n",argv[1]);
        exit(1);
    }

/* display the file's guts */
    while(fgets(buffer,BUFSIZE,viewfile))
        printf("%s",buffer);
    fclose(viewfile);
    return(0);
}
```

Carelessly type this source code into your editor. This program is designed to read text — not binary information — from a file. The way that's done is via the fgets() function, which is the disk-reading counterpart to the gets()

function. Unlike `gets()`, two additional items are in the parentheses with `fgets()`:

```
string = fgets(buffer,size,handle);
```

A *buffer* is a holding bin for the characters that `fgets()` reads from disk, which is the same option you use when reading text from the keyboard with `gets()`. The *buffer* is a `char` array, an empty string.

The *size* value indicates how many characters `fgets()` reads from disk. The `fgets()` function stops reading characters from disk when it encounters the newline (`\n`) character or the `EOF`.

The *handle* variable is a `FILE` handle pointer returned from an `fopen()` function. The file must be opened in read mode for `fgets()` to work.

If `fgets()` cannot read a string from disk, it returns a NULL pointer.

Save the source code to disk as VIEW.C. Compile! Run!

```
Missing filename!
Here is the format:
VIEW filename
```

Okay, okay. Type **view view.c** or **./view view.c** at the command prompt to view the VIEW.C source code file.

In addition to storing the string read from disk in the *buffer*, `fgets()` returns a pointer to the string that's read. So, you can get away with a trick like this:

```
puts(fgets(buffer,80,myfile);
```

The storage space `fgets()` uses must be *one byte larger* than the amount of characters read from disk. That extra byte enables `fgets()` to stick a NULL (`\0`) on the end of the text, making it an official C string.

Taking a dump

Dump is an inelegant term, but one that programmers are stuck with. At its roots, *dump* is a verb that means to transfer information from one place to another, usually without messing with the information along the way. It's information in the raw — not cooked.

In the old days, *screen dumps* were common on a PC to send a copy of all the text on the screen to a printer. This was done with the extant Print Screen key.

In Unix, a *core dump* is a copy of memory saved to disk whenever the system panics. The idea behind that is that some guru could examine the raw data and determine what went wrong.

And now, you can dump too! You don't even need a special program; the VIEW.C program you create earlier in this chapter can do it. All you need to do is display the contents of a non-text file.

In Windows, type **view view.exe** to display the binary data stored inside the VIEW program itself. In Unix, type **./view view**. (This assumes, of course, that you named the program file VIEW when it was compiled).

What's displayed on the screen is a hunk of funny characters and symbols — not readable text. In fact, you may notice that only a handful of the characters are displayed; that's because VIEW.C assumes the file to be text and perhaps one of the binary values that was read was the EOF "character." That happens. The way to avoid it is to open a file for *binary* reading instead of plain text — raw versus cooked:

```c
#include <stdio.h>
#include <stdlib.h>

int main(int argc,char *argv[])
{
    FILE *dump_me;
    int i;
    int x = 0;

/* Check for filename argument */
    if(argc<2)
    {
        puts("Format: DUMP filename");
        exit(1);
    }

/* Open the file argv[1] in read-binary mode */
    dump_me = fopen(argv[1],"rb");
    if(dump_me==NULL)
    {
        printf("Error opening %s\n",argv[1]);
        exit(1);
    }

/* Display file's contents in hex */
    while((i=fgetc(dump_me))!= EOF)
    {
        printf("%0.2X ",i);
        x++;
```

```
        if(!(x%16)) putchar('\n');
    }
    fclose(dump_me);

/* file trivia display */
    printf("\n%s: size = %u bytes\n",argv[1],x);
    return(0);
}
```

Crack your knuckles, and open a new sheet in your text editor. Carefully type the preceding source code. It differs from the VIEW.C program in that the file is opened for binary reading:

```
dump_me = fopen(argv[1],"rb");
```

Specifying a b after the file-opening mode tells the compiler that the file should be treated as a binary file rather than as text.

Note in the code that characters are read from the file via fgetc() and displayed in hexadecimal, not in ASCII (readable) text.

Save the file to disk as DUMP.C:

Compile. Fix any errors, which you should be used to by now.

Run it: In Windows, type **dump dump.exe**, and in Unix, type **./dump dump**. You see something like this:

```
80 08 00 06 64 75 6D 70 2E 63 2B 88 18 00 00 00
14 54 43 38 36 20 42 6F 72 6C 61 6E 64 20 43 2B
2B 20 35 2E 30 F9 88 05 00 00 F9 03 01 76 88 0E
```

Blah blah blah blah blah, until you finally see

```
4C 55 44 45 5C 73 74 64 6C 69 62 2E 68 00 28 74
20 32 88 04 00 00 E8 01 8B 8A 02 00 00 74
dump.exe: size = 16190 bytes
```

What you're looking at is raw data, binary stuff that text-viewing programs such as VIEW.C would utterly choke over. Because you open the file in binary mode and display the information as hexadecimal values rather than as text, the program doesn't choke.

Why hex? Because hex numbers can be displayed using two digits, whereas decimal values require one, two, or three. The %0.2X placeholder in the printf() function formats each value to be displayed as a 2-digit hexadecimal number.

The DUMP program is similar to the Unix hexdump command.

Exercise 5.3.4

Modify the DUMP.C source code so that the b is removed from the fopen() statement. How does this affect the program?

Chapter 4: More Formal File Writing and Reading

In This Chapter

✔ **Writing info to disk with** `fprintf()`

✔ **Reading info from disk with** `fscanf()`

✔ **Reading and writing arrays to disk**

✔ **Using** `fwrite()` **to put structures to disk**

✔ **Reading structures from disk with** `fread()`

✔ **Creating a database program**

Although you do some programming that involves writing long expanses of text to disk or reading in raw binary data, most of the stuff you save to disk in your programs is *formatted*. For example, if you want to read in a graphics file, you must properly interpret the graphics file format so that the image's binary data can be displayed correctly.

Formatting information for disk access isn't difficult. The simplest tool for doing so is your old pal the `printf()` function. Or, more accurately, it's `printf()`'s disk-related cousin, `fprintf()`. (All those *F*s, remember?) Plus, you have other ways to read and write formal file chunks to and from disk. This chapter covers all that territory.

Formatted File Input and Output

Formatted output to disk is the same as formatted output to the screen; it's just information displayed in a friendly, organized way.

As an example, consider the basic difference between a value and a number — a lesson that hearkens back to your early days of learning the C language. A value is, for example, 42. But a number is the text string "42," which is composed of the two characters 4 and 2. One important aspect of formatting file input and output is being able to save a value to disk and read it back as a value — ditto for a number — and be able to tell the difference between the two.

Writing formatted output

As an example of formatted output, consider the desire your program has to save a high score value to disk. Observe this source code:

```
#include <stdio.h>

int main()
{
    FILE *scores;
    int s = 1000;

    scores=fopen("scores.dat","w");
    if(scores==NULL)
    {
        puts("Error creating file");
        return(1);
    }

    fprintf(scores,"%d",s);
    fclose(scores);
    puts("High score saved to disk!");
    return(0);
}
```

Let your fingers dance on the key caps as you whack in this source code. Save it to disk as HISCORE.C (it's pronounced "high score," not "his core").

Note that the SCORES.DAT file is opened in "w" mode. For this reason, any existing file by that name is overwritten. That's okay — you want the new high scores to replace the old ones.

Compile and run:

```
High score saved to disk!
```

That's all the visual feedback you get. Otherwise, a file named SCORES.DAT is created on disk and the value 1000 written to that file. The score is now etched in silicon for all to marvel at and attempt to defeat.

To see the file, use the VIEW program you create in Book V, Chapter 3; type **view scores.dat** in Windows or **./view scores.dat** in Unix:

```
1000
```

True to form, fprintf() prints the number 1,000 to disk. If you look back at the program, however, you see that 1000 was stored in a *numeric* variable. The fprintf() function translates that value into text characters to be stored on disk. Hmmm.

Reading formatted information from disk

Honestly, it really doesn't matter whether you write a high score to disk as a value or a number. As long as you use the proper formatting methods to read that value back in from disk, you get that high score exactly as you want it:

```c
#include <stdio.h>

int main()
{
    FILE *scores;
    int s;

    scores=fopen("scores.dat","r");
    if(scores==NULL)
    {
        puts("Error opening file");
        return(1);
    }

    fscanf(scores,"%d",&s);
    fclose(scores);
    printf("The high score is %d\n",s);
    return(0);
}
```

Enter this source code into your editor. Save it to disk as SCORE.C.

This program reads the file SCORES.DAT, which is assumed to already exist on disk. It was created in the preceding section by the HISCORE program.

Compile and run:

```
The high score is 1000.
```

No biggie, right? But, consider that the value 1000 is stored to disk as a *string*. The fscanf() function reads it in that way — just as scanf() reads keyboard input — but it stores it in the s variable, an integer. Both fscanf() and scanf() are similar, but fscanf() has one extra option in its parentheses:

```c
fscanf(handle,"%s",&var);
```

Handle is a file handle variable returned from an fopen() function. *Handle* identifies the open file from which scanf() reads its formatted information.

Note that fscanf() returns the value EOF (as defined in the STDIO.H file) if it encounters the end of the file while reading from disk.

Writing an array to disk

Anyone who has ever played a computer game (at least a game worthy of boasting about) knows that the game never has only one high score. The following modification to the HISCORE.C program compensates for that situation by writing an entire array of scores to disk:

```
#include <stdio.h>

int main()
{
    FILE *scores;
    int s[10] = { 1000, 990, 985, 960,
        955, 950, 945, 945, 945, 930 };
    int x;

    scores=fopen("scores.dat","w");
    if(scores==NULL)
    {
        puts("Error creating file");
        return(1);
    }

    for(x=0;x<10;x++)
    {
        fprintf(scores,"%d\n",s[x]);
    }
    fclose(scores);
    puts("High scores saved to disk!");
    return(0);
}
```

Update the source code to HISCORE.C (from earlier in this chapter), modifying it to match what you see here. This new variation is essentially the same as the original HISCORE.C, but an array of ten items is written to disk rather than to a single item. Save the new source code to disk as HISCORES.C.

Compile. Run. Although the ten scores are written to disk by the `fprintf()` function, the only feedback you see is the final message:

```
High scores saved to disk!
```

Of course, the proof is whether the values can be read back from disk. That thrill happens in the next section.

Reading an array from disk

Saving scores to disk, as shown in the preceding section, is only half the battle. The other half is reading the scores back in, which is done with code sort of like this:

```
#include <stdio.h>

int main()
{
    FILE *scores;
    int s[10];
    int x;

    scores=fopen("scores.dat","r");
    if(scores==NULL)
    {
        puts("Error opening file");
        return(1);
    }

    for(x=0;x<10;x++)
        fscanf(scores,"%d",&s[x]);
    fclose(scores);

    puts("High scores:");
    for(x=0;x<10;x++)
        printf("%d\n",s[x]);
    return(0);
}
```

Modify the original SCORE.C source code in your editor to resemble the following source code. Save the file to disk as SCORES.C.

Compile.

Run:

```
High scores:
1000
990
985
960
955
950
945
945
945
930
```

The program reads information from the SCORES.DAT file by using `fscanf()`, just as a similar program would have read values from the keyboard with `scanf`.

Be mindful that you properly write information to disk so that it can properly be read. In this case, the key is to include a newline (\n) after each value in the array is written, way back in the HISCORES.C program:

```
fprintf(scores,"%d\n",s[x]);
```

That newline serves as a break when reading the data back in with the fscanf() function:

```
fscanf(scores,"%d",&s[x]);
```

Had you forgotten the newline, only one line of text would have been written to disk. The SCORES.DAT file would have then looked like this:

```
10099098596095595097597597930
```

So, if you ever try to read multiple values from disk and things don't seem to be coming out properly, first check the file on disk to see whether the information looks right. You can use the VIEW or DUMP programs you create in Book V, Chapter 3 to help you. If the information isn't being written to disk as you expect, the problem lies with the disk-writing program or function, not with the disk-reading program or function.

Reading and Writing File Chunks

Formatted input and output are okay for some data. Most of the time, however, you probably will write complex information to disk, such as a list of high scores along with the winners' names. Although you could use fprintf() for that task, whenever you're working with two different types of variables as a unit, you should be using a structure.

Writing and reading structures to and from disk makes your program truly database-like. You write a chunk of information to disk and then read it back — just like any other file-reading and -writing program, although when you work with structures to and from disk, the files tend to get a little long.

Sadly, the C language has no specific function for writing a structure to disk. But, because a structure is stored in a chunk of memory, you can use the handy fwrite() function to put a function to disk; the fwrite() function writes a chunk of memory to disk.

The counterpart to fwrite() is fread(), which is used to read a chunk of information from a disk file, and that chunk can carefully be placed back into a structure. Cinchy. Big programs. But cinchy.

The basic skeleton for your structure-to-disk program

If you're going to write more than one structure to disk, you need some type of complex program to create, write, and then read the structures — a sort of minidatabase nightmare project!

The following code is the beginning of a program that creates and writes structures to disk and then reads them back in. This segment is merely the basic skeleton for the program, which consists of a switch-case thing that acts as a menu. You fill in the meat later, but first make sure that this part works properly:

```c
#include <stdio.h>
#include <stdlib.h>
#include <ctype.h>

#define FALSE 0
#define TRUE !FALSE

struct stock_data {
    char name[30];
    float buy_price;
    float current_price;
};

void write_info(void);
void read_info(void);

int main()
{
    char c;
    int done=FALSE;

    while(!done)
    {
        puts("\nStock Portfolio Thing\n");
        puts("A - Add new stock\n");
        puts("L - List stocks\n");
        puts("Q - Quit\n");
        printf("Your choice: ");

        c = getchar();
        fflush(stdin);              /* fpurge(stdin) */
        c = toupper(c);
        switch(c)
        {
            case('A'):
                puts("Add new stock\n");
                write_info();
                break;
```

```
            case('L'):
                puts("List stocks");
                read_info();
                break;
            case('Q'):
                puts("Quit\n");
                done = TRUE;
                break;
            default:
                puts("?");
                break;
        }
    }
    return(0);
}

void write_info(void)
{
}

void read_info(void)
{
}
```

Type this skeleton into your editor. It's basically the start of the menu system minus the disk access statements. That's fine. Baby steps!

In Line 31, you must replace `fflush(stdin)` with `fpurge(stdin)` for some Unix systems.

Save the code to disk as STOCKS.C.

Compile. Run:

```
Stock Portfolio Thing

A - Add new stock

L - List stocks

Q - Quit

Your choice:
```

Make sure that it all works. Press **A**. Press **L**. Press the **K** or Escape key to see whether unwanted input is handled properly. Then, press **Q** to quit.

Writing a structure to disk

Because C has no `fwritestructure()` function, you have to settle for one of the other disk-writing functions. The best one you have is `fwrite()`, which writes a chunk of memory to disk. Here's how:

```
c = fwrite(&buffer,size,items,handle);
```

Buffer is a pointer divulging the location of a chunk of memory you want to write to disk. It can be the start of a string in memory or the location of a structure.

Size is the size of the buffer in bytes (or characters). It can be a constant value or the size of a variable or structure as returned by the `sizeof` operator.

Items refers to the number of items (from the memory location *buffer* and of the size *size*) that you want to write. This value is usually 1.

Handle refers to the file handle that's returned from a file opened for writing or appending.

The `fwrite()` function returns a value, c, which is equal to the value of *size* (typically, 1), indicating the number of chunks written to disk. If a disk error occurs, `fwrite()` returns 0 or some value less than the value of *size*.

In the STOCKS.C source code, the `write_info()` function is used to create a structure of the `stock_data` type, fill in the structure, and then write it to disk. That's done by using the `fwrite()` function, as shown here:

```
void write_info(void)
{
    FILE *stocks;
    struct stock_data stock;

    printf("Enter stock name:");
    gets(stock.name);
    printf("How much did you pay for it? $");
    scanf("%f",&stock.buy_price);
    stock.current_price = stock.buy_price/11;

    stocks = fopen("stock.dat","a");
    if(stocks==NULL)
    {
        puts("Error opening file");
```

```
        exit(1);
    }

    fwrite(&stock,sizeof(stock),1,stocks);

    fclose(stocks);
    puts("Stock added!");
    fflush(stdin);              /* fpurge(stdin) */
}
```

Update the STOCKS.C source code in your editor to match what's shown here. Remember to use the proper input stream flushing command at the end of the function (as shown in this example). Save STOCKS.C, updating the source code on disk. Compile and run.

Press **A** and Enter when you see the program's menu:

```
Add new stock

Enter stock name:
```

Type **Blorfus Industries** and press Enter:

```
How much did you pay for it? $
```

Type **153.89** and press Enter:

```
Stock added.
```

You return to the main menu. Press **Q** to quit.

Now, you can look at the data structure as it sits in the disk file. First, use the `view` command you create in Book V, Chapter 3. In Windows, type **view stock.dat**; in Unix, type **./view stock.dat**:

```
Blorfus Industries||_A
```

Ugh. Not beautiful! That's because, unlike `fprintf()`, the `fwrite()` function writes binary data to disk — just the way the information is stored in memory in the `stocks` structure. This capability makes reading the information from disk easier, but it makes looking at it on disk painful.

Better write the rest of the program to see what the data really looks like.

Reading a structure from disk

Because you can't readily get at the information in any other way, you should finish the STOCKS.C program (begun earlier in this chapter) by completing the `read_info()` function. Only by using that function and `fread()` can you get your precious data back into the computer:

```
void read_info(void)
{
    FILE *stocks;
    struct stock_data stock;
    int x;

    stocks = fopen("stock.dat","r");
    if(stocks==NULL)
    {
        puts("No data in file");
        return;
    }

    while(TRUE)
    {
        x = fread(&stock,sizeof(stock),1,stocks);

        if(x==0) break;

        printf("\nStock name: %s\n",stock.name);
        printf("Purchased for: $%.2f\n",stock.buy_price);
        printf("Current price: $%.2f\n",stock.current_price);
    }

    fclose(stocks);
}
```

Load the STOCKS.C source code back into your editor. Complete the `read_info()` function as just written. The only new item is the `fread()` function, which isn't utterly new if you know about `fwrite()`. Save the source code to disk to complete the STOCKS.C source code.

Compile and run.

Press **L** on the menu to list the stocks you have saved to disk. You may see them displayed, looking something like this:

```
Stock name: Blorfus Industries
Purchased for: $153.89
Current price: $13.99

Stock name: Toxic Waster, Inc.
Purchased for: $100
Current price: $9.09
```

Then you see the main menu again. The `read_info` function properly reads the values from disk. Press **Q** to quit the STOCKS.C program.

The final STOCKS.C program

Here's the final result of your labor. The STOCKS.C program should look like this in your editor:

```c
#include <stdio.h>
#include <stdlib.h>
#include <ctype.h>

#define FALSE 0
#define TRUE !FALSE

struct stock_data {
    char name[30];
    float buy_price;
    float current_price;
    };

void write_info(void);
void read_info(void);

int main()
{
    char c;
    int done=FALSE;

    while(!done)
    {
        puts("\nStock Portfolio Thing\n");
        puts("A - Add new stock\n");
        puts("L - List stocks\n");
        puts("Q - Quit\n");
        printf("Your choice: ");

        c = getchar();
        fflush(stdin);          /* fpurge(stdin) */
        c = toupper(c);
        switch(c)
        {
            case('A'):
                puts("Add new stock\n");
                write_info();
                break;
            case('L'):
                puts("List stocks");
                read_info();
                break;
```

```
            case('Q'):
                puts("Quit\n");
                done = TRUE;
                break;
            default:
                puts("?");
                break;
        }
    }
    return(0);
}

void write_info(void)
{
    FILE *stocks;
    struct stock_data stock;

    printf("Enter stock name:");
    gets(stock.name);
    printf("What did you buy it for? $");
    scanf("%f",&stock.buy_price);
    stock.current_price = stock.buy_price/11;

    stocks = fopen("stock.dat","a");
    if(stocks==NULL)
    {
        puts("Error opening file");
        exit(1);
    }

    fwrite(&stock,sizeof(stock),1,stocks);

    fclose(stocks);
    puts("Stock added!");
    fflush(stdin);          /* fpurge(stdin) */
}

void read_info(void)
{
        FILE *stocks;
    struct stock_data stock;
        int x;

    stocks = fopen("stock.dat","r");
    if(stocks==NULL)
    {
        puts("No data in file");
```

```
        return;
    }

    while(TRUE)
    {
        x = fread(&stock,sizeof(stock),1,stocks);

        if(x==0) break;

        printf("\nStock name: %s\n",stock.name);
        printf("Purchased for $%.2f\n",stock.buy_price);
        printf("Current price: $%.2f\n",stock.current_price);
    }

    fclose(stocks);
}
```

You don't have to stop here. You can keep modifying the program, if you like. Add functions to search through the records on disk or sort the stocks by name or price. This is how most crazy programs start and how most programmers come to realize that 4 o'clock comes twice a day!

Chapter 5: Random Access Files

In This Chapter

- ✔ **Reading and writing file chunks**
- ✔ **Understanding the file pointer**
- ✔ **Using** `fseek()` **to find a file chunk**
- ✔ **Discovering the file pointer's position with** `ftell()`
- ✔ **Replacing a chunk in the middle of a file**
- ✔ **Building a disk-based database**

Nothing about random file access is really *random*. It's just another way of getting to information on disk. The first way, demonstrated in earlier chapters of this book, is officially known as *sequential* disk access. That means that information is read from disk sequentially, one chunk after another, from the start of the file to the end.

With random access, you control which part of the file information is written from or read to. That way, you can store a database or sorts on disk, reading and writing specific records to and from disk without having to read in and write out the entire file every time.

This chapter assumes that you have read Book V, Chapter 4 and created the STOCKS.C program source code listed at the end of Chapter 4.

The Random Access Demonstration

Random file access works best when you use `fwrite()` to write chunks of a given size to a file. That way, the entire file looks like a database full of records of a given size. You can then work with the file in those chunk-size pieces, reading and writing individual chunks as you please. This all works out nice and tidy, as long as all the chunks are of the same size.

Creating the FROOT file

For demonstration purposes, the following code creates a file on disk composed of 25 types of fruit. Each fruit name is stored in a chunk that is 14 bytes long, written to disk with the fwrite() function. Here's the code:

```c
#include <stdio.h>

int main()
{
    char froot[25][14] = {
        "Apple", "Avocado", "Banana", "Blackberry",
    "Boysenberry",
        "Cantaloupe", "Cherry", "Coconut", "Cranberry",
    "Cumquat",
        "Grape", "Guava", "Mango", "Marionberry", "Melon",
        "Orange", "Papaya", "Peach", "Pear", "Persimmon",
        "Pineapple", "Plum", "Raspberry", "Strawberry",
    "Watermelon"
    };
    FILE *f;
    int x;

    if(!(f = fopen("froot.txt","w")))
    {
        puts("Error creating file");
        return(1);
    }

    for(x=0;x<25;x++)
        fwrite(froot[x],14,1,f);
    fclose(f);
    return(0);
}
```

Save this code to disk as FROOT.C. Compile Run.

The program has no visible output, but it does create the file FROOT.TXT on the hard drive. You can best view that file by using the dump command you create in Book V, Chapter 3. At the command prompt, in Windows, type **dump froot.txt**; in Unix, type **./dump froot.txt**. You see something like this:

```
41 70 70 6C 65 00 00 00 00 00 00 00 00 00 41 76
6F 63 61 64 6F 00 00 00 00 00 00 00 42 61 6E 61
6E 61 00 00 00 00 00 00 00 00 42 6C 61 63 6B 62
65 72 72 79 00 00 00 00 42 6F 79 73 65 6E 62 65
72 72 79 00 00 00 43 61 6E 74 61 6C 6F 75 70 65
00 00 00 00 43 68 65 72 72 79 00 00 00 00 00 00
00 00 43 6F 63 6F 6E 75 74 00 00 00 00 00 00 00
43 72 61 6E 62 65 72 72 79 00 00 00 00 00 43 75
6D 71 75 61 74 00 00 00 00 00 00 00 47 72 61 70
```

```
65 00 00 00 00 00 00 00 00 00 47 75 61 76 61 00
00 00 00 00 00 00 00 00 4D 61 6E 67 6F 00 00 00
00 00 00 00 00 00 4D 61 72 69 6F 6E 62 65 72 72
79 00 00 00 4D 65 6C 6F 6E 00 00 00 00 00 00 00
00 00 4F 72 61 6E 67 65 00 00 00 00 00 00 00 00
50 61 70 61 79 61 00 00 00 00 00 00 00 00 50 65
61 63 68 00 00 00 00 00 00 00 00 00 50 65 61 72
00 00 00 00 00 00 00 00 00 00 00 50 65 72 73 69 6D
6D 6F 6E 00 00 00 00 00 00 50 69 6E 65 61 70 70 6C
65 00 00 00 00 50 6C 75 6D 00 00 00 00 00 00 00
00 00 00 00 52 61 73 70 62 65 72 72 79 00 00 00
00 00 53 74 72 61 77 62 65 72 72 79 00 00 00 00
57 61 74 65 72 6D 65 6C 6F 6E 00 00 00 00
froot.txt: size = 350 bytes
```

See all those zeroes in there? That's the padding after each fruit's name. That padding ensures that each fruit is stored in a chunk of disk space exactly 14 bytes long.

Also note that there's no EOF marker or even a newline (\n) code anywhere in the dump. That's because fwrite() wrote chunks of memory, not strings of text, to disk. Remember that random file access works best when chunks of stuff have been written to disk.

In Unix, the hexdump command can be used to better view a *dump* of the FROOT.TXT file. Type **hexdump -C froot.txt** and press Enter. The output is shown in Figure 5-1.

Figure 5-1:
How the
FROOT.TXT
file is stored
on disk
(courtesy
of the
hexdump
command).

```
00000000  41 70 70 6c 65 00 00 00  00 00 00 00 00 00 41 76  |Apple.........Av|
00000010  6f 63 61 64 6f 00 00 00  00 00 00 00 42 61 6e 61  |ocado.......Bana|
00000020  6e 61 00 00 00 00 00 00  00 00 42 6c 61 63 6b 62  |na........Blackb|
00000030  65 72 72 79 00 00 00 00  42 6f 79 73 65 6e 62 65  |erry....Boysenbe|
00000040  72 72 79 00 00 00 43 61  6e 74 61 6c 6f 75 70 65  |rry...Cantaloupe|
00000050  00 00 00 00 43 68 65 72  72 79 00 00 00 00 00 00  |....Cherry......|
00000060  00 00 43 6f 63 6f 6e 75  74 00 00 00 00 00 00 00  |..Coconut.......|
00000070  43 72 61 6e 62 65 72 72  79 00 00 00 00 00 43 75  |Cranberry.....Cu|
00000080  6d 71 75 61 74 00 00 00  00 00 00 00 47 72 61 70  |mquat.......Grap|
00000090  65 00 00 00 00 00 00 00  00 00 47 75 61 76 61 00  |e.........Guava.|
000000a0  00 00 00 00 00 00 00 00  4d 61 6e 67 6f 00 00 00  |........Mango...|
000000b0  00 00 00 00 00 00 4d 61  72 69 6f 6e 62 65 72 72  |......Marionberr|
000000c0  79 00 00 00 4d 65 6c 6f  6e 00 00 00 00 00 00 00  |y...Melon.......|
000000d0  00 00 4f 72 61 6e 67 65  00 00 00 00 00 00 00 00  |..Orange........|
000000e0  50 61 70 61 79 61 00 00  00 00 00 00 00 00 50 65  |Papaya........Pe|
000000f0  61 63 68 00 00 00 00 00  00 00 00 00 50 65 61 72  |ach.........Pear|
00000100  00 00 00 00 00 00 00 00  00 00 50 65 72 73 69 6d  |..........Persim|
00000110  6d 6f 6e 00 00 00 00 00  50 69 6e 65 61 70 70 6c  |mon.....Pineappl|
00000120  65 00 00 00 00 00 50 6c  75 6d 00 00 00 00 00 00  |e.....Plum......|
00000130  00 00 00 00 52 61 73 70  62 65 72 72 79 00 00 00  |....Raspberry...|
00000140  00 00 53 74 72 61 77 62  65 72 72 79 00 00 00 00  |..Strawberry....|
00000150  57 61 74 65 72 6d 65 6c  6f 6e 00 00 00 00        |Watermelon....|
0000015e
```

Introducing the file pointer

Given a file composed of chunk-size records or elements or pieces, you can direct the operating system to read any specific chunk from the file. You do that by positioning something called the file pointer.

The file pointer isn't the same thing as a pointer variable. It's just an example of how limited some folks can be when thinking of new names for computer things. In this case, a *file pointer* indicates a position or offset inside the file at which information is being read.

For example, when you open a file, the file pointer is at offset 0 — the start of the file. If you read in 80 bytes, the file pointer is at offset 80, ready to read the 81st byte in the file.

In C, you can use a handful of functions to manipulate or query the file pointer. For example, the ftell() function reports the file pointer's current position. Here's an update to the FROOT.C source code that demonstrates ftell() and shows you how the file pointer slogs through a file as its written to disk:

```
#include <stdio.h>

int main()
{
    char froot[25][14] = {
        "Apple", "Avocado", "Banana", "Blackberry",
    "Boysenberry",
        "Cantaloupe", "Cherry", "Coconut", "Cranberry",
    "Cumquat",
        "Grape", "Guava", "Mango", "Marionberry", "Melon",
        "Orange", "Papaya", "Peach", "Pear", "Persimmon",
        "Pineapple", "Plum", "Raspberry", "Strawberry",
    "Watermelon"
    };
    FILE *f;
    int x;

    if(!(f = fopen("froot.txt","w")))
    {
        puts("Error creating file");
        return(1);
    }
    printf("After file opened, file pointer =
%d\n",ftell(f));

    for(x=0;x<25;x++)
    {
        fwrite(froot[x],14,1,f);
        printf("Wrote record %d, file pointer = %d\n",
x,ftell(f));
    }
```

```
        fclose(f);
        return(0);
}
```

In this modification to the FROOT.C source code, two `printf()` statements have been added (along with braces on the `for` loop), both of which display the file pointer by using the `ftell()` function. Note that `ftell()` takes as an argument the file handle.

Save these changes to the FROOT.C source code. Compile and run:

```
After file opened, file pointer = 0
Wrote record 0, file pointer = 14
Wrote record 1, file pointer = 28
Wrote record 2, file pointer = 42
Wrote record 3, file pointer = 56
```

And so on. The `ftell()` function properly reports the offset into the file, the position at which the file pointer is writing information to disk.

Exercise 5.5.1

You can also use the `ftell()` command to check the file pointer while reading from a file. Modify the source code to VIEW.C (refer to Book V, Chapter 3) so that the `while` loop that display's the file's contents also displays the file pointer position.

Exercise 5.5.2

Write a program, SHOWFROOT.C, that displays each record in the FROOT.TXT file. Use `fread()` to read in each file chunk. Have each chunk displayed along with its record number using this format:

```
14: Melon
```

Seeking out a specific record

Another C language function you can use to goof with the file pointer is `fseek()`. The `fseek()` function positions the file pointer at a specific offset, from either the file's start or end or from the present position of the file pointer. Here's the format:

```
x = fseek(handle, offset, whence)
```

Handle is the file handle pointer that's returned whenever a file is opened on disk.

Offset sets the file pointer's position. It's the number of bytes from either the file's start or end or from the file pointer's current position. The *whence* value determines how *offset* is read.

Whence tells `fseek()` where to start seeking information inside a file. Three values are defined in STDIO.H:

✦ Specify `SEEK_SET` to tell `fseek()` to start reading data relative to the file's start.

✦ Specify `SEEK_END` to direct `fseek()` to start reading data relative to the file's end.

✦ Specify `SEEK_CUR` to tell `fseek()` to start reading data based on where the last chunk of data was read.

`fseek()` returns the value 0 if successful; otherwise, -1.

Ideally, you want to use `fseek()` on a file that contains chunks of a constant size so that you can hoppity-skippity between the chunks in a file. To move to a specific record or chunk in the file, you must know the record number as well as the chunk size to calculate the offset.

The following source code demonstrates how you can use `fseek()` to obtain the name of the 13th record in the FROOT.TXT file. Note in Exercise 5.5.2 (refer to the preceding section) that the records in the file start with Record 0, so the 13th record is really the 12th "element" in the file, or "Mango." Here's some source code for you:

```
#include <stdio.h>

#define RECSIZE 14

int main()
{
    FILE *f;
    char froot[RECSIZE];
    int record,offset;

    if(!(f = fopen("froot.txt","r")))
    {
        puts("Error opening file");
        return(1);
    }

/* Get record 12, record size = RECSIZE */
    record = 12;
    offset = record * RECSIZE;
    fseek(f,offset,SEEK_SET);
    fread(froot,RECSIZE,1,f);
    printf("%2d: %s\n",record,froot);
```

```
        fclose(f);
        return(0);
}
```

The program calculates the 12th (or 13th) item's offset by setting the variable `record` equal to 12 and then setting `offset` equal to that value multiplied by the `RECSIZE`, or record size, value. The result of that calculation is put into the `fseek()` function to position the file pointer at the start of that record. Then, `fread()` reads in only that record.

Save the source code to disk as FROOT12.C. Compile. Run:

```
12: Mango
```

As predicted, the `fseek()` function found and displayed the 12th (13th) chunk in the file. Yee-haw.

Exercise 5.5.3
Modify the FROOT12.C source code so that it uses `fseek()` to display every other record in the file. You have two ways to accomplish this. See whether you can think of them both: FROOT12A.C and FROOT12B.C.

Changing a record
Silly. Silly. Silly. Hopping and skipping around in a file and reading stuff is really silly. The pure power of random file access comes not from hopping around and reading, but, rather, from hopping around and *writing!* Witness this potent example:

```
#include <stdio.h>

#define RECSIZE 14

int main()
{
    FILE *f;
    char newfroot[RECSIZE] = "Snozberry";
    int record,offset;

    if(!(f = fopen("froot.txt","r+")))
    {
        puts("Error opening file");
        return(1);
    }

/* Replace record 12, record size = RECSIZE */
    record = 12;
    offset = record * RECSIZE;
    fseek(f,offset,SEEK_SET);
```

```
fwrite(newfroot,RECSIZE,1,f);
fclose(f);
return(0);
}
```

This code seeks out Record 12 (Element 13, or "Mango") in the file and *replaces* that record with a new record. To do this, you use `fseek()` to position the file pointer at the proper place inside the file, and then you use `fwrite()` to put a new chunk of data there. Oh, and the file must be opened for both reading and writing (`"r+"`).

Carefully type the preceding code into your editor. Save it to disk as NEW12.C. Compile. Run.

It has no output, but the record has been changed. To view the new Record 12, you can use either the FROOT12 or SHOWFROOT program you create earlier in this chapter. You see that the new fruit listed in Item 12 is now `Snozberry`.

Starting all over

I have one more file pointer function to mention: `rewind()`. Not as flashy as `ftell()` or `fseek()`, `rewind()` resets the file pointer back to position 0 at the start of a file. That's necessary sometimes when you may not be certain of where the pointer is or when you just need to start over.

The `rewind()` function takes only an open file's pointer variable as its argument. Also note that, unlike all other file commands, `rewind()` doesn't start with an *f*. Weird!

Building a Disk-Based Database

You can combine the `fseek()` function with `fread()` or `fwrite()` to actively change chunks of a file, which is ideal for managing a disk-based database. Using the information already covered in this chapter, this section adds to the STOCKS.C source code (from Book V, Chapter 4) to start the process of building a database.

Load the source code for STOCKS.C into your editor. The complete source code is listed at the end of Book V, Chapter 4. You need to define a new function in the code, `replace_info()`, which is in charge of fetching a specific record from disk and then replacing it with something new. To make it happen, fix up the code as I describe here.

Add the prototype for `replace_info()` to the other prototypes at the start of the code:

```
void replace_info(void);
```

Modify the menu display so that Option R appears between Options L and Q:

```
puts("R - Replace stock\n");
```

Then, add a new case in the `switch-case` thing to handle the R key press:

```
case('R'):
    puts("Replace stock");
    replace_info();
    break;
```

Finally, you need to create the new `replace_info()` function. The following code has `replace_info()` use `fseek()` and `fread()` to find and read in a specific record from disk. That record is then displayed — but not modified. That comes later:

```
void replace_info(void)
{
    FILE *stocks;
    struct stock_data stock;
    int record,x;
    long offset;

    printf("Which record number do you want to find? ");
    scanf("%d",&record);

    stocks = fopen("stock.dat","r");
    if(stocks==NULL)
    {
        puts("Error opening file");
        return;
    }

    offset = (long)(record-1)*sizeof(stock);
    x = fseek(stocks,offset,SEEK_SET);
    if(x != 0)
    {
        puts("Error reading from file");
        return;
    }

    x = fread(&stock,sizeof(stock),1,stocks);
    if(x==0)
    {
        puts("Error reading record");
        return;
    }

    printf("\nRecord: %d\n",record);
    printf("Stock name: %s\n",stock.name);
    printf("Purchased for $%.2f\n",stock.buy_price);
```

```
        printf("Current price: $%.2f\n",stock.current_price);
        fclose(stocks);
        fflush(stdin);          /* fpurge(stdin) */
}
```

Add this function to the rest of the code modifications. Save the sucker to disk. Compile. Fix any errors. Then, recompile. And so on.

Run!

It helps to add a few records, so use the A command to add new stocks until you get about three or four. Then, use the new R command to view individual stocks.

After pressing **R** (and Enter) from the menu, you should see something like this:

```
Replace stock
Which record number do you want to find?
```

Type **2** for Record 2 (note that the code subtracts 1 from the value input to equal the true record number on disk):

```
Record: 2
Stock name: Beta Potato
Purchased for: $1.98
Current price: $0.18
```

Hopefully, that worked for you! `fseek()` finds the record and `fread()` reads it. The next step is to update the structure and use `fwrite()` to put the new information to disk.

Exercise 5.5.4

It's time to finish the update for STOCKS.C. Based on information gleaned from the FROOT.TXT series of programs, finish STOCKS.C so that the `replace_info()` function asks for the new stock data (name and purchase price) and then writes that information to disk to replace the old record. This works just like replacing Record 12 in FROOT.TXT, though a structure is used rather than a string of text.

After replacing the record, you should be able to use the menu's L command to list all the stocks, and all of them should be there; the new one along with the old ones that are unchanged.

Good luck!

Chapter 6: Folder Folderol

In This Chapter

✓ Understanding how directories work

✓ Reading file trivia with the `stat()` function

✓ Opening and closing a directory

✓ Reading files from a directory

✓ Reading the current working directory

✓ Changing directories

✓ Introducing recursion

✓ Reading subdirectories

If you want to find a file on disk, you can always use the `fopen()` command just to see whether it exists. Of course, `fopen()` may not return an error because the file is missing. The file could be busy, or it could be living in another folder or perhaps even hiding from you. No, there must be a better way to find files on disk.

In both Windows and Unix, files are organized on disk using folders or directories. I prefer the term *directory* because it's the original, technical term, existing long before the feel-good graphical era of folders. As you would suspect, just as you have tools for reading files on disk, you have tools for reading directories and discovering which files they contain. This chapter covers the whatnots and howtos of all that folder folderol.

Who Knows What Lurks on Disk?

I have to get it off my chest: Directories are a myth. A *directory* is nothing more than a small database file on a disk listing, one that contains information about other files. The database keeps track of the file's name, date, time, size, permissions, attributes, and other trivial information. It also contains information necessary for the operating system to locate the file's data elsewhere on disk.

When the operating system tells you what's on disk, it's merely reporting information stored in the directory or database. It doesn't list all the information, mostly because humans don't need to know *all* the details, but it lists enough.

A *subdirectory* is merely another database located elsewhere on the disk. It has a directory entry just as a file does, but it's really just a reference to another directory or database file located elsewhere on the disk.

The C language comes with a smattering of tools that let you access the directory or database. You can use these tools to find specific files, list available files on disk, or gather specific technical information about files. The following sections disclose the details.

Grabbing Information about a File with `stat()`

The operating system knows all, sees all. . . .

The amount of detail the operating system stores about a file is huge. But it's also trivial. In most cases, the information that's stored is really only for the operating system and is of little use to you and your programs. Still, you can examine that information, if you want.

One handy C language function you can use to gather information about a file is the `stat()` function. Here's how it works:

```
x = stat(*filename,&stat_buf)
```

Filename is a string constant or a pointer to the name of the file you want to peek at. It can be an individual filename or a full pathname to some file elsewhere on disk.

&stat_buf is the location of a `stat` structure in memory, one that the `stat()` function fills in with information about the file.

If everything works properly, `stat()` returns 0; otherwise, it returns -1 with the official error stored in the `errno` variable; refer to your compiler's documentation for the details.

The `stat()` function requires the SYS/STAT.H and SYS/TYPES.H header files for it to properly "funct."

The following source code demonstrates the `stat()` function. In this code, the `stat()` function examines the FILEINFO.C program — its own source code, returning that information in the `stat` structure. Although a wealth of information is returned by the `stat()` function, the real details depend on your operating system. Refer to your compiler's documentation for a full description of what's offered in the `stat` structure:

```
#include <stdio.h>
#include <sys/stat.h>
#include <sys/types.h>
#include <time.h>

int main()
{
    struct stat fbuf;
    int x;

    x = stat("fileinfo.c",&fbuf);
    if(x != 0 )
    {
        puts("Error reading file");
        return(1);
    }

    puts("Some file stats on FILEINFO.C:");
    printf("File size is %d bytes\n",fbuf.st_size);
    printf("File last modified %s\n",ctime(&fbuf.st_mtime));
    return(0);
}
```

Save this source code to disk as FILEINFO.C. Compile. Run:

```
Some file stats on FILEINFO.C:
File size is 406 bytes
File last modified Sat May 08 22:00:37 2004
```

(The statistics you see may be subtly different, of course.)

Here's what happened:

✦ The stat() function reads information about the named file, fileinfo.c (the source code), storing it in the stat structure's fbuf variable.

✦ Although many interesting things are available in the stat structure, two are common between Windows and Unix and are rather easy values to interpret: st.size, which is the size of the file in bytes, and st_mtime, which is the time stamp for the last time the file was modified.

✦ The st_size value can be displayed directly, as shown in Line 19.

✦ The st_mtime value is stored in seconds according to the Unix Epoch. The ctime() function translates that into a readable text string.

✦ Refer to Book IV, Chapter 9 for more information on time functions in C.

Note that stat() is a reporting function. It doesn't modify the trivial tidbits associated with a file.

Exercise 5.6.1

Modify the FILEINFO.C source code so that the user specifies which file to examine on the command line.

Reading a Directory

A directory is nothing more than a special database file on disk, one that lists information about other files — as well as other directories. To access the special directory file a handful of directory-reading functions are used in C. This section introduces these functions, as well as describe how to read and display a directory of files in C.

Opening and closing the directory

Reading a directory involves opening a directory "file" on disk. Because the directory is a special type of file, you cannot use the standard file reading functions (fopen(), fread(), fclose())to read the directory's contents. Instead, specific directory-reading functions are used.

The opendir() function is used to open a directory database for reading. Here's the format:

```
handle = opendir(pathname)
```

pathname is the name of the directory you want to open and examine. You can use the . shortcut to represent the current working directory in both Unix and Windows. Otherwise the full directory path needs to be specified.

Windows uses backslashes as directory separators in the path. Because the backslash is also an escape character, you must specify *two* of them in a path. So, to specify the \WINDOWS directory, you must write \\windows.)

If the directory file can be opened, a memory address is returned and stored in the pointer handle. Just as you use a FILE type of pointer for opening a file, you need a DIR type of pointer for opening a directory (see the following source code).

If opendir() returns NULL, the directory was unable to be opened.

Note that in order to properly "funct,"opendir() requires both the SYS/TYPES.H and DIRENT.H header files.

After the directory is opened, information can be read from it by using specific directory-reading functions. (I tell you more about that in the next section.) When all is done, just as you would close an open file, you need to close an open directory. You do that by using the `closedir()` function:

```
x = closedir(handle)
```

Handle is the pointer variable that's returned when the directory is opened.

This function returns 0 if the directory was successfully closed. Otherwise, -1 is returned and the `errno` variable is set equal to the proper operating system error (refer to your compiler's documentation on `errno` for the details):

```
#include <stdio.h>
#include <sys/types.h>
#include <dirent.h>

int main()
{
    DIR *dhandle;

    dhandle = opendir(".");
    if(dhandle == NULL)
    {
        puts("Error opening directory");
        return(1);
    }

    puts("Directory successfully opened!");

    closedir(dhandle);
    return(0);
}
```

Type this source code into your editor. Save it to disk as DODIR.C. Compile. Run:

```
Directory successfully opened!
```

The program uses the `opendir()` function to open the current working directory, represented by `"."` in Line 9. Nothing is read from the directory, so it's just closed up with a `closedir()` function at the end of the code.

Note how the directory handle variable is created:

```
DIR *dhandle;
```

This approach is similar to the way file handle variables are created with the FILE typedef, though the DIR typedef is used instead. Note that dhandle is a pointer variable, though it's never used with an asterisk outside of its declaration.

Reading files from the directory

After the directory is opened, files are read from it one chunk at a time. Indeed, the file-reading functions have quite a random access nature. A *directory pointer* is used to march through the directory file's database, pointing at a specific structure that contains information about files listed in the directory.

The main function used to read files from the directory database is readdir(). It works like this:

```
*dirent = readdir(handle);
```

Handle is the DIR pointer variable associated with an open directory file. It's returned by the opendir() function.

Dirent is a pointer to a directory entry structure named dirent. When the readdir() function is successful, the directory entry structure is filled with information about the file entry in the directory database. When a boo-boo occurs, a NULL is returned.

The readdir() function requires the same header files as opendir(): SYS/TYPES.H and DIRENT.H.

Here's the source code for a program that lists all the files in the current directory:

```
#include <stdio.h>
#include <sys/types.h>
#include <dirent.h>

int main()
{
    DIR *dhandle;
    struct dirent *drecord;

    dhandle = opendir(".");
    if(dhandle == NULL)
    {
        puts("Error opening directory");
```

```
        return(1);
    }

    while( (drecord = readdir(dhandle)) != NULL)
        printf("%s\n",drecord->d_name);

    closedir(dhandle);
    return(0);
}
```

Open the DODIR.C source code in your editor. Modify it so that it resembles what you see here. You're adding a `dirent` structure pointer named `drecord` to store the file information that's read from the directory. Plus, a `while` loop is used to read and display the file names found in the directory. Save the changes to disk. Compile and run.

(The contents of the current directory are displayed.)

I have looked high and low, and I can't find any detailed information about the `dirent` structure or its contents. The only element that seems to be used from that structure is `dirent->d_name`, which is the name of the file. So, if you want more information about the file, you need to use a function such as `stat()` (covered earlier in this chapter).

Exercise 5.6.2

Modify the DODIR.C source code again. This time, use the `stat()` function on each file that's found to return its size in bytes and then display that size along with the filename in the program's output.

Regular files versus directory files

If you completed Exercise 5.6.2, you noticed that any directory entries in the program's output show a file size of zero bytes. That's not really true, of course; directories have a size as well as files do. But that's not my point.

You could replace the file size value with the text `<DIR>`, which is what Windows does in its output. But, to do that, you need to recognize when a file is a regular file and when it's a directory entry. You can pry that information from the `stat()` function's `stat` structure by using the `S_ISDIR` macro.

Assume that you have created a `stat` structure, such as

```
struct stat sbuf;
```

Then, you use the stat() command to read information about a file, something like this:

```
stat(drecord->d_name,&sbuf);
```

One element of the stat structure is st_mode, which you can use to evaluate which type of file the name (drecord->d_name) represents. To see whether the file is a directory, the S_ISDIR macro is used:

```
S_ISDIR(sbuf.st_mode)
```

This command evaluates to TRUE if the file is in fact a directory. It returns FALSE otherwise, indicated by a nondirectory entry.

Here's an update to the DODIR.C source code that accounts for and displays information about directory entries. This update is combined with my solution for Exercise 5.6.2:

```
#include <stdio.h>
#include <sys/types.h>
#include <dirent.h>
#include <sys/stat.h>

int main()
{
    DIR *dhandle;
    struct dirent *drecord;
    struct stat sbuf;

    dhandle = opendir(".");
    if(dhandle == NULL)
    {
        puts("Error opening directory");
        return(1);
    }

    while( (drecord = readdir(dhandle)) != NULL)
    {
        stat(drecord->d_name,&sbuf);
        if(S_ISDIR(sbuf.st_mode))
            printf("%-16s %-9s\n",drecord->d_name,"<DIR>");
        else
            printf("%-16s %9d\n", drecord->d_name,
    sbuf.st_size);
    }
    closedir(dhandle);
    return(0);
}
```

Load the DODIR.C source code from earlier in this chapter into your editor. Modify the code so that it matches the preceding source code, noting that some of the lines may have wrapped in this text; they don't need to wrap the same in your editor. Save the thing back to disk. Compile. Run.

The output lists files and their size, but specifies <DIR> by directory entries, such as

```
.                       <DIR>
..                      <DIR>
a.exe                        12288
alive.txt                       58
```

And so on. . . .

It's important to know which "files" are really directories, especially if you want to write a program that searches through directories. You read more about that toward the end of this chapter.

Exercise 5.6.3

Modify DODIR.C one last time. This time, have it keep track of the total number of files and their sizes so that you can display a summary after the last line of output:

```
nnn file(s) for a total of nnnn bytes
```

Directories Hither, Thither, and Yon

Back in the old, primitive days of personal computing, you had only one directory per disk. That made sense: When you had only 180 kilobytes of storage, there was no point in "organizing" the information on that disk much beyond properly naming the files. But, as storage devices grew larger, the notion of directories and subdirectories became not only popular but also necessary.

The command prompt in both Windows and Unix has commands for reporting the current directory, changing to a new directory, and creating and removing a directory. Each of these commands has a similar function in the C language, functions you can use to manipulate which directories your program can visit and even create directories of its own.

"Where the heck am I?"

Just as users are "logged" to certain directories, so can programs. Normally, a program starts and runs in the directory it lives in — but that's not a rule I would rely on.

When I use the command line, I configure my command prompt to display the current working directory. In Windows, it looks like this:

```
C:\Documents and Settings\Dan\My Documents\prog\c\disk>
```

In Unix, it's

```
/home/dang/prog/c/disk $
```

And, in my C programs, it's the `getcwd()` function that conjures up a string telling me just where the heck I am. Here's the format:

```
string = getcwd(&buffer,size);
```

Like the `cd` command in Windows or `pwd` in Unix, the `getcwd()` function in C reports the current working directory.

Buffer is a character pointer to a storage location in your program. *Size* is the size of *buffer* in characters. After the call to `getcwd()`, the buffer contains a string representing the current working directory. The function also returns a pointer to that *string* (which is simply the address of *buffer*).

If the `getcwd()` command fails, it returns a NULL. Note that this function requires the UNISTD.H header file in order to properly "funct":

```
#include <stdio.h>
#include <unistd.h>

#define BUFSIZE 128

int main()
{
    char buffer[BUFSIZE];

    getcwd(buffer,BUFSIZE);
    printf("The current working directory
is:\n\t%s\n",buffer);

    return(0);
}
```

Carefully type the preceding source code into your editor. Save it to disk as GETCWD.C. Compile and run.

Here's the output I witnessed:

```
The current working directory is:
        C:\Documents and Settings\Dan\My
    Documents\prog\c\disk
```

Note that I didn't do any error checking in the program. I was bad. Although it's true that `getcwd()` should always return a working directory, the problem may be in the buffer size. If the pathname is too large for the buffer, NULL is returned.

Pathnames can be incredibly long. Although the operating system may have a size limit (which is about 256 characters in Windows), note that it's common for URLs to be used as path names, in which case the real size can be quite enormous.

Pulling up your digs

Suppose that your program really needs to be in a specific directory. If so, it can change to that directory just as a user would change or log to a specific directory. The command that makes that happen in both Unix and Windows is `cd`, followed by the new directory name. In the C language, the `chdir()` function switches directories:

```
x = chdir(path);
```

Path is the full pathname of the directory to which you want to change — just like the pathname that follows the `cd` command. You can even use the `..` shortcut (for the parent directory), if you like.

Windows uses backslashes as directory separators in a pathname. Because the backslash is also an escape character, *two* must be specified in a pathname.

The `chdir()` function returns 0 upon success; otherwise, -1. The `errno` variable is then set to the specific operating system error; for the specifics, refer to the `errno` documentation for your compiler:

```
#include <stdio.h>
#include <unistd.h>

#define BUFSIZE 128

int main()
{
    char orgdir[BUFSIZE];
    char newdir[BUFSIZE];
    int x;

    getcwd(orgdir,BUFSIZE);
    printf("The current working directory
is:\n\t%s\n",orgdir);

    puts("Changing to the root directory...");
    x = chdir("\\");        /* x = chdir("/"); */
```

```
if( x != 0)
{
    puts("Error changing directories");
    return(1);
}

getcwd(newdir,BUFSIZE);
printf("The current working directory is
now:\n\t%s\n",newdir);

return(0);
}
```

Type this source code into your editor. Remember to use the proper command in Line 16: \\ for the root in Windows or / for the root in Unix. Save it to disk as CHANGED.C. Compile and run:

```
The current working directory is:
    C:\Documents and Settings\Dan\My Documents\prog\c\disk
Changing to the root directory...
The current working directory is now:
    C:\
```

Other directory commands I don't have space to completely write about

Just as there's a `mkdir` command for creating new directories, the C language sports a `mkdir()` function. To compare with `rmdir` for removing directories, there's also a C language `rmdir()` function. You can use either of these functions in your source code to create or remove directories and, O, just have lots of fun.

The `mkdir()` function takes on this format:

```
x = mkdir(path,mode);
```

Path is the pathname of the new directory to create; *mode* is the permissions for that directory. Refer to your compiler's documentation for properly setting the *mode* value.

The `rmdir()` function takes on this format:

```
x = rmdir(path);
```

Path is the pathname of the directory to remove. It must be an empty directory, containing no files or subdirectories.

The `mkdir()` function requires the SYS/STAT.H header file; `rmdir()` requires UNISTD.H.

Both functions return 0 upon success; upon failure, -1, with the `errno` variable set to a value indicating what has offended the operating system.

And, in Unix:

```
The current working directory is:
      /usr/home/dang/prog/c/disk
Changing to the root directory...
The current working directory is now:
      /
```

Note that the working directory doesn't change. Only the directory the program uses changes; as a user, you still remain logged to the same directory regardless of which directory the program changes to using the chdir() function.

Exercise 5.6.4
Modify CHANGED.C so that the program changes back to the original directory when it's done.

The Art of Recursion

I must admit that I'm terrified of recursion. It's something that baffles most beginners to their wits' end. But, recursion does have its place. I find that it can easily be understood when it comes to the topic of scanning directories. With that example, most every beginner can comprehend what it means to recurse. But, first, I give you the bad examples.

The boring recursive demo program
Recursion is the art of a function calling itself. In a way, you can almost envision it like those Russian Matrioshka dolls: Open up one doll and you find another, smaller doll. Open up the smaller doll, and you see another, smaller doll inside. Keep that up until you're opening up molecule-size Russian dolls. Oh, what fun! Yet, that is the essence of recursion.

Recursion is really nothing more than a function calling itself.

Of course, there's a method to this madness. Consider this:

```
void endless(void)
{
    printf("Endless!\n");
    endless();
}
```

The endless() function continues to call itself, over and over and over, essentially putting the computer into an endless loop (though, generally, the program runs out of something called *stack space* and eventually crashes and dies).

So, the object of recursion is to have a function call itself, yet know a way out when it's done. Truly useful examples of this process are rare in the C language; indeed, recursion isn't something the C language is known for. The following program demonstrates a silly example. You can see the true power of recursion in the next section, about digging through directories. For now, puzzle yourself with this source code:

```c
#include <stdio.h>

int doubler(int v)
{
    if( v < 1000)
        return(doubler(v*2));
    else
        return(v);
}

int main()
{
    int x;

    x = doubler(1);
    printf("The final value of X is %d\n",x);

    return(0);
}
```

Type this source code into your editor. Save it to disk as DOUBLER.C. Compile. Run:

```
The final value of X is 1024
```

Here's what happens:

- ✦ The doubler() function is called with the value 1 used as its variable v.

- ✦ When the value of variable v is less than 1000, the function returns.

- ✦ The value the function returns is equal to what the doubler() function returns, with v multiplied by 2, or doubled. If your eyes are crossed and smoke is coming out of your ears, you're doing okay. That's normal.

✦ The net effect of return(doubler(v*2)) is that the doubler() function is called again; this time, double the previous value. That action is repeated until the value of v is geometrically grown to be greater than 1000. At that point, the entire thing begins to unravel.

✦ When v is greater than or equal to 1000, the return(v) statement is executed. The function then returns, returns, returns, returns — and so on — until the unraveling is complete and control returns to the main() function.

A better example of recursion

The following code uses recursion to count the number of characters in a string. See whether you can figure out how it works before you run the program:

```c
#include <stdio.h>

int string_count(char *s)
{
    int count = 1;

    if(*s++)
        count += string_count(s);
    else
        count--;

    return(count);
}

int main()
{
    char *string = "Count me! Count me, you fool!";
    int length;

    length = string_count(string);
    printf("The string:\n\t%s\nis %d characters long\n",
    string,length);
    return(0);
}
```

Type this source code into your editor with vigor. Save it to disk as COUNTER.C. Compile and run:

```
The string:
        Count me! Count me, you fool!
is 29 characters long
```

And so it is.

Each call to the `string_count()` function doesn't increase the value of `count`; that variable is incremented as the function *returns*. So, the `count` variable is increased based on how many times the `string_count()` function is called. That number itself is based on the length of the string, which is unraveled by `*s++`.

It may not make a whole heck of a lot of sense, but it works. I believe that you will find that the more you study it, the more it makes sense.

In your travels, if you encounter any code that uses recursion, flag it for long-term storage. Often, programmers clever enough to use recursion can teach you a thing or two with their code. For those few times that recursion works well, it's worth keeping the code just to learn something.

Using recursion to dig through directories

The first time I ever saw recursion used and understood what the heck was going on was while reading files from disk. That's because there really is no other elegant way for a program to dig through directories than to use recursion.

As an example, consider the DODIR.C source code, from an earlier section in this chapter. That code displays the contents of a directory, listing all the files that are present.

When DODIR encounters a directory rather than a file (in the source code's final incarnation), it flags the directory with the text `<DIR>` and then keeps on processing. But, what if the program instead changes to that directory and then begins listing files there? That way, the program could systematically scan all files in a given branch of the directory structure. And, it all happens thanks to recursion.

The first step in adding recursion to the directory-reading routine is to make it a function. The function, named `dir()`, accepts the name of a directory as its option. Here's the updated source code:

```
#include <stdio.h>
#include <stdlib.h>
#include <sys/types.h>
#include <dirent.h>
#include <sys/stat.h>

void dir(char *path);

int main(int argc, char *argv[])
{
    if(argc != 2)
        dir(".");        /* default: current dir. */
```

```
      else
          dir(argv[1]);
      return(0);
}

void dir(char *path)
{
    DIR *dhandle;
    struct dirent *drecord;
    struct stat sbuf;
    int x;

    dhandle = opendir(path);
    if(dhandle == NULL)
    {
        printf("Error opening directory '%s'\n",path);
        exit(1);
    }

    x = chdir(path);
    if( x != 0)
    {
        printf("Error changing to '%s'\n",path);
        exit(1);
    }

    printf("Directory of '%s':\n",path);
    while( (drecord = readdir(dhandle)) != NULL)
    {
        stat(drecord->d_name,&sbuf);
        if(S_ISDIR(sbuf.st_mode))
        {
            printf("%-16s",drecord->d_name);
        }
        else
        {
            printf("%-16s",drecord->d_name);
        }
    }
    putchar('\n');
    closedir(dhandle);
}
```

Start with your DODIR.C source code in your editor. Change it so that it reads as just shown. After making the necessary modifications, save the source code to disk as SCANDIR.C. Note that the program doesn't do recursion just yet.

Compile. Run.

The program's output displays the contents of the current directory. If you specify a path to another directory, the program lists that directory's contents as well.

Eliminating the . and .. entries

The SCANDIR.C program is almost ready for you to add recursion, which allows the program to display files in any subdirectories that are found. Before you can do that, however, you need to deal with the two special directories . and ...

Each directory has two special shortcut directory entries:

. is a shortcut specifying the current directory.

.. is a shortcut specifying the parent directory.

Together, these two entries help keep the directory database linked to other directory databases in the disk hierarchy system. However, if you use recursion on them, the program ends up in an endless loop; it starts in the current directory, finds the . entry and changes to that (again, the current directory), and then repeats those steps infinitely.

To fix the problem, you must direct the program to ignore the . and .. entries. You can do that by modifying the if statements at and after Line 43 in the code:

```
if(S_ISDIR(sbuf.st_mode))
{
    if( strcmp(drecord->d_name,".") == 0 ||
        strcmp(drecord->d_name,"..") == 0 )
            continue;
    printf("%-16s",drecord->d_name);
}
```

The inserted if statement compares the filename that's found, drecord->d_name, with either the . or .. entries. If strcmp() equals 0 in either case, the continue command is executed and the while loop spins again.

Also, be sure to add this line at the top of your source code:

```
#include <string.h>
```

Make these two changes to the SCANDIR.C source code. Compile and run.

The program's output should be the same, though the . and .. directory entries no longer appear.

With the two shortcut directory entries eliminated from the output, you're now ready to add recursion to the SCANDIR.C source code. I cover this topic in the next section.

Finally, adding recursion

Giving the SCANDIR.C source code the ability to dig through subdirectories as they're found is only one line away in your source code. If you have been following along with the modifications so far, you have only one line to change in the SCANDIR.C source code to enable recursion and have the program scan subdirectories.

Change Line 49 to read:

```
dir(drecord->d_name);
```

This line replaces the old `printf()` statement that displayed the sub-directory's name. Now, rather than that name, the directory's contents are displayed.

Next, insert this line just above the new Line 49:

```
putchar('\n');
```

Finally, after returning from an episode in recursion, the `dir()` function must pop back up to the previous directory. That's done with this command placed just before the final `closedir(dhandle)` statement in the `dir()` function:

```
chdir("..");
```

All told, here's the final source code:

```
#include <stdio.h>
#include <stdlib.h>
#include <sys/types.h>
#include <dirent.h>
#include <sys/stat.h>
#include <string.h>

void dir(char *path);

int main(int argc, char *argv[])
{
    if(argc != 2)
        dir(".");     /* default: current dir. */
```

```
        else
            dir(argv[1]);
        return(0);
    }

void dir(char *path)
{
    DIR *dhandle;
    struct dirent *drecord;
    struct stat sbuf;
    int x;

    dhandle = opendir(path);
    if(dhandle == NULL)
    {
        printf("Error opening directory '%s'\n",path);
        exit(1);
    }

    x = chdir(path);
    if( x != 0)
    {
        printf("Error changing to '%s'\n",path);
        exit(1);
    }

    printf("Directory of '%s':\n",path);
    while( (drecord = readdir(dhandle)) != NULL)
    {
        stat(drecord->d_name,&sbuf);
        if(S_ISDIR(sbuf.st_mode))
        {
            if( strcmp(drecord->d_name,".") == 0 ||
                strcmp(drecord->d_name,"..") == 0 )
                    continue;
            putchar('\n');
            dir(drecord->d_name);
        }
        else
        {
            printf("%-16s",drecord->d_name);
        }
    }
    putchar('\n');
    chdir("..");
    closedir(dhandle);
}
```

Modify your SCANDIR.C source code to match what's shown here. Be careful! Save it to disk.

Compile. Fix any errors. Run.

Try running the program on a higher directory. For example, type the path to your home directory. Or, specify the `prog` directory beneath which all your C programs are stored.

The SCANDIR program dutifully scans each folder for files, listing them and then digging down and displaying the contents of the files in any subfolders — and even sub-subfolders beneath them.

Note that there's a point beyond which SCANDIR doesn't function. Because it has to keep opening new directory handles, eventually system resources may dry up, and you get an error. Or, perhaps SCANDIR will encounter problems as it attempts to open a directory to which it doesn't have full privileges. You have ways to fix this, ways that I happily let you discover on your own!

Chapter 7: Under New File Management

In This Chapter

- ✔ Giving a file a new name
- ✔ Using the `errno` variable
- ✔ Killing off a file
- ✔ Making a copy or duplicate of a file
- ✔ Relocating a file to a new directory

*B*ehold the file! Oops! Now it's gone!

As master of your computer, you have life-and-death power over the peon files that dwell on its spinning disks. You can breathe life into them, duplicate them, destroy them, rename them, and modify them at will.

Most of the commands you use to lord over your files belong to the operating system. You can issue the commands at the command prompt (hence, its catchy name) via the graphical part of your operating system or, in the C language, via the handy commands disclosed in this chapter.

Renaming a File

Renaming a file is a snap in C. The `rename()` function makes it happen:

```
x = rename(current,new)
```

Current is a string representing the file's current name. *New* is the new name to be given to the file.

The `rename()` function returns 0 when it happily completes its task. Otherwise, it returns -1 with the official error code stored in the `errno` variable. Refer to your compiler's documentation for the details on `errno`.

Happily, `rename()` is prototyped in the STDIO.H header file.

Grant that file a new name!

The following code renames the file YOURNAME.TXT to ZOOMBA.TXT. The code assumes that the file YOURNAME.TXT already exists (you create it in Exercise 5.3.1, in Book V, Chapter 3):

```c
#include <stdio.h>

int main()
{
    int x;

    x = rename("yourname.txt","zoomba.txt");
    if( x != 0 )
    {
        puts("Some kind of error renaming the file!");
        return(1);
    }
    puts("File renamed!");
    return(0);
}
```

Carefully type this source code into your editor. Save it to disk as NEWNAME.C. Compile. Be sure that you have a file named YOURNAME. TXT on disk before you run it, and then run it:

```
File renamed!
```

Use the `dir` or `ls` command to display the local directory and confirm that the file ZOOMBA.TXT exists. Congratulations!

Checking for errors when renaming (errno)

If you have been reading this book for the past few chapters, you have noticed that I refer to the `errno` variable when certain disk operations return -1 as a result. This source code demonstrates briefly how to use `errno` in an update to the NEWNAME.C program:

```c
#include <stdio.h>
#include <errno.h>

int main()
{
    int x;

    x = rename("yourname.txt","zoomba.txt");
    if( x != 0 )
    {
        printf("ERROR: ");
```

```
        switch (errno) {
            case 1:
                printf("Operation not permitted");
                break;
            case 2:
                printf("No such file");
                break;
            case 13:
                printf("Permission denied");
                break;
            case 30:
                printf("Read-only file");
                break;
            case 63:
                printf("Filename too long");
                break;
            default:
                printf("Other strange error encountered");
                break;
        }
        return(1);
    }
    puts("File renamed!");
    return(0);
}
```

Load the source code for NEWNAME.C into your editor. Update it as shown here.

The ERRNO.H header file defines the `errno` variable, which is set when certain system operations fail. A variety of values can be returned, though I have specified only the few that may result directly from a botched file rename in the preceding source code. (For the full list, see your compiler's documentation.)

Save the changes to disk. Compile. Don't worry about whether the YOURNAME.TXT file exists — just run the sucker! Here's what I saw:

```
ERROR: No such file
```

The truth! The truth!

Adding a similar `switch-case` structure, or even a similar function, to your source code can provide your program's users with more detail on the errors encountered. Or, you could even customize your program so that it responds in a specific, intelligent way when certain types of errors are encountered.

Deleting a File

It's much easier to destroy than it is to create. Witness the `unlink()` function.

Yes, `unlink()`. It could have been named `delete()` or `remove()`, but it's `unlink()`. Here's the format:

```
x = unlink(filename)
```

Filename is the name of the file you want to obliterate. It can be a path to a specific file, a string variable, or the name of a file in the current directory.

If the file is successfully killed off, `unlink()` returns 0; otherwise, -1. The `errno` variable contains the specific error number or reason (refer to the preceding section).

The `unlink()` function requires the UNISTD.H header file in order to properly compile:

```
#include <stdio.h>
#include <unistd.h>

int main()
{
    int x;

    x = unlink("zoomba.txt");
    if( x != 0 )
    {
        puts("Some kind of file error!");
        return(1);
    }
    puts("File killed!");
    return(0);
}
```

Carefully type this source code into your editor. Name it KILLFILE.C.

Note that KILLFILE tries to remove the file named ZOOMBA.TXT, which you create (rename) earlier in this chapter.

Save. Compile. Run:

```
File killed!
```

And, it's gone.

Copying or Duplicating a File

Copying a file is easy: You open one file and then open or create a second file. You read from the first file and write to the second file. When the last byte is read from the first file, you close both files. The code for doing this is surprisingly brief:

```c
#include <stdio.h>

int main()
{
    char original_file[] = "copyfile.c";
    char duplicate_file[] = "copyfile.dup";
    FILE *org,*dup;
    char ch;

    org = fopen(original_file,"r");
    dup = fopen(duplicate_file,"w");
    if( org == NULL || dup == NULL)
    {
        puts("Error copying file");
        return(1);
    }

    while( (ch=fgetc(org)) != EOF )
        fputc(ch,dup);

    fclose(org);
    fclose(dup);
    puts("File copied!");
    return(0);
}
```

Vigilantly copy this source code into your editor. Save it to disk as COPYFILE.C. Yes, it's the same COPYFILE.C that's copied to the file named COPYFILE.DUP. How handy.

Compile. Run:

```
File copied!
```

Now, type the **dir copyfile*** or **ls -l copyfile*** command for Windows or Unix, respectively, to see the original file and the duplicate listed in the directory. Note that both files are the same length. They also have the same contents. Amazing.

Moving a File (The Secret)

Moving a file is the same thing as copying a file, though the original is deleted. Of course, within a single directory, that's the same thing as renaming a file, which is why the Unix command for renaming a file is the mv (move) command.

No, moving a file happens only when you need to move it from one directory to another. First, the original file is duplicated in the target directory, and then that original file is deleted.

The following source code solves the directory issue by querying users and getting them to properly enter the destination directory. It's also a rather fancy program, if I may say so:

Suspiciously type this source code into your editor. Be mindful of the subtle items that change between Windows and Unix; they're noted in the source code's comments. (You can also download this source code from the Unofficial *C For Dummies* Web site, at www.c-for-dummies.com.)

Save the code to disk as MOVEFILE.C. Compile. Fix those typos. Then, recompile and run.

Obey the instructions on the screen.

```c
#include <stdio.h>
#include <ctype.h>
#include <string.h>
#include <stdlib.h>

void error_exit(char *message);

int main(int argc, char *argv[])
{
    char original_file[256];
    char duplicate_file[256];
    char new_name[256];
    FILE *org,*dup;
    char ch;
    int len;

/* gather information */
    puts("MoveFile - a moving file utility");
    printf("Enter the name of the original file: ");
```

```
    scanf("%255s",&original_file);
    if(strlen(original_file) == 0)
        error_exit("Missing filename");

    printf("Move file '%s' to directory: ",original_file);
    scanf("%255s",&duplicate_file);
    if(strlen(duplicate_file) == 0)
        error_exit("Missing destination directory");
        /* fix path, if necc. */
    len = strlen(duplicate_file);
    if(duplicate_file[len-1] != '\\')    /* '/' in unix */
        strcat(duplicate_file,"\\");     /* add trailing \ */

    printf("Give the file a new name? (Y/N): ");
    fflush(stdin);                /* fpurge(stdin) */
    ch = getchar();
    ch = toupper(ch);
    if(ch == 'Y')
    {
        printf("Enter new name: ");
        scanf("%255s",&new_name);
        if(strlen(new_name) == 0)
            error_exit("No new name specified");
        strcat(duplicate_file,new_name);
    }
    else
        strcat(duplicate_file,original_file);

    printf("\nMoving file '%s' to '%s'\n\n",
    original_file,duplicate_file);

/* First, copy the file */
    org = fopen(original_file,"r");
    dup = fopen(duplicate_file,"w");
    if( org == NULL || dup == NULL)
        error_exit("Error opening or creating file");

    while( (ch=fgetc(org)) != EOF )
        fputc(ch,dup);

    fclose(org);
    fclose(dup);

/* Now, delete the original */
    unlink(original_file);
```

```
/* And we're done */
    puts("File moved!");
    return(0);
}

/*
 * Display error message and exit the program
 */

void error_exit(char *message)
{
    printf("ERROR: %s\n",message);
    exit(1);
}
```

Book VI

The Joy of Linked Lists

"Now, when someone rings my doorbell, the current goes to a scanner that digitizes the audio impulses and sends the image to the PC where it's converted to a Pict file. The image is then animated, compressed, and sent via high-speed modem to an automated phone service that sends an e-mail message back to tell me someone was at my door 40 minutes ago."

Contents at a Glance

Chapter 1: Why Linked Lists?

In This Chapter

✔ **Understanding the database**

✔ **Linking structures with pointers**

✔ **Creating the first structure in the list**

✔ **Using the** `first_item`, `current_item`, **and** `new_item` **pointers**

✔ **Capping the linked list with a NULL**

*O*ne thing that strikes terror into the hearts of any computer science student — especially the nonmajors — is the *linked list*. It's nothing to be afraid of. A linked list is simply the dawn of database programming inside C. It's the answer to the question "Why can't I resize an array after my program starts?" Because it's mostly university students who ask that question, you would think that they would be delighted with linked lists. Sadly, it's just not so.

This chapter provides an introduction to the concept of the linked list. I think that linked lists are rather fun. I hope that you will learn to enjoy them as well, and you can, if you stick with this chapter and read the exciting, thrilling installments that follow.

Source code and programs that you create for this part of the book should be saved in the LLIST folder or directory on your computer's hard disk.

A Review of Database Programming in C

If you have read this book from cover to cover, you probably recall that the best way to do a database in C — to organize your Collection o' Stuff — is to use structures.

Structures are the multivariables. They let you cluster a bunch of information together and slap a single variable name on the thing. In Book III, Chapter 4, you may have worked with a structure like this:

```
struct oz {
    char actor[18];
    int age;
    char roll[16];
    };
```

The oz structure stores information used to track the folks who starred in the 1939 movie *The Wizard of Oz*. Like a record in a database, the oz structure has space to store the actor's name, the actor's age at the time, and the role that person played, as just shown.

The only limit to the number of items you can store in a structure is your computer's memory. You can have a structure with only one item, or you can have a structure with dozens of elements. You can even have structures within structures, as in

```
struct person {
    char first[64];
    char last[64];
    char middle[64];
};

struct music {
    struct person artist;
    char title[64];
    char album[64];
    int year;
    time_t length;
};
```

In this example, the music structure is defined as containing a person structure variable named artist.

I have seen some operating system structures that have structures within structures within structures — pretty scary stuff! But the point is that the compiler lets you do it, and it helps keep things organized — á la the database.

One limitation placed on a database of structures, however, is their total number. Most programmers simply create an array of structures, guessing the maximum number they need:

```
struct music song[300];
```

Creating an array of 300 music structures — the song[] array — is fine if you have exactly 300 songs to catalog. If you have fewer songs, you're wasting memory. And, if you have more than that number, you need to reedit the source code and recompile the program because *C does not let you dynamically reallocate arrays*.

You may recall from Book IV, Chapter 8 that you can create new arrays from thin electrons by using the malloc() function and then using pointers to reference the array's contents. But you still need something to keep track of all those structures, either an array of structure pointers or some other monstrosity.

With an array of pointers, you still have the same basic problem: *C does not let you dynamically reallocate arrays.* So the solution must be some other monstrosity. And that other monstrosity is the *linked list.*

How Linked Lists Work

Linked lists are quite an easy concept to grasp; it's their implementation that boggles the minds of most humans. Simply speaking, a *linked list* is simply a bunch of structures. Each structure contains a pointer. That pointer contains the memory address of the next structure in the list.

In a way, linked lists work like that old treasure map game you may have played as a kid. The first map or note gave instructions on how to find the next map. The second map had instructions for finding the third map. And so on it goes, with each map giving instructions for finding the location of the next map, until the last map — and the treasure — is finally located.

In C programming, the linked list works just like the treasure map system of finding goodies. The list is composed of structures. One element of each structure is a pointer that stores (or divulges) the memory location for the next structure in the list:

✦ The pointer inside each structure is the *link.*

✦ The group of all the structures linked together is the *list.*

✦ The list is linked by all the pointers.

To help imagine how this works, consider Figure 1-1. I'm using as an example a database of actors who have played James Bond. Each box in the figure represents a complete structure — a record — describing the actor who's listed. Along with the actor's name, films, dates, and other tidbits is one special element in the structure. That element is a pointer variable showing where you can find the next structure in the list. In Figure 1-1, the pointer is shown as a memory addresses value.

In Figure 1-1, the first structure in the database contains information about Sean Connery, and among its elements is a pointer to the next structure in the list, found at memory location 2C0 (hex), according to the figure.

Each structure in the list links to the next, with the final structure containing a NULL pointer, which flags the end of the list (the treasure!).

Though each structure stores the address of the next structure, knowing the address isn't necessary; you merely use the pointer variable to reference the structure and use those fun -> doodads to reference the structure's data. (Refer to Book IV, Chapter 8 if you don't recognize the -> doodad.)

Book VI Chapter 1

Why Linked Lists?

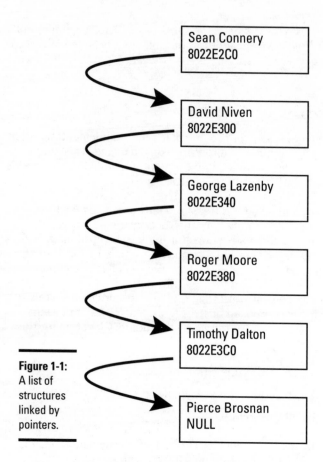

Figure 1-1:
A list of
structures
linked by
pointers.

Building the first structure

Now that I'm thinking about James Bond, why not create the start of a linked list database that uses him as an example? All linked lists must have a first entry, and then entries in the middle, and then a final last entry. This first part of the sample program concentrates on making that important first entry.

Why is the first entry important? Because the first entry is where you start the linked list. You can't "follow the map" unless you have that one, solid reference to the first item in the list:

```
#include <stdio.h>
#include <stdlib.h>
#include <string.h>

int main()
{
```

```
    struct jb {
        char actor[25];
        struct jb *next;
    };
    struct jb *bond;

/* Create the first structure in the list */
    bond = (struct jb *)malloc(sizeof(struct jb));

/* Fill the structure */
    strcpy(bond->actor,"Sean Connery");
    bond->next = NULL;    /* End of list */

/* Display the results */
    printf("The first structure has been created:\n");
    printf("\tbond->actor = %s\n",bond->actor);
    printf("\tnext structure address = %p\n",bond->next);

    return(0);
}
```

Cautiously type this source code into your text editor. Yes, you add to it later, so it's best to write it all down now while it's nice and small. Save the code to disk as BOND.C.

Compile. Run.

```
The first structure has been created:
        bond->actor = Sean Connery
next structure address = 00000000
```

The only truly new thing in the code is the structure pointer inside the structure. That may confuse you, but remember that a pointer can be a legitimate member of a structure, just as any other type of variable in C can.

A pointer is a variable that holds a memory address. The pointer in the following line references a jb structure at some unknown location in memory:

```
struct jb *next;
```

It helps to think of this thing as a *link* and not really as a "pointer structure of the same type." For example:

```
struct jb {
    char actor[25];
    link_to *next_structure;
};
```

The jb structure contains a text string named actor. Then it contains a link to the next structure in the list. But — shhh! — the link is really just a pointer. And the pointer variable is of the same type as the structure. (You could use typedef to create the link_to variable type — but I wouldn't recommend it at this "learning" stage.)

Anyway, here's a review of what has happened in the program so far:

✦ To build the linked list, you need a structure, which is declared starting at Line 7.

✦ To link the lists, the structure must contain a pointer variable to the same type of structure. This happens in Line 9.

✦ To build the first structure, you use malloc() to dish up a chunk of memory and then refer to the structure by using pointers. (I cover this topic in Book IV, Chapter 8.)

✦ The structure is filled in by using strcpy() in Line 17.

✦ Line 18 creates the link to the next structure, but because this is the only (and therefore last) structure in the list, NULL is used.

✦ The rest of the code displays information about the structure.

✦ Note that knowing the specific address isn't necessary; I merely display it in Line 23 to keep the output similar to what you see in Figure 1-1, earlier in this chapter.

Don't worry about this stuff not making complete sense just yet. The idea of the linked list is to have different items to link to. That begins in the next section.

Adding another structure and linking to it

The BOND.C source code in the preceding section is good for setting up the linked list, but it lacks foresight. For example, if you want to create pointers to all the items in the list, it seems like you would need some sort of — dare I say it? — *array* to hold all those pointers! But aren't linked lists about avoiding the limitations of arrays?

The solution is to create reusable pointers. To avoid forcing you to ruminate, here are the traditional three:

```
*first_item;
*current_item;
*new_item;
```

The first_item variable is used to reference the first item in the list. It doesn't change; it always refers to the first item in the list.

The `current_item` variable always points to the current item in the list, whichever item that may be.

The `new_item` variable is used whenever a new item is created.

You could name the variables `first`, `current` and `new`, but `new` is a reserved word in C++, so although it would compile just fine in a regular C program, it would make that code incompatible with a C++ compiler, which is a bad idea.

The following source code begins to show how these three pointer variables can be used by adding a second structure to the list:

```
#include <stdio.h>
#include <stdlib.h>
#include <string.h>

int main()
{
    struct jb {
        char actor[25];
        struct jb *next;
    };
    struct jb *first_item;
    struct jb *current_item;
    struct jb *new_item;

/* Create the first structure in the list */
    first_item = (struct jb *)malloc(sizeof(struct jb));

/* Fill the first structure */
    strcpy(first_item->actor,"Sean Connery");
    new_item = (struct jb *)malloc(sizeof(struct jb));
    first_item->next = new_item;

/* Fill the second structure */
    current_item = new_item;
    strcpy(current_item->actor,"David Niven");
    current_item->next = NULL;        /* end of the list */

/* Display the results */
    printf("The first structure:\n");
    printf("\tfirst_item->actor = %s\n",first_item->actor);
    printf("\tnext structure address = %p\n",
    first_item->next);

    printf("The second structure:\n");
    printf("\tcurrent_item->actor = %s\n",
    current_item->actor);
```

```
        printf("\tnext structure address = %p\n",
    current_item->next);

        return(0);
}
```

Load the BOND.C source code into your editor. Make these modifications and additions. Save it back to disk. Recompile. Run it again:

```
The first structure:
        first_item->actor = Sean Connery
        next structure address = 003D37F8
The second structure:
        current-item->actor = David Niven
        next structure address = 00000000
```

The `first_item` pointer always points to the first item in the list. After that, the `new_item` and `current_item` pointers are juggled to create and reference additional items in the list.

At this stage, with only two items in the list, it's difficult to see the benefits. In the next section, though, you add the rest of the elements and use a loop, where the two variables — `new_item` and `current_item` — are used over and over.

Adding the rest of the structures

The best way to fill a structure, such as the James Bond linked list, is by using a loop. The first step there is to cheat and create an array of the actors' names so that you don't have to manually code all that stuff. After that's done, you can use a loop to not only create the elements of the linked list but also fill them.

No, this isn't cheating. In fact, in "real life," you would probably type the information manually. So at least this trick saves you from that step:

```
#include <stdio.h>
#include <stdlib.h>
#include <string.h>

#define RECORDS 6

int main()
{
    struct jb {
        char actor[25];
        struct jb *next;
```

```
        };

        char *bonds[RECORDS] = {
            "Sean Connery",
            "David Niven",
            "George Lazenby",
            "Roger Moore",
            "Timothy Dalton",
            "Pierce Brosnan"
        };

        struct jb *first_item;
        struct jb *current_item;
        struct jb *new_item;
        int index = 0;

/* Create the first structure in the list */
        first_item = (struct jb *)malloc(sizeof(struct jb));
        current_item = first_item;

/* Fill the structures */
        while(index < RECORDS)
        {
            strcpy(current_item->actor,bonds[index]);
            new_item = (struct jb *)malloc(sizeof(struct jb));
            current_item->next = new_item;

            current_item = new_item;
            index++;
        }

/* Display the results */
        /* to come ... */

        return(0);
}
```

Update your BOND.C source code as shown. Save it to disk. Compile. Run.
You see no output. Yet.

After setting up the first_item in the list, a while loop churns through the
rest of the structures. Note how it works:

```
strcpy(current_item->actor,bonds[index]);
new_item = (struct jb *)malloc(sizeof(struct jb));
current_item->next = new_item;
```

First, the string from the *bonds* array is stored in the new structure. After that, a chunk of memory for a new structure is created and its address saved in the `new_item` variable. Then, that address is saved in the structure's `next` variable.

In the preceding chunk, `current_item` refers to the current structure. It contains the address of the current structure.

The `new_item` variable contains the address for the next structure in the list. That comes into play in the next chunk of statements inside the `while` loop:

```
current_item = new_item;
index--;
```

To advance through the list, the `current_item` variable is assigned to the value of `new_item`. That way, the program advances to the next structure in the linked list. The loop is repeated.

Only one thing is missing from the list: the NULL pointer marking the last item. The program doesn't have that now, mostly because I want to keep the `while` loop simple. In the next section, I address that minor problem.

Marking the end with a NULL

The BOND.C program cheats a bit by defining the RECORDS constant. It's an admitted cheat so that you don't have to repeatedly type all those names every time you run the program. But that cheat can also be a crutch because you know the maximum number of items in the linked list.

Be wary of using `typedef`

When it comes to structures, university professors (and the graduate students who teach their classes) love to show off the `typedef` keyword, and, O, what a great shortcut it makes. Please, O, please, don't fall into that trap.

At this stage, it's important that you find out how a linked list works: how to create one and how to use one and to understand why things are done. If you use `typedef` to create shortcut words for defining structures at this point, your brain is dealing with not *one* strange thing, but, rather, *two* strange things. That's too much strangeness for most folks.

My advice is this: If you want to make shortcuts using `typedef`, wait until you have the linked list concept down cold. Then go back and use `typedef` to shorten your code and make things all cute and whatever. For understanding linked lists, `typedef` unnecessarily gets in the way.

In the real world (wherever that is), you may never know how many items are in your linked list. You have to keep the thing flexible, so declaring a constant like RECORDS doesn't work. Instead, you put a cap on the end of the list in the form of a NULL pointer. That way, any loop can find the end of the list by simply comparing the next element with NULL.

Here's an update to the code:

```
#include <stdio.h>
#include <stdlib.h>
#include <string.h>

#define RECORDS 6

int main()
{
    struct jb {
        char actor[25];
        struct jb *next;
    };

    char *bonds[RECORDS] = {
        "Sean Connery",
        "David Niven",
        "George Lazenby",
        "Roger Moore",
        "Timothy Dalton",
        "Pierce Brosnan"
    };

    struct jb *first_item;
    struct jb *current_item;
    struct jb *new_item;
    int index = 0;

/* Create the first structure in the list */
    first_item = (struct jb *)malloc(sizeof(struct jb));
    current_item = first_item;

/* Fill the structures */
    while(1)
    {
        strcpy(current_item->actor,bonds[index]);

        index++;
        if(index < RECORDS)
        {
            new_item = (struct jb *)malloc(sizeof(struct
jb));
```

```
            current_item->next = new_item;
            current_item = new_item;
        }
        else
        {
            current_item->next = NULL;
            break;
        }
    }

/* Display the results */

    current_item = first_item;          /* start over */
    index = 1;
    while(current_item)
    {
        printf("Structure %d: ",index++);
        printf("%s\n",current_item->actor);
        current_item = current_item->next;
    }
    return(0);
}
```

Carefully update your BOND.C source code to match what's shown here. Save the changes to disk when you're done. Compile. Run:

```
Structure 1: Sean Connery
Structure 2: David Niven
Structure 3: George Lazenby
Structure 4: Roger Moore
Structure 5: Timothy Dalton
Structure 6: Pierce Brosnan
```

The main while loop has been updated to detect when the last item was entered. Yes, it's a cheat: The RECORDS constant is used. But the idea is solid: When the last record is encountered, a new_item obviously doesn't need to be created. So, the current_item->next value is simply set to NULL, tagging the end of the linked list.

To display the results, a simple while loop is used with current_item as its condition. The value of current_item is always some memory address — except for the last structure in the linked list. In that case, the value is NULL, stopping the while loop. (The index variable is used only for display, not to count the loop.)

Chapter 2: Dawn of the Database

In This Chapter

✔ Creating a database using linked lists

✔ Adding items to the database

✔ Listing items in the database

✔ Removing a record from a linked list

✔ Modifying a record

*L*inked lists are really all about databases. The structure itself is like a record in a database, and the variables in the structure are fields. I can't see how it could get any more obnoxiously obvious. And, if that's all true, the linked list is really just another term for a database — an endless database that can grow as you need it to without the limitations of an array in C.

This chapter opens up the view on linked lists as a database of sorts. The programs are more flexible than the example in Book VI, Chapter 1 because all the information is typed at the keyboard. That's a bit more realistic, and it illustrates how flexible linked lists can be in a more real-world perspective.

The Ubiquitous Bank Account Program

It seems like the last few times that I have gotten questions from readers about linked lists, the questions had to do with banking programs. You know the type: They lose track of you and your money — unless you owe them money, in which case they're on you like a hyperactive terrier on a mailman in shorts. I could go into my banking program conspiracy theory, but I dread the e-mail I would get for that.

Because of its database-like nature, I refer to the structures in a linked list as records. The nerdy thing to do is to refer to the structures as *nodes,* which I find an annoying and confusing term. For example, node is also used to refer to network thingamabobs. Although I don't use *node* in this book, be aware that other books and C language resources use the term — often to the point of being annoying.

The BANK program

The following code begins your journey into the world of high finance. It's the foundation of what will eventually be a rather large program that manages a linked list. But, like everything else in this book, the program starts small and builds:

```c
#include <stdio.h>
#include <stdlib.h>
#include <string.h>
#include <ctype.h>

void clearInput(void);
void addNewAccount(void);

struct account {
    int number;
    char lastname[15];
    char firstname[15];
    float balance;
    struct account *next;
    };
struct account *firsta,*currenta,*newa;
int anum = 0;

int main()
{
    char ch;
    firsta = NULL;

    do
    {
    clearInput();
        puts("\nA - Add a new account");
        puts("Q - Quit this program\n");
        printf("\tYour choice:");
        ch = getchar();
    ch = toupper(ch);
        switch(ch)
        {
            case 'A':
                puts("Add new account\n");
    clearInput();
                addNewAccount();
                break;
            case 'Q':
                puts("Quit\n");
            default:
                break;
        }
```

```
    }
    while(ch != 'Q');

    return(0);
}

/*
 * This function clears any text from the input stream
 */

void clearInput(void)
{
    fflush(stdin);                    /* fpurge(stdin) */
}

void addNewAccount(void)
{
    newa = (struct account *)malloc(sizeof(struct account));

/*
 * Check to see if this is the first record
 * If so, then initialize all the pointers to this
 * first structure in the database
 */

    if(firsta==NULL)
        firsta = currenta = newa;

/*
 * Otherwise, you must find the end of the structure list
 * (easily spotted by the NULL pointer) and add on the
 * new structure you just allocated memory for
 */

    else
    {
        currenta = firsta;        /* make first record current */
                                  /* loop through all records: */

        while(currenta->next != NULL)
            currenta = currenta->next;
                /* the last record is found */
        currenta->next = newa;    /* save the address of new */
        currenta = newa;          /* make current record new */
    }

/* Now, you just fill in the new structure */

    anum++;
    printf("%27s: %5i\n","Account number",anum);
    currenta->number = anum;
```

```
    printf("%27s: ","Enter customer's last name");
    gets(currenta->lastname);

    printf("%27s: ","Enter customer's first name");
    gets(currenta->firstname);

    printf("%27s: $","Enter account balance");
    scanf("%f",&currenta->balance);
/*
 * Finally, cap the new record with a NULL pointer
 * so that you know it's the last record:
 */

    currenta->next = NULL;
}
```

Quickly type this code into your editor. Be careful to replace `fflush` with `fpurge` in Line 56 if you're using Unix. Double-check! Save it to disk as BANK.C.

Compile. Fix those errors! Recompile.

Run:

```
A - Add a new account
Q - Quit this program

        Your choice:
```

You have only two options at this stage. Press **A** to add a record:

```
Add new account

            Account number:     1
    Enter customer's last name:
```

Fill in the items as you're prompted: last name, first name, and an outrageous account balance. After that, you return to the main menu.

The program lacks any method for reviewing the records that are created; that function is added later. Before that, a review of what this program does is in order.

The promised review that's in order

The BANK program is set up to work properly with a linked list that has no elements in it or any unknown number of elements. All the action happens in the `addNewAccount()` function.

First, storage is allocated for a new structure. After all, that's the basic task of the addNewAccount() function, so it's done right away:

```
newa = (struct account *)malloc(sizeof(struct account));
```

The only real question to answer is "Is this the first record or, if not, where's the end of the list so that this record can be tacked on?"

The next group of statements determines whether there's a first record:

```
if(firsta==NULL)
    firsta = currenta = newa;
```

If there's no first record, the newa record created becomes the first record (and the current record).

When there's a first record, the next step is obviously to find the *last* record in the list so that the next record can be appended. Before that, the first record is made current. After all, you have to start somewhere:

```
currenta = firsta;      /* make first record current */
```

After you initialize the currenta pointer to the first structure in the linked list, you can use a simple while loop to quickly flip through all the records until the last one is found. The last record has NULL as the value of its next element:

```
while(currenta->next != NULL)
    currenta = currenta->next;
```

The condition that while examines is to see whether the next element of the current record is NULL. If not, the current record becomes the next record: currenta->next is the address of the next structure in the list. So, after the line currenta = currenta->next, the value of currenta is equal to the next record.

When the last record is found, the values of the necessary pointer variables are

✦ firsta: Always points to the first record in the list

✦ currenta: Points to the last record in the list

✦ currenta->next: NULL; marks the end of the list

✦ newa: Contains the address of the newly created structure in memory

Because a new record is being appended, `currenta->next` needs to point to it rather than to NULL. So:

```
currenta->next = newa;   /* save the address of new */
```

And then, the new record becomes the current record:

```
currenta = newa;         /* make current record new */
```

Figure 2-1 attempts to illustrate how the preceding statement works.

After the new record is linked in, the structure is filled with data using various prompts and text-reading functions.

Finally, the new addition is capped with a NULL pointer, indicating the end of the list:

```
currenta->next = NULL;
```

After that, control returns to the main part of the program, the menu.

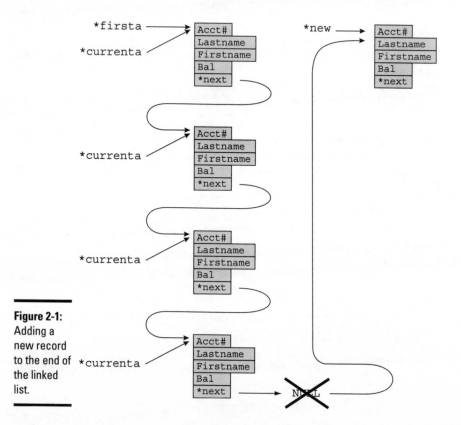

Figure 2-1:
Adding a
new record
to the end of
the linked
list.

Exercise 6.2.1

Add to the program a function named `listAll()`. The function's job is to list all records in the database. Be sure to add a link to `listAll()` from the `main()` function's menu; have it be menu command **L** to *l*ist all records in the database.

Removing Records from a Linked List

Back in the old days, databases were kept on paper, such as a drawer full of 3 x 5 cards. Adding a new record simply meant pulling up a new 3 x 5 card and filling it in. Sorting the records meant that you needed a good, large tabletop — and that took time. One task that didn't take time was the easy way in which records were deleted: The 3 x 5 card was simply removed from the box and tossed away — simple.

Now suppose that your database isn't a stack of 3 x 5 cards, but, rather, an array of structures in memory. You need to remove `array[7]`.

The first thing you would do, of course, is to zero out all the data in the structure at `array[7]`. But then you would have an empty structure. So, the next thing you would do is rebuild the array, copying element `array[8]` down to `array[7]`, `array[9]` down to `array[8]`, and so on until you hit the end of the list.

What a pain!

What about removing records in a linked list? How painful is that? Well, it turns out that removing a record from a linked list is about the easiest thing you can do.

Offing deadbeat records

Unlike an array, a linked list stores its records in memory, with each structure in the list keeping track of where the next structures lives. In reality, most of the time the structures are created sequentially in memory. But they don't have to be; the structures could exist anywhere in memory. Thanks to the pointers, it isn't a problem for you to reckon with.

Figure 2-2 illustrates how strangely records in the BANK.C program may be stored in memory. Thanks to pointers linking everything up, however, the list is presented sequentially inside the program.

Deleting a structure from the list is then as easy as removing its pointer; the pointer from the previous record then simply references the next structure in the list. Figure 2-3 illustrates how it might look.

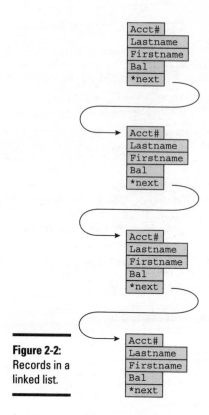

Figure 2-2:
Records in a
linked list.

In Figure 2-3, the pointer in the first structure now references the third structure in the list; the second structure is skipped over. In effect, it's deleted.

Sadly, the record still exists in memory. So, before you remove the final reference (pointer) to that memory chunk, you should use the free() function to free up, or release, that memory for something else. That would finally, and fatally, remove the record from memory and clean up the list.

Adding the deleteAccount() *function*

To delete a structure from the BANK.C program, you need to write a deleteAccount() function. That function needs to do five things:

1. Ask the user which record to remove from the list. Call that record the "current" record.

2. Locate the current record's memory address, found in the previous record's *next pointer.

3. Locate and save the next record's address.

4. In the previous record, replace the current record's address with the next record's address.

5. Free the memory used by the current, now deleted, record.

Here's the `deleteAccount()` function I concocted to get the job done:

```
void deleteAccount(void)
{
    int record;
    struct account *previousa;

    if(firsta==NULL)
    {
        puts("There are no records to delete!");
        return;
    }

    listAll();          /* show all records first */
    printf("Enter account number to delete: ");
    scanf("%d",&record);

    currenta = firsta;
    while(currenta != NULL)
    {
        if(currenta->number == record)
        {
            if(currenta == firsta)    /* special condition */
                firsta=currenta->next;
            else
                previousa->next = currenta->next;
            free(currenta);
            printf("Account %d deleted!\n",record);
            return;
        }
        else
        {
            previousa = currenta;
            currenta = currenta->next;
        }
    }
    printf("Account %d was not found!\n",record);
    puts("Nothing deleted.");
}
```

Update your BANK.C source code to add the function just shown. Remember to update the prototype and add the menu text and item D for "Delete account." A description of what happened in this example follows shortly.

Save the sucker back to disk. Compile. Run.

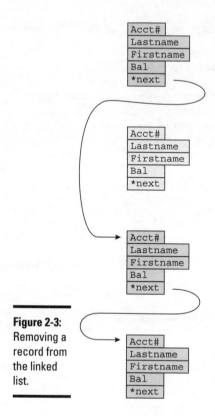

Figure 2-3:
Removing a
record from
the linked
list.

You need to add a few records first. Then press D to delete an account:

```
Delete account

Acct# Last          First              Balance
    1: Washington    George        $     1.00
    2. Lincoln       Abraham       $     5.00
    3. Hamilton      Alexander     $    10.00
    4. Jackson       Andrew        $    20.00
    5. Grant         Ulysses       $    50.00
Enter account number to delete:
```

Choose a number to delete — 3, for example: Type **3** and press Enter:

```
Account 3 deleted.
```

You return to the main menu after deleting an item. You can then use the L
command to list the records and see how things have changed.

Be sure to delete the first and last records, to be sure that those functions work as well!

How the `deleteAccount()` *function works*

From the preceding section, the `deleteAccount()` function is used to remove a record from the list. The record is referenced by the structure's `number` variable, which is equal to the bank's account number. You could also delete structures by naming names or listing account balances, but integers are much easier to search for.

First, the function needs a way to reference the previous structure in the linked list. To do that, a `previousa` pointer variable is declared:

```
struct account *previousa;
```

As needed, that variable holds the value of the previous record in the linked list. Combined with the `currenta` pointer for the current record, both variables are used to remove a record.

Next, the function tests to see whether the list is empty:

```
if(firsta==NULL)
{
    puts("There are no records to delete!");
    return;
}
```

After all, if the list is empty — which means that the pointer `firsta` is still initialized to NULL — there's no point in trying to delete anything.

Next, the function displays the full list of accounts by using the `listAll()` function. Then the user is prompted for an account to delete:

```
listAll();          /* show all records first */
printf("Enter account number to delete: ");
scanf("%d",&record);
```

After determining which record to delete, the program merely needs to cull through the database, looking for a match. First, the `currenta` variable is initialized to the `firsta` variable, pointing to the start of the list:

```
currenta = firsta;
```

Then, a `while` loop is used to scan through the list, repeating until the NULL at the end of the list is found:

```
while(currenta != NULL)
```

Inside the loop. an `if` statement tests to see whether the current record's account number matches what was entered. If so, the record is deleted. If not, the next record is viewed.

A special case is made for the first record. That's because the first record has no previous record:

```
if(currenta == firsta)     /* special condition */
    firsta=currenta->next;
```

When the first record needs to be deleted, the program merely resets the `firsta` variable to point to the next record in the list. Note that the `currenta` variable continues to point at the deleted record.

If the record to be deleted isn't the first, the `previousa` pointer is used:

```
previousa->next = currenta->next;
```

The pointer from the previous record leaps over the current record and is reset to reference the next record. Note again that the `currenta` variable continues to point at the deleted record.

After deleting either the first record or any subsequent record, the next bit of code does three things:

```
free(currenta);
printf("Account $d deleted\n",record);
return;
```

First, the old record's memory is freed by the `free()` function. Remember that the `currenta` pointer still contains the memory address of the deleted record.

Second, a confirmation message is printed.

Finally, the function returns to the caller, the main menu.

When nothing is deleted, the `else` part of the `if-else` structure moves the pointers merrily down the linked list:

```
else
{
    previousa = currenta;
    currenta = currenta->next;
}
```

The previousa pointer is updated or set equal to the currenta, or current, record. Then, the currenta pointer references the next record in the list. These two pointers essentially inch up through the list; previousa references the previous record and currenta references the current record. Remember that this happens every time the proper account number to delete hasn't been found.

Finally, if the while loop scans the entire list and doesn't find a matching account number to delete, you can safely assume that a bogus account number was entered. The final statements of the function deal with that situation:

```
printf("Account %d was not found!\n",record);
puts("Nothing deleted.");
```

Exercise 6.2.2

Add another function to the BANK.C program. Base the function on how the deleteAccount() function works, but call this function modifyAccount(). Have it ask the user for an account number to modify or change. Then have the function prompt the user for new values and update the specific record. Don't' forget to add this function to the main menu as "M - Modify account."

Chapter 3: Storing a Linked List on Disk

In This Chapter

✔ Using `fwrite()` to put a linked list to disk

✔ Reading in linked list records

✔ Completing the BANK.C source code

*W*hen I originally wrote up a series of online linked list lessons, I thought that I had covered it all. I mean, after an example such as the BANK.C program in the preceding chapter, how much more can you do with a linked list?

Well, it turns out that there's quite a bit more. The question I was asked most often from my students was "How do I save a linked list to disk?" Honestly, I didn't think that the question was really worthy of an answer. But the students persisted, and I must admit that they're correct: The BANK.C program from Book 6, Chapter 2 isn't really worth anything when you have to continually type information into the sucker by hand.

The solution to the problem, and what my students yearned to know about, is to save the linked list to disk. This may sound like something easy to do — as I thought it was — but apparently it needs a bit more hand-holding and tender care, which is what this chapter offers.

From Memory to Disk and Back Again

Saving and loading all your database information to and from disk is a real time-saver and makes sense. It's also far more safe than manually typing information and praying that you never experience a power outage.

Honestly, saving a linked list to disk works just like saving structures to disk. I cover this topic in Book V, Chapter 4. The action works exactly the same for a linked list, as this section demonstrates.

Note that this chapter uses the BANK.C program, introduced in Book VI, Chapter 2. For a complete and final listing of BANK.C (including the file-saving and -loading functions), read the end of this chapter.

Saving your linked list to disk

Saving a linked list to disk works just like saving an array of structures or, really, any individual structure. The key is to use the `fwrite()` function to write the structure-size chunk of information to disk. Coding it isn't really much work — especially if you have run through the examples and lessons in Book VI, Chapter 2.

For the BANK.C database, I make saving an automatic operation, taking place whenever the program quits. This action is easier to implement than some scheme to save the information under a specific filename or routines that save only specific records.

Load the BANK.C source code into your editor.

At the start of the `main()` function, add these two variable declarations:

```
FILE *datafile;
char *filename = "bank.dat";
```

The `datafile` variable is used to open and reference the file, which is named in the `filename` variable.

At the end of the `main()` function, between the lines `while(ch != 0)` and `return(0)`, add this chunk of code:

```
/*
 * Save the records to disk
 */
    currenta = firsta;
    if(currenta == NULL)
        return(0);         /* no data to write
                              END OF PROGRAM */
    datafile = fopen(filename,"w");
    if(datafile == NULL)
    {
        printf("Error writing to %s\n",filename);
        return(1);
    }
                    /* Write each record to disk */
    while(currenta != NULL)
    {
        fwrite(currenta,sizeof(struct account),1,datafile);
        currenta = currenta->next;
    }
    fclose(datafile);
```

The code has three parts:

✦ The first part sets the current record equal to the first record, resetting the linked list to start over. This part also checks to see whether any data is in the list. If not, a `return(0)` statement ends the program right there.

✦ The second part of the code opens the file BANK.DAT for writing and displays an error message if a problem occurs.

✦ The final part loops through the linked list, writing each record to disk by using the `fwrite()` function. Then, the file is closed and the program quits.

**Book VI
Chapter 3**

At the core is `fwrite()`, which puts each record to disk, writing a chunk of memory at a time to the BANK.DAT file.

Storing a Linked
List on Disk

Update your BANK.C source code to match the preceding instructions. Save. Compile. Run.

You have to create a list of accounts again — but this time your efforts aren't wasted. When you quit the program, the list is written to disk and saved.

You can prove that the data has been written by viewing the BANK.DAT file on disk. Use either the **dir bank.dat** or **ls -l bank.dat** command (for Windows or Unix, respectively) to confirm that the file is there and that it doesn't have a zero length. (A zero length means that the file was opened, but no data was ever written.)

In Windows, you can use the `type` command to view the file: **type bank.dat**. In Unix, use the `hexdump` command to get a better idea of how the file is stored on disk: **hexdump bank.dat**.

Reading a linked list from disk

If you can handle writing structures to disk, you can handle reading them back. The same is true for linked lists, with the `fread()` command used to read a chunk of information from disk and then store that chunk in a structure.

The only thing you need to remember when reading in a linked list from disk is that the pointer information stored in the `next` variable is useless. After all, who knows where the program puts the structures in memory?

If you read the structures in from disk properly, you must reallocate memory for each structure as it's read from disk. For that reason alone, the `next` variable must point to a new and different location than the one stored on disk.

In fact, the only pointer that doesn't change when read from disk is the final NULL. You can even use that NULL as a trigger to know when to stop reading from disk.

You need to modify the BANK.C source code so that it automatically reads the BANK.DAT file and loads the structures from disk when the program starts. To do this, summon BANK.C into your editor.

In the main() function, between the variable declarations and the do loop that works the main menu, add this bit of code:

```
datafile = fopen(filename,"r");
if(datafile)     /* file opened; doesn't exist otherwise */
{
    firsta = (struct account *)malloc(sizeof(struct
account));
    currenta = firsta;
    while(1)
    {
        newa = (struct account *)malloc(sizeof(struct
account));
        fread(currenta,sizeof(struct account),1,datafile);
        if(currenta->next == NULL)
            break;
        currenta->next = newa;
        currenta = newa;
    }
    fclose(datafile);
    anum = currenta->number;
}
```

Carefully update your source code to include this hunk of code. Watch out! The malloc() functions may wrap here, but need not wrap inside your editor.

Save! Compile! Run!

When you first run the program, try the L command to list the records that were saved the last time you quit. They should all be there, just as you left them. You can go ahead and add records, modify them — whatever. When you quit the program, the records are automatically saved. Restarting the program automatically loads them into memory again.

How the file-reading routine works

Reading in a database of saved linked list records from disk is simple. As long as you remember not to pay attention to any next value that's read from disk, you're fine.

Here's how I tackled the problem in the BANK.C source code. First, the file is opened:

```
datafile = fopen(filename,"r");
if(datafile)    /* file opened; doesn't exist otherwise */
```

If the file exists, the program automatically processes the file's data. Otherwise, the program assumes that the file doesn't exist and the file-reading routine is skipped.

The first thing to do is to set up the linked list, just as though the information were being read from the keyboard. The first record's pointer is initialized, pointing to a properly sized chunk of memory:

**Book VI
Chapter 3**

**Storing a Linked
List on Disk**

```
firsta = (struct account *)malloc(sizeof(struct account));
```

Next, that location is referred to by the current pointer's variable, `currenta`, so that a `while` loop can be used to march through all the records stored on disk:

```
currenta = firsta;
```

The `while` loop is endless:

```
while(1)
```

The key to breaking the loop is reading in the last record from disk, which contains a NULL in its next variable. But, first, space must be allocated for the next record in the list:

```
newa = (struct account *)malloc(sizeof(struct account));
```

Then, a record is read from disk:

```
fread(currenta,sizeof(struct account),1,datafile);
```

The data is transferred from disk into the memory chunk allocated and referenced by `currenta`. Next, a test is made for the last record:

```
if(currenta->next == NULL)
    break;
```

If the last record has been read from disk, its `next` value is NULL. The `while` loop then stops. (And, it should free up the space allocated to `newa`, but that's something I forgot to do.) When the last record hasn't been found, the pointers need to be updated. First, the next pointer must reference the next record in the list:

```
currenta->next = newa;
```

Then, the current pointer must "hop up one" to reference the new and next structure to be read from disk:

```
currenta = newa;
```

When all is done, the file is closed with `fclose(datafile)` and the account number variable, `anum`, is read and made current:

```
anum = currenta->number;
```

Above all, the key is *not* to reference, or even use, the `next` pointer that was stored on disk. Although you can test for yourself whether the program uses the same addresses, it's not worth the trouble to trust those old addresses. I wouldn't.

The Final Code Listing for BANK.C

Here's the complete source code listing for the BANK.C program, including all updates and additions from this chapter and Book VI, Chapter 2:

```c
#include <stdio.h>
#include <stdlib.h>
#include <string.h>
#include <ctype.h>

void clearInput(void);
void addNewAccount(void);
void listAll(void);
void deleteAccount(void);
void modifyAccount(void);
int prompt(void);

struct account {
    int number;
    char lastname[15];
    char firstname[15];
    float balance;
    struct account *next;
};
struct account *firsta,*currenta,*newa;
```

```
int anum = 0;

int main()
{
    FILE *datafile;
    char *filename = "bank.dat";
    char ch;
    firsta = NULL;

    datafile = fopen(filename,"r");
    if(datafile)    /* assume doesn't exist otherwise */
    {
        firsta = (struct account *)malloc(sizeof(struct
account));
        currenta = firsta;
        while(1)
        {
            newa = (struct account *)malloc(sizeof(struct
account));
            fread(currenta,sizeof(struct account),1,
datafile);
            if(currenta->next == NULL)
                break;
            currenta->next = newa;
            currenta = newa;
        }
        fclose(datafile);
        anum = currenta->number;
}

    do
    {
        clearInput();
        puts("\nA - Add a new account");
        puts("D - Delete account");
        puts("L - List all accounts");
        puts("M - Modify account");
        puts("Q - Quit this program\n");
        printf("\tYour choice:");
        ch = getchar();
        ch = toupper(ch);
        switch(ch)
        {
            case 'A':
                puts("Add new account\n");
                clearInput();
                addNewAccount();
                break;
            case 'D':
                puts("Delete account\n");
```

```
                    deleteAccount();
                    break;
                case 'L':
                    puts("List all accounts\n");
                    listAll();
                    break;
                case 'M':
                    puts("Modify an account\n");
                    modifyAccount();
                    break;
                case 'Q':
                    puts("Quit\n");
                default:
                    break;
            }
        }
        while(ch != 'Q');

/*
 * Save the records to disk
 */
        currenta = firsta;
        if(currenta == NULL)
            return(0);           /* no data to write
                        END OF PROGRAM */
        datafile = fopen(filename,"w");
        if(datafile == NULL)
        {
            printf("Error writing to %s\n",filename);
            return(1);
        }
                        /* write each record to disk */
        while(currenta != NULL)
        {
            fwrite(currenta,sizeof(struct account),1,datafile);
            currenta = currenta->next;
        }
        fclose(datafile);
        return(0);
}


/*
 * This function clears any text from the input stream
 */

void clearInput(void)
{
    fflush(stdin);                /* fpurge(stdin) */
}


void addNewAccount(void)
{
```

```
        newa = (struct account *)malloc(sizeof(struct account));

/*
 * Check to see if this is the first record
 * If so, then initialize all the pointers to this
 * first structure in the database
 */

    if(firsta==NULL)
        firsta = currenta = newa;

/*
 * Otherwise, you must find the end of the structure list
 * (easily spotted by the NULL pointer) and add on the
 * new structure you just allocated memory for
 */

    else
    {
        currenta = firsta;      /* make the first current */
                                /* loop through all records */

        while(currenta->next != NULL)
            currenta = currenta->next;
                                /* last record found */
        currenta->next = newa;  /* save the address of new */
        currenta = newa;        /* make current new */
    }

/* Now, you just fill in the new structure */

    anum++;
    printf("%27s: %5i\n","Account number",anum);
    currenta->number = anum;

    printf("%27s: ","Enter customer's last name");
    gets(currenta->lastname);

    printf("%27s: ","Enter customer's first name");
    gets(currenta->firstname);

    printf("%27s: $","Enter account balance");
    scanf("%f",&currenta->balance);

/*
 * Finally, cap the new record with a NULL pointer
 * so that you know it's the last record:
 */

    currenta->next = NULL;
}
```

```c
void listAll(void)
{
    if(firsta==NULL)
        puts("There are no records to print!");
    else
    {
        printf("%6s %-15s %-15s %11s\n",
"Acct#","Last","First","Balance");
        currenta=firsta;
        do
        {
            printf("%5d: %-15s %-15s $%8.2f\n",
                currenta->number,
                currenta->lastname,
                currenta->firstname,
                currenta->balance);
        }
        while((currenta=currenta->next) != NULL);
    }
}

void deleteAccount(void)
{
    int record;
    struct account *previousa;

    if(firsta==NULL)
    {
        puts("There are no records to delete!");
        return;
    }

    listAll();          /* show all records first */
    printf("Enter account number to delete: ");
    scanf("%d",&record);

    currenta = firsta;
    while(currenta != NULL)
    {
        if(currenta->number == record)
        {
            if(currenta == firsta)     /* special condition */
                firsta=currenta->next;
            else
                previousa->next = currenta->next;
            free(currenta);
            printf("Account %d deleted!\n",record);
            return;
        }
        else
        {
```

```
                previousa = currenta;
                currenta = currenta->next;
            }
        }
    printf("Account %d was not found!\n",record);
    puts("Nothing deleted.");
}

void modifyAccount(void)
{
    int record;

    if(firsta==NULL)
    {
        puts("There are no records to modify!");
        return;
    }

    listAll();          /* show all records first */
    printf("Enter account number to modify or change: ");
    scanf("%d",&record);

    currenta = firsta;
    while(currenta != NULL)
    {
        if(currenta->number == record)
        {
            printf("Account $%d:\n",currenta->number);
            printf("Last name: %s\n",currenta->lastname);
            if(prompt())
                gets(currenta->lastname);
            printf("First name: %s\n",currenta->firstname);
            if(prompt())
                gets(currenta->firstname);
            printf("Balance %8.2f\n",currenta->balance);
            if(prompt())
                scanf("%f",&currenta->balance);
            return;
        }
        else
        {
            currenta = currenta->next;
        }
    }
    printf("Account %d was not found!\n",record);
}

int prompt(void)
{
    char ch;
```

```
    clearInput();
    printf("Update?");
    ch = getchar();
    ch = toupper(ch);
    clearInput();
    if(ch == 'Y')
    {
        printf("Enter new: ");
        return(1);
    }
    else
        return(0);
}
```

Chapter 4: The Nightmare of the Double-Linked List

In This Chapter

✔ Creating a double-linked list

✔ Linking to the next and preceding records

✔ Displaying a double-linked list backward

✔ Removing a record from a double-linked list

If you thought that double-linked lists were a myth, like being double-jointed, you're woefully wrong. In fact, just ruminating on the possibilities of whatever a double-linked list could possibly be infuses my brain with a host of nightmares and unbearable mental agony. Praise your favorite deity if the topic of double-linked lists isn't a requirement at your university or place of business.

Anyway, scary notes aside, a *double-linked list* is really nothing more than a linked list with one extra redundant link in it. Some folks prefer to write their linked lists in this unusual manner, probably because they don't trust only one link. No matter. For whatever reason, this chapter provides you with a teensy insight into the obtuse subject of double-linked lists.

The Theory of the Double-Linked List

If you have been reading the chapters in Book VI sequentially, you're most likely fairly comfortable with the concept of linked lists and have a good — if not solid — understanding of how they work and why they're necessary. In case you forgot why they're necessary:

A linked list is better than a fixed array in C. Arrays cannot be resized, although linked lists can be as big or as small as needed (or as memory allows).

Linked lists work thanks to pointers. A new structure-size chunk of memory is created, and then a series of pointers helps you fill, reference, and organize the linked list. From the previous chapters, you may recognize the pointers as

✦ `first`, constantly referencing the first item in the list

✦ `current`, always referencing the current item in the list

✦ `current->next`, referencing the next item in the list or NULL for the last item

✦ `new`, referencing a new structure to be added to the list

You can't really use `new` as a variable name in C any more; that's because `new` is a reserved word in the C++ language, so you have to use some variation on a theme for the four standard linked-list variable names.

Into this mix come three more pointer variables in the double-linked list:

✦ `current->previous` references the previous item in the list

✦ `prior` is used to reference the previous record, just as `current` references the current record

✦ `last` is used to point to the last record, just as `first` points at the first record

If you have toiled through the first three chapters in Book VI, the concept of a previous pointer may seem rather silly. But what it does is let you refer to the previous structure in a list, allowing a program to sift through the structures in both forward and reverse order, if need be.

Then again, just getting down the basics of a single-linked list is enough for some people. Why bother exploding your brain by adding another dratted pointer to the mix?

An Example of a Double-Linked List

Suppose that you want to keep a database of winning lottery numbers. The rank amateur C language programmer would probably do something like this:

`lotto[52][6];`

That would be an array of 52 groups of six numbers: six numbers per drawing at 52 weeks per year. But the clever C programmer would recognize that this lotto ball nonsense is the stuff of structures and make a storage gizmo that may look like this:

```
struct lotto {
    int balls[6];
};
```

Rather than declare an array of lotto structures, just modify it into a linked list:

```
struct lotto {
    int balls[6];
    struct lotto *next;
};
```

Beyond that, modify it into a *double*-linked list:

```
struct lotto {
    int balls[6];
    struct lotto *previous;
    struct lotto *next;
};
```

Scary? Perhaps. You definitely have more junk to keep track of this way.

Building the double-linked list

The following sample code creates a small double-linked list of lotto ball drawings. Because it's is only an example, the lotto balls are simply drawn randomly; no sorting is done, nor is any checking done to confirm that the same numbers aren't drawn twice. Also, the list is limited to only 10 structures, whereas in practice, you need no limitation on any linked list:

```
#include <stdio.h>
#include <malloc.h>
#include <time.h>
#include <stdlib.h>

#define RANGE 52
#define BALLS 6

int getBall(void);

struct lotto {
    int ball[BALLS];
    struct lotto *previous;
    struct lotto *next;
    };
struct lotto *f,*c,*n,*p,*l;

int main()
{
    int x,y;
```

```
    srandom((unsigned)time(NULL));    /* seed randomizer */

/* fill first record */
    f = (struct lotto *)malloc(sizeof(struct lotto));
    for(x=0;x<BALLS;x++)
        f->ball[x] = getBall();
    f->previous = NULL;
    f->next = NULL;
    c = f;

/* fill middle records */
    for(y=0;y<9;y++)
    {
        p = c;
        n = (struct lotto *)malloc(sizeof(struct lotto));
        c->next = n;
        c = n;
        for(x=0;x<BALLS;x++)
            c->ball[x] = getBall();
        c->previous = p;
    }

/* fix in the last record */
    c->next = NULL;
    l = c;

    return(0);
}

int getBall(void)
{
    return(random() % RANGE + 1);
}
```

Copy this source code into your editor. I apologize for the cryptic nature of the variables; I hope that it makes it easier to type them (descriptions follow).

Be sure to replace srandom( ) with srand( ), and random( ) with rand( ) if your compiler doesn't support the newer random-number-generating functions (refer to Book II, Chapter 4.)

Save the sucker to disk as LOTTO.C. Compile. Run.

There's no output, but, hopefully, a double-linked list of 10 items was created. Here's how that happened:

```
struct lotto {
    int ball[BALLS];
```

```
struct lotto *previous;
struct lotto *next;
};
```

The lotto structure contains the ball array — the balls drawn for the lotto. They're supplied by the random-number generator. Then come the two pointers, one to the next record and the other to the previous, both aptly named.

To make the double-linked list work, you need five pointer variables of the lotto structure type:

```
struct lotto *f,*c,*n,*p,*l;
```

**Book VI
Chapter 4**

**The Nightmare of
the Double-Linked
List**

f is for the first record in the list; c references the current record; n references a new record called out of memory via the malloc() function; p references the preceding record; and, finally, l references the last record in the linked list.

After seeding the randomizer, the main() function goes about creating the first record. This record is unique and is usually created outside of a loop. That's because it must be flagged as the first record — a special record in the list:

```
f = (struct lotto *)malloc(sizeof(struct lotto));
for(x=0;x<BALLS;x++)
    f->ball[x] = getBall();
f->previous = NULL;
f->next = NULL;
c = f;
```

In the first record, the previous variable is always NULL, marking the start of the list, just as NULL for the next record marks the end of the list.

For this record, the next variable is also set to NULL, though that value is reset as the second record is added.

Finally, to prepare for the loop, the first record is referenced as the current record with c = f.

To fill the rest of the records, a for loop is used. This is done simply to expedite things. The loop creates a new record, references it as the current record, fills it, and then moves on to the next record. Note how the p variable helps keep track of the preceding record just as c helps keep track of the current record:

```
/* fill middle records */
    for(y=0;y<9;y++)
    {
```

```
    p = c;
    n = (struct lotto *)malloc(sizeof(struct lotto));
    c->next = n;
    c = n;
    for(x=0;x<BALLS;x++)
        c->ball[x] = getBall();
    c->previous = p;
}
```

To complete the last record, the next element is set to NULL, and then the l
pointer is set so that the last record can quickly be found:

```
c->next = NULL;
l = c;
```

Sadly, none of this can be proved without a little output. That happens in the
next section.

Scanning through the double-linked list

Marching through a double-linked list is the same as displaying data in a regular linked list. This bit of code helps the LOTTO.C program display its list:

```
/* Display all records forward */
    y = 1;
    for(c = f;c !=NULL;c=c->next)
    {
        printf("Lotto pix %d: ",y++);
        for(x=0;x<BALLS;x++)
            printf(" %d",c->ball[x]);
        putchar('\n');
    }
```

The y variable is used only to tick off the lotto results. Otherwise, the for
loop quickly sifts through the linked list in a manner that you should pay
attention to. The rest of the routine merely displays the lotto results.

Insert this chunk of code between the l = c statement and return(0) in
the main() function of LOTTO.C. Save your changes to disk. Recompile. Run:

```
Lotto pix 1:    3 37 4 7 27 27
Lotto pix 2:    21 27 21 33 29 28
Lotto pix 3:    19 21 11 13 3 22
Lotto pix 4:    3 18 30 11 20 39
Lotto pix 5:    9 16 51 40 28 24
Lotto pix 6:    36 17 34 4 48 42
Lotto pix 7:    37 15 3 49 14 6
Lotto pix 8:    23 22 18 30 5 20
Lotto pix 9:    34 28 16 2 24 52
Lotto pix 10:   39 13 44 21 33 28
```

A special look at that `for` loop

I'm utterly impressed with the `for` loop that quietly and efficiently whips through a linked list. No, I didn't make it up. (Hardly!) But I truly admire its proficiency.

Here's the loop in generic, linked-list language:

```
for(current = first;current
    !=NULL;current=current
    ->next)
```

The first part of the loop initializes the pointer list, setting the `current` pointer equal to the `first` record in the list. This is the loop's setup.

Next comes the "while true" part of the `for` loop. The loop continues to repeat until the `current` variable is equal to NULL.

The final part is the "do this" part of the loop, the part that's repeated after each iteration of the `for` loop's statements. In this example, that part sets the `current` record equal to the `next` record, effectively hopping up one notch in the list.

Amazing.

Of course, the numbers you see are different, but the results should be the same: Each item in the linked list is displayed.

Exercise 6.4.1

Add another chunk of code to the LOTTO.C source code, this one just before the `return` statement. Use this code to set up a `for` loop to display all the records in the linked list, from the last one to the first one.

Deleting an Item from a Double-Linked List

Just like deleting an item from a regular linked list, deleting an item from a double-linked list is done by removing the pointer references to that item and then freeing its memory. The complexity here is that two pointers, not just one, are referencing each item in the list.

Figure 4-1 illustrates how double-linked lists work, using the lotto structure as an example. I dared not show you this illustration earlier, for fear that it would induce palpitations and possibly even death in some people. And, it helps to illustrate that "needlessly complicated" aspect of double-linked lists.

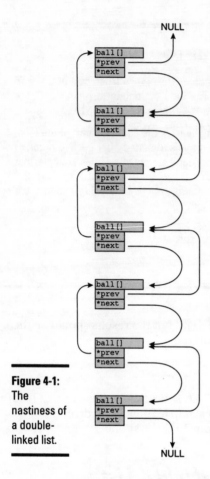

Figure 4-1:
The
nastiness of
a double-
linked list.

Anyway, Figure 4-2 shows you how an element in the linked list would be removed and which pointers need to be fixed up. Unlike in a regular linked list, where only one structure is affected, deleting a record from a double-linked list affects two structures.

The following bit of code removes a record from the LOTTO.C source code. The code isn't as nasty or tangled as it would seem from the figures nearby:

```
/* delete a record */
    printf("Enter a record to delete: ");
    scanf("%d",&y);
    for(x=1,c=f;x<y;x++)        /* find the record */
        c = c->next;
                                /* c is the record */
    p = c->previous;
    n = c->next;                /* borrow n here */
    if(p != NULL)
```

```
        p->next = n;        /* update references */
else
        f = n;              /* new first */
if(n != NULL)
    n->previous = p;
else
        l = p               /* new last */
free(c);                    /* remove record */
```

After the record number is obtained, a for loop is used to find that record in the linked list. (Note how the for loop initializes both the value of x and the c pointer to the f pointer.)

When the deleted record is found, the p and n pointers are borrowed to reference the previous and next structures. These values then help reset the pointers in those structures. Then comes the massive swapping.

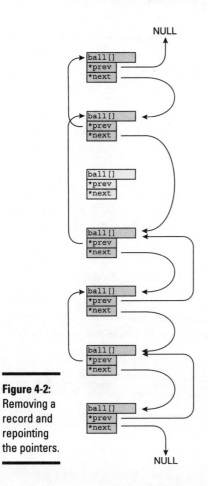

Figure 4-2:
Removing a
record and
repointing
the pointers.

Update your LOTTO.C source code with the preceding snippet. In my editor, I removed the portion of the program that displays the list in reverse order. I also copied the chunk that displays the list, putting it after the preceding code to display the results. Here's my complete code, for your reference:

```c
#include <stdio.h>
#include <malloc.h>
#include <time.h>
#include <stdlib.h>

#define RANGE 52
#define BALLS 6

int getBall(void);

struct lotto {
    int ball[BALLS];
    struct lotto *previous;
    struct lotto *next;
    };
struct lotto *f,*c,*n,*p,*l;

int main()
{
    int x,y;

    srand((unsigned)time(NULL));    /* seed randomizer */

/* fill first record */

    f = (struct lotto *)malloc(sizeof(struct lotto));
    for(x=0;x<BALLS;x++)
        f->ball[x] = getBall();
    f->previous = NULL;
    f->next = NULL;
    c = f;

/* fill middle records */
    for(y=0;y<9;y++)
    {
        p = c;
        n = (struct lotto *)malloc(sizeof(struct lotto));
        c->next = n;
        c = n;
        for(x=0;x<BALLS;x++)
            c->ball[x] = getBall();
        c->previous = p;
    }
```

```
/* fix in the last record */
    c->next = NULL;
    l = c;

/* display all records forward */
    y = 1;
    for(c = f;c !=NULL;c=c->next)
    {
        printf("Lotto pix %d: ",y++);
        for(x=0;x<BALLS;x++)
            printf(" %d",c->ball[x]);
        putchar('\n');
    }

/* delete a record */
    printf("Enter a record to delete: ");
    scanf("%d",&y);
    for(x=1,c=f;x<y;x++)      /* find the record */
        c = c->next;
                              /* c is the record */
    p = c->previous;
    n = c->next;             /* borrow n here */
    if(p != NULL)
        p->next = n;         /* update references */
    else
        f = n;               /* new first */
    if(n != NULL)
        n->previous = p;
    else
        l = p;               /* new last */
    free(c);                 /* remove record */

/* display all records forward */
    y = 1;
    for(c = f;c !=NULL;c=c->next)
    {
        printf("Lotto pix %d: ",y++);
        for(x=0;x<BALLS;x++)
            printf(" %d",c->ball[x]);
        putchar('\n');
    }
    return(0);
}


int getBall(void)
{
    return(rand() % RANGE + 1);
}
```

Update your LOTTO.C source code so that it matches what's shown here. Save to disk. Compile. Run.

Choose a record to delete by using the reference numbers. After deleting that record, the list of lotto winnings is displayed again, minus the record you deleted. (The numbering doesn't reflect the missing record, however.)

Book VII

Appendixes

The 5th Wave   By Rich Tennant

Contents at a Glance

Appendix A: The Stuff You Need to Know before Reading Everything Else in This Book

You need a few things before C programming is possible on your computer. The purpose of this appendix is to outline what you need and how to use it in order to work with the sample programs in this book. It's not that hard, but it may be something you're not used to, so pay attention!

Setting Things Up

You need two things to program in C on your computer:

+ A compiler

+ A place to put your programs

For Unix, which includes Linux, FreeBSD, the Mac OS X operating system, plus other similar operating systems, your C language compiler is already included; it comes with the operating system. For Windows and older Mac systems, you must obtain a compiler. That's not as difficult as it sounds.

The C language compiler

Thanks to the C language's popularity, many compilers are available for you to use with this book. I do, however, recommend the following:

In Windows: If you're using Windows, I recommend that you get a GCC or GNU-compatible C compiler. A list of these compilers is provided on this book's Web page, at www.c-for-dummies.com.

For this book, I used the MinGW compiler that comes with the Dev-C++ IDE (Integrated Development Environment). It's free and available from www.bloodshed.net or www.mingw.org.

Whichever compiler you use, note its location on your PC's hard drive. You need to use this location to modify your system's path so that you can access the compiler from any folder in your disk system. More on that later.

+ Other compilers are out there as well, including the best-selling Microsoft Visual C++ (MSVC). If you have MSVC, fine; you should be okay with running the programs in this book, but note that I'm not familiar with the current version of MSVC and don't reference it in this book, nor can I answer questions about it via e-mail. If you don't have MSVC, you have no reason to buy it.

+ I was once a big fan of the Borland compilers, but I haven't installed or used one for about 10 years. As with MSVC, I'm certain that the compiler works well with this book, although I'm unable to answer any e-mail questions you may have about your Borland compiler.

+ Plenty of free, shareware, and open-source C compilers are available on the Internet.

+ If you have other books on the C language, check the back for a free compiler.

+ Any GCC or GNU-compatible C compiler works best with this book.

In Unix (Linux, FreeBSD, or the Mac OS X): If you're using any of these or other variations of Unix, you should already have the GCC compiler installed and ready to use. To confirm it, open a terminal window and type the following line at the command prompt:

```
gcc -v
```

The GCC version number and other information is displayed on the screen. If you get a `command not found` error, GCC isn't installed; you need to update your operating system to include GCC as well as all the C programming libraries and other materials. (You can generally do this through your operating system's setup or configuration program.)

On the Mac (before OS X): Older versions of the Mac lack a built-in C language compiler. I recommend the Code Warrior compiler, though you should also check the Apple Web site to see whether any other (free) compilers are available: `http://developer.apple.com/`.

The place to put your stuff

When you figure out how to program, you create scads of files. These include the original text "source code" files and also the final program files and perhaps even object code files, depending on the compiler. Obviously, you want to keep those files organized and separate from your regular junk.

For this book, I recommend creating a `prog` folder or directory. Create this folder off your main folder — the `$HOME` folder in Unix or the `My Documents` folder in Windows. The `prog` folder is designed to hold all your programming projects.

Beneath `prog`, you should put the `c` folder, for all your C language programming projects.

Beneath the `c` folder, you create separate folders for each of the "books" in this multivolume tome. Table A-1 gives you the breakdown:

Table A-1	Suggested Folders or Directories for This Book	
Book Number	*Title*	*Folder or Directory*
Book 1	"Hello, C"	`prog/c/basic`
Book 2	"Middle C"	`prog/c/middle`
Book 3	"Above C Level"	`prog/c/above`
Book 4	"Advanced C"	`prog/c/advanced`
Book 5	"Disk Drive C"	`prog/c/disk`
Book 6	"The Joy of Linked Lists"	`prog/c/llists`

In Windows: To create a folder for your C language projects, open the My Documents icon on the desktop. Use the File⇨New⇨Folder command to create the `prog` folder and then the `c` folder inside the `prog` folder. Finally, use the File⇨New⇨Folder command to create individual folders for each book, according to the names listed in the preceding table. (The names are also repeated in each book's Chapter 1.)

Refer to a Windows reference book for more information on creating, naming, and using folders in Windows.

In Linux, FreeBSD, the Mac OS X, or Unix: You can create the folders by using your operating system's graphical shell, or you can use the command prompt or a command-prompt window.

From your home directory, use the `mkdir -p` command to create a full branch of folders, if necessary:

```
mkdir -p prog/c/learn
```

In this example, the `mkdir` command creates the `prog/c` folder branch — two folders at once. You can then use `mkdir` to create each book's folder.

Refer to a Unix reference book for more information on working with folders and directories at the command prompt. I believe that you will find it a more efficient way to manage your files than struggling with a graphical interface.

On the Mac (before OS X): Alas, the old Mac operating system lacked a "home folder" for all your stuff. If you have such a folder, use it as a base to create the subfolders as described in this book. Otherwise, you can create these folders right on the desktop for handy access: Use the ⌘+N command to create a new folder. First, create `prog` and then a folder inside `prog` named `c`. Then, create folders for each book, as shown in the table nearby.

When using your compiler, remember to save all your files in the `learn` folder.

Making Programs

To build programs, you need two tools: an editor and a compiler. You use the editor to create or edit the source code — which is merely a text file. Then, you use the compiler to magically transform that text into the language the computer understands, stuffing it all into a program file.

This book teaches programming by using small programs targeted to showcase specific examples of the C language. Because of that, using the command prompt for compiling programs is easier than using the IDE that may have come with your compiler. I recommend that you become familiar with the command prompt.

The steps in the following section don't apply to programming on the Macintosh earlier than version OS X. If you're using an older Mac, refer to your compiler's documentation to find out how to edit and compile programs. Remember to use the proper folder for each book as you create and save your source code and programs.

Finding your directory or folder

The first step to programming is to navigate your way to the proper folder or directory by using the command prompt:

1. **Start a terminal or command-prompt window.**

In Windows, run the CMD.EXE program, also known as the MS-DOS prompt.

This program is on the Accessories or, often, main Programs menu, off the Start button. Or, you can type **CMD** in the Run dialog box to start the command-prompt window.

In Unix, open a terminal window if you're using a graphical shell. Otherwise, any terminal display will do.

2. **Change to your home directory.**

   In Windows XP or Windows 2000, type this command:

   ```
   cd "my documents"
   ```

   In other versions of Windows, type this command:

   ```
   cd "\My Documents"
   ```

   The command prompt should now reflect that you're using the My Documents folder, similar to

   ```
   C:\Documents and Settings\Dan\My Documents>
   ```

   or

   ```
   C:\My Documents>
   ```

   (The last part of the prompt reads "My Documents.")

   In Unix, type the **cd** command to change to your home directory. That one command does the job.

3. **Change to the c directory.**

   Everyone type this line:

   ```
   cd prog/c
   ```

   except in older versions of Windows, where it's

   ```
   cd prog\c
   ```

   (Note the backslashes, not forward slashes.)

4. **Change to or create the proper directory for the book you're reading.**

   At the start of each book, in Chapter 1, you're given directions on the name of the directory to create for storing your source code files and creating your programs. Create that specific directory, and then change to it using the necessary commands from your operating system.

5. **Confirm that you're in the proper directory.**

   You do this in Windows by typing the **cd** command; in Unix, type **pwd**. The current directory is displayed, which should be the directory that's noted for whichever book you're reading.

You must be in the proper folder for whichever book you're reading because many of the programs share common names between books. If you're not in the proper folder, you may end up overwriting source code that you would otherwise want to keep.

Running an editor

To concoct your C language source code, you need to use a text editor. In Windows you can use the EDIT command to summon the MS-DOS Editor. It's rather simple to understand and use, it works with the mouse, and it's free and available.

For the various Unix operating systems, you have multiple editor choices. The simplest text editor is Easy Editor, activated with the ee command. Otherwise, you can use any of the Unix editors — and quite a few of them are available.

My favorite editor for working with C is vim, a variant on the infamous vi editor in Unix (see Figure A-1).

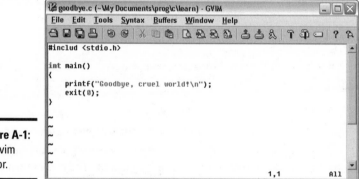

Figure A-1:
The vim editor.

Unlike vi, vim uses colors to code text. When you edit your source code in vim, you see keywords, values, and other parts of the C language highlighted in color.

✦ Versions of vim are available for Linux, FreeBSD, Mac OS X, Windows, and even the older Macs. You can pick it up at www.vim.org.

✦ Windows XP may not like the EDIT command. As an alternative, you can use Notepad to edit your source code. For example, to edit the GOOD-BYE.C text file, you would type this command at the prompt:

```
NOTEPAD GOODBYE.C
```

Notepad opens in another window, where you can edit the text file. Simply close the window when you're done.

Compiling and linking

After the source code text file is created, your next step is to compile and link. This step is what transforms the meek and mild text file into a robust and useable program on your computer.

Refer to the proper subsection for compiling and linking specifics for your operating system. For Macs before OS X, see the reference material that came with your compiler.

Making GCC work in Windows

Heck, for all the advances made with Windows, you may as well be using DOS when it comes to compiling programs at the command prompt. Anyway . . .

Windows compilers are not designed to be friendly for command line compiling. Because of that, it's up to you to make the compiler work at every command prompt and in every folder in your computer system. The best way to do that is to add your compiler's directory name to the Windows search path. This is done differently, depending on your version of Windows.

One thing that's the same, no matter which version of Windows you have, is taking note of which the directory the compiler is in. This is very important!

For example, if you have installed MinGW's GCC, it may be in this directory:

```
C:\MinGW\bin
```

Or, it may be installed in the Program Files folder, in which case this is the directory:

```
C:\Program Files\MinGW\bin
```

Or, perhaps you have installed another compiler and this is the folder it lives in:

```
C:\Program Files\OtherGCC\bin
```

Whatever that folder is, make a note of it! You *must* remember that full path name: disk drive, parent folders, and then the folder containing the gcc command. Write that path down or memorize it.

Your second step is to modify the system's path variable. You want to put your compiler's location into the path variable so that Windows can run the gcc command from any directory and on any hard drive. You have two ways to do this, depending on your version of Windows.

In Windows XP, follow these steps:

1. **Open the Control Panel's System icon to display the System Properties dialog box.**

2. **Click the Advanced tab.**

3. **Click the Environment Variables button.**

4. **Click to select the Path variable in the bottom part of the Environment Variables dialog box.**

5. **Click the Edit button.**

6. **In the Edit System Variable dialog box, click the Variable value text box to select it.**

7. **Press the End key on your keyboard.**

8. **Type a semicolon (;).**

9. **Type the full path name to the GCC compiler, such as** c:\mingw\bin.

10. **Double-check that you entered everything properly!**

11. **Click OK to close the dialog box, and then continue to click the OK buttons to close previously opened dialog boxes. Eventually, you close the System Properties window. You're done.**

In Windows 98, follow these steps:

1. **From the Start menu, choose the Run command.**

2. **In the Run dialog box, type** MSCONFIG.

3. **Click OK to run the System Configuration Utility.**

4. **Click the Autoexec.bat tab in the System Configuration Utility's window.**

5. **Click to select the line in the window that begins with** PATH=.

6. **Click the Edit button.**

7. **At the end of the existing path, type a semicolon (;).**

8. **Add to the end of the path (after the semicolon) the full path name to your GCC compiler, such as** c:\mingw\bin.

9. **Confirm that you didn't make any typing boo-boos.**

10. **Click OK to save this item, and then close the System Configuration Utility's window.**

11. **Restart your computer.**

After fixing the path, you want to test to ensure that GCC works. To do so, follow the steps from earlier in this appendix for changing to the `prog/c` directory in the command-prompt window. After you're there, type this line at the prompt:

```
gcc -v
```

If you see a whole lotta blech appear on the screen, congratulations! You got it to work!

If it doesn't work, review the preceding steps. You probably didn't copy the path name properly. If so, you need to repeat the steps so that the proper path to the `gcc` command is included with the system's `PATH` variable.

Windows: Compiling, linking, and running

After setting up the path and the `gcc` command, you're ready to start creating programs. You will repeat the following steps often enough that you will no longer need to refer to this appendix for help:

1. **Ensure that you're in the proper folder.**

    Refer to the section "Finding your directory or folder," earlier in this appendix.

2. **Use your text editor to create your source code file.**

    Refer to Book I, Chapter 1 for the listing of the DUMB.C program. Follow the instructions in that chapter to type that text into your editor.

3. **Compile and link the source code.**

    You do this with the `gcc` command, both steps at once. Here's the command to type:

    ```
    gcc dumb.c -o dumb
    ```

    You type four things:

    - `gcc`, the command to compile and link the source code
    - `dumb.c`, the name of the source code file
    - `-o`, the output switch
    - `dumb`, the name of the final program

If you leave off the -o switch and its option, GCC creates in Windows the program file named A.EXE. I don't recommend this. Instead, remember the -o option and specify a name for the output program. The name can be the same as the source code file. (C language source code files end in .C, and program files end in .EXE.)

4. Run the program.

Type the program file's name at the prompt. For the example, type **dumb** and press Enter. This command executes that program's code and displays something on the screen or does something interesting, depending on what the program is supposed to do.

Those are the basic steps you take (all in the same folder) to create the program examples in this book. As I have said, eventually, all this becomes second nature to you.

✦ If you get an error message, such as the compiler cannot find its files or some installation problem has occurred, please refer to the compiler's documentation or Web site for help. I cannot help you with problems related to the compiler or its installation.

✦ For each program you create, there are two files: the source code file (a text file) and the program file. That's generally how things go in this book.

✦ I recommend keeping the programs around for reference; don't delete them until you have been programming a while and really no longer need them.

Unix: Compiling, linking, and running

The main thrust of programming the individual examples in this book involves the following steps. Eventually, you will have repeated them often enough that you won't have to return here to see what's next:

1. Ensure that you're in the proper folder.

Heed the steps in the section "Finding your directory or folder," earlier in this appendix.

2. Use your text editor to create your source code file.

Use vi, ee, or whatever your favorite text editor is to create and save the source code file. For an example, you can check the listing of the DUMB.C source in Book 1, Chapter 1; type that text into your editor.

3. Compile and link the source code.

Compiling and linking are both handled by the gcc command. As an example, here's what you need to type to compile and link the DUMB.C source code you create in Step 1:

```
gcc dumb.c -o dumb
```

You see four items:

- gcc, the command to compile and link the source code
- dumb.c, the name of the source code file
- -o, the output switch
- dumb, the name of the final program

If you leave off the -o switch and its option, GCC creates the program file named a.out. I don't recommend this. Instead, remember the -o option and specify a name for the output program. The name can be the same as the source code file, but without the .c extension.

4. **Run the program.**

Alas, your operating system doesn't run your program if you type its name at the prompt. The reason is that Unix runs only programs found on the path, and I don't recommend putting any of your C source code directories on the path. (If you create your own programs that you want to run, copy them to a bin directory beneath your home directory, and put that directory on the search path.)

To get the operating system to notice your program, you have to be specific about where the program lives, (in the current folder, for example). You do this by prefixing ./ to the program's name. So, to run the dumb program, type this line at the prompt:

```
./dumb
```

And, the program runs.

Those are the basic steps you take (all in the learn folder) to create the program examples in this book. As I have said, eventually this procedure becomes second nature to you.

✦ Filename extensions are optional in Unix, but I recommend that you use .c to suffix all your C language source code files. This helps you keep them straight. As a bonus, the vim editor, GCC, and other programs recognize the .c and treat the file accordingly.

✦ For each program you create, there are two files: the source code file (a text file) and the program file. That's generally how things go in this book.

✦ The GCC compiler automatically sets the permission bits on the resulting program file, allowing it to be run. The permission bits are `-rwxr-xr-x`, or the equivalent of a `chmod 755` command.

✦ I recommend keeping the programs around for reference; don't delete them until you have been programming a while and really no longer need them.

Appendix B: ASCII Table

Code	Character	Hex	Binary	Notes
0	^@	00	0000 0000	Null character, \0
1	^A	01	0000 0001	
2	^B	02	0000 0010	
3	^C	03	0000 0011	
4	^D	04	0000 0100	Exit key (Unix)
5	^E	05	0000 0101	
6	^F	06	0000 0110	
7	^G	07	0000 0111	Bell, \a
8	^H	08	0000 1000	Backspace, \b
9	^I	09	0000 1001	Tab, \t
10	^J	0A	0000 1010	Line feed
11	^K	0B	0000 1011	Vertical tab, \v
12	^L	0C	0000 1100	Form feed, \f
13	^M	0D	0000 1101	Enter key, \n (or \r)
14	^N	0E	0000 1110	
15	^O	0F	0000 1111	
16	^P	10	0001 0000	
17	^Q	11	0001 0001	
18	^R	12	0001 0010	
19	^S	13	0001 0011	
20	^T	14	0001 0100	
21	^U	15	0001 0101	
22	^V	16	0001 0110	
23	^W	17	0001 0111	
24	^X	18	0001 1000	
25	^Y	19	0001 1001	
26	^Z	1A	0001 1010	End of File (DOS)
27	^[	1B	0001 1011	Escape
28	^\	1C	0001 1100	
29	^]	1D	0001 1101	
30	^^	1E	0001 1110	

(continued)

Code	Character	Hex	Binary	Notes
31	^_	1F	0001 1111	
32		20	0010 0000	Space
33	!	21	0010 0001	
34	"	22	0010 0010	
35	#	23	0010 0011	
36	$	24	0010 0100	
37	%	25	0010 0101	
38	&	26	0010 0110	
39	'	27	0010 0111	
40	(	28	0010 1000	
41	)	29	0010 1001	
42	*	2A	0010 1010	
43	+	2B	0010 1011	
44	,	2C	0010 1100	
45	-	2D	0010 1101	
46	.	2E	0010 1110	
47	/	2F	0010 1111	
48	0	30	0011 0000	(Numbers)
49	1	31	0011 0001	
50	2	32	0011 0010	
51	3	33	0011 0011	
52	4	34	0011 0100	
53	5	35	0011 0101	
54	6	36	0011 0110	
55	7	37	0011 0111	
56	8	38	0011 1000	
57	9	39	0011 1001	
58	:	3A	0011 1010	
59	;	3B	0011 1011	
60	<	3C	0011 1100	
61	=	3D	0011 1101	
62	>	3E	0011 1110	
63	?	3F	0011 1111	
64	@	40	0100 0000	
65	A	41	0100 0001	(Uppercase alphabet)

Code	Character	Hex	Binary	Notes
66	B	42	0100 0010	
67	C	43	0100 0011	
68	D	44	0100 0100	
69	E	45	0100 0101	
70	F	46	0100 0110	
71	G	47	0100 0111	
72	H	48	0100 1000	
73	I	49	0100 1001	
74	J	4A	0100 1010	
75	K	4B	0100 1011	
76	L	4C	0100 1100	
77	M	4D	0100 1101	
78	N	4E	0100 1110	
79	O	4F	0100 1111	
80	P	50	0101 0000	
81	Q	51	0101 0001	
82	R	52	0101 0010	
83	S	53	0101 0011	
84	T	54	0101 0100	
85	U	55	0101 0101	
86	V	56	0101 0110	
87	W	57	0101 0111	
88	X	58	0101 1000	
89	Y	59	0101 1001	
90	Z	5A	0101 1010	
91	[	5B	0101 1011	
92	\	5C	0101 1100	
93	]	5D	0101 1101	
94	^	5E	0101 1110	
95	_	5F	0101 1111	
96	'	60	0110 0000	
97	a	61	0110 0001	(Lowercase alphabet)
98	b	62	0110 0010	
99	c	63	0110 0011	

**Book VII
Appendix B**

ASCII Table

(continued)

Code	Character	Hex	Binary	Notes
100	d	64	0110 0100	
101	e	65	0110 0101	
102	f	66	0110 0110	
103	g	67	0110 0111	
104	h	68	0110 1000	
105	i	69	0110 1001	
106	j	6A	0110 1010	
107	k	6B	0110 1011	
108	l	6C	0110 1100	
109	m	6D	0110 1101	
110	n	6E	0110 1110	
111	o	6F	0110 1111	
112	p	70	0111 0000	
113	q	71	0111 0001	
114	r	72	0111 0010	
115	s	73	0111 0011	
116	t	74	0111 0100	
117	u	75	0111 0101	
118	v	76	0111 0110	
119	w	77	0111 0111	
120	x	78	0111 1000	
121	y	79	0111 1001	
122	z	7A	0111 1010	
123	{	7B	0111 1011	
124	|	7C	0111 1100	
125	}	7D	0111 1101	
126	~	7E	0111 1110	
127		7F	0111 1111	Delete (or "rubout")

Appendix C: Answers to Exercises

The numbers after the filenames in this appendix aren't required for your own source code. For example, INTEGER3.C is merely the third variation of the original INTEGER.C source code. I use those numbers in this appendix, and in the online source code files, so that you can keep each variation of a source code file. On your computer, though, you don't need to rename the source code files.

You can find the source code library for this book on the Web at this address:

www.c-for-dummies.com/source.code/

Book 1: Hello, C

Exercise 1.3.1

MINE.C

```
/* MINE.C by Dan Gookin. Written 3/4/2004
 * This program displays my name so that if
 * I lose this computer and someone finds it
 * they'll remember to enter the command
 * prompt and type the MINE command to see
 * who the computer belongs to
 */

#include <stdio.h>

int main()
{
    printf("This computer belongs to:\n");
    printf("Dan Gookin\n");
    printf("P.O. Box 2697\n");
    printf("CDA, ID  83816\n");
    printf("(208) unlisted\n");
    return(0);
}
```

You can also use puts() rather than printf(), in which case you don't need the \n escape sequence.

Exercise 1.4.1

INTEGER3.C

```
#include <stdio.h>

int main()
{
    printf("Sigmund will be 75 in the year %d.\n",1952+75);
    return(0);
}
```

The text string can vary, but the answer should still be 2027.

Exercise 1.4.2

CREAM3.C

```
#include <stdio.h>

int main()
{
    printf("The new crematorium is %f miles further
    away.\n",19.2-13.5);
    return(0);
}
```

Exercise 1.4.3

WEIGHT.C

```
#include <stdio.h>

int main()
{
    int weight;

    weight = 210;              /* put your weight here */
    weight = weight - 20;
    printf("You weigh %d? That's not what your driver's
    license says!\n",weight);
    return(0);
}
```

Exercise 1.4.4

MOON3.C

```
#include <stdio.h>

int main()
```

```
{
    float duration,days;
    float distance = 378921.46;
    float speed = 140;

    duration =  distance / speed;
    days = duration / 24;

    printf("The moon is %f km away.\n",distance);
    printf("Traveling at %f kph, ",speed);
    printf("it would take %f hours to drive to the
moon.\n",duration);
    printf("That's %f days.\n",days);
    return(0);
}
```

This is only one of many possible solutions. As long as the output says that it takes 112 (plus change) days, you got it correct.

Exercise 1.5.1

SPONSOR1.C
```
#include <stdio.h>

int main()
{
    printf("This program is sponsored by the letter
'%c'\n",'P');
    return(0);
}
```

**Book VII
Appendix C**

**Answers to
Exercises**

Single quotes are simply added into printf()'s formatting string, as shown here; one tick is put on each side of the %c placeholder.

Exercise 1.5.2

OZ1.C
```
#include <stdio.h>

int main()
{
    char oz = 'O';

    printf("This book covers subjects from %c",oz);
    oz = 'Z';
    printf(" to %c.\n",oz);
    return(0);
}
```

Exercise 1.5.3

The AGE.C program may have been modified, so showing the exact source code here would be tough. Instead, the only modification needed to the program is in Line 5:

```
char age;
```

Replacing int with char turns the trick.

This works because most people are younger than the maximum value that can be stored in a char variable, 128. If you know anyone older than that, first contact *The Guinness Book of World Records,* and then use an int variable instead.

Exercise 1.5.4

YOUARE1.C

```
#include <stdio.h>

int main()
{
    char firstname[20];
    char lastname[20];

    printf("What is your first name?");
    gets(firstname);
    printf("What is your last name?");
    gets(lastname);
    printf("Pleased to meet you, %s
%s!\n",firstname,lastname);
    return(0);
}
```

Be sure to specify %s twice in the printf() statement; it's hard to see in this exercise because the line wraps.

Exercise 1.5.5

YOURDATA1.C

```
#include <stdio.h>
#include <stdlib.h>

int main()
{
    char input[20];
    int age;
```

```
    float height;

    printf("Enter your age in years:");
    age = atoi(gets(input));

    printf("Enter your height in inches:");
    height = atof(gets(input));

    printf("You are %d years old\n",age);
    printf("and %f inches tall.\n",height);
    return(0);
}
```

Exercise 1.5.6

YOURDATA2.C

```
#include <stdio.h>
#include <stdlib.h>

int main()
{
    char input[20];
    int age;
    float height;

    printf("Enter your age in years:");
    age = atoi(gets(input));
    age = age * 12;

    printf("Enter your height in inches:");
    height = atof(gets(input));
    height = height * 2.2;

    printf("You are %d months old\n",age);
    printf("and %f centimeters tall.\n",height);
    return(0);
}
```

Don't forget to change the text in the final two `printf()` statements to reflect the new values that are computed!

Exercise 1.5.7

YOURDATA3.C

```
#include <stdio.h>

int main()
{
```

```
char input[20];
int age;
float height;

printf("Enter your age in years:");
scanf("%d",&age);
age = age * 12;

printf("Enter your height in inches:");
scanf("%f",&height);
height = height * 2.2;

printf("You are %d months old\n",age);
printf("and %f centimeters tall.\n",height);
return(0);
}
```

Did you remember to remove the #include <stdlib.h> line? You don't
need it any more! And, if you forgot the ampersands in the scanf() statements, did your computer crash?

Exercise 1.6.1

MYFAV1.C

```
#include <stdio.h>

int main()
{
    int fav;

    printf("Enter your favorite number, 1 thru 10:");
    scanf("%d",&fav);
    if(fav == 7)
    {
        printf("That's my favorite number, too!");
    }
    return(0);
}
```

If you goofed, you probably put the number between single quotes rather
than specify an immediate value (shown as 7 here). You could have also
used gets() to read the input and then atoi() to convert it.

Exercise 1.6.2

RETIRE1.C

Change Line 9 to read

```
if(age >= 65)
```

Exercise 1.6.3

RETIRE2.C

```
int main()
{
    int age;

    printf("How old are you?");
    scanf("%d",&age);
    if(age >= 65)
    {
        printf("You're %d years old.\n",age);
        printf("How's your retirement?\n");
    }
    else
    {
        printf("You're %d years old.\n",age);
        printf("You have to keep on working!\n");
    }
    return(0);
}
```

The two printf() statements belonging to else can be anything in your code. The point is to add the else below if's statements and then use curly braces to contain the statements belonging to else.

Exercise 1.6.4

CHILLY4.C

```
#include <stdio.h>

int main()
{
    float temp;

    printf("What is the temperature outside?");
    scanf("%f",&temp);
    if(temp < 65)
    {
        printf("My but it's a bit chilly out!\n");
    }
    else if(temp >= 80)
    {
        printf("My but it's hot out!\n");
    }
    else if(temp == 72)
    {
        printf("It's perfect out!\n");
    }
```

```
    else
    {
        printf("My how pleasant!\n");
    }
    return(0);
}
```

Exercise 1.7.1

TICK1.C

```
#include <stdio.h>

int main()
{
    int tick;

    printf("Variable tick is uninitialized.\n");
    for(tick=1;tick<11;tick=tick+1)
    {
        printf("\tIn the loop, tick = %d\n",tick);
    }
    printf("After the loop, tick = %d\n",tick);
    return(0);
}
```

Basically, you just change Line 8. The value of tick starts at one, but to loop 10 times, you must use tick<11. You could also use this for statement:

```
for(tick=1;tick<=10;tick=tick+1)
```

Give yourself an extra point if you thought of that!

Exercise 1.7.2

BLASTOFF.C

```
#include <stdio.h>

int main()
{
    int countdown;

    for(countdown=10;countdown>0;countdown=countdown-1)
    {
        printf("%d\n",countdown);
    }
    printf("%d, Blastoff!\n",countdown);
    return(0);
}
```

Exercise 1.7.3

ENDLESS1.C

You need only fix Line 8 so that it reads properly:

```
for(packet=0;packet<1000;packet=packet+1)
```

Replace the = sign with <.

Exercise 1.7.4

ENDLESS2.C

This is a tricky one, but it's a trick that's good to know. Because the project manager is concerned only with the output, you need only modify the statement that produces the output. In this case, it's the printf() statement in Line 10 that needs to be changed:

```
printf("Doing amazing things with packet#%d\n",packet+1);
```

The value of the packet variable *is not* changed in the preceding statement. However, by adding the immediate value 1 to packet, the printf() statement displays numbers one greater than the values used internally by the program. This technique tweaks the output the way the project manager wants without extensively overhauling your code. Remember this trick!

Book VII
Appendix C

Exercise 1.7.5

TICK2.C

```c
#include <stdio.h>

int main()
{
    int tick;

    printf("Variable tick is uninitialized.\n");
    for(tick=0;tick<=10;tick=tick+1)
    {
        printf("\tIn the loop, tick = %d\n",tick);
        if(tick>5) break;
    }
    printf("After the loop, tick = %d\n",tick);
    return(0);
}
```

Answers to
Exercises

Note that the loop repeats six times before it stops. That's because the value of `tick` must be *greater than* 5. So, whenever `tick` equals 6, it's greater than 5, and the loop stops with the `break` statement.

Exercise 1.7.6

NAMES1.C

```c
#include <stdio.h>

int main()
{
    char a,b,c,d,e;

    for(a='A';a<='Z';a=a+1)
        for(b='A';b<='Z';b=b+1)
            for(c='A';c<='Z';c=c+1)
                for(d='A';d<='Z';d=d+1)
                    for(e='A';e<='Z';e=e+1)
                        printf("%c%c%c%c%c\t",a,b,c,d,e);
    return(0);
}
```

This program creates 11,881,376 permutations. It took more than six minutes to run on my Pentium III test computer. (And the stars still didn't wink out!)

Exercise 1.8.1

TICKETS1.C

```c
#include <stdio.h>

int main()
{
    int total,fine,speeding;
    int speedlimit,rate,first_ticket,second_ticket,
    third_ticket;

    speedlimit = 55;
    rate = 15;
    first_ticket = 85;
    second_ticket = 95;
    third_ticket = 100;

    puts("Speeding Tickets\n");

/* first ticket */
```

```
    speeding = first_ticket - speedlimit;
    fine = speeding * rate;
    total = total + fine;
    printf("For going %d in a %d zone: $%d\n",
    first_ticket,speedlimit,fine);

/* second ticket */

    speeding = second_ticket - speedlimit;
    fine = speeding * rate;
    total = total + fine;
    printf("For going %d in a %d zone: $%d\n",
    second_ticket,speedlimit,fine);

/* third ticket */
    speeding = third_ticket - speedlimit;
    fine = speeding * rate;
    total = total + fine;
    printf("For going %d in a %d zone: $%d\n",
    third_ticket,speedlimit,fine);

/* Display total */

    printf("\nTotal in fines: $%d\n",total);
    return(0);
}
```

Did you remember to replace the values in the `printf()` statements? That's also part of the deal, and it's necessary if you want to exploit the full power of constants in your program.

Exercise 1.8.2

TICKETS3.C

Thanks to the power of constants, you have only three changes to make to alter the entire program, to Lines 3, 4, and 7:

```
#define SPEEDLIMIT 65
#define RATE 26

#define THIRD_TICKET 110
```

Despite the higher speed limit, the high rate makes the total fine much greater! Better mind that speedometer!

Exercise 1.8.3

MOON4.C

```
#include <stdio.h>

#define DISTANCE 378921.46
#define SPEED 140

int main()
{
    float duration,days;

    duration =  DISTANCE / SPEED;
    days = duration / 24;

    printf("The moon is %f km away.\n",DISTANCE);
    printf("Traveling at %f kph, ",SPEED);
    printf("it would take %f hours to drive to the
moon.\n",duration);
    printf("That's %f days.\n",days);
    return(0);
}
```

Note that you don't need to define DISTANCE as a floating-point number. Remember that it's not a variable — it's a constant. You can have immediate floating-point values, which is how the constant DISTANCE is treated.

Exercise 1.9.1

ANSWER1.C

```
#include <stdio.h>

int main()
{
    int answer;

    answer = 7 + 8 - 3 * 4 / 2;
    printf("The answer is %d\n",answer);
    return(0);
}
```

Exercise 1.9.2

ANSWER2.C

The only line that needs to be modified is Line 7. Here's a solution:

```
answer = (4 + 5 - 2) * (6 / 3);
```

Exercise 1.9.3

B1GEARS2.C
Only Line 7 needs to be changed, as in

```
for(c=0;c<100;c++)
```

Exercise 1.9.4

BLASTOFF1.C
Only Line 7 needs to be changed:

```
for(countdown=10;countdown>0;countdown--)
```

Exercise 1.9.5

PREPOST2.C
You want to make this modification to Line 8:

```
beta = alpha--;
```

Exercise 1.9.6

AGE3.C
```
#include <stdio.h>

int main()
{
    int age;

    printf("Enter your age in years:");
    scanf("%d",&age);
    printf("You are %d years old.\n",age);
    age += 25;
    if(age>100)
    {
        printf("In 25 years you'll probably be dead!\n");
    }
    else
    {
        printf("In 25 years you'll be %d years old!\n",age);
    }
    return(0);
}
```

Exercise 1.10.1

TYPING2.C
Modify Line 12 to read

```
if(ch=='~' || ch=='`')
```

And. you may also think about changing Line 8:

```
puts("Type away; press '~' or '`' to quit:");
```

Exercise 1.10.2

CHILLY5.C
```
#include <stdio.h>

int main()
{
    float temp;

    printf("What is the temperature outside?");
    scanf("%f",&temp);
    if(temp >= 68 && temp <= 75)
    {
        printf("My how pleasant!\n");
    }
    else
    {
        printf("The temperature could be better.\n");
    }
    return(0);
}
```

Book 11: Middle C

Exercise 2.1.1

IQ1.C
The modification includes two if statements to be added after Line 16 in the original code. Here's a possible snippet:

```
iq = number/first;
if(iq<50)
    iq+=100;
```

```
if(iq>50 && iq<=80)
    iq*=2;
/* Rest of the program continues here: */
printf("This computer guesses your IQ to be %f.\n",iq);
```

You need *two* if statements, not one and an else if. The first if checks to see whether the value of iq is less than 50. If so, the variable iq is increased by 100. Give yourself a bonus point if you used iq+=100 rather than iq=iq+100.

The second if statement uses a logical AND to compare two conditions: when the value of iq is greater than 50 *and* less than or equal to 80. If the value of iq falls within that range, it's doubled. Again, give yourself a bonus point if you wrote iq*=2 rather than iq=iq*2 or iq=iq+iq.

Exercise 2.1.2

MONOPOLY2.C

Either it runs or it doesn't. If you're using GCC, as this book recommends, the ints should be long by default.

Exercise 2.1.3

MOONM.C

```
#include <stdio.h>

#define DISTANCE 378921.46       /* in kilometers */
#define PI 3.141
#define MILES 0.621371195

int main()
{
    float orbit;

    orbit = DISTANCE * 2 * PI * MILES;
    printf("The moon travels %f miles in one orbit.\n",
    orbit);
    return(0);
}
```

I've defined MILES as a constant in Line 5, representing the number of miles in a kilometer. This value is multiplied with the other values in Line 11. Line 12 is also changed to reflect the result. Here's what I got:

```
The moon travels 1479102.375000 miles in one orbit.
```

Exercise 2.1.4

MOON2.C

On my computer, the answer appears like this:

```
The moon travels 2380833.750047 km in one orbit.
```

Exercise 2.1.5

CHUCK.C

Here's one possible solution:

```c
#include <stdio.h>

#define START 65
#define END 90

int main()
{
    long int humongous;
    char chuck;

    for(humongous=START;humongous<=END;humongous++)
    {
        chuck = (char)humongous;
        putchar(chuck);
    }
    putchar('\n');          /* for the end of the line display */
    return(0);
}
```

The extra `putchar('\n')` is added for display purposes only.

(The program works correctly without the typecasting in Line 13, though not every program in C is as lucky.)

Exercise 2.2.1

BASES3.C

You need only modify Line 11 as follows:

```c
    printf("I must deliver 0x%X pods to 0x%X locations.\n",
PODS, LOCATIONS);
```

Exercise 2.2.2

AGEHEX.C

Anything along these lines is correct:

```c
#include <stdio.h>

int main()
{
    int age;

    printf("Enter your age in years:");
    scanf("%d",&age);
    printf("You are %X hexadecimal years old!\n",age);
    return(0);
}
```

Note that I didn't prefix 0x before the value in Line 9 because the output already tells the user that it's a hexadecimal number.

Exercise 2.2.3

BASES5.C

```c
#include <stdio.h>

#define PODS 50
#define LOCATIONS 0xBA3C

int main()
{
    puts("Base 10:");
    printf("I must deliver %d pods to %d locations.\n",PODS,
    LOCATIONS);
    puts("Base 16:");
    printf("I must deliver 0x%X pods to 0x%X locations.\n",
    PODS, LOCATIONS);
    puts("Base 8:");
    printf("I must deliver %o pods to %o locations.\n",PODS,
    LOCATIONS);
    puts("Scientific notation:");
    printf("I must deliver %G pods to %G locations.\n",PODS,
    LOCATIONS);
    return(0);
}
```

Yes, this is the solution. But the output from the new Line 15 is probably not what you expected:

```
I must deliver 1.101168E-309 pods to 1.78006E-307 locations.
```

Return to Chapter 2 to see what's up.

Exercise 2.2.4

CURRENCY2.C

Change the two `printf()` statements in Lines 17 and 18 so that `.3` comes between % and the f:

```
printf("%c%.3f\n",POUNDS,bp);
printf("%c%.3f\n",YEN,jy);
```

Here's the output:

```
Enter the amount in dollars: $450
Currency Conversion
£243.315
¥48055.500
```

Exercise 2.2.5

CURRENCY3.C

Here's the output with `%12.2f`:

```
Enter the amount in dollars: $450
Currency Conversion
£       243.32
¥     48055.50
```

Here's the output with `%5.2f`:

```
Enter the amount in dollars: $450
Currency Conversion
£243.32
¥48055.50
```

The value really depends on the input. For this example, a width value of 9 works best, assuming that the yen result doesn't get too large.

Exercise 2.2.6

TWOS2.C

```
#include <stdio.h>

int main()
{
    int a,b;

    printf("Here is your two's table:\n\n");
    for(a=1,b=2;b<=20;a=a+1,b=b+2)
        printf("2 * %2d = %2d\n",a,b);
    return(0);
}
```

Now the output is all lined up:

```
Here is your two's table:
2 *  1 =  2
2 *  2 =  4
2 *  3 =  6
2 *  4 =  8
2 *  5 = 10
2 *  6 = 12
2 *  7 = 14
2 *  8 = 16
2 *  9 = 18
2 * 10 = 20
```

Exercise 2.3.1

SQRT21.C

Non-integer values in C have decimal points in them:

```
sqroot2 = sqrt(2.0);
```

Exercise 2.3.2

SQRT22.C

Modify Lines 8 and 9 to read

```
sqroot2 = sqrt(3.0);
printf("The square root of 3 is %f.\n",sqroot2);
```

Book VII
Appendix C

Answers to
Exercises

You could have also changed the name of sqroot2 to sqroot3. If so, give yourself a bonus point.

```
The square root of 3 is 1.732051
```

Exercise 2.3.3

WHATEVER.C

```c
#include <stdio.h>
#include <math.h>

int main()
{
    double answer;

    answer = pow(5.0,399.0);
    printf("5 to the 399th power is %G\n",answer);
    return(0);
}
```

Tell me that you chose to use %G to display the value. If not, please read Chapter 2 in Book II and do the program again. Here's the answer:

```
5 to the 399th power is 7.74518E+278
```

Exercise 2.3.4

FIVE.C

```c
#include <stdio.h>
#include <math.h>

int main()
{
    double s,p;

    s = sqrt(5.0);
    p = pow(5.0,0.5);          /* 0.5 is one half */
    printf("The square root of 5 is %f\n",s);
    printf("5 to the 1/2 power is %f\n",p);
    return(0);
}
```

Of course, the two values that are displayed are equal.

Exercise 2.3.5

CUBE31.C

The cube root is any value raised to the 1/3 power. Modify Line 8 of the source code to read

```
cube = pow(2.0,(double)1/3);
```

I've used immediate integer values to calculate 1/3 and then typecast that result as a double for the pow( ) function.

Exercise 2.3.6

DEG2RAD.C

```
/* convert degrees to radians */

#include <stdio.h>

#define RAD 57.2957795

int main()
{
    float degrees,radians;

    puts("Convert degrees to radians");
    printf("Enter a value in degrees: ");
    scanf("%f",&degrees);

    radians = degrees/RAD;

    printf("%.3f degrees is %.5f radians.\n",
    degrees,radians);
    return(0);
}
```

Book VII
Appendix C

Answers to
Exercises

Exercise 2.3.7

ROOT1.C

Remember that C works from the inside out:

```
root = sqrt((double)abs(value));
```

First, the result of abs(value) is computed. Then that value is typecast as a double. Finally, the sqrt( ) function operates on that value, sending the result into the root variable.

Exercise 2.3.8

ROOT2.C

```c
#include <stdio.h>
#include <math.h>

int main()
{
    int value;
    double root;

    printf("Enter a value: ");
    scanf("%d",&value);
    if(value<0)
    {
        puts("I cannot compute the root of a negative
number.");
    }
    else
    {
        root = sqrt((double)value);
        printf("The square root of %d is %f.\n",value,root);
    }
    return(0);
}
```

Without the `abs()` function, you don't need to include the STDLIB.H library.

Exercise 2.4.1

RAND100.C

```c
#include <stdio.h>
#include <stdlib.h>

int main()
{
    long int hat;
    int loop;

    for(loop=0;loop<100;loop++)
    {
        hat = random();
        printf("%10d\t",hat);
    }
    return(0);
}
```

Give yourself a bonus if you right-justified the numbers by using `%10d`; if you used the `rand()` function instead, right-justify them with `%6d`.

Exercise 2.4.2

RAND100D.C

This is a +1 solution you can apply in two ways. The first and easiest is simply to change the `printf()` statement :

```
printf("%d\t",hat+1);
```

Because only the *display* needs to be changed, this fix works; 1 is added to the value of `hat`, and then that result is displayed. The original value of `hat` is unchanged, so it could be used elsewhere.

You can also just modify the value of `hat`, by adding this statement before `printf()`:

```
hat = hat + 1;
```

I prefer this method over `hat++` because the issue is adding, not incrementing, 1. That way, if the program needs to be fixed later, you can more easily find out where +1 was added; ++ may be overlooked.

Exercise 2.4.3

DICE1.C

```
#include <stdio.h>
#include <stdlib.h>
#include <time.h>

int main()
{
    int d1,d2,total,loop;

    srandom((unsigned)time(NULL));

    for(loop=1;loop<=16;loop++)
    {
        d1 = random() % 6 + 1;
        d2 = random() % 6 + 1;
        total = d1 + d2;
        printf("You rolled %d and %d: Total %d\n",
    d1,d2,total);
    }
    return(0);
}
```

Note that you don't need to reseed the randomizer with `srandom()` for each turn of the loop. The randomizer needs to be seeded only once.

Exercise 2.5.1

WHILE100.C

This is one way to do it:

```c
#include <stdio.h>

int main()
{
    int a = 1;

    while(a<=100)
    {
        printf("%3d\t",a);
        a++;
    }
    return(0);
}
```

Bonus points for you if you used %3d to format the output!

Exercise 2.5.2

BABELON1.C

You need to change only Lines 21 and 22:

```c
alpha = 'a' + (char)r;
if(alpha=='q') done=TRUE;
```

Line 7 need not be changed because the value of 'Z' - 'A' is identical to the value of 'z' - 'a'.

Exercise 2.5.3

GUESS1.C

This is one of many possible solutions:

```c
#include <stdio.h>
#include <stdlib.h>
#include <time.h>

#define RANGE 100
#define GUESSES 5

int main()
{
    int guess,number,turn;
```

```
    srandom((unsigned)time(NULL));

    puts("Guessing Game!");

    number=random() % RANGE + 1;  /* value from 1 to RANGE */

    printf("I'm thinking of a number from 1 to %d.\n",RANGE);
    printf("Can you guess what it is in less than %d
guesses?\n",GUESSES+1);

    turn=0;
    while(turn < GUESSES)
    {
        printf("Enter guess $%d: ",turn+1);
        scanf("%d",&guess);
        if(guess == number)
        {
            puts("You got it!");
            break;
        }
        else if(guess < number)
            puts("Too low!");
        else
            puts("Too high!");
        turn++;
    }
    printf("The number was %d\n",number);
    return(0);
}
```

Exercise 2.5.4

The line to delete should be obvious: It's Line 11, containing the `continue`
command. The single character to change is an = to a ! in Line 10:

```
if(count%5 != 0)
```

Exercise 2.6.1

Here's just one example of how you can do it. As long as your program uses
a switch case loop and it works, you've passed this exercise.

```
#include <stdio.h>

int main()
{
    char party;

    printf("Which is your political party?\n");
```

```
        printf("D, I, R or something else: ");
        scanf("%c",&party);

        switch(party)
        {
            case 'd':
            case 'D':
                puts("Democratic. ");
                break;
            case 'i':
            case 'I':
                puts("Independent ");
                break;
            case 'r':
            case 'R':
                puts("Republican");
                break;
            default:
                puts("Something else");
        }
        return(0);
}
```

The biggest mistake made here is forgetting to put the single quote ticks around the immediate characters used by `case`.

Exercise 2.7.1

OHNO1.C

```
#include <stdio.h>

int main()
{
    int naughty;

    for(naughty=0;naughty<10;naughty++)
        puts("Naughty, naughty");
    return(0);
}
```

Book III: Above C Level

Exercise 3.1.1

1Q.C

Here's one possible solution:

```
#include <stdio.h>

int main()
{
    float iq[] = { 20.0, 55.6, 100.3, 119.8, 27.1 };
    int worker;

    puts("My Co-Worker's Iqs:");
    for(worker=0;worker<5;worker++)
    {
        printf("Worker #%d, %5.1f\n",worker+1,iq[worker]);
    }
    return(0);
}
```

Give yourself a bonus point if you formatted the floating-point output, as shown here (in Line 11).

Remember that immediate floating-point values should have a decimal place in them.

Exercise 3.1.2

TEMPS.C

Here's just one possible solution:

```
#include <stdio.h>

#define COUNT 5

int main()
{
    float temps[COUNT];
    float total,average;
    int c;

/* initialize the array */

    for(c=0;c<COUNT;c++)
    {
        printf("Input the temperature for day %d: ",c+1);
        scanf("%f",&temps[c]);
    }

/* display the array */

    total = 0.0;
    printf("Temperatures for the page %d days:\n",COUNT);
```

```
        for(c=0;c<COUNT;c++)
        {
            printf("Day %d, %5.1f\n",c+1,temps[c]);
            total += temps[c];
        }

        average = total/(float)COUNT;
        printf("The average temperature was %5.1f\n",average);
        return(0);
    }
```

Bonus points and kudos to you if you included all the junk that I did in this program. If not, try again!

Exercise 3.1.3

SORTME1.C
Change the > in Line 19 to <.

Exercise 3.2.1

GREETINGS1.C

```
#include <stdio.h>

int main()
{
    char prompt[] = "Please enter your first name:";
    char gratis[] = "Thanks!";
    char first[25];
    char last[25];

    printf(prompt);
    gets(first);
    printf("Please enter your last name:");
    scanf("%s",&last);
    puts(gratis);
    printf("Pleased to meet you, %s %s!\n",first,last);
    return(0);
}
```

You can also choose to have the `Please enter your last name:` prompt be a string variable rather than an immediate constant. But your `scanf()` and final `printf()` statements should look like the ones in this exercise.

Exercise 3.2.2

SUSHI3.C

```
include <stdio.h>

int main()
{
    char phrase[] = "sushi is mooshi";
    char ch;
    int x = 0;

    puts(phrase);
    while(ch = phrase[x])
    {
        if(ch == ' ')
            phrase[x] = '-';
        x++;
    }
    puts(phrase);
    return(0);
}
```

Exercise 3.2.3

BOOBOO1B.C

```
#include <stdio.h>

int main()
{
    char yours[25];
    char mine[25];
    int x = 0;

    printf("What is your name?");
    gets(yours);
    while(mine[x] = yours[x])
        x++;
    printf("My name is %s just like your name is %s!\n",
    mine,yours);
    return(0);
}
```

Did you remember to remove the #include <string.h>?

Exercise 3.2.4

PASSWORD1.C

```
#include <stdio.h>
#include <string.h>

int main()
{
    char string[16];
    char password[] = "please";

    printf("Enter your secret password:");
    gets(string);

    if(!strcmp(string,password))
        puts("Entry granted!");
    else
        puts ("Sorry. Wrong password.");
return(0);
}
```

If you don't put the ! (not) before the strcmp() function, you have to switch the puts() statements between if and else. That's okay, but the format in this exercise reads more logically.

Exercise 3.2.5

NAMES1.C

It's not as bad as you think! Just change the order of the two for statements:

```
for(b=0;b<3;b++)
    for(a=0;a<4;a++)
```

Exercise 3.3.1

WASTEOFTIME.C

```
#include <stdio.h>
#include <ctype.h>

int main()
{
    char input[128];
    int x,numbers;

    x = numbers = 0;
```

```
    printf("Enter your street address:");
    gets(input);

/* scan the text */
    while(input[x])
    {
        if(isdigit(input[x]))
            numbers++;
        x++;
    }
    printf("Your address has %d numbers in it.\n",numbers);
    return(0);
}
```

The key is to use the isdigit() CTYPE function, as shown in Line 17 in this exercise.

Exercise 3.3.2

STRIPPER.C

You have a number of ways to do this. Here's just one:

```
#include <stdio.h>
#include <ctype.h>

int main()
{
    char input[128];
    int x = 0;

    puts("Enter some text:");
    gets(input);

    while(input[x])
    {
        if(isalnum(input[x]))
            input[x] = tolower(input[x]);
        else
            input[x] = '*';
        x++;
    }
    puts(input);
    return(0);
}
```

I chose to use the `isalnum()` function, which is TRUE whenever a letter or a number is encountered, but FALSE for spaces and punctuation. Other functions can work in there as well. As long as your program can take a string like this:

```
This is just Some Sample Text! Here!
```

and produce results like this:

```
this*is*just*some*sample*text**here*
```

consider the exercise passed.

Exercise 3.4.1

Note that Margaret Hamilton's name changes the size of things somewhat. Be sure to make all the changes noted. First, change the `define` to allow for the longer name:

```
#define LINE_LENGTH 40
```

Next, modify the data so that it reads:

```
char actor[6][18] = {
    "Judy Garland",
    "Ray Bolger",
    "Bert Lahr",
    "Jack Haley",
    "Margaret Hamilton",
    "Frank Morgan"
};
int age[6] = { 17, 35, 44, 40, 37, 49 };
char roll[6][16] = {
    "Dorothy",
    "Scarecrow",
    "Cowardly Lion",
    "Tin Woodsman",
    "Wicked Witch",
    "The Wizard"
};
```

Make this change in the table heading to accommodate Margaret:

```
printf("%-18s %3s   %-15s\n","Actor","Age","Roll");
```

And, remember to change the `for` loop as well:

```
for(x=0;x<6;x++)
    printf("%-18s %3d   %-15s\n", actor[x],age[x],roll[x]);
```

Exercise 3.4.2

MYSTUFF2.C

```c
#include <stdio.h>

int main()
{
    char input[10];

    struct stuff
    {
        char letter;
        int number;
    } my, his, her;

/* Here is his info */

    his.letter = 'Y';
    his.number = 199;

/* Here is her info */

    his.letter = 'A';
    his.number = 21;

    puts("Your Own Stuff");

    printf("Enter your favorite letter: ");
    my.letter = getchar();

    printf("Enter your favorite number: ");
    scanf("%d",&my.number);

    printf("Your favorite letter is %c\n",my.letter);
    printf("and your favorite number is %d.\n",my.number);
    printf("His favorite letter is %c\n",his.letter);
    printf("and his favorite number is %d.\n",his.number);
    printf("Her favorite letter is %c\n",her.letter);
    printf("and her favorite number is %d.\n",her.number);
    return(0);
}
```

Exercise 3.4.3

OZ7.C

Shame on you if you peeked without attempting this problem on your own!

```c
#include <stdio.h>

#define LINE_LENGTH 40
```

```
int main()
{
    struct oz {
        char actor[18];
        int age;
        char roll[16];
        };

    struct oz cast[6] = {
        "Judy Garland", 17, "Dorothy",
        "Ray Bolger", 35, "Scarecrow",
        "Bert Lahr", 44, "Cowardly Lion",
        "Jack Haley", 40, "Tin Woodsman",
        "Margaret Hamilton", 37, "Wicked Witch",
        "Frank Morgan", 49, "The Wizard"
        };
    struct oz temp;
    int line,x,a,b;

/* Sort the list by age*/
    for(a=0;a<6-1;a++)
        for(b=a+1;b<6;b++)
            if(cast[a].age > cast[b].age)
            {
                temp = cast[a];
                cast[a] = cast[b];
                cast[b] = temp;
            }

    puts("Wizard of Oz Database!");

/* draw the table heading */
    printf("%-18s %3s    %-15s\n","Actor","Age","Roll");
    for(line=0;line<LINE_LENGTH;line++) putchar('-');
    putchar('\n');

/* display the data */
    for(x=0;x<6;x++)
        printf("%-18s %3d    %-15s\n",
            cast[x].actor,\
            cast[x].age,\
            cast[x].roll);
    return(0);
}
```

Exercise 3.5.1

SECNUM1.C

```
#include <stdio.h>
#include <stdlib.h>
#include <time.h>
```

```
void separator(void);

int main()
{
    srandom((unsigned)time(NULL));

    puts("Here are today's secret number values:");
    separator();
    separator();
    separator();
    return(0);
}

void separator(void)
{
    int x;
    long int r;

    for(x=0;x<10;x++)
        putchar('*');
    putchar('\n');
    r = random();
    printf("%d\n",r);
}
```

(The whole thing can be done with copy and paste.)

Exercise 3.5.2

LINEMOD.C

```
#include <stdio.h>
#include <string.h>

void shout(void);
void showline(void);
void dashes(void);

char line[81];
int linelen;

int main()
{
    puts("Enter a line of text:");
    gets(line);
    linelen = strlen(line);

    puts("Here is the line you entered:");
    showline();
    puts("Here is the line in upper case");
```

**Book VII
Appendix C**

**Answers to
Exercises**

```
        shout();
        return(0);
}

void shout(void)
{
    int x = 0;

    dashes();              /* line above */
    while(line[x])
    {
        putchar(toupper(line[x]));
        x++;
    }
    putchar('\n');
    dashes();              /* line below */
}

void showline(void)
{
    dashes();
    puts(line);
    dashes();
}

void dashes(void)
{
    int x;

    for(x=0;x<linelen;x++)
        putchar('-');
    putchar('\n');
}
```

Did you remember to prototype shout()?

I added the dashes() function above and below the modified output, just as the showline() function does.

The while(line[x]) type of thing is covered in Chapter 2.

toupper() is covered in Book II, Chapter 3.

Exercise 3.5.3

MODLINE1.C

```
#include <stdio.h>
#include <string.h>

void showline(void);
```

```
void dashes(char c);

char line[81];
int linelen;

int main()
{
    puts("Enter a line of text:");
    gets(line);
    linelen = strlen(line);

    puts("Here is the line you entered:");
    showline();
    return(0);
}

void showline(void)
{
    dashes('*');
    puts(line);
    dashes('*');
}

void dashes(char c)
{
    int x;

    for(x=0;x<linelen;x++)
        putchar(c);
    putchar('\n');
}
```

Remember to change the prototype for `dashes()` and to use the character variable (c, in this exercise) in the `puchar()` function inside `dashes()`.

Exercise 3.5.4

ROLLEM.C
Here's what I came up with:

```
#include <stdio.h>
#include <stdlib.h>
#include <time.h>

void line(int length);
int throw(void);

int main()
{
    int dice,x,roll;
```

```
    int total = 0;

/* seed randomizer */

    srandom((unsigned)time(NULL));

/* Game title and prompt */
    puts("R O L L ' E M !");
    do
    {
        printf("How many dice would you like to roll (1 to
12)? ");
        scanf("%i",&dice);
    }
    while(dice < 1 || dice > 12);

    printf("Rolling %d...\nHere they come!\n",dice);

/* process / display */
    for(x=0;x<dice;x++)          /* first row */
        printf(" %2d ",x+1);
    putchar('\n');

    line(dice);                  /* fancy line row */

    for(x=0;x<dice;x++)          /* third row */
    {
        roll = throw();
        total += roll;
        printf("| %d ",roll);
    }
    printf("|\n");

    line(dice);                  /* fancy line row last */

    printf("Total = %d\n",total);

    return(0);
}

int throw(void)
{
    int die;

    die = random() % 6 + 1;
    return(die);
}

void line(int length)
{
    int x;
```

```
    for(x=0;x<length;x++)
        printf("+---");
    printf("+\n");
}
```

Exercise 3.6.1

MODLINE2.C

```
#include <stdio.h>
#include <string.h>

void showline(void);
void dashes(char c);

char line[81];
int linelen;

int main()
{
    puts("Enter a line of text:");
    gets(line);
    linelen = strlen(line);

    puts("Here is the line you entered:");
    showline();
    return(0);
}

void showline(void)
{
    dashes(' ');
    puts(line);
    dashes('*');
}

void dashes(char c)
{
    int x;

    if(c == ' ')
    {
        putchar('\n');
        return;
    }
    for(x=0;x<linelen;x++)
        putchar(c);
    putchar('\n');
}
```

Exercise 3.7.1

ENOCH1.C

Here's the output:

```
X = 100
X = 101
X = 102
X = 103
X = 104
X = 105
X = 106
```

Exercise 3.7.2

STATIC2.C

Something like this works for the new request() function:

```
void request(void)
{
    static int i = 0;

    puts("\New Request!");
    printf("\tPrevious request was \"%d\"\n",i);
    printf("\tEnter new request: ");
    scanf("%d",&i);
    fflush(stdin);
    puts("\Thank you!");
}
```

Note the addition of the fflush(stdin) or fpurge(stdin) statement. It's required in order to "eat" the Enter key press after entering the number.

Book IV: Advanced C

Exercise 4.1.1

ODDLITL4.C
Sixty-four bytes! Woo-hoo!

Exercise 4.1.2

ODDLITL6.C
Here's the program's output on my system:

```
Memory location of char variable c = 0022FF87
Memory location of int variable i = 0022FF84
Memory location of long variable x = 0022FF80
Memory location of float variable f = 0022FF7C
Memory location of double variable d = 0022FF70

Memory location of temp[0] = 0022FF58
Memory location of temp[1] = 0022FF5A
Memory location of temp[2] = 0022FF5C
Memory location of temp[3] = 0022FF5E
Memory location of temp[4] = 0022FF60
Memory location of temp[5] = 0022FF62
Memory location of temp[6] = 0022FF64
Memory location of temp[7] = 0022FF66
```

The integer values are now separated by twos. Figure C-1 shows you the memory map:

Exercise 4.1.3

Here are my declarations:

```
char *k;
int *s,*e;
float *sc;
```

As long as you have met the following requirements, your answers are okay:

+ You must declare one chars, two ints, and one float. You don't have to declare both int variables on the same line.

+ Each variable name *must* be prefixed by an asterisk. That creates a pointer variable. Otherwise, you're not creating pointers, but, rather, just regular variables.

+ You can give the pointer variables any name, but the name *cannot* be the same as existing variables. So, if you did this:

    ```
    char *key;
    int *start,*end;
    float *seat_cushion;
    ```

    you were wrong.

+ According to Hungarian notation, you could have done this:

    ```
    char *pcKey;
    int *pnStart,*pnEnd;
    float *pfSeatCushion;
    ```

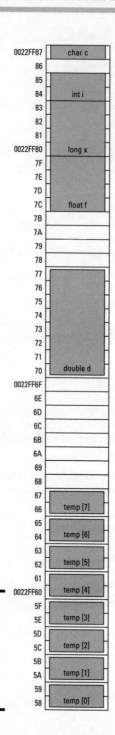

Figure C-1:
Variables
stored in
memory,
short
integer
array.

Exercise 4.1.4

METRIC3.C

Here's what I came up with — 10:15 in the morning and stone-cold sober. I know: That's rare for an author.

```c
#include <stdio.h>

#define KPM 1.609344

int main()
{
    float miles,kilometers;
    float *pmiles,*k_address;

    printf("Enter a value in miles:");
    scanf("%f",&miles);

    kilometers = miles*1.609;

    printf("%.2f miles works out to %.2f kilometers.\n",
    miles,kilometers);

    pmiles = &miles;                    /* initialize pointer */
    k_address = &kilometers;
    printf("Variable 'miles' is %d bytes long at %p
    address\n",sizeof(miles),pmiles);
    printf("Variable 'kilometers' is %d bytes long at %p
    address\n",sizeof(kilometers),k_address);
    return(0);
}
```

Book VII
Appendix C

Answers to
Exercises

Exercise 4.1.5

HELLO2.C

It goes something like this:

```c
#include <stdio.h>

int main()
{
    char array[] = "Hello!\n";
    char *a;
    int x;

    for(x=0;x<sizeof(array);x++)
    {
```

```
        a = &array[x];
        printf("array[%d] at %p = %c\n",x,a,array[x]);
    }
    return(0);
}
```

Here's the output (specific address values vary):

```
array[0] at 0022FF88 = H
array[1] at 0022FF88 = e
array[2] at 0022FF88 = l
array[3] at 0022FF88 = l
array[4] at 0022FF88 = o
array[5] at 0022FF88 = !
array[6] at 0022FF88 =

array[7] at 0022FF88 =
```

Array element 6 is the \n (newline), and array element 7 is the NULL character.

Exercise 4.2.1

TEENY1.C

```
#include <stdio.h>

int main()
{
    float teeny;
    float *t;

/* initialize variables */
    teeny = 1.414213;
    t = &teeny;

/* use and abuse variables */
    printf("Variable teeny = %f\n",teeny);
    printf("Variable t = %p\n",t);
    printf("Variable *t = %f\n",*t);
    return(0);
}
```

Here's some sample output:

```
Variable teeny = 1.414213
Variable t = 0022FF8C
Variable *t = 1.414213
```

Exercise 4.2.2

MOON.C

Here's one way to do it:

```c
#include <stdio.h>

int main()
{
    float duration;
    float distance = 378921.46;
    float speed = 140;
    float *d;

    duration =  distance / speed;

    d = &distance;
    printf("The moon is %f km away.\n",*d);
    d = &speed;
    printf("Traveling at %f kph, ",*d);
    d = &duration;
    printf("it would take %f hours to drive to the
moon.\n",*d);
    return(0);
}
```

Exercise 4.3.1

BEC83D7.C

```c
#include <stdio.h>

int main()
{
    printf("0xBEC83D7 is %d\n",0xBEC83D7);
    return(0);
}
```

The answer is 200,049,623, which is the original value used in the section.

Exercise 4.3.2

SHIFTR1.C

```c
#include <stdio.h>

int main()
{
```

```
    int v,r;

    printf("Enter an integer value: ");
    scanf("%d",&v);
    r = v >> 2;      /* shift bits two notches right */
    printf("%d cut in quarter is %d\n",v,r);
    return(0);
}
```

Try entering even values first, such as 1000 or 6392. And then try 70 or 9.
Remember that integers don't have fractions.

Exercise 4.3.3

Nope. Don't even try it. Because floating-point values are carefully stored
inside a long word (or double long word), shifting them destroys the original
value and yields something unpredictable.

Exercise 4.3.4

X10.C

Although you cannot shift bits left to multiply by 10, you can shift left to multiply by 8 and multiply by 2. Adding those two values then gets you the 10
you were looking for. Here's my method:

```
#include <stdio.h>

int main()
{
    int value,v8,v2,total;

    printf("Enter an integer value: ");
    scanf("%d",&value);

/* First multiply by 8 */
    v8 = value << 3;

/* Next, multiply by 2 */
    v2 = value << 1;

/* Then add the values */
    total = v8 + v2;

    printf("%d * 10 = %d\n",value,total);

    return(0);
}
```

Exercise 4.3.5

SPLIT1.C

```
#include <stdio.h>

int main()
{
    unsigned long int hex,h4,h3,h2,h1;

    printf("Enter an eight-digit hex value: ");
    scanf("%x",&hex);

    h1 = hex & 0x000000FF;
    h2 = hex & 0x0000FF00;
    h3 = hex & 0x00FF0000;
    h4 = hex & 0xFF000000;
    h2 >>= 8;
    h3 >>= 16;
    h4 >>= 24;

    printf("0x%08X is composed of %02X %02X %02X %02X\n",
    hex,h4,h3,h2,h1);

    return(0);
}
```

Exercise 4.3.6

OAR1.C

```
#include <stdio.h>

int main()
{
    int twos =  1;
    int x,r;
    unsigned short int v = 0;

    for(x=0;x<16;x++)
    {
        r = v | twos;
        printf("0x%04X | %5d = 0x%04X\n",v,twos,r);
        twos += twos;
    }
    return(0);
}
```

The statement twos += twos effectively doubles the value of the variable twos each time the for loop is spun.

Exercise 4.4.1

PRIMES.C

Here's the program I came up with:

```c
#include <stdio.h>

int main()
{
    int primes[] = { 2, 3, 5, 7, 11, 13, 17, 19, 23, 29 };
    int x;

    for(x=0;x<10;x++)
    {
        printf("%d\n",primes[x]);
    }
    return(0);
}
```

Exercise 4.4.2

CENT1.C

```c
#include <stdio.h>

int main()
{
    int cent[8];
    int *c;
    int x;

    c = cent;
    for(x=0;x<8;x++)
    {
        *c = (x+1) * 100;
        printf("cent[%d] = %d\n",x,*c);
        c++;
    }
    return(0);
}
```

Did you remember to initialize the pointer? Did you remember to increment the pointer?

Exercise 4.4.3

CENT2.C

Modify the `printf()` line to read

```
printf("cent[%d] = %d\n",x,*c++);
```

Then, remove the line with c++;.

Exercise 4.4.4

PRIMES4.C

This is entirely acceptable, unless you've read ahead or already know the better shortcut:

```
#include <stdio.h>

int main()
{
    int primes[] = { 2, 3, 5, 7, 11, 13, 17, 19, 23, 29 };
    int *p;

    p = primes;

    p++; p++; p++; p++;
    printf("The fifth prime number is %d\n",*p);
    p++; p++;
    printf("and the seventh is %d\n",*p);

    return(0);
}
```

Exercise 4.5.1

GETNAME.C

Here's one possible solution:

```
#include <stdio.h>

int main()
{
    char name[64];
    char *n;

    printf("Enter your name: ");
    gets(name);

    n = name;

    while(putchar(*n++))
        ;
    return(0);
}
```

Exercise 4.6.1

And, here you go:

```
char *prompts[] = {
    "Type something:",
    "C:\>",
    "."
};
```

Exercise 4.6.2

SNOW1.C

Change Line 17 to read

```
printf("%s\n",*(seven+x));
```

Exercise 4.6.3

I said "*Never mind!*"

Exercise 4.6.4

```
*(*(seven+x)+0)
```

Surround the memory location, `*(seven+x)+0`, with parentheses, and then prefix an asterisk. Ta-da!

Exercise 4.6.5

SNOW4.C

```
#include <stdio.h>

int main()
{
    const char *seven[] = {
        "bashful",
        "doc",
        "dopey",
        "grumpy",
        "happy",
        "sneezy",
        "sleepy"
    };
    int x,c;
```

```
    for(x=0;x<7;x++)
    {
        c = 0;
        while(*(*(seven+x)+c))
        {
            putchar(*(*(seven+x)+c));
            c++;
        }
        putchar('\n');
    }
    return(0);
}
```

If you condensed the while loop down to this:

```
while(putchar(*(*(seven+x)+c++)))
    ;
```

give yourself a bonus point!

Exercise 4.6.6

PSORT1.C

```
#include <stdio.h>

#define SIZE 8

int main()
{
    char *names[] = {
        "Mickey",
        "Minnie",
        "Donald",
        "Daisy",
        "Goofy",
        "Chip",
        "Dale",
        "Pluto"
    };
    char *temp;
    int x,a,b;

    for(a=0;a<SIZE-1;a++)
        for(b=a+1;b<SIZE;b++)
        {
            if(**(names+a) > **(names+b))
            {
                temp = *(names+a);
```

```
                        *(names+a) = *(names+b);
                        *(names+b) = temp;
                }
        }

    for(x=0;x<SIZE;x++)
        printf("%s\n",*(names+x));
    return(0);
}
```

Exercise 4.6.7

SORTER1.C

```
#include <stdio.h>

#define SIZE 10

int main()
{
    int input[SIZE];
    int *isort[SIZE];
    int *temp;
    int x,a,b;

/* Get the SIZE number of integers */
    printf("Enter %d numbers:\n",SIZE);
    for(x=0;x<SIZE;x++)
    {
        printf("#%d: ",x+1);
        scanf("%d",&input[x]);
        isort[x] = &input[x];     /* Get address not value */
    }

/* Sort the values via pointers */
    for(a=0;a<SIZE-1;a++)
        for(b=a+1;b<SIZE;b++)
            if(*isort[a] > *isort[b])       /* values! */
                {
                    temp = isort[a];
                    isort[a] = isort[b];
                    isort[b] = temp;
                }

/* print the results */
    printf("Sorted list:\tOriginal list:\n");
    for(x=0;x<SIZE;x++)
        printf("%12d\t%12d\n",*isort[x],input[x]);

    return(0);
}
```

There are differences between strings and values! You must use & and * in the source code with values; when working with strings these things were optional! Most notably: In Line 18, the pointer array is initialized to the *location* of the value in the int array. And, in Line 24, the values are compared, not the locations. If you failed the first time, review the preceding source code and check your mistakes.

Exercise 4.7.1

PUKE1.C

```
#include <stdio.h>

void peasoup(int green);

int main()
{
    int turn;
    int *head;

    head = &turn;

    turn=13;
    peasoup(*head);
    return(0);
}

void peasoup(int green)
{
    while(green--)
        puts("Blech!");
}
```

Exercise 4.7.2

ARRAY2.C

```
printf("Element %d: %d\n",x,*(array+x));
```

If this notation helps further your understanding of how arrays are passed to functions, *bravo!* I find pointer notation better than using array notation inside functions anyway.

Exercise 4.7.3

ARRAY4.C

When you use sizeof(primes), the value that's returned is the number of bytes used by the whole array. In ARRAY.C, it yields the value 24 on modern computers; there are 4 bytes per int and six elements in the array, or 4 × 6 = 24. So, the real solution is to divide that answer by the size of an int:

```
elements = sizeof(primes)/sizeof(int);
```

This result holds true for any computer system and for any type of array. As long as the array name is given and the type of variable is examined, the result is the number of elements in the array.

Here's the proper code:

```
#include <stdio.h>

void showArray(int *array, int size);

int main()
{
    int elements;
    int primes[] = { 2, 3, 5, 7, 11, 13 };

    elements = sizeof(primes)/sizeof(int);
    showArray(primes,6);
    return(0);
}

void showArray(int *array, int size)
{
    int x;

    for(x=0;x<size;x++)
        printf("Element %d: %d\n",x,*(array+x));
}
```

Note that there's no reason to typecast the division (see Line 10) as a float. Because the size of the array is always a multiple of the size of the variable type, no remainder ever appears in the calculation.

Exercise 4.7.4

STRLEN.C

```
#include <stdio.h>

int strlength(char *string);

int main()
{
    char input[64];
```

```
    int len;

    printf("Enter some text: ");
    gets(input);
    len = strlength(input);
    printf("That text is %d characters long.\n",len);
    return(0);
}

int strlength(char *string)
{
    int x = 0;

    while(*string)
    {
        x++;
        string++;
    }
    return(x);
}
```

Exercise 4.7.5

REVERSE.C

I hope that you didn't give up. It was a tougher challenge, you probably thought, but the exercise is a good thinking one. Here's my solution:

```
#include <stdio.h>

char *reverse(char *string);

int main()
{
    char input[64];
    char *backwards;

    printf("Enter some text: ");
    gets(input);
    backwards = reverse(input);
    printf("That would be \"%s\" backwards!\n",backwards);
    return(0);
}

char *reverse(char *string)
{
    static char back[64];
    int len = 0;
    int x;
```

```
/* Get the string's length and set the last/first char */
    while(*string)
    {
        len++;
        string++;
    }

    string--;               /* backup over NULL */

/* Fill the array */
    for(x=0;x<len;x++)
    {
        back[x] = *string;
        string--;
    }
    back[x] = '\0';         /* ending NULL char */
    return(back);
}
```

Exercise 4.8.1

HOWDY2.C

```
#include <stdio.h>
#include <string.h>
#include <stdlib.h>

int main()
{
    char input[64];
    char *string;
    int size;

    printf("Enter some text: ");
    gets(input);
    size = strlen(input) + 1;       /* remember the NULL! */
    string = (char *)malloc(size);
    if(string==NULL)
    {
        puts("Not enough memory");
        return(0);
    }

    strcpy(string,input);
    printf("Original string: %s\nDuplicate: %s\n",
    input,string);
    return(0);
}
```

Exercise 4.8.2

OZ1.C

Here are the code snippets you need to modify:

```
struct cast {
    char actor[18];
    int age;
    char role[16];
};
typedef struct cast OZ;          /* create typedef shortcut OZ */
```

I prefer to keep my `typedef` statements on a line by themselves, which helps avoid confusion. In this exercise, the new variable type `OZ` is created. It's basically a shortcut or alias for the `cast` type of structure:

```
OZ *star;          /* create structure pointer */
```

In this line, the `star` pointer variable is created. It uses the `OZ` typedef, which replaces the `struct cast *star` statement. The `typedef` makes it easier to deal with, especially for the following:

```
star = (OZ *)malloc(sizeof(OZ));
```

This is the niftiest `typedef` shortcut. See how it compares with the original:

```
star = (struct cast *)malloc(sizeof(struct cast));
```

The `typedef` `OZ` not only makes the line shorter, but it's also easier to read.

Exercise 4.9.1

TODAY1.C

Just change Line 10 to read

```
now = time(NULL);
```

The program's output is the same (or is unaffected).

Exercise 4.9.2

WEEKDAY1.C

Just testing to see whether you're awake. This part of the code is the only part that needs to be changed:

```
char *wdays[] = {
    "Sun",
    "Mon",
    "Tue",
    "Wed",
    "Thu",
    "Fri",
    "Sat"
};
```

Exercise 4.9.3

TTIME1.C

```
#include <stdio.h>
#include <time.h>

int main()
{
    struct tm *t;
    time_t now;
    int hour,min,sec;
    char ap;

    time(&now);             /* get the current time */
    t = localtime(&now);    /* get the tm structure */

/* fill variables with time values */
    hour = t->tm_hour;
    min = t->tm_min;
    sec = t->tm_sec;

/* convert 12/24 time format */
    if(hour > 12)
    {
        hour -= 12;         /* subtract 12 from hour */
        ap = 'P';           /* PM */
    }
    else
        ap = 'A';           /* AM */

    printf("It is now %d:%02d:%02d %cM\n",
```

```
        hour,
        min,
        sec,
        ap);
    return(0);
}
```

Obviously, you can handle the AM/PM notation in other ways than what I've done. My solution is based on my years of assembly language programming, which taught me to be byte-clever. If you had another solution, that's okay — as long as the output works.

Exercise 4.9.4

DDATE.C

I'll bet that you had more trouble with the year than anything else. Here's my solution. I hope that it doesn't cause a lot of hair-pulling:

```
#include <stdio.h>
#include <time.h>

int main()
{
    struct tm *t;
    time_t now;

    time(&now);               /* get the current time */
    t = localtime(&now);      /* get the tm structure */
    printf("%d/%d/%02d\n",
        t->tm_mon + 1,
        t->tm_mday,
        t->tm_year % 100);
    return(0);
}
```

Note that you have to add 1 to the month value (t->tm_mon in Line 12) because the month values start with 0 for January.

Exercise 4.10.1

GAMMA.C
Here's one way to do it:

```
#include <stdio.h>

void c(void)
```

```
{
    int x = 5;
    while(x--)
        puts("I'm having fun now");
}
```

Also, you need to modify ALPHA.C to call the c() function:

```
#include <stdio.h>

int main()
{
    printf("Hello ");
    b();
    c();
    return(0);
}
```

Here's the command to glue them all into one program:

```
gcc alpha.c beta.c gamma.c
```

Exercise 4.10.2

GAMMA.C
```
#include <stdio.h>

void c(int count)
{
    while(count--)
        puts("I'm having fun now");
}
```

And the modification to ALPHA:

c(5);

Book V: Disk Drive C

Exercise 5.1.1

UNDERLINE.C
```
#include <stdio.h>

int main()
{
    char ch;
```

```
    while( (ch = fgetc(stdin)) != EOF)
    {
        if(ch == ' ')
            ch = '_';
        fputc(ch,stdout);
    }
    return(0);
}
```

Exercise 5.1.2

CAPS.C

Here's one way to do it:

```
#include <stdio.h>
#include <ctype.h>

int main()
{
    char ch;

    while( (ch = fgetc(stdin)) != EOF)
    {
        if(isalpha(ch))
            ch = toupper(ch);
        fputc(ch,stdout);
    }
    return(0);
}
```

Exercise 5.2.1

REQUIRED1.C

```
#include <stdio.h>

int main(int argc, char *argv[])
{
/* check for proper number of arguments */
    if(argc == 1)
    {
        puts("This program requires you to type");
        puts("some text after the program name.");
        return(1);
    }
    if(argc > 2)
    {
        puts("This program requires only one option.");
        puts("The extra options will be ignored.");
```

```
    }

/* Program continues here */
    printf("I shall now work on the \"%s\"
    option.\n",argv[1]);
    return(0);
}
```

Note that this solution warns the user, but continues processing. You could have also answered correctly by modifying Line 6 to read

```
if(argc != 2)
```

and then adjusting the error message to explain why the program is quitting.

Exercise 5.2.2

REQUIRED2.C

Here's one way to do it:

```
#include <stdio.h>

int main(int argc, char *argv[])
{
/* check for proper number of arguments */
    if(argc != 3 )
    {
        if(argc == 1)
            puts("ERROR: No options detected!");
        if(argc == 2)
            puts("ERROR: Too few options!");
        if(argc > 3)
            puts("ERROR: Too many options!");
        puts("This program requires you to type");
        puts("two options exactly or it will not work.");
        return(1);
    }

/* Program continues here */
    printf("Working on %s and %s...\n",argv[1],argv[2]);
    return(0);
}
```

Exercise 5.2.3

ALPHA.C

```
#include <stdio.h>
#include <stdlib.h>
#include <string.h>
```

```
int main()
{
    char name[64];
    char command[64];

    printf("Please enter your name: ");
    gets(name);
    strcpy(command,"beta \"");
    strcat(command,name);
    strcat(command,"\"");
    system(command);
    return(0);
}
```

Note how I've used strcpy() and strcat() to build the system() function's command. I wanted the command to look like this:

```
beta "name in quotes"
```

This way, the BETA program needs to worry only about printing one argument:

BETA.C
```
#include <stdio.h>

int main(int argc, char *argv[])
{
    if(argc == 1)
    {
        puts("No name specified!");
        return(1);
    }
    printf("Is your name %s?\n",argv[1]);
    return(0);
}
```

Exercise 5.3.1

YOURNAME.C
```
#include <stdio.h>

int main()
{
    char yourname[65];
    FILE *f;

    printf("Enter your name: ");
    gets(yourname);
```

```
    f = fopen("yourname.txt","w");
    if(!f)
    {
        puts("Some kind of file error!");
        return(1);
    }

    fprintf(f,"%s\n",yourname);
    fclose(f);
    return(0);
}
```

Exercise 5.3.2

CONSUME.C

```
#include <stdio.h>

int main()
{
    FILE *myfile;
    char c;

    myfile = fopen("consume.c","r");

    while((c = fgetc(myfile)) != EOF)
        putchar(c);

    fclose(myfile);
    return(0);
}
```

I opted not to check myfile for NULL; after all, if the source code doesn't exist, the program doesn't exist, eh?

Exercise 5.3.3

EVENMORE.C

```
#include <stdio.h>

int main()
{
    FILE *myfile;

    myfile = fopen("alive.txt","a");
    if(!myfile)
    {
        puts("Some kind of file error!");
```

```
        return(1);
    }

    fprintf(myfile,"Alive, I tell you! Alive!\n");
    fclose(myfile);
    return(0);
}
```

Exercise 5.3.4

By removing the b from fopen( ), you direct the operating system to open the file in text mode rather than in binary mode. The output is then truncated, and you have no guarantee that DUMP displays the entire file's contents. The reason is that the EOF character, although acceptable as a valid character in a binary file, marks the end of a text file.

Exercise 5.5.1

VIEW1.C

One way to do this is to modify the printf( ) statement in the while loop to read

```
printf("%d: %s",ftell(viewfile),buffer);
```

Exercise 5.5.2

SHOWFROOT.C

Here's one solution:

```
#include <stdio.h>

int main()
{
    FILE *f;
    char froot[14];
    int x;

    if(!(f = fopen("froot.txt","r")))
    {
        puts("Error opening file");
        return(1);
    }

    for(x=0;x<25;x++)
    {
        fread(froot,14,1,f);
```

```
        printf("%2d: %s\n",x,froot);
    }
    fclose(f);
    return(0);
}
```

Exercise 5.5.3

FROOT12A.C

In this example, `fseek()` is used in a loop to find and display every other element from the start of the file:

```
#include <stdio.h>

#define RECSIZE 14

int main()
{
    FILE *f;
    char froot[RECSIZE];
    int record,offset;

    if(!(f = fopen("froot.txt","r")))
    {
        puts("Error opening file");
        return(1);
    }

    for(record=0;record<25;record+=2)
    {
        offset = record * RECSIZE;
        fseek(f,offset,SEEK_SET);
        fread(froot,RECSIZE,1,f);
        printf("%2d: %s\n",record,froot);
    }
    fclose(f);
    return(0);
}
```

FROOT12B.C

In this example, `fseek()` finds every other record by using the `SEEK_CUR` option and then skipping over a `RECSIZE` chunk on disk. Observe:

```
#include <stdio.h>

#define RECSIZE 14
```

```
int main()
{
    FILE *f;
    char froot[RECSIZE];
    int record,offset;

    if(!(f = fopen("froot.txt","r")))
    {
        puts("Error opening file");
        return(1);
    }

    for(record=0;record<25;record+=2)
    {
        fread(froot,RECSIZE,1,f);
        fseek(f,RECSIZE,SEEK_CUR);
        printf("%2d: %s\n",record,froot);
    }
    fclose(f);
    return(0);
}
```

Exercise 5.5.4

STOCKS.C

Here's the final STOCKS.C source code:

```
#include <stdio.h>
#include <stdlib.h>
#include <ctype.h>

#define FALSE 0
#define TRUE !FALSE

struct stock_data {
    char name[30];
    float buy_price;
    float current_price;
    };

void write_info(void);
void read_info(void);
void replace_info(void);

int main()
{
    char c;
    int done=FALSE;
```

```
        while(!done)
        {
            puts("\nStock Portfolio Thing\n");
            puts("A - Add new stock\n");
            puts("L - List stocks\n");
            puts("R - Replace stock\n");
            puts("Q - Quit\n");
            printf("Your choice: ");

            c = getchar();
            fflush(stdin);              /* fpurge(stdin) */
            c = toupper(c);
            switch(c)
            {
                case('A'):
                    puts("Add new stock\n");
                    write_info();
                    break;
                case('L'):
                    puts("List stocks");
                    read_info();
                    break;
                case('R'):
                    puts("Replace stock");
                    replace_info();
                    break;
                case('Q'):
                    puts("Quit\n");
                    done = TRUE;
                    break;
                default:
                    puts("?");
                    break;
            }
        }
        return(0);
}

void write_info(void)
{
    FILE *stocks;
    struct stock_data stock;

    printf("Enter stock name:");
    gets(stock.name);
    printf("What did you buy it for? $");
    scanf("%f",&stock.buy_price);
    stock.current_price = stock.buy_price/11;

    stocks = fopen("stock.dat","a");
```

```
        if(stocks==NULL)
        {
            puts("Error opening file");
            exit(1);
        }

        fwrite(&stock,sizeof(stock),1,stocks);
        fclose(stocks);
        puts("Stock added!");
        fflush(stdin);
}

void read_info(void)
{
        FILE *stocks;
    struct stock_data stock;
        int x;

    stocks = fopen("stock.dat","r");
    if(stocks==NULL)
    {
        puts("No data in file");
        return;
    }

    while(TRUE)
    {
        x = fread(&stock,sizeof(stock),1,stocks);

        if(x==0) break;

        printf("\nStock name: %s\n",stock.name);
        printf("Purchased for $%.2f\n",stock.buy_price);
        printf("Current price: $%.2f\n",stock.current_price);
    }

    fclose(stocks);
}

void replace_info(void)
{
        FILE *stocks;
    struct stock_data stock;
        int record,x;
    long offset;

    printf("Which record number do you want to find? ");
    scanf("%d",&record);

    stocks = fopen("stock.dat","r");
```

```
        if(stocks==NULL)
        {
            puts("Error opening file");
            return;
        }

        offset = (long)(record-1)*sizeof(stock);
        x = fseek(stocks,offset,SEEK_SET);
        if(x != 0)
        {
            puts("Error reading from file");
            return;
        }

        x = fread(&stock,sizeof(stock),1,stocks);
        if(x==0)
        {
            puts("Error reading record");
            return;
        }

        printf("\nRecord: %d\n",record);
        printf("Stock name: %s\n",stock.name);
        printf("Purchased for $%.2f\n",stock.buy_price);
        printf("Current price: $%.2f\n",stock.current_price);
        fclose(stocks);
        fflush(stdin);          /* fpurge(stdin) */

/* read in new stock information */
        printf("Enter new stock name: ");
        gets(stock.name);
        printf("Enter purchase price: ");
        scanf("%f",&stock.buy_price);
        stock.current_price = stock.buy_price/9;

/* write stock information back to disk */
        stocks = fopen("stock.dat","r+");
        if(stocks==NULL)
        {
            puts("Error opening file for update");
            return;
        }

        offset = (long)(record-1)*sizeof(stock);
        x = fseek(stocks,offset,SEEK_SET);
        if(x != 0)
        {
            puts("Error finding record");
            return;
```

```
    }
    x = fwrite(&stock,sizeof(stock),1,stocks);
    if(x==0)
    {
        puts("Error writing record");
        return;
    }
    fclose(stocks);
    fflush(stdin);    /* fpurge(stdin); */
}
```

Exercise 5.6.1

FILEINFO1.C

```
#include <stdio.h>
#include <sys/stat.h>
#include <sys/types.h>
#include <time.h>

int main(int argc, char *argv[])
{
    struct stat fbuf;
    int x;

    if(argc != 2)
    {
        puts("Error! Format:");
        puts("FILEINFO filename");
        return(1);
    }

    x = stat(argv[1],&fbuf);
    if(x != 0 )
    {
        puts("Error reading file");
        return(1);
    }

    printf("Some file stats on '%s':\n",argv[1]);
    printf("File size is %d bytes\n",fbuf.st_size);
    printf("File last modified %s\n",ctime(&fbuf.st_mtime));
    return(0);
}
```

Exercise 5.6.2

DODIR2.C

```
#include <stdio.h>
#include <sys/types.h>
#include <dirent.h>
#include <sys/stat.h>

int main()
{
    DIR *dhandle;
    struct dirent *drecord;
    struct stat sbuf;

    dhandle = opendir(".");
    if(dhandle == NULL)
    {
        puts("Error opening directory");
        return(1);
    }

    while( (drecord = readdir(dhandle)) != NULL)
    {
        stat(drecord->d_name,&sbuf);
        printf("%-16s %9d\n",drecord->d_name,sbuf.st_size);
    }
    closedir(dhandle);
    return(0);
}
```

Remember that stat() requires the SYS/STAT.H header file and uses the stat structure. I set up the printf() statement to print filenames with only a 16-character-wide field. Longer filenames mess that up, of course.

Bonus points to you if you used fields in your printf() statement!

Exercise 5.6.3

DODIR4.C

```
#include <stdio.h>
#include <sys/types.h>
#include <dirent.h>
#include <sys/stat.h>

int main()
{
    DIR *dhandle;
    struct dirent *drecord;
```

```
        struct stat sbuf;
        int file_count = 0;
        long total_size = 0;

        dhandle = opendir(".");
        if(dhandle == NULL)
        {
            puts("Error opening directory");
            return(1);
        }

        while( (drecord = readdir(dhandle)) != NULL)
        {
            stat(drecord->d_name,&sbuf);
            if(S_ISDIR(sbuf.st_mode))
                printf("%-16s %-9s\n",drecord->d_name,"<DIR>");
            else
            {
                printf("%-16s %9d\n", drecord->d_name,
    sbuf.st_size);
                file_count++;
                total_size += sbuf.st_size;
            }
        }
        closedir(dhandle);
        printf("%d file(s) for a total of %d bytes\n",
    file_count,total_size);
        return(0);
}
```

Exercise 5.6.4

CHANGED1.C

```
#include <stdio.h>
#include <unistd.h>

#define BUFSIZE 128

int main()
{
    char orgdir[BUFSIZE];
    char newdir[BUFSIZE];
    int x;

    getcwd(orgdir,BUFSIZE);
    printf("The current working directory
    is:\n\t%s\n",orgdir);
```

```
    puts("Changing to the root directory...");
    x = chdir("\\");     /* x = chdir("/"); */
    if( x != 0)
    {
        puts("Error changing directories");
        return(1);
    }

    getcwd(newdir,BUFSIZE);
    printf("The current working directory is
now:\n\t%s\n",newdir);

    puts("Changing back to original directory...");
    x = chdir(orgdir);
    if( x != 0)
    {
        puts("Error changing directories");
        return(1);
    }

    puts("Done!");

    return(0);
}
```

Book VI: The Joy of Linked Lists

Exercise 6.2.1

listAll ( )
```
void listAll(void)
{
    if(firsta==NULL)
        puts("There are no records to print!");
    else
    {
        printf("%6s %-15s %-15s %11s\n",
    "Acct#","Last","First","Balance");
        currenta=firsta;
        do
        {
            printf("%5d: %-15s %-15s $%8.2f\n",
                currenta->number,
                currenta->lastname,
                currenta->firstname,
                currenta->balance);
        }
```

```
        while((currenta=currenta->next) != NULL);
    }
}
```

Granted, you may not have come up with the same solution, but remember these points and how the preceding code addresses them:

+ First, there must be a test to see whether the list is empty. That's done simply by comparing the `firsta` pointer with NULL. Obviously, if the list is empty, there's no need to print any records.

+ A `do-while` loop was chosen because if there are any records, the loop has to spin at least once. A `while` loop would work just as well.

+ Inside the loop is a simple `printf()` statement, though I've split it on multiple lines in this exercise. `printf()` formats its output to display each field in each record. Note that the account number is used as an index for the records, so there's no need to use and display a separate `index` type of variable.

+ The loop continues to spin until the end-cap NULL is found. That's the condition that `while` examines.

Here's a sample of the output from the preceding routine, when it's included in the BANK.C source code, compiled, and run:

```
Acct# Last          First              Balance
    1: Simpson       Homer          $    0.98
    2: Simpson       Marge          $  250.00
    3: Simpson       Bart           $    9.87
    4: Simpson       Lisa           $ 9687.14
    5: Simpson       Maggie         $    0.01
```

Exercise 6.2.2

modifyAccount ()

```
void modifyAccount(void)
{
    int record;

    if(firsta==NULL)
    {
        puts("There are no records to modify!");
        return;
    }

    listAll();          /* show all records first */
    printf("Enter account number to modify or change: ");
```

```c
    scanf("%d",&record);

    currenta = firsta;
    while(currenta != NULL)
    {
        if(currenta->number == record)
        {
        printf("Account $%d:\n",currenta->number);
        printf("Last name: %s\n",currenta->lastname);
        if(prompt())
            gets(currenta->lastname);
        printf("First name: %s\n",currenta->firstname);
        if(prompt())
            gets(currenta->firstname);
        printf("Balance %8.2f\n",currenta->balance);
        if(prompt())
            scanf("%f",&currenta->balance);
        return;
        }
        else
        {
            currenta = currenta->next;
        }
    }
    printf("Account %d was not found!\n",record);
}

int prompt(void)
{
    char ch;

    clearInput();
    printf("Update?");
    ch = getchar();
    ch = toupper(ch);
    clearInput();
    if(ch == 'Y')
    {
        printf("Enter new: ");
        return(1);
    }
    else
        return(0);
}
```

Note that I created *two* functions in this exercise; the second is prompt(),
which prompts users yes-or-no to modify a record. This method simply
makes more efficient the approach I chose to use for modifying records. You
can do this in other ways too; as long as your routine modifies the records
and doesn't screw up the results, consider that you passed the exercise.

Exercise 6.4.1

Here's my solution:

```
/* display all the records reverse */
    y = 10;
    for(c = 1;c != NULL;c=c->previous)
    {
        printf("Lotto pix %d: ",y--);
        for(x=0;x<BALLS;x++)
            printf(" %d",c->ball[x]);
        putchar('\n');
    }
```

The key is getting the for loop correct, as shown in this exercise. The y variable is simply used to track the output; allowing you to compare the records forward and reverse to ensure that they match up.

Appendix D: C Language Keywords and Operators

C Language Keywords, ISO C Standard

auto	double	int	struct
break	else	long	switch
case	enum	register	typedef
char	extern	return	union
const	float	short	unsigned
continue	for	signed	void
default	goto	sizeof	volatile
do	if	static	while

Older Reserved Words, No Longer ISO Standard

asm	entry	fortran

C++ Keywords You May Consider Reserved Too

asm	false	private	throw
bool	friend	protected	true
catch	inline	public	try
class	mutable	reinterpret_cast	typeid
const_cast	namespace	static_cast	using
delete	new	template	virtual
dynamic_cast	operator	this	

C Language Operators

Operator	Duty
=	Assignment (equals)
+	Mathematical, addition
-	Mathematical, subtraction
*	Mathematical, multiplication

(continued)

C Language Operators *(continued)*

Operator	Duty
/	Mathematical, division
%	Mathematical, modulo
>	Comparison, greater-than
>=	Comparison, greater-than or equal to
<	Comparison, less-than
<=	Comparison, less-than or equal to
==	Comparison, is equal to
!=	Comparison, is not equal to
&&	Logical, AND
||	Logical, OR
!	Logical, NOT
++	Mathematical, increment by one
--	Mathematical, decrement by one
&	Bitwise, AND
|	Bitwise, inclusive OR
^	Bitwise, exclusive OR (XOR or EOR)
<<	Bitwise, shift bits left
>>	Bitwise, shift bits right
~	Bitwise, one's complement
+	Unary, positive
-	Unary, negative
*	Unary, pointer
&	Unary, address
sizeof	Unary, returns the size of an object
.	Structure, element access
->	Structure, pointer element access
?:	Conditional expression (funky if operator)

Assignment Operators

Operator	Shortcut for
+=	Addition
-=	Subtraction
*=	Multiplication
/=	Division

Operator	Shortcut for
%=	Modulo
<<=	Shift left (bitwise)
>>=	Shift right (bitwise)
&=	Bitwise AND
|=	Bitwise inclusive OR
^=	Bitwise exclusive OR

The assignment operators allow you to take an equation, such as

```
alpha = alpha + beta;
```

And shorten it to

```
alpha += beta;
```

The + and += can be substituted with any assignment operator.

Sacred Order of Precedence

Operators	Read from
Unary operators: ! ~ ++ -- + - * & (*typecast*) sizeof	Left to right
* / %	Right to left
+ -	Left to right
<< >>	Left to right
< <= > >=	Left to right
== !=	Left to right
&	Left to right
^	Left to right
|	Left to right
&&	Left to right
||	Left to right
?:	Right to left
= += -= *= /= %= &= ^= |= <<= >>=	Right to left
,	Left to right

✦ The unary operators come first; note that there's a difference between +
  and –, which make a value negative or positive, and + addition or – subtraction. And, the * unary operator is the pointer, not multiplication.

✦ Parentheses are used to prioritize precedence; things in the parentheses
  are always done first.

✦ The comma operator (the last table entry) is used in the `for` statement
  to separate items in the first and third part of `for`'s parentheses.

Appendix E: C Language Variable Types

Type	Value Range		Comments
char	−128	to 127	
unsigned char	0	to 255	
int	−32,768	to 32,767	16-bit
	−2,147,483,648	to 2,147,483,647	32-bit
unsigned int	0	to 65,535	16-bit
	0	to 4,294,967,295	32-bit
short int	−32,768	to 32,767	
unsigned short int	0	to 65,535	
long int	−2,147,483,648	to 2,147,483,647	
unsigned long int	0	to 4,294,967,295	
float	1.17×10^{-38}	to 3.40×10^{38}	6-digit precision
double	2.22×10^{-308}	to 1.79×10^{308}	15-digit precision

Some compilers treat the char type as signed, and others treat it as unsigned. To be sure, use the signed or unsigned prefix if you absolutely need a signed or unsigned char variable.

The size of the basic integer depends on the microprocessor. For most modern microprocessors, a 32-bit width is used. Older computers used only a 16-bit width. To ensure a 16-bit value, define your ints as short. To ensure the 32-bit value, use long ints.

Appendix F: Escape Sequences

Escape Sequence	Character
\a	Bell (speaker beeps)
\b	Backspace (non-erase)
\f	Form feed/clear screen
\n	New line
\r	Carriage Return
\t	Tab
\v	Vertical tab
\\	Backslash
\?	Question mark
\'	Single quote
\"	Double quote
\x*nn*	Hexadecimal character code *nn*
\o*nn*	Octal character code *nn*
nn	Octal character code *nn*

Appendix G: Conversion Characters

Conversion Character	Displays
%%	The percent character, %
%c	Single character (char) value
%d	Integer (int, short int, long int) value
%e	Floating-point (float or double) value in scientific notation with a little E
%E	Floating-point (float or double) value in scientific notation with a big E
%f	Floating-point (float or double) value in decimal notation
%g	Either %f or %e is used, depending on which is shorter
%G	Either %F or %E is used, depending on which is shorter
%i	Integer (int, short int, long int) value
%o	Unsigned octal value (no leading 0)
%p	Memory location or address in hexadecimal (pointer)
%s	String constant or variable (char *)
%u	Unsigned integer (unsigned int, unsigned short int, unsigned long int) value
%x	Unsigned hexadecimal value, lowercase a-f, no leading 0 or x
%X	Unsigned hexadecimal value, uppercase A-F, no leading 0 or X

Index

Special characters and numbers

B

C

D

J

K

P

Q

R

W

Notes

Notes

FOR DUMMIES®

The easy way to get more done and have more fun

PERSONAL FINANCE

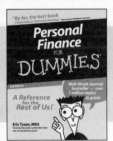

0-7645-5231-7

0-7645-2431-3

0-7645-5331-3

Also available:

Estate Planning For Dummies
(0-7645-5501-4)
401(k)s For Dummies
(0-7645-5468-9)
Frugal Living For Dummies
(0-7645-5403-4)
Microsoft Money "X" For
Dummies
(0-7645-1689-2)
Mutual Funds For Dummies
(0-7645-5329-1)

Personal Bankruptcy For
Dummies
(0-7645-5498-0)
Quicken "X" For Dummies
(0-7645-1666-3)
Stock Investing For Dummies
(0-7645-5411-5)
Taxes For Dummies 2003
(0-7645-5475-1)

BUSINESS & CAREERS

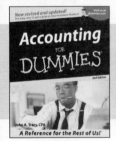

0-7645-5314-3

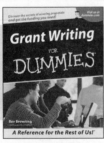

0-7645-5307-0

0-7645-5471-9

Also available:

Business Plans Kit For
Dummies
(0-7645-5365-8)
Consulting For Dummies
(0-7645-5034-9)
Cool Careers For Dummies
(0-7645-5345-3)
Human Resources Kit For
Dummies
(0-7645-5131-0)
Managing For Dummies
(1-5688-4858-7)

QuickBooks All-in-One Desk
Reference For Dummies
(0-7645-1963-8)
Selling For Dummies
(0-7645-5363-1)
Small Business Kit For
Dummies
(0-7645-5093-4)
Starting an eBay Business For
Dummies
(0-7645-1547-0)

HEALTH, SPORTS & FITNESS

0-7645-5167-1

0-7645-5146-9

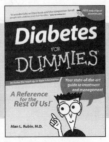

0-7645-5154-X

Also available:

Controlling Cholesterol For
Dummies
(0-7645-5440-9)
Dieting For Dummies
(0-7645-5126-4)
High Blood Pressure For
Dummies
(0-7645-5424-7)
Martial Arts For Dummies
(0-7645-5358-5)
Menopause For Dummies
(0-7645-5458-1)

Nutrition For Dummies
(0-7645-5180-9)
Power Yoga For Dummies
(0-7645-5342-9)
Thyroid For Dummies
(0-7645-5385-2)
Weight Training For Dummies
(0-7645-5168-X)
Yoga For Dummies
(0-7645-5117-5)

Available wherever books are sold.
Go to www.dummies.com or call 1-877-762-2974 to order direct.

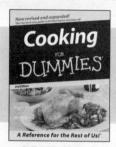

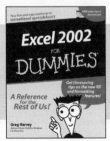

FOR DUMMIES®

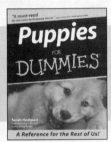

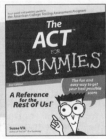